Egypt
& the Sudan
a travel survival kit
Scott Wayne

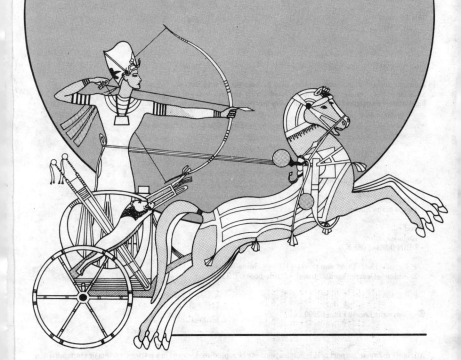

Egypt & the Sudan - a travel survival kit
   2nd edition

Published by
   Lonely Planet Publications
   Head Office: PO Box 617, Hawthorn, Victoria 3122, Australia
   US Office: PO Box 2001A, Berkeley, CA 94702, USA

Printed by
   Singapore National Printers Ltd, Singapore

Photographs by
   Glenn Beanland (GB)
   Dan Burton (DB)
   Caroline Matthew (CM)
   Scott Wayne (SW)
   Tony Wheeler (TW)
   Helen Williams (HW)
   Front cover: Abu Simbel (SW)
   Back cover: Temple of Hatshepsut (GB)

First Published
   November 1987

This Edition
   July 1990

National Library of Australia Cataloguing in Publication Data

Wayne, Scott
   Egypt & the Sudan, a travel survival kit.

   2nd ed.
   Includes index.
   ISBN 0 86442 082 X.

   1. Egypt – Description and travel – 1981– – Guide-books.
   2. Sudan – Description and travel – Guide-books. I. Title.

   916.20455

Scott Wayne

Scott Wayne is an American who has lived, studied and travelled in the Middle East, Africa and Europe. He graduated from Georgetown University's School of Foreign Service with a degree in International Relations. He also did graduate studies at the Royal Institute of International Affairs in London and the University of Southern California. His studies at Georgetown included a long stint at the American University in Cairo and many adventures up and down the Nile. He later returned to Egypt and the Sudan to write this guide. Scott is also the author of Lonely Planet's *Egyptian Arabic – a language survival kit* and *Baja California – a travel survival kit*, and co-author of *Mexico – a travel survival kit*.

From the Author

I am grateful to many organisations and individuals for help in researching this book.

For the Sudan section many thanks to the people of LALMBA, the Colorado-based relief organisation – especially Jenny Demeaux, Charlotte Geier, Jody Meador and Cathy Matthews (USA); also special thanks to Lydi Ravensbergen (NETH) for reports on her year in the Sudan. Thanks also to Elsabet Mesfin of *USA for Africa – United Support of Artists for Africa* for information about various organisations in the Sudan.

In Egypt, I am grateful to the Kamal family – Ashraf, Raymonda, Hany, Ayman and their parents – of Shubra, Cairo, who welcomed me into their home and tolerated my frequent late night sessions with a Toshiba laptop computer. Thanks to Julie Javernick (USA) for sharing a Cairo research stint, Ingrid Peters (West Germany), Simon Dickerson (UK) for the *Times* and sharing adventures to Siwa, Ruth Zelickman (UK), Ayman Ahmed El Samun of Luxor, Noury Dawi Mohammed of Aswan, Mohammed and Ingrid Kabany of the Dahab New Diving Centre for their hospitality and guidance

to Dahab's dive spots, Gordon Robinson (USA) for his friendship and write-up about the boat to Jeddah, Alain Sobol of the Aquamarine Diving Centre in Na'ama Bay for information about diving in the Red Sea and for showing me some of the underwater sites, Iman Bibars for insights on life in Egypt, Kris Greiber (USA) for her story about the night train to Cairo, Ahmed Safwat (Egypt) and Amina Zaghloul (Egypt).

On the home front, this book is dedicated to my mother, Jolyn Wayne. Also, of course, great pyramids of thanks to my wife, Shirley, for her love, patience and understanding.

Lonely Planet Credits

Editor	Michelle de Kretser
Cover design, design & illustrations	Glenn Beanland
Maps	Trudi Canavan
	Greg Herriman
	Valerie Tellini
	David Windle
Typesetting	Ann Jeffree

Thanks also to: Mark Ellis, Sharan Kaur, David Meagher, Jenny Missen and Allison White for copy-editing; Alan Tiller for proofing; Lindy Cameron and Susan Mitra for proofing and sound advice; Sharon Wertheim for indexing; Ann Jeffree for additional illustrations; and Trudi Canavan and Tamsin Wilson for map corrections.

A Warning & a Request

Things change – prices go up, schedules change, good places go bad and bad places go bankrupt – nothing stays the same. So if you find things better or worse, recently opened or long since closed, please write

and tell us and help make the next edition better!

Your letters will be used to help update future editions and, where possible, important changes will also be included as a Stop Press section in reprints.

All information is greatly appreciated and the best letters will receive a free copy of the next edition, or any other Lonely Planet book of your choice.

Contents

EGYPT

Introduction

Ever since Herodotus, the ancient Greek historian and traveller, first described Egypt as 'the gift of the Nile', she has been capturing the imagination of all who visit her.

The awe-inspiring monuments, left by the Pharaohs, Greeks and Romans as well as by the early Christians and Muslims, attract thousands of visitors every year – but the pyramids, temples, tombs, monasteries and mosques are just part of this country's fascination.

Modern Egypt – where mud-brick villages stand beside Pharaonic ruins surrounded by towering steel, stone and glass buildings – is at the cultural crossroads of East and West, ancient and modern. While TV antennae decorate rooftops everywhere, from the crowded apartment blocks of Cairo to the mud homes of farming villages and the goatskin tents of the Bedouins, the fellahin throughout the Nile's fertile valley still tend their fields with the archaic tools of their ancestors.

In the gargantuan city of Cairo the sound of the muezzin summoning the faithful to prayer or the mesmerising voice of Om Kolthum, the 'Mother of Egypt', compete with the pop music of ghetto blasters and the screech of car horns. And everywhere there are people: swathed in long flowing robes or Western-style clothes, hanging from buses, weaving through an obstacle course of animals and exhaust-spewing traffic or spilling from hivelike buildings.

Spectacular edifices aside, the attraction of this country lies in its incredible natural beauty and in the overwhelming hospitality of the Egyptian people.

Through everything the Nile River flows serene and majestic, the lifeblood of Egypt as it has been since the beginning of history.

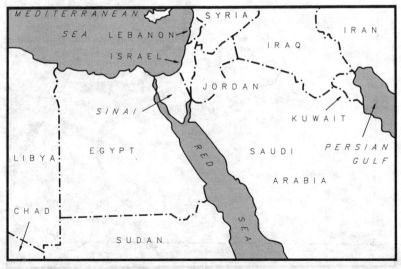

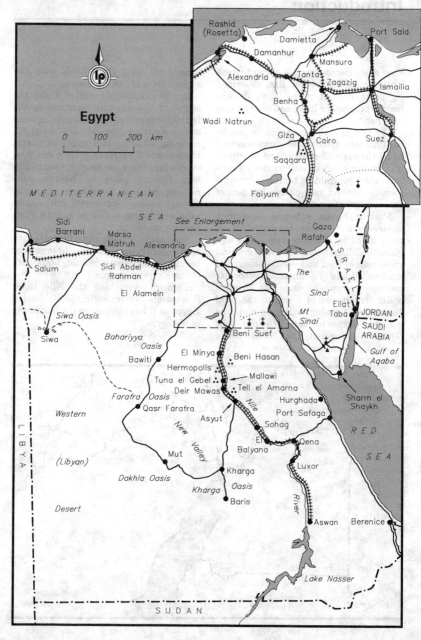

Facts about the Country

HISTORY

About 5000 years ago an Egyptian king named Menes unified Upper and Lower Egypt for the first time. No-one is quite sure how he did this, but it is known that his action gave rise to Egypt's first relatively stable dynasty of kings. Menes' powerful and civilised reign suggests that civilisation must have been developing in the Nile Valley for many centuries before this time.

The history of Egypt is inextricably linked to the Nile. Ever since the earliest known communities settled the Nile Valley, the river has inspired and controlled the religious, economic, social and political life of Egyptians. For many centuries the narrow, elongated layout of the country's fertile lands hampered the fusion of those early settlements, which held fast to their local independence. But once again it was the river, this time as a common highway, which broke the barriers by providing an avenue for commercial traffic and communication. The small kingdoms eventually developed into two important states, one covering the valley as far as the delta, the other consisting of the delta itself. The unification of these two states, by Menes in about 3000 BC, set the scene for the greatest era of ancient Egyptian civilisation. More than 30 dynasties, 50 rulers and 2700 years of indigenous – and occasionally foreign – rule passed before Alexander the Great ushered in a long, unbroken period of foreign rule.

Fifty centuries of history! Obviously, it is not within the scope of this book to cover it in great detail. To give some idea of the major events in Egypt's history, the last 5000 years, from the time of Menes, can be divided roughly into seven periods:

Pharaonic times (3000-341 BC)
Greek rule (332-30 BC)

Roman & Byzantine rule (30 BC-638 AD)
The Arab conquest & the Mamelukes (640-1517)
Turkish rule (1517-1882)
British occupation (1882-1952)
Independent Egypt (1952 onwards)

Pharaonic Times (3000-341 BC)

Little is known of the immediate successors of Menes except that, attributed with divine ancestry, they promoted the development of a highly stratified society, patronised the arts and built many temples and public works.

As you travel through Egypt, it is easy to be overwhelmed by the many names and dates of Pharaonic rule. Some of the books listed in the Facts for the Visitor chapter offer a detailed account of the long period encompassing the Old, Middle and New kingdoms.

In the 27th century BC, Egypt's pyramids began to appear. King Zoser and his chief architect, Imhotep, built what may have been the first, the Step Pyramid at Saqqara. Zoser ruled from the nearby capital of Memphis. Until his reign, most of the royal tombs had been built of sun-dried bricks. The construction of Zoser's massive stone mausoleum, therefore, was not only a striking testimony to his power and the prosperity of the period but the start of a whole new trend. It was also during the period of Zoser's rule that the sun-god Ra became the most important of the deities worshipped by Egyptians.

For the next three dynasties and 500 years – a period called the Old Kingdom – the power of Egypt's Pharaohs and the size of their pyramids and temples greatly increased. The size of such buildings symbolised the Pharaoh's importance and power over his people. The pyramid also gave the Pharaoh steps to the heavens, and the ceremonial wooden

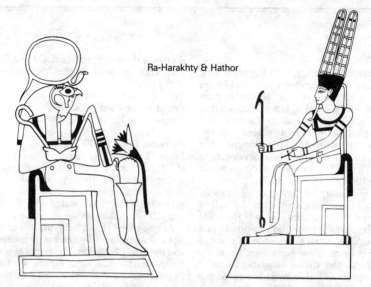

Ra-Harakhty & Hathor

barques buried with him provided him with symbolic vehicles to the next life.

Not long after Zoser's Step Pyramid was completed, 4th dynasty Pharaohs built several more in the relatively short period between 2650 and 2500 BC.

Pharaoh Sneferu built the Pyramid of Meidum in El Faiyum and the Red Pyramid of Dahshur near Saqqara, and took royal power and the accompanying artistic and commercial development of Egypt to even greater heights. During his time, trading vessels nearly six metres long began plying the waters of the Nile. He brought back thousands of prisoners from successful campaigns against the Nubians in the south, and defeated all enemies who threatened the country.

The last three Pharaohs of the 4th dynasty, Cheops, Chephren and Mycerinus, built the three Great Pyramids of Giza. Cheops took the throne when the Pharaonic era was reaching the apex of its prosperity and culture, and if his colossal pyramid is any indication he must have been one of the greatest of all the Pharaohs. Its sheer size and mathematical

precision is not only a monument to the extraordinary development of Egyptian architecture; it also suggests, as many Egyptologists believe, that the era of Cheops saw the emergence, for the first time in human history, of an organisational principle. Under his rule, and through the enormous labour and discipline involved in the construction of the pyramid, Egypt became a highly organised state.

As the centuries passed and the 5th dynasty (about 2490-2330 BC) began, there were changes in the power and rule of the Pharaohs. One of the first indications of this was the comparatively small pyramids built at Abu Sir, 12 km south of Giza. The Pharaohs had begun to share power with various high officials and nobles in the vast bureaucracies they had created, so, unlike their predecessors, they were no longer absolute monarchs and did not have the same resources for the construction of immense funerary monuments.

As control became even more diffused during the 6th and 7th dynasties (about 2330-2170 BC), a number of small local principalities popped up around the country, and a second capital was established at Heracleopolis (near present-day Beni Suef) during the 9th and 10th dynasties. The princes of these small dynasties ruled Egypt for many years, but their constant feudal struggles prevented any possibility of economic or artistic development. With the collapse of the Old Kingdom a state of disunity succeeded the unparalleled grandeur of the early Pharaonic dynasties.

Civil war at the beginning of the 11th dynasty finally put an end to the squabbling. An enterprising member of the Intef family rallied all the principalities of the south against the weakness of Heracleopolis, and established an independent kingdom with Thebes (present-day Luxor) as its capital. Under Mentuhotep II the north and south were again united under the leadership of a single Pharaoh. The princes of Thebes became rulers of all Egypt, and the Middle Kingdom period began.

With political order came economic stability and social and artistic development. Thebes prospered for about 250 years. Tombs and temples were built throughout Egypt; their remains can be seen today in almost every Egyptian town. The Pharaohs Mentuhotep, Amenemhet and Sesostris built monuments at Lisht, Dahshur, Hawara and Lahun – all of which are near El Faiyum and Saqqara. Their building frenzy diminished as the governors and nobles of the nomarchs (provinces) once again began squabbling among themselves and demanding more control (around 1780-1660 BC). Royal power was weakened by this lack of unity; the empire was divided and ripe for conquest by an outside power.

These invaders came from the north-east. The Egyptians called them the Hyksos, which means 'princes of the foreign lands'. They ruled Egypt for more than a century, but are remembered for little more than having introduced the horse-drawn chariot to Egypt. By about 1550 BC the Egyptians had routed the Hyksos and expelled them from power. A new kingdom, with its capital first at Thebes and thereafter at Memphis, was established and Egypt truly entered the ranks of the great powers.

The New Kingdom represented a blossoming of culture and empire in Pharaonic Egypt. For almost 400 years, from the 18th to the 20th dynasties (1550-1150 BC), Egypt was a great power in north-east Africa and the eastern Mediterranean. Renowned kings and queens ruled an expanding empire from Memphis, and built monuments which even today are unique in their immensity and beauty.

The temple complex of Karnak at Thebes became an important symbolic power centre for the empire. The temple seemed to grow as the empire expanded. Each successive Pharaoh of the 18th and 19th dynasties added a room, hall or pylon, with intricately carved hieroglyphic inscriptions on every wall and pillar. Some of what is known about Egyptian life during this time comes from the stories told by these inscriptions.

Significant expansion of the empire began with the reign of Tuthmosis I in 1528 BC. He grabbed Upper Nubia, and became the first Pharaoh to be entombed in the Valley of the Kings on the west bank across from Thebes. His daughter, Hatshepsut, became one of Egypt's few female rulers. A spectacular mortuary temple was built for her at Deir el Bahri on the west bank.

Tuthmosis III, Hatshepsut's nephew, was next in line; he became Egypt's greatest conqueror. He expanded the empire past Syria and into western Asia. He built and contributed to temples at Thebes, Buhen, Amada and other locales throughout Egypt.

Empire expansion and temple/tomb building continued under the next three Pharaohs – Amenophis II, Tuthmosis IV and Amenophis III – and reached its peak in 1417 BC under Amenophis III. He built the Luxor Temple and a massive mortuary temple, of which the only remains are the Colossi of Memnon on the west bank at Luxor. During this period the country was relatively prosperous and stable.

Amenophis IV quarrelled with the priesthood of the god Amun – the leading god of Thebes – and took the name Akhenaten in honour of Aten, the disc of the rising sun. Akhenaten and his wife, Nefertiti, were so devoted to the worship of Aten that they established a new capital called Akhetaten devoted solely to the worship of the new god. Some historians believe that this worship represented the first organised form of monotheism. Today, the scant remains of Akhenaten's capital can be seen at Tell el Amarna, near the town of El Minya.

After Akhenaten's death, the priests of Thebes went on a rampage and destroyed any signs of his rule and his monotheism. This included the Temple of the Sun at Karnak. (Recently, an American archaeological team photographed the hieroglyphic inscriptions on more than 35,000 stone blocks from the temple which had been scattered around the world. From the photographs, the archaeologists were able to reconstruct the temple and learn more about the lives of Akhenaten and Nefertiti.)

Akhenaten's young son-in-law, Tutankhamun, ruled for about nine years and died just before reaching manhood. His tomb was discovered in 1922 with almost all its treasures untouched.

For the next few centuries, Egypt was ruled by generals: Ramses I, II and III, and Seti I. Like good Pharaohs and military leaders they built massive monuments, such as the temples at Abydos and Abu Simbel, and waged war against the Hittites and Libyans. However, by the time Ramses III came to power (1198 BC) as the second king of the 20th dynasty, disunity had begun to set in. The empire continued to shrink, and Egypt was subsequently subjected to attack from outsiders. This was the state of affairs when Alexander the Great arrived in the 4th century BC.

Queen Nefertiti & Pharaoh Akhenaten

Greek Rule (332-30 BC)

Egypt was a mess when Alexander arrived in 332 BC. Over the previous several centuries Libyans, Ethiopians, Persians and Assyrians had invaded the country at different times. Alexander promptly established a new capital, which he named Alexandria after himself. After his death, Egypt was eventually ruled by a Macedonian general, who established a new dynasty as Ptolemy I.

The Ptolemies ruled Egypt for 300 years. Alexandria became a great Greek city, housing a famous library, among other things. The temples of Dendara, Philae and Edfu, which were built further south, are still in excellent shape, with most of their walls and roofs extant. There was a melding of the Greek and Egyptian religions.

Despite the prosperity, however, the Ptolemies' rule was not without its share of murder, intrigue and threats from abroad. While they bickered, expelled and assassinated one another, the overall weakness and instability of their reign attracted the interest of the rulers of the expanding Roman Empire. For a while, the Romans supported various Ptolemies, but this seemed to lead to more rivalry and assassination rather than peace and stability. The litany of events leading to complete Roman rule over Egypt reads like a bloody soap opera.

From 51 to 48 BC Cleopatra VII and her younger brother Ptolemy XIII together ruled Egypt, under Roman protection. Pompei, one of Julius Caesar's rivals, was sent from Rome to watch over them. Ptolemy had Pompei killed and Cleopatra banished. However, in the same year (48 BC), Caesar gave his all to Cleopatra and on arrival in Egypt threw Ptolemy in the Nile, appointing another of Cleopatra's brothers, Ptolemy XIV, as coruler. Cleopatra gave birth to Julius Caesar's son in 47 BC and had her brother killed in 45 BC. A year later Caesar was also assassinated. (Are you lost yet?) Marc Antony arrived from Rome, fell in love with Cleopatra, and moved in with her for 10 years of bliss, an arrangement the Roman senate wasn't too thrilled about. They declared Antony an enemy of the people and sent Octavian to deal with him. Antony and Cleopatra preferred bliss to strife. They both committed suicide in 30 BC and Egypt became a Roman province.

Roman & Byzantine Rule (30 BC-638 AD)

Octavian was the first Roman ruler of Egypt. He ruled as Emperor Augustus for a few years and made Egypt the granary of the Roman Empire. Except for a brief invasion by Ethiopia in 24 BC, Egypt was basically stable and peaceful for about 30 years.

Although the Bible tells us that Mary, Joseph and their young baby fled from Bethlehem to Egypt, where Jesus grew up before returning to Palestine to spread the word of God, it was not until St Mark started preaching the gospel, around 40 AD, that Egyptians began converting to Christianity. The Roman emperor Nero capitalised on this renewed sense of religious unity by developing Egypt as a trade centre between Rome and India in 54 AD.

A national Egyptian, or Coptic, Church was founded, despite the persecution of Christians throughout the Roman Empire during the following centuries. Egypt prospered, but by the 3rd century the Roman Empire had begun to succumb to war, famine and power struggles. In the 4th century, not long after Christianity was declared the state religion, the Roman Empire cracked in half. The eastern half became what was later known as the Byzantine or Eastern Empire. It was ruled from Constantinople (now Istanbul), while the Western Roman Empire remained centred in Rome.

The empire was too weak to rule its dominions effectively, so Egypt was left to invaders – Nubians from the south and North Africans from the west. Egypt was also left to develop the Coptic Church independently of the Byzantines. The Copts' adoption of a Monophysitic doctrine (the belief that Christ is divine, rather than both human and divine) was deemed heretical by the Byzantine and Roman orthodoxy, so they expelled the Coptic Church from the main body of Christianity. That doctrine, however, and a tradition of monasticism, greatly influenced later developments in European Christianity and are still an integral part of the Christian church in Egypt.

Aside from a few wars with Nubians, a famine and a couple of Persian invasions, life in 'Byzantine' Egypt was relatively sedate. Then, in 640 AD, the Arabs arrived.

The Arab Conquest & the Mamelukes (640-1517)

The Arab conquest brought Islam to Egypt. By 642 the new Arab rulers had established Fustat as a military base and seat of government – the precursor of Cairo. Although it didn't last long as the seat of government, it grew quickly as a city of Muslims. The ruins of Fustat can still be seen just south of Cairo.

In 658 the Omayyads, an Arab dynasty based in Damascus, snatched control of Egypt and stayed until 750. During the 92 years of their rule, Islamic faith and the Omayyad Empire extended from Spain all the way to central Asia. Theological splits were inevitable in such a large empire. One of the main splits concerned the spiritual leadership of the descendants of Ali, the Prophet Mohammed's son-in-law. Two groups – the Sunni and the Shi'ite – evolved because of this dispute, and conflict between them continues today. More than 1200 years ago, this same conflict led to the downfall of the Omayyad dynasty and the decapitation of Marwan, the last Omayyad caliph, or ruler. Persian troops paraded his head around the burnt remains of Fustat. For the next 108 years Egypt was ruled by the Baghdad-based Abbasid dynasty.

The Abbasids ruled Egypt a little differently from their predecessors. They brought in outsiders, Turkish-speaking soldier slaves known as Mamelukes, to protect their interests throughout the empire. One of these fighting nomads, Bayikbey, eventually gained enough power and influence to become a threat to the caliph. The caliph gave him Egypt, but Bayikbey preferred to remain in Turkey, where the caliph eventually had him killed. Bayikbey's stepson Ibn Tulun, or 'son of Tulun', was sent to Egypt as governor in his place.

Ibn Tulun wanted Egypt to be an independent state, not an Abbasid province, so he fought and defeated the Abbasids and established a dynasty. He erected one of the largest mosques in the Middle East: the Mosque of Ibn Tulun was large enough to accommodate all his cavalry – both horses and men.

After Ibn Tulun's death, Egypt was unable to keep its independence. Various leaders and invaders followed, including the Abbasids, Byzantines, Ikhshids and, finally, the Fatimids. The Fatimids came from a kingdom of rulers in north-west Africa who claimed descent from Mohammed's daughter, Fatima, and Ali. They quickly established a dynasty of independent caliphs which lasted for just over 200 years (968-1169).

Egypt flourished under the first Fatimid rulers. At the behest of the mysterious caliph Al Móizz, a Greek named Gohar spent four years building the new city of Cairo. Desmond Stewart writes in his book *Great Cairo: Mother of the World* that Al Móizz:

. . . rule[d] mysteriously, as befitted an imam, from behind the curtain of awe. For Fatimid power was based on an idea: the sense that God allows an aspect of himself to be incarnate in an infallible ruler.

Gohar's construction work in Cairo befitted an imam imbued with godliness, and his greatest work was the Al Azhar Mosque. This immense structure, which resembles a fortress, became one of the world's greatest centres of Islamic studies. Today it continues to function as both a mosque and a major university. After Al Móizz's death, Egypt continued to flourish under his son, Al Aziz, but the good times ended with the rule of Al Aziz's crazy son, Al Hakim (996-1021).

At first, Al Hakim ruled Egypt as an absolute monarch with beneficence and grace. A magnificent mosque was built at the northern wall of Cairo between the gates of Bab al Futuh and Bab al Nasr. Al Hakim began to share his rule with a council of advisers and also attempted to understand the problems of Cairenes by touring the city on a mule and talking to his people. All of this paled into insignificance, however, when the young Al Hakim began ruling like a lunatic.

At the age of 15 he murdered his tutor. He then decided he didn't like his advisers any more so he murdered them too. He loved the night and took to riding after dark on Moon, his pet mule, so it became illegal and punishable by death to work during the day and sleep at night. Al Hakim also hated merchants who cheated their customers, so if he found one during his nightly mule rides he would have his slave Masoud sodomise the merchant. Sometimes Al Hakim would help by standing on the merchant's head.

Al Hakim hated women as well. He tried to impose a 24 hour curfew on them, and when that didn't work he imposed a ban on the manufacture of women's shoes. He figured that without shoes women would not want to plod through the manure and open sewers on the streets.

This lunacy continued until one night in 1021, when Al Hakim mounted Moon and rode off into the Moqattam Hills near Cairo. The mule was found but Al Hakim had disappeared, never to be heard from again. He left a group of disciples who maintained the mystical belief that Al Hakim was a divine incarnation. This group became the Druse. Although they still exist in Lebanon, Syria, Jordan and Israel, very little is known of their beliefs

and practices, as it is blasphemous for a Druse to reveal his people's secrets to outsiders.

Over the next 150 years several Fatimid caliphs ruled Egypt. Apart from a relatively brief spate of plague and famine, and a few power squabbles, battles and wars, Egypt was prosperous. Food was plentiful in the souks, or markets, and apartment buildings with as many as 10 floors (sometimes more) rose in Cairo. This prosperity, however, could not be maintained in those parts of the empire outside Egypt.

Around this time the Christians of Western Europe began a crusade to spread Christianity and rescue the Holy City of Jerusalem from the Muslims.

The Crusaders seized Jerusalem from the Fatimids in 1099. Tripoli, in Lebanon, fell in 1109 and so did several other parts of the Fatimid Empire. By 1153 all of Palestine was under Christian control, and rather than suffer a similar fate the weakened Fatimid state decided to cooperate with the Crusaders. The Muslim Seljuk dynasty of Syria was not happy about this, as the balance of power was upset – a balance which had begun to tip increasingly in their favour. So the Seljuks sent in an army led by a Kurdish warrior named Shirkoh and his nephew Salah al Din (known to the West as Saladin).

Salah al Din eventually gained control of Egypt and founded his own dynasty, the Ayyubids, in 1171. The Crusaders attacked and partly burned Cairo in 1176, so Salah al Din immediately began fortifying the city. He built part of the city walls and the Citadel; the latter became a small town of shops, stables and workshops. His reign marked the heyday of medieval Egypt and in 1187 he drove the Crusaders from Jerusalem.

Above all, Salah al Din sought power. He purchased Mamelukes (whose name comes from an Arabic word for 'owned' or 'held') to assist him. Most Mamelukes were Turkish mercenaries, sold by their parents when they were boys to be trained solely to fight for the sultan. In his book *Travels through Syria & Egypt in the Years 1783, 1784 & 1785*, M Volney describes the Mamelukes as follows:

Strangers among themselves. . .Without parents. . .the past has done nothing for them; they do nothing for the future. Ignorant and superstitious by upbringing, they become fierce through murders, mutinous through tumults, deceitful through intrigues, corrupt through every species of debauch.

After a certain period of servitude and military service, many Mamelukes were free to own land and raise families. Yes, despite their violent nature some did choose to settle down quietly. Other Mamelukes, however, began to seek positions of power and influence within the state. Their efforts brought about the demise of Shagarat al Durr, the last Ayyubid ruler and the first woman to reign over Egypt since Cleopatra, and ushered in more than 2½ centuries of Mameluke rule.

Two dynasties of Mamelukes ruled Egypt. The Bahri Mamelukes were the first: in their 132 years of rule there were more than 25 sultans. Murder, intrigue and war were rife. In between fighting and conspiring, however, the Mamelukes developed a distinctive style of architecture and several mosques were built, including those of Sultan Hassan, El Zahir and Qalaun.

The sultans of the next dynasty were equally given to construction. This dynasty began when a Circassian slave named Barquq seized power from the Bahri ruler, a six year old Mameluke (not difficult!). More than 21 Circassian Mamelukes became sultan before Egypt fell to the Turks in 1517.

Turkish Rule (1517-1882)

Since most of the Mamelukes were either of Turkish descent or from Turkey and the surrounding areas, rule over Egypt by the Ottoman sultans of Constantinople was not difficult. In fact, their rule basically consisted of collecting taxes from Egypt, while the rest of the governing business was left to the Mamelukes. This continued until Napoleon invaded Egypt in 1798.

Napoleon and his army routed the Mameluke army, supposedly as a show of support for the Ottoman sultan. In reality, Napoleon wanted eventually to strike a blow at British trade in the Indian Ocean by gaining control of the land and sea routes to India. He was also keen to 'civilise' Egypt.

Napoleon established a French-style government, revamped the tax system and implemented public works projects – canals were cleared, streets were cleaned of garbage and temporary bridges spanned the Nile. Through his Institut d'Egypte he put a variety of French intellectuals to work on a history of ancient Egypt and a record of the ancient monuments. The French were also responsible for the planting of new crops, establishing a new system of weights and measures, and reorganising the hospitals. However, as Alan Moorehead writes in his book *The Blue Nile*:

Everything these new conquerors proposed was a strain; it was a strain *not* to throw rubbish in the streets, *not* to bribe witnesses and officials, and it was upsetting to be obliged to undergo medical treatment where prayers had always served in the past. [The Egyptians] had been getting on very well, they felt, as they were before. They had no need for new canals, new weights and measures, and new schools. . . They did not believe Bonaparte's protestations of his respect for Muhammad, nor were they much impressed by his dressings-up in turban and caftan. . .

Napoleon's Egyptian adventure seemed doomed from the beginning. Less than a month after he arrived, the British navy, under Admiral Nelson, appeared off the coast of Alexandria. Nelson quickly destroyed the French fleet and cut off Napoleon's forces from France. A year later the British sent an army of 15,000 Turkish soldiers to expel the French from

Egypt. The resulting battle at Abu Qir was a victory for the French; 5000 Turks were killed. Nevertheless, the British returned in 1801 and compelled the French to leave.

Although brief, the French occupation significantly weakened Egyptian political stability. After a period of internal strife, the headstrong Mohammed Ali became viceroy. A lieutenant in the Albanian contingent of the Ottoman army, he rose to power after the Albanian soldiers mutinied against their Turkish rulers. With Mameluke help, he temporarily expelled the British from Egypt. The Mameluke leaders, however, also posed a threat to Mohammed Ali, so he invited them to a sumptuous banquet and then had them massacred on their way home. A charming host!

Mohammed was power-hungry. He sent his troops on successful forays into the Sudan, Greece, Syria and Arabia, and by 1839 he controlled most of the Ottoman Empire. However, the British intervened again and forced him into sharing power with the sultan in Istanbul. Mohammed died in 1848 and was succeeded by his grandson Abbas, who was in turn succeeded by his son Said.

Said began implementing many government reforms and projects, foremost of which was the establishment of the railway system and the digging of the Suez Canal.

Pasha Ismail succeeded Said, and followed in his path by establishing factories, a telegraph and postal system, canals and bridges. The fledgeling cotton industry of Egypt prospered as the American Civil War disrupted cotton production in America's southern states. Ismail opened the Suez Canal in 1869 and achieved political independence for Egypt in 1873. With independence, Ismail confidently spent more state money than he had. The national debt became so great that he was forced to abdicate in 1879.

British Occupation (1882-1952)

The debt and abdication brought greater British control over Egyptian affairs. With pressure from the British, Ismail's son Tawfiq reorganised Egypt's finances, and British and French controllers installed themselves in the government.

With the outbreak of WW I the Egyptian government threw in its lot with the Allies. When Turkey entered the war, and made an abortive attack on the Suez Canal, the British Foreign Office placed Egypt 'under the protection of His Majesty', effectively terminating the suzerainty of Turkey over Egypt. The khedive, Abbas Hilmi, was deposed for his Turkish sympathies, Prince Hussein Kamil became sultan and martial law was proclaimed throughout the country.

During this time, several groups in Egypt, in particular the Ulama, or Muslim elite, and Egyptian civil servants, military officers and landowners, were disturbed by the increase in foreign influence, especially within the Egyptian government and civil service. A movement to expel Europeans from these areas evolved from a coalition of opposition groups, but the plan backfired and the British remained in such positions until 1952.

The British did, however, eventually allow the formation of a nationalist political party, called the Wafd, and a monarchist party. The first elections were held in 1922, independence was granted,

Allied soldiers – WW I

and King Fuad 1 was elected to head a constitutional monarchy. For the next 30 years the British, monarchists and Wafdists jockeyed for power and influence. Egypt was left in chaos following WW II and defeat in Israel's 1948 War of Independence. By 1952 only a group of dissident military officers had the wherewithal to take over the government.

Post-Revolution Egypt (1952-1981)

The Free Officers, led by Colonel Gamal Abdel Nasser, overthrew King Farouk, Fuad's son, in a bloodless coup. The coup was quickly dubbed the Revolution of 1952. The first independent Arab Republic of Egypt was formed and Nasser, as head of state, wasted no time in getting embroiled in international politics. He became one of the architects of the nonaligned movement, an association of countries which sought closer relations with the USSR and the People's Republic of China and more distant relations with the West. Through his role in the movement Nasser criticised the West; this cost him Western assistance in building the Aswan High Dam, so he turned to the Soviets instead. In 1956, Nasser nationalised the Suez Canal Company. The British, French and Israelis promptly invaded. The United Nations successfully urged the invaders to leave and installed a UN peacekeeping force to guarantee safe passage through the canal. Nasser became a hero, especially in the Arab world.

The Suez Crisis of 1956 made Nasser head of a pan-Arab nationalist movement which emphasised Arab unity. Unsuccessful attempts were made to unite Egypt, Syria and Yemen in a United Arab Republic. As Egypt's economy worsened, under Nasser's 'Arab socialist' policies of nationalisation, he began diverting attention from the internal problems by emphasising Arab unity and making Israel a scapegoat. He asked the UN force to leave the Sinai and then closed the Straits of Tiran, Israel's only outlet to the Indian Ocean. On 5 June 1967 Israel attacked, and in just six days destroyed the Egyptian air force, captured the Sinai and closed the Suez Canal. Despite this devastating defeat, the Egyptian people insisted that Nasser remain in power, which he did until his death in 1970. Arabs continue to revere him, and his photograph can still be found in many homes and shops.

Anwar el Sadat succeeded Nasser and attempted to repair Egypt's economy by becoming friendlier with the West, particularly the USA, at the expense of relations with the Soviets. Sadat also realised that to truly revitalise Egypt's economy he would have to deal with Israel – but first he needed bargaining power, a basis for negotiations. So, on 6 October 1973, the Jewish holiday of Yom Kippur, he launched a surprise attack across the Suez Canal. Although Egypt actually lost the war, Sadat's negotiating strategy succeeded.

On 19 November 1977, Sadat travelled to Jerusalem to begin making peace with Israel, and a peace treaty based on the

Camp David Agreement was eventually signed in 1979. Most of the Sinai was returned to Egyptian control by 1982 and relations between Egypt and Israel were normalised. Egypt was immediately ostracised by the rest of the Arab world and most socialist and developing countries. But for most Egyptians the treaty promised future peace and prosperity. However, radical groups of fundamentalist Muslims were opposed to the price of peace: normalisation of relations with Israel and alignment with the West. A member of one such group assassinated Sadat during a military parade on 6 October 1981.

Egypt Today

Hosni Mubarak, Sadat's vice president since 1974, was sworn in as president and has had his hands full of problems ever since. The prosperity promised by the treaty has been difficult to obtain, partly because of a vicious circle of demographic and economic problems that has grown since political independence in 1952.

During his presidency, from 1952 to 1970, Nasser sought economic independence for Egypt, which meant less dependence on the Western import of Egypt's agricultural products. He was a visionary, who imagined Egypt as a proud, powerful nation with jobs and a share of the economic pie for all citizens. Translated, this meant the industrialisation of Egypt through immense, state-run, somewhat paternalistic enterprises.

Nasser wanted a better life for Egyptians. He thought that he could accomplish this by 'catching up' with the industrialised world and making Egypt self-sufficient. Unfortunately, this was pursued at the expense of Egypt's strongest sector and main source of employment – agriculture. Capital resources were increasingly diverted to state-run industries, which were generally fledgeling enterprises, overly bureaucratic and mismanaged and with an excess of employees.

Mismanagement and bureaucratisation within these enterprises and related government ministries made many of the businesses unprofitable and inefficient. Since they were government-run, the government had to foot the bill rather than risk dismantling the business and causing many people to lose their jobs. Consequently, a huge system of subsidies that also extended (and extends today) to certain commodities and foodstuffs, such as bread, was spawned. The stage was set for the vicious circle of problems that President Mubarak and his government must deal with today.

The circle goes something like this: as the population increases by one million every nine months, more new jobs, schools and land are needed. Only 4% of Egypt is arable land – along the Nile and in the delta. This is being farmed to capacity with almost no room to accommodate population increases. Desert and oasis regions, such as the Western Oases and cultivated desert land between Cairo and Alexandria, offer some hope, but only on a relatively limited scale. Imports have soared in order to both feed and educate the growing population and to expand the economy, but this has also helped spawn an inflation rate of at least 30% a year. The foreign debt is now more than US$43 billion, which greatly increases whenever there's the slightest increase in interest rates.

To make its payments to creditors – obviously a necessary condition for continued foreign aid – and to continue purchasing imports, Egypt needs hard currency (US$, DM, UK£, etc). This comes from selling Egypt's exports (mainly oil), attracting foreign tourists to Egypt, Suez Canal revenues and – Catch 22! – foreign aid in the form of loans and grants (US aid totals more than US$2 billion annually). Hard currency also comes from money sent home by the hundreds of thousands of Egyptians who are working in other countries. Egypt's economy has become dependent on these rather unreliable sources of hard currency for its very survival.

President Hosni Mubarak

These pillars of Egypt's economy weaken whenever, among other things, the price of oil drops, a terrorist incident scares away tourists, debt and interest payments are delayed or import prices increase.

There have been substantial increases in manufactured exports and the amount of desert land made arable, particularly around the Western Oases. However, the government's efforts to encourage people from the crowded Nile Valley to resettle in the oases haven't been completely successful.

As I discovered on a crowded bus between the oases of Dakhla and Kharga while researching this edition, parents in the oases still send their teenage sons to work in Cairo to earn money for the family. I was surrounded by boys who were all headed to Cairo to work at *fuul* and *ta'amiyya* (felafel) stands. One boy, who claimed to be 14, but who had the height and voice of someone much younger, told me that he had already been to Cairo 10 times for work. I asked him about school. He shrugged and smiled, but didn't have an answer.

In a way, his smile was symbolic of an unflappable Egyptian spirit that is somewhat difficult, perhaps, for a foreigner to grasp. For Egyptians, living can be difficult, but life is like the Nile – simple and straightforward. You can put obstacles such as dams in its path or even try to divert it, yet it somehow keeps right on flowing. And life goes on in Egypt, even if you are heading off to dish out fuul and ta'amiyya in Cairo.

GEOGRAPHY

Egypt is almost square in shape. The distance from north to south is 1030 km (640 miles); from east to west it's 965 km (600 miles). For most Egyptians the Nile Valley is Egypt. To the east of the valley is the Eastern (Arabian) Desert – a barren plateau bounded on its eastern edge by a high ridge of mountains. To the west is the Western (Libyan) Desert – a plateau punctuated by huge clumps of bizarre geological formations and luxuriant oases.

North of Cairo, the Nile splits into several tributaries, the main two being the Rosetta and the Damietta branches. The valley becomes a delta, a wide green fan of fertile countryside, and the tributaries eventually flow into the Mediterranean.

Along the northern coast to the west of Alexandria there are hundreds of km of brilliant white-sand beaches. Some have been, or are being, developed as resorts, but a good deal of this coast is still fairly isolated. However, if you're a sun-worshipper in search of the perfect beach, be careful about wandering off the beaten track. The coast from El Alamein to the Libyan border was the scene of the WW II standoff between field marshals Rommel and Montgomery. Land mines were laid throughout this area and many have still not been recovered.

To the east, across the Suez Canal, is another former battlefield – the Sinai. Terrain here varies from Mt Sinai in the south to desert coastal plains and lagoons in the north. The jagged mountains and wadies (watercourses) around Mt Sinai appear to change shape and colour as the sun passes overhead, and a climb to the top offers a commanding view of this spectacle. Moses certainly chose the right mountain to climb.

CLIMATE

Egypt's climate is easy to summarise. Most of the year, except for the winter months of December, January and February, it is hot and dry. Temperatures increase as you travel south from Alexandria. Alexandria receives the most rain – approximately 19 cm a year – while far to the south in Aswan any rain at all is rare.

Summer temperatures range from a scorching 50°C (122°F) in Aswan to 31°C (87°F) on the Mediterranean coast. At night in winter the temperatures sometimes plummet to as low as 8°C, even in the south.

Be prepared for the temperature extremes. Sweaters are useful in the evenings throughout the country, all year around, though evenings will tend to be warmer the farther south you go. It can be a bit cool (some would say cold) all day in winter, especially in Cairo and Alexandria, and you will definitely need warm clothing at night.

The Sinai has unique weather. The desert is typically hot during the day and cold at night, but the mountains can be freezing, even during the day. See the Sinai chapter for further information.

POPULATION & PEOPLE

In 1981, Egypt's population was estimated at 41 million. Medical care has improved, birth rates have increased, mortality rates have declined and consequently the population has increased almost fivefold since 1907. Today, it is estimated that there are more than 51 million people in Egypt, nearly 25% of whom live in Cairo (some recent estimates put this figure closer to 40%). The population is now increasing at a rate of one million every eight to nine months. One result is that 50% of the population is now under 18 years. The government hasn't been able to construct schools and train teachers quickly enough to keep up with the population growth, so an increasing segment of the population – about 50% – is functionally illiterate. Those who are literate have usually received inferior education because classes are often too large for individual attention.

Until this past decade Egypt had the agricultural resources to support its burgeoning population; however, with a growth rate of almost 2.7%, Egypt can no longer feed itself. The population is too large for the mere 4% of the country which is cultivable. In order to feed the people, almost all of Egypt's foreign exchange reserves are now spent on food imports, especially cereals. Normally these reserves would be used for long-term investments – projects such as new industrial plants and improved transportation – but capital works have taken a back seat to the basic task of providing enough food. If the money were not spent on food imports the potential for civil strife and political upheaval would be very great.

Potential religious conflict is another problem resulting from Egypt's economic troubles. As the economy worsens, more Egyptians are beginning to look to Islamic fundamentalism for answers to the country's woes. The fellahin, the peasant farmers who form Egypt's largest economic group, have been most affected by the economic climate. A theocratic state similar to Iran seems highly unlikely, because most of Egypt's Muslim leaders appear to be preaching moderation and dialogue rather than radicalism. However, if the economy continues to decline, Egyptians may want more than talk and promises.

The Copts, who comprise only about 13% of the total population, are understandably threatened by the rise in fundamentalism, because any additional Islamicisation in Egypt would make life even more difficult for Egypt's Christians. There are ongoing attempts by the government to defuse potential conflict between Copts and Muslims (see the Religion section in this chapter).

Egypt's economic problems have also begun to affect the Bedouins, the country's most isolated population group. Nearly 500,000 Bedouins survive in the harshest, most desolate parts of the Western and Eastern Deserts and the Sinai. The Western Desert oases have long been slated for massive agricultural development and resettlement to ease urban overcrowding. There are also plans to increase tourism in this region. Tourism is also important to the Sinai, particularly the south-eastern coast, which is rapidly becoming a stretch of tourist resorts. With the influx of outsiders into their previously isolated domains, the Bedouins are gradually becoming more settled and less self-sufficient.

CULTURE

Egyptians are fond of telling jokes about the government, about other Arabs and, most of all, about themselves. Every other Egyptian you meet seems to be a walking encyclopedia of jokes. One of the most common quips about themselves concerns IBM's control of Egypt.

An Egyptian taxi driver once said to me: 'Hey, you know, Egypt controlled by IBM. You know, big company, IBM.'

'What do you mean?' I asked, since in all my time in Egypt I had seen only one IBM electric typewriter.

"'I' for *insha-allah*; 'B' for *bukra*; 'M' for *malaysh*,' he chortled, and quickly swerved to the left to avoid clipping a donkey cart full of garbage. A banana peel slid across the hood. The driver knew he was right.

Although these three words can't completely sum up life in Egypt, they tell a lot about Egyptians: insha-allah means 'if God wills it'; bukra means 'tomorrow'; and malaysh means 'never mind', 'it doesn't matter'. You will probably hear them used like this:

You are walking down Sharia Talaat Harb, one of Cairo's main streets. An Egyptian with an ear-to-ear smile and an outstanding American accent begins walking and talking next to you. You are in an adventurous mood.

Egyptian: Hello, hello. Welcome to Egypt. Change money, change money?
Traveller: No.
Egyptian: You have girlfriend? Yes? Good, then come to my bazaar and perfume shop. Many things there.
Traveller: OK, but I don't have any money. I just want to look.
Egyptian: Fine. No problem. Here is bazaar.

By now you know that the guy's name is Mohammed (every other Egyptian seems to be named Mohammed). Mohammed sits you down on a couple of big velvet cushions and takes a vial of purple liquid from a glass case.

Egyptian: You want perfume for girlfriend, yes? (Mohammed's smile seems even bigger now.)
Traveller: No, actually I need a money pouch. I was on the bus to the pyramids yesterday and mine was taken. Can you get me another?
Egyptian: Yes, yes. I get money pouch. Bukra, bukra. I get money pouch. Tomorrow. Now, perfume for your girlfriend.

'Yes' is a favourite response. Mohammed doesn't really know if he can get the pouch but, like many Egyptians, he won't say 'no' because it looks bad to say 'no'. This can cause a lot of problems, especially when you ask for directions. Back to Mohammed and the perfume.

Before you know it, he is dabbing purple perfume on your arm: 'Smell, smell; smell the essences of jasmine.' Clutching the open vial, Mohammed pushes it up to your nose. Purple perfume splashes on your shirt.

Traveller: (Jumping to his feet.) Hey, you got the stuff all over my shirt.
Egyptian: (As if nothing has happened.) Ach, malaysh. Don't worry. Malaysh.
Traveller: (Fuming.) What do you mean, don't worry? Will this stuff come out?
Egyptian: (Looking to the ceiling with an open

palm as if expecting rain.) Insha-allah, insha-allah. It is how Allah wants it. Here, have some mint tea.

It's hot, smoggy and dusty outside, but the sweet mint tea cools your temper and temperature. And, even though you smell like a field of jasmine, you're again ready for Egypt and the Egyptians.

This nonchalance, fatalism, apathy – call it what you wish – comes from the Nile. Well, not exactly. Like the Nile, life in Egypt has flowed with relatively few interruptions. Life is simpler here, living is not. The main events of life – birth, marriage and death – and the main concerns of daily life – family, friends and food – are most important. The future is not important because it has not been and will not be much different from the past or present. Life goes on in Egypt irrespective of lost money pouches, spilled perfume or a thousand and one other mishaps and inefficiencies which you might encounter. However, this is all beginning to change.

Western technology and life styles have come to Egypt. The fellahin in the countryside, who make up the majority of Egypt's population, have begun using tractors and diesel-powered irrigation pumps in place of ploughs and ancient ox-driven water wheels. Despite these innovations, however, Egypt can no longer feed itself and great quantities of food must be imported. Along with the food and agricultural machines, other imports have arrived which have significantly affected Egyptian life.

TV programmes from the West, particularly the USA, have had an incredible impact. At the flick of a switch, a family of fellahin is transported from a mud-brick house in an Upper Egypt village to places like the streets of San Francisco or the living rooms of the Ewing family in Dallas. A life style of previously unimaginable luxury suddenly comes alive on a little screen in front of them and the seed of possibility, the chance of living a better life, is planted.

The impact has at least two consequences. First, young people have begun to realise that life doesn't have to be limited to the village and the farm. They can go to the city, earn more money, and live better lives; hence the second major consequence.

Egyptian cities like Cairo, Alexandria and Aswan are all experiencing population explosions. Population growth is skyrocketing because people are generally healthier and living longer. But the increase is straining public services such as housing construction, transportation, water supplies and sewerage. Industrial growth can't keep up, and unemployment and underemployment are becoming more common.

TV and tractors aren't the only Western imports which have affected Egyptian society. Egypt is gradually being 'Coca-Cola-ised' by the trappings of Western life. Things such as Coca-Cola, colour TVs, VCRs and blue jeans are quite popular, not only for what they are, but, more importantly, for what they symbolise. For the average Egyptian these things that can be bought 'over the counter' represent a slice of the better life – life at the Ewing's ranch or even life among the relatively few upper-crust Egyptians. The average person will either be motivated to try and go beyond these small things to a bigger and better life or become frustrated in the attempt. The ranks of both frustrated *and* motivated people are growing.

Egypt's Coptic Christians, estimated at around 13% of the population, seem to be one of the most motivated groups in the country. Perhaps this is because Coptic Christianity is more similar to Western religion and more amenable to change than Islam. For whatever reasons, Coptic Christians seem to have welcomed the 'Coca-Cola-isation' of Egypt and have become an economically powerful minority.

Some Egyptian Muslims have also welcomed the country's modernisation, but the vast majority, the Muslim fellahin, are distressed by the possibility of sudden changes to a way of life which has remained virtually unchanged for so many centuries. A few Muslim fundamentalist groups feel that traditional Egypt is threatened by the 'Coca-Cola and blue jeans revolution'. As the economy worsens, they argue that the answers to Egypt's problems do not lie outside, in the import of Western technology and life styles, but inside, in a return to traditional Islam and culture. The fundamentalists, however, are perhaps overestimating the impact of the West on life in Egypt. Like the Nile, life flows practically unchanged here and many things, such as music and dance, have changed very little over the centuries.

ARTS
Music
It's 5 pm. Radios throughout Egypt are turned up. A female voice is heard. At first it is soft and quiet, like a mother whispering and humming a bedtime story; then come the flutes, a gentle wailing which induces you to breathe and gyrate in time with the music, like a mesmerised snake. The rest of the orchestra picks up – the violins, drums, organs, and traditional wind and string instruments. You inhale deeply as the drums beat faster and the violins resound in powerful unison. The voice returns with a clear booming resonance. The voice of Om Kolthum – the 'Mother of Egypt' – has got you by the ears.

Om Kolthum died in 1975 but her music lives on. For Western ears it epitomises and simplifies the mystery and complexity of Arabic music. As you walk down a street in Cairo or any other Egyptian city, the music lends a certain mystique to the street life. It's then, when it begins resounding in your ears, that you really know you haven't accidentally landed in a Hollywood movie studio. You have, in a sense, landed back in time.

Dance

Dance in Egypt is equally alluring. However, unlike with music, it is a bit more difficult to see the real thing. Although belly-dancing shows can be seen in most of Cairo's major hotels, that is when you *will* think you have landed on that Hollywood set. Many of the dancers will be European or American, because it is not considered proper for an Arab woman to dance in public. Still, even though the performances are usually full of Hollywood glitter and hype, the dancing is often quite authentic. A talented dancer, even if she is American, will capture your eyes with her alluring gyrations and flowing silk scarves.

Dancing is generally considered promiscuous by Egyptians. Nevertheless, there are a few Egyptian dance troupes of both men and women who perform in Cairo, Luxor and Aswan during the winter and in Alexandria during the summer. Egyptians also dance at weddings, private parties and other family gatherings. Get yourself invited to an Egyptian wedding (which is not difficult) and you will experience Egypt and Egyptians at their best.

RELIGION
Islam

Thousands of thin towering minarets, some as high as 80 metres, are some of the first things people notice in Egypt. Five times a day, the mosque officials known as muezzins bellow out the call to prayer through speakers on top of the minarets. Faithful Muslims follow the call and fill the mosques below for several minutes of elaborate prayers. With these prayers an Egyptian reaffirms his or her faith in Islam, the predominant religion of Egypt.

Islam shares its roots with two of the world's other major religions - Judaism and Christianity. Adam, Abraham (Ibrahim), Noah, Moses and Jesus are all accepted as Muslim prophets, although Jesus is not recognised as the son of God. Muslim teachings correspond closely to the Torah, the Old Testament and the Gospels, but the essence of Islam is the Qur'an (Koran) and the Prophet Mohammed.

Islam means 'submission' - submission to Allah (God). Mohammed was the last and truest prophet to deliver this and other messages from Allah to the people. He was born in 570 AD in Mecca (now in Saudi Arabia) and had his first revelation from Allah in 610. He began to preach against the idolatry that was rampant in the region, particularly in Mecca, and proved to be a powerful and persuasive speaker. He quickly gained a devoted following.

The Muslim faith was more than just a religion: it also called on its followers to spread the word - by the sword if necessary. Within two decades of the Prophet's death, most of Arabia had converted to Islam, and in succeeding centuries it spread over three continents. Mecca became Islam's holiest city because it was there that Abraham built the first shrine to Allah. The building, known as the Kabah, is still the holiest pilgrim shrine in Islam; it contains the black stone given to Abraham by the Angel Gabriel.

More than 10 years after Mohammed's death in 632 AD, his messages and revelations were compiled into the Muslim holy book, the Qur'an. No changes to that text have been permitted since 651 AD.

According to the Qur'an, faithful Muslims must carry out five acts, known

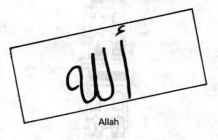

Allah

formally as the Five Pillars of Faith. They must:

Publicly declare that 'there is no God but Allah and Mohammed is his Prophet'.

Pray five times a day: at sunrise, 12 noon, mid-afternoon, sunset, and night.

Give *zakah*, or alms, for the propagation of Islam and for help to the needy.

Fast during the day for the month of Ramadan.

Make the *haj*, or pilgrimage to Mecca.

The first pillar is accomplished through prayer, which is the second pillar. Since you will probably see quite a lot of praying during your travels in Egypt and the Sudan, here is a brief description of what happens:

When a Muslim enters a mosque he takes off his shoes and carries them, sole to sole, in his left hand. It is considered offensive to wear shoes in the house of God. He enters with his right foot

first and then washes himself in a certain way before proceeding to pray.

Prayers are performed in one to two minute cycles called *rek'ah*. Each worshipper faces the mihrab, the niche which indicates the direction of Mecca. In fact, the entire mosque is built so that it points towards Mecca. The first rek'ah goes something like this:

The worshipper says: *Bism-allah wisallahtu wisalaamu rasulallah allahum ergferrli zenubi waftahli abwaba rahmatik.*

Then he prays silently, and bows his head a number of times. This is followed by certain actions and prayers said aloud:

  Alla-hu akbar, which means 'Allah is great'.

  The first chapter of the Qur'an.

  Verses from another chapter.

  Alla-hu akbar.

Then he bows, kneels and places his palms on the ground, followed by his nose and forehead. The foreheads of the most faithful Muslims have a slight but noticeable indentation created by this genuflection.

  'I extol the perfection of Allah the Great' (said three times).

The worshipper stands:

  Alla-hu akbar.

Back to the ground, saying the same thing as before.

That is one rek'ah, and a good Muslim performs several in a single prayer session. The rek'ah requires a lot of concentration. To create the right conditions for this, the interior of most mosques is simple and devoid of elaborate decorations.

Visiting Mosques Before traipsing through mosques there are a few rules you should be aware of. You cannot visit during prayer time, but any other time is fine. Nor can you visit all mosques; only those designated by the Ministry of Tourism as 'tourist sites'. You'll know if you have stumbled into one of the nontouristic mosques because someone will probably tell you to leave.

You must dress modestly. For men that means no shorts; for women that means no shorts, tight pants, shirts that aren't done up, or anything else even remotely suggestive. Just use your common sense. Lastly, you must either take off your shoes or use the shoe coverings available for a few pt at most mosques.

Egyptian Coptic Christianity

Before the arrival of Islam, Christianity was the predominant religion in Egypt. St Mark, one of the 12 apostles of Jesus, began preaching Christianity in Egypt in 35 AD, although it didn't become the official religion of the country until the 4th century. The word 'Copt' is derived from the Greek word for Egyptian, which the Arabs transliterated and eventually shortened to Copt. The term 'Coptic Church' originally referred to the native Egyptian Christian Church, but by the 5th century a different meaning had evolved.

Egyptian Christians split from the orthodox church of the Eastern (or Byzantine) Empire, of which Egypt was then a part, after the main body of the Church described Christ as both human and divine. Dioscurus, the patriarch of Alexandria, refused to accept this description. He embraced the theory that Christ is totally absorbed by His divinity and that it is blasphemous to consider Him human. Since that time, Egyptian Christians have been referred to as Coptic Christians.

The Coptic Church is ruled by a patriarch, other members of a religious hierarchy, and an ecclesiastical council of laymen. The Coptic Church has a long history of monasticism and can justly claim that the first Christian monks, St Anthony and St Pachomius, were Copts. The Coptic language is still used in religious ceremonies, sometimes in conjunction with Arabic for the benefit of the congregation. It has its origins in a combination of Egyptian hieroglyphics and Ancient Greek. Today, the Coptic language is centred around the Greek alphabet with an additional seven characters taken from hieroglyphics.

The Copts comprise about 13% of Egypt's population. The precise number has been a subject of much controversy. The Muslims and the Copts have each done a census and come up with very different figures. Muslim extremists continuously harassed the Copts. In the late 1970s the government further Islamicised the legal system, a move which infuriated the Copts but pleased Muslim extremists. By 1981 relations between the two were very tense. A Coptic church in Cairo was bombed, and to avoid further conflict Sadat sent the Coptic pope, Shenuda III, into internal exile. He stayed at one of the monasteries of Wadi Natrun until Mubarak allowed him to return in early 1985.

In 1989, relations between the two groups seemed to be improving thanks, in part, to theatre presentations sponsored by the Ministry of Culture. In Asyut, traditionally a centre of strained Muslim-Coptic relations, Adel Iman, a nationally renowned comedian, and his theatre group were presenting comedy routines that poked fun at cultural conflict. However, the presence of significant numbers of police outside the theatre was a sign, perhaps, that it may take more than comedy to quell tension between the two groups.

Judaism

Until 1948 more than 80,000 Jews lived in Egypt. However, with the independence of Israel and subsequent wars between the two countries, many Jews had to leave. Today, there are fewer than 500 Jews, mostly elderly, scattered through Alexandria, Cairo and El Minya. The marble-pillared synagogues of Alexandria and Cairo are open to the public and are an interesting vestige of what must once have been a thriving community.

Pharaonic Religion

The religion of Pharaonic Egypt is difficult to describe because so much about it is still unknown. The stories behind the many gods and goddesses

Horus

Anubis

depicted in hieroglyphics tell more about how, rather than what, ancient Egyptians actually worshipped. But Egyptologists have been able to solve a few of the mysteries and, at the very least, it is known what most of the ancient deities symbolised.

The sun shines through cloudless skies during the day almost always in Egypt. Thus, it is no surprise that a sun-god became one of Egypt's most important deities. The sun-god was usually known as Ra; Aten was the name of the visible disc of the sun. Ra was the creator and ruler of other deified elements of nature. There was Nut, the sky-goddess, Shu, the god of air and Geb, the earth-god.

Nut was a particularly interesting goddess. She was always depicted (either as a woman or a cow) stretched across the ceilings of tombs, swallowing the sun and creating night. The next morning she would give birth to the sun.

Animals were also important to the ancient Egyptians. Several were considered sacred, especially the Apis bulls of

Memphis, the cats of Beni Hasan, the rams of Elephantine (part of ancient Aswan), and the crocodiles of Kom Ombo. Animals were also often associated with various gods and goddesses; eventually many deities were portrayed in a combined animal-human form.

The human aspects of the gods were often presented like ancient soap operas. Only a few of these 'soaps' have survived Egypt's long history. One of the most celebrated starred the godly heavyweights Osiris, Isis and Horus.

Osiris was the benevolent 'ruler' of Egypt. His brother Seth, the epitome of evil, talked him into testing the inside of a crate by lying in it. Once Osiris was in the crate, evil Seth promptly locked it and tossed it into the Nile. Isis, the sister and wife of Osiris, searched all over the world until she found the crate and smuggled it back to Egypt. Seth discovered the crate, cut Osiris into 14 pieces and distributed the bits throughout the country. Loyal Isis managed to find all the pieces, built temples dedicated to Osiris, and put him back together again. Isis and Osiris then begat Horus who slew Seth. End of story.

If you wish to learn more about religion in ancient Egypt, refer to the section on Books in the Facts for the Visitor chapter.

HOLIDAYS & FESTIVALS

Egypt's holidays and festivals are primarily Islamic or Coptic religious celebrations. The Islamic calendar moves up 11 Western calendar days each year, so, if you're calculating by a Western calendar, holiday dates will seem to change each year. The Islamic calendar has 12 lunar months, which are:

1st   Moharram
2nd   Safar
3rd   Rabei el Awal
4th   Rabei el Tani
5th   Gamada el Awal
6th   Gamada el Taniyya
7th   Ragab
8th   Shaaban
9th   Ramadan
10th Shawal
11th Zuu'l Qeda
12th Zuu'l Hagga

Islamic Holidays

The following is a list of the main Muslim holidays:

Ras al Sana
   New Year's Day; celebrated on 1 Moharram
Mulid al Nabi
   Birthday of the Prophet Mohammed; celebrated on 12 Rabei el Awal. The streets of Cairo are a feast of lights and food on this day.
Ramadan
   The ninth month of the Islamic calendar, Ramadan is considered the fourth of Islam's five fundamental pillars of faith. For the entire month, faithful Muslims fast from dawn to sunset in order to gain strength against evil spirits. No food and water are allowed until sunset. The *feeter*, or breaking of the fast, occurs the moment the sun has set. Try to attend a feeter at an Egyptian family's home. Everyone counts the minutes and seconds until it's time to eat, then chicken bones, scraps of bread and

pieces of vegetables fly as the family descends upon the feast dish. You need to be quick – a feast for 10 is consumed in less than 10 minutes.
Eed al Fitr
   The end of Ramadan fasting; the celebration lasts from 1 to 3 Shawal
Eed al Adhah
   The time for Muslims to fulfil the fifth pillar of Islam, the pilgrimage to Mecca. Every Muslim is supposed to make the haj at least once in his or her lifetime. This special period for making the haj lasts from 10 to 13 Zuu'l Hagga.

Ramadan It is more difficult to travel around Egypt during Ramadan than during the rest of the year. Almost everything, closes in the afternoon or has shorter daytime hours; this does not apply to businesses that cater mostly to foreign tourists, but some restaurants and hotels may be closed the entire month of Ramadan.

Transportation schedules, which are usually erratic even at the best of times, become even crazier and sometimes it is more difficult to buy reserved seats. *Never* travel during Eed al Fitr, which marks the end of Ramadan. All of Egypt is travelling at that time, so practically all buses and trains are dangerously crowded – especially on the last day of the *eed*, or feast, when everyone is returning home.

The starting date of Ramadan slips forward 10 to 12 days each year on the Western calendar. For the next few years Ramadan starts on: 17 March 1991; 5 March 1992; and 23 February 1993.

Coptic Christian Holidays

These are a mixture of religious and commemorative holidays.

Christmas
   7 January
Epiphany
   19 January
Annunciation
   23 March
Easter
   celebrated on different dates each year

Sham el Nessim (Sniffing the Breeze)
 A special Coptic holiday with Pharaonic origins. It falls on the first Monday after the Coptic Easter and is celebrated by all Egyptians, with family picnics and outings.

Other Holidays

The following are also public holidays:

New Year's Day
 1 January
Union Day
 28 February
Evacuation Day (the day the British left Egypt)
 18 June
Revolution Day
 23 July
National Day (a day of military parades and air displays)
 6 October
Suez National Day (commemoration of the Suez Crisis)
 23 October
Victory Day
 23 December

LANGUAGE

Arabic is the official language of Egypt. However, the Arabic spoken on the streets is different from the Arabic written in newspapers, spoken on the radio or recited in prayers at the mosque.

Egyptian street Arabic – colloquial Egyptian Arabic – is fun, but difficult to learn. Unlike most languages, there is no official written version of colloquial Arabic. In other words, the Arabic which you learn to speak, you won't be able to write using written Arabic. You will either have to devise your own system of transliteration or use someone else's. This is one of the main reasons so few non-Arabs and non-Muslims study Arabic. Nevertheless, if you take the time to learn even a few words and phrases, you will discover and experience much more while travelling through the country.

Pronunciation

Pronunciation of Arabic can be somewhat tongue-tying for someone unfamiliar with the intonation and combination of sounds. Pronounce the transliterated words and phrases slowly and clearly.

The following guide should help, but it isn't complete because the myriad rules governing pronunciation and vowel use are too extensive to be covered here.

Vowels In spoken Egyptian Arabic, there are five basic vowel sounds that can be distinguished:

a   as the 'a' in 'had'
e   as the 'e' in 'bet'
i   as the 'i' in 'hit'
o   as the 'o' in 'hot'
u   as the 'oo' in 'book'

The ‾ symbol over a vowel gives it a long sound. For example:

ā   as the 'a' in 'father'
ē   as the 'e' in 'ten', but lengthened
ī   as the 'e' in 'ear', only softer
ō   as the 'o' in 'for'
ū   as the 'oo' in 'food'

Combinations Certain combinations of vowels with vowels or consonants form other vowel sounds:

aw   as the 'ow' in 'how'
ay   as the 'i' in 'high'
ei   as the 'a' in 'cake'

Consonants Most of the consonants used in this section are the same as in English. However, a few of the consonant sounds must be explained in greater detail.

Three of the most common are the glottal stop ', the 'ayn' sound ", and the 'rayn' **gh**. These are some of the most difficult sounds in Arabic, especially for a non-native speaker, so don't be discouraged if you aren't being understood, just keep trying.

The glottal stop is the sound you hear between the vowels in the expression 'oh oh!'. It is actually a closing of the glottis at the back of the throat so that the passage of air is momentarily halted. It can occur anywhere in the word – at the beginning, middle or end.

The ", or 'ayn', and the **gh**, or 'rayn', are two of the most difficult sounds in Arabic. Both can be produced by tightening your throat and sort of growling, but the **gh** requires a slight 'r' sound at the beginning. When the " occurs before a vowel, the vowel is 'growled' from the back of the throat. If it is before a consonant or at the end of a word, it sounds like a glottal stop. The best way to learn these sounds is to watch a native speaker pronounce their written equivalents.

Other common consonant sounds include the following:

g	as the 'g' in 'gain' or 'grab' (Egyptian Arabic is the only Arabic dialect with this sound)
H	a strongly whispered 'h', almost like a sigh of relief
q	a strong guttural 'k' sound, almost like a glottal stop
kh	a slightly gurgling sound, like the 'ch' in Scottish 'loch'
r	a rolled 'r', as in the Spanish 'para'
s	pronounced as in English 'sit', never as in 'wisdom'
sh	as the 'sh' in 'shelf'
ẑ	as the 's' in pleasure; rarely used in Egyptian Arabic

Double Consonants In Arabic, double consonants are both pronounced. For example the word *istanna*, which means 'wait', is pronounced 'istan-na'.

Greetings & Civilities

Arabic is more formal than English, especially with greetings; thus even the simplest greetings, such as 'hello', vary according to when and how they are used. In addition, each greeting requires a certain response that varies according to whether it is being said to a male, female or group of people.

Hello. (literally 'peace upon you')
salām "alēkum
And hello to you. ('and peace upon you')
wa "alēkum es salām

Hello/How do you do?/Welcome/Pleased to meet you.
ahlan wa sahlan
Hello. (in response)
ahlan bīk　(to male)
ahlan bīkī　(to female)
ahlan bīkum　(to group)

Greetings. (used as both 'hello' and 'goodbye', either alone or with *ahlan wa sahlan*)
sa"īda

Pleased to meet you. (formal, used when first meeting)
tasharrafna
Nice meeting you. (less formal, said as you are leaving to someone whom you have met for the first time)
forsa sa"īda
How are you? (this is unique to the Egyptian dialect)
izzayyak?　(to m)
izzayyik?　(to f)
izzayyukum?　(to grp)

Fine. (literally 'fine, thanks be to God')
kwayyis ilHamdu lillah　(said by m)
kwaysa...　(f)
kwaysīn...　(grp)
On their own, *kwayyis*, *kwaysa* and *kwaysīn* literally mean 'good' or 'fine', but they are rarely heard alone in response to 'how are you?'

Good morning.
sabāH el khēr
Good morning. (in response)
sabāH el nūr
Good evening.
misa' el khēr
Good evening. (in response, also 'good afternoon' in the late afternoon)
misa' el nūr

Good night.
tisbaH "ala khēr (to m)
tisbaHī "ala khēr (to f)
tisbaHu "ala khēr (to grp)

Good night. (in response)
wenta bikhēr (to m)
wentī bikhēr (to f)
wentū bikhēr (to grp)

Good bye. (literally 'go with peace')
ma"as salāma

Excuse me.
"an iznak, esmaHlī (to m)
"an iznik, esmaHīlī (to f)
"an iznukum, esmaHūlī (to grp)

Thank you.
shukran

Thank you very much.
shukran gazīlan

You are welcome.
"afwan, el "affu

No thank you.
la' shukran

There are three ways to say please in Egyptian Arabic, each of which is used somewhat differently:

When asking for something in a shop, for example, say:
min fadlak (to m)
min fadlik (to f)
min fadlukum (to grp)

Under similar, but more formal circumstances, say:
law samaHt (to m)
law samaHtī (to f)
law samaHtu (to grp)

When offering something to someone, for example a chair or bus seat, say:
itfaddel (to m)
itfaddelī (to f)
itfaddelū (to grp)

Small Talk

My name is...
ismī...

What is your name?
ismak ēh? (to m)
ismīk ēh? (to f)

I understand.
ana fāhem

I do not understand.
ana mish fāhem

Do you speak English?
enta bititkallim inglīzī? (to m)
entī bititkallimī inglīzī? (to f)

Yes.
aywa (heard only in the Egyptian dialect)
na"am (more formal)

No.
la'

One of the most useful words to know is *imshī*, which means 'go away'. Use this at the pyramids or at other tourist sites when you are being besieged by children. Do not use it on grown-ups; instead, just say 'no thank you' (*la' shukran*).

Accommodation

Where is the hotel...?
fein el fonduk...?

Can you show me the way to the hotel...?
mumkin tewarrīnī el tarīk le fonduk...?

I'd like to see the rooms.
ana "awiz ashūf el owad bita"ak

May I see other rooms?
mumkin ashūf owad tēnī?

How much is this room per night?
kam el taman lemoddit yōm?

Do you have any cheaper rooms?
fī owad arkhas?

That's too expensive.
da ghālī 'awī

This is fine.
da kwayyis

Getting Around

Where is the...?	*fein...?*
bus station for...	*maHattit el otobīs le...*
train station	*maHattit el 'atr*
ticket office	*maktab el tazēker*

street	*el shēri"*	boat	*markib*
city	*el medīna*	camel	*gamal*
village	*el qarya*	car	*sayyāra*
bus stop	*maHuttit el*	crowded	*zaHma*
	otobīs	daily	*kull yōm*
station	*el maHatta*	donkey	*Humār*
		early	*badrī*
How far is...?	*ma hiyya el*	horse	*Husān*
	masāfa le...?	late	*mut'akhar*
When does the	*Emta...yeghāder/*	left side	*"alash shimēl*
...leave/arrive?	*yewassel?*	number	*nimra*
bus	*el otobīs*	right side	*"alal yimīn*
train	*el 'atr*	this address	*el "enwān da*
boat	*el markib*	ticket	*tazkara*
		where?	*fein?*
		wait	*istanna*

Which bus goes to...?
otobīs nimra kam berūH...?

Does this bus go to...?
el otobīs da yerūH le...?

How many buses per day go to...?
kam otobīs fil yōm yerūH le...?

Please tell me when we arrive at...
min fadlak, ullī emta Hanūsel le...

I want to go to...
ana "awiz arūH...

What is the fare to...?
bikam el tazkara le...?

Stop here, please.
wa'if hena, min fadlak

Please wait for me.
mumkin tentezernī

May I/we sit here?
mumkin eglis/neglis hena?

Where can I rent a bicycle?
fein e'aggar "agala?

air-conditioning	*takyīf hawa*		
airport	*matār*		
bicycle	*"agala, bīcīklēt*		

Around Town

Where is the...?	*fein...?*
bank	*el bank*
barber	*el Hallē'*
beach	*el plāž*
embassy	*es safāra*
ladies' room	*twalēt el Harīmī?*
market	*es sūq*
men's room	*twalēt el ragel*
mosque	*el gāme"*
museum	*el matHaf*
old city	*el medīna el*
	qadīma
palace	*el qasr*
police station	*el bolīs*
post office	*el bōsta*
restaurant	*el mat"am*
synagogue	*el ma"bad el*
	yehūdī
university	*el gam"a*
zoo	*Hadīqat el*
	Hayawēn

مسيرات

Women

رجال

Men

I want to change...	*ana "aiwiz aghayyar...*	11	*Hidāshar*
money	*fulūs*	12	*itnāshar*
US$	*dolār amrikānī*	13	*talattāshar*
UK£	*gineh sterlīnī*	14	*arba"tāshar*
A$	*dolār ostrālī*	15	*khamastāshar*
DM	*mārk almānī*	16	*sittāshar*
travellers' cheques	*shīkēt siyaHiyya*	17	*saba"tāshar*
		18	*tamantāshar*
		19	*tisa"tāshar*
		20	*"ishrīn*

Shopping

Where can I buy...?
fein aqdar ashtirī...?
How much is this/that...?
bikam da...?
It costs too much.
da ghālī 'awī
Do you have...?
fī "andak?

21	*itnein wi "ishrīn*
30	*talatīn*
40	*arba"īn*
50	*khamsīn*
60	*sittīn*
70	*sab"īn*
80	*tamanīn*
90	*tis"īn*
100	*miyya*
101	*miyya wi wāHid*
110	*miyya wi "ashara*
1000	*'alf*
2000	*'alfein*
3000	*talattalēf*
4000	*arba"talēf*
5000	*khamastalēf*

Numbers

English	Arabic	Pronunciation
0	•	*sifr*
1	١	*wāHid*
2	٢	*itnein*
3	٣	*talāta*
4	٤	*arba"a*
5	٥	*khamsa*
6	٦	*sitta*
7	٧	*sab"a*
8	٨	*tamanya*
9	٩	*tis"a*
10	١٠	*"ashara*

Ordinal Numbers		third	*tēlit*
first	*'awwel*	fourth	*rābi''*
second	*tēnī*	fifth	*khēmis*

The Preparation for Life Eternal

It was death, of course, that prompted the construction of the Egyptian pyramids but the incredible amount of resources, effort and time that went into them was indicative of many aspects of life in those days. The tombs served a variety of purposes, not the least of which was to provide the final resting place of the owner and a repository for his worldly possessions.

Obviously the size and grandeur of the tomb was designed to enhance the owner's greatness in the eyes of his people during his lifetime, but his tomb also became a place of worship for his subjects after his death.

The pyramids were also a symbol of life and death, of life over death and of life after death, serving to preserve the Pharaoh in the memory of his people and to ensure his continued existence in the afterlife. It was not a fear of death, or even an obsession with it, that guided the ancient Egyptians; rather it was a belief in life eternal and the desire to be one with the gods and their universe that inspired such extremes.

The pyramid was seen as an indestructible sanctum for the preservation of the Pharaoh's ka. This spirit, or life force emanating from the gods, was the 'double' of a living person but gained its own identity with the death of that person. The Pharaoh's ka would either continue to exist in his tomb – hence the need for all his worldly belongings – or would journey off to join the gods. The survival of the ka, however, depended on the continued existence of the body, so the process of mummification developed alongside the technology of tomb building.

In Pre-Dynastic times the dead were simply buried in shallow graves on the edge of the desert and covered with sand. Because of the dry atmosphere and hot sand this practice often caused the bodies to dehydrate before the tissues decomposed and this natural method of preservation did not go unnoticed.

As the ancient Egyptians changed their burial rituals and introduced coffins, the technique of mummification was developed to artificially preserve the dead bodies of those who could afford the process, as well as to preserve an incredible number of sacred birds, reptiles and animals.

For humans the mummification process took about 70 days. The most important aspect was the removal of the vital organs and the drying of the body using a dehydrating agent called natron (a mineral of hydrated sodium carbonate). The actual wrapping of the body in bandages played no role in the preservation of the corpse.

The treatment took place in six main stages:

The brain was extracted by being broken up and removed through the nose.

The viscera (except for the heart and kidneys) were removed through an incision in the lower left abdomen. The intestines, stomach, liver and lungs were dehydrated with natron, treated with resin and stored separately in canopic jars.

The body was sterilised and the internal cavities were temporarily packed with natron and fragrant resins.

The body then underwent the main preservative treatment of being covered with natron for about 35 days.

The temporary packing was then removed; the limbs were packed, under the skin, with clay; and the body cavities were permanently packed with linen soaked in resin, bags of cinnamon and myrrh, and sawdust.

The body was then anointed with fragrant oils and ointments, the abdominal incision was covered with an amulet of the Eye of Horus, and the skin was treated with molten resin.

Finally the body was wrapped up, with pieces of jewellery and protective amulets being placed among the bandages.

Facts for the Visitor

VISAS & DOCUMENTS

All foreigners entering Egypt, except nationals of Malta and Arab countries other than Libya, must obtain visas from Egyptian consulates overseas or at the airport or port upon arrival. A three month multiple-entry tourist visa from the consulate costs US$13 for USA passport holders, US$25 for West German passport holders, UK£17 for British passport holders and about US$20 for others. Processing of your visa application seems to vary according to nationality and where the application is made. In the USA and the UK, processing takes about 24 to 48 hours if you drop your application off in person, or about 10 days to six weeks if you mail it. Be sure to include one passport-size photograph, a money order or certified cheque (not a personal cheque), a stamped self-addressed envelope with enough postage to send it registered (if you are mailing it) and, of course, your passport with the application. Visa applications in the UK, and possibly in some other countries, don't require photographs.

If you wait until you get to the airport or port, processing is usually quick and easy. A photograph is not required. At the airport, any of the numerous money exchange windows, which are just before you get to the immigration/passport control booths, will sell you the necessary government stamps for the visa – E£15 in taxes and US$2 for the 'upkeep of the monuments'. When you exchange money with them, they will deduct the cost of the stamps from the total amount exchanged.

However, if you are coming from Israel, you can't get a visa at the border. You must get it at the Egyptian Consulate in Eilat or Tel Aviv, or elsewhere. Your passport will be stamped with the name of the Egyptian border post.

Most people are given a three month tourist visa with either single or multiple entries. If you plan to return to Egypt after, for example, visiting Israel, Jordan or the Sudan, then you should request the multiple entry visa.

WARNING: don't be duped by the fact that your visa is valid for 'three months'. All it means is that you have three months from the time the visa was issued to actually enter Egypt. Register with the government within one week of arrival. You will then be issued a permit which is valid for a one month stay from the date of entry.

To extend your visa beyond one month, you must present bank receipts showing that you exchanged at least US$180 the previous month. Credit card receipts showing payment in E£ can also be presented for visa extensions.

Note that if you plan to purchase an air or ferry ticket in Egypt you will also need to present bank receipts, but you can't use these same receipts for the visa extension or vice versa.

Embassies

Following are the addresses and telephone numbers of Egyptian embassies in major cities around the world:

Australia
   1 Darwin Avenue, Yarralumla, Canberra, ACT 2600 (tel (062) 734437)
Canada
   3754 Côte des Neiges, Montreal, Quebec H3H 7V6 (tel (514) 936 7781)
   454 Laurier Ave, Ottawa, Ontario K1N 6R3 (tel (613) 234 4931)
Greece
   3 Ave Cassilissi Sosias, Athens (tel 612954)
Sudan
   Sharia el Gama'a, Mogran, Khartoum (tel 77646/7, 72836)
UK
   South Audley St, London W1 (tel (01) 291 3209)

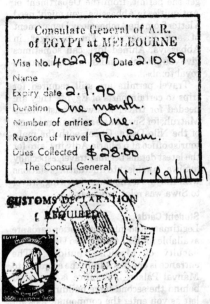

Consulate General of A.R.
of EGYPT at MELBOURNE

Visa No. 4022/89 Date 2.10.89

Name

Expiry date 2.1.90

Duration One month.

Number of entries One.

Reason of travel Tourism.

Dues Collected $28.00

The Consul General N.T.Rahim

CUSTOMS DECLARATION
REQUIRED

USA

1110 2nd Ave, New York, NY 10022 (tel (212) 757 7120)

2300 Decatur Place NW, Washington DC 20008 (tel (202) 234 3903)

3001 Pacific Ave, San Francisco, CA 94415 (tel (415) 346 9700)

2000 West Loop South, Houston, TX 77027 (tel (713) 961 4915)

505 North Shore Lake Drive, Chicago, IL 60611 (tel (312) 670 2633)

There are also Egyptian consulates in Australia (Melbourne), West Germany, France, Italy, Kenya, Jordan, Turkey and Israel (Tel Aviv and Eilat).

Greece An Egyptian visa can be obtained in one day from the Egyptian Embassy in Athens for Dr 2650 (US$20); one photograph is required.

Holland For Dutch passport holders, visa

processing reportedly takes three days and costs f65 at the Egyptian Embassy (tel (070) 542000) in The Hague.

Israel In Tel Aviv the Egyptian Embassy is at 50 Rehov Basel; take bus No 5 from Tel Aviv Central Bus Station. If you get there before 9 am you can probably beat the long queues and pick up your passport at 12 noon. If you don't have any passport-size photos (you need two for the visa) you can have your photograph taken just outside the embassy for a couple of dollars. Visa fees also vary – you'll pay at least US$20, plus varying amounts of shekels.

The Egyptian Consulate (tel (059) 76115) in Eilat issues visas in 20 minutes for about US$20. The consulate is at 34, The Moore Centre, near the Melony Tower. Bring spare photographs with you.

Remember that if you have an Israeli stamp in your passport, then you will not be permitted to enter Jordan, Syria, the Sudan or most other Arab countries.

Jordan There is an Egyptian Consulate in Aqaba. Visas cost JD7 and take 1½ hours. One photograph is required.

Registration

You must register with the police within one week of your arrival in Egypt. Most hotels will take care of this, some for a small fee. It's worth having the hotel do it for you, unless you are really anxious to have the cultural experience of visiting the labyrinthine Mogamma building. The bigger hotels complete the registration formality without being asked to do so – most package tourists don't even know it happens.

The Mogamma is a mammoth government building on Midan Tahrir in central Cairo. If you have to go there, enter through the right side of the main entrance, not the left, or you will be stampeded by the exiting herd. Climb the stairs on your right and go to window No 50 on the 2nd floor. It is near there that you also go for re-entry visas and visa extensions. (See the Information section in the Cairo chapter.)

In Alexandria the Passport Registration Office is on Sharia Talaat Harb. Both offices are open from 8.30 am to 2 pm.

Visa Extensions

Extensions can be obtained for periods of from one to four weeks. Normally, you must show bank receipts proving that you've changed another US$180 for the second month. The amount remains at US$180 even if you're only getting an extension for an extra week or two. The officials keep the bank receipts, so you can't use them if you need to buy a plane or ferry ticket.

As mentioned previously, credit card receipts showing payment in E£ can be used for visa extensions. You also need one photograph, E£2 for each two week period and the usual amount of patience.

Transit & Temporary Visas

Transit and temporary visas, valid for 48 hours, are issued at the airport, free of charge. If you stay longer than one week, then you must register with the police before the end of the week.

Vaccination Certificate

A vaccination certificate proving that you have been vaccinated for yellow fever and/ or cholera is only necessary if you are coming from an infected area (such as most of sub-Saharan Africa and South America). Occasionally they do ask travellers coming from these areas for their certificate. To be on the safe side, it is still a good idea to have these vaccinations.

Some countries, such as Kenya, require yellow fever vaccination certificates if you are coming from Egypt.

See the section on Health in this chapter for more information.

Permits

An antiquities permit is a useful thing to have, as it allows you easier access to many of Egypt's archaeological sites. To get the permit, from the Department of Antiquities in Abbassiya, you might need a letter from the Archaeology Department of any university. The manager in Abbassiya, Ahmed Idri, can sometimes give you special permission to visit certain royal tombs.

Travel permits are still required for trips to certain parts of Egypt. They are needed for travel westward past Marsa Matruh, for Siwa Oasis and for some parts of the Nile Delta. Check with the main tourist office at 5 Sharia Adly in Cairo for the latest details because travel, especially to Siwa, is subject to fluctuating relations with Libya. At the time of writing, travel to Siwa was relatively easy.

Student Cards

Legitimate student identification cards are available for E£7 from Cairo University's Faculty of Medicine building. The entrance is one block from the entrance to Manyal Palace. The office is in a shed behind the second large building to your left as you enter the compound; look for the 'SSS' sign. It's not difficult to find, as there's often a line of foreigners waiting for student cards. As a little experiment, ask some of the people in line if they are actually students. Don't be surprised if most say they aren't. Student cards are notoriously easy to obtain here, so I wouldn't be surprised if someday the International Student Identity Card people suspended this particular issuance of student cards. Proof of student status is rarely requested, but you need a photograph. Hours are 11.30 am to 12.30 pm daily, except Friday.

It's also easy to obtain student identification cards in Turkey and Greece.

Some travellers who have written to Lonely Planet claim that sometimes they also received student discounts by showing their International Youth Hostel Association cards, Youth International Educational Exchange cards and even Eurail cards. Discounts were received on train fares and entry fees to temples and tombs.

Business Cards

Another source of identification is a business card. A business card can also give you a certain degree of credibility in Egypt and, depending what's on it, can be a great help in obtaining assistance.

CUSTOMS

The Egyptian government issues a list of articles which are duty-free, dutiable, prohibited or restricted. The following information comes from that list:

Duty-Free Articles

The following articles can be brought into Egypt without duty being charged: personal clothing and toiletries, equipment and tools for use during work, one bottle of liquor and 100 cigarettes.

Dutiable Articles

Customs duty will be levied on articles in excess of the duty-free allowance. Duty will have to be paid on the following items regardless of whether or not they have been used previously: cars, motorcycles and video cameras.

Prohibited & Restricted Articles

Books, printed matter, motion pictures, phonographs and materials that are considered subversive or constituting a national risk or incompatible with the public interest.

Articles for espionage or intelligence activities. (They didn't specifically say what they meant by this.)

Explosives.

Sometimes, Customs Declaration Form D is given to arriving tourists to fill out. You are supposed to list all cameras, jewellery, cash, travellers' cheques and electronics (Walkmen, computers, radios, VCRs, etc). I have never heard of anyone being asked for this form upon departure. On the other hand, I have heard of travellers being asked to register their video cameras.

It's easy to make a little profit on duty-free liquor. If you haven't already bought some, drop into the duty-free shop when you arrive at the Cairo airport (it's just off to the left before you walk down the last hallway). It's quite easy to resell well-known brands of whisky and cognac to the hustlers in front of the Egyptian Museum in Cairo.

WORKING IN EGYPT

More than 40,000 foreigners already live and work in Egypt. That figure alone should give you some idea of the immense presence foreign companies have in the country. It is possible to find work with one of these companies if you are committed and motivated. Begin your research before you leave home. *Cairo: A Practical Guide*, published by The American University in Cairo Press, has a relatively up-to-date list of all foreign companies operating in Egypt. There's also a directory listing all foreign companies, subsidiaries and represent-atives in Egypt that's available in most hotel bookstores (eg, the Nile Hilton). If you know some Arabic, you will definitely be in an advantageous position. Once you have an employer, securing a work permit through an Egyptian Consulate or, in Egypt, from the Ministry of the Interior, should not be difficult.

In addition to working for foreign companies, there are also many oppor-tunities for teaching English as a second language. The Institute of International Education has information on teaching opportunities abroad. Contact them at 809 United Nations Plaza, New York, NY 10017 (tel (212) 888 8200).

The International Living Language Institute (ILLI) is often looking for teachers of English, French and German as second languages in its various branch centres. According to a British teacher with ILLI, one of the branch directors prefers British to American teachers, but this isn't always the case. If your accent and qualifications are acceptable, they will put you in a two week training programme and pay you E£5 per day.

Payment rates for teaching vary and often include a room in a shared flat.

If you look European and want to earn a few extra pounds in Egypt while you're travelling, you can appear in Egyptian TV commercials, as the local advertising agencies are always looking for Western faces. A Dutch traveller appeared in a shaving cream commercial and the advertising people dressed him up as a cowboy and had him get on and off a horse at the pyramids. It took about three hours and he received E£60. Not bad! To arrange something like this, you might try the following agencies in Cairo:

AMA – Leo Burnett
    49 Sharia Shahab, Mohandiseen (tel 807891, 805570)
Americana
    32H Sharia Radwan Ibn el Talib, Giza (tel 720707)
Arab Graphic Centre
    4 Sharia Molla, Matria
Intermarkets
    17 Sharia Gamal al Din Abdul Mahassen, Garden City (tel 31138)

Notices for cameo parts in commercials and TV soap operas are sometimes put on the bulletin board at the Oxford Pensione.

STUDYING IN EGYPT
American University in Cairo

The American University in Cairo is one of the premier universities in the Middle East. The campus, on Midan Tahrir, is in the heart of Cairo. The curriculum, and half the faculty of 160, are American and accredited in the USA. Four types of programmes are offered.

AUC offers nondegree and summer school programmes. The nondegree programmes are designed primarily for American university students who wish to take their third year of studies in Egypt. Any of the regular courses offered can be taken. Popular subjects include Arabic Language, Arab History & Culture, Egyptology, Middle East Studies and social science courses on the Arab world.

Up to 15 unit hours can be taken per semester at the undergraduate level.

Summer programmes offer similar courses. The term lasts from mid-June to the end of July. Two three-unit courses can be taken and several well-guided field trips throughout Egypt are usually included.

The largest programmes at AUC are for bachelor's and master's degrees; they offer more than 20 subjects ranging from Anthropology to Teaching English as a Foreign Language.

AUC is also home to the Arabic Language Institute. This independent wing of the university offers intensive instruction in Arabic language at beginning, intermediate and advanced levels. There are courses on both colloquial Egyptian Arabic and modern standard Arabic. I heard a few complaints from students in this programme because they wanted most of their coursework in colloquial Egyptian Arabic, but the programme emphasised classical written Arabic. Apparently, you must specify what you want and insist on it.

Applications for programmes with the Arabic Language Institute and undergraduate and graduate studies at the university are separate. Specify which you want when requesting an application. A current catalogue and programme information can be obtained from: The Office of Admissions, The American University in Cairo, 866 United Nations Plaza, New York, NY 10017-1889; or PO Box 2511, Cairo, Egypt (tel 354 2964, extension 5011/12/13). Tuition in 1989 was US$6800 for the year.

Egyptian Universities

It is also possible to study at Egyptian universities such as Al Azhar, Alexandria, Ain Shams and Cairo. Courses offered to foreign students include Arabic Language, Islamic History, Islamic Religion and Egyptology. For information on courses, tuition fees and applications, contact: The Cultural Counsellor, The Egyptian

Educational Bureau, 2200 Kalorama Rd NW, Washington DC 20008.

Language Programmes

Short intensive programmes in Arabic language are offered through several language institutes in Cairo. The Berlitz School (tel 915096), 165 Sharia Mohammed Farid, offers personalised colloquial Arabic courses. The Egyptian Centre for International Cooperation (tel 815419), 11 Shagarat al Durr, Zamalek, offers courses in classical Arabic.

The International Language Institute (tel 666704), 3 Sharia Mahmoud Azmy, Medinat al Sahafeyeen, offers a variety of courses at all levels. They are quite flexible and, apparently, the instructors are quite good. This school now seems to be the favourite among the local diplomatic community and journalists for learning both classical and colloquial Arabic.

Refer also to the Arabic Lessons entry in the Cairo Information section.

MONEY

The official currency of Egypt is called the pound (E£). In Arabic it is called a *guinay*. A pound = 100 piastres (pt – sometimes indicated by ‮ﻗ‬). The Arabic word for piastre is *irsh* or *girsh*. There are notes in denominations of 5, 10, 25 and 50 pt (rarely if ever around) and E£1, 5, 10, 20 and 50. Avoid the E£50 notes: a few years ago the police discovered counterfeit E£50 notes in circulation.

Although new notes have been issued for most denominations because so much of the money was literally falling apart, you will still come across bills held together by bits of packing tape.

Coins in circulation are for denominations of ½ pt (5 millims), 1, 5 and 10 pt, but the 1 pt and ½ pt coins are now rarely seen.

The low values of both coins and notes are one of the first signs that prices in Egypt are relatively low. However, prices are rising at an average annual inflation rate of 30% with estimates for some items as high as 50%. Prices can be written with or without a decimal point. For example, E£3.33 can also be written as 333 pt.

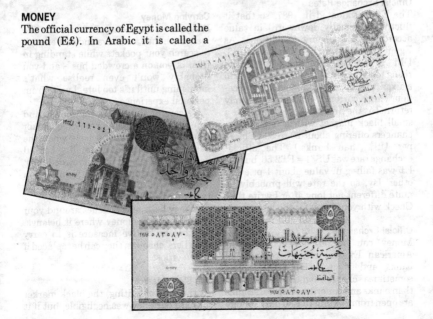

There is a severe shortage of small change in Egypt. The notes for amounts less than E£1 seem to have disappeared and there are never enough coins around. As a result, you're often offered 'change' in the guise of boxes of matches, sweets, aspirins (at pharmacies) and the like. The only answer is to be ruthless: when you're told there's no change, don't scrape around and find it yourself – insist that they do the scraping around, else you'll always end up without change when you really need it. Remember that taxi drivers are never going to have change if the fare can be rounded up against you. An E£8 taxi fare will always be E£10 if you don't have exactly E£8 to give the driver.

It is illegal to import or export any more than E£20. Even so, a lot still ends up overseas. If you have more than E£20 when entering the country, there is a risk – albeit slim – of having the excess confiscated.

Official Exchange Rates
The E£ was floated in 1987, so that it fluctuates (usually downward) in value according to economic conditions. As Egypt's demands for hard currency (US$, DM, FFr, UK£, etc) increase with its rising foreign debts, the E£ may revert to a fixed rate. If that happens, the once-flourishing currency black market may return. (At the time of writing, there was a small black market with a few money-changers offering about 20 to 30 pt more per US$ than banks.) The official exchange rate was US$1 = E£2.56, but the E£ was falling in value about 1 pt every other day, so the rate will probably be quite different not long after I write this. Check with your bank for the latest rate.

Official Exchanges
Money can be officially changed at American Express offices, commercial banks and some hotels. The hotels sometimes charge higher commissions than banks and American Express. Banks are open from 8.30 am to 1.30 pm Monday to Thursday. On Sunday banks are usually open from 10 am to 12 noon. Banking services are available 24 hours a day at the airport and in major luxury hotels. (See the section on Business Hours further on in this chapter as well.)

Foreign banks are closed on Friday and Saturday, while most Egyptian banks are open on Saturday. During Ramadan, banks are open between 10 am and 1.30 pm.

If you have an American Express card and travellers' cheques or personal cheques, you can exchange or cash them for hard currency at American Express offices. American Express charges a 2% commission and writes the amount obtained in the back of your passport.

Official Re-Exchange
Excess E£ can be exchanged into hard currency at the end of your stay, if you can show bank and credit card receipts which indicate that you spent the equivalent of US$30 per day.

Carrying Money
Pickpockets like money. In fact, some like it so much they are brave and deft enough to search your pockets while standing in front of you on a crowded bus – and you probably won't even realise what's happening until it's too late. I write from personal experience.

Be careful about carrying money and valuables in a day pack or handbag. Razor blades work wonders on bags when the dastardly perpetrator is standing behind you in a queue or on a crowded bus. Passengers on bus No 900 from Midan Tahrir to the pyramids are a favourite target for these stealthy fingers.

Money belts and pouches around your neck keep your money where it belongs. Another protective measure is to carry travellers' cheques; they can be replaced if stolen or lost.

The Black Market
At the time of writing, the black market for hard currency was negligible, but if it

should return, the following will probably again be relevant:

The words 'black market' conjure up images of dark alleyways where mumbling, shifty-eyed characters count wads of notes. Well, in Egypt that's a fairly accurate image. The characters do have shifty eyes and mumble, but they also bumble. Most of the action takes place on the street and in bazaars full of papyrus paintings and fake antiquities. The bumblers will constantly approach you chanting 'change money, change money'. Ignore them. When you want to change money, compare the rates yourself at a few bazaars. Large amounts of hard currency, and cash rather than travellers' cheques, bring higher rates.

After the black market transaction has been made, always sit down and count the money directly in front of the person who did the exchange. Changing money on the black market is officially illegal but relatively small transactions are unofficially tolerated. Nevertheless, exercise caution.

Money from Home

There are two convenient ways to receive money from home. If you have an American Express card and personal cheques, American Express will cash your cheques. If you have an American Express green card, however, you are not permitted to cash more than US$400 each 21 days without authorisation from their offices in London or the USA. If you have a Visa or MasterCard, you can get a cash advance from the Bank of America in Cairo or the Commercial Bank of Egypt.

It is also possible to have money wired from home through American Express, the Bank of America and the following banks:

Manufacturers Hanover
  3 Sharia Ahmed Nessim, Giza, Cairo (tel 988266)
Chase Manhattan
  9 Sharia Gamal al Din Abdul Mahassen, Garden City, Cairo (tel 26111)
Chemical Bank
  2nd floor, 14 Sharia Talaat Harb, Cairo (tel 740707)

Citibank
  4 Sharia Ahmed Pasha, Garden City, Cairo (tel 27246)

COSTS

Travel in Egypt is cheap. It is easily possible to get by on US$12 a day or even less if you're willing to endure certain inconveniences. Foregoing hot water or showers, and taking 3rd class trains packed to the hilt with screaming babies, chicken cages and half the Egyptian army, will save you quite a bit in daily expenses. For the most part, the amount of convenience and comfort varies according to how much you are willing to pay. Yet, even at the 1st class level, Egypt is cheap compared to similar travel amenities in Western countries.

Prices

Prices change, especially as the development of Egypt's tourist industry skyrockets. New hotels, resorts, restaurants and tour companies are appearing almost daily, which possibly means both additional price-fixing by the government in government-controlled or managed establishments, and price competition among private enterprises.

Prices are also subject to changing economic conditions – fluctuating exchange rates, an inflation rate of at least 30%, the rise and fall of the price of oil, the amount of interest owed on Egypt's foreign debt, etc. When comparing the prices indicated in this book, which were accurate at the time of writing, to prices during your trip, keep in mind such possible effects on them. Most other guidebooks covering less developed countries should be regarded in the same way. Prices are not, therefore, as some travellers apparently believe, written in stone like the Ten Commandments.

TIPPING

Tipping in Egypt is called baksheesh, although it is more than just a reward for having done a service properly. Salaries and wages in Egypt are much lower than in Western countries, so baksheesh is regarded as a means of supplementing income – an often essential means. For example, a cleaner in a one or two star hotel earns only about E£50 to E£60 per month (about US$20 to US$24 at current rates), so E£1 a day in baksheesh would mean quite a lot to him or her.

For Western travellers who are not used to almost continual tipping, demands for baksheesh for doing anything from opening a door to being unwillingly guided through an ancient site can be quite irritating. But it is the accepted way of getting things done in Egypt. Don't be intimidated into paying baksheesh when you don't think the service warrants it, but remember that more things warrant baksheesh here than anywhere in the West.

Services such as opening a door or carrying your bags warrant 25 pt to 50 pt. A personal guide to, for example, the Egyptian Museum costs about E£5 per hour in baksheesh. A guard who shows you something off the beaten track at an ancient site should receive about 50 pt to E£1. Baksheesh is not necessary when asking for directions.

In tombs and temples, if you're alone or with one or two others, the guards will whisper to you about some supposedly Pharaonic secret that they want to reveal only to you. Their English usually amounts to only a few words, which means that they can't really explain anything they're showing you. In one tomb, I was taken back and shown a deteriorating panel of hieroglyphics that depicted a basket of fruit and a couple of dogs. The guard looked around to make sure no one else was listening and whispered, 'Ah food. Ah dog. Yes,' and shook his head with a big smile. That Pharaonic 'secret' cost me 50 pt.

Unfortunately, in several tourist areas, many children have become baksheesh brats, screaming and clawing at you, demanding baksheesh and pens. Many tourists give something to them, just to shut them up. DON'T DO IT! You will only perpetuate what has already become a gigantic nuisance. If you really want to give money or gifts to impoverished children, you will have a much greater impact by making a donation through a school, orphanage, medical clinic or any number of other social welfare organisations.

A last tip on tipping: carry lots of small change with you, but keep it separate from bigger bills, so that baksheesh demands don't increase when they see that you could supposedly afford more.

TOURIST INFORMATION

The Egyptian government has tourist information offices in nine countries and throughout Egypt. The tourist offices outside Egypt are more helpful than the ones within, with the exception of the head office in Cairo where several languages, including English and French, are spoken by the very helpful staff. If they don't know the answer to a question they will call someone who does. They have maps of Cairo and Egypt, as well as brochures on various sites around the country. The information tends to be a bit faulty, but the photographs should give you a better idea of what you might visit.

Local Tourist Offices

Following is a list of the tourist offices within the country:

Cairo
    Head Office, 5 Sharia Adly (tel 923000)
    Airport Office (tel 966475)
    Pyramids Office, Pyramids Rd, near Hotel Mena House (tel 850259)
Alexandria
    Sharia Nabi Daniel, just off Midan Saad Zaghloul and across from the express buses to Cairo (tel 807611)
Aswan
    Corniche el Nil, two blocks north of the Abu Simbel Hotel, behind a small park (tel 32329)
Ismailia
    Governorate building
Luxor
    Tourist Bazaar, across from the Luxor Temple

Marsa Matruh
    corner of Sharia Alexandria & the Corniche
Port Said
    43 Sharia Palestine

Overseas Reps

Following is a list of Egyptian tourist offices outside the country:

Canada
    Egyptian Tourist Authority, Place Bonaventure, 40 Frontenac, Montreal, Quebec H5A 1V4 (tel (514) 861 4420)
    PO Box 304, Montreal, H5A 1V4
France
    Bureau de Tourisme, Ambassade de la RAE, 90 Ave des Champs Elysées, Paris (tel 45 62 94 42)
Germany
    Aegyptisches Fremdenverkehrsamt, 64A Kaiserstrasse, 6 Frankfurt am Main, West Germany (tel 252319)
Greece
    Egyptian State Tourist Office, 6th floor, 10 Amerikas St, Athens 134 (tel 360 6906)
Italy
    Ufficio Informazioni Turistiche, 19 Via Bissolati, 00187 Rome (tel 475 1985)
Japan
    Egyptian State Tourist Office, Akasaka 2-Chome Annexe, 19-18 Akasaka 2 Chome, Minato Ku, Tokyo (tel 58 90 65 31)
Switzerland
    Office du Tourisme d'Egypte, 9 Rue des Alpes, Geneva (tel (022) 329132)
UK
    Egyptian State Tourist Office, 168 Piccadilly, London W1 (tel (01) 493 5282)
USA
    Egyptian Tourist Authority, 630 5th Ave, New York, NY 10020 (tel (212) 246 6960)
    Egyptian General Authority for the Promotion of Tourism, Suite 608, 323 Geary St, San Francisco, CA 94102 (tel (415) 781 7676)

Foreign Embassies

For information on foreign embassies in Egypt see the Information section in the Cairo chapter.

GENERAL INFORMATION
Post

The Egyptian postal system is slow but

eventually most mail gets to its destination. Letters are slow in coming and going; post cards are even slower; and packages... well, bring out the camel express, it may be faster. Receiving and sending packages through customs can cause tremendous headaches, but I've sent many letters and postcards from Egypt to the USA, Australia, Singapore and the UK without any problems; they took anywhere from four to seven days for the UK and two to three weeks for the USA. It takes about the same time for a letter to arrive from the USA and one to two weeks from Europe.

Postal Rates Airmail letters cost 10 pt to Arab countries and 50 pt to all other countries. Postcards to non-Arab countries cost 45 pt. Postage for packages is relatively inexpensive. Stamps are available at souvenir kiosks, reception desks of major hotels, some shops, newsstands and, of course, post offices.

Sending Mail Post offices in Egypt are open from 8.30 am to 3 pm every day except Friday. The GPO at Midan Ataba in Cairo is usually open somewhat longer; it used to be open 24 hours. Sending mail from the post boxes at major hotels instead of from the post offices seems to be quicker.

Packages will probably have to be sent via the GPO with an export licence. Most curio shops will send your packages for a fee. See the Information section in the Cairo chapter for details about the formalities.

Receiving Mail Mail can be received at American Express offices or at the poste restante in most Egyptian cities.

American Express offices are the better option if you have an American Express card or travellers' cheques. Have mail sent to the American Express office in central Cairo. The address is: 15 Sharia Kasr el Nil, Cairo, Egypt. Sending mail to other American Express offices is less reliable because it's often forwarded to the central office anyway.

The poste restante in Egypt functions remarkably well. If you plan to pick up mail there, have the clerk check under Mr/Ms/Mrs in addition to your first and last names. The main poste restante section is at window No 16 on the Sharia el Bedak side of the GPO in Midan Ataba in Cairo.

Supposedly, the Royal Bank of Canada, which is on the 10th floor of the Abu el Feda building at 3 Sharia Abu el Feda, Cairo, will also hold mail for travellers. However, you should double-check this with the bank before you have mail sent to you here.

Telecommunications

Telephone The phones in Egypt are a test of one's patience and sense of humour. If you're lacking in either, then be prepared for frustration and grumpiness. Making long-distance or international telephone calls is often easier than just ringing down the street. Fortunately, this is changing.

In 1986 the Egyptian government began the process of revamping the system. Lines and connections are being upgraded. Most importantly, some numbers have already been changed and others were supposed to change soon. In Cairo the situation is especially confusing because not all parts of the city have been converted to the new numbering system. I tried to find out which parts of the city have changed and which haven't. Well, unfortunately, there's no easy answer because some parts of the same street have new numbers and others don't. Older establishments tend to have four to six digit numbers and newer places five to seven digits.

For those Cairo numbers listed in this book which do not function, first try dialling a 3, 5 or 7 and then the number. If that doesn't work, consult a copy of the 5th edition of *Cairo: A Practical Guide*, which lists many (not all) updated telephone numbers. There's also a Cairo 'yellow pages' telephone directory, available at most of the major hotels, published by Hawk Publishing (tel 698818), 23A Sharia Ismail Mohammed, Zamalek, Cairo. As a last resort, you can ask someone to look up a number in the multivolume Egyptian telephone directory; however, even that seems to be missing some numbers.

Local telephone calls cost 10 pt (or sometimes old 5 pt pieces which are the same size as the new 10 pt pieces). Calls can be made from cigarette kiosks, major hotels and telephone offices. There are a few pay phones in the lobby of the Nile Hilton. Telephone office locations are mentioned throughout the book.

International calls must be made from a hotel or telephone office. At the telephone office you pay for the call in advance. You can either use one of the booths in the office or have the operator call you at a private number. A few private lines (very few) have direct connections to international lines.

There are different rates for day (8 am to 7.59 pm) and night (8 pm to 7.59 am) calls. Three-minute calls to the USA cost approximately E£17 at the day rate and E£13 at night; to Australia and New Zealand, E£24.20/18.20 for day/night; the

UK, E£15.20/11.50; Canada, E£18.20/13.70; and France, E£18.20/13.70. Collect calls cannot be made from Egypt.

In Cairo, the central telephone and telegraph offices at Sharia Adly, Midan Tahrir, Sharia Ramses and Sharia Alfi Bey are open 24 hours a day. Other telephone offices are open from 7 am to 9 pm.

Telex & Telegraph Telegrams in English or French can be sent from the telephone and telegraph offices in central Cairo. The rate to North America is 60 pt per word.

Telex machines are available at the telephone and telegraph offices on Sharia Adly and Sharia Alfi Bey, and at major hotels. Rates vary.

Fax Fax machines are available for sending and receiving documents at the telephone and telegraph office on Sharia Alfi Bey in Cairo, and at most five star hotels. A one page fax to the USA costs about E£12 from the Sharia Alfi Bey office; hotel rates are approximately double.

Electricity
Electric current is 220 volts AC, 50 Hz everywhere, except Alexandria and the Cairo suburbs of Maadi and Heliopolis, where the current is 110 to 120 volts, 50 Hz. Wall plugs are the round, two prong European type. Bring adapter plugs and transformers if necessary; travel-size transformers are difficult to obtain in Egypt.

Time
Egypt is two hours ahead of Greenwich Mean Time and daylight saving time is observed. So, without allowing for variations due to daylight saving, when it's 12 noon in Cairo it is: 10 am in London; 5 am in New York and Montreal; 2 am in Los Angeles; 1 pm in Moscow; and 7.30 pm in Melbourne and Sydney.

Business Hours
Money Banking hours are from 10 am to 12 noon on Sunday and from 8.30 am to 1.30 pm Monday to Thursday. Bank Misr at the Nile Hilton in Cairo is open 24 hours. Foreign banks are shut on both Friday and Saturday, while Egyptian banks are usually open on Saturday.

Many banks, in Cairo and elsewhere, seem to open for exchange transactions in the evening – typically between 5 and 8 pm but sometimes later as well.

During Ramadan, banks are open between 10 am and 1.30 pm.

Shops Generally, shops have different hours at different times of the year. In summer most shops are open from 9 am to 1 pm and from 5 to 8 pm. Winter hours are from 10 am to 6 pm. Hours during Ramadan are from 9.30 am to 3.30 pm and from 8 to 10 pm.

Weights & Measures
Egypt is on the metric system. Basic conversion charts are given at the end of this book.

Laundry

There are a few self-service laundries around Cairo. Another option is to take your clothes to one of Egypt's many 'hole-in-the-wall' laundries where they wash and iron your clothes by hand. The process is fascinating and entertaining to watch. The ironing man, or *mukwagee*, takes an ancient iron which opens at the top, places hot coals inside and then fills his mouth with water from a bottle on the table. The water is sprayed from his mouth over the clothes as he vigorously irons.

Your last option, and the most common, is to do your own laundry. You can buy powdered laundry soap throughout Egypt. Bring a nail brush for scrubbing, a flat rubber stopper for the sink and some nylon cord and clothes pegs (pins) for hanging up your wet clothes.

MEDIA

Newspapers & Magazines

The *Egyptian Gazette* is Egypt's daily English-language newspaper. It is difficult to find outside of Cairo and Alexandria, and the news coverage varies from mediocre to good. That is due, in part, to government censorship. At the very least, though, it gives you some idea of what is happening in Egypt and the rest of the world. The Saturday issue is called the *Egyptian Mail*.

Cairo Today, another English-language publication, is a monthly magazine which covers a variety of subjects including the arts and sport in Egypt. Feature articles regularly focus on different parts of Egypt. Every issue has a guide to nightlife in Cairo and, often, Alexandria.

Middle East Times is a weekly English-language newspaper that offers excellent coverage of events and issues in Egypt and the rest of the Middle East.

The *Middle East Observer* is also found

Episode in a laundry – fellow takes a mouthful of water and spits it out as a fine mist over your laundry, then he irons this to perfection using a massive two handed hot plate heated over glowing coals.

THE IRON

The Egyptian Gazette

ذى لجشـــيان جازيـ

at newsstands in Cairo, but it covers mostly news about African and Middle Eastern financial markets, so it really isn't much use to travellers.

Almost every major Western newspaper and news magazine can be found in Cairo and Alexandria, including *Newsweek* and *Time*. They're available in major hotels and at a few newsstands and bookstores.

For the latest international news there are wire service teletype machines in the lobby of the Cairo Sheraton. It's on the opposite bank of the Nile from Midan Tahrir. The news printouts are hung on a bulletin board next to the machines. The Nile Hilton also has wire service teletype machines.

Radio & Television
There are daily English-language programmes on radio and TV. Check the *Egyptian Gazette* for the latest programme information. Normally, the news can be heard in English on a radio frequency of 557 kHz at 7.30 am, 2.30 pm and 8 pm. On 640 kHz news from the BBC World Service can be heard at 8 am in winter and 9 am in summer. The Voice of America can also be heard.

TV news in English is usually shown at 8 pm. Several American and British TV series appear on Egyptian TV. At the time of writing, *Knot's Landing* was a big hit in Egypt. Sometimes the programmes are shown with Arabic subtitles, other times they're dubbed.

HEALTH
Travel health depends on your pre-departure preparations, your day-to-day health care while travelling and how you handle any medical problem or emergency that may develop. While the list of potential dangers can seem quite frightening, with a little luck, some basic precautions and adequate information, few travellers experience more than upset stomachs.

Don't forget that you should always see your doctor for medical advice before heading off for a trip overseas.

Travel Health Guides
There are a number of books on travel health:

Staying Healthy in Asia, Africa & Latin America, Volunteers in Asia. Probably the best all-round guide to carry, as it's compact but very detailed and well organised.

Travellers' Health, Dr Richard Dawood, Oxford University Press. Comprehensive, easy to read, authoritative and also highly recommended, although it's rather large to lug around.

Travel with Children, Maureen Wheeler, Lonely Planet Publications. Includes basic advice on travel health for younger children.

Pre-Departure Preparations
Health Insurance Get some! You may never need it, but if you do you'll be very glad you got it. There are many different travel insurance policies which cover medical costs for illness or injury, the cost of getting home for medical treatment, life insurance and baggage insurance. Some protect you against cancellation penalties on advance purchase tickets should you have to change travel plans because of illness. Most travel and insurance agents should be able to recommend a policy, but

check the fine print before you decide which one to take out.

Medical Kit It is always a good idea to travel with a small first-aid kit. Some of the items which should be included are: Band-aids, a sterilised gauze bandage, Elastoplast, cotton wool, a thermometer, tweezers, scissors, antibiotic cream or ointment, an antiseptic agent (Dettol or Betadine), burn cream (Caladryl is good for sunburn, minor burns and itchy bites), insect repellent and multivitamins.

Don't forget water sterilisation tablets or iodine, antimalarial tablets, any medication you're already taking and contraceptives, if necessary.

Recommended traveller's medications include diarrhoea tablets, such as Lomotil or Imodium, paracetamol for pain and fever, and a course of antibiotics (check with your doctor). Erythromycin is recommended for respiratory, teeth and skin infections and is a safe alternative to penicillin. Metronidazole (Flagyl) is recommended for the treatment of amoebic dysentery and giardia. Again, check with your doctor before leaving home.

Most of these items, other than contraceptives, water sterilisation tablets and insect repellent, are readily available in Egyptian pharmacies.

General Thoughts Make sure your teeth are in good shape before you leave home. If you have an emergency, however, there are English-speaking dentists in most of Egypt's cities and towns. In Cairo, consult your embassy.

If you wear eyeglasses, carry a second pair or at least a copy of your prescription in case of loss or breakage.

Public toilets are bad news: fly-infested, dirty and stinky. Some toilets are still of the squat-over-a-hole-in-a-little-room variety. Always carry a roll of toilet paper with you; it's easy to buy throughout Egypt.

Vaccinations
These should be obtained before you arrive in Egypt. However, if you have to get a vaccination in Egypt, buy a sterilised syringe at a pharmacy and go to the government Public Health Unit, at the back of the lobby of the Continental Savoy Hotel in Midan Opera, Cairo.

The recommended vaccinations are cholera, typhoid, yellow fever and tetanus. You might also consider gamma globulin for protection against infectious hepatitis if you plan to be in Egypt for more than two months. You should check with your doctor for up-to-date details. If you are in Melbourne, Australia, the Travellers' Medical & Vaccination Centre (tel (03) 650 7600) can help you.

A pre-exposure rabies vaccine is advised for people planning an extended stay or on working assignments.

Food & Water
Tap water in Egypt's cities is generally safe to drink. It is so heavily chlorinated that most microbes and other little beasties are annihilated. Unfortunately, the excessive chlorination can sometimes be hard on your stomach. If the tap water makes you feel sick it is possible to buy bottled water. Make sure that the bottles have been properly sealed before you pay for them, as there used to be a scam of refilling them with tap water.

In the countryside the water is not so safe. You should only drink tap water which has been boiled for at least 10 minutes. Simple filtering won't remove all dangerous organisms, so if you can't boil water it should be treated chemically. Chlorine tablets (Puritabs, Steritabs or other brand names) will kill many but not all pathogens. Iodine is very effective in purifying water and is available in tablet form (such as Potable Aqua), but follow the directions carefully and remember that too much iodine can be harmful.

If you can't find tablets, tincture of iodine (2%) or iodine crystals can be used. Two drops of tincture of iodine per litre of clear water is the recommended dosage; the water should then be left to stand for 30 minutes. Iodine crystals can also be used to purify water but this is a more complicated process, as first you have to prepare a saturated iodine solution. Iodine loses its effectiveness if exposed to air or damp, so keep it in a tightly sealed container. Flavoured powder will disguise the taste of treated water and is a good idea if you are travelling with children.

There are also a few common-sense precautions to take with food in Egypt. You should always wash and peel fruits and vegetables and avoid salads. Egyptians sometimes fertilise their fields with human excrement and this waste has a way of sticking to the produce. The food isn't always well washed before it reaches your plate. If you can't wash or peel it, don't eat it. On the other hand, many travellers – including myself – have eaten salads regularly in Egypt with few ill effects. If you think that you are particularly susceptible to stomach troubles, then you should avoid salads.

Meat is safe as long as it has been thoroughly cooked. If you favour raw meat, keep in mind that conditions in Egypt can make the meat a nice and tasty home for worms. Your stomach and intestines are an even better habitat. Similar precautions should be taken with fish, which is more perishable than meat.

Avoid milk that hasn't at least been boiled; the same goes for cream. Milk in sealed cartons is usually imported and safe to drink because it has been pasteurised and homogenised. Most processed and packaged ice cream is safe.

Avoid anything raw, especially shellfish.

Contaminated food or water can cause dysentery, giardia, hepatitis A, cholera, polio and typhoid – all of which are best avoided!

Medical Problems & Treatment
Common Ailments Almost every traveller who stays in Egypt for more than a week seems to be hit with Pharaoh's Revenge, more commonly known as diarrhoea. There is usually nothing you can do to prevent the onslaught; it is simply your system trying to adjust to a different environment. It can happen anywhere. There is no 'cure', but following certain regimens will eventually eliminate or suppress the problem. Avoid taking drugs if possible, as it is much better to let it run its course.

The regimen to follow is fairly basic: drink plenty of fluids but not milk, coffee, strong tea, soft drinks or cocoa. Avoid eating anything other than dried toast or, perhaps, fresh yogurt. Yogurt is recommended by Egyptians, but I'm not absolutely convinced about it as a remedy.

If you are travelling, it may be difficult to follow this path. That is when Lomotil, Imodium, codeine phosphate tablets, a liquid derivative of opium prescribed by a doctor, or a medicine with pectin (like kaopectate) can be useful. Lomotil is convenient because the pills are tiny. If you are still ailing after all of this, then you might have dysentery. See a doctor.

Breathing can sometimes be troublesome in Egypt. I know that sounds odd because, of course, you have to breathe. However, the lack of humidity, the contrast of heat outside and air-conditioning indoors, and the abundance of dust can aggravate your eyes, nose and throat. Eyedrops and throat lozenges can be helpful, although you can survive without them while travelling through Egypt. During hot periods, try not go in and out of air-conditioned rooms too frequently or you'll catch a cold – which is particularly miserable when the weather is hot.

Dysentery This is, unfortunately, quite common among travellers. There are two types of dysentery, characterised by diarrhoea containing blood and lots of mucus. Seek medical assistance if you have these symptoms.

Bacillary dysentery, the most common

variety, is short, sharp and nasty but rarely persistent. It hits suddenly and lays you out with fever, nausea, cramps and diarrhoea but, as it's caused by bacteria, it responds well to antibiotics.

Amoebic dysentery, which, as its name suggests, is caused by amoebic parasites, is much more difficult to treat, is often persistent and is more dangerous. It builds up more slowly, cannot be starved out and if untreated will get worse and permanently damage your intestines. Metronidazole (Flagyl) is the recommended drug for the treatment of amoebic dysentery; it should be taken under medical supervision only.

Hepatitis This is a liver disease caused by a virus. There are two types – infectious hepatitis (Type A) and serum hepatitis (Type B). Type A, the more common, can be caught from eating food, drinking water or using cutlery or crockery contaminated by an infected person. Type B can only be contracted by having sex with an infected person, by using the same syringe or having a contaminated blood transfusion. Symptoms appear 15 to 50 days after infection (generally around 25 days) and consist of fever, loss of appetite, nausea, depression, lack of energy and pains around the base of the ribcage. Your skin turns yellow, the whites of your eyes turn yellow to orange and your urine will be deep orange or brown. Do *not* take antibiotics.

There is no cure for hepatitis except complete rest and good food. You should be over the worst in about 10 days but continue to take it easy after that. A gamma globulin injection is said to provide protection against Type A for three to six months, but its effectiveness is still debatable.

Cholera This can be extremely dangerous, as it is very contagious and usually occurs in epidemics. The symptoms are: very bad but painless watery diarrhoea (commonly known as 'rice-water shits'),

vomiting, quick shallow breathing, fast but faint heart beat, wrinkled skin, stomach cramps and severe dehydration. Do not attempt to treat cholera yourself – see a doctor immediately. Cholera vaccinations are valid for six months and if you're revaccinated before the expiry date it is immediately valid. The vaccine doesn't give 100% protection but if you take the usual precautions about food and water as well you should be safe.

Polio This is another disease spread by unsanitary conditions and found more frequently in hot climates. There is an oral vaccine against polio – three doses of drops taken at four to eight week intervals. If you were vaccinated as a child you may only need a booster. Once again, take care with food and drink while travelling.

Typhoid Typhoid fever is a dangerous infection which starts in the gut and spreads to the whole body. It can be caught from contaminated food, water or milk and, as its name suggests, the main symptom is a high temperature. Another characteristic is rose-coloured spots on the chest and abdomen which may appear after about a week. Two vaccinations, a month apart, provide protection against typhoid for three years. Seek medical assistance if you think you've been infected.

Malaria Malaria is spread by mosquitoes. The disease has a nasty habit of coming back in later years – and it can be fatal. You must start taking precautions before you travel. Although malaria is uncommon in Egypt, you should exercise caution in rural areas of the Nile Delta, the El Faiyum region, the Nile Valley and the Western Oases. Sleeping near a fan (mosquitoes hate fast-moving air) and using insect repellent are usually adequate; antimalarial protection has not always been regarded as essential.

The disease is common in the Sudan and becomes more so the further south you travel. Common symptoms are: headache, fever, chills and sweats.

According to the World Malaria Risk Chart published by the IAMAT, malaria is 'present' in Egypt. You should consult your doctor about the latest recommended methods of prevention. Note that Fansidar is no longer recommended as a prophylactic.

The IAMAT chart also indicates that June to October is the period of highest risk for contracting malaria. However, the risk level is quite low compared to the Sudan.

In the Sudan, malaria is present in both urban and rural areas all year. There are chloroquine-resistant mosquitoes that carry falciparum malaria – the most dangerous strain – so special precautions are essential. According to the IAMAT:

It is mandatory to remain in well-screened areas after sunset and to use mosquito bednets at night. Wear light-coloured clothing that covers most of your body. Do not use perfume or aftershave lotion. Use mosquito repellents (containing DEET) on your body and pyrethrin insecticides to spray the room at night.

This advice is also pertinent to travel in Egypt, just to avoid getting bitten, regardless of malaria risk. Mosquito coils are available throughout Egypt.

Yellow Fever A serious, often fatal, disease transmitted by the mosquito. It is caused by a virus that produces severe inflammation of the liver. Yellow fever is entirely preventable. It requires one injection, at least 10 days before departure, which is valid for 10 years.

Bilharzia Bilharzia, also called schistosomiasis, is prevalent in Egypt. The Nile and Nile Delta are infested with the bilharzia parasite and the microscopic snail which carries them; both prefer warm, stagnant pools of water. Do not drink, wash, swim, paddle or even stand in water that may be infected. The parasites, minute worms, enter humans by burrowing through the skin. They inhabit and breed in the blood vessels of the abdomen, pelvis and sometimes the lungs and liver. The disease is painful and causes persistent and cumulative damage by repeated deposits of eggs.

The main symptom is blood in the urine, and sometimes in the faeces. The victim may suffer weakness, loss of appetite, sweating at night and afternoon fevers. If you have contracted bilharzia, you will begin noticing these symptoms anywhere from one to four weeks after contact. Treatment is possible, so see a specialist in tropical medicine as quickly as possible.

Do *not* swim in the Nile! However, if you must, then swim in the middle, where the risk of being infected is much lower than along the banks.

Rabies If you are bitten, scratched or even licked by a rabid animal and do not start treatment within a few days, you may die. Rabies affects the central nervous system and is certainly an unpleasant way to go. Typical signs of a rabid animal are: mad or uncontrolled behaviour, inability to eat, biting at anything and frothing at the mouth. If you are bitten by an animal, react as if it has rabies – there are no second chances. Get to a doctor and begin the course of injections that will prevent the disease from developing. Remember that a pre-exposure rabies vaccine is now available.

Meningococcal Meningitis Sub-Saharan Africa is considered the 'meningitis belt', but there are recurring epidemics in other places, including the Nile Valley. The disease is spread through close contact with people who carry it in their throats and noses, spread it through coughs and sneezes, and may not be aware that they are carriers.

This very serious disease attacks the brain and can be fatal. A scattered blotchy rash, fever, severe headache, sensitivity to light and neck stiffness that prevents forward bending of the head are the first symptoms. Death can occur within a few hours, so immediate treatment is vital.

Treatment is large doses of penicillin given intravenously or, if that is not possible, intramuscularly. Vaccination offers good protection for over a year, but you should also check for reports of current epidemics.

Tetanus Tetanus is a killer disease, but it can easily be prevented by immunisation. It is caught through cuts and breaks in the skin caused by rusty or dirty objects, animal bites or contaminated wounds. Even if you have been vaccinated, wash the wound thoroughly.

Sexually Transmitted Diseases Sexual contact with an infected person spreads these diseases. While abstinence is the only 100% preventative, use of a condom is also effective. Gonorrhoea and syphilis are the most common of these diseases, and sores, blisters or rashes around the genitals, discharges or pain when urinating are common symptoms. Symptoms may be less marked or not observed at all in women. The symptoms of syphilis eventually disappear completely but the disease continues and can cause severe problems in later years. Treatment of gonorrhoea and syphilis is by antibiotics.

There are numerous other sexually transmitted diseases, for most of which effective treatment is available. However, there is no cure for herpes and there is also currently no cure for AIDS. The latter is common amongst heterosexuals in parts of Africa. Using condoms is the most effective preventative.

AIDS can also be spread through infected blood transfusions (most developing countries cannot afford to screen blood for transfusions) or by dirty needles – vaccinations, acupuncture and tattooing can potentially be as dangerous as intravenous drug use if the equipment is not clean. If you do need an injection buy a new syringe, as suggested in the Vaccinations section.

Coping with the Heat

Protect yourself against the heat of the sun in Egypt and the Sudan. It is difficult, especially in Egypt, to gauge how quickly you are losing body water, because the climate is dry. Headaches, dizziness and nausea are signs that you have lost too much water and might have heat exhaustion. To prevent this, take a bit of extra salt with your food, drink plenty of fluids and wear a hat and sunglasses. The salt helps keep you from getting dehydrated. Incidentally, the caffeine in coffee and tea also contributes to dehydration.

Sunscreen will prevent the sun from frying your skin. Wearing pants and long sleeves is cooler than shorts and short sleeves because your body moisture stays closer to your skin. Lastly, remember that when you're on the beach or in the water you will burn you quite quickly, so wear a shirt while snorkelling or swimming.

Prickly Heat Prickly heat is an itchy rash caused by excessive perspiration trapped under the skin. It usually strikes people who have just arrived in a hot climate whose pores have not yet opened sufficiently to cope with greater sweating. Keeping cool and bathing often, using a mild talcum powder or even resorting to air-conditioning may help until you acclimatise.

Women's Health

Gynaecological Problems Poor diet, lowered resistance due to the use of antibiotics for stomach upsets and even contraceptive pills can lead to vaginal infections when travelling in hot climates. Keeping the genital area clean, and wearing cotton underwear and skirts or loose-fitting trousers will help to prevent infections.

Yeast infections, characterised by a rash, itch and discharge, can be treated with a vinegar or even lemon juice douche or with yogurt. Nystatin suppositories are the usual medical prescription. Trichomonas is a more serious infection; symptoms are a discharge and a burning sensation when urinating. Male sexual partners must also be treated and if a vinegar douche is not effective medical attention should be sought. Flagyl is the prescribed drug.

Pregnancy Most miscarriages occur during the first three months of pregnancy, so this is the most risky time to travel. The last three months should also be spent within reasonable distance of good medical care, as quite serious problems can develop at this time. Pregnant women should avoid all unnecessary medication, but vaccinations and malarial prophylactics should still be taken where possible and if recommended by your doctor.

Doctors & Hospitals

There are hospitals throughout Egypt. Most of the doctors are well trained and often have to deal with a greater variety of diseases and ailments than their Western counterparts. On the other hand, most medical facilities are *not* well equipped and, consequently, it is not unusual for diagnoses to be inaccurate. If you need an operation, don't have it here. London or other European cities are only a few hours away by plane.

Before you leave for Egypt or the Sudan it is worthwhile writing to the International Association for Medical Assistance to Travellers (IAMAT) for their worldwide directory of English-speaking doctors. Doctors who belong to this organisation charge fair and reasonable standard fees for their services. The fees are set by IAMAT. Their membership addresses are:

Canada
    40 Regal Rd, Guelph, Ontario N1K 1B5
New Zealand
    PO Box 5049, Christchurch 5
Switzerland
    57 Voirets, 1212 Grand-Lancy, Geneva
USA
    417 Center St, Lewiston, NY 14092

In Cairo there are IAMAT centres at the following locations:

87 Road 9, Maadi (tel 350 3105, 351 0230); coordinator: Dr Sherif Doss

13 Sharia Wakf el Kharboutly (tel 901816, 243 4653); coordinator: Dr Nabil Ayad el Masry

11 Sharia Imad el Din (tel 910816, 916424); coordinator: Dr Samir B Bassily

1 Midan Roxy, Heliopolis (tel 258 2729); coordinator: Dr Amin Iskander Fakry

There's also a centre in Luxor at 51 Sharia Saad Zaghloul (tel 82442); the coordinator is Dr Sabry S Sefein.

The British, Canadian and American embassies can also help you find a doctor.

WOMEN TRAVELLERS

Egyptians are conservative, especially about matters concerning sex and women; Egyptian women that is, not foreign women.

Unlike many Middle Eastern Muslims, the majority of Egyptian women don't wear veils but they are still, for the most part, quite restricted in what they can do with their lives. They do not have the same degree of freedom, if any at all, that Western women have. Egyptian men see this not as restraint and control, but as protection and security. For many Egyptians, both men and women, the role of a woman is specifically defined: she is simply mother and matron of the household, and it is this which the men seek to protect – they don't want their wives to have to work. Ironically, in maintaining this position a woman actually works very hard. Even if she can afford domestic help and doesn't do any household work herself, her husband's view is still that she doesn't have to work for pay. It is *his* role to provide for the family.

There is obviously a consideration lacking here: maybe some women want to do more than play the dutiful mother and wife. But while this may be so in a few cases, most Egyptian women are still raised to want or expect nothing else. Consequently, very few have broken away from the house and family. The traditional role is still taken very seriously by the women themselves as well as by their men.

Premarital sex is considered a violation of this role – for women that is. So, enter the foreign woman. In Western TV programmes and films shown in Egypt, she is presented, by Egyptian standards, as a walking billboard for sex. It doesn't actually take much in the way of presentation to promote and perpetuate this belief – bare shoulders or shorts on a woman are 'proof' enough.

For the woman traveller from the West, this could mean harassment, even if she is dressed in jeans and a long-sleeved shirt. Although Cairo and beach areas (such as the Sinai and Hurghada) are becoming somewhat more liberal about Westerners' dress habits, most of the rest of the country is not. And as far as many Egyptian men are concerned, the misconception about the sexual availability of foreign women seems to be something they'd rather not have disproved. The two go together – Western women and sex.

I say 'could mean harassment' because it all depends on how a Western woman carries herself. Physical harassment and rape are not significant threats in Egypt. You can travel independently if you follow a few tips: avoid direct eye contact with an Egyptian man unless you know him; try not to respond to an obnoxious comment from a man – act as if you didn't hear it; be careful in crowds where you are crammed between people, as it is not unusual for crude things to happen behind you; if you're in the countryside (off the beaten track) it's often a good idea to wear a scarf in your hair; and, most of all, be careful about behaving in a flirtatious or suggestive manner – it could create more problems than you ever imagined.

Generally, if you're alone or with other women, the amount of harassment you get will be directly related to how you dress – the more skin that is exposed, the more harassment you'll get. As hot as it gets in Egypt, you'll have fewer hassles if

you don't dress for hot weather in the same way as you might back home.

An entire book could be written from the comments and stories I've heard from women travellers about their adventures and misadventures in Egypt. Most of the incidents they recounted were non-threatening nuisances, in the same way a fly buzzing in your ear is a nuisance: you can swat him away and keep him at a distance, but he's always out there buzzing around.

Here are just a few of the comments and tips I've heard from women travellers:

Wear a wedding band. Generally, Egyptian men seem to have more respect for a married woman.

Expect to be asked out constantly to discos and offered to be shown around Cairo.

Be wary when guys at the pyramids want to take you riding. A guy'll ride really close to you and grab your horse, among other things. After the ride he apologises and asks, 'You want to stay at my house?' When this happened to me I said 'No', and told him he was crazy. If you tell these guys that they are dirty old men, they will just laugh at you.

Egypt isn't the place for a full suntan.

From a woman traveller's letter: The Egyptian man sees the Western woman as an exotic object usually associated with sex. He will try anything in order to be able to conduct a conversation or, better yet, have a drink or a meal with her. This leads to endless calls of 'Hello, I love you', 'You're beautiful', etc. On any stroll you may wish to take, if you decide to chat with an Egyptian man, expect many personal questions and perhaps offers of marriage... If you don't wish to be friendly with any of the many men who approach you on the street, ignore them and, if that doesn't work, be blunt and say 'I want to be alone'. This is usually enough to leave you in peace.

If you need help for any reason (directions, etc), ask a woman first. Egyptian women are very friendly and will not threaten or follow you. Lastly, do not be overly fastidious about Egyptian men. Many of them are very kind and sincerely interested in simply conversing with someone from another country.

Another recommendation for women travellers is to befriend an Egyptian girl. Apart from having someone totally nonthreatening to show you around, you will probably also learn much more about life in Egypt from her. Many speak at least some English from high school.

Lastly, if you need any more information and tips, refer to an article by Ludmilla Tüting titled 'The Woman Traveller', which has appeared in both the *The Globe-trotters Handbook* and *The Traveller's Handbook*. Another good source of information and tips, particularly the section on travel in Middle Eastern countries, is a British book entitled *The Guidebook for Women Travellers*.

See the Books section in this chapter for details of books which offer insights into Egyptian women's lives.

FILM & PHOTOGRAPHY

Film

In Cairo, colour print processing is E£1 plus 30 to 40 pt per print depending on film size. B&W processing is not recommended, but colour processing is usually adequate for nonprofessional purposes. Film prices are E£25 for Kodachrome 64 (36 exposures) including processing, Kodacolor Gold 100 (36 exposures) E£6.50, Kodacolor 200 (36 exposures) E£7.50, Kodacolor 400 E£8.50 and Agfa 100 (36 exposures) E£6.

One hour photo machines/labs can be found in Cairo and a few other cities around the country. The average processing fee per roll of print film is about E£1.50 plus 35 pt per print.

Photography

Egypt is full of opportunities for great photography. Early morning and late afternoon are the best times to take photographs. During the rest of the day, the sunlight can be too bright and the sky too hazy and your photos will look washed out. There are a few remedies for this: a polarisation filter will cut glare and reflection off sand and water; a lens hood will cut some of the glare; Kodachrome film, with an ASA of 64 or 25, and Fujichrome 50 and 100 are good slide films to use when the sun is bright.

Cameras and lenses collect dust quickly in Egypt. Lens paper and cleaner are difficult to find, so bring your own. A dust brush is also useful.

Be careful when taking photos of anything other than tourist sites, the Nile, the Suez Canal and beaches. It is forbidden to photograph bridges, train stations, anything military, airports and other public works. Signs are usually posted. You can take photos of the interior of mosques, temples and a few tombs, though at some sites the government now charges E£5 or E£10 for the privilege.

It can sometimes be a bit tricky taking photos of people, so it's always better to ask first. Children will almost always say yes, but their parents or other adults might say no. Some Muslims believe that by taking photos of children you might be casting an 'evil eye' upon them. Similar attitudes sometimes apply to taking photos of women, especially in the countryside. Egyptians are also sensitive about the negative aspects of their country. It is not uncommon for someone to yell at you when you're trying to take photos of things like a crowded bus, a donkey cart full of garbage or a beggar – so exercise discretion.

ACCOMMODATION

Accommodation in Egypt ranges from cheap to expensive and rough to luxurious. There are hotels, pensions, youth hostels and a few camping grounds.

The majority of travellers seem to fly first to Cairo, arriving in the late evening or early morning. For most, the first Egyptians they meet will be the infamous 'tourism officials'. Because I have received many complaints about them, the following information should be useful.

Upon arrival at either the new or old airport terminals, you will probably be approached by a person wearing an official-looking badge that says 'Egyptian Chamber of Tourism' or something similar. Such people claim to be 'tourism officials' who will gladly help you find a hotel room 'free of charge'. Many travellers think they are government officials because they are approached in the customs and passport control areas. Wrong!

After shunting you through officialdom, they will take arrivals at the old terminal to a row of shabby little travel company offices on one side of the arrivals hall to arrange accommodation; arrivals at the new terminal are put into taxis and sent to a hotel.

These touts do offer what could be a useful service, especially during the high season – calling hotels for you to arrange rooms – but they are quite devious about it.

No matter which hotel you ask for, they usually say something like 'No, that hotel is no good', 'I know they don't have rooms, I just called them for another foreigner', 'That hotel is very expensive', or 'It is impossible to get a room for that price'.

Some hotel rates might be greater than those quoted in this book; like much of the world, Egypt isn't immune from rising prices. However, it's unlikely that these prices will have doubled or tripled, which is what the touts will claim when they supposedly call the hotel you want. Often they will pretend to call a hotel by dialling with their finger on the cradle button. Or else they call the wrong number and say it's the right one.

When they finally do book a room for you, it will sometimes be at a hotel that isn't, as they claim, in or near central Cairo, but across the river in the neighbourhoods of Dokki, Giza or Mohandiseen. In addition, the rate you are quoted may be higher than the hotel's usual rate because the tout's commission is included.

If you really wish to have them help you find a room, then insist on making the call yourself and offer to pay 25 pt to 50 pt for the call.

Hotels

At the five star end of the price range are hotels representing most of the world's major chains: Hilton, Sheraton, Holiday Inn, Marriott, Jolie Ville and the Meridien. Prices at these hotels typically start at about US$125 to US$150 per night, not including a 14% service charge and tax. There are also a few privately owned Egyptian hotels in this range.

In the next price range – four stars – there are mostly Egyptian hotels managed and owned by a government organisation, the Egyptian Hotels Company, or private groups of Egyptian and/or foreign investors. These hotels range upwards in price from US$45 per night and also charge the 14% tax and service charge. Standards are still fairly high at this price.

Next come the three star hotels. They are clean, comfortable and good for someone who wants most of the comforts of the fancier hotels but doesn't want to spend as much money. Rooms cost from US$15 to US$45 per night.

Taxes and service charges may be only two of the 'extras' that get added on to your final bill. Egyptian hotels are very keen on giving you breakfast but it's often 'compulsory' rather than included. Sometimes the fridge and TV in your room may incur an extra charge as well. In this way you can take an ordinary double room, add E£4 each for two breakfasts, E£2 for the fridge you never used and E£2 for the TV you never turned on, whack 12% service on the whole lot and then 6% government tax on top of that, and your E£30 room suddenly costs you E£50 a night.

The two, one and no star hotels form the budget group. Often the ratings mean nothing at all, as a hotel without a star can be equally as good as a two star hotel, only cheaper. You can spend as little as E£4 per night for a clean room with hot water and a shower or as much as E£10 for a dirty room without a shower. Pensions are in this range and tend to be fairly good. No extra charges and taxes are levied by these hotels.

Youth Hostels

Hostels are cheaper than the cheapest hotels in Egypt. They are located in Cairo, Alexandria, Port Said, Aswan, Asyut, Damanhur, Marsa Matruh, Sohag and Suez and range in price from E£1.50 to E£5. The youth hostels at Sharm el Shaykh and Hurghada charge E£5 per night because they are more comfortable than the average hostel and have air-conditioning. Having an International Youth Hostel card is not absolutely necessary, as nonmembers are admitted. A card will save you about E£1 or E£2. The youth hostels tend to get noisy, crowded and a bit grimy. Reservations are not usually needed.

The Egyptian Youth Hostel Association office (tel 758099) at 7 Sharia Dr Abdel Hamid (near Cinema Odeon), Cairo, can give you the latest information.

Camping

Officially, camping is allowed at only a few places around Egypt: in Cairo, at Giza near the pyramids; on the Mediterranean coast at Sidi Abdel Rahman; at Hurghada almost on the beach; and at Marsa Matruh, Luxor and Aswan. Outside the plots specifically set aside for camping, almost all the land is either desert or cultivated fields. And even at the official sites, with a few exceptions, facilities tend to be rudimentary.

FOOD

Egyptian food varies from exotic to mundane, and sampling the various types of Egyptian food should be part of the adventure of your visit. Be open-minded, don't look at the kitchens, and remember that you can have a uniquely great meal here for very little money.

Egyptian restaurants often include a 12% service charge at the bottom of the bill, but the money probably goes into the till rather than the waiter's pocket. Really the menu is just 12% more expensive than you think – if you want to tip the waiter you have to add the baksheesh afterwards.

Appetisers

Fuul and *ta'amiyya* are unofficially the national staples of Egypt. Fuul is *fava* beans, with a variety of things such as oil, lemon, salt, meat, eggs and onions added to spice it up. Ta'amiyya is a concoction of mashed chickpeas and spices fried into little balls, similar to felafel. A fuul and ta'amiyya sandwich on pita bread with a bit of tomato makes a tasty snack or light lunch.

It's also popular to substitute *tahina* for fuul in pita bread sandwiches. Another national staple, tahina is a delicious sesame spread spiced with oil, garlic and lemon. In addition to putting it on ta'amiyya, you can also order a plate of tahina to eat as a dip with pita bread. With a couple of sandwiches, pita bread, a plate of tahina and some fruit from the market, you have a decent meal for about 50 pt.

Hoummos and *baba ghanough* are two other popular spreads which can be eaten in the same way as tahina. Hoummos is a chickpea spread which is especially tasty with a bit of oil and a few pinenuts on top. Baba ghanough is a mix of mashed eggplant and tahina.

Sandwich stands also serve – you guessed it – the *sandweech*. However, they aren't quite sandwiches as you and I know them. Most Egyptian sandweeches are small rolls with an equally small piece of meat, cheese or *basturma*, a smoked meat which resembles pastrami. Nothing else. Add some mustard to perk it up. Other popular sandwiches include: grilled, crumbed or fried *kibda* (liver) served with spicy green peppers and onions; *mokh*, or crumbed cow's brains; and tiny shrimp.

Shwarma is also good for sandwiches and is the Egyptian equivalent of the Greek *gyros* sandwich. Throughout Egypt you will see the shwarma spits with rotating legs of lamb. Hot strips of lamb are cut from the spit and placed in a pocket of pita with tomatoes to make a sandwich fit for pigging out.

Another appetiser which you will often be served is *torshi*, which is a mixture of pickled vegetables such as radishes, carrots and cucumbers. They look somewhat strange and discoloured but taste great if they're pickled properly.

There are several other quick, cheap dishes available, such as the following. *Fiteer* is a cross between pizza and pastry and is served at a place called a *fatatri*. It's flat and flaky, and contains sweet things like raisins and powdered sugar, or something spicy like white cheese, ground meat or eggs. One fiteer is almost filling enough to be an entire meal.

Shakshooka is a mixture of chopped meat and tomato sauce with an egg tossed on top. You must taste this; the combination is delicious. It's rather like a Spanish omelette with meat.

Makarone is a clump of macaroni baked into a cake with ground meat and tomato sauce inside and *pashamel* (white sauce or gravy). It is very filling and costs from 50 pt to E£1.

Mahshi are various vegetables such as vine leaves (in summer), cabbage (in winter), tomatoes, and white and black aubergines (*dolma*), usually stuffed with minced meat, rice, onions, parsley, green herbs and, sometimes, tomatoes.

Main Dishes

Kufta and *kebab* are two of the most popular dishes in Egypt. Kufta is ground meat peppered with spices, skewered and grilled over a fire just like shish kebab. Kebab is similar, but the meat isn't ground. Grilled tomatoes and onions are also served. Both dishes are ordered in Egyptian restaurants by weight.

Molokhiyya is also very popular and is one of the few truly Egyptian dishes. It's a green, slimy, delicious soup made by stewing a strange leafy vegetable, rice and garlic together in chicken or beef broth.

Firakh, or chicken, is something you'll probably be eating quite often. It is usually grilled or stewed and served with a vegetable. Takeaway spit-roasted chickens are available from many small restaurants for about E£3.50 to E£5 depending on the weight. They are easy to spot – just look for a case of brown spinning chickens.

Grilled *samak* (fish) is tasty. The best fish comes from the Mediterranean and south Sinai coasts. The restaurants along the Mediterranean serve their fish by the kg. You choose it yourself from a large ice tray near the kitchen and the price usually includes a salad, bread and dips like tahina and baba ghanough.

WARNING: fish spoils quickly in the summer heat. Before ordering your fish, be sure that it's fresh. It shouldn't smell like the inside of a locker room and shouldn't feel spongy.

Another grilled dish is *hamam*, or pigeon. Pronounce the word carefully because another 'm' makes the word *hammam*, which means bathroom. Hamam is served grilled on charcoal or sometimes stuffed with *freek* (wheat stuffing). It's also served as a stew cooked with onions, tomatoes and rice or freek in a deep clay pot known as a *tajine* or *ta'gell*.

Another popular dish is *kushari*, a combination of noodles, rice, black lentils, fried onions and tomato sauce. Each item is cooked separately and piled high in the windows of kushari joints, which are never street stands because the tomato sauce spoils quickly in the sun. A bowl of kushari is healthy and very filling and costs only about 25 pt to 50 pt. The fried onions are usually extra.

For those who find themselves on long train or bus rides, it is also essential to know about bread and cheese – the easily transportable staple of the traveller. Bread, including pita, is called *aysh*. In Egypt aysh also means 'life'. Egyptians say that life without aysh isn't life. Most of the aysh which you'll see and eat is *aysh baladi*, also called country bread or pita. The other main type is called *aysh fransawi*, or French bread (for obvious reasons).

There are also two main types of cheese: *gibna beyda*, or white cheese, which tastes like Greek feta, and *gibna rumi*, or Roman cheese, which is a hard, sharp, yellow-white cheese. Imported processed French cheeses such as Ki-Ri and La Vache qui Rit are also quite common.

Here are some more food words which could be helpful as you eat your way around Egypt:

Soup

soups	*shurba*
chicken soup	*shurbit firakh*
lentil soup	*shurbit 'aads*
tomato soup	*shurbit tamatim*

Fish & Shellfish

fish	*samak*
Nile perch	*ishr bayad* (try it grilled)
flatfish	*samak musa*
red mullet	*mourgan*
fried fish	*samak maklee*
crab	*kaboria*
prawns, shrimps	*gambari*
squid	*calamari*

Vegetables

aubergine	*badingan*
cabbage	*khroumbe*
carrots	*gazar*
cauliflower	*arnabeet*
green vegetables	*khudrawat, khudar*
green beans	*fasulya*
lentils	*'aads*
maize	*durra* (try it charcoal grilled from a sidewalk vendor)
okra	*ba'amiyya*
peas	*baseelah*
potatoes	*batatas*
turnips	*lift*
dry green wheat	*fareek*

Salad Items

salad	*salata*
cucumber	*khiyaar*
garlic	*tum*
lettuce	*khass*
onion	*bassal*
green winter pepper	*sabanekh*
hot pepper	*shattah*
sweet pepper	*filfil*
tomato	*tamatim, uta*

Meat & Poultry

meat	*al-luhum*
beef	*lahma kanduz, lahma ba'aree*
camel	*lahma gamali*
chicken	*firakh*
kidney	*kalawwi*
lamb	*lahma danee*
liver	*kibda*
turkey	*deek roumee* (usually found only at Christmas)
veal	*lahma beetalu*

Desserts

cornflour pudding	*mahalabiyya*
milk dish with nuts, raisins & wheat	*bilaylah*
ice cream	*ays krim, gelati*
flaky pastry & nuts in honey	*baklawah*
shredded wheat pastry with nuts	*atayf*
pastries dipped in rosewater	*zalabiyyah, lomet el addee*
Turkish delight	*malban*
semolina cake	*basboosah*
cornflour pudding with nuts & cream	*om ali*
stringy pastry with honey & nuts	*khounafa*
baked rice & milk pudding	*ruz bi laban*
flaky pastry with nuts & honey or cheese	*ghoulash*

Fruit

fruit	*fawakah, fakha*
apricots	*meesh-meesh*
apples	*toofa*
bananas	*mohz*
dates	*balah*
figs	*teen*
grapes	*einab*
guavas	*guafa*
limes	*limuun*
mangoes	*manga*
oranges	*burtuaan*
peaches	*khukh*
pears	*kumitrah*
pomegranates	*ruman*
strawberries	*farawleh*
tangerines	*yusuf affandi*
watermelons	*bateekh*

Miscellaneous Items

bread	*aysh, khubz*
pita bread	*aysh baladi*
butter	*zibda*
cheese	*gibna*
cream	*ishta*
eggs	*bayd*
jam	*murabbah*
honey	*asal*
milk	*laban*
mint	*nannah*
salt	*malh* (pronounced almost as 'malha')
sugar	*sukur*
yogurt	*zabadi*
water	*miyya*
watermelon seeds	*lib* (roasted, a national passion)

DRINKS
Tea & Coffee

Shy and *ahwa* – tea and coffee – head the list of things to drink in Egypt. Both are usually made strong enough to be major contenders for the title of most caffeinated drink in the world.

Tea is served in glasses at traditional Egyptian cafes and in teacups at Western-style restaurants. At cafes, the tea leaves are boiled with the water. Unless you

enjoy chomping on tea leaves, wait until they settle back down to the bottom. Tea bags are appearing in the Western-style places.

If you don't specify how much sugar you want, two or three big teaspoons of sugar will be automatically plopped into your glass. If you only want a bit of sugar in your tea, ask for *shy ma'ah shwayya sukur*. If you don't want any sugar at all ask for *shy meen reer sukur*. Egyptians are always amazed that Westerners don't like as much sugar as they do. Try *shy bi-nannah* (mint tea) or *shy bi-laban* (tea with milk).

If you ask for coffee, you will probably get *ahwa turki*, Turkish coffee, which is served throughout the Middle East. It bears a strong resemblance to mud and it's quite a surprise to find your spoon doesn't actually stand up in it. Don't be deceived by the size of the tiny porcelain cups; this coffee is *very* strong. Let the grains settle before drinking it, in small sips. As with tea, you have to specify how much sugar you want if you don't want to suffer an overdose. *Ahwa ziyadda* is for those who seek the ultimate sugar and caffeine high – it is extra sweet. *Ahwa*

mazboota comes with a moderate amount of sugar but still fairly sweet and *ahwa saada* is without sugar. Egyptians drink the latter when a relative or close friend has died.

Western-style instant coffee is called Nescafe. It comes in a small packet with a cup of hot water.

Another popular hot drink is *hoummos el shem*, which is made from boiled chickpeas, tomato sauce, lemon and cumin.

Fruit Juices

On practically every street corner in every town throughout Egypt there is a juice stand, where you can get a drink squeezed out of just about any fruit or vegetable you want. Standard *asiir*, or juices, include:

banana	*mohz*
guava	*guafa*
hibiscus	*karkaday*
lime	*limuun*
mango	*manga*
orange	*burtuaan*
pomegranate	*ruman*
strawberry	*farawleh*
sugar cane	*asiir asab*
tamarind seed	*tamr hindi*
tangerine	*yusuf affandi*

Other Nonalcoholic Drinks

Soft drinks are extremely popular in Egypt and most major brands are sold here, including Coca-Cola, Sport Cola, Seven-Up, Fanta, Schweppes and Pepsi. Schweppes drinks come in various fruit flavours such as orange, lemon, mandarin and apple. If you drink at the soda vendor's stand, you won't have to pay a deposit on the bottle. Soft drinks are cheap – only 25 pt – but it's not unusual to pay as much as E£1 in hotels and at tourist sites. The short squat bottles cost about 50 pt each and don't have to be returned. Cans of drink can cost as much as E£1 each, though, because the can isn't reusable. Diet soft drinks are becoming quite popular in Egypt, especially Diet Coke, Pepsi and Seven-Up. Remember that when it's hot, a soft drink will not quench your thirst. In fact, if anything, the sugar in it will make you more thirsty.

Sahleb is a sweet, milky drink made from rice flour, grapes, coconut and various nuts, including hazelnuts and pistachios. Cheap juice stands sell a simpler version.

A few other *shirbat*, or drinks, which you might encounter are:

carob	*carob*
cocoa	*kakaw*
aniseed	*yansun*
licorice	*arasus*
caraway seed	*karawiyya*

Tap water is generally safe to drink throughout Egypt, but some travellers prefer to begin drinking it gradually rather than immediately. See the Health section in this chapter for more details.

Alcohol

Egypt also has several indigenous alcoholic beverages. The beer, which can be

excellent, is called Stella, and is served in huge one litre bottles. There is also Stella Export, which comes in smaller bottles, has double the alcohol content of regular Stella and also costs more. Few things can beat a cold bottle of Stella on a hot day. It has a rich, smooth taste that makes it easy to drink a lot in a short amount of time. Be wary of expiry dates, however. A non-alcoholic beer called Birelli is also available, but it seems to be little more than a concoction of hops and soda water. It's often used as a prescribed remedy for people with kidney stones.

Try the Egyptian wines too. One of the best medium-dry white wines is called Ganaklis Village; it comes from a village of the same name in the Nile Delta. A good dry white wine is Patalomai. There's only one type of rosé wine – Robi d'Egypte. For red wines, the best dry one is Omar Khayyam, the best medium-dry is Ganaklis Château, and the sweetest is Nefertiti. They don't exactly compare with Western wines, but they aren't bad.

For hard liquor, go to the bars at major hotels rather than to small street bars because the latter have been known to doctor the contents with potentially dangerous additives.

BOOKS

The following is a short list of books which can further introduce you to Egypt and the Egyptians. Most can be found at bookshops in Egypt or in the library and bookshop of the American University in Cairo. Outside Egypt, many of them can be ordered through local bookshops.

People & Society

Shahhat: An Egyptian, Richard Critchfield, Syracuse University Press, 1984. Critchfield lived and worked for an extended period in a west bank village near Luxor to write this in-depth portrait of a young man named Shahhat and his life in an Egyptian village.

Egypt: Burdens of the Past, Options for the Future, John Waterbury, Indiana University Press, 1978. An excellent comprehensive portrayal of Egyptian society by a leading scholar of North Africa.

An Account of the Manners & Customs of the Modern Egyptians, Edward Lane, first published 1839; reprinted by the State Mutual Book & Periodicals Service, New York, 1986. Lane's wonderful classic continues to offer insight into the traditional Arab culture of Egypt.

Journey to the Orient, Gerard de Nerval, first published in the 19th century and now distributed by Kampmann & Company, Moyer Bell Ltd, Mt Kisco, New York (1986 reprinting). This book will prime you for exploration of the mysteries of Egypt.

The Other Nile, Charlie Pye-Smith, Penguin Books, 1987. A highly readable and incisive account of a leisurely ramble up the Nile through Egypt and into the Sudan, where internal strife stopped the author going any further. He contrasts the trip with an earlier one he made right through the Sudan and Ethiopia in the mid-70s.

The Hidden Face of Eve: Women in the Arab World, Nawal El Saadawi, Zed Press, 1980, and Beacon, 1981. This, the first of the author's numerous works to be translated into English, considers the role of women in world history, Arab history and literature, and contemporary Egypt. Nawal El Saadawi is a psychiatrist, feminist, novelist and writer of nonfiction. She is the founder and president of the Arab Women's Solidarity Association. All her books, many of which have been translated into several languages, are well worth reading for the insight they provide into the lives of women in the Arab world.

Khul-Khaal: Five Egyptian Women Tell their Stories, edited by Nayra Atiya, The American University in Cairo Press, 1984. The life stories of five contemporary Egyptian women from a variety of backgrounds. Fascinating information for anyone interested in understanding Egyptian life.

Fiction

Midaq Alley, Miramar and *The Thief & the Dogs*, Naguib Mahfouz, The American University in Cairo Press. These novels, by Egypt's first Nobel Prize-winning author, provide insightful perspectives on life in Egypt. *Midaq Alley* portrays a poor back-alley neighbourhood in Islamic Cairo. The book focuses on the life of a girl who gets engaged to the local barber but becomes a prostitute while her fiancé is off earning money for their future together. *Miramar* presents a microcosm of Egyptian society through the story of a young girl from the countryside who flees to Alexandria to avoid an arranged marriage. The relationships she develops with her neighbours in the city form a revealing picture of life in a fairly typical urban neighbourhood in Egypt. *The Thief & the Dogs* is a critical, somewhat cynical, psychological study of a man who was wrongfully imprisoned for several years and then set free. His new life becomes a symbolic quest for justice.

Mahfouz, who has written 40 novels and short story collections and 30 screenplays, was awarded the 1988 Nobel Prize in Literature for works that many compare to Dickens or Balzac. According to the Swedish Academy, his works are 'rich in nuance – now clear-sightedly realistic, now evocatively ambiguous. . . his work speaks to us all'.

History

The Penguin Guide to Ancient Egypt, William J Murnane, Penguin Books, 1983. Murnane has given us one of the best overall books on the life and monuments of ancient Egypt. There are plenty of illustrations and descriptions of almost every major monument in the country. *The Ancient Egyptians: Religious Beliefs & Practices*, Rosalie David, Routledge & Kegan Paul, 1982. This is one of the first books to trace the evolution of religious beliefs and practices in ancient Egypt. It is a very thorough and comprehensible treatment of a complex subject.

The Gods & Symbols of Ancient Egypt, Manfred Lurker, Thames & Hudson, 1984. This is an illustrated dictionary which offers brief explanations and descriptions of the most important aspects of ancient Egypt. It can be helpful in understanding some of the hieroglyphics.

The Blue Nile and *The White Nile*, Alan Moorehead, New English Library, 1982, and Random House, 1983. Both books are classics which cover the history of the Nile during the 19th century. *The Blue Nile* deals with the period 1798 to 1856; *The White Nile* is concerned with events from 1856 to the end of the century. Moorehead's detailed descriptions of events and personalities are superb. These two should definitely be read.

In Search of Identity, Anwar Sadat, Harper & Row, 1979. Sadat's autobiography is a good introduction to the events leading up to and following Egypt's 1952 Revolution.

Great Cairo: Mother of the World, Desmond Stewart, The American University in Cairo Press, 1981. This covers 55 centuries of Cairo's history; the descriptions of the many diabolical rulers are wonderful.

Nagel's Encyclopedia Guide to Egypt, Passport Books, National Textbook Company, Illinois, 1987. This is an expensive but extremely thorough guide to Egypt's ancient monuments.

The History of Egypt, P J Vatikiotis, Johns Hopkins University Press, Baltimore, 1986. This is one of the best books on the history of Egypt. It emphasises the 19th and 20th centuries with a focus on political and social development since 1805 and the 'new social order' that has evolved since the 1952 Revolution.

A Short History of Modern Egypt, Afaf Lutfi al Sayyid Marsot, Cambridge University Press, Cambridge, 1985. For a more concise history of Egypt from 639 AD read this book, which is by one of Egypt's foremost historians. It offers a great introduction to Egyptian history.

Travel Guides

The Blue Guide, Veronica Seton-Williams & Peter Stocks, W W Norton, 1988. This massive tome is one of the most comprehensive guides to Egypt. It describes every place of even the slightest historical interest and has excellent sections on Egypt's natural history. However, it is a bit heavy to lug around in a backpack.

Alexandria: A History & a Guide, E M Forster, Michael Haag Ltd, 1985. First published in 1922, this is still one of the best guides to the sights and history of Alexandria.

Cairo: A Practical Guide, The American University in Cairo Press. Almost every bit of practical information from auctions to toy shops is contained in this annual guide. The maps are some of the best you will find.

Discovery Guide to Egypt, Michael Haag Ltd, 1990. A comprehensive guide with plenty of detail about the monuments and their place in history, as well as practical information for getting around.

Let's Go Israel & Egypt, St Martin's Press. Put together by Harvard Uni students, the Let's Go series provides plenty of background info, tells you about things to see, places to stay, etc, and is updated annually. This one also covers Jordan.

Language

Those who want a comprehensive guide to colloquial Egyptian Arabic should check at the American University in Cairo bookstore for the latest textbooks. Otherwise, my Lonely Planet phrasebook *Egyptian Arabic – a language survival kit* should suffice. It's small enough to easily fit in your pocket.

Bookshops

Cairo and Alexandria both have several English language bookshops where you can find most of the books mentioned here. For addresses refer to the Cairo and Alexandria sections. In Cairo there are also several excellent second-hand bookstalls in Ezbekiya Gardens selling some of the most unlikely books and magazines, including three year old copies of *Time*.

MAPS

Michelin map No 154 covers Egypt, the Sudan and the Sinai. The Sudan section is excellent but there are better maps on Egypt and the Sinai. The best is published by Kummerly & Frey, a Swiss company. It covers all of Egypt and the Sinai, on a scale of 1:750,000, and sells for US$6.95.

Another map publisher, Freytag & Berndt, publishes a map which includes a plan of the Great Pyramids and covers all of Egypt except the western quarter. The scale is 1:1,000,000 and it sells for US$5.95.

The Macmillan Publishers *Map of Egypt* has a 1:1,000,000 map of the Nile Valley and a small map of all Egypt, plus good maps of Cairo, Alexandria and a variety of enlargements, temple plans and the like.

Clyde Surveys, of England, has an excellent map of eastern Egypt. It covers the Nile region from the coast to Aswan, and has detailed maps of Cairo, Alexandria, Luxor and Thebes, and the Great Pyramids, with notes in English, French and German. Titled *Clyde Leisure Map No 6: Egypt & Cairo*, it sells for around US$7.

The Bartholomew World Travel Map of Egypt is also quite good, though it is very inaccurate in the Sinai. The scale is 1:1,000,000; it costs US$6.95.

THINGS TO BUY

Egypt is a budget souvenir and kitsch shopper's paradise. Hieroglyphic drawings of Pharaohs, queens, gods and goddesses embellish and blemish everything from ashtrays to engraved brass tables. Brass plates engraved with various Pharaonic

scenes are well done and sometimes cost no more than E£5. Similar scenes are precisely and colourfully painted on cotton wall-hangings.

Since cotton is one of Egypt's major crops it is no surprise that cotton clothing is very popular. Cotton shirts, pants and *galabiyyas* (the loose gowns worn by many Egyptians) can be made to your specifications. Many Cairene tailors can work from photographs of the clothing. Gold and silver jewellery can also be made to specification for not much more than the cost of the metal. A cartouche with the name of a friend or relative spelled in hieroglyphics makes a great gift.

The best thing about souvenir hunting in Egypt is not, however, the souvenirs. They are secondary to the excitement of the expedition up and down the back alleyways of the bazaars, past pungent barrels of basil and garlic and through medieval caravanserais. Take your sense of humour and curiosity with you, and if

you want to buy something, be prepared to bargain for it; it is expected.

Everyone seems to have a different bargaining strategy. I have found that one of the best is to not show too much interest in the thing that you want to buy. Start the bargaining with a price which is much lower than you really want to pay and then barter up to that point. When you state your first price the shopkeeper will inevitably huff about how absurd that is and then tell you his 'lowest' price. If it is still not low enough, then be insistent and keep smiling. Tea might be served as part of the bargaining ritual; accepting it doesn't place you under obligation to buy. If you still can't get your price, then just walk away. There are hundreds of shops in the bazaars.

It would be impossible to list everything that you can buy in Egypt but the specialities of a few regions are: El Faiyum – baskets of all sizes; the Sinai, especially around El Arish – colourfully embroidered Bedouin dresses; Port Said – duty-free electronic goods from Japan; Giza, at the village of Kerdassa – tapestries; Aswan – spices.

Things to Avoid

Unfortunately, ivory is also sold in Egypt's souvenir shops. Most of the ivory comes from the Sudan and Kenya where the elephant populations are being decimated to meet tourists' demands for ivory jewellery, trinkets and bookends. Perhaps, if people stop buying ivory, the elephant slaughter will also end. The slaughter prompted President George Bush to initiate a ban on all ivory imports to the USA and to call for similar bans in other countries. Ivory brought into Australia without a permit from Australian National Parks & Wildlife *and* the country of origin will be detained by customs.

WHAT TO BRING

Bring sunglasses, flashlight, a collapsible drinking cup, a water bottle/canteen, sun screen, a hat, a flat drain stopper (not a plug), a pocket knife, two to three metres of nylon cord, plastic clothes pegs (pins), a day pack, a small sewing kit and a money belt or pouch (leather pouches can be made to order in the bazaars).

Although most toiletries can be found in Cairo, Luxor and Aswan (especially at major hotels), certain items can be expensive or difficult to find in Egypt. So you may want to bring your own contact lens solution, tampons, contraceptives,

shaving cream in a can (in a tube it's readily available), or any favourite brand of shampoo or deodorant, as such items are expensive in Egypt.

STOP PRESS

Entrance fees for several archae-ological sites in Egypt are set to rise in October 1990. For example, the admission fee for the Great Pyramids will rise from E£3 to E£8.

Getting There

If you're heading to Egypt or the Sudan from Europe, you have the choice of either flying direct or going overland to one of the Mediterranean ports and taking a ferry to North Africa. If you're coming from any other continent, it can sometimes be cheaper to fly first to Europe, and then make your way to Egypt, than to fly direct. There are also the overland combinations of bus, taxi and ferry from other countries in Africa, and from Jordan, Kuwait, Saudi Arabia and Israel (and, as of June 1989, from Libya).

Whichever route you take there is always the inescapable search for the cheapest ticket and the certainty that no matter how great a deal you find, there's always someone out there with a better one.

AIR

Egypt has several airports but only six are international ports of entry: Cairo, Alexandria and, increasingly, the 'international' airports at Luxor, Aswan, Hurghada (Ghardaka) and Sharm el Shaykh. Most air travellers enter Egypt through Cairo.

Condor, the charter subsidiary of Lufthansa German Airlines, is operating direct flights from several cities in Germany to the five airports other than Cairo. During the high season (October to April), Condor has several flights each week to Sharm el Shaykh. For more information, see the From Europe section in this chapter.

Cairo

The airport is 25 km, or a 45 to 60 minute drive, from central Cairo. There are now two terminals – old and new – about 3 km apart. Most of the world's major airlines fly through the new terminal. Check out the duty-free stores on your arrival or departure, as they supposedly offer some of the best deals in the world on perfumes

and liquor. Refer to the Getting Around section in the Cairo chapter for notes on airport transport.

WARNING: on arrival at Cairo Airport, if you're not with a group, the chances are that you will be approached in the baggage claim area by a man or woman with an official-looking brass or laminated badge that says 'Egyptian Chamber of Tourism' or something similar. Such people are not government tourism officials, they are hotel touts. See the Accommodation section in the Facts for the Visitor chapter for more details of their operating methods.

Alexandria

The international airport in Alexandria is much smaller than in Cairo. A few flights to and from North Africa and southern Europe are serviced there. Lufthansa German Airlines is one of the few major international carriers with direct flights in and out of Alexandria.

Luxor

Charter companies fly directly from Europe, especially Germany, to Luxor International Airport. The charter flights are often part of package deals that include discounted accommodation at hotels such as the Jolie Ville and the Sheraton, among others.

Fares

Fares change every day, so those given here are simply an indication of what was available at the time of writing. The types of discounted tickets already mentioned are those which the airlines officially sanction. There are, however, unofficially discounted tickets available through certain travel agents around the world. The cheapest fares are always those offered by these so-called 'bucket shops', which sell an airline's unsold tickets at discounts of up to 50% off the 'official' fares. Despite the airlines' protestations to the contrary these tickets are actually released by them to selected travel agents. After all, it's better to fill all the seats even if some of the passengers are only paying half-price.

Many of the bucket shops are well established and reputable, but there are exceptions, so you need to exercise a little caution. When you pay your deposit make sure you get all the details of the flight in writing and never hand over the full amount until you have the ticket in your hand. If you change the flight, also get the changes in writing. Ask about provisions for getting your money back or a new ticket if you change your plans.

The best places in the world for bucket shops are London, Amsterdam and Hong Kong. They can also be found in other European cities and the USA. Use the official airline fare as a guide and shop around.

When booking your flight consider using an American Express card, as they have a special travel plan called 'Sign & Travel' which allows you to charge airline tickets and pay for them over a period of 20 months. The bad news is that they also charge a whopping 18% annual interest (or sometimes more depending on current interest rates).

With flying there are a bewildering number of possibilities, ticket types and jargon to get used to. The best thing to do first is arm yourself with as much general info and fare details as you can. One of the best sources of information about cheap fares all over the world is the monthly magazine *Business Traveller*. It's available from most newsstands or direct from 60/61 Fleet St, London EC4 ILA, UK, or 13th floor, 200 Lockhart Rd, Hong Kong. Other very useful magazines are: *Trailfinder*, from Trailfinders Travel Centre, 46 Earls Court Rd, London W8 6EJ, UK; and *Time Out*, London's weekly entertainment guide available direct from the publisher at Tower House, Southampton St, London WC2E 8QW, UK. In the USA, the Sunday travel sections of big city

newspapers such as the *Los Angeles Times* and the *New York Times* are also good sources of advertisements for discounted flights.

Advance Purchase These tickets must be bought from 14 days to two months in advance. They're usually only available on a return basis, have minimum and maximum stay requirements, allow no stopovers and carry cancellation charges.

Excursion Fares These are priced midway between advance purchase and full economy class. There are no advance booking requirements but a minimum stay abroad is often mandatory. Their advantage over advance purchase is that you can change your bookings and/or stopover without a surcharge.

Point-to-Point This is a discount ticket that can be bought on some routes in return for passengers waiving their rights to stopover.

ITX An 'independent inclusive tour excursion' (ITX) is often available on tickets to popular holiday destinations. Officially it's a package deal combined with hotel accommodation, but many agents will sell you one of these for the flight only. They'll give you phoney hotel vouchers in the unlikely event that you're challenged at the airport.

Economy Class Symbolised by 'Y' on the airline ticket, this is the full economy fare. Tickets are valid for 12 months.

Budget Fare These can be booked at least three weeks in advance but the actual travel date is not confirmed until seven days prior to travel. There are cancellation charges.

MCO A 'miscellaneous charge order' (MCO) is a voucher which looks just like an airline ticket but carries no destination or date. It is exchangeable with any IATA airline for a ticket on a specific flight. Its principal use for travellers is as an alternative to an onward ticket in those countries which demand one, and it's much more flexible than an ordinary ticket if you're not sure of your route.

Round-the-World An RTW ticket is just that. You have a limited period in which to circumnavigate the globe and you can go anywhere the carrying airlines go, as long as you don't backtrack. These tickets are usually valid for one year, the number of stopovers or total number of separate flights is worked out before you set off and they often don't cost much more than a basic return flight.

Standby This is one of the cheapest ways of flying. You simply turn up at the airport – or sometimes the airport's city terminal – without a ticket and take your chances that there will be a seat on the flight you want. The discount is quite considerable, but get there early as it's first come, first served.

From the UK

London is one of the best centres in the world for discounted air tickets. The price of RTW tickets, especially, is about the best available anywhere. An RTW ticket on TWA, Singapore Airlines or Japan Airlines will take you via Cairo for UK£900 (bought through Trailfinders in London).

For the latest fares, check out the travel page ads of the *Sunday Times*, *Time Out*, *LAW*, or the *News & Travel Magazine* (*TNT*). All are available from most London newsstands.

Two of the most reliable London agents are STA, at 74 Old Brompton Rd, London SW7 and 117 Euston Rd, London NW1; and Trailfinders, 46 Earls Court Rd, London W8. The latter also offers inexpensive inoculations and travel insurance as well as discounts on Budget Rent-a-Car and a few hotels in Cairo.

As of June 1989, Trailfinders was

offering a London to Cairo fare for UK£176 one way and UK£318 return.

The cheapest, but most unpredictable, way to fly to Cairo from London is for free as a courier for DHL or another air courier service. I met an elderly Hungarian woman in Cairo who had been spending her retirement travelling all over the world as a courier for DHL. She claimed that it was particularly easy to arrange from London.

From Europe

West Germany One of the most popular European carriers for flights between North Africa and the rest of the world is Lufthansa German Airlines. If your trip is originating in Germany, or if you wish to stop over in Germany before or after visiting Egypt, Lufthansa and its charter subsidiary Condor offer some of the most frequent connections with flights to and from Egypt. There are direct scheduled flights from Munich and Frankfurt to Cairo, Luxor and Alexandria. During the high season (October to April), there are several flights weekly to Sharm el Shaykh.

In Munich, a great source of travel information and equipment is the Därr Travel Shop (tel (089) 282032) at Theresienstrasse 66, D-8000, Munich 2. Aside from producing one of the most comprehensive travel equipment catalogues I've ever seen, they also run an 'Expedition Service' with current flight information available.

Amsterdam This is another popular departure point. Some of the best fares are offered by the student travel agency NBBS Reiswinkels (tel (020) 237686), Dam 17, Amsterdam. They offer a return fare from Amsterdam to Nairobi, with a stopover in Cairo or a return extension to Bombay. Their fares are comparable to London bucket shop fares.

Athens Bucket shop agencies around the Plaka and Syntagma Square in Athens charge about the lowest fares you can find for flights from Athens to Cairo. Fantasy Travel at 10 Xenofontas St (near Syntagma Square), Speedy Ways Travel Agency and Lin Travel (tel 322 1681), at 39 Nikis St, have all been recommended by travellers. At Lin Travel, Yorgos Akepsimidis has been recommended as the person to ask about cheap fares.

Standard excursion fares are available with airlines such as TWA for US$234 return. This fare requires a stay of at least 10 days.

Brussels From Brussels you can fly to Cairo, or Khartoum via Cairo, for reasonable fares that are comparable to those from London bucket shops, if you buy your tickets through NBBS Reiswinkels (student travel agency) or Acotra (tel 513 4480), 38 Rue de la Montagne, Brussels.

Paris A small French-Egyptian company called Djoser International (tel 42 45 46 24), at 6 Impasse du Curé, Paris 75018, seems to be acquiring a reputation for arranging budget flights to Egypt. Their speciality, however, is in organising small group adventures and expeditions to off-the-beaten-track destinations as well as more popular ones throughout Egypt. Unlike most other adventure travel operators, they maintain an office and their own minibuses and trekking equipment in Cairo. In 1989, they offered everything from one day visits to Saqqara and El Faiyum to camping adventures through the Western Oases and the Sinai. Their prices seem to be much lower than most of their competition because their overheads are lower.

From Israel

Air Sinai and El Al regularly fly between Cairo and Tel Aviv for about US$120 one way. El Al offers a 'Cairo extension' fare for half the regular price if you fly into Tel Aviv with them from somewhere else. If you have the time, however, travelling overland between Egypt and Israel is much cheaper and more adventurous.

From the Sudan

Flights on a variety of airlines leave Khartoum every day for Cairo. Sudan Airways flies from Khartoum to Cairo. The one-way flight costs about US$205 plus a few other charges that the Sudanese government seems to impose summarily.

From Tunisia

Tunis Air and EgyptAir offer student discounts on flights between Cairo and Tunis. Consult the offices of each airline for the latest information.

From the USA

An RTW ticket which includes a stopover in Cairo is a possibility: it will cost from about US$1699 to US$1899. Check the travel sections of Sunday newspapers for the latest deals.

EgyptAir flies from New York and Los Angeles to Cairo. Advance purchase and youth fares are available. An advance purchase ticket must be booked at least 14 days in advance. You must stay in Egypt a minimum of six days and a maximum of two months. The youth fare is valid all year, but you must be between 12 and 26 years old and book at least 72 hours in advance. The advance purchase fares from New York and Los Angeles are US$1049 and US$1079 respectively.

Lufthansa has connections to Cairo via Frankfurt from Anchorage, Chicago, Los Angeles, New York, San Francisco and Seattle. As of June 1989, there was also a service to Cairo from Los Angeles via Dusseldorf and Munich.

From Australia

Some of the best fares from Australia to Cairo are offered by STA. Fares start at A$875/1505 one way/return from Melbourne or Sydney, and A$820/1450 one way/return from Perth. RTW fares, which include a stopover in Cairo, cost between A$1775 and A$2120, depending on the season. STA has offices throughout Australia.

From Asia

Cheap tickets to Cairo are available in Hong Kong and Singapore, usually as part of an RTW ticket. From Hong Kong, an RTW ticket on EgyptAir costs approximately HK$12,900 or US$1655. From Bangkok, EgyptAir offers a one-way fare of around US$834 (US$627 for those under 26 years). Investigate bucket shop deals on EgyptAir and other airlines in both Hong Kong and Bangkok.

OVERLAND

From Israel

Egypt can be entered from two points in Israel. If you are crossing from the town of Eilat, you will go through the Egyptian borderpost in Taba. From Taba there are buses and collective, or service (pronounced 'ser-vees'), taxis which go south to Nuweiba, Dahab and Sharm el Shaykh. A few of these buses also continue on to Cairo via St Catherine's or Sharm el Shaykh. The four hour bus ride to Sharm el Shaykh costs E£7.

The other entry point is through the border post at Rafah in the south-western section of the Gaza Strip. *Sheruts*, the Israeli version of a service taxi, will take you and seven others to Rafah. Public buses also travel to the border, though changing buses could be a bit of a hassle.

Several Israeli tour operators offer bus transportation from Tel Aviv, Jerusalem or Eilat to Cairo with relatively quick processing through customs. Tickets cost from about US$25/36 one way/return, and some of the agents offer packages which include a few nights in a clean and comfortable Cairo hotel. There are a few agents near the Egyptian Embassy in Tel Aviv which have been recommended, including: Neot Hakikar (tel (03) 403111), 252 Hayarkon St; Masada Tours, Ibn Gvirol St (if you get a group together for the trip, you'll receive a discount); Galilee Tours, 142 Hayarkon St (they offer a package for US$60 return, including three nights at a Cairo hotel); VIP Tours (tel (03) 244181), 130 Hayarkon St; and Egged, the national bus company of Israel, which also puts together travel packages to Cairo. In Eilat, Neot Hakikar has an office across from the Shekhem Etzion Square.

If you plan to return to Israel, buy an open return ticket before you travel to Egypt. The return portion is often valid for up to six months. Don't forget the Israeli exit fee of about US$11 and the Egyptian entry fee of US$5, both of which can be paid in either the local or Western currencies.

Egyptian visas can be obtained from the embassy in Tel Aviv or the consulate in Eilat. For more information see the section on Visas in the Facts for the Visitor chapter.

A few travellers have reported that it was easier getting through Israeli passport control and customs in twos or threes rather than as individuals.

There are several possibilities for travel to Israel from Cairo. Travco (tel 342 0488), 13 Sharia Mahmoud Azmy, near the Cairo Marriott in Zamalek, has daily buses to Jerusalem and Tel Aviv for E£57/98 one way/return, daily except Saturday. The bus departs from the Cairo Sheraton at 5 am and from the Sheraton at Heliopolis at 5.30 am. The office is open from 9 am to 4 pm daily.

The Eastern Delta Transportation Company (tel 824773) has buses that depart daily, except Tuesday, Friday and Saturday, at 7.30 am; you must be at Abbassiya Station (Sinai Terminal) in Cairo before 7 am. The fare is E£61 one way (approximately US$23) and E£122 return. The ticket should be purchased at least a day in advance.

The cheapest way to go between Egypt and Israel is to take service taxis and/or local buses, but you really don't save that much money. From Cairo, take a service taxi from Midan Ulali (which is behind Ramses Station) between 4.30 and 6 am to El Qantara. It should cost about E£5 and take two hours. At El Qantara a ferry takes you across the Suez Canal (free), and on the east bank another service taxi will take you to the border at Rafah, for about E£6. That trip takes takes about 2½ hours. A bus takes you between the Egyptian and Israeli border posts, and after going through Israeli customs you have a choice of shared taxi or public bus. Buses depart at 12.30 and 3 pm for Ashkelon, where you can easily change for Tel Aviv or Jerusalem.

From the Sudan

There are two ways to travel overland from the Sudan to Egypt, but they're not very practical for foreign travellers – unless you're already a practised camel herder or have your own 4WD vehicle.

The camel herders, following an age-old caravan route known as Darb al Arba'een, or 'The 40 Day Road', bring their camels up from western Sudan through the Sahara Desert to Aswan, where they sell them. With a bit of negotiation and an adventurous spirit, you might be able to join a caravan.

If you have a tough 4WD vehicle, it is possible to drive up from the Sudan along the Red Sea coast. The border is seldom crossed, though, because the roads are very rough.

From Libya

Another way to enter Egypt overland is from Libya. At the time of writing the border had just been reopened, so details were unavailable. Minibuses and service taxis regularly travel from Marsa Matruh to Salum, which is on the Egyptian-Libyan border. In June 1989, Egyptian officials had begun discussing plans to widen the road between Marsa Matruh and Salum.

BOAT

From Europe

Adriatica Line operates a weekly ferry between Venice, Iraklion (Crete), Piraeus and Alexandria. Their Venice office can be contacted through Adriatica di Navigazione (tel 29133), 1412 Zattere. Other agents for Adriatica Line include: Extra Value Travel (tel (212) 758800), 437 Madison Ave, New York, NY 10022; Gilnavi Agencies (tel 452 4517), Akti Miaouli 97, Piraeus; Menatours (tel 740864), 14 Sharia Talaat Harb, Cairo; and Menatours (tel 809676), Midan Saad Zaghloul, Alexandria.

There are other companies that operate boats/ferries from Piraeus, Rhodes, Limassol (Cyprus), Corfu, Odessa (USSR), Varna (Bulgaria), Istanbul, Latakia (Syria) and Larnaca (Cyprus) to Alexandria and sometimes Port Said. For more information see the Alexandria Getting There section.

From the Sudan

The most common way of travelling between the Sudan and Egypt is by steamer from Wadi Halfa up Lake Nasser to Aswan. For more details on this, refer to the sections on Wadi Halfa and Aswan.

From Jordan & Saudi Arabia

It is possible to travel by boat between Jeddah (Saudi Arabia) and Suez via Aqaba (Jordan). The trip takes three days.

Arranging passage from Jeddah to Suez can be somewhat complicated and expensive. In Jeddah tickets are sold by the Red Sea Shipping Company, on Mina'a St across from the service taxi stand, and by Misr Travel on Al Malek Abd al Aziz St in the commercial centre across from the Corniche. First class is SR 500 and deck class is SR 250.

It's possible to buy a combination bus/ferry ticket that will take you from Jeddah and Riyadh via Aqaba and Nuweiba all the way to Cairo for SR 250. Buses depart Jeddah at least three times a week from the international bus terminal on Ba'ashan St, next to the SAPTCO terminal and across from the GPO. In Riyadh, tickets can be bought from most of the agencies near the SAPTCO terminal, just off Al Bathaa St. Finding someone around these terminals who speaks English can be difficult, if not impossible.

A similar bus/ferry ticket is possible from Amman (Jordan) via Aqaba to Nuweiba in the Sinai; you travel on air-conditioned buses for US$35, including the ferry ticket, which is cheaper than the ferry ticket alone. The ferry runs twice a day between Aqaba and Nuweiba.

An Egyptian visa can be issued 'on the spot' at the Egyptian Consulate in Aqaba.

From Kuwait

A bus travels from Kuwait across Saudi Arabia to Aqaba, Jordan. From Aqaba you can take the ferry to Nuweiba and then a bus to Cairo. The bus leaves Kuwait on Thursdays and Mondays at 1.30 pm and arrives in Aqaba at 11 am on Saturdays and Wednesdays. You're allowed 70 kg of luggage per person and this is checked thoroughly by the customs officials when you cross the Saudi border. The bus only takes 15 people, stops every four hours for a break, and costs about US$125 per person.

Getting Around

Egypt has a very extensive public and private transport system. If you don't suffer from claustrophobia, have plenty of patience and a tough stomach, you can travel just about anywhere in Egypt for relatively little money.

AIR

In Egypt, air fares are about average by international standards, but probably out of the range of most low-budget travellers. For example, the one-way air fare from Cairo to Luxor is E£135; E£70 for the 40 minute flight to Alexandria. In general, it is only worth flying if your time is very limited.

If you do have to go by plane, EgyptAir flies from Cairo to Hurghada (Ghardaka), Sharm el Shaykh, St Catherine's Monastery, Luxor, Kharga Oasis, Aswan and Abu Simbel.

During the high season (October to April), many of these flights are full. In 1989, EgyptAir had to rent Kuwaiti and Yugoslavian planes (with crews) to meet domestic flight demands.

Air Sinai has frequent, but occasionally delayed, flights from Cairo to Hurghada, Luxor, St Catherine's Monastery and Sharm el Shaykh. There are also flights from Sharm el Shaykh to Luxor and St Catherine's, Hurghada to St Catherine's and Sharm el Shaykh, and Luxor to St Catherine's and Sharm el Shaykh.

In 1989 a small charter company called ZAS had begun competing with Air Sinai and EgyptAir for domestic routes. By the time you read this, they will probably be a fully fledged airline with regularly scheduled flights for very competitive fares.

BUS

Buses service just about every city, town and village in Egypt and, on average, they're cheaper than the trains. Inter-city buses tend to become quite crowded, and even if you are lucky enough to get a seat in the first place, you'll probably end up with something or somebody on your lap. It's a great way to meet Egyptians!

Deluxe buses travel between some of the main towns. For instance, the Golden Rocket bus company runs deluxe buses between Cairo and Alexandria daily. Air-conditioned, comfortable buses with a few less amenities also run between Cairo, Ismailia, Port Said, Suez, St Catherine's Monastery, Luxor and Hurghada. Tickets cost a bit more than on standard buses but they're still cheap. Information about these buses will be given in the appropriate sections.

Tickets can be bought at windows at the bus stations or, sometimes, on the bus. Hang on to your ticket until you get off, as controllers sometimes board the bus to check fares.

TRAIN

Trains travel to almost every major city and town in Egypt from Aswan to Alexandria. Services range from relatively cheap (compared to the USA and Europe) 1st class wagons-lits (cars with deluxe sleeper compartments) to ridiculously cheap 3rd class cars. If you have an International Student Identification Card (ISIC) discounts as high as 50% are granted on all fares except wagon-lit fares. I have also heard about travellers getting a 50% discount with International Youth Hostel Association cards and Youth International Educational Exchange cards. It is possible to travel from Cairo to Aswan for 90 pt if you have an ISIC and are willing to take a beating in the 3rd class cars.

Wagons-Lits

Trains with wagons-lits are the best and fastest in Egypt. The cars are the same as those used by trains in Europe and only

sleeper compartments are available. Two wagon-lit trains travel between Cairo, Luxor and Aswan every day. Both are express trains. The schedule is:

Cairo	Luxor	Luxor	Aswan
Depart	*Arrive*	*Depart*	*Arrive*
7 pm	5.38 am	6.06 am	10 am
7.35 pm	7.38 am	8.30 am	12.35 pm

Aswan	Luxor	Luxor	Cairo
Depart	*Arrive*	*Depart*	*Arrive*
2 pm	5.50 pm	7.30 pm	6.40 am
5.45 pm	9.35 pm	10.35 pm	9.50 am

Wagon-lit trains are air-conditioned, and each compartment has hot and cold water. There are lounge cars, and dinner and breakfast are served in the compartments. A double compartment costs about E£140 one way, per person, including the sleeper ticket, meals, service and taxes. For slightly less, you can take a 50 minute flight to Luxor.

Reservations can be made at: the Wagon-Lit Central Reservation Office (tel 842367), 48 Sharia Giza, Cairo; or, as a last resort, the wagon-lit office at Ramses Station. You will need to show your passport.

I once bought a wagon-lit ticket at Ramses Station and had to wait for an hour while the woman behind the counter painted her nails and played with the intercom. After being told to wait 10 minutes four times, I went next door to the Tourist Police and complained. Within 20 minutes, although the woman's nails were still wet, I had a ticket.

Other Trains

There are other trains which travel to Luxor and Aswan from Cairo. Regular night trains with sleeper compartments and meals included leave every day and cost much less than the wagon-lit fares. To Luxor, the 1st class fare is about E£24 without a sleeper and E£40 with one. Reservations must be made in advance at Ramses Station in Cairo.

Night trains without sleepers also go to Luxor and Aswan from Cairo.

Always check the timetables posted at stations for the latest train schedules.

TAXI

Travelling by 'ser-vees' taxi is the fastest way to go from city to city. In most places the service taxis and their drivers congregate near bus and train stations. Each driver waits with his Peugeot taxi until he has six or seven passengers; he won't leave before his car is full unless you and/or the other passengers want to pay more money. If you want to go somewhere these taxis don't usually go, you can either hire a whole taxi for yourself or coax other travellers into joining you.

On the other hand, service taxi rides are really only for those with strong stomachs and blind faith in a driver who, if you are unlucky, might seem blind himself. Most of Egypt's main Nile road has only two lanes, so one ambling donkey cart can cause an immense traffic jam. This prompts everyone to try passing everyone else, even though the oncoming traffic usually prevents a clean, smooth pass. It's a modern joust where, fortunately, the jousters usually miss each other. Occasionally they don't, however, and the metal scraps of past accidents litter the roadside all over the country.

BOAT

Feluccas, the ancient sailboats of the Nile, are still the most common means of transport up and down the river. Sunset is one of the best times to take a felucca ride, but you can arrange a few hours peaceful sailing at any time from just about anywhere on the Nile. The best trip to make, however, is the journey between Aswan and Esna, Edfu or Kom Ombo; this takes from one to three days. See the Aswan Getting There & Away section for more information on how to arrange a trip.

DRIVING

Several car rental agencies have offices in Egypt, including Avis, Hertz and Budget. Their rates are similar to American rates and you need an international driving licence. Drivers in Cairo are complete maniacs, so think seriously before you decide to rent a car there. However, driving in other parts of the country isn't necessarily so bad. It would be great to have a car – or better still a 4WD – in the

Sinai, where the traffic is very light and there are lots of fascinating places to visit. Refer to the Getting Around section in the Cairo chapter for car rental costs.

MOTORCYCLE

Motorcycle would be an ideal way to travel around Egypt. The only snag is that you have to bring your own and the red tape involved is extensive. Ask your country's automobile association and the Egyptian Consulate about regulations. You must ride very carefully because the roads are often sandy and pocked with potholes. At Bahariyya, in the Western Oases, I met a German couple who were touring Egypt on BMW motorcycles. They had both fallen off en route to Bahariyya when their cycles hit a pocket of sand on the road. The man was only slightly bruised, but his girlfriend suffered mild concussion and temporary memory loss.

BICYCLE

Bicycles are a practical way of getting around a town and its surrounding sites. In most places, particularly Luxor, you can rent a bicycle quite cheaply; prices start at around E£5 per day.

Bicycles are, however, somewhat impractical for travelling long distances. The biggest problem is the possibility of getting flattened by one of Egypt's crazy drivers, who are not the slightest bit accustomed to cyclists on the roads.

HITCHING

It is easy to hitch in Egypt, but drivers are used to being paid for giving you a ride. You'll probably not save very much money by hitching, but it could be a good way to meet people. On the other hand, in Egypt, as elsewhere, hitching can be a dangerous practice, especially for women travellers.

CAMEL

Yes, it is actually possible to travel around Egypt by camel. While the more intrepid

If you're less adventurous (or more sensible!) there are easier and less physically and financially draining ways to realise your camel fantasies. It's easiest to hire a camel for a couple of hours and take a tour around the pyramids at Giza or the temple complex at Saqqara. A guide usually accompanies you. It is also easy to arrange a camel safari in the Sinai from near Nuweiba. More information about such treks is given in the Sinai chapter.

DONKEY

Donkeys are a very popular means of transport and you'll see them everywhere in Egypt except, perhaps, in restaurants. *Don't* buy one of these critters. They are cheap enough to rent for a couple of hours, or a few days, for getting you around some of Egypt's ancient sites.

LOCAL TRANSPORT

Bus

Cairo and Alexandria are the only cities in Egypt with their own bus systems, although neither one ever seems to have enough vehicles. If this is your first visit to a developing country, it will probably be the first time you have ever seen buses as crowded as these. The typical city bus has had its windows popped out and doors yanked off so that passengers can make use of the extra space by hanging from the door and window frames.

When I first arrived in Cairo I took photographs of this spectacle, but several Egyptians yelled at me for doing it. In a way they were right for berating me, because I was treating them like a sight for tourists. So, if you're tempted to take photos of crowded buses, consider your reasons for doing so.

Metro

Cairo is the only city in Egypt with a metro system. It's a single line of 33 stations that stretches for 43 km from the southern suburb of Helwan to El Marg near Heliopolis. The five stations in central Cairo are the only ones underground.

travellers will probably want to buy their own 'ship of the desert' there are easier and less costly alternatives.

Camels are brought, in caravans, from the Sudan to Egypt's two main camel markets at Daraw, near Kom Ombo, and Imbaba, near Cairo. If you're serious about owning your own, note that the camels are cheaper at Daraw, as it's closer to the end of the caravan route. They cost about US$200 there, while in Imbaba the price rises to as much as US$1000 per animal. This US$ price, of course, depends on the current exchange rate. In mid-1989, a medium-size camel was selling for E£1000 at Imbaba, while a bigger one was E£2000.

Once you've purchased your camel you then have to buy a proper saddle and appropriate kit bags. It all gets somewhat costly and complicated. It would be a good idea to try and get hold of an article by Rene Dee called 'Travel by Camel', which appeared in *The Traveller's Handbook*.

Another line is planned between Shubra and Giza.

The metro is fast, inexpensive (25 pt from Midan Tahrir to Ramses Station) and usually not crowded. It seems to have significantly reduced traffic in central Cairo.

Tram

Cairo and Alexandria are also the only two cities with tram systems. Alexandria's trams are relatively efficient and go all over the city but they also get quite crowded. Cairo's trams are similar, but as Cairo's subway system expands they're gradually being phased out. The trams are as cheap as, and sometimes cheaper than, the buses.

Taxi

There are taxis in most cities in Egypt. The most common and cheapest are the black-and-white taxis in Cairo and the black-and-orange ones in Alexandria. Almost all of them have meters but most of the meters don't work, so you have to pay what you think is right and be prepared to argue and bargain. The best method for paying is to get out of the cab when you arrive at your destination, stick the money through the front passenger's side window and walk away.

If you have to argue the price with the driver and he seems to be trying to cheat you, then just mention the police, and the taxi driver will probably accept your price

to avoid any hassle. Don't be intimidated by the driver's yelling; it's usually just an act to get you to cough up more money. If he agrees with you about seeing the police, then the fare you offered is probably too low. Sometimes, as one traveller reports, the driver may even jump out of the car, rip open his shirt like Superman and pound on his chest. Fortunately, this latter tactic rarely occurs.

The taxis marked 'Special' charge more than other taxis; these are almost always Peugeots that can hold up to seven passengers. Although their meters usually work, it makes little difference to the price because the fares are so inflated. The advantage of these taxis, though, is that you can get a group together and commandeer one for a trip to the pyramids or Saqqara for less than a black-and-white taxi might charge.

Whichever type of taxi you choose, if you're uncertain about the fare, then first consult a local or, as a last resort, negotiate the price before you get in. For long trips, such as to the pyramids or the airport, the driver will usually insist on first setting a fare. If possible, however, the best strategy whenever you take a taxi is to pretend that you know the fare, and pay after you've left the taxi.

When you want a taxi, stand where a driver can see you and wave your arm. When he slows down, yell out your destination so that, if he feels like it, he can stop for you. It's quite common to share a taxi with other passengers.

Cairo

Cairo is a seething, breathing monster of a city that swallows new arrivals and consumes those who return. All are destined to be captured and captivated in some small way by its incredible past and vibrant present. There are few, if any, cities in the world where the clash between old and new, modern and traditional, and East and West is more evident. Tall, gleaming hotels and office buildings overlook streets where cars and buses rumble and weave past donkey carts and their stubborn drivers. Less than one km from a computer store and supermarket in central Cairo there are mud-brick houses where goats still wander through 'living rooms' and water is obtained from spigots down the street.

Cairo is still the heart of Egypt and is allegorically called the Mother of the World. Since its rise in the 10th century, under Ibn Tulun, Egyptians have known Cairo as Al Qahira, which means 'the victorious'. They also call it Al Misr, which means 'Egypt'. For Egyptians this is the centre of their country; a centre which has been attracting them in ever-increasing numbers for centuries. No-one is quite sure just how many people have been drawn in from the countryside, even over the last few years, but the city has grown to mammoth proportions. Estimates of Cairo's population range from 11 to 15 million – roughly one quarter of Egypt's total.

The massive and continual increase in the number of people has overwhelmed the city. Housing shortages are rife; buses are packed to the hilt; snarled traffic paralyses life in the city; and broken pipes spew water and sewage into the streets. Everything is discoloured – buildings, buses and footpaths are brown and grey from smog and desert dust.

Amidst this chaos, the city government is trying to do what it can. A new metro rail system with 33 stations, including five in central Cairo, has been built to alleviate some of the traffic problems. Satellite suburbs such as Nasser City have been, or are being, built to alleviate housing shortages, and there have been somewhat futile attempts to ban donkey carts from the city streets.

Finding your way through this chaos is, remarkably, not as complicated as you may first think, and Cairo is a great city for walking around because it's not too spread out.

Orientation

Almost all travellers find themselves in Midan Tahrir at the beginning of their trip through Egypt. From Midan Tahrir north-east to Midan Talaat Harb and Ezbekiya Gardens you will find most of Egypt's Western-style shops and many of the budget hotels.

Further east there are Cairo's poorest districts, the market and medieval neighbourhoods of Muski, Darb al Ahmar and the City of the Dead. South of Darb al Ahmar is the ancient Citadel. Continuing farther east towards the airport you will enter Heliopolis, also called Masr Gidida or New Cairo.

North of Midan Tahrir are the neighbourhoods of Bulaq and Shubra. In the 1800s, under Mohammed Ali, Bulaq became Cairo's industrial centre. Today, it's one of Cairo's most densely populated areas and the industrialisation has spread northward to Shubra. Ramses Station is at the junction of the two districts.

West of Midan Tahrir is Gezira Island, the home of Cairo's elite, including diplomats and one of Egypt's foremost soccer teams. On the northern end of Gezira and the adjacent west bank is the central Cairo district of Zamalek, with its embassies, modern apartment buildings and a large private sports club.

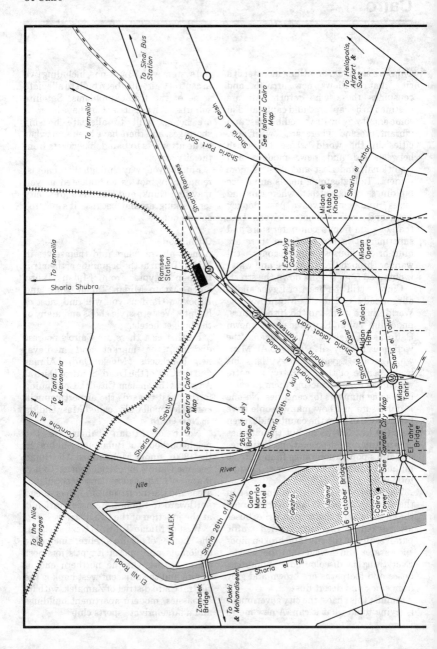

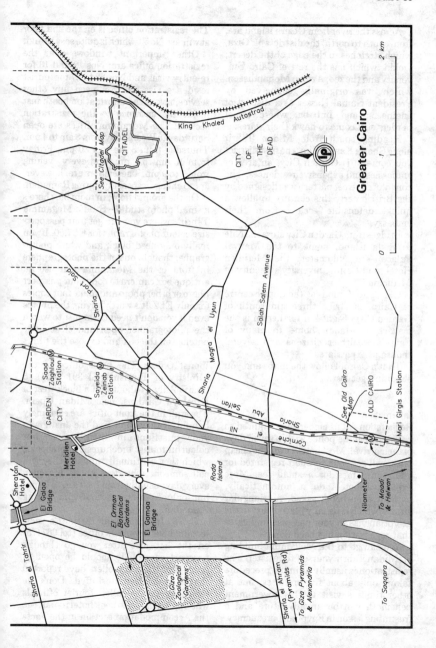

Greater Cairo

King Khaled Autostrad

CITADEL

See Citadel Map

CITY
OF
THE
DEAD

0   1   2 km

Sharia Port Said

Saad
Zaghloul
Station

Sayeida
Zeinab
Station

Salah Salem Avenue

Sharia Magra el Uyun

GARDEN
CITY

Sheraton
Hotel

El Galaa
Bridge

Meridien
Hotel

El Orman
Botanical
Gardens

El Gamaa
Bridge

Sharia el Tahrir

Sharia Abu Seitan

Corniche el Nil

Roda
Island

Nilometer

See Old Cairo
Map

OLD
CAIRO

Mari Girgis Station

To Maadi
& Helwan

Giza
Zoological
Gardens

Sharia el Ahram
(Pyramids Rd)

To Giza Pyramids
& Alexandria

To Saqqara

Across the river from Gezira Island are, from south to north, the districts of: Giza, which stretches to the edge of the desert; Dokki, which has the rest of Cairo University and the zoo; Aguza; Mohandiseen, which was originally conceived by President Gamal Nasser as a district of engineers; and Imbaba, where camel herders still come to hawk their wares.

Heading south from Midan Tahrir along Sharia Kasr el Eini, the first district you come to is Garden City, an area of embassies and expensive residences. The convoluted street pattern was designed by the British early this century to allow a quick, defensible escape from their embassy.

Bridges from Garden City cross the Nile to Roda Island, home to the Manyal Palace, the Nilometer, the Meridien Hotel, and Cairo University's Faculty of Medicine.

Old Cairo, famous as the Coptic centre of Cairo, is about three km south of Garden City. Eight km further on is the district of Maadi, home to many of Egypt's wealthier citizens and several thousand expatriates.

That's Cairo. Follow the maps and you shouldn't get lost.

Information

Registration All foreigners are required to register with the police within seven days of their arrival. Most hotels, even the cheap ones, will get your passport registered for you, sometimes for a small fee. More expensive hotels do it automatically, without even being asked. A triangular stamp, which is usually placed next to the Egyptian visa in your passport, indicates that registration has been done.

You can go to the Mogamma building on Midan Tahrir yourself to register. The registration is usually a simple procedure taking only about five minutes, but at other times a visit to this government behemoth can be an adventure and a frustrating lesson in Egyptian bureaucracy.

The registration office is on the 2nd floor at window No 50, which is quite easy to find.

Other important windows near the registration office are: Nos 12 and 13 for re-entry visas and Nos 22 to 27 for tourist residence visas. If you need any other service, ask at the information booth just inside the entrance to the registration section. The Mogamma offices are open Saturday to Wednesday from 8 am to 4 pm, Thursday from 8 am to 1.30 pm, Friday from 10 am to 1 pm, and every evening from 7 to 9 pm. These hours are, however, apt to change, especially during Ramadan.

On the ground floor, in room 99, there's a small photo studio – Studio Mogamma Tahrir – where you can get four passport-size colour photographs for E£7.50. If you really only need black and white photographs, though, one of the photographers in front of the Mogamma will use an antique box camera to copy your passport photo or other photo and make four copies for only E£2. It's worth buying the photos even if you don't need them just to watch the photographer open and close little hatches on the box and expose the film.

Tourist Offices The head office of the Ministry of Tourism (tel 391 3454), 5 Sharia Adly, is about half a block west of Ezbekiya Gardens, near Midan Opera. The staff in the front office are extremely helpful. If they can't find the answers to your questions in their sparse but colourful tourist brochures or notebooks, which they continually update, they will call someone who does know. It's open every day: usually from 8.30 am to 7 pm, but only from 9 am to 5 pm during Ramadan.

Cairo International Airport's new terminal has a tourism office (tel 667475) on the left just after you go through passport control. It should be open 24 hours, but some travellers have reported that it was often unstaffed. Don't be fooled by the so-called tourist officials who approach you to book hotel rooms; see the Accommodation section in the Facts for the Visitor chapter for more on these airport hotel touts.

There's also a tourist office (tel 950259) at the pyramids; it's on Pyramids Rd (also known as Sharia al Ahram), on the left just after the junction with the Desert Road to Alexandria. It's usually open from 8.30 am to 5 pm every day.

Misr Travel, the official Egyptian government travel agency, is at 1 Sharia Talaat Harb.

Post Cairo's GPO, in Midan Ataba near Midan Opera and the Ezbekiya Gardens, is open 24 hours a day except on Fridays and certain holidays. If you want to mail a package, be prepared for a time-consuming process. Do not seal your package before letting a customs official see the contents.

First, go to the GPO Parcel & Customs area (there is a sign in English outside the door) and pay 40 pt to an official to complete the necessary forms for you. Someone behind the counter will approve the forms and slap on a few stamps, and the package is weighed and sewn up for E£3.50. The average rate for postage is about E£4 per kg. Packages must not weigh more than 20 kg and must not total more than 1½ metres when you add the height, width and depth together. If the items you are sending are worth more than E£100, you may need an export licence from the Ministry of Economy & Foreign Trade (tel 919661), 8 Sharia Adly.

The easiest way to send a package is to pay someone else a small fee and have them do it for you. Some shopkeepers will provide this service, especially if you've bought the article in their bazaar. It should include obtaining an export licence, packaging and mailing.

There are post office branches at: Cairo International Airport (in the departures section); on Midan Falaki; in the grounds of the Egyptian Museum; and at Ramses Station. You can only send packages from the GPO, the airport branch, or the Ramses Station branch. Hours are 8.30 am to 3 pm, except Friday.

The branches tend to be crowded most of the day, so it's much easier to buy stamps from hotel bookstores or cigarette/postcard kiosks. They charge about 5 pt more than the post office. Airmail postage to countries outside the Arab world is 50 pt for a letter and 45 pt for a postcard.

An express mail service is also available through a few post office branches – two days to Europe, three to the USA. Rates are E£20 to Europe and North America for packages less than 100 grams; E£22 for an additional half kg and E£7 for every half kg after that.

Other express mail services are available through Federal Express (tel 355 0427), 1079 Corniche el Nil, Garden City; Middle East Courier Service (tel 245 9281), 1 Sharia Mahmoud Hafez, Heliopolis; and Skypac International Express (tel 348 8204). These courier services are also possible sources of free or discounted air tickets to various destinations outside Egypt, because they often need couriers to transport their packages.

Letters deposited in the reception desk mail box at any major hotel seem to take less time to arrive at an overseas destination than if they were sent directly through a post office box. If you wish to use the post office boxes, remember that red is for domestic mail, green is for Cairo and Cairo express mail, and blue is for international air mail.

Telecommunications Since 1986, Cairo has been revamping its telephone system and changing the numbering system. It's hard to know which parts of the city have changed and which haven't, and which will and which won't. Some parts of the same street, for example, have new numbers while others don't. Older establishments tend to have four to six digit numbers, and newer places have five to seven digits. The new numbers have usually gained another digit at the beginning – either a 3, 5 or 7.

Local telephone calls cost 10 pt, but you can supposedly use the old 5 pt coins for pay phones. They are usually in front of telephone offices, in metro stations, and in the lobbies of major hotels. Perhaps I just had bad luck, but I was unable to get any of the three pay phones I tried to work, even the only one at the five star Semiramis Hotel. If you don't have old 5 pt pieces you're out of luck, because neither the bank nor the hotel cashiers have these coins.

Many kiosks and small shops have telephones for public use, for 25 to 50 pt per call. The Nile Hilton, right by Midan Tahrir, has a bank of pay phones for which they sell 50 pt tokens.

Direct long-distance calls can be made from some home phones, but most are made from hotels or telephone offices. Most hotels, but not the very cheap ones, have direct international lines, but they'll charge more than the telephone offices. At either place the connections are usually quite good. It's impossible to make collect calls from Egypt.

Calls booked at telephone offices must be paid for in advance. They can either be taken in a booth at the office or directed to an outside number such as a private home or hotel. If you opt for the latter, keep the receipt just in case you need a refund for an incomplete call.

There are telephone offices in several places around Cairo; just look for the sign with a telephone dial on it. There's an office on the north side of Midan Tahrir, one in Sharia Adly near the tourist information office, and one in Sharia Mohammed Mahmud in the Telecommunications building. All main telephone offices are open 24 hours a day. Branch offices are open from 7 am to 9 pm.

Rates for international calls are cheapest between 8 pm and 7.59 am. Three minute calls to the USA are (8 am to 7.59 pm/8 pm to 7.59 am) E£17/13; UK E£15.20/11.50; Australia E£24.20/18.20; Canada E£18.20/13.70; West Germany E£15.20/11.50; and France E£18.20/13.70.

Telegrams can be sent from most of the telephone offices. The charge for a telegram to the USA is 60 pt per word. Each word in an address is also counted.

Money Most of the world's major banks have branches in Cairo. Cash advances in US$ are available at the Bank of America and Citibank if you have a Visa card or MasterCard. Advances might also be available with the same cards through Chase Manhattan, Chemical Bank and Manufacturers Hanover. Money can be wired through all of these banks. Their addresses in Cairo are:

Bank of America
    106 Sharia Kasr el Eini, Garden City (tel 354 7788); open from 8.30 am to 2 pm, but only from 10 am to 1.30 pm during Ramadan
Barclays International
    Banque du Caire, 12 Midan el Sheikh Yusuf, Garden City (tel 354 2195). Personal banking services are available, but the office specialises in corporate banking. Mail must be addressed to PO Box 2325, Cairo.
Lloyds Bank International
    44 Sharia Mohammed Mazhar, Zamalek (tel 341 8366). Personal and corporate banking facilities are available.
Manufacturers Hanover
    3 Sharia Ahmed Nessim, Giza (tel 726703)
Chase Manhattan
    9 Sharia Gamal al Din Abdul Mahassen, Garden City (tel 26111)
Chemical Bank
    14 Sharia Talaat Harb (tel 740707)
Citibank
    4 Sharia Ahmed Pasha, Garden City (tel 355 1873/7)
Royal Bank of Canada
    10th floor, Abu el Feda building, 3 Sharia Abu el Feda, Zamalek (tel 698128)
Misr America International Bank
    8 Sharia Ibrahim Neguib, Garden City (tel 756341). This is the head office of an Egyptian bank that is affiliated with the Bank of America.

Bank hours are Monday to Thursday from 8.30 am to 1.30 pm and Sunday from 10 am to 12 noon. Most Egyptian banks are also open on Saturdays, and there are Bank

Misr exchange offices at the Nile Hilton and outside Shepheard's Hotel which are open 24 hours a day.

American Express American Express has several offices in Cairo. They can provide US$ cash for US$ travellers' cheques, exchange money, cash personal cheques or sell travellers' cheques. An American Express card is necessary for cashing personal cheques and purchasing travellers' cheques.

You should change money for a visa extension at a commercial bank, although this rule is subject to change. If you're exchanging money at an American Express office for the purchase of an airline ticket, be sure that they don't invalidate your exchange receipt with an Arabic stamp that translates as 'not for airline tickets'.

There are American Express offices at:

Central Cairo
    Egypt Head Office, 17 Sharia Mohammed Bassiuni (tel 764244)
    15 Sharia Kasr el Nil, between Midan Tahrir and Midan Talaat Harb (tel 750444, 750455). Open from 8.30 am to 4.30 pm, but only from 9 am to 4 pm during Ramadan. The client letter service is closed on Friday. This is one of the best places in Cairo to receive mail and to have money wired from overseas. To qualify for the mail service you should have an American Express card or travellers' cheques.
Ramses Hilton
    1115 Corniche el Nil, Garden City (tel 773690)
Nile Hilton
    Corniche el Nil (tel 743383)
Sheraton Hotel
    Sharia el Nil, Dokki (tel 348 8937)
Cairo Marriott
    Sharia Gezira, Zamalek (tel 341 0136)
Residence Hotel
    Road 18, Maadi (tel 350 7817)
Meridien Cairo
    Corniche el Nil (tel 844017)
Cairo International Airport (tel 670895)

Thomas Cook Thomas Cook has four offices in Cairo, and a foreign exchange

counter at Cairo International Airport. The offices are at:

Central Cairo
    17 Sharia Mohammed Bassiuni (tel 743955)
Maadi
    88 Road 9 (tel 350 2651)
Dokki-Giza
    Shops 9 & 10, Sharia 26th of July (tel 346 2429)
Heliopolis
    7 Sharia Baghdad (tel 670622)

Airline Offices Most airlines which operate in and out of Egypt will only sell you air tickets if you can show them bank receipts which prove that you officially changed enough money for the ticket. They will also keep the receipts so you can't reuse them for visa extensions. Airlines which are not part of IATA (the International Airlines Transport Association) usually don't require receipts, so you can buy a ticket through them, at discounts of up to 30%, with black market money. Some of these airlines also offer student and youth discounts but this changes quite often, so you'll have to check for yourself. Most of the Eastern European airlines, such as Yugoslav Airlines (JAT), Polish Airlines (LOT) and Balkan Airlines, don't belong to IATA.

The addresses of airlines which operate in and out of Cairo are:

Air France
    2 Midan Talaat Harb (tel 743300)
    Cairo International Airport (tel 668903)
Air India
    1 Sharia Talaat Harb (tel 754864/73/75)
    Cairo International Airport (tel 966756)
Air Sinai
    Nile Hilton (tel 760948)
    12 Sharia Kasr el Nil
Balkan Airlines
    13 Sharia Mohammed Sabri Abu Alam (tel 751211)
British Airways
    1 Sharia Abdel Salam Aref (tel 759977, 772981)
Bulgarian Airlines
    17 Sharia Kasr el Nil (tel 751152)

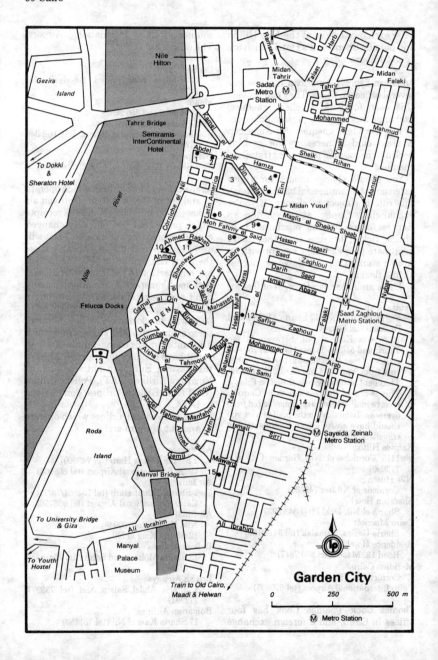

Nile Hilton

Gezira Island

Midan Tahrir

Sadat Metro Station

Midan Falaki

Tahrir

Talaat

Harb

Ramses

Kamel

Mohammed

Mahmud

Gendi

Yusef

Tahrir Bridge

Semiramis InterContinental Hotel

Sheik Rihan

Abdel
1   2

Kader

Din Selah

Hamza

4

Eini

5

To Dokki & Sheraton Hotel

River

3

Latin America

Midan Yusuf

Mansur

Corniche el Nil

6

Maglis el Sheikh Shaab

Moh Fahmy el Said

7

9

8

Hassan Hegazi

Nile

Ahmed Ragheb

Saad Zaghloul

10

11

Darih Saad

Ahmed

el Shennawi

Serag el Kubra

Ismail Abaza

Felucca Docks

GARDEN CITY

Saray el Gezira

Haras

Saad Zaghloul Metro Station

Gamal el Din

Kamel

Abdul

Mahassen

Safiya

Zaghoul

Falaki

Nubar

Birgas

Hasan Mura

12

Tolumbat

Sufia

Arab

Aisha

el Tahmouria

Walda

Mohammed Izz el Arab

Roda Island

Dar

Zein Hemdol

Salamlek

Amir Sami

Abdel Rahman Manfahmy

Kasr

14

Ahmed Gemil

Ismail Sirri

Sayeida Zeinab Metro Station

Manyal Bridge

Mawara

15

To University Bridge & Giza

Ali Ibrahim

Ali Ibrahim

To Youth Hostel

Manyal Palace Museum

13

Train to Old Cairo, Maadi & Helwan

Garden City

0   250   500 m

M Metro Station

1	Shepheard's Hotel
2	Ministry of Industry
3	US Embassy
4	Bank of America
5	Barclay's Bank Building
6	Sit In Restaurant
7	UK Embassy
8	Canadian Embassy
9	Sudan Embassy
10	Nile Hotel
11	US Cultural Center
12	Garden Palace Hotel
13	Meridien Cairo Hotel
14	French Cultural Centre
15	Abu Shakra Restaurant

Czechoslovak Airlines (CAS)
    9 Sharia Talaat Harb (tel 751416)
EgyptAir
    Nile Hilton (tel 759771)
    Reservations(tel 747 4444)
    Cairo International Airport (tel 244 5982)
    6 Sharia Adly (tel 922444)
    Flight information (tel 872122)
El Al Israel Airlines
    5 Sharia Mazriki, Zamalek (tel 341 1620)
Ethiopian Airlines
    Nile Hilton (tel 740911)
Hungarian Airlines
    12 Sharia Talaat Harb (tel 753111)
Japan Airlines (JAL)
    Nile Hilton (tel 740621/809)
    Cairo International Airport (tel 660843)
KLM (Royal Dutch Airlines)
    11 Sharia Kasr el Nil (tel 740648/999)
    Cairo International Airport (tel 662226)
Kenya Airways
    Nile Hilton (tel 747428)
Lufthansa German Airlines
    9 Sharia Talaat Harb (tel 393 0343)
    Cairo International Airport (tel 666975)
Olympic Airways
    23 Sharia Kasr el Nil (tel 393 1318/277)
    Cairo International Airport (tel 664503)
PanAm
    Emeco Travel, 2 Sharia Talaat Harb (tel 747302)
Polish Airlines (LOT)
    1 Sharia Kasr el Nil (tel 747312)
Singapore Airlines
    Nile Hilton (tel 762702)
    Cairo International Airport (tel 291 5144)
Sudan Airways
    1 Sharia el Bustan (tel 747251)

Trans World Airlines (TWA)
    1 Sharia Kasr el Nil (tel 749900)
    Cairo International Airport (tel 344 1050)
Yugoslav Airlines (JAT)
    9 Sharia el Sherifien (tel 742166)

Embassies The addresses of some of the foreign embassies in Cairo are:

Algeria
    14 Sharia Hassan Sabri, Zamalek (tel 341 7782, 340 7709)
Australia
    Cairo Plaza, 1097 Corniche el Nil (tel 777990/999/273); hours are from 8 am to 3 pm, Sunday to Thursday.
Canada
    6 Sharia Mohammed Fahmy el Said, Garden City (tel 354 3110); hours are from 7.30 am to 3 pm, Sunday to Thursday
Central African Republic
    15A Corniche el Nil, Maadi (tel 35 09 23 37)
Ethiopia
    12 Midan Bahlawi, Dokki (tel 755133, 705372)
France
    29 Sharia el Giza, Giza (tel 728649, 728346). This street has changed names several times, so there are several variations – it's also known as Sharia Taha Hussein, Sharia Dr Taha Hussein , and Sharia Bahyi al Din Barakat, which is actually an extension southward of Sharia el Giza.
India
    5 Sharia Aziz Abaza, Zamalek (tel 340 1000/6168)
Iran
    Embassy of Switzerland Interests Section
    12 Sharia Rifa'a, Dokki (tel 348 7508)
Iraq
    9 Sharia Mohammed Mazhar(tel 340 9815)

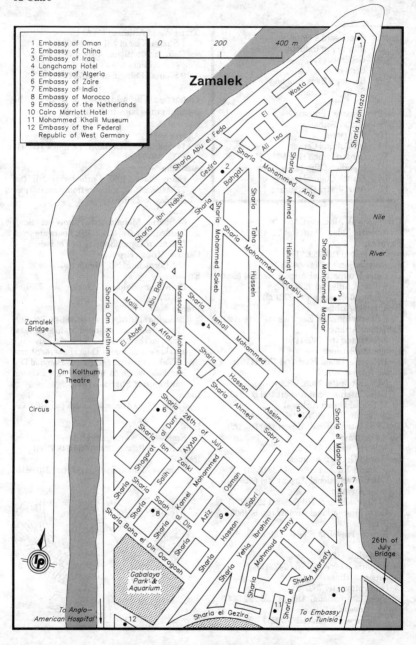

1 Embassy of Oman
2 Embassy of China
3 Embassy of Iraq
4 Longchamp Hotel
5 Embassy of Algeria
6 Embassy of Zaire
7 Embassy of India
8 Embassy of Morocco
9 Embassy of the Netherlands
10 Cairo Marriott Hotel
11 Mohammed Khalil Museum
12 Embassy of the Federal
   Republic of West Germany

0   200   400 m

Zamalek

Nile

River

Sharia Montaza

El Wosta

Ali Isa

Sharia

Sharia Mohammed Anis

Sharia Ahmed Hishmat Marashly

Sharia Abu el Feda

Gezira

Sharia Bahgat

Sharia Toha Hussein

Sharia Mohammed Mazhar

Sharia Ibn Nabik

Sharia

Sharia Mohammed Sakeb

Sharia Mohammed

Sharia

Abu Bakr

Mansour

Sharia Ismail Mohammed

Malik

El Abdel el Affal

Mohammed

Sharia Hassan Assim

Sharia Ahmed Sabry

Zamalek
Bridge

Sharia Om Kolthum

Om Kolthum
Theatre

Circus

Sharia al Durr

26th of July

Shagarat Ibn Zanki

Ayyub Kamel Mohammed

Osman

Sharia Salih al Din

Aziz

Hassan Sabri

Sharia Salah al Din

Sharia Qaragosh

Sharia Baha el Din

Sharia Yehia Ibrahim

Sharia Mahmoud Azmy

Sharia el Sheikh Marsafy

Sharia el Maahad el Swissri

26th of
July
Bridge

Gabalaya
Park &
Aquarium

Sharia el Gezira

To Anglo—
American Hospital

To Embassy
of Tunisia

Israel
    6 Sharia Ibn al Malek, Giza (tel 726000,
    727706); hours are from 10 am to 2.30 pm
    daily
Jordan
    6 Sharia Gohaina, Dokki (tel 348 5566);
    hours are from 9 am to 2 pm, Saturday to
    Thursday. The embassy is two blocks west
    of the Sheraton Hotel. Visas are free and
    take about three hours to process. You'll be
    denied a visa if your passport indicates that
    you've been to Israel, which will be shown by
    Egyptian border stamps from Rafah or Taba.
Kenya
    20 Sharia Boulos Hanna, Dokki (tel 704455,
    704546). One traveller reports that a 30 day
    visa was granted while he waited.
Netherlands
    18 Sharia Hassan Sabri, Zamalek (tel
    698744, 698936)
New Zealand
    New Zealand's affairs are handled by the
    UK Embassy
North Yemen
    28 Sharia Amin al Rafi'i, Dokki (tel 348 6754).
    For a visa you will need two photographs
    and a letter of recommendation from your
    embassy. You must travel within 14 days of
    the issuance date of the visa, otherwise the
    visa becomes invalid. Visas are usually
    issued within two days of applying. Upon
    arrival you will be granted a one month visa.
Sudan
    3 Sharia al Ibrahimy, Garden City. The
    consulate is around the corner at 1 Sharia
    Mohammed Fahmy el Said, Garden City
    (tel 354 5043). Visa applications can usually
    be filed from 9 am to 12 pm from Sunday to
    Thursday at a visa window on Sharia
    Mohammed Fahmy el Said, just around the
    corner from the petrol station on Sharia
    Kasr el Nil. Five copies of the application,
    five passport size photos, and a letter of
    recommendation from your embassy are
    required before the visa can be issued. At
    the time of writing, it was taking about 15
    days to issue a visa. For more details on visas
    and travel restrictions, refer to the Facts for
    the Visitor chapter in the Sudan section of
    this book.
Tunisia
    26 Sharia el Gezira, Zamalek (tel 698962)
Uganda
    9 Midan el Missaha, Dokki (tel 980329,
    981945)

UK
    corner Sharia Ahmed Ragheb and Sharia
    Latin America, Garden City (tel 354 0850);
    hours are from 8 am to 1 pm, Sunday to
    Thursday
USA
    5 Sharia Latin America, Garden City (tel
    355 7371); hours are from 8.30 am to 2 pm,
    Sunday to Thursday
West Germany
    8 Sharia Hassan Sabri, Zamalek (tel
    403687, 406017)
Zaire
    5 Sharia el Mansour Mohammed, Zamalek
    (tel 341 1069, 341 7954)

Cultural Centres There are several cultural
centres in Cairo sponsored by other
countries. Most run libraries, show films
and sponsor various lectures, exhibits and
performances. They are great places to
catch up on the latest news from home or
to watch a free movie or video.

The American Cultural Center (tel 355
0532) is at 4 Sharia Ahmed Ragheb, Garden
City, opposite the UK Embassy. The
library holds more than 200 periodicals
and 10,000 books and also shows video-
taped news, from the ABC *Nightline*
programme, twice a week. You can
arrange to see a video tape on your own
when the facilities are not being used for
public presentations. Used book sales are
also arranged occasionally. The reading
rooms are open from 10 am to 8 pm on
Monday and Wednesday, and from 10 am
to 4 pm the rest of the week except on
Saturday and American and Egyptian
holidays, when it's closed.

The British Council Library (tel 345
3281), which is in a villa near the circus
grounds at 192 Sharia el Nil, Zamalek,
carries most major daily and weekly
newspapers. It has more than 30,000 books
and 120 periodicals, and the reading
rooms are open daily, except Sunday,
from 9 am to 1 pm and from 5 to 8 pm.

The West German centre, known as the
Goethe Institute (tel 759877), 5 Sharia
Abdel Salam Aref, near the Cleopatra
Hotel and Midan Tahrir, presents

interesting seminars and lectures on Egyptology and other topics in German. There are also performances by visiting music groups and special art exhibits. The library has rather erratic hours, so phone first.

Other cultural centres include:

Canada
    Canadian Embassy, 6 Sharia Mohammed Fahmy el Said, Garden City (tel 23110)
France
    Madrasat el Houquq al Fransiyya, Mounira (tel 27679)
Italy
    Italian Cultural Institute, 3 Sharia el Sheikh Marsafy, Zamalek (tel 808791)
Japan
    Japanese Cultural Centre, 10 Sharia Ibrahim Neguib, Garden City (tel 339624)
India
    Information Service of India, 37 Sharia Talaat Harb (tel 747702). If you don't have Lonely Planet's *India – a travel survival kit*, this is the next best source of information on India.

Film There are several camera stores in Cairo where you can buy and process film and have certain types of cameras repaired. Actina Photo, which is on Sharia Talaat Harb between Midan Talaat Harb and Midan Tahrir, charges E£1 for colour print processing and 30 to 40 pt per print depending on the size. Supposedly, if you give them the film by 10 am, you can have the prints by 4 pm the same day. Film prices are E£25 for Kodachrome 64 (36 exposures) including processing, Kodacolor Gold 100 (36 exposures) E£6.50, Kodacolor 200 (36 exposures) E£7.50, Kodacolor 400 E£8.50 and Agfa 100 (36 exposures) E£6. They can repair all cameras other than Yashica and Russian models.

There's also a one hour photo shop next to the Grand Hotel.

Books The American University in Cairo Press publishes a few books about Cairo which can be very helpful. Their *Cairo: A Practical Guide* has already been mentioned. They also publish a *Guide to the Islamic Monuments of Cairo*, which is probably one of the best of its kind available. *The Blue Guide to Egypt* describes almost everything in Cairo and the rest of Egypt in more detail than you probably want, though it's useful for finding some of Cairo's lesser known monuments.

For a perceptive look into life on Cairo's back streets, read the short novel *Midaq Alley* by Naguib Mahfouz, one of Egypt's foremost authors and a Nobel Prize winner. It was written in the 1940s, but much of what it portrays about life on a small street near Khan el Khalili is still relevant.

Bookshops & Newsstands One of the best bookshops in Cairo is Shourouk, on Midan Talaat Harb and at 16 Sharia Gawad Husni. They have a great selection of books in English, French and German about Egypt, including translations of contemporary Egyptian literature such as books by Mahfouz. In front, there are several major news magazines and newspapers.

The Readers' Corner Bookshop, 33 Sharia Abdel Khaliq Sarwat (near Sharia Sherif and Sharia Mustafa Kamel), has a fairly good selection of English language books and newspapers. There's also a branch in the Nile Hilton.

The American University in Cairo Bookstore, on the corner of Sharia Mohammed Mahmud and Sharia Yusuf el Gendi, carries an excellent selection of books in English, including a wide range of books and guides about life in Egypt. The bookstore also carries many Lonely Planet titles (including this book), periodicals and newspapers from Europe and the USA. It's closed in August.

In front of Groppi's on Midan Talaat Harb is the best newspaper and magazine stand in Cairo. It carries the most recent editions of major newspapers and magazines from around the world, including *Time*, *Newsweek*, the *Times* and the *International Herald Tribune*. You can also find most of the English-language Cairo publications here.

Across the street at 15 Sharia Kasr el Nil is L'Orientaliste, one of only three bookstores in the world specialising in Egyptology. L'Orientaliste has an excellent collection of antiquarian books and prints of 19th century Egypt.

Nearby in Midan Talaat Harb, Madbouly (or Madbouli) bookshop has an extensive collection of books in English, French and German. Anything you can't find in the other bookshops, you should be able to find here.

A few other good bookshops around Cairo are Garden City Bookstore, 1103 Corniche el Nil, between the British Embassy and Shepheard's Hotel; Lehnert & Landrock, 44 Sharia Sherif; Al Ahram Bookstore, in the outside arcade of the the Nile Hilton; and the Anglo-Egyptian Bookshop, 165 Sharia Imad el Din. There are also bookshops in most of the major hotels.

Look around the bookstalls at Ezbekiya Gardens. Their collections of second-hand books and magazines in English are remarkable. You will find some of the most unlikely books here – everything from Dickens to Plato.

For the latest wire service news reports, check the wire copy in the lobby of the Sheraton Hotel in Giza, or in the Nile Hilton across from the business centre.

Arabic Lessons Several organisations offer Arabic lessons in Cairo. Most of the programmes available are listed in the Studying in Egypt section of the Facts for the Visitor chapter.

Arabic lessons are also offered through cultural centres. The French Cultural Centre, Madrasat el Houquq al Fransiyya, Mounira, offers a nine month course for E£1250. Classes are held for four hours, Monday to Friday. (In winter classes are held for one month at a ramshackle hotel on the west bank in Luxor.)

The Goethe Institute, 5 Sharia Abdel Salam Aref, also offers relatively inexpensive Arabic lessons. Check the magazine *Cairo Today* for a listing of other organisations which occasionally offer Arabic courses.

Dive Clubs The Cairo Diving Club organises monthly diving trips, rents equipment and offers plenty of information on the dive sites. The club meets on the first Monday of each month in the Arusa room of the Nile Hilton. Dues are E£25 a year and PADI instruction is available.

The British Sub-Aqua Club, also in Cairo, offers BSAC and PADI certification and instruction. Members meet on the third Monday of each month at 7.30 pm in the recreational centre of the British Petroleum building, 31 Lebanon St, Mohandiseen.

Diving equipment is also available at Bas Khalides on Sharia Champollion. They sell masks, snorkels, scuba gear and fishing tackle.

Emergency Some important numbers in Cairo are:

Ambulance
    Cairo Ambulance Service (tel 123, 770123, 770227); possibly slow
Police
    Emergency (tel 122)
    Garden City (tel 20781)
    Zamalek (tel 80179)
Fire
    all districts (tel 125)

Medical Information
Hospitals There are three hospitals in Cairo with more modern facilities than most of Egypt's other hospitals: Cairo Medical Centre (tel 695168) in Heliopolis; Anglo-American Hospital (tel 806163), next to the Cairo Tower in Zamalek; and Al Salaam International Hospital (tel 350 7350/267), Corniche el Nil, Maadi, which has 24 hour facilities.

24 Hour Pharmacies There are a number of pharmacies in Cairo that operate day and night. These include Gomhuriyya, which has one branch (tel 816424) at 3 Sharia Shagarat el Durr, Zamalek, one (tel 748835) on Sharia Mazloum, Bab el Louk, and one (tel 743369) on the corner of Sharia Ramses and Sharia 26th of July; and Abul Ezz (tel 843772), which is at 49 Sharia Kasr el Eini.

Almost anything can be obtained without a prescription from Egypt's pharmacies.

Doctors & Dentists Enquire at your embassy for the latest list of recommended doctors and dentists or consult *Cairo: A Practical Guide* published by The American University in Cairo Press.

There are International Association for Medical Assistance to Travellers (IAMAT) centres at:

Central Cairo
  13 Sharia Wakf el Kharboutly (tel 901816, 243 4653); coordinator Dr Nabil Ayad el Masry
  11 Sharia Imad el Din (tel 910816, 916424); coordinator Dr Samir B Bassily
Maadi
  87 Road 9 (tel 350 3105, 351 0230); coordinator Dr Sherif Doss
Heliopolis
  1 Midan Roxy (tel 258 2729); coordinator Dr Amin Iskander Fakry

Vaccinations Vaccinations against cholera, yellow fever, tetanus, hepatitis, and a few other diseases are available at the Mogamma building and the former Hotel Continental. At the Mogamma building on Midan Tahrir, go to the public health section just inside the entrance on the left side. One traveller who got vaccinations here claimed that the 'place looked dirty, but they do use sterile needles'.

At the old Hotel Continental, on Sharia el Gomhurriya facing the Ezbekiya Gardens, is the International Vaccination Centre; it's at the back of the lobby on the right side. They give you the standard yellow International Certificate of Vaccination card free. If you are getting a yellow fever vaccination, keep in mind that protection doesn't become effective until 10 days after vaccination. The centre is open from 8 am to 2 pm.

Central Cairo

Most travellers begin their Egyptian experience in the vicinity of Midan Tahrir and Sharia Talaat Harb. It's the bustling, noisy centre of central Cairo where you'll find an amazing variety of shops as well as most of the budget hotels and eating places, banks, travel agents and cinemas. Central Cairo also has a number of museums, art galleries, markets, gardens and scenic views of the Nile.

Egyptian Museum
This museum is in a huge building a little north of Midan Tahrir. Also called the Egyptian Museum or the Museum of Egyptian Antiquities, it is one of the greatest museums you will ever see; it should not be missed. In fact, it's a good idea to visit this place at least twice – at the beginning of your visit to familiarise yourself with Egypt's ancient history, and at the end to understand better all you have seen throughout the country.

More than 100,000 relics and antiquities from almost every period of ancient Egyptian history are housed in the museum. This vast collection was first gathered under one roof in 1858 by Auguste Mariette, a French archaeologist who excavated the temples of Edfu, Dendara, Deir el Bahri, Amun (at Karnak in Luxor) and a few others.

The exhibits are arranged chronologically from the Old Kingdom to the Roman Empire. Each room could easily be a museum in its own right; if you spent only one minute at each exhibit it would take more than nine months to see everything. The sheer number and variety of things to see, while fascinating, is quite overwhelming. To help you deal with this

Top: Cairo skyline from Zamalek (GB)
Left: Cairo backstreets (SW)
Right: Bab Zuweila, one of several medieval gates in Islamic Cairo (SW)

Top: Market scene, Cairo (TW)
Left: Market scene (TW)
Right: Market scene (TW)

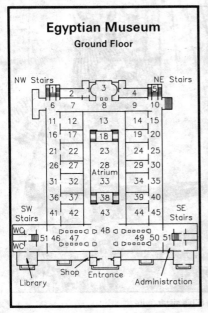

Egyptian Museum
Ground Floor

will take you around for about E£5 per hour.

The following is an abbreviated guide to some of the most popular exhibits. If you wish to learn more about a particular period or set of antiquities, check out the selection of Egyptology books in the library of the American University in Cairo.

Tutankhamun Without doubt, the exhibit that outshines everything else in the museum is the treasure of the comparatively insignificant New Kingdom Pharaoh Tutankhamun.

The tomb and treasures of this young king, who ruled for only nine years during the 14th century BC, were discovered in 1922 by English archaeologist Howard Carter. Its well-hidden location in the Valley of the Kings, below the much grander but ransacked tomb of Ramses VI, had prevented tomb robbers and, later, archaeologists from finding it any

labyrinth there are a couple of guidebooks available.

A Guide to the Egyptian Museum, a 300 page list of the museum's artefacts, is available at the museum's ticket window or the gift shop for E£5. It's organised by catalogue number rather than by room, with little description of each item. The *Blue Guide* is a costlier alternative but it describes the museum room by room in excellent detail. *The Egyptian Museum Cairo – Official Catalogue* costs E£60 and has descriptions and excellent photographs, most of them in colour, of 270 important exhibits at the museum.

Admission to the museum is E£4, or E£2 for students with a student card. It's open from 9 am to 4 pm daily but closes between 11.15 am and 1.30 pm on Friday. Bags and cameras have to be left at the front desk unless you wish to pay an extra E£10 for permission to use your camera in the museum. There are official guides who

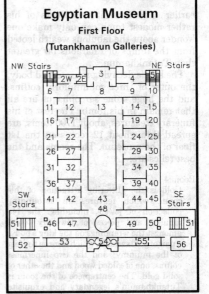

Egyptian Museum
First Floor
(Tutankhamun Galleries)

Tutankhamun & his sister/wife

earlier. The incredible contents of his rather modest tomb can only make one wonder about the fabulous wealth looted from the tombs of Pharaohs far greater than Tutankhamun.

The king's decaying mummified body, the outer of three mummiform coffins, and the huge stone sarcophagus are all that remain in his tomb. The rest of his funerary treasures, about 1700 items, are spread throughout 12 rooms on the 1st floor of the museum. The rooms and the best relics are:

Room 4
Gold is the glittering attraction of this room, which features an astounding collection of jewels, including: the 143 amulets and pieces of jewellery found amongst the wrappings on the king's body; a pair of gold sandals, which were on the feet of the mummy; and the two innermost coffins, one of gilded wood and the other of solid gold. The centrepiece of the room is Tutankhamun's legendary and exquisite

mask of beaten gold inlaid with lapis lazuli and other gems.

Rooms 7, 8 & 9
The gilded wooden shrines which fitted inside each other and held the gold sarcophagus of Tutankhamun at their centre are in these rooms.

Room 15
King Tutankhamun's bed befits a Pharaoh; it is covered with sheet gold, with string stretched across the frame. Beautifully rigged model ships, to be used by the Pharaoh on his voyage through the afterworld, are also found in this room.

Room 20
A gilded copper trumpet is the feature of this room; it was once 'played' in 1939.

Room 24
Here you will see the originals of the papyrus paintings that you find in bazaars throughout Cairo.

Room 30
The most interesting items in this room are a beautiful wooden clothing chest and Tutankhamun's wooden throne. Covered with sheet gold, silver, gems and glass, the

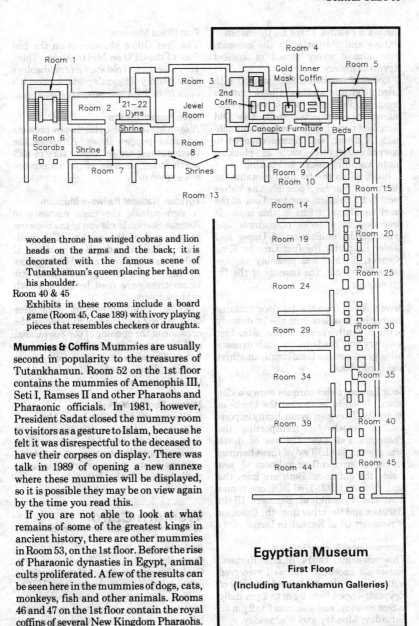

Room 1
Room 2
21–22 Dyns
Shrine
Room 3
Jewel Room
2nd Coffin
Room 4
Gold Mask
Inner Coffin
Canopic Furniture
Beds
Room 5
Room 6 Scarabs
Shrine
Room 8
Shrines
Room 7
Room 13
Room 9
Room 10
Room 15
Room 14
Room 19
Room 20
Room 24
Room 25
Room 29
Room 30
Room 34
Room 35
Room 39
Room 40
Room 44
Room 45

Egyptian Museum

First Floor

(Including Tutankhamun Galleries)

wooden throne has winged cobras and lion heads on the arms and the back; it is decorated with the famous scene of Tutankhamun's queen placing her hand on his shoulder.

Room 40 & 45

Exhibits in these rooms include a board game (Room 45, Case 189) with ivory playing pieces that resembles checkers or draughts.

Mummies & Coffins Mummies are usually second in popularity to the treasures of Tutankhamun. Room 52 on the 1st floor contains the mummies of Amenophis III, Seti I, Ramses II and other Pharaohs and Pharaonic officials. In 1981, however, President Sadat closed the mummy room to visitors as a gesture to Islam, because he felt it was disrespectful to the deceased to have their corpses on display. There was talk in 1989 of opening a new annexe where these mummies will be displayed, so it is possible they may be on view again by the time you read this.

If you are not able to look at what remains of some of the greatest kings in ancient history, there are other mummies in Room 53, on the 1st floor. Before the rise of Pharaonic dynasties in Egypt, animal cults proliferated. A few of the results can be seen here in the mummies of dogs, cats, monkeys, fish and other animals. Rooms 46 and 47 on the 1st floor contain the royal coffins of several New Kingdom Pharaohs.

Statues & Palettes There are thousands of statues and statuettes in the museum from almost every period of ancient Egyptian history.

Room 47 on the 1st floor is lined with sarcophagi and statues. Check out the centre exhibit cases, which have several interesting statuettes from the Old Kingdom period. These include a hunchback, a dwarf, and figures engaged in everyday activities such as plucking birds, kneading dough and baking.

Room 42 on the 1st floor contains the Palette of Narmer, possibly the oldest record of a political event and one of the most significant items in this room. It describes, in a series of pictures and symbols, the unification of Upper and Lower Egypt for the first time by King Narmer. Narmer was probably another name for Menes, the founder of the 1st dynasty.

Jewels Room 3 on the 1st floor contains interesting jewellery from the 1st dynasty to the Byzantine period. Some of the best jewellery was made in the 12th dynasty using gems such as lapis lazuli, amethyst and turquoise.

Solar Barques Solar barques were wooden boats placed in or around the tombs of Pharaohs. They were symbolically important as vessels for transporting the Pharaoh's soul over the sea of death beneath the earth. Two of these barques are on the ground floor in Room 43, just inside the entrance. Both are from the 12th dynasty (1990-1780 BC); one comes from the Pyramid of Senusert III in Dahshur and the other from the Colossus of Senusert III at Karnak in Luxor.

Entomological Society Museum

This museum, at 14 Sharia Ramses, houses an excellent and well-preserved collection of the birds and insects of Egypt. It's open from 9 am to 1 pm daily except Sunday, and also from 6 to 9 pm on Saturday, Monday and Wednesday.

Post Office Museum

The Post Office Museum is on the 2nd floor of the GPO on Midan Ataba. There are collections of old stamps and displays of the history of Egypt's postal service. It's open from 9 am to 1 pm.

Cairo Puppet Theatre

Also on Midan Ataba, this theatre presents colourful puppet shows. Although the presentations are in Arabic they're still worth seeing, as most of the actions are self-explanatory.

Egyptian National Railways Museum

A sign outside the main entrance to Ramses Station leads you to the museum at one end of the station. This well-organised museum displays the history of railways and railway-related architecture in Egypt. On the ground floor are locomotives once used by Egypt's 19th century rulers.

A beautifully preserved locomotive built in 1862 for Princess Eugénie on the occasion of the opening of the Suez Canal still has its original upholstery and oil lamps. The museum is open daily except Monday, Friday and holidays from 8 am to 1 pm. Admission is 50 pt.

Military Surplus Market

While you are at the Railways Museum, visit the military surplus market next door, on the far side of the station. They sell an interesting assortment of surplus military boots, pants, shirts, blankets, duffle bags and other items.

Western Cairo

Gezira Island

Opera House Just over Tahrir Bridge on Gezira Island is the Opera House, which is far from being a mere house. It's a US$30 million arts complex that includes a museum, library, art gallery, and music halls with modern technical equipment and superb acoustics. The complex was built using traditional Islamic designs, visible in both the geometrical layout of the courtyards and the styles of the windows and doors. The main music hall and opera house has hosted groups from all over the world, including theatre groups from the USA and dance troupes from Spain and Portugal. There's always something happening here; check *Cairo Today* and the *Egyptian Gazette* for the latest details.

Cairo Tower One of the best places for a panoramic view of Cairo is the 185 metre high tower. Early in the morning, when you can usually see the pyramids at Giza, or late afternoon are the ideal times for taking photographs. There's a revolving restaurant on top which is a bit expensive by Egyptian standards, but there's also a cafeteria where you can have the same revolving view of Cairo with much cheaper drinks. The entrance fee for the tower, if you're going to the top, is E£3. Hours for the viewing area are 9 am to 12 midnight, daily.

Mohammed Khalil Museum This museum, at 1 Sharia el Sheikh Marsafy, is opposite the entrance to the Gezira Club. The collection includes several sculptures by Rodin, some French Impressionist paintings, and contemporary works by Egyptian artists. The contemporary exhibits offer an interesting insight into the minds of modern Egyptians. The museum is open from 9 am to 3 pm and 5 to 8 pm, and admission is E£1, or 50 pt for students.

Gabalaya Park & Aquarium Gabalaya Park, near Sharia el Gezira, includes an aquarium. This cute place, where the fish inhabit aquariums built into tunnels that look like they were once bomb shelters, seems to be practically unknown to foreigners. Even if fish don't interest you, the park is still worth a visit for the respite it offers from the chaos of Cairo.

Moukhtar Museum This museum, also known as the National Centre for Fine Arts, is on the left side of Sharia Tahrir, just before you cross Al Galaa Bridge to Dokki. Moukhtar (1891-1934) was the sculptor laureate of Egypt, and this museum contains most of his major works. It is open from 9 am to 1.30 pm daily, except Monday. The entrance fee is E£2, or E£1 for students.

Dokki, Zamalek & Imbaba
Museum of Modern Art This museum, at 18 Sharia Ismail Abou Foutuh, Dokki, is around the corner from the Indiana Hotel. It will give you some idea of contemporary culture and changing life in Egypt. The watercolour room is especially good; have a look at the painting of the temple complex at Philae by an artist named Zaky. To find the room, look for the stone crocodile on the floor and go in the direction of its big nose. The garden in front is overgrown with weeds and dotted with statues. The museum is open from 9 am to 2 pm, Sunday to Thursday; 9 am to 1 pm on Friday. Admission is E£1, or 50 pt for students.

Agricultural & Cotton Museums This complex in Dokki is off Sharia Wisaret el Ziraa, at the foot of the overpass on Sharia 6th of October. The Agricultural Museum contains lots of stuffed animals and exhibits that show life in Egyptian villages. The Cotton Museum has displays of the history of cotton production in Egypt. In winter it's open from 9 am to 4 pm, Sunday to Thursday; 9 to 11.30 am and 1 to 4 pm on Friday. There's a small entrance fee.

Cairo Circus This small big top is at the foot of Zamalek Bridge, off Sharia 26th of July in Zamalek. Check with the tourist office or *Cairo Today* for a schedule of performances.

Camel Market The camel market, or Souk el Gahmell, is just off Sharia Sudan, near

1 Agricultural and Cotton Museums
2 Museum of Modern Art
3 West German Embassy
4 Cairo Sheraton Hotel
5 Jordanian Embassy
6 Soviet Embassy
7 Presidential Residence
8 Ugandan Embassy

Dokki

0   250   500 m

the Imbaba airport. It is the largest of its kind in the country. Amongst the growing urban sprawl the market looks rather like a mirage – which is probably why it's one of the most interesting things to see in this part of Cairo.

The camels are brought up the 40 Day Road from the Sudan to Aswan by camel herders from Western Sudan. Then they are crammed into trucks in Aswan for the 24 hour journey to Imbaba, where they're traded or sold for other livestock such as goats, sheep and horses. If you're interested in buying a camel, smaller ones cost about E£1000 while the bigger ones are E£2000. Early Friday or Sunday between about 6.30 and 8 am are the best times to visit, although the market does seem to last well into the late morning hours.

Enterprising young men at the entrance gate will attempt to charge you a E£1 entrance fee. There is no official entrance fee; just walk in and ignore them.

Getting to the market is as much of an adventure as the market itself. The easiest way is to take a taxi, but the more scenic route is a one to 1½ hour walk from central Cairo. From Midan Tahrir walk across the 6th of October Bridge through Zamalek to Sharia Gamal Abdel Nasser, turn right and walk along the Nile to Midan Kit Kat (also called Midan Khalid Ibn al Walid). Turn left on Sharia Sudan, which starts at the midan, and follow it to the train tracks. Veer left, cross the tracks to Sharia Matar on the other side and continue walking in the same direction. You'll cross another set of tracks to the main street, where the market is on the left side.

If you don't want to walk, there are minibuses from Midan Tahrir, Midan Giza and the pyramids (Saqqara and Pyramids roads) to Midan Kit Kat for 35 pt. From Midan Kit Kat, there's another minibus to the camel market for 15 pt; ask for the Souk el Gahmell. The waterbus also stops near Imbaba.

To get back to town, flag down a minibus in front of the market and ask for Midan Kit Kat – most of them are going there – then take another minibus to central Cairo. See the Getting Around section in this chapter for a list of buses around Cairo.

Islamic Cairo

Islamic Cairo is an area replete with medieval mosques, apartment buildings, and the greatest density of people in the country – and probably the Middle East.

It is easy to get lost in this district. In the back alleyways and streets of neighbourhoods with names like Darb al Ahmar and Baatiniyya you'll suddenly find yourself back in the Cairo of six or seven centuries ago; in a time when donkeys and camels transported people and goods, buildings were like shaky wooden pyramids, and exotic foods were hawked from pavement stalls. Be prepared for this passage to the past because it hits all your senses.

Splendid mosques and imposing buildings still loom over narrow, crowded streets and bustling squares; the sweet, pungent aromas of turmeric, basil and cumin drift from open barrels, mix with the offensive odours of livestock, and grab at your nose like invisible fingers; and people go about their daily business as they have done, it seems, forever. This could be the medieval Cairo of Ibn Tulun or Salah al Din, except that the age-old aromas now mingle with petrol fumes as donkeys and camels compete with cars for space; and an awful lot of poverty offsets the grandeur of the architecture throughout what was once the intellectual and cultural centre of the Arab world.

Your tour can begin anywhere in the area, but the following describes two different walking tours. Before you begin, you may want to buy a specialised guide to the monuments in the area. *A Practical Guide to Islamic Monuments in Cairo*, by

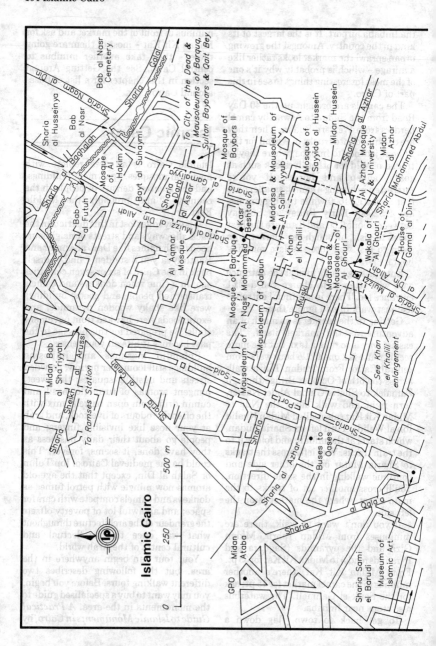

Islamic Cairo

To City of the Dead &
Mausoleums of Barquq,
Sultan Baybars & Qait Bey

Bab al Nasr
Cemetery

Sharia Nagm al Din

Calal

Sharia al Husseinya

Bab
al Nasr

Sharia
al Husseinya

Baghalah

Sharia

Bab
al Nasr

Mosque
of Al
Hakim

Bayt al Suhaymi

Sharia Darb
al Astar

Sharia
Gamaliyyo

Mosque of
Baybars II

Mosque of
Sayyida al Hussein

Midan Hussein

Sharia

Al Azhar Mosque
al Azhar

Midan
al Azhar

Al Azhar Mosque
& University

Midan
Mohammed Abdul

Bab
al Futuh

Sharia Muizz al Din Allah

Kasr
Beshtak

Madrasa & Mausoleum of
Al Salih Ayyub

House of
Gamal al Din

Al Aqmar
Mosque

Mosque of Barquq

Mosque of
Al Nasir Mohammed

Khan
el Khalili

Wakala of
Al Ghouri

Sharia al Din Allah

Mausoleum of Qalaun

Madrasa &
Mausoleum of
Al Ghouri

Sharia al Muizz

Sharia al Muski

See Khan
el Khalili
enlargement

Midan Bab
al Sha'riyyah

Sheikh al Arussi

To Ramses Station

Sharia al Geish

Sharia Port Said

Sharia al Azhar

Buses to
Oases

Sharia

500 m

250

Islamic Cairo

0

Midan
Ataba

GPO

Sharia al Azhar

Sharia al Qalaa

Sharia Sami
el Barudi

Museum of
Islamic Art

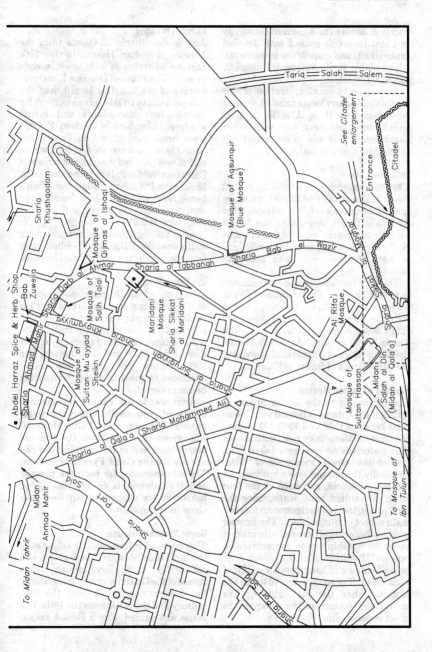

Parker & Sabin (The American University in Cairo Press), is packed with detailed explanations and maps of the monuments. It's available at the American University in Cairo Bookstore.

As you begin your exploration of this part of Cairo, carry lots of small change for baksheesh. You'll need it for tipping guards and caretakers, who will expect baksheesh if you ask to see something special, such as a minaret.

WALKING TOUR 1

The first walking tour begins at Midan Salah al Din at the foot of the Citadel, in front of the mosques of Sultan Hassan and Al Rifa'i. To get there, take bus No 72 (usually extremely crowded) or minibus No 54 (not crowded) from Midan Tahrir, or walk there (it will take about 45 minutes).

There are several interesting monuments to visit in the area. On this walk of five or six hours en route to the Citadel, you can visit the Mosque of Sultan Hassan, Al Rifa'i Mosque, an open-air market, Ibn Tulun Mosque, Gayer-Anderson House, the Mausoleum of Shagarat al Durr, and the Mausoleum of Imam al Shafi'i.

Mosque of Sultan Hassan

The mosque is to the left of Sharia al Qala'a if the Citadel is behind you. It was built between 1356 and 1363 AD, during the time of Mameluke rule, with stones that historians believe were taken from one of the Great Pyramids of Giza. Originally the mosque was a *madrasa*, or theological school, and each of the four *liwan*, or vaulted halls, surrounding the central court served as classrooms for each main school of Sunni Islam. The interior is typically devoid of decoration to make it easier for worshippers to concentrate on prayers. Hundreds of chains which once held oil lamps still hang from the ceiling of each liwan. Try to visit this place in the morning when the sun lights up the mausoleum portion of the mosque; the effect is quite eerie.

Al Rifa'i Mosque

Just across Sharia al Qala'a from the Mosque of Sultan Hassan is this 19th century imitation of a Mameluke-style mosque. The Princess Dowager Khushyar, mother of the Khedive Ismail, had the mosque built in 1869 to serve as a tomb for herself, her descendants and future khedives. Members of modern Egypt's royal family, including King Farouk, are buried here – as is the Shah of Iran, whose casket was paraded through the streets of Cairo from Abdin Palace to the mosque in 1980, with President Sadat, the Shah's family and Richard Nixon leading the cortege. Hours are 8 am to 6 pm and admission is E£1.

After visiting these two mosques, walk south-west down Sharia al Salibah away from the Citadel to the Ibn Tulun Mosque.

Ibn Tulun Mosque

This is one of the largest mosques in the world. Ibn Tulun was sent to rule Cairo in the 9th century by the Abbasid Caliph of Baghdad. He had the mosque built in 876, with an inner courtyard large enough for most of his army and their horses. The 13th century fountain in the centre continues to provide water for washing before prayers.

After wandering around the massive courtyard, you should climb the spiral minaret (see map of Ibn Tulun Mosque). The views of Cairo from the top are magnificent and in the morning you can usually see the Great Pyramids at Giza. The admission fee for both the mosque and the minaret is 50 pt, plus 25 pt baksheesh for slippers to put over your shoes in the mosque.

Gayer-Anderson House

This museum is immediately adjacent to the Ibn Tulun Mosque. The house is also called Bayt al Kritliyya, which means 'house of the Cretan woman'. It is actually two houses, one dating from the 16th century and the other from the 18th. The house was named after a British major,

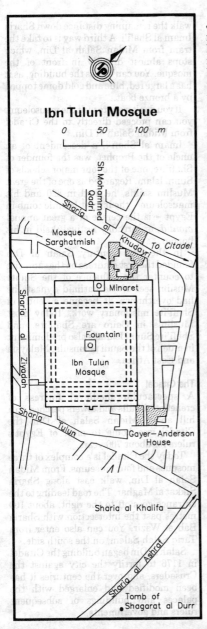

Ibn Tulun Mosque

0   50   100 m

Sharia Mohammed al Qadri

Sharia al Khudayri   To Citadel

Mosque of Sarghatmish

Minaret

Sharia al Ziyadah

Fountain

Ibn Tulun Mosque

Sharia Tulun

Gayer–Anderson House

Sharia al Khalifa

Sharia al Ashraf

Tomb of Shagarat al Durr

John Gayer-Anderson, who occupied and restored it between 1935 and 1942. In 1942 he bequeathed the house and exotic furnishings to Egypt for use as a museum. Each room has a different exotic theme – the Persian Room, the Queen Anne Room, the Chinese Room, the Mohammed Ali Pasha Turkish Room and the Harem Room of Amina Bint Salem el Gazzar.

Most of the rooms have windows with intricately carved wooden *mashrabiyya* screens, which enabled the women of the harem to discreetly observe the goings-on of any male visitors without being seen themselves. Hours are 9 am to 4 pm from Sunday to Thursday, and 11.15 am to 1.30 pm on Fridays. Admission is E£1, or 50 pt for students.

When you leave Gayer-Anderson House turn right on the street parallel to the Ibn Tulun Mosque and walk to Sharia Tulun. Turn left and walk the short distance to the intersection with Sharia al Khalifa, then turn right. Sharia al Khalifa becomes Sharia al Ashraf, and you continue walking down this street into a district called the Southern Cemetery. This is the beginning of a vast Muslim necropolis which stretches all the way to the suburb of Maadi, about five km south. After about 250 metres you will come to the Mausoleum of Shagarat al Durr on the left.

Mausoleum of Shagarat al Durr

Built in 1250, this is a small simple tomb which has Byzantine glass mosaics gracing the prayer niche. The most interesting thing, however, is the story of the woman whose remains are entombed here.

Shagarat al Durr was a slave from a nomadic tribe who managed, albeit briefly, to become the only female Muslim sovereign in history. She secured this position fairly easily and in the process instigated Mameluke rule, which was to last for the next 200 years; however, she came to a very nasty end.

Salih Ayyub, the last ruler of the Ayyubid dynasty, married Shagarat al

Durr at a time when the soldiers of the 7th Crusade had taken control of Damietta, in the Nile Delta. Knowing that Ayyub was sick and dying, the Crusaders were prepared to wait out his death and attack Cairo when the government collapsed. So when he died in 1249, Shagarat al Durr hid his corpse, and for three months managed to pretend that he was still alive and passing on orders to his generals through her. She waited for her son to come back from Mesopotamia and take control, but when he did return he proved to be a weak ruler, so she had him killed.

She then declared herself Sultana of Egypt and ruled for 80 days – the only woman to rule over Muslims until Queen Victoria. But the Abbasid caliph of Baghdad refused to recognise her position, so she married a Mameluke, the leader of her slave warriors, and ruled through him. When he decided that he needed an extra wife, Shagarat al Durr had him killed and threw his second wife into prison. When the Mameluke warriors discovered Shagarat al Durr's part in the assassination, she offered to marry their new leader but was imprisoned instead. She was eventually turned over to her husband's second wife who, along with several other women, beat Shagarat al Durr to death with wooden clogs. They hung her body from the side of the Citadel as food for the dogs. What was left of her was salvaged and entombed.

Mausoleum of Imam al Shafi'i
This mausoleum is two km south of the Midan Salah al Din, in the Southern Cemetery. To get there, walk south from the Citadel along Sharia Mabarrat Mustafa Kamel to Tariq Salah Salem. Turn right and then left off the square into Sharia al Qadiriyyah, which becomes Sharia Imam al Shafi'i. The mausoleum is a little over one km further on.

You can also take bus No 405 from Midan Salah al Din, get off before it turns left towards the Moqattam Hills, and

walk the remaining distance down Sharia Imam al Shafi'i. A third way is to take the tram from Midan Salah al Din, which stops almost directly in front of the mosque. You can't miss the building, as it has a large red, blue and gold dome topped by a bronze boat.

If you don't want to visit the mausoleum, you can proceed directly to the Citadel from Midan Salah al Din.

Imam al Shafi'i, a descendent of an uncle of the Prophet, was the founder of Shafi'ite, one of the four major schools of Sunni Islam. Regarded as one of the great Muslim saints, he died in 820 and his mausoleum – the largest Islamic tomb in Egypt – is the centre of a great annual *moulid*, or birthday festival, held in his honour.

In the 12th century Salah al Din founded the first madrasa on the same site to counter the influence of the Shi'ite Muslim sect of the Fatimid dynasty he had overthrown. It became a centre of Shafi'ite missionary work. Today most Muslims in Cairo are Shafi'ite, and Shafi'ite Sunni Islam is also predominant in much of the Saudi peninsula, Malaysia and East Africa.

The Citadel
A spectacular medieval fortress of crenellated walls and towers perched on a hill above Midan Salah al Din, the Citadel was home to most of Egypt's rulers for about 700 years.

Today the Citadel is a complex of three mosques and four museums. From Midan Salah al Din, walk east along Sharia Sikkat al Maghar. The road leading to the entrance goes off to the right, about 100 metres past the intersection with Sharia Bab el Wazir. You can also enter from Tariq Salah Salem, on the south side.

Salah al Din began building the Citadel in 1176 to fortify the city against the Crusaders, and over the centuries it has been modified and enlarged with the palaces and buildings of subsequent rulers and governments.

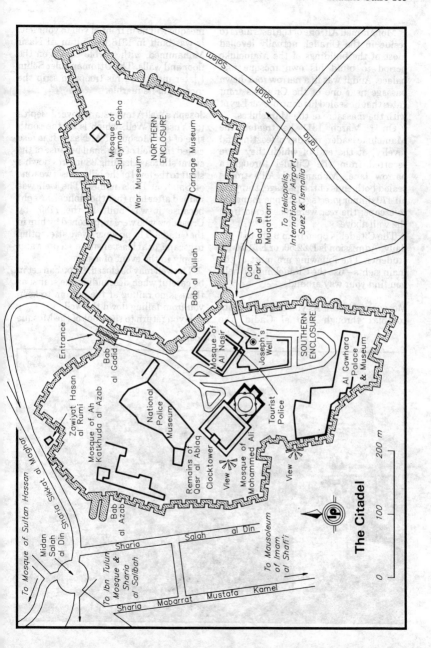

The Citadel

0   100   200 m

Mohammed Ali, one of the last rulers to reside in the Citadel, actually levelled most of the buildings of the Mameluke period to build his own mosque and palace. And it was in a narrow rock-hewn passage near one of the Citadel's front gates that he sealed his control over Egypt with the massacre of the Mamelukes.

On 1 March 1811 he treated the Mameluke leaders to a day of feasting and revelry, at the end of which they were escorted from the Citadel through a narrow lane. Mohammed Ali's troops sealed both ends of the passage, trapping all 470 dinner guests. Only one managed to escape; the rest were massacred from the wall above.

The Citadel is open from 9 am to 5 pm daily. Admission is E£2.50, or E£1.50 for students. The following are most of the main sights – use the Citadel map to help you find your way around.

Mosque of Al Nasir As you enter the main complex through Bab al Gadid, the mosque will be in front of you to your left. It was built in 1318 by Sultan Al Nasir Mohammed, with marble panels on the floor and walls. The Ottoman ruler Selim I later instructed his troops to strip the mosque of its marble.

Joseph's Well A tower stands over Joseph's (or Yusef's) Well, which is on the south side of the Mosque of Al Nasir. It is also called the Well of the Snail because of the spiral staircase leading 88 metres down a shaft to the level of the Nile. Yusef was one of Salah al Din's names. The well was named after him (not the biblical Joseph) because it was built in the 1180s by Crusaders who were imprisoned by him in the Citadel. The prisoners were attempting to escape, or at least ensure a secure water supply in the event of a siege.

The well may be closed; if you can get in be careful when descending the stairs, as there is no railing at the bottom to keep you from falling down the well.

If you return to the front of the Mosque

The Citadel

of Al Nasir, the National Police Museum is straight ahead and the Mosque of Mohammed Ali is the large building on your left. Walk to your left and between these two mosques, then cross to the edge of the parapet, and you'll see all of Islamic Cairo beneath you – the medieval mosques and minarets, winding alleyways, and countless shaky, ramshackle buildings. In the distance you can see the tall buildings of central Cairo and, sometimes, the Great Pyramids at Giza.

Al Gawhara Palace & Museum With the view behind you, the palace is on your right. It was built in 1814 by Mohammed Ali, but after the 1952 Revolution it was used as a museum for the jewels of the khedives. In 1972 thieves attempted to make off with that valuable collection, and in doing so set part of the palace on fire. Today the museum contains a diorama of palace life.

Mosque of Mohammed Ali Also known as the Alabaster Mosque, this mosque and mausoleum was built by Mohammed Ali between 1830 and 1848. His gilt tomb is on the right as you enter. Although the interior is vast, it is badly decorated. The gingerbread clock in the central court has never worked; it was given to Mohammed Ali by King Louis-Philippe of France in return for a Pharaonic obelisk from Luxor that still stands in the Place de la Concorde in Paris. The most spectacular features of the mosque are outside – its huge dome and half-domes and tall, slim minarets are very impressive.

National Police Museum This museum has an interesting collection of exhibits covering such subjects as 'the police struggle', 'police in Islamic and Pharaonic times', and 'the confiscations of antiquities'. There is also an Assassination Room, where descriptions and photographs tell the stories of the attempted assassination of President Nasser and the assassination of Sir Lee Stack.

Northern Enclosure There are three sights worth seeing in the northern enclosure of the Citadel. The entrance to the enclosure, Bab al Qullah, faces the north-east side of the Mosque of Al Nasir. Inside are the Archaeological Garden Museum, the War Museum and the Carriage Museum.

The Archaeological Garden Museum is really neither a garden nor a museum, but this area does have an interesting collection of statues and pieces of monuments spread out among the park benches. Just follow the signs.

The Carriage Museum, next to the garden, contains a small but interesting collection of 19th century horse-drawn carriages and painted wooden horses.

The War Museum contains lots of swords, rifles, military uniforms and cannons in the various exhibits detailing Egypt's military history, from Pharaonic times through the Greco-Roman and Islamic periods to the present. The museum is open only from 9 am to 2 pm, daily except Tuesday.

Leaving the Citadel If you've had enough sightseeing for the day, you can take a bus or minibus back to the city centre from Midan Salah al Din. Minibus No 54 goes to Midan Tahrir; and bus Nos 81, 83, 84 and 604 go to Midan Opera.

Otherwise you can continue to the next part of the walking tour.

From the Citadel to Al Azhar
This part of the walking tour takes you through one of Cairo's oldest and poorest districts. It is called Darb al Ahmar, which means 'red road'. It almost seems like time stopped here several centuries ago; poverty and conservatism have kept the district isolated from many of the changes, both good and bad, that other parts of Cairo have experienced.

I recommend that you begin your exploration at either the Citadel or the Al Azhar Mosque. The following section, which is written as if you are starting at the Citadel, describes some of the main sights.

Leave the Citadel by the main entrance and go downhill and left into Sharia Sikkat al Maghar, then take the first right onto Sharia Bab el Wazir, the 'street of the gate of the vizier'. About 550 metres up the street on the east side there is a unique mosque – the Mosque of Aqsunqur.

Mosque of Aqsunqur Also called the Blue Mosque, this was built in 1347 and then rebuilt in 1652 by a Turkish governor, Ibrahim Agha, who added the blue tiles on the walls. Agha imported the decorated tiles from Damascus, but apart from making the mosque unique in Egypt they do little for the aesthetics of the place.

Behind the mosque you can see part of Salah al Din's city walls which ran from north to south. Across the street from the mosque there is a Turkish apartment building which dates from 1625 and is still inhabited. However, unless by some strange stroke of luck you happen to know one of the inhabitants, this building is not open to tourists.

Maridani Mosque Continue walking up Sharia Bab el Wazir another 350 metres as it becomes Sharia al Tabbanah. The Maridani Mosque will be on your left where a small street, Sharia Sikkat al Maridani, meets Sharia al Tabbanah. Built in 1339, the mosque is one of the oldest buildings in the area.

Several styles of architecture were used in its construction: eight granite columns were taken from a Pharaonic monument; the arches were made from Roman, Christian and Islamic designs; and the Ottomans added a fountain and wooden housing. There are several other decorative details inside. There won't be any hands thrust at you for baksheesh here because very few foreigners visit the mosque.

Mosque of Qijmas al Ishaqi Further along, Sharia al Tabbanah changes name again and becomes Sharia Darb al Ahmar. The

beautiful little Mosque of Qijmas al Ishaqi is about 200 metres north of Maridani Mosque, on the other side of the street. Qijmas was Master of the Sultan's Horses and took charge of the annual pilgrimage to Mecca. His mosque is one of the best examples of architecture from the 15th century Burgi Mameluke period.

The plain exterior of the building is quite deceiving, as inside there are beautiful stained-glass windows, inlaid marble floors and stucco walls. The floor under the prayer mats in the eastern liwan is a fantastic marble mosaic. Ask the guard to lift the mat for you.

Mosque of Salih Talai This small but intriguing building, 150 metres further up on the left, is one of the best examples of the Fatimid style of architecture, with strangely shaped arches, classical columns and wooden beams. The mosque is directly opposite Bab Zuweila, one of the original city gates. Ask the guard to show you up to the roof, as the views of the surrounding neighbourhood are great. The guard will expect some baksheesh; 25 pt should be appropriate.

Sharia Khayamiyya This is the 'street of the tentmakers', which intersects Sharia Darb al Ahmar at the Mosque of Salih Talai. About 400 metres further south, it becomes Sharia al Surugiyyah, the 'street of the saddlemakers'. Part of this thoroughfare is a wooden arcade that has stood for several centuries. Medieval apartments with mashrabiyya screens on the windows jut out over the street. The tentmakers here make the appliqué panels used throughout Egypt on the ceremonial tents that are set up for funerals, wakes, weddings and holiday celebrations.

Bab Zuweila Of the original 60 gates of the medieval city of Cairo, Bab Zuweila, built in 1092, is one of only three that remain. The other two, Bab al Nasr and Bab al Futuh, were built at about the same time,

Top: Mosque of Al Hakim, Cairo (TW)
Left: Mosque of Mohammed Ali, The Citadel (GB)
Right: Mausoleum of Barquq, Cairo (TW)

Top: Overview of Islamic Cairo (TW)
Left: Souk, Cairo (SW)
Right: Entrance to the Egyptian Museum, Cairo (GB)

and even as recently as the late 19th century were used to close off the city. Bab Zuweila, the southern gate, was also often the site of public executions. The last Mameluke sultan, Tumanbay, was hanged here three times – he survived the first two attempts! You can climb up to the top of the gate through the adjoining Mosque of Sultan Mu'ayyad Sheikh.

Mosque of Sultan Mu'ayyad Sheikh This was built between 1416 and 1420 by the Burgi Mameluke Mu'ayyad Sheikh, a freed Circassian slave who eventually rose through the ranks of the Mamelukes to become Sultan of Egypt. Mu'ayyad had a drinking problem before becoming sultan, and his fellow Mamelukes considered beatings and incarceration just therapy for such a weakness. Mu'ayyad was imprisoned on this site and vowed that one day he would replace the prison with a mosque. Although it's not a terribly impressive building there is a magnificent view of Cairo from its minaret, which is on top of Bab Zuweila, not the mosque.

If you climb the minaret, be careful on both the first set of stairs, where the wooden railing is very shaky, and on the second set, which is steep and very dark in parts. The guard will insist on giving you a tour and showing you the entrance to the minaret. This is not necessary, but be careful if you refuse his offers of assistance or don't give him baksheesh. I made this mistake, found the entrance myself and mounted the stairs to the roof. When I returned to the door at the bottom of the stairs it was locked. Believe me, being trapped in a medieval minaret is not all that much fun, so watch out!

The entrance fee is 50 pt, or 25 pt for students, with an additional 50 pt of baksheesh to the guard for showing you the minaret.

Old Turkish Baths In front of the Mosque of Sultan Mu'ayyad Sheikh there is a small door which leads to the Old Turkish Baths. There is no sign – you just have to guess

which door is the entrance. The admission fee is E£2, for which you'll get a massage and traditional Turkish steam bath.

Abdel Harraz Spice & Herb Shop For another change from mosques and minarets, go back through Bab Zuweila onto Sharia Darb al Ahmar, turn right, and walk another 400 metres. The street changes name again, to Sharia Ahmad Mahir. On the right side, one block before the Museum of Islamic Art, there is a very special shop which has everything imaginable in the way of herbs, spices and exotic concoctions. In the store window there is even a jar of desiccated crocodiles for use by people who are oversexed. The crocodiles are ground up, boiled into a potion and then drunk.

Museum of Islamic Art With the treasures of the Pharaohs being the main objective of most tourists to Cairo, this museum, which has one of the world's finest collections of Islamic art, is rarely crowded. The museum is on the north side of Midan Ahmad Mahir, where Sharia al Qala'a, Sharia Port Said and Sharia Ahmad Mahir all meet.

Some exhibits are arranged chronologically to show the influence of various eras, such as the Fatimid, Ayyubid or Mameluke periods, on Islamic art in Egypt; others are in special displays dealing with a particular subject. The latter include collections of textiles, glassware, calligraphy, tapestries and pottery from throughout the Islamic world. The intricate woodwork in the collection of mashrabiyya window screens is the best you will see in Egypt. There is also one room of inlaid metalwork, another with a collection of magnificent Oriental carpets, a wonderful exhibit of medieval weapons and suits of armour, and a collection of superb illuminated books and ancient Qur'anic manuscripts.

The museum is open Saturday to Thursday from 9 am to 4 pm, and on

Friday from 11.15 am to 1.30 pm. Admission is E£2, or E£1 for students.

This is the end of the first walking tour through Islamic Cairo. You can return to Midan Tahrir by walking the 1½ km west along Sharia Sami el Barudi, Sharia el Bustan, and Sharia Tahrir.

WALKING TOUR 2 The second walking tour around Islamic Cairo begins at the Al Azhar Mosque and University. The first set of things to see is south of Al Azhar Mosque, back towards Bab Zuweila, and the second set takes you from the mosque to Bab al Nasr.

Al Azhar & Khan el Khalili

Al Azhar Mosque & University The oldest university in the world, and one of the first mosques, Al Azhar was built in 970 AD for the study of Qur'anic law and doctrine. There are more than 80,000 Islamic manuscripts in its libraries. While the basic curriculum in theology has changed very little since the time of the Mamelukes, the university has expanded to cover subjects such as medicine, physics and foreign languages.

Courses in Islamic theology sometimes last as long as 15 years, and the traditional Socratic method of teaching with one tutor and a small group of students is still practised. Over 4000 students from all over the Islamic world receive free board and tuition and live all year on mats around the courtyard of the mosque. On the eastern side there is also a Chapel of the Blind, which accommodates blind students.

The university is open daily from 9 am to 3 pm except on Friday, when it is closed from 11 am to 1 pm. Admission is E£1, and for an extra 50 pt the guard will show you up the minaret for a great view of the complex. Women must cover their heads with scarves.

Wakala of Al Ghouri This ancient caravanserai, at 3 Sharia al Sheikh Mohammed Abdul, just around the corner from the Al Azhar Mosque, is excellently preserved and now serves as a cultural centre. It was built in 1505 as a merchants' hotel. The merchants would sleep in rooms above where their animals were stabled, and business would be carried out in the courtyard around the fountain.

The courtyard now serves as a theatre and concert hall; the hotel rooms house a permanent exhibition of peasant and Bedouin crafts, and workshops for teaching traditional crafts are held there. There are Sufi dance performances three times a week. Ask at the tourism office for the latest schedule. The *wakala* is open from 9 am to 5 pm daily except during Ramadan, when it's open from 9 to 11 am and 2 to 4 pm. The entrance fee is E£2.

Madrasa & Mausoleum of Al Ghouri Opposite each other, at the intersection of Sharia al Muizz al Din Allah and Sharia al Azhar, are two of the last great Mameluke structures built before the Ottomans took control of Egypt. Al Ghouri, the penultimate Mameluke sultan, went all out to ensure that he left his architectural mark on the city. During his 16 years of rule he managed, quite well, to perpetuate the Mamelukes' reputation for being thieves, murderers and tyrants. His madrasa, though elegant and peaceful, was apparently partly built from materials extorted or just simply stolen from other buildings.

Al Ghouri, who was killed in a battle against the Turks near Aleppo in Syria when he was well into his 70s, is not entombed in his mausoleum. The body there is that of his successor, the almost-lucky Sultan Tumanbay, who was hanged three times from Bab Zuweila before the rope held together long enough to kill him.

Both monuments can be visited anytime the doors are open. Inside the madrasa there is a library, with a beautifully carved dome, and a community centre. In the 16th century, one part of the library was used as a bedroom; it's now a centre for typing lessons.

House of Gamal al Din This restored upper-class 16th century merchant's house is worth visiting. It is at 6 Sharia Khushqadam, which runs east off Sharia al Muizz al Din Allah, just south of Sharia al Azhar. Enter through the mammoth wooden door and continue into the courtyard through the foyer, where horses used to be tied up. Then call out for the guard, who will show you around. Don't miss the beautiful mashrabiyya and stained-glass windows of the 'business

room'; when the sun shines through them, the effect is brilliant. The house is open from 9 am to 2 pm, and admission is 50 pt, or 25 pt for students.

Khan el Khalili To reach this famous bazaar, return to Sharia al Muizz al Din Allah, turn right, and walk north past the Madrasa of Al Ghouri, then continue along Sharia al Muizz al Din Allah to Sharia al Muski.

The Khan is one of the largest bazaars in the Middle East, if not the world. It stretches from Sharia al Muski, between Sharia Port Said and Midan Hussein, up

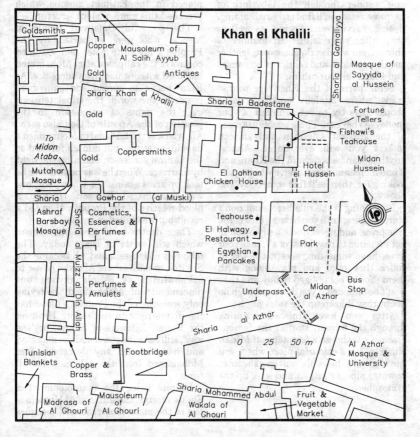

Sharia al Muizz al Din Allah and Sharia al Gamaliyya, to the Mosque of Al Hakim.

The bazaar began as a caravanserai built in 1382 by Garkas el Khalili, Sultan Barquq's Master of Horses. When the Ottomans gained control of Egypt, the caravanserai changed from a fairly simple inn where caravans rested and a little trade was carried out to a fully fledged Turkish bazaar which attracted traders and customers from throughout the world.

Today the Khan is an immense conglomeration of shops and markets. As you wander through the labyrinth of narrow streets you'll find artisans building, dyeing, carving and sewing, as well as shop after shop selling all manner of things from woodwork, glassware, leather goods, perfumes and fabrics to souvenirs and Pharaonic curiosities.

Some parts of the Khan are tourist traps where anxious and aggressive shopkeepers try to get as much of your money as they can. These people are some of the greatest salesmen and smooth talkers you will ever meet. Almost anything can be bought in the Khan, and if one merchant doesn't have what you're looking for, then he'll find somebody who does.

Bargaining is the rule here – but don't start haggling until you have an idea of the true price, and never quote a price you're not prepared to pay. Most of all, take your time, have some fun, accept the tea or coffee they offer and play along with them. You're not obliged to buy and they won't be offended if you don't – though no doubt they'll keep up the sales pitch.

After you have finished roaming through the bazaar, stop at the famous *Fishawi's* teahouse a few steps off Midan Hussein. It's a colourful place where you can chat with the locals, puff on a *sheesha*, or water pipe, or just sit and soak up the atmosphere.

From Al Azhar to Bab al Nasr

This is almost the last set of the recommended sights in Islamic Cairo; it begins with the Mosque of Sayyida al Hussein.

Mosque of Sayyida al Hussein Opposite the Al Azhar Mosque, next to the bazaar, is one of the most sacred places of Muslim worship in Cairo. The Mosque of Sayyida al Hussein is revered as the final resting place of the head of Al Hussein, grandson of the Prophet. In 1153, almost 500 years after his death, Al Hussein's head was brought to Cairo in a green silk bag and placed in the Fatimid mosque which preceded this more modern structure.

The powerful Umayyad family of Mecca, who were supported by the Prophet's favourite wife, had assumed control of the caliphate after Mohammed had died without naming a successor. As Islam began to spread and gain more power in the world, the tribal tensions over the rights of succession to the position of the Apostle of God also grew. Ali, who was the husband of Mohammed's daughter Fatima, put himself forward as the natural successor, claiming the right by marriage. When he was passed over he took up arms against the Umayyads, but was assassinated. His son, Hussein, a blood relative of the Prophet, then led a revolt but was killed in battle.

Their deaths resulted in the schism which still exists in Islam today. The followers of Hussein and Ali became the Shi'ites, or partisans of Ali, who refuse to acknowledge as caliph anyone but descendants of Mohammed, believing only someone of the Prophet's blood has the divine right to succession. However the Sunni, followers of Sunna, or 'the way', still have the power and the majority, and have banned any descendants of Mohammed from the caliphate for all time.

Despite being the mausoleum of a Shi'ite martyr, the shrine of Al Hussein is one of the main congregational mosques in Cairo. Even the president of Sunni Egypt prays there on special religious holidays. The mosque is only open to Muslims, though others can look in from the entrance. The best time to visit it is during Ramadan, when the breaking of the fast each evening is a major event. The square in front of the mosque comes alive with festive celebrations when all the restaurants lay out their food.

Muski This bazaar stretches on both sides of Sharia al Muski (which is also called Sharia Gawhar) between Sharia al Muizz al Din Allah and Sharia Port Said, one block in and parallel to Sharia al Azhar. Almost always jammed with a solid moving mass of people, Muski is the bazaar where the locals shop for things like bolts of colourful cloth, plastic furniture, wedding portraits, toys, spices and food. Although Muski is less exotic than Khan el Khalili, it's still interesting to wander through.

Souk al Attarin A true delight for all the senses is the Souk al Attarin, or spice bazaar, where dried and crushed flowers and fruit add their aromas to those of saffron, cinnamon, ginger, pepper, cloves, and other exotic or easily recognisable spices. The bazaar is just off Sharia al Muizz al Din Allah, south of Sharia al Muski.

It will cost you about E£2 for 100 grams of saffron – easily 100 times cheaper than it would be outside Egypt.

Sharia al Muizz al Din Allah Also called the Street of the Coppersmiths, Sharia al Muizz al Din Allah is the thoroughfare which takes you north out of Khan el Khalili. During the times of the Fatimids and Mamelukes it was the major avenue through the heart of Cairo, and it was along this street that parades of pilgrims marched on their return from Mecca. It is still easy to imagine how life may have been here several centuries ago.

Madrasa & Mausoleum of Al Salih Ayyub The madrasa is just off Sharia al Muizz al Din Allah, on a small alley on the right about 125 metres north of Sharia al Muski. The entrance is marked by an arch but there is not much left to see. The mausoleum can be entered by going back to Sharia al Muizz al Din Allah and turning right. The door, below the dome on your right, will probably be locked, but there will be someone around who can find the keeper.

The madrasa and mausoleum were built in the 13th century by the last sultan of Salah al Din's Ayyubid dynasty. Al Salih Ayyub died before his complex was finished, so it was completed by his wife, Shagarat al Durr, who became one of Egypt's few female rulers. During the following Mameluke period the complex became Cairo's central court. Executions were conveniently carried out just outside the doors, on Sharia al Muizz al Din Allah.

Mausoleum of Qalaun There is a hospital, madrasa and mausoleum in this late 14th century complex opposite the Mausoleum of Al Salih Ayyub. Qalaun, one of the most successful Mameluke sultans and also one of the longest-lived (1220-1290), founded a dynasty which lasted nearly a century.

A *maristan*, or hospital and insane asylum, has stood on this site for more than 700 years, but a modern facility has been built within the boundaries of the original. Sultans like Qalaun built the facilities that enabled enlightened care for the sick and insane. Hospitals and separate clinics were established, and even delicate surgery such as the removal of cataracts was performed here.

The interior of the mausoleum is beautifully decorated, especially near the entrance, and once your eyes become accustomed to the soft rainbow effect of sunlight through the stained-glass windows the tomb seems to be much larger than it is. Mashrabiyya screens, inlaid stone and carved stucco add to the overall feeling of peace and tranquillity that pervades the entire Qalaun complex.

Mausoleum of Al Nasir Mohammed Except for the facade, doorway and courtyard, there is very little left of this 14th century tomb. It is just north of the Mausoleum of Qalaun, in Sharia al Muizz al Din Allah. It was one of several public works projects undertaken by Qalaun's son, Al Nasir Mohammed, who also built the Mosque of Al Nasir in the Citadel and the aqueduct from the Nile. His 40 year reign marked the pinnacle of Egyptian culture and prosperity under the Mamelukes.

The Gothic doorway was taken from a church in Acre, which is in present-day Israel, when Al Nasir and his Mameluke army ended Crusader domination there in 1290. Not many many people visit the mausoleum; Al Nasir is actually buried in his father's tomb next door.

House of Uthman Katkhuda Katkhuda was an 18th century city official who built his house from a 14th century palace. His house is opposite the tomb of Qalaun, on a small street which runs east from Sharia al Muizz al Din Allah. The doorway is about halfway down on the left side and you either knock or go upstairs and ask for someone to show you around. Baksheesh is expected, but wait until you have seen all you want to see.

Despite Katkhuda's renovations the house is still a fine example of Mameluke domestic architecture, and what's left of the decor of the spacious interior shows the influences of both the 14th and 18th centuries. One of the best things about the house is that there won't be hordes of tourists around. In fact you may be the only one there, and the view from the roof is fantastic.

Mosque of Barquq This mosque is just north of the Mausoleum of Al Nasir Mohammed, in Sharia al Muizz al Din Allah. Barquq, the first Burgi Mameluke sultan, came to power like most of the

Mamelukes – through a series of plots and murders. His beautifully restored mosque, with its black and white marble entrance way and silver-inlaid bronze door, was built in 1386 as a madrasa. The colourful ceiling over part of the inner courtyard is supported by four Pharaonic columns made of porphyry quarried from near the Red Sea coast. Barquq's daughter is buried in the splendid domed tomb chamber, which is decorated with marble walls and floors and stained-glass windows, while the sultan himself rests in his mausoleum in the City of the Dead.

Kasr Beshtak Only a small part of this splendid 14th century palace remains. It's on Sharia al Muizz al Din Allah, just north of the Mosque of Barquq on the east side, and was built on the foundations of an earlier Fatimid palace. The Emir Beshtak was a very wealthy man who was married to the daughter of Sultan Al Nasir. When he built this palace in 1334 it had five storeys, each with running water.

Sabil Kuttab of Abdul Katkhuda Also on Sharia al Muizz al Din Allah, where the street forks, is a *sabil kuttab* built in 1744 by Uthman Katkhuda's son, Abdul. The porches of the *kuttab*, a Qur'anic school for children, overhang the street on both sides of the fork. The kuttab is still used as a local school. The remains of the great *sabil*, a covered public drinking fountain, are underneath, and behind the kuttab is a 14th century apartment building.

Bayt al Suhaymi This superb merchant's house, built in the 16th and 17th centuries, is one of Cairo's greatest houses. To find it, turn right on Sharia Darb al Asfar, which runs east off Sharia al Muizz al Din Allah. It's No 19, on the left; just knock on the big wooden door. The house is in rather decrepit condition and only partially furnished but it has a peaceful and elegant atmosphere that invites you to linger as long as possible. Mashrabiyya screens, lattice windows, beautiful tiling and arched galleries abound. Ask the self-appointed guides to show you the women's bedroom and the harem reception room which overlooks the garden courtyard. Admission is E£1, or 50 pt for students.

Bab al Futuh One of the original 60 gates of medieval Cairo, Bab al Futuh is at the end of Sharia al Muizz al Din Allah. It was built in 1087, and was often called the Gate of Conquests. Through this entrance thousands of pilgrims returned from Mecca. Of the three remaining gates of Cairo, Bab al Futuh has the most interesting interior. Wide stonecut stairs lead to a large room with a high ceiling. There are narrow slits, just wide enough for arrows, cut in the sides of the room and along the tunnel, which leads to Bab al Nasr. Soldiers were once housed in this tunnel while awaiting their next battle. There's a wonderful view of the Fatimid wall, Bab al Futuh, Bab al Nasr and the minarets of the Mosque of Al Hakim. You can walk either through the tunnel or along the wall linking the two gates. Admission is 50 pt, or 25 pt for students. The caretaker usually sits in front of a cafe opposite the gate.

Bab al Nasr Still attached to Bab al Futuh by a tunnel inside the old wall, this is the 'gate of victory'. If you're in the tunnel above this gate, look for the hole over the entrance. Boiling oil was poured through this aperture to discourage unwelcome visitors from entering the city. Wandering through the passageways between the gates is quite an eerie experience. Climb the stairs to the roof and the minaret of the adjoining Mosque of Al Hakim. Outside the gate and walls you can see the vast City of the Dead, with its tombs stretching for several km across the horizon. On the other side, walk across the roof to the Mosque of Al Hakim.

Mosque of Al Hakim The haunting mosque of the ruthless and paranoid Al Hakim has

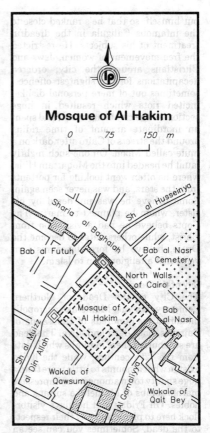

Mosque of Al Hakim

0   75   150 m

rarely been used as a place of worship. Completed in 1010, it has been used as a prison for Crusaders, as one of Salah al Din's stables, and as a warehouse by Napoleon. It is being repaired by members of the Ismaili sect of Shi'ite Islam, who claim the Fatimids as their religious ancestors and the Agha Khan as their spiritual leader.

Al Hakim was the third of the Fatimid caliphs, who ruled with absolute political, religious and military authority. His name means 'he who rules at the command of God', which was something he did with complete disregard for anyone but himself, so that he's ranked close to the infamous Caligula in the dreadful treatment of his subjects. He restricted the free movement of women, Jews and Christians around the city; ordered decapitations for the slightest offences, sometimes out of mere personal dislike; incited riots which resulted in huge sections of the city being burnt; and spent an inordinate amount of time riding around the streets of Cairo after dark on a mule called Moon. On one such nightly jaunt he headed into the Moqattam Hills, where he often went looking for portents from the stars, and was never seen again. Some believe he was murdered by his sister, whom he planned to marry. The Copts believe he had a visitation from Christ, while others, later to become the Druse, believe he formulated his own version of a religion akin to Islam.

City of the Dead

The City of the Dead, or Northern Cemetery, is a vast Mameluke necropolis inhabited by hundreds of thousands of Cairenes, both dead and alive. The dead are still buried there in tombs which date from the 12th century, while the living exist in what amounts to little more than a huge shanty town amongst the impressive marble tombs of Mameluke sultans and nobles. On Friday and holidays visitors flock here to picnic and pay their respects to the dead. Sometimes you can see an entire family feasting on top of a tomb and, wandering around this area, you often have to remind yourself that, yes, you really are in a cemetery. The City of the Dead begins outside and to the right of Bab al Nasr and Bab al Futuh. As you leave Bab al Nasr turn right down Sharia Galal and walk about 1½ km; you'll cross Tariq Salah Salem before entering the cemetery.

Mausoleum of Barquq You will be able to see the minarets of this mausoleum, 1½ km from Bab al Nasr, long before you cross into the City of the Dead. From the outside the effect of its domes is reduced by the surrounding architecture but the interior of these high vaulted structures is quite splendid. The building was completed in 1411 and the tomb chambers contain the bodies of Barquq, who was moved from his mosque, his sons and the women of the family. Don't miss the beautiful marble *minbar*, or pulpit. For a little baksheesh the caretaker will take you up the northern minaret; there is a magnificent view of Cairo, including the necropolis. Admission fee is 50 pt.

Mausoleum of Sultan Baybars The interior of the decorated dome and the mosaics on the floor and minbar are the highlights of this mausoleum, which was built in 1432. It is 50 metres down the road from Barquq's tomb, on the left side. Look for the guard or have one of the children in the area find him; he'll let you in for a bit of baksheesh.

Mausoleum of Qait Bey Completed in 1474 and rated as one of the greatest buildings in Cairo, Qait Bey's tomb is also featured on the E£1 note. The exquisite dome and the finely tapered minaret, with its three intricately decorated tiers, stand out among the mausoleums in the area. The splendid, refined interior is equally beautiful.

Sultan Qait Bey, a prolific builder, was the last Mameluke leader with any real power in Egypt. He ruled for 28 years and, though he was as ruthless as the Mameluke sultans before him, he had a reputation for fairness. He also had a great love of beautiful architecture. The tomb contains the cenotaphs of Qait Bey and his two sisters, as well as two stones which supposedly bear the footprints of the Prophet.

Southern Cairo

Roda Island

Roda Island is south of Gezira Island. In

the 13th century, Sultan Al Salih Ayyub built an immense fortress here for his army of Mamelukes. The fortress had barracks, palaces, mosques and more than 50 towers. Various sultans used the facilities until the 18th century, by which time other, stronger fortresses in Egypt had replaced this one. Today the island is home to an eclectic palace built in the early 20th century; the Nilometer; a small art museum; and several thousand Cairene apartment dwellers.

Manyal Palace Museum The Manyal Palace Museum is on your left after you take Sharia Ali Ibrahim across the canal to Roda Island.

It was built in the early part of this century as a residence for Prince Mohammed Ali Tewfik. The government converted it into a museum in 1955. Apparently the prince couldn't decide which architectural style he preferred for the palace, so each of the five main buildings is different. The styles include Persian, Syrian, Moorish and Ottoman.

After you enter the palace grounds, walk along the path on the right to the Mosque of Mohammed Ali and the hunting museum of the royal family. The hunting museum was added to the complex in 1962 to house King Farouk's huge collection of stuffed animal trophies. This is not a place for animal lovers. The heads of several hundred gazelles line the walls along with a variety of other animals shot by the royal family, and there's also a strange table constructed from elephant ears.

Return to the path leading from the palace entrance and follow it to the other buildings. The Residence Palace is the next one you will see. Each room is ornately decorated with hand-painted geometric shapes – a traditional design in Islamic art. Several of the doors are inlaid with carved pieces of ivory, and the windows feature intricate mashrabiyya screens.

There is rather an odd view from one of the bedroom windows on the 2nd floor. You can see over the fence into the swimming pool area of Club Méditerranée, which now occupies half of the palace grounds. It's a bit of a surprise while touring rooms steeped in the art, history and traditions of Islam to be suddenly yanked back to the 20th century with views of scantily clad Club Med vacationers!

The largest building contains Mohammed Ali's fascinating collection of manuscripts, clothing, silver objects, furniture, writing implements and other items dating from medieval times to the 19th century. A self-appointed guide likes to show you around this part of the museum object by object. If you don't want his services let him know.

The palace is open daily from 9 am to 3 pm, and admission is E£1, or 50 pt for students.

Nilometer This interesting ancient monument is on the southern tip of Roda Island. Built in the 9th century to measure the rise and fall of the Nile, it helped predict the state of the annual harvest. If the Nile rose to 16 cubits, approximately equal to the length of a forearm, this would hold great promise for the crops, and the people would celebrate.

The conical dome was added when the Nilometer was restored in the 19th century. The measuring device, a graduated column, is well below the level of the Nile in a paved area at the bottom of a flight of steps. The structure is often locked but the caretaker lives in small house on the left side of the building and there are usually lots of kids around who'll get him for you. The admission fee is 25 pt.

Centre for Art & Life This small but interesting art and crafts museum, next to the Nilometer, occupies a former palace. Every form of local art, from batik, ceramics, glass, pottery, textiles and handicrafts to photography, is on display. There are also more traditional Persian, Islamic and Coptic art objects.

Old Cairo

Originally a Roman fortress town called Babylon, this part of Cairo was of great importance to the early Christians. Egypt was one of the first countries to embrace the new Christian faith in the 1st century AD. The fortress was built about 900 years before the Fatimids founded Cairo, on a then-strategic point on the Nile. The river has since shifted its course about 400 metres west.

The development of Coptic Christianity, and the monastic tradition it adopted after Paul of Thebes chose a life of solitude in the Egyptian desert, greatly influenced early European Christianity. But for Egypt the Christian period was merely one of transition from Pharaonic times to the Islamic era.

During the several centuries that Christianity did predominate in Egypt, this town, only five km south of where the Muslims would later build their city, became quite a metropolis. It was considered a holy place not only by the Copts but by the Jews and later the Muslims who lived in the area. At one time there were 20 churches and a synagogue there. The Christian monuments of Old Cairo that have survived the centuries are still very important to the Copts. There are also several mosques in the area, and Cairo's small Jewish population still worships at the ancient synagogue.

Old Cairo is 5½ km south of central Cairo. To get there you can take either a bus, a taxi – ask for Masr el Qadima – or the metro from Midan Tahrir (get off at Mari Girgis Station, which is above ground); the metro only costs 25 pt, but during rush hours, 8 to 9.30 am and 2 to 4 pm, it can get quite crowded.

The easiest bus to take is a water bus from the Radio & Television building, which just north of the Nile Hilton and Midan Tahrir. Before boarding, ask for the Masr el Qadima bus. Get off at the Mari Girgis stop and walk the rest of the way. The normal bus is easier to take

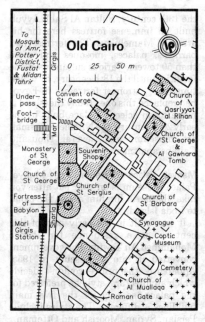

from, rather than to, Old Cairo, as it's usually empty when it makes the return trip to Midan Tahrir. The Old Cairo terminus is north of the Coptic Museum, on the main street near the Mosque of Amr. Ask for *otobees li* Midan Tahrir.

Fortress of Babylon The only remaining part of the fortress, built in 30 AD by Emperor Augustus, is a tower that was part of the waterside Roman battlements. The tower originally overlooked an important port on the Nile before the river shifted course, and excavations directly below the tower have revealed part of the ancient quay, several metres below street level.

Coptic Museum The fortress's tower now marks the entrance to the tranquil courtyards and lush, verdant gardens of the Coptic Museum. The museum building is paved with mosaics and decorated with elegant mashrabiyya screens from old Coptic houses, and is bright and airy. Its exhibits cover Egypt's Christian era from 300 to 1000 AD, showing the Pharaonic, Greco-Roman and Islamic influences on the artistic development of the Copts. It is the world's finest collection of Coptic religious and secular art. The icons and textiles are particularly interesting, and there are also splendid examples of stonework, manuscripts, woodwork, metalwork, glass, paintings and pottery.

The museum is open from 9 am to 4 pm from Sunday to Thursday, and from 9 to 11 am and 1 to 4 pm on Friday. Admission is E£2, or E£1 for students.

Church of Al Muallaqa Dubbed the Hanging Church, this is one of the oldest Christian places of worship in Egypt. It was built on top of one of the old fortress gatehouses with its nave suspended over the passage. Dedicated to the Virgin Mary and properly known as Sitt Mariam, or St Mary, the Church of Al Muallaqa is also one of Cairo's most beautiful churches.

Just inside the entrance, through a doorway in the walls just south of the Coptic Museum, there is an interesting 10th century icon of the Virgin and the Child. The inner courtyard is adorned with icons and the interior of the church, renovated many times over the centuries, is quite beautiful. In the centre, standing on 13 slender pillars that represent Christ and his disciples, is a beautiful pulpit which is used only on Palm Sunday every year.

There is no admission fee because the church is still in use. Coptic Mass is held on Friday from 8 to 11 am and on Sunday from 7 to 10 am. The ancient liturgical Coptic language is still used in most of the services.

Monastery & Church of St George When you leave the Church of Al Muallaqa, head back towards the train tracks and turn right on Sharia Mari Girgis, the street in front of the station. You will pass the Church of St George, one of the few remaining circular churches in the Middle East. The interior is a bit gutted from past fires, but the stained-glass windows are bright and colourful. The monastery next door is closed to the public, but it can sometimes be entered if you ask permission at the church or monastery.

Convent of St George This is an especially interesting place to visit because of a rather strange ritual that is practised there. To get there follow the sign on Sharia Mari Girgis for the Church of St Sergius and descend the stairs that are about 50 metres north of the Monastery of St George, on the right. On the other side of the short underground passage you'll see a wooden door leading to the courtyard of the Convent of St George.

On the left side of the convent there's a small room still used for the chain-wrapping ritual, in which visitors are welcome to participate. Remove your shoes before entering. The chains are symbolic of the persecution of St George during the Roman occupation. A nun oversees the wrapping and says the requisite prayers while standing next to a 1000 year old icon. Several of the nuns speak English and are thrilled when you ask them questions about their beliefs. They will gladly wrap you up in chains. Photographs are permitted.

Church of St Sergius To get to St Sergius, also called Abu Serga, leave the Convent of St George by the same door you entered, turn left and walk down the lane to the end. Pass under the low archway on the right and enter the church on the left side.

This is supposedly one of the places where the Holy Family rested after fleeing from King Herod. Every year, on 1 June, a special mass is held here to commemorate the event. At the turn of the century this little church, which dates from the 10th century, was the most important pilgrimage spot in Old Cairo for visiting Christian tourists. There are 24 marble columns lining the central court, and a series of 12th century icons above an iconostasis (a partition screen bearing icons) depicting the 12 apostles.

Church of St Barbara To get to this church, also known as Sitt Barbara, turn right as you leave the Church of St Sergius. When you get to the end of the alley turn left, and the Church of St Barbara is in front of you. This church is dedicated to the saint, who was beaten to death by her father for trying to convert him to Christianity. The church, which is similar to the church of St Sergius, was restored during the Fatimid era. St Barbara's relics supposedly rest in a small chapel to the right of the nave, and the remains of St Catherine, after whom the famous monastery in the Sinai was named, are also said to rest here.

Ben Ezra Synagogue This synagogue, one of the oldest in Egypt, is a few metres south of the Church of St Barbara. Turn left when leaving the church and enter the first gate on your left, marked by a Star of David. Although there is no rabbi and services are rarely held, it is used by the 42 Jewish families that reside in the area.

Set in a shady garden, it was built on the site of a 4th century Christian church, which the Copts had to sell in the 9th century to enable them to pay taxes to Ibn Tulun for the construction of his mosque. The synagogue, named after a 12th century Rabbi of Jerusalem, Abraham Ben Ezra, was severely damaged by Arabs after the 1967 war with Israel, but it has been almost completely renovated.

There are also many legends about the synagogue. It is said that the temple of the prophet Jeremiah once stood on the same spot and that Jeremiah is actually buried under a miracle rock in the grounds. There is also a spring which is supposed to mark the place where the Pharaoh's daughter found Moses in the reeds, and where Mary drew water to wash Jesus.

Mosque of Amr

This mosque is a few blocks north of the Old Cairo fortress, but isn't all that interesting. The original mosque, of which nothing remains, was the first place of Muslim worship built in Egypt. It was constructed in 642 AD by the victorious invader Amr, the general who is said to have founded Fustat on the site where he had pitched his tent. However, according to Coptic history books, the mosque was built over the ruins of a Coptic church. The present mosque structure probably dates back to 827. Admission is E£1, or 50 pt for students. Don't forget to take off your shoes before entering the mosque.

Pottery District

Behind the mosque, nestled beneath smouldering mounds that are actually workshop roofs and kilns, is a community of potters. You can wander around and watch them make and fire pottery vessels and utensils.

Fustat

This was where Cairo first rose as a city. To get there from Old Cairo, head north up Sharia Mari Girgis till you see the Mosque of Amr on the right. Take Sharia Ain al Sira, just south of the mosque, over a crossroad and then go left along a short lane to the Fustat site.

The site has been excavated by an archaeological team from the American University in Cairo. Although the remains are scanty, you can make out traces of alleyways, houses, wells and water pipe systems surrounded by a low wall. Part of the original wall of Cairo has also been restored here. Several families in the area make pottery.

Fustat started out in about 640 AD as a tent city, a garrison town for the conquering Muslim army. It became the first Islamic capital in Egypt and for three centuries it continued to grow and prosper. At the height of its glory, before the conquering Fatimids founded the neighbouring city of Cairo in 969 AD,

Fustat had a water supply, sewerage and sanitation facilities far superior to anything that was known in Europe before the 18th century.

The city was destroyed and abandoned in 1168 to prevent it falling into the hands of the invading Crusader, King Amalric of Jerusalem.

Giza

The Giza district begins opposite the west side of Roda Island and stretches 18 km westward to the Great Pyramids. Most of the things of interest are either near the Nile or at the western end of Pyramids Rd (also known as Sharia al Ahram).

For the mere pittance of 10 pt you can have the bone-crushing experience of riding bus Nos 8, 9 or 900 almost all the way to the pyramids. All three leave from the terminal on Midan Tahrir and drop you at the Hotel Mena House Oberoi on Pyramids Rd. From Ramses Station you can take bus No 30 to Midan Giza for 10 pt, and then bus Nos 3 or 103 to the pyramids. From Midan Tahrir you can take bus Nos 108 or 173 to Midan Giza. Buses are much easier to take in the other direction, from the pyramids to central Cairo, because they start off empty; get a seat near the front so you'll be able to get out more easily.

A much more practical and comfortable alternative is to take a minibus. Most of the minibuses are converted Volkswagen or Toyota vans. They leave from in front of the Mogamma building; the fare to the pyramids is 35 pt. Look for the men standing next to minibuses and shouting *ahram, ahram*, which means 'pyramids, pyramids'.

The minibus actually leaves you at Saqqara Rd, so you will have to walk the rest of the way to the pyramids – about 15 minutes walk. On the way, you'll pass the tourist office, where you can check on the rates for horse and camel rides (about E£6

per hour, or E£20 per person for the ride to Saqqara). However, it's not uncommon for prices to be higher or lower. The office is open from 8 am to 5 pm daily, except Friday, when it open from 9 am to 4 pm.

Another way to get through Giza and out to the pyramids is to take a taxi, which should cost between E£7 and E£10, although you may have to bargain with the driver to get this price. Ask locals for the latest estimate.

Pyramids Road

The road to the pyramids, also called Sharia al Ahram, was built in the 1860s so that Empress Eugénie could travel the 11 km from Cairo in her carriage. The road was another in a long list of public works projects initiated by Khedive Ismail. However, it wasn't paved until US president Jimmy Carter visited the pyramids. The khedive also had a palace (now the Cairo Marriott Hotel) built for the empress, so that she would have a place to stay while attending the ceremonies for the opening of the Suez Canal. Pyramids Rd intersects Sharia el Giza about 500 metres south of Cairo Zoo.

Before you go to the pyramids, you might want to first turn left at Midan al Galaa from Sharia Tahrir, into Sharia el Giza, to see a couple of interesting buildings. The first big building on your left after you pass the Cairo Sheraton is the Embassy of the Soviet Union. The official residence of the president of Egypt is next to it. About one km further south along Sharia el Giza you will see the entrance to the zoo. The buses to the pyramids pass by here.

Great Pyramids of Giza

The ancient Greeks considered the Great Pyramids to be one of the Seven Wonders of the World. They are Egypt's most visited monuments, and among the world's greatest tourist attractions. For centuries the Great Pyramids of Giza have intrigued and puzzled visitors and,

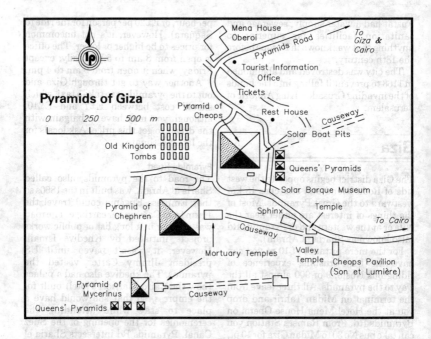

Pyramids of Giza

0   250   500 m

Mena House
Oberoi

To
Giza &
Cairo

Pyramids Road

Tourist Information
Office

Tickets

Rest House

Pyramid of
Cheops

Causeway

Solar Boat Pits

Old Kingdom
Tombs

Queens' Pyramids

Solar Barque Museum

Pyramid of
Chephren

Sphinx

Temple

To Cairo

Causeway

Mortuary Temples

Valley
Temple

Cheops Pavilion
(Son et Lumière)

Pyramid of
Mycerinus

Causeway

Queens' Pyramids

even in the 20th century, it is difficult to stand before them and not be overwhelmed. For 4½ millennia, surviving the rise and fall of great dynasties and outlasting Egypt's many conquerors, they have shared the desert plateau of Giza with other monuments: smaller attendant pyramids, some for royal wives; rows of mastabas, the tombs of 4th and 5th dynasty princes and nobles; and the imposing figure of the Sphinx.

It was not an obsession with death, or a fear of it, on the part of the ancient Egyptians that led to the construction of these incredible mausoleums; it was their belief in eternal life and their desire to be one with the cosmos. A Pharaoh was the son of a god, and the sole receiver of the ka, or life force, that emanated from the god. The Pharaoh, in turn, conducted this vital force to his people, so in life and death he was worshipped as a god.

A pyramid was thus not only an indestructible sanctum for the preservation of a Pharaoh's ka, nor simply an incredible, geometric pile of stones raised over the mummified remains of a Pharaoh and his treasures to ensure his immortality. It was the apex of a much larger funerary complex that provided a place of worship for his subjects, as well as a visible reminder of the absolute and eternal power of the gods and their universe.

The age of the pyramids lasted only a few hundred years. Egypt's first pyramid, in Pharaoh Zoser's mortuary complex at Saqqara, was a 62 metre high marvel of masonry completed in the 27th century BC. It was a product of the technical brilliance of Imhotep, the Pharaoh's chief architect. This was the first time stone had been used to such an extent and with such artistry and precision. Imhotep's architectural genius changed the face of Egypt. Less than 100 years after his tribute to his Pharaoh there arose from the sands of Giza the perfection of the Great Pyramid of Cheops.

The mortuary complexes of Cheops, Chephren and Mycerinus, who were father, son and grandson, included the following: a pyramid, which was the Pharaoh's tomb as well as a repository for all his household goods, clothes and treasure; a funerary temple on the east side of the pyramid; pits for the storage of the Pharaoh's solar barques, which were his means of transport in the afterlife; a valley temple on the banks of the Nile; and a causeway from the river to the pyramid. The entrance passageways, as with all 80 royal pyramids found in Egypt, face north towards the Pole Star; the tomb chambers inside face west, towards the Kingdom of the Dead; and the mortuary temples outside face east, towards the rising sun.

The pyramids and temples at Giza were built from stone quarried locally and from the Moqattam Hills. Napoleon estimated that there would be enough stones in the three main pyramids alone to build a wall, three metres high, all around France.

There's an admission fee of E£3 (E£1.50 for students) for the pyramids area. The fee permits you to enter three pyramids (including the Pyramid of Cheops), four tombs, and the Sphinx area. Admission to the Solar Boat Museum is an extra E£5, but it's worthwhile.

Plan on spending at least half a day around the pyramids. The site is open from 8 am to 4.30 pm daily, though the interior chambers usually close at about 3.30 pm. The best times to visit are at sunrise, sunset and night. During the day it can get very hot and crowded, and the hazy sky makes it difficult to take photographs.

Getting Around Every visit to the Great Pyramids includes a stroll, or sometimes a run, through a veritable obstacle course of extra things to spend money on.

The Sphinx

hustlers, souvenir shops, alabaster factories, papyrus museums, and self-appointed, and usually unwanted, guides. But don't despair; escape from this maddening onslaught is possible.

The best strategy is just to ignore them, though this is not always easy. An alternative is to hire a horse or camel and gallop, glide, or jolt through the desert around the pyramids. There are stables near the tourist office on Pyramids Rd. You can also try approaching one of the many camel and horse owners around the pyramids. It is better to approach them first rather than vice versa because then you have more chance of being the one who determines what will be negotiated.

If you don't set a price before you set off, the camel driver will begin doing extra things for you, like taking a more scenic route to another tomb or two, and at the end of your ride he'll list all the extra charges. So set a price before you even touch the animal, and if your guide offers extra things en route find out the price. A camel should cost about E£6 an hour.

The best time to go for a ride is at sunset, ending at the Cheops Pavilion just as the sound & light show illuminates the pyramids and the Sphinx.

Pyramid of Cheops This great pyramid, the oldest at Giza and the largest in Egypt, stood 146.5 metres high when it was completed around 2600 BC. After 46 centuries its height has been reduced by only nine metres. Approximately 2½ million limestone blocks, weighing around six million tonnes, were used in the construction. It supposedly took 10 years to build the causeway and the massive earth ramps used as a form of scaffolding, and 20 years to raise the pyramid itself. The job was done by a highly skilled corps of masons, mathematicians, surveyors and stonecutters as well as about 100,000 slaves who carried out the back-breaking task of moving and laying the stones. The blocks had to be exactly placed to prevent excess pressure building up on any one

point and causing the collapse of the whole structure.

Although there is not much to see inside the pyramid, the experience of climbing through such an ancient structure is unforgettable. The entrance, on the north face, leads to a descending passage which ends in an unfinished tomb (usually closed) about 100 metres along and 30 metres below the pyramid. About 20 metres from the entrance, however, there is an ascending passage, 1.3 metres high and one metre wide, which continues for about 40 metres before opening into the Great Gallery, which is 47 metres long and 8.5 metres high. There is also a smaller horizontal passage leading into the so-called Queen's Chamber.

As you ascend the Great Gallery to the King's Chamber at the top notice how precisely the blocks were fitted together. Unlike the rest of the pyramid, the main tomb chamber, which is just over five metres wide and 10 metres long, was built of red granite blocks. The roof, which weighs more than 400 tonnes, consists of nine huge slabs of granite, above which are another four slabs separated by gaps designed to distribute the enormous weight away from the chamber. There is plenty of air in this room, as it was built so that fresh air flowed in from two shafts on the north and south walls.

Climbing the outside of the Great Pyramid has been a popular adventure for centuries. It is officially forbidden, and guards will do what they can to stop you, but it is still possible. But be careful, especially coming down again. There are plenty of 'guides' to show you the way: make sure you follow one, because each year a few people fall off and are killed. It takes about 20 minutes to get to the top and it's quite a climb, as many of the blocks are taller than you are. The view of Cairo and the surrounding desert from the summit is magnificent.

Back on the ground, around the pyramid, are five long pits which once contained the Pharaoh's boats. These

Top: The Great Pyramids, Giza (TW)
Left: The Sphinx and Pyramid of Chephren, Giza (GB)
Right: The Great Pyramids, Giza (GB)

Top: Pyramid of Cheops, Giza (TW)
Bottom: Zoser's Step Pyramid, Saqqara (GB)

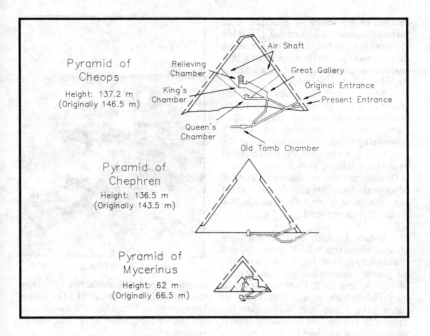

Pyramid of
Cheops

Height: 137.2 m
(Originally 146.5 m)

Air Shaft

Relieving
Chamber

Great Gallery

King's
Chamber

Original Entrance

Present Entrance

Queen's
Chamber

Old Tomb Chamber

Pyramid of
Chephren

Height: 136.5 m
(Originally 143.5 m)

Pyramid of
Mycerinus

Height: 62 m
(Originally 66.5 m)

solar barques may have been used to bring the mummy of the dead Pharaoh across the Nile to the valley temple, from where it was brought up the causeway and placed in the tomb chamber. The boats were then buried around the pyramid to provide transport for the king in the next world. One of these ancient wooden vessels, possibly the oldest boat in existence, was unearthed in the 1950s. The sacred barge was restored and a glass museum built over it to protect it from damage from the elements.

On the eastern side of the pyramid are the Queens' Pyramids, three small structures about 20 metres high, which resemble little more than pyramid-shaped piles of rubble. They were the tombs of Cheops' wives and sisters.

Pyramid of Chephren South-west of the Great Pyramid, and with almost the same

dimensions, is the Pyramid of Chephren. At first it seems larger than his father's, because it stands on higher ground and its peak still has part of the original limestone casing which once covered the whole structure. It is 136.5 metres high (originally 143.5 metres).

Although the chambers and passageways are less elaborate than those in the Great Pyramid, they are also less claustrophobic. The entrance leads down into a passage and then across to the burial chamber, which still contains the large granite sarcophagus of Chephren.

One of the most interesting features of this pyramid is the substantial remains of Chephren's mortuary temple outside to the east. Several rooms can be visited, and the causeway, which originally provided access from the Nile to the tomb, still leads from the main temple to the valley temple.

Pyramid of Mycerinus At a height of 62 metres (originally 66.5 metres), this is the smallest pyramid of the three. Extensive damage was done to the exterior by a 16th century caliph who decided he wanted to demolish all the pyramids.

Inside, a hall descends from the entrance into a passageway, which in turn leads into a small chamber and a group of rooms. There is nothing particularly noteworthy about the interior, but at the very least you can have the adventure of exploring a seldom-visited site.

Outside are the excavated remains of Mycerinus' mortuary temple and, further east, the ruins of his valley temple, still lying beneath the sand.

The Sphinx Legends and superstitions abound about this relic of antiquity, and the mystery surrounding its long-forgotten purpose is almost as intriguing as the sight of the structure itself. Known in Arabic as Abu Hol, which means 'the father of terror', the feline man was called the Sphinx by the ancient Greeks, because it resembled the mythical winged monster with a woman's head and lion's body who proposed a riddle to the Thebans and killed all who could not guess the answer.

Carved almost entirely from one huge piece of limestone left standing in the quarry from which Cheops had the stones cut for his pyramid, the Sphinx is about 50 metres long and 22 metres high. It is not known when it was carved but one theory is that it was Chephren who thought of shaping the rock into a lion's body with a god's face, wearing the royal headdress of Egypt. Another theory is that it is the likeness of Chephren himself that has been staring out over the desert sands for so many centuries.

One legend about the Sphinx is associated with the fact that it was engulfed by sand and hidden completely for several hundred years. The sun-god Ra appeared to the man who was to become Tuthmosis IV and promised him the

The Sphinx

crown of Egypt if he would free his image, the Sphinx, from the sand. The stelae (stone tablets) found between the paws of the Sphinx recorded this first known restoration.

During the period of the Ottoman Empire the Turks used the Sphinx for target practice, and its nose and beard, which are now in the British Museum, fell off. A team of American and Egyptian archaeologists is restoring parts of the Sphinx, and negotiations are underway to have his nose and beard returned.

Tomb of Khenthawes This rarely visited but imposing structure, opposite the Great Pyramid and north of Mycerinus' causeway, is the tomb of the daughter of Pharaoh Mycerinus. Khenthawes became queen of Userkaf and founder of the 5th dynasty. The tomb is a rectangular building cut into a small hill. You can go down a corridor at the back of the chapel room to the burial chambers, but the descent is a bit hazardous, so be careful.

Cemeteries Around the pyramids are private cemeteries with several rows of tombs organised in a grid pattern. Most of the tombs are closed to the public, but those of Qar, Idu and Queen Mersyankh III, in the eastern cemetery, are accessible, although it's sometimes difficult to find the guard who has the keys.

The Tomb of Iasen, in the western cemetery, contains interesting inscriptions and wall paintings which show life and work during the Old Kingdom.

Sound & Light Show The Sphinx takes the role of the narrator in this sound & light show, which is designed with the tourist in mind but definitely worth seeing. The booming narrative which accompanies the colourful illumination of the pyramids and Sphinx is an entertaining way to learn a little of Egypt's ancient history.

The are two shows every evening with various languages scheduled for different nights of the week, as follows:

Day	1st show (sunset)	2nd show (7.30 pm)
Monday	English	French
Tuesday	French	Italian
Wednesday	English	French
Thursday	Arabic	English
Friday	English	French
Saturday	English	Spanish
Sunday	French	German

There is open-air seating on the terrace of the Cheops Pavilion, near the Sphinx and facing Chephren's valley temple. Admission costs E£10.

In summer the sunset show has the same schedule, but there is no second show, except on Friday (in French) and Sunday (in German). During Ramadan the first show starts at 8.30 pm.

Ride to Saqqara If you're after adventure you could rent a camel, donkey or horse for the ride across the desert to Saqqara. This trip is not really for inexperienced riders. By the end of the day you will have spent about six or seven hours atop a horse or camel and a few more hours roaming around the sites at Saqqara.

The trip takes about three hours each way, and costs about E£15 for a horse and E£20 for a camel. These prices haven't changed in a few years, so don't be surprised if they have increased somewhat since I was last there. Don't forget that a camel can carry two people.

Cairo Zoo
The zoo is near Cairo University, between Sharia Gamiat el Qahira (Cairo University St) and Sharia el Giza; it is worth a visit,

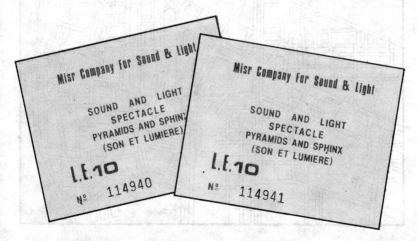

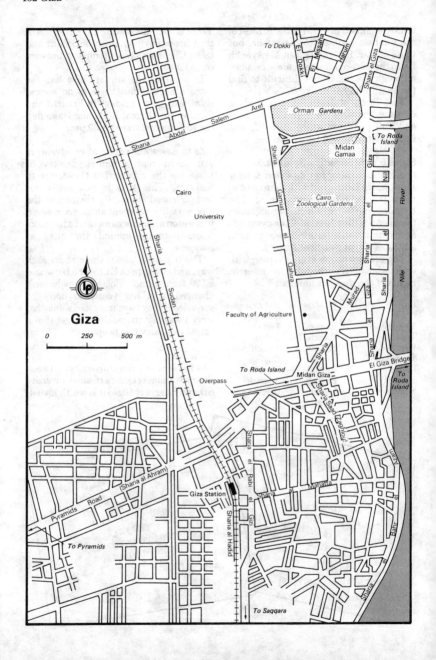

To Dokki

El Messaha
Harun
Sharia el Giza

Orman Gardens

Salem
Aref

Sharia
Abdel

Sharia
Gamal
el
Qahira

To Roda Island

Midan Gamaa

Giza
el
Nil

Cairo University

Cairo Zoological Gardens

Sharia el Nil

Giza

0   250   500 m

Sudan

Faculty of Agriculture

Murad
Giza
Sharia

To Roda Island

Overpass

Midan Giza

El Giza Bridge
To Roda Island

Sharia Saad Zaghloul

Pyramids Road (Sharia al Ahram)

Sharia el Rabi

Giza Station

Sharia al Mahatta

Sharia el Gizi

Sharia al Hadid

To Pyramids

To Saqqara

River Nile

especially if you've had an overdose of ancient tombs and medieval mosques. The animals aren't the healthiest, but it's still pleasant to get away from the Cairo chaos and walk around the grounds. Avoid the zoo on Friday, Saturday and holidays, when it becomes extremely crowded. There's a restaurant on an island in the centre of the park. Hours are 9 am to 5 pm and admission costs 10 pt.

Faculty of Agriculture

Just south of the zoo, near Midan Giza, is one of Mohammed Ali's palaces, now the home of Cairo University's Faculty of Agriculture. The building is worth visiting if you can get permission from the Tourist Police. The large swimming pool was used by Mohammed Ali's harem, and downstairs in the basement the remnants of his torture chambers are still visible.

Kerdassa

Many of the galabiyyas, scarves, rugs and weavings sold in the bazaars and shops of Cairo are made in this village near Giza. To get there, head down Pyramids Rd towards the pyramids, turn right at the second canal, and follow the road to the village. The minibus to the pyramids begins and ends its trips at the junction of the canal and Pyramids Rd. Many tourists visit this village in search of bargains, so it's probably no longer the great place it once was for special deals.

The camel trail across the Western Desert to Libya begins in Kerdassa. If you're looking for an incredibly challenging adventure join a caravan here – but it's definitely only for the experienced!

Places to Stay – bottom end

Cairo is full of inexpensive hotels and pensiones. The prices can be deceiving, because they aren't always accurate indicators of the hotel's quality, and because prices can sometimes be negotiated. So consider the room rates given here as estimates; although they were obtained

directly from the hotels, travellers have reported paying different prices for the same accommodation. The Manyal Youth Hostel on Roda Island is the cheapest place to stay in Cairo.

Unless otherwise indicated, the prices quoted include breakfast. Don't have great expectations about these breakfasts. They usually consist of no more than a couple of pieces of bread, a chunk of frozen butter, a dollop of jam, and tea or coffee. Beyond this, you have to pay extra.

Central Cairo The *Golden Hotel* (tel 742659), 3rd floor, 13 Sharia Talaat Harb, is in a great location – between Midan Tahrir and Midan Talaat Harb. It was once something of an institution among travellers, but it has deteriorated over the years and gets few recommendations. The polish has long worn off the wood furniture and floors, bed bugs are rife, and the elevator is usually broken. A double with shower costs E£10, and a single costs E£5. The use of a refrigerator and stove is included, and bottles of mineral water are sometimes on sale.

The *Tulip Hotel* (tel 758433), 3rd floor, 3 Midan Talaat Harb, is right on the midan. It is excellent value. There is a range of rooms, with and without bathrooms, from about E£12 to E£25. The rooms with balconies are lighter and cooler than the inside rooms. For E£1 one of the hotel clerks will register your passport for you at the Mogamma building. The staff can seem somewhat curt at first, but they are all quite friendly. They have seen and heard everything imaginable from budget travellers, especially when it comes to paying the bill. Ask Mahmoud, a serious man with a good sense of humour who works as the night clerk, to tell you about his first week on the job and the frightful encounter with a huge naked woman.

The *Hotel Beau Site* (tel 392 9916), 5th floor, 27 Sharia Talaat Harb, is actually down a small alley just off Sharia Talaat Harb. Reports about this hotel are mixed.

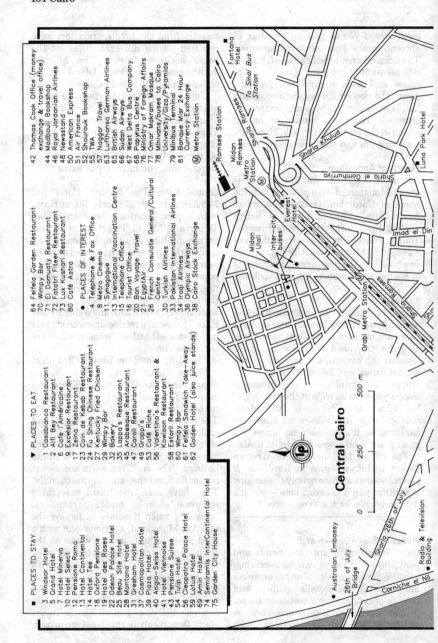

■ PLACES TO STAY

3 Windsor Hotel
5 Grand Hotel
7 Hotel Minerva
10 Hotel Select
12 Pensione Roma
13 Hotel Continental
14 Hotel Tee
18 Oxford Pensione
19 Hotel des Roses
22 Odeon Palace Hotel
25 Beau Site Hotel
28 Montana Hotel
31 Gresham Hotel
37 Cosmopolitan Hotel
39 Plaza Hotel
40 Anglo-Swiss Hotel
41 Hotel Viennoise
43 Pensione Suisse
54 Tulip Hotel
56 Cleopatra Palace Hotel
59 Lotus Hotel
69 Amin Hotel
74 Semiramis InterContinental Hotel
75 Garden City House

▼ PLACES TO EAT

1 Casablanca Restaurant
6 Aifi Bey Restaurant
8 Cafe L'Américaine
17 Excelsior Restaurant
23 Zeina Restaurant
24 Coin de Kebab Restaurant
27 Fu Shing Chinese Restaurant
29 Kentucky Fried Chicken
32 Bakery
35 Lappa's Restaurant
45 Arabesque Restaurant
47 Caroll Restaurant
49 Groppi's
53 Café Riche
55 Valentino's Restaurant & Kowloon Restaurant
58 Estoril Restaurant
60 Wimpy Bar
61 Felfela Sandwich Take-Away
62 Golden Hotel (also juice stands)
64 Felfela Garden Restaurant
70 Wimpy Bar
71 El Damucty Restaurant
72 Fatatri Fiteer Restaurant
73 Lux Kushari Restaurant
80 Café Astra

● PLACES OF INTEREST

4 Telephone & Fox Office
8 Metro Cinema
11 Synagogue
13 International Vaccination Centre
15 Telephone Office
16 Tourist Office
20 Bon Voyage Travel
21 EgyptAir
26 French Consulate General/Cultural Centre
30 Turkish Airlines
33 Pakistan International Airlines
34 Iraqi Airlines
36 Olympic Airways
38 Cairo Stock Exchange
42 Thomas Cook Office (money exchange & travel office)
44 Maddouli Bookshop
46 Royal Jordanian Airlines
48 Newsstand
50 American Express
51 Air France
52 Shourouk Bookshop
55 TWA
57 Naggar Travel
63 Lufthansa German Airlines
65 British Airways
66 Sudan Airways
67 West Delta Bus Company
68 Papyrus Centre
76 Ministry of Foreign Affairs
77 Omar Makram Mosque
78 University/Giza/Pyramids Minivans/buses to Cairo
79 Minibus Terminal
81 Banque Misr 24 Hour Currency Exchange
Ⓜ Metro Station

Central Cairo

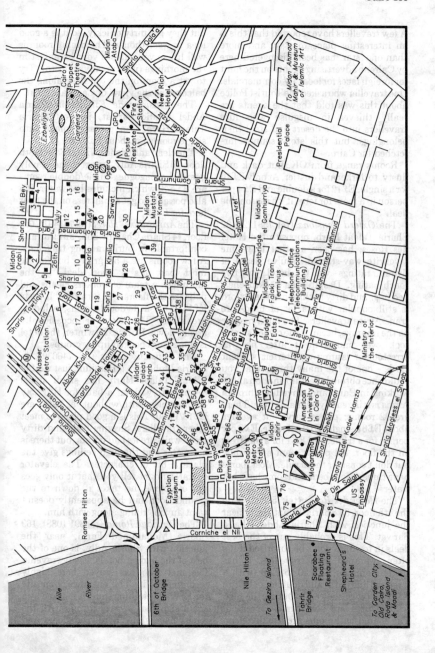

A few travellers have reported that this is an interesting place to stay, and more than one 'star' has been discovered here by Cairene advertising agents on the hunt for foreign faces for local TV commercials. One traveller who asked the Tourist Police about this was told that the agents are really thieves in disguise who lure travellers into the desert and steal their belongings; but this story sounds far-fetched for Cairo.

Rooms range from OK, but dark and dusty, to darker and dustier. At only E£10 for a single, E£12 for a double and E£4 per person in a room for four, it's a reasonable deal.

The *Oxford Pensione* (tel 758172), 32 Sharia Talaat Harb, opposite the Hotel des Roses, has been another long-time favourite way-station. You've heard of five star ratings – well this hotel gets a five roach rating. Despite the cockroaches, bed bugs and dirty bathrooms, the Oxford is still popular with a lot of hard-core trans-Africa travellers. The hotel may be on the improve, because the owner's sister took over management after he was arrested for issuing counterfeit student cards – one of the many things that you could once obtain here. Information about working in Cairo and travelling through Africa is still readily available here. There are 32 rooms; prices vary, but average about E£6 a single, E£9 a double, E£3 per person for a triple, and E£1 for a mattress on the floor. All prices seem negotiable, but don't consider this a rule. Most rooms have three to four beds and some have hot water.

The *Hotel des Roses* (tel 758022) is on the 4th floor, 33 Sharia Talaat Harb, near the junction with Sharia Abdel Khaliq Sarwat. This is probably one of the best deals in town, so don't be surprised if it's often swamped with travellers. It has single rooms for E£6.50 to E£9 (with a large bed and bath) and doubles for E£8 to E£11.50 (with showers). During the high season rates are sometimes increased. The shared bathrooms are usually clean but they get dirty quickly, so it is a good idea to wear thongs. The dining room is well lit, so you can see your breakfast in the mornings (if you really want to). Try to get a room on the top floor along the balcony, as the views of Cairo are great.

The *Pensione de Famille* in Sharia Abdel Khaliq Sarwat, just off Sharia Talaat Harb, is a pleasant place with single rooms for about E£4.50.

The clean and friendly *Hotel Select*, 8th floor, 19 Sharia Adly, is next to the heavily guarded synagogue. Single/double rooms are E£5/8, which includes hot water. It's also possible to get a mattress on the floor here for E£2.

The *Anglo-Swiss Hotel* (tel 751491), 6th floor, 14 Sharia Champollion, is a clean and comfortable favourite among travellers. A few rooms are a bit grimy, but for the most part it's a good deal. In the mornings, a team of workers cleans and polishes the floors and furniture. It costs E£13/25 for single/double rooms, including breakfast. The elevator occasionally breaks down. During the winter, the hotel is sometimes booked up by groups.

The *Pensione Swiss* (tel 746639), in Sharia Mohammed Bassiuni, just west of Midan Talaat Harb, has small single rooms with/without a bath for E£12.50/10. Doubles with/without a bath are E£18/14.50. This is a good place to meet other travellers. Sagging beds and dirty green walls are its bad points, but there is hot water and the high ceilings give the place a bit of character. The elevator operator might tell you that it only goes up; of course, he takes it down to the ground floor, but he apparently doesn't want anyone riding along with him.

The *Pensione Roma* (tel 391 1088), 169 Sharia Mohammed Farid, near the junction with Sharia Adly, is one of the best of the budget hotels. Every traveller I've met who has stayed here highly recommends it. The entrance, opposite the El Walid clothing store, is marked by a small sign that is easy to miss. All the rooms have shiny hardwood floors and beautiful antique furniture. Single/double rooms without a bath are E£10.50/21.50. It is best to make reservations here, especially during the high season, because a few adventure travel companies have discovered it.

The *Luna Park* (tel 918626), 65 Sharia el Gomhurriya, between Midan Ramses and Midan Opera, is a good clean place for the budget traveller. Each room is supplied with soap, towels, toilet paper, and a sink with hot and cold water. A small cafe and bar are attached to the hotel. Singles/doubles are E£8/14.

The *Plaza Hotel*, 8th floor, 32 Sharia Kasr el Nil, is next to the Galion children's store, near Midan Mustafa Kamel. It's a good clean place with hot water. Rooms are E£5/8.50 for singles/doubles, including breakfast.

The *Hotel Tee* on Sharia Adly, near the synagogue, has small single/double rooms for E£15/20 with baths, hot water and dirty carpets. The hotel has a bar where good music is often played.

Hidden in an alley off Sharia 26th of July, just across the road from the Grand Hotel, is the entrance to the *Hotel Minerva*. It has big clean rooms and cold showers that are cleaned every day. The elevator is broken, but don't be discouraged by the dark, gloomy staircase. Most rooms have wooden floors and Queen Anne furniture. Single/double rooms are E£4/7.50.

The nearby *Claridge Hotel*, near the corner of Sharia Talaat Harb and Sharia 26th of July, is a place to stay away from. For E£15 a double you get a dirty room and a lousy breakfast.

The *Amin Hotel* (tel 393 3813), 38 Midan Falaki, Bab el Louk, has fully carpeted rooms all with fans and some with bathrooms. The shared bathrooms tend to get somewhat messy. Single rooms with/without a bath are E£15/13.50, and doubles with/without a bath are E£19/17.50.

Around Midan Ramses The *Everest Hotel* (tel 742707), on Midan Ramses, is in the tallest building opposite Ramses Station.

Its 80 rooms are on the 14th, 15th and 16th floors, and the reception desk, restaurant and cafeteria are on the 15th floor. The rooms are cheap and dusty. Doubles with/without a bath cost E£14.50/10. The low prices, its proximity to the train station, and the fantastic views from the balcony have made this a popular place, but the deteriorating condition of some of the rooms has begun to discourage people from staying here.

Roda Island The *Manyal Youth Hostel* (tel 840729), 135 Sharia Abdel Aziz al Saud, is near the Manyal Palace. It used to be a dump, but has now been cleaned up and there are meals, locks on the doors and clean bathrooms. It's a good place to pick up information from other travellers. Mosquitoes and cats are plentiful enough to ensure constant companionship of a sort. This is definitely the cheapest place to stay in the city, and it's only a 30 minute walk from Midan Tahrir. It costs between E£3 and E£4, depending on your age and on whether you have IYHA membership. IYHA membership costs E£12. To get there you take bus Nos 8 or 900 from Midan Tahrir and get off at the University Bridge, or bus No 95 from Ramses Station.

Camping *Camping Salma* is next to the Wissa Wassef carpet school in Giza. It is owned by an Egyptian with a Swiss-German education. Camping costs E£2 per person with your own tent, or you can get a four-person cabin for E£20. There are 12 toilets and cold showers; the one hot shower costs E£1 per person. An outdoor restaurant and bar offers grilled pigeon, kufta and kebab. Overland tour companies use this campground, which has views of the pyramids from the back area.

To get there, take a minibus west along Pyramids Rd to the Obelisk and the junction with Saqqara Rd. From there, take another minibus six km to the campground. You'll see the signs. Be prepared for a mosquito attack at sunset.

Places to Stay – middle

Central Cairo The *Garden City House* (tel 354 4969), 23 Sharia Kamel el Din Salah, Garden City, is around the corner from the American Embassy, opposite the Semiramis Hotel. Look for the small sign outside the 3rd floor and the bronze plaque at the front of the building. This hotel has long been a favourite among Egyptologists and Middle East scholars. You can get a medium-size room without a bath, a large room without a bath, or a large room with a bath. They cost, in that order, E£23, E£25 and E£29 for singles, and E£38, E£41 and E£45.50 for doubles. All prices include compulsory half-board and taxes. It is best to make reservations. Better rooms can be found for slightly lower rates at other hotels, but you can't beat the hotel's riverfront location and often fascinating guest list.

The *Lotus Hotel* (tel 750627), 12 Sharia Talaat Harb (opposite Felfela Garden), is one of the best hotels in this price range. The elevator to the reception desk is reached through an arcade which almost faces Sharia Hoda Shaarawi. The rooms are clean and comfortable. You'll pay E£17 for a single without a bath, and E£20 for a single with a bath and air-conditioning. Doubles with/without bathrooms are about E£27.50/23, and triples are E£35/33.

The mattresses sag, but the management claimed to be buying new ones and getting the rooms ready for new paint and wallpaper. Hot water is only available from 6 to 9 am and 6 to 9 pm. There's a restaurant, bar and a quasi-sundeck on the top floor. A few travellers have reported that the food can barely be called food, especially at what they believed were absurdly high prices.

The *Hotel Viennoise* (tel 743103), 11 Sharia Mohammed Bassiuni, is a little west of the Pensione Swiss. It is not representative of anything related to the beautiful city of Vienna. Big, dusty single rooms with hot water, TVs, and telephones are E£18, and doubles are E£23. This place is overpriced at any price. Until they scrape the grime and peeling paint off their walls and sweep the floors, there are much better deals.

The *Cosmopolitan Hotel* (tel 393 3531, 392 3956; telex 21451 COSMO UN) is in Sharia Ibn Taalab, just off Sharia Kasr el Nil. It is an upper-middle range hotel that's quite popular with various tour groups, so getting a room here can sometimes be difficult. It has beautifully plush old rooms with dark lacquered furniture, central air-conditioning, and tiled bathrooms with tubs. Some rooms have balconies and there's a wonderful old open elevator. Singles/doubles cost E£75/100 and despite the hotel's very central location it's surprisingly quiet.

The *Gresham Hotel* (tel 762094, 759043), 20 Sharia Talaat Harb, is a relatively new hotel. Singles are E£35/25 with/without a bath, and doubles are E£40/30 with/without a bath. Unfortunately, the arabesque decor in the reception area falsely raises one's expectations about the rooms, which are quite clean and adequate, but slightly overpriced for what you can get at other hotels. The staff are friendly and willing to help you get around Cairo. This is also one of the few hotels in this price range that accepts American Express cards.

The *Odeon Palace Hotel* (tel 767971, 776637), 6 Sharia Abdel el Hamid Said, is about 1½ blocks north-west of Sharia Talaat Harb. It is an upper-middle range hotel, but lacks the old Victorian character of the Cosmopolitan. The rooms are quite clean and comfortable. Each has a minifridge, TV, telephone and air-conditioning. Single/double rooms are E£76/98. All credit cards are accepted here.

The *Grand Hotel* (tel 757509), 17 Sharia 26th of July, at the intersection with Sharia Talaat Harb, has clean and comfortable rooms with hardwood floors and antique armoires. You'll find a wide variety of rooms, with and without bathrooms or air-conditioning. Singles cost from E£25 to E£40, doubles from E£40 to E£55.

Lunch or dinner costs from about E£8 to E£12. The Valley of the Kings Restaurant on the 1st floor has a great view over the busy streets below and an exotic-looking fountain in the centre. The food is quite good.

Unfortunately the hotel's staff are not always as communicative as they should be and they are notoriously bad about taking messages or putting through phone calls.

The *New Rich Hotel* (tel 900145), 47 Sharia Abdel Aziz, near Midan Ataba and the GPO, is a new hotel with single rooms for E£30, including shower and air-conditioning.

The *Hotel Montana*, 7th floor, 23-25 Sharia Sherif, was being renovated at the time of writing, and sparkling new showers were being installed. The management expected prices to be about E£18 for a single and E£23 a double.

The *Windsor Hotel* (tel 915277), 19 Sharia Alfi Bey (near Ezbekiya Gardens), was once a great place with lots of class and comfort, but it has deteriorated. The Windsor has an interesting history. During the time of the Ottoman Empire it was the private bathhouse of the Turkish leaders; it was used to house Russian engineers during the construction of the Aswan Dam; and it was set on fire during the 1952 Revolution because it was the British Officers' Club.

Several travellers have written to complain about the Windsor. One claimed to have been charged double rates, and another said their room had bed bugs. There is a wide variety of rooms, with and without bath or shower, with prices ranging all the way from E£57 for a bathless single to E£90 for a double with bath.

Around Midan Ramses The *Fontana Hotel* (tel 922321), Midan Ramses, is on your left (east) as you leave the train station. There are clean double rooms for E£32 or singles for E£20. Even the sheets are clean

and towels are provided. There are fans in all rooms, and air-conditioning is available for E£3. There's a swimming pool and disco on the 8th floor.

The two star *Capsis Palace Hotel* (tel 754219, 754188), 117 Sharia Ramses, is conveniently situated near the train station and inter-city bus terminals (Midan Ulali and Midan Ahmed Helmi). The rooms are small, but there are hot showers with towels and soap and toilets with toilet paper provided. Single/double rooms are E£17/20.

Islamic Cairo The *Hotel el Hussein* (tel 918089), in Midan Hussein, is the closest hotel to the centre of Islamic Cairo and the Khan el Khalili bazaar. The rooms are clean and well maintained, and the restaurant on the roof has a fantastic view of medieval Cairo. Prices with/without bathrooms are E£15/10 for singles and E£20/18 for doubles. Air-conditioning, a telephone and hot water are included, but a TV or fan and the 14% service and taxes are extra.

Giza & Dokki The *Indiana Hotel* (tel 714503), 16 Sharia Hasan Rostom, around the corner from the Museum of Modern Art, has very clean singles for E£45 and doubles for E£55. Some rooms have TVs and refrigerators.

The *Tiab House Hotel* (tel 709170, 709805), 24 Sharia Mahmoud Khalaf, is a fair place to stay if you can't find or don't want a room in central Cairo. It's across the Nile from the city centre, near major thoroughfares in Dokki, but this is inconvenient for visiting some parts of Cairo. Rooms are clean, carpeted and comfortable. Single/double/triple rooms are E£32/38/45.

Places to Stay – top end
Almost all the world's major hotel chains have hotels in Cairo. Their prices, standards and amenities are usually on a par with their hotels in other countries. Most of these hotels distribute detailed

brochures about their facilities and amenities. If your local travel agent doesn't have current information, check the *International Hotel Guide*, which can be found in major libraries. Most agents should also be able to check the current rates and package deals.

A few of the more expensive hotels are interesting to visit and pleasant places to seek refuge from the chaos and cacophony of Cairo's streets.

Central Cairo The centrally located five star *Shepheard's Hotel* (tel 355 3800, 355 3900) was recently renovated and has all but lost its British Empire atmosphere. The old dining room was closed when I visited, but it will supposedly retain some of the hotel's original charm. Founded in 1841 by an Englishman, Samuel Shepheard, it was one of the first European-style tourist hotels in Cairo. It was renovated in 1891, 1899, 1904, 1909 and 1927, and completely rebuilt in 1957. During the British occupation of Egypt, the hotel and its rooftop terrace bar were favourites with British military officers and administrators. Alas, yet another renovation has transferred the terrace bar to the lobby – the Nile view from the bar is now hardly the same. Rates for single/ double rooms are US$95/105, a little cheaper than its newer competitors.

Right across the road from Shepheard's is the *Semiramis InterContinental Hotel* (tel 355 7171), one of the newest and best hotels in Egypt. It's right on the Nile and the rooms and amenities in this large hotel are exactly what you would expect from the lines of Mercedes and even Rolls-Royces parked outside. Singles/doubles are US$115/145, singles with a view of the Nile are slightly more and there are also a variety of suites with costs heading up towards the sky.

The *Nile Hilton* (tel 740777, 750666), on the Corniche el Nil, also has terrific views across the Nile. It is very centrally located, backing onto Midan Tahrir right by the Egyptian Museum, and is one of the most popular hotels with Westerners, but don't expect it to be up to the standard of Hiltons in other countries. It was one of Egypt's first five star hotels and the rooms are large and clean although the plumbing is unreliable. Prices for the better single/ double rooms are about US$100/125.

Just north of the Nile Hilton, and also right by the river, is the newer *Ramses Hilton*.

Zamalek The *Cairo Marriott* (tel 340 8888) is in Sharia el Gezira, just south of the 26th of July Bridge. It is in a palace built in 1869 by Khedive Ismail to accommodate Empress Eugénie during the opening of the Suez Canal. The hotel is 19th century elegance at its best: polished marble floors, engraved brass lamps and ornately carved mashrabiyya screens. Have a Stella beer in the garden next to the swimming pool. Single/double rooms are US$130/145.

Roda Island, Gezira Island & Dokki The *Cairo Meridien Hotel* (tel 845444), Corniche el Nil, Roda Island, is right on the river, and the views are magnificent. Spacious single/double rooms with all facilities are US$110/140.

The views from the Meridien are matched only by those from the *El Gezira Sheraton*, right across the river from the Meridien at the southern end of Gezira Island. The *Cairo Sheraton* is across the river in Dokki.

Giza The *Hotel Mena House Oberoi* (tel 855444, 856222) is the closest hotel to the pyramids, but it is a long way from the other places of interest in Cairo. It's one of the grand old hotels of the world, with an abundance of elegance and opulent Oriental decor. It has served an important role in Middle East history as a base for the British in WW II and the site of peace negotiations between Egypt and Israel. Prices are about US$80/100 for single/ double rooms. There's also a *Holiday Inn* near the Pyramids.

Places to Eat

Eating in Cairo can be a real treat. There are thousands of cafes, teahouses and market stalls where you can find exotic or plain food and where it's easy to have a very filling meal for less than E£2. On the more expensive side there are plenty of restaurants serving European dishes and places where you can get Western imports like hamburgers.

Breakfast Almost all the major hotels offer all-you-can-eat breakfast buffets which are fairly good deals.

The Nile Hilton has a buffet from 6 to 10.30 am for E£7 (continental breakfast) and E£14 (all-you-can-eat hot and cold buffet). The latter is a wonderful treat, particularly after a long, dusty tour around Egypt. They serve everything from freshly squeezed juices and corn flakes to hot croissants and pastries.

The *Cairo Meridien Hotel* buffet, from 7 to 10 am, is great value for E£15 and is a favourite among expatriate students. The views of the Nile from the dining room are incredible, the chocolate croissants are great, and there are free newspapers in French or English.

The *Hotel Mena House Oberoi* is a wonderful place to have breakfast before touring the pyramids. At E£7.20 their continental breakfast is skimpy, but their special breakfasts are fair deals for E£13.10. The 'Oberoi' breakfast includes fruit juice, croissants and pancakes, while the 'Egyptian' breakfast gets you yogurt with honey and fuul with eggs.

Budget Eats – north of Midan Talaat Harb
The *Casablanca*, opposite the Grand Hotel on Sharia Talaat Harb, does good chicken, chips, tahina, tomatoes and pickled vegetables for E£5. Sharia Tawtiqiyya, beside the Casablanca and also opposite the Grand Hotel, is a wonderful market street with some great-looking fruit stalls which operate until late at night. Close to the corner of Sharia Talaat Harb and Sharia 26th of July, in an

alley running off this street, is *Al Shams* (the sign is only in Arabic). This traditional teahouse is a colourful place, with waiters hustling back and forth carrying water pipes and trays of tea glasses while in the background there's a constant clatter of domino tiles and backgammon pieces.

The *Cafe l'Américaine*, at the intersection of Sharia 26th of July and Sharia Talaat Harb, is a place to avoid for meals. They serve a veal cutlet for about E£4.20 that I wouldn't even give to my dog. The chicken was greased up enough for a sun tan, and great for using as a table-top hockey puck. Maybe I ate there on a bad day. The desserts, especially those served with ice cream, are reputedly much better.

Ali Hassan el Hatti (tel 918829), 8 Midan Halim (off Sharia 26th of July), is another kebab and kufta place. Try their speciality called *moza*, which is roast lamb on rice. A meal of moza costs about E£8. The prices are comparable to other cheap kebab restaurants.

Alfi Bey Restaurant, Sharia Alfi Bey, one block north of Sharia 26th of July and one block east of Sharia Talaat Harb, has a relaxing 1940s' style. Some of the staff claim to have worked here since the '40s! They serve tender, juicy chicken with rice for less than E£5. There are a few other dishes, but nothing really outstanding. Their soups are like vaguely flavoured dishwater.

Excelsior, on the corner of Sharia Talaat Harb and Sharia Adly, is a great place for people-watching. You can eat here for between 90 pt and E£6. Try their mixed grill for E£5.75, or one of the chicken dishes for E£4.50. Service is excellent, but not included in the prices. A waiter comes to your table with a bread-basket and carefully serves your choice of breads (usually only two) with a set of tongs. The hungry cats milling around the place will gladly scoop up what you don't eat.

Zeina Restaurant, 34 Sharia Talaat

Harb, is next to the Oxford Pensione. You can get a simple meal of chicken, vegetables, rice and bread for under E£5. Eating at the counter is cheaper. The food is on display so all you need to do is point. There's also an English menu on the wall. Sometimes the meat dishes are a bit greasy but the makarone is fairly good and filling. One serving makes a great lunch. The shwarma sandwiches are also good and inexpensive, and there's also a fair selection of traditional Egyptian pastries. This is one of the few low-budget restaurants in Cairo where you can find turkey.

The *Coin de Kebab* (or Kebab Corner) is about one block off Sharia Talaat Harb, near the Odeon Palace Hotel (see the Central Cairo map). You can get excellent kebab and tahina here for about E£12. Be prepared for generous portions of meat.

Budget Eats - south of Midan Talaat Harb

The *Felfela Garden* (tel 392 2751, 392 2833), 15 Sharia Hoda Shaarawi just off Sharia Talaat Harb, is the best all-round restaurant in Cairo. This is the original Felfela Restaurant, founded in 1963 by Madame Amina Zaghloul as a small vegetarian restaurant serving mostly fuul and ta'amiyya. A vegetarian, she started the restaurant because she was dismayed by the lack of clean, inexpensive vegetarian restaurants in Cairo. To earn a four star government tourism rating, she eventually had to add various meat and poultry dishes such as pigeon and kufta.

It's a favourite among Egyptians and foreigners alike, and there are also a great many cats (which ensure that mice and rats don't make it their favourite place too). Your dinner of fuul, ta'amiyya, tahina, and tea can cost as little as E£3, especially if you come with a small group and share various dishes. Try the desserts: om ali, a pastry baked with milk, raisins and nuts; baked rice with milk; and the 'Felfela cocktail' of ice cream, rice

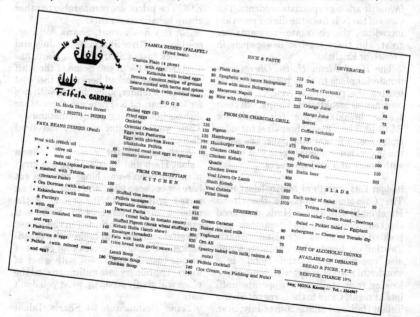

pudding and nuts. Check out the fish and turtles in the aquariums. Overall, this is a good, very reasonably priced restaurant for sampling typical Egyptian dishes.

Felfela Sandwich Take-Away, just around the corner from the main restaurant, has excellent ta'amiyya sandwiches for less than 50 pt. There are signs in English, including a strange one that says 'foul fava begins by egg'. A couple of ta'amiyya and fuul (they spell it 'foul') sandwiches make a filling light lunch or snack. They also serve kufta sandwiches for 70 pt and chicken or beef shwarma sandwiches for 80 pt.

Café Riche, 17 Sharia Talaat Harb, was supposedly a favourite haunt of Gamal Nasser and other military officers while they planned the 1952 Revolution. Today it's a popular place to get a cheap meal inside or sip a Stella beer while people-watching outside under a long awning on the side. The E£3 to E£4 breakfast special includes an omelette, bread, honey and cheese. For lunch or dinner there is soup for about E£1.30, spaghetti with a bizarre bolognaise sauce, an omelette for E£3, grilled fish for E£8 and tahina. There are mixed reports about the service, food and prices.

Abu Aly, in the courtyard of the Nile Hilton on Midan Tahrir, has some of the best fuul, ta'amiyya, kushari and shwarma around, served from the fanciest carts in Egypt. The prices are much higher than street prices, but where else in the world can you get a meal at a Hilton for US$0.40! Fuul and ta'amiyya sandwiches cost E£3, shwarma and kufta are E£5.50. It's open from 10 am to 11 pm but the carts only operate until 5 pm.

The *Pizzeria* (tel 750651) in the Nile Hilton serves good small pizzas (12 types) and various Italian dishes such as spaghetti with basil and garlic sauce for about E£6 to E£9. It's open from 12 noon to 2 am.

At 166 Sharia Tahrir, east of Midan Tahrir, is *Fatatri el Tahrir*, an excellent place for fiteer – E£3 for medium ones,

E£4 for large. A little further east along Sharia Tahrir, right by the Midan Falaki tram terminus, there's another good place for kushari – lentils, rice, noodles and fried onions. It's called *Lux*, and you can get a big bowl of kushari for only 50 pt here.

El Domuaty is a cheap restaurant on the north side of Midan Falaki. Look across the tram tracks for the pale orange awning at the foot of the blue pedestrian overpass. They serve an incredible amount of food for E£2: you get a plate of fuul, a few patties or balls of ta'amiyya, pickled vegetables and tahina.

The block of Sharia Mansur that stretches from Midan Falaki to Sharia Mohammed Mahmud has a wonderful variety of cheap eats possibilities. It's easy to find Sharia Mansur, as the pedestrian footbridge over the Midan Falaki tram lines is on the street. There are several small, nameless restaurants and an interesting market. This area is a great place to introduce yourself to Egyptian food and shopping strategies. There's everything from sandwich places to fiteer restaurants, juice stands, bakeries, fuul and ta'amiyya stands and kushari restaurants.

At the Midan Falaki end of the street there are juice stands where you can get a freshly squeezed drink from almost any kind of fruit or vegetable for between 50 pt and E£1. Pay the cashier first; he'll hand you a token which you give to the juice-squeezer. Having stood next to a toothless man with a hacking cough who sucked on his glass as he drank, I recommend that you bring your own drinking vessel – the glasses here are only rinsed.

At the fiteer restaurant you can get sweet fiteers with raisins, nuts, coconut and powdered sugar, or savoury ones with cheese, tomatoes and onions. One fiteer, which costs about E£3, is plenty for a meal or big dessert. You'll recognise the kushari restaurant by the mounds of kushari in the front window waiting to be consumed. A very filling bowl of this dish is only 50 pt but you may need to ask for extra onions. Pay at the cashier on your way out.

Next door there is a fuul and ta'amiyya stand. Try the fuul in a bowl, or throw it together with the small balls of ta'amiyya and pita bread for a great sandwich. Makarone is also served and all these dishes cost about 50 pt.

The open market on Sharia Mansur is not all that open, considering it's in a converted warehouse just off the street. Each stall and shop in the market specialises in something different like eggs, fruit or flowers. Watch out for the huge hunks of meat that the meat man hangs on high hooks. You probably won't see them until something wet and red drips on you. Most prices are posted, but it's not uncommon to bargain. Go early in the morning before the stench of old meat and chicken gets too strong. Shopping here, or at least having a look around, is an adventure which everyone should have at least once, if only to get a taste of daily life in Cairo.

Round the corner on Sharia Mohammed Mahmud there's a 24 hour sandwich shop across the street from the old Bab el Louk Station, near the new Telecommunications building. Sandwiches of basturma, cheese and olives or egg cost between 50 pt and E£1. They also serve makarone and torshi.

A bakery a couple of doors along from the sandwich shop sells small loaves of French bread or hot pieces of pita straight from the oven for about 15 pt. The almond cookies are good, but the pastries are only for those looking for intense sugar highs.

Budget Eats - Garden City The *Sit-In Restaurant* (tel 554341), 1 Sharia Latin America, serves cheap sandwiches, hamburgers, grilled chicken and other main dishes. It's open from 8 am to 12 midnight. Look for the big Donald Duck sign across from the British Embassy and just south of the American Embassy.

At *Abou Shakra*, 69 Sharia Kasr el Eini (about 1½ km south of Midan Tahrir), you will find some of the best kufta and kebab in Cairo. To get there from Midan Tahrir, either walk or take bus Nos 8 or 900 and get off when it turns right. A half-order is plenty of food for one person. The prices are moderate to high, and a 10% service charge is added. One speciality, pigeon and rice, costs E£6. There are seven types of salads and a takeaway service. It's open from 1 to 5 pm and 7 to 11 pm. There are quite a few cheap eating places and teashops just around here.

Budget Eats - Islamic Cairo *El Hussein Restaurant*, right in Khan el Khalili in Islamic Cairo, is a rooftop restaurant in the hotel of the same name, near the Mosque of Sayyida al Hussein. The views of the Citadel and surrounding area are great and compensate somewhat for the lousy food. During Ramadan this is one of the most popular places in the area. It's open from 8 am to 12 midnight.

There are a host of other restaurants and cafes along this side of Midan Hussein. The next street over, which runs off Sharia al Muski, has a popular teahouse and excellent fiteer at *Egyptian Pancakes*.

Ahzab's Place is close to Bab Zuweila, just off the main drag near the El Ganabki Mosque. It's a hole-in-the-wall sort of place with a painting of Mickey Mouse on the wall and Stella beers in the cooler. Ahzab, the cook, serves cheap juicy kebab straight from the grill. This is a fantastic place to do lots of people-watching.

Budget Eats - Dokki One of the greatest juice stands in Cairo is near the junction of sharias Dokki, Tahrir and Amin Bey el Rafi'i in Dokki. Next door is a cheap fish restaurant. While you're there, check out the mausoleum for saints across the street.

Cafes & Tea Rooms *Groppi's*, on Midan Talaat Harb, used to be one of the most popular places in Cairo for sipping coffee, munching on baklawa, and watching a unique assortment of people troop in and

A COMMON SIGHT — TEA HOUSE DELIVERY BOY ON THE CITY SIDEWALKS.

out. However, the management changed and it's not quite like it used to be. There's a minimum charge of E£1 per person and their display of cakes and sweets is positively mind-blowing. There is also a *Garden Groppi's* on Sharia Adly, opposite the tourist office.

Lappa's, on Sharia Kasr el Nil just the other side of Midan Talaat Harb, is similar to Groppi's, but the atmosphere isn't quite as intriguing; not as many people flow in and out of here.

Cafe Astra, on the corner of Sharia Mohammed Mahmud and Midan Tahrir, used to be popular with bureaucrats from the Mogamma. Although it is gradually being inched out of existence by neighbouring travel agencies, it is still a good place for tea and a water pipe.

Western Fast Food There are several *Wimpy* bars in Cairo where you can partake of the Egyptian version of these very British hamburgers. The local combinations are a little weird: eg, hamburgers with strange ice cream concoctions, and hot dogs wrapped in fried eggs! I visited one in Sharia Talaat Harb and was told that it costs about E£1 to E£2 to eat in, so I opted for a takeaway. Naturally, the takeaway menu is much shorter – neither 'Wimpy burgers' nor 'Maxi-burgers' are available, only 'half-pounders', which are the most expensive and seem to weigh far less than half a pound. If you really can't live without a Wimpy burger, you can find them on Sharia Taha Hussein in Zamalek, Sharia Medinat Mohandiseen in Dokki and on Pyramids Rd in Giza. In Central Cairo there are Wimpys on Sharia Hoda Shaarawi near Midan Falaki, on Sharia Talaat Harb opposite Felfela Garden and on Sharia Sherif opposite the Montana Hotel.

There are a few *Kentucky Fried Chicken* places in Cairo offering the Colonel's usual menu. There's one in Sharia el Batal Ahmed Abdel Aziz, Mohandiseen, and one on Sharia Abdel Khalla Sarwat just off Sharia Talaat Harb in Central Cairo.

Restaurants – central Cairo *Fu Shing* (tel 756184), 28 Sharia Talaat Harb, is actually in a lane; look for the sign on the main street. It is one of Cairo's few Chinese restaurants, and it has a menu in English. For between E£10 and E£15 you can get a full meal that could include chop suey, shark fin soup and various fried noodle dishes.

The *Valley of the Kings Restaurant* (tel 757509) on the 1st floor of the Grand Hotel, 17 Sharia 26th of July, has a great view over the busy streets below and an exotic-looking fountain in the centre. The food is quite good.

The *Caroll Restaurant* (tel 246434), 12 Sharia Kasr el Nil, is a popular place for European and Egyptian food. It's opposite the American Express office. Across the road is *Estoril*; the address is 12 Sharia Talaat Harb, although it's actually in a lane next to the American Express office. Meals are a combination of French and Middle Eastern food and cost about E£15. Dishes include grilled beef, veal cutlets, roasted chicken and pan-fried sea bass (E£9.50). It's open from 12 noon to 3.15 pm and 7.15 to 10.15 pm.

Taverne du Champs de Mars (tel 740777), on the ground floor of the Nile Hilton, is a great bar that's good for lunch and dinner. The entire interior was transported from Belgium and reassembled.

Arabesque, 6 Sharia Kasr el Nil, between Midan Talaat Harb and Midan Tahrir, is the only restaurant in Egypt which is also an art gallery. It's a small gallery, but sometimes there are interesting works displayed. The food is mediocre at best and seems quite overpriced for what you get, which isn't much. What you're really paying for, apparently, is the pleasant Oriental decor and not the food.

Paprika (tel 749744), 1129 Corniche el Nil, just south of the Radio & Television building, serves various European dishes, including pizza. Prices start at about E£10 for a meal and it's open from 12 noon to 12 midnight. Radio and TV personalities like to hang out here.

The *Peking* (tel 912381), 14 Sharia el Ezbekiya, near Sharia Mohammed Farid, serves Cantonese food for about E£15.

The *Kowloon* in the Cleopatra Palace Hotel, Sharia el Bustan (near Midan Tahrir), is a popular Korean and Chinese restaurant which serves dinner from 7.30 to 11.30 pm. In the same hotel is *Valentino's*, a friendly Italian restaurant which serves reasonable pizza at E£6 to E£7 or pasta dishes at around E£5 to E£7.

Restaurants – Zamalek The *Four Corners* (tel 341 2961, 340 7510), 3rd floor, 4 Sharia Hassan Sabri is a real treat – four restaurants in one. One is a classic French restaurant called *Justine* that serves typical *haute cuisine*; another is *La Piazza*, which has an international menu with Italian pasta specialities; the third is

Matchpoint, an American-style snackbar and bar with American sports videos and music; and the fourth is *Max's*, a disco for couples only. Hours are 1 to 3 pm and 8 to 11 pm (Justine); 12 noon to 12 midnight (La Piazza); 1 pm to 1 am (Matchpoint); and 10.30 am to 2 am (Max's).

Angus, in the New Star Hotel building, Sharia Yehia Ibrahim, specialises in Argentine dishes, particularly steaks. *El Patio*, at 5 Sharia el Sayed el Bakry, is part of the same small restaurant chain and has pretty good pasta dishes at around E£11 and good desserts. Count on about E£20 per person.

Restaurants – Mohandiseen The *King Grill* is opposite the Atlas Zamalek Hotel on Sharia Gamiat al Dowal el Arabiya. Their speciality is tasty grilled chicken with 15 different spices, all which affect your stomach in strange and mysterious ways. At E£6 per dish it's a bit overpriced, because it's mainly a takeaway restaurant.

Le Chalet, downstairs from the chic Swissair Restaurant at 10 Sharia al Nakhil, serves European-style food in a pseudo-Swiss coffee shop atmosphere. Their club sandwich for E£7.80 is good, as are the spaghetti and lasagne.

The *Tandoori* (tel 348 6301) at 11 Sharia Shelab, just off Sharia Gamiat al Dowal el Arabiya, serves tandoori chicken, *kema* (a curry of minced lamb with potatoes and peas) and *jhinga* (curried prawns cooked in a special sauce). A meal costs about E£15 to E£20 per person. Service is excellent. It's open from 12.30 to 4.30 pm and from 7.30 to 11.30 pm. Bus No 167 runs along Sharia 26th of July from central Cairo to the restaurant.

Prestige at 43 Sharia Geziret al Arab is, as its name indicates, Cairo's chic restaurant. Actually, it's two restaurants in one: a dapper, romantic (when the lights and rock music are turned down) pizzeria on one side; a full Italian restaurant with cloth serviettes and candles on the other. The pizzeria serves various types of individual pizzas that are reasonably cheap. Beer is served inside only. The Italian restaurant is more expensive, but still reasonable by international standards.

The *Taj Mahal* is on Midan Ibn Afaan, just across Sharia Ibn al Waleed from the Singapore Embassy. It is, according to expatriates, one of the best restaurants in Cairo. You'll walk away feeling stuffed and satisfied with the tandoori chicken, papadums, curried vegetables and other typically Indian foods. An average meal costs between E£20 and E£30.

Restaurants - Dokki *Tia Maria*, in Sharia Jeddah, is an Italian restaurant that serves some of the best spaghetti in Cairo. They make their own pasta every day and their prices are reasonably cheap.

Restaurants - Maadi The *Four Seasons*, 12 Sharia Mustafa Kamel, is a Korean/Chinese restaurant which serves several exotic dishes such as shark fin soup and sauteed *kimchi*. It's open from 12 noon to 12 midnight every day.

The Seahorse (tel 988499), opposite El Salam Hospital on the Corniche el Nil, is a seafood restaurant right by the Nile. It's open from 12.30 pm to 1.30 am.

Restaurants - Giza *Andrea's Chicken & Fish Restaurant* (tel 851133), 60 Sharia Maryutia, is one km from Pyramids Rd, opposite Saqqara Rd. A full meal of chicken, fish or kebab, served with salads, dips and fruit, costs about E£13.50. It is usually a bit overrun by tour groups.

Felfela Village (tel 854209) is down the road and across the canal from Andrea's, next to the Holiday Inn. The address is 27 Desert Rd. If you're after a packaged Middle Eastern atmosphere with everything that is supposedly exotic, then this is the place. This restaurant and circus has everything: dancing horses, camel rides, acrobats, snake charmers, and a playground and small zoo for the kids. However, despite the kitsch tourist atmosphere, this place seems to be more

popular with Arabs than Westerners, which in itself is a reason for coming here.

One of the most memorable performers was a happy woman with a powerful singing voice whose ballads lured young women to the stage to perform traditionally snaky and alluring dances. After a few minutes the singer bellowed, in Arabic, 'But she's not Saudi' - so off went one woman and on came another. Finally, a chubby Saudi man with a white headdress and robe climbed on stage and moved as best as he could in time to the music, until the singer finished and the band ushered in a juggler. The band was also somewhat of a spectacle - Arabs in bright floral print Hawaiian shirts and red tarbooshes.

Come here with a group, because massive amounts of traditional Egyptian food are served. Try the paper-wrapped baked meat and tomatoes or the baked rice and chicken. Sunday and Friday are the most popular days; get here by 1 pm on those days, because it's completely full by early afternoon.

Auberge des Pyramides, 325 Pyramids Rd, is one of Cairo's most popular tourist nightclubs and restaurants. Western and Middle Eastern entertainment shows which include music and belly dancing start at 11 pm.

Restaurant el Dar (tel 852289) is on Saqqara Rd, about four km from the junction with Pyramids Rd. It's quite reasonably priced - about E£10/15 (lunch/dinner) for a full spread of traditional Egyptian dishes. It's better to come here with a small group because of the great amount of food they serve. The restaurant is outdoors under thatched roofs in a pseudo-Egyptian village atmosphere, with women baking bread in the corner.

Floating Restaurants The *Omar Khayyam Restaurant* is aboard a houseboat on the Nile, opposite the Gezira Club in Zamalek. It's a fairly formal place with a full Oriental grill.

Scarabee is moored alongside Corniche el Nil, next to Shepheard's Hotel. It sails twice a day, at 2.30 pm for lunch and 9.30 pm for dinner. The Scarabee is affiliated with the French Wagons-Lits company.

The *Kamar el Zaman* is moored on the east bank, just south of the El Gamaa Bridge. It costs E£28 for dinner and a short cruise on the Nile, or you can just take the boat trip.

Pharaoh, moored on the west bank, is a bit jazzier and more expensive than the others. Dinner and a Nile cruise cost E£36.50. It departs at 8 and 10 pm.

Entertainment

Nightclubs with floor shows, Western-style discos and movie theatres with English-language movies abound in Cairo.

Nightclubs A night out on the town in a club usually includes a lavish feast, folkloric dance performances, belly dancers and Arabic music. Expect to spend at least E£20 just to watch the show. All the major hotels have floor shows, as do many of the clubs along Pyramids Rd.

Discos Discos are discos – lots of bright, twirling lights and loud music. However, *Jackie's* at the Nile Hilton is interesting if you can get in. It's a private club where, in dark corners at candle-lit tables, Egyptian couples momentarily forget their conservatism and get a bit cosy. Outside on the street, such displays of affection are scorned.

Another popular but much less exclusive disco is sponsored every Thursday at *Hotel Longchamp*, next to the Cypriot Embassy, by a loose-knit group known as the African Students of Cairo. They play a combination of African, reggae and soul music and charge a E£6 entrance fee.

Bars If you're missing the typical pub or bar scene, then try *Pub 28*, a pseudo-British pub complete with tattooed

expatriates, peanuts on the table and a good choice of foreign beers.

Cinemas Going to a movie in Cairo is an interesting and inexpensive cultural experience. Tickets are sold in advance by section and cost about E£1; the price differs from section to section. Most foreign-language movies have subtitles in Arabic and French, but because the audience doesn't have to listen to the soundtrack they usually talk all the way through the movie. The same applies to the multitude of hawkers plying the aisles with buckets of soda bottles, boxes of candy and trays of small sandwiches.

Don't be surprised if a scene in a movie suddenly disappears. Censorship is common in all movies except those shown at the Cairo International Film Festival during the autumn. The same five censors who decide which parts of a movie millions of Egyptians won't see also scrutinise music tapes, video cassettes, books, magazines and anything else which they feel might not be appropriate for local consumption.

Activities

Feluccas are the ancient broadsail boats

Feluccas on the Nile

seen everywhere up and down the Nile. Taking a felucca ride while you're in Egypt is an absolute must; there's no better way to see the Nile, especially at sunset. If you don't have the time or inclination to spend five days on one between Luxor and Aswan, the next best thing is to hire one in Cairo and take a leisurely cruise for a few hours. It costs about E£10 per hour to hire a felucca (along with its captain). This rate is, of course, subject to haggling and could be higher or lower depending on your negotiating (or arguing) skills. Feluccas congregate at several quays along the river, but one of the most popular departure points is in Garden City, opposite the Meridien Hotel.

Things to Buy

The Things to Buy section in the Facts for the Visitor chapter outlines some of the Egyptian shopping possibilities. If it's available anywhere in Egypt it will be available in Cairo.

For regular, run-of-the-mill tourist souvenirs the sprawling Khan el Khalili bazaar is definitely the place to head for. The confusing maze of alleys is packed with places selling brassware, inlaid boxes, T-shirts, papyrus paintings and every possible souvenir of a visit to Egypt. Unfortunately a great deal of it is simply tourist junk, cheap and amusing bits of souvenir kitsch but nothing more. You'll find the same sort of items in the tourist shops in the major hotels or in the surprisingly large souvenir shop opposite the Church of St Sergius in Old Cairo.

Although they're mass produced in such numbers that you soon become heartily sick of them, the papyrus paintings make attractive and easily packed little gifts. They're certainly clearly Egyptian.

The Egyptian Museum has a great series of posters including a fine one of Tutankhamun's tomb. They're available from the shops just inside the museum entrance but you'll often find them cheaper at other outlets, such as the Lehnert & Landrock bookshop on Sharia Sherif.

Getting There & Away

Air EgyptAir flies between Cairo and several places within Egypt, including Hurghada, Sharm el Shaykh, St Catherine's Monastery, Luxor, the Kharga Oasis, and Aswan. Fares are fairly reasonable by international standards but a lot more expensive than surface transport. A one-way ticket to or from Luxor costs about E£135, Sharm el Shaykh E£155, St Catherine's E£125 and Hurghada E£165.

Several travel agencies specialise in reduced fares for international flights from Cairo. I met several travellers who were pleased with Bon Voyage Travel at 16 Sharia Adly. They will reportedly give you up to 32% off ticket prices if you give them bank receipts showing that you changed an equivalent amount of hard currency into E£.

Bus Cairo has several long-distance bus stations. Buses to Alexandria and the Mediterranean coast leave from Midan Tahrir. The West Delta bus company (tel 759751) has a kiosk for buses to Marsa Matruh across from the Nile Hilton in Midan Tahrir; it's the last one you come to heading towards the Mogamma building. Kiosks for buses to Alexandria are nearby. There are buses to Alexandria at least every hour from 5 am to 7 pm (fares E£7 to E£10). Several buses run each day to Marsa Matruh during summer, and every day at 8 am during the rest of the year; the fare costs between E£10 and E£20, depending on the type of bus. Not all of them are air-conditioned, although it is claimed that all the buses to Marsa are.

The best buses to and from Alexandria are run by the Golden Rocket company. They are sleek and comfortable, with shaded windows and powerful air-conditioning (except in the back seat, where the engine heat can be overpowering). During the three hour trip you can order tea, coffee, soft drinks, sandwiches, and snacks, but beware of the 'stewardess' – you must pay for everything she gives you. We thought that the 12 packets of biscuits she piled in our laps were free, and that she was just trying to get rid of them. Rather than refuse them, we began munching away, but as we approached Cairo she returned and demanded E£6. We gagged on our remaining biscuits and had to pay up.

Buses to other destinations are as follows:

Nile Delta, Suez Canal, Red Sea and Upper Egypt
   Big yellow buses leave from Midan Ulali (see the Central Cairo map).
El Minya, Asyut, Luxor and Aswan
   Buses leave from Ahmed Hilmi Station, behind Ramses Station.
Sinai
   Buses leave from Abbassiya Station (commonly known as the Sinai Terminal), just off Midan Abbassiya.
Western Oases
   Buses leave from 45 Sharia al Azhar, near Midan Ataba.
Israel
   Buses to Tel Aviv and Jerusalem usually depart daily, except Saturday, from Midan Tahrir and various hotels at about 4.30 am. The return fare is E£60. Several travel agencies around Cairo, including Ashour Travel and Travco Travel in Zamalek and some places in the Midan Talaat Harb area, can arrange tickets.

Train Ramses Station, on Midan Ramses, is Cairo's main train station. Everything and everyone seems to be moving all at once, and at first it can be a bit confusing trying to buy tickets from the right window. The Tourist Police have an office just inside the entrance and the officer on duty usually speaks some English and can be very helpful.

Sometimes, representatives of the Tourist Friends Association roam around the station, and they will help you buy tickets. The Friends will probably find you before you find them if you look lost

enough. They're quite sincere when they say they only want to help you and practise their English. They will show you their official papers to prove that they are legitimate and not asking for baksheesh.

Most tickets for destinations south of Cairo, including Luxor and Aswan, are bought on the far side of the station, not in the main building near the Tourist Police office. The wagon-lit tickets are an exception – they're sold in the office right next to the Tourist Police. For other south of Cairo tickets follow the crowd towards the outside tracks, turn right and go through the tunnel under the tracks. When I was there last the tunnel to the left was blocked, and many people were scampering over the tracks and between the trains.

There are two adjacent rooms where you buy tickets. With the main station behind you, the room on the left is for all 1st class tickets, except wagon-lit tickets. The room on the right is for other tickets. I attempted to find out exactly which windows in the second room were for which classes and destinations, but the Friends informed me that this occasionally changes. Don't be surprised if you get bounced from window to window, and if Egyptian women push their way to the front of the lines – that's acceptable practice here, and foreign women are able to do the same.

Tickets for Alexandria trains are bought from the ticket windows in the main Ramses Station building. As you pass the Tourist Police and telephone offices on your left in the station, these windows are just ahead of you, again on your left. Although one of the staff at the Alexandria information ticket window claimed otherwise, I think you can also buy tickets for destinations in the Nile Delta and Suez Canal areas from these windows.

If you have an International Student Identification Card you are eligible for a discount of up to 50% on all tickets, except those for wagons-lits. Other forms of student or quasi-student identification have sometimes been successfully used by travellers.

Not all trains have 1st and 2nd class air-conditioned carriages, but basically there are five classes: 1st class deluxe (wagons-lits); 1st class ordinary; 2nd class with air-conditioning; 2nd class ordinary; and 3rd class.

Some examples of fares to or from Cairo are: El Minya E£9.50/5.15 (1st class/2nd class air-conditioned) and Luxor E£40 (1st class with sleeper).

The overnight trains to Luxor and Aswan are the ones most commonly taken by foreigners. They are among the best trains in Egypt (see the Luxor Getting There & Away section for fares).

There are at least four overnight trains from Cairo to Luxor and Aswan. The express trains (Nos 84 and 86) from Cairo to Aswan via Luxor have sleepers and a dining car. (See the Wagon-Lit section in the Egypt Getting Around chapter for schedules.) Train No 88 has sleepers, a dining car, buffet and air-con, and No 868 has 1st and 2nd class and air-con. Train Nos 88 and 868 stop for between five and 45 minutes at stations en route.

Trains from Cairo to Alexandria via Tanta and Damanhur depart at least every hour, almost 24 hours a day. Fares from Cairo are: E£2.25/0.30 for 1st/3rd class to Tanta; E£3.60/0.45 for 1st/3rd class to Damanhur; and E£9.50/6 for 1st/2nd class to Alexandria.

Four trains make the trip from Cairo to Port Said: Nos 7, 27, 61 and 941. The trains stop at Zagazig, Ismailia and Qantara, and No 941 travels to Port Said via Suez.

Other trains to Suez run via Qubba Palace, on the outskirts of Cairo. The fare is 70 pt in 2nd class and 35 pt in 3rd class. Train Nos 311, 313 and 315 have air-conditioning.

Schedules for all trains do change from time to time, so always check the timetables posted at stations for the latest information.

Taxi Cairo's service taxis depart from various places around the city. Fares are determined by the distance travelled, so check with the local tourist office for official prices beforehand, and negotiate a price with the driver before you start. Just to give you an idea, the fare to Alexandria is E£6.

Most taxis going to the Nile Delta and the Suez Canal leave from Midan Ahmed Hilmi, behind Ramses Station. Service taxis for Alexandria also leave from in front of Ramses Station and the Nile Hilton. Taxis for destinations in and around El Faiyum leave from Midan Giza in Giza. Taxis for Helwan leave from Bab el Louk Station, opposite the Tele-communications building.

Getting Around

Getting around Cairo can be a confusing and frustrating experience, but several modes of transport are available. Buses are the most common form of transport for the majority of Cairenes, but minibuses are equally popular, less crowded, and increasingly prevalent. Taxis are everywhere at any time of the day or night. There's a partially underground metro train service between Helwan and El Marg, near Heliopolis, and there's also a waterbus that travels the Nile from Maadi to Qanater, north of Cairo. Private donkey carts and horse-drawn carriages continue to weave through the streets and alleyways, along with an occasional camel laden with goods for the market.

Airport Transport If you arrive at the new airport terminal, the only way to get to central Cairo is by taxi, unless you want to walk or persuade a taxi to take you three km to the old terminal. Although one traveller I met claimed that there's a shuttle service between the old and new terminals, I couldn't find it. Most international air carriers use the new terminal. Only EgyptAir and a few Gulf State airlines use the old terminal. The official taxi fare from the new terminal to central Cairo was E£17.

From the old terminal, there are several ways to get to central Cairo. You can get a taxi for around E£15 to E£20, depending on your bargaining skills. It seems that the closer you are to the arrival hall, the higher the taxi fare. As I walked away from the hall and approached the minibus stop, the fares that drivers shouted to me quickly fell; the last fare I heard before hopping on the bus was E£4! If the drivers have plenty of business, this undoubtedly won't occur.

There is also a limousine taxi service next to the Misr Travel stand that takes a maximum of four passengers for E£14 per person.

Another alternative is the Misr Travel airport service bus, which you catch from in front of the international arrivals hall. The bus takes a minimum of five passengers to any hotel in central Cairo for E£12.50 per person; E£3.50 extra for hotels in Giza.

Bus No 400 (15 pt) and minibus No 27 (50 pt) depart frequently round the clock; they leave from the lot in front of the old airport terminals. Going to the airport, you can take the same bus (No 400) from the central Cairo terminal behind the Nile Hilton, or minibus No 27 from the stands in front of the Mogamma building.

For more information about arrival details, see the Accommodation section in the Facts for the Visitor chapter.

Bus If you're really planning on squeezing in and out of Cairo's crowded buses, buy the small book which lists all the city's bus and minibus routes. The book is sold at some newsstands, including the one directly opposite the American University in Cairo campus on Sharia Mohammed Mahmud. Although this little book is in Arabic, you can easily find someone to translate the routes for you.

Riding a bus in Cairo requires more than just the slippery eel-like qualities necessary for claiming your space. Route numbers are usually indicated in Arabic numerals on small signs behind the windscreen. You have to be able to recognise the numerals quickly, because the buses hardly stop. They roll into the station, sometimes already full, and a few seconds later roll out the other side, seemingly with even more passengers and less space. If there are lots of people waiting for the bus, the strategy for boarding is to push, shove and grunt. Watch your wallets and money pouches because it is during this crunch that a lot of things tend to disappear. Once you're on the bus, try to squeeze your way up towards the front door, which is the exit. At some point during the trip, a man with a long wooden box will collect the 10 pt fare.

There are two parts to Cairo's main bus terminal, which is in the area around Midan Tahrir. Directly in front of the Nile Hilton, buses and minibuses leave for Islamic Cairo, Heliopolis, Cairo Airport, and Shubra. Taking a minibus is one of the best ways to travel. It costs only 20 pt to 50 pt (depending on your destination) for a seat. Passengers are not allowed to stand and crowd each other, and each minibus leaves as soon as every seat is taken. A minibus is easily recognised by its smaller size and orange and white stripes.

The other part of the main bus terminal is in front of the Mogamma building. Most of the buses from there go across the river to Giza, Mohandiseen and Imbaba.

Following is a list of some of the bus numbers and their destinations.

From the Nile Hilton terminal
No 400
    Cairo Airport
No 510
    Heliopolis
Nos 173 & 403
    Citadel and Mosque of Sultan Hassan
No 75
    Islamic Museum and Bab Zuweila
No 63
    Mosque of Al Azhar and Khan el Khalili

Nos 170 & 95
    Ramses Station and Zamalek
No 500
    Masr Gidida (Heliopolis)
Nos 44, 128 & 350
    Ain Shams
No 330
    Medinat Issalam
No 302
    Shubra
No 99
    Midan Lubman
No 60
    Aguza
Minibus No 24
    Midan Roxy and Masr Gidida

Minibus No 2
    Shubra

From the Mogamma terminal
No 900
    Kasr el Eini, Manyal Palace, Cairo
    University, Giza and the Great Pyramids
No 8
    Kasr el Eini, Manyal Palace, Giza and the
    Great Pyramids
No 174
    Sayeida Zeinab, the mosques of Ibn Tulun
    and Sultan Hassan, and the Citadel
Nos 83, 86, 182
    Mausoleum of Shafi'i in the Southern
    Cemetery

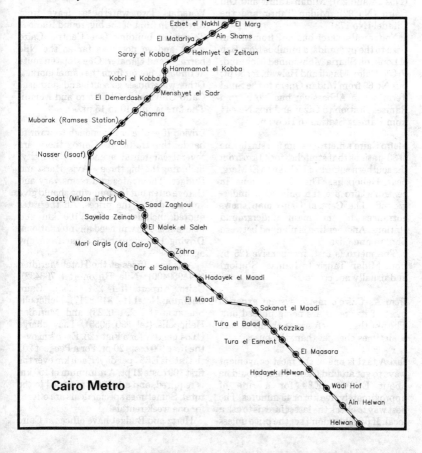

Cairo Metro

El Marg
Ezbet el Nakhl
Ain Shams
El Matariya
Helmiyet el Zeitoun
Saray el Kobba
Hammamat el Kobba
Kobri el Kobba
Menshyet el Sadr
El Demerdash
Ghamra
Mubarak (Ramses Station)
Orabi
Nasser (Isaaf)
Sadat (Midan Tahrir)
Saad Zaghloul
Sayeida Zeinab
El Malek el Saleh
Mari Girgis (Old Cairo)
Zahra
Dar el Salam
Hadayek el Maadi
El Maadi
Sakanat el Maadi
Tura el Balad
Kozzika
Tura el Esment
El Maasara
Hadayek Helwan
Wadi Hof
Ain Helwan
Helwan

No 140
  Midan Ramses and Ramses Station
Nos 6, 803
  Midan Giza
No 166
  Ula Daqar
Minibus No 27
  Cairo Airport (old terminal)

There are also private minibuses which go to Giza and the pyramids for 30 pt. Other minibuses run between Midan Tahrir and Midan Ramses (Nos 70 and 95); Midan Ramses and Midan Ataba (Nos 65 and 80); Midan Ataba and Midan Ramses (Nos 24 and 25); Midan Tahrir and Old Cairo (No 92); Midan Tahrir and the Citadel (No 173).

You can also catch bus No 3 from Midan Giza to the pyramids; a minibus from Bab el Louk, on Sharia Mohammed Mahmud, to Old Cairo, Maadi and Helwan, for 50 pt; bus No 69 from Midan Opera to the Sinai Terminal in Abbassiya; bus No 9 from Ramses Station to Giza; and bus No 444 from Ramses Station to Helwan.

Metro Cairo's metro system is a single line of 33 stations that stretches for 43 km from the southern suburb of Helwan to El Marg, near Heliopolis. The five stations in central Cairo are the only ones underground. The Central Cairo map shows entrances to the main underground stations. Another line is planned between Shubra and Giza.

The metro is fast, inexpensive (25 pt from Midan Tahrir to Ramses Station) and usually not crowded.

Tram As Cairo's metro system expands most of its trams are being phased out. The few that are left are as cheap as, and sometimes cheaper than, the buses.

Taxi A taxi is one of the most convenient ways to get around Cairo. Fares should be about E£2 to E£4 for a ride of approximately five km or 45 minutes. The best way to check the latest fares is to ask a local. If possible, don't set the price unless

the ride is especially long, such as from central Cairo to the airport or the pyramids. Wait until you arrive at your destination, get out of the car, pay the driver through the window, and walk away. Sometimes the driver will yell for more money or even (rarely) jump out of the car, rip open his shirt like Superman and pound on his chest. If he adopts the latter technique then it's possible you really have underpaid him!

For more information on the different sorts of taxis and how to flag them down, see the Getting Around chapter.

Waterbus Two waterbuses leave from directly in front of the big, round Radio & Television building (see Central Cairo map) and go north as far as the Nile barrages and Qanater. One stops en route at Imbaba, not far from the camel market. Other waterbuses go south and stop near Cairo University, Old Cairo and Maadi. The fare is only 10 to 15 pt.

Driving If you're crazy enough to want to battle the traffic in Cairo, there are several car rental agencies in the city, including the 'big three' – Avis, Hertz and Budget. Their rates and terms vary and change often but the following should give you an idea of the prices. All the rates quoted include the first 100 km and insurance. You will need an International Driving Permit to rent a car from any agency.

Avis has offices at the Hotel Meridien (tel 989400), Nile Hilton (tel 766432), Cairo Airport (tel 291 4255), Cairo Sheraton Hotel (tel 348 8717), Heliopolis Sheraton (tel 291 0223) and Meridien Heliopolis (tel 290 5055). They charge E£54 per day for a Fiat 128. Each km over the first 100 costs 20 pt. For a Peugeot 205 the rate is E£57 per day. Each km over the first 100 costs 21 pt. A minimum of 100 km is required, and a 12% tax is added to the total. Sometimes special deals are offered for one week rentals.

Hertz and Budget have offices at Cairo

Airport (tel 291 4277, extension 2395), Zamalek (tel 341 3790, 340 9474), the Semiramis InterContinental Hotel (tel 355 7171, extension 8991), Heliopolis (tel 291 8244) and the Ramses Hilton (tel 777444). Their most inexpensive car is a Superfuera 127, which costs E£67.20 per day. Each km over the first 100 costs 20 pt. A 12% tax is added to the total.

One of the cheapest agencies is Europcar Rent-a-Car, which has offices at the Marriott Hotel (tel 340 1152, 340 1125), Sheraton Gezira Hotel (tel 341133, extension 5337), Cairo Airport (tel 665166, extension 4344), and a 24 hour service at 8 Sharia Kasr el Nil (tel 774330). They rent a Fiat 127 for E£50.60 per day. Each km over the first 100 costs 20 pt.

Around Cairo

The region around Cairo offers some of Egypt's most interesting attractions, including the ancient tombs and pyramids of Saqqara, El Faiyum – one of the world's largest oases – and the medieval monasteries of Wadi Natrun. Most of the destinations described in this chapter can be visited on day trips from Cairo.

MEMPHIS

Memphis, once the glorious Old Kingdom capital of Egypt, has almost completely vanished. It is believed that the city was founded around 3100 BC, probably by King Menes, when Upper and Lower Egypt were first united. It had many splendid palaces and gardens, and was one of the most renowned and populous cities of the ancient world. Like most Egyptian cities with any degree of importance, Memphis also had its own deity, the all-powerful creator-god Ptah, who formed the world with words from his tongue and heart.

Even as late as the 5th century BC, long after Thebes had taken over as capital of Egypt, Memphis was described by the Greek historian Herodotus as a 'prosperous city and cosmopolitan centre'. Its enduring importance, even then, was reflected in the size of its cemetery on the west bank of the Nile, an area replete with royal pyramids, private tombs and sacred animal necropolises. This city of the dead, centred at Saqqara, covers 30 km along the edge of the desert, from Dahshur to Giza.

Centuries of annual floods have inundated the city with Nile mud, while other ancient buildings and monuments have long since been ploughed over and cultivated by the fellahin. Today there are few signs of the grandeur of Memphis: in fact, it's extremely difficult to imagine that a city once stood where there is now only a small museum and some statues in

a garden. The museum contains a colossal limestone statue of Ramses II, similar to the one which stands at the centre of Midan Ramses in Cairo. This one, however, is a lot more neglected and damaged.

In the garden there are more statues of Ramses II, an eight tonne alabaster sphinx, the sarcophagus of Amenhotep and the alabaster beds on which the sacred Apis bulls were mummified before being placed in the Serapeum at Saqqara.

Getting There & Away

Memphis is 24 km south of Cairo and three km from Saqqara. The cheapest way to get there from Cairo is to take the 3rd class train from Ramses Station at about 10.20 am from platform No 8 to El Manashy, and get off at El Badrashein village; the trip takes about two hours (that's right – two hours to go 24 km!). From the village, you can either walk for about 15 to 20 minutes or take a taxi. The most common way of getting to Memphis is to gather six or seven people and hire a service taxi (Peugeot 504) for about E£50 to E£60 for a day trip that also includes Saqqara.

A more expeditious way to arrange this trip is with a member of the Kamal family – brothers Ashraf, Ayman and Hany (tel 751126). They pick you up at your hotel in a minibus in the morning and take you to Saqqara, Memphis and whatever other stops you wish to make along the way. More energetic travellers also like to include Giza, although that is a bit much for one day. Usually, the Kamals can get you back to central Cairo by about 5 pm. To arrange this trip, call them at least two days in advance and, if necessary, leave a message on the answering machine. At about US$7 per person it's a good deal, particularly since you are accompanied by one of these English-speaking brothers.

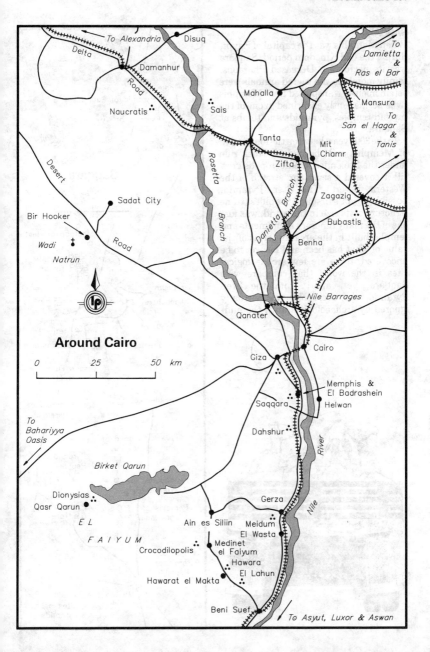

To Alexandria
Disuq
Delta
Road
Damanhur
To Damietta & Ras el Bar
Mahalla
Naucratis
Sais
Mansura
To San el Hagar & Tanis
Tanta
Mit Chamr
Zifta
Desert
Zagazig
Sadat City
Bubastis
Bir Hooker
Benha
Wadi
Natrun
Road
Nile Barrages
Qanater
Cairo
Giza
Memphis & El Badrashein
Saqqara
Helwan
Dahshur
To Bahariyya Oasis
River
Birket Qarun
Dionysias
Gerza
Qasr Qarun
Ain es Siliin
Meidum
El Wasta
Crocodilopolis
Medinet el Faiyum
Hawara
El Lahun
Hawarat el Makta
Beni Suef
To Asyut, Luxor & Aswan

Around Cairo

0   25   50 km

SAQQARA

When Memphis was the capital of Egypt, during the Old Kingdom period, Saqqara was its necropolis. Deceased Pharaohs, family members and sacred animals were ceremoniously transported from Memphis to be permanently enshrined in one of the myriad temples, pyramids and tombs at Saqqara.

In the 3000 years between the foundation of Memphis and the end of Greek rule under the Ptolemies, the necropolis grew till it covered a seven km stretch of the Western Desert. The Step Pyramid, possibly Egypt's first and the oldest stone structure of its size in the world, was just one of the many funerary monuments and temples built in the area. In terms of the value of what has been and has yet to be uncovered, there are few archaeological sites in the world that compare with Saqqara; yet, apart from the Step Pyramid, the necropolis was virtually ignored by archaeologists until the mid-

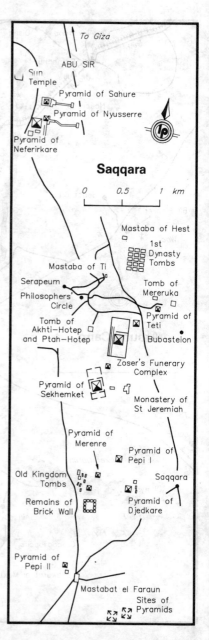

19th century, when Auguste Mariette found the Serapeum. Even the massive mortuary complex surrounding Zoser's Step Pyramid wasn't discovered and reclaimed from the sand until 1924, and it is still being restored.

A worthwhile visit to Saqqara will take more than one day. Because of its size it seems that other visitors are few and far between, apart from the organised tour groups that are rushed through in the mornings. You'll find here, in the middle of the desert, a peaceful quality rarely found at other ancient sites in Egypt.

The main places of interest are in North Saqqara, with other sites scattered between South Saqqara, Dahshur (a closed military area) and Abu Sir. Most travellers start their visit in North Saqqara (Zoser's Step Pyramid area) and, if they are up to it, continue by taxi, donkey or camel to Abu Sir and/or South Saqqara. However, ask first at the ticket office, which is at the base of the plateau of North Saqqara, about which monuments are open. There's usually a list indicating which ones are accessible.

Most of the pyramids and tombs at Saqqara can be 'officially' visited between 7.30 am and 4 pm. The guards start locking the monument doors at about 3.30 pm. The admission fee for all North Saqqara sights is E£3, or E£1.50 for students.

Step Pyramid

When it was constructed by Imhotep, the Pharaoh's chief architect, in the 27th century BC, the Step Pyramid of King Zoser was the largest stone structure ever built. It is still the most noticeable feature of Saqqara. Imhotep's brilliant use of stone, and his daring break with the tradition of building royal tombs as underground rooms with the occasional mud-brick mastaba, was the inspiration for Egypt's future architectural achievements.

The pyramid began as a simple mastaba, the flat tomb superstructure common at the time, but Imhotep added to it five times. With each level of stone he

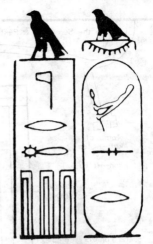

Zoser's Cartouche

gained confidence in his use of the new medium and mastered the techniques required to move, place and secure the huge blocks. This first pyramid rose to over 62 metres, in six steps, before it was sheathed in fine limestone.

The Step Pyramid dominates Zoser's mortuary complex, which is 544 metres long and 277 metres wide and was once surrounded by a magnificent bastioned and panelled limestone wall. Part of the enclosure wall survives, to a height of over 4.5 metres, and a section near the south-eastern corner has been restored, with stones found in the desert, to its original 10 metre elevation. In the enclosure wall, the many false doors which were carved and painted to resemble real wood with hinges and sockets allowed the Pharaoh's ka, or attendant spirit, to come and go at will.

For the living there is only one entrance, on the south-eastern corner, via a vestibule and along a colonnaded corridor into the broad Hypostyle Hall. The 40 pillars in the corridor are the original 'bundle columns', ribbed to resemble a bundle of palm stems. The walls have been restored, but the protective ceiling is modern concrete. The roof of the

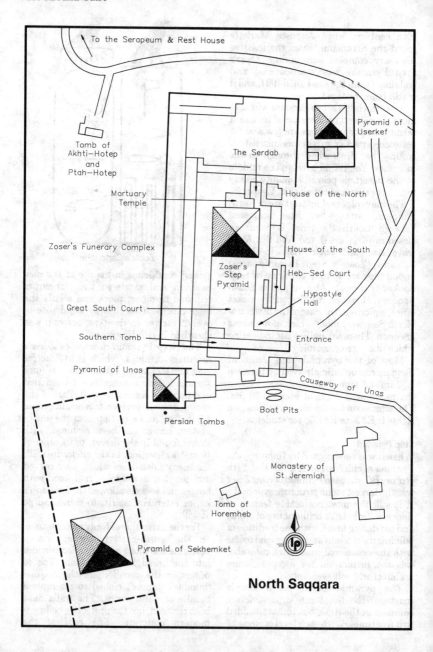

To the Serapeum & Rest House

Tomb of
Akhti–Hotep
and
Ptah–Hotep

Pyramid of
Userkef

The Serdab

Mortuary
Temple

House of the North

Zoser's Funerary Complex

House of the South

Zoser's Step
Pyramid

Heb–Sed Court

Great South Court

Hypostyle
Hall

Southern Tomb

Entrance

Pyramid of Unas

Causeway of Unas

Persian Tombs

Boat Pits

Monastery of
St Jeremiah

Tomb of
Horemheb

Pyramid of Sekhemket

North Saqqara

Hypostyle Hall is supported by four impressive bundle columns and there's a large, false, half-open ka door.

The hall leads into the Great South Court, a huge open area flanking the south side of the pyramid, with a rebuilt section of wall featuring a frieze of cobras. The cobra, or uraeus, was a symbol of Egyptian royalty, a fire-spitting agent of destruction and protector of the king. A rearing cobra, its hood inflated, always formed part of a Pharaoh's headdress.

Near the frieze is a shaft that plunges 28 metres to the floor of Zoser's Southern Tomb, which is similar in decoration to the main tomb beneath the Step Pyramid. Originally, it probably stored the canopic jars containing the Pharaoh's preserved internal organs.

In the centre of the Great Court are two stone altars representing the thrones of Upper and Lower Egypt. During the 30th year of a Pharaoh's reign it was traditional for him to renew his rule by re-enacting his coronation. In a ritual called the Heb-Sed Race, he would sit first on one throne and then on the other to symbolise the unification of Egypt. He would also, during the five day jubilee, present all the provincial priests with gifts, obliging them to recognise his supremacy over their local gods. The jubilee would actually have been held in Memphis, while these altars in the Great Court perpetuated in stone the cosmic regeneration of the Pharaoh's power and ka.

On the eastern side of the pyramid are two 'houses' representing the shrines of Upper and Lower Egypt, which symbolise the unity of the country. The House of the South, which is faced with proto-Doric columns, features the oldest known examples of tourist graffiti. The vandalism of visiting 12th century BC Theban scribes, who scrawled their admiration for Zoser on the wall in a cursive style of hieroglyphics, is now protected under a piece of transparent plastic just inside the entrance. The House of the North is similar to its southern counterpart, except that sculpted papyrus flowers grace the capitals of its columns.

The Serdab, a stone structure right in front of the pyramid, contains a slightly tilted wooden box with two holes drilled into its north face. Look through these and you'll have the eerie experience of coming face to face with Zoser himself. Inside is a life-size, lifelike painted statue of the long-dead king, gazing stonily out towards the stars. Although it's only a copy (the original is in the Egyptian Museum), it is still quite haunting. Serdabs were designed so that the Pharaoh's ka could communicate with the outside world. The original entrance to the Step Pyramid is directly behind the Serdab, but is closed to the public.

Pyramid & Causeway of Unas

What appears to be a big mound of rubble to the south-west of Zoser's tomb is actually the Pyramid of Unas, the last Pharaoh of the 5th dynasty. This is one of the easiest pyramids to visit at Saqqara, which means if there's a tour group in the area it will probably be crowded. The entrance is on the north face along a 1.4 metre high passage.

Only 350 years after the inspired creation of the Step Pyramid, and after the perfection of the Great Pyramids, this unassuming pile of loose blocks and dirt was built. In fact, despite the tomb's exterior, it marked the beginning of a trend in design. Until Unas' time (24th century BC), pyramid interiors had been unadorned – so while the outside of his tomb looks more like Zoser's than Cheops', the inside is of immense historical importance.

In 1881, Thomas Cook & Sons sponsored the excavation of the tomb by Gaston Maspero, who found the walls covered in hieroglyphs. Carved into the huge slabs of white alabaster, these so-called Pyramid Texts are the earliest known examples of decorative writing in a Pharaonic tomb chamber. The texts record the rituals, prayers and hymns that accompanied the

Pharaoh's burial to enable the release of his ka, and list the articles, like food and clothing, necessary for his existence in the afterlife.

Part of the one km causeway, which ran from the east side of the Pyramid of Unas, has been restored. On either side of it more than 200 mastabas have been excavated and there are several well-preserved tombs, some of which can be visited. The beautiful tomb of the 5th dynasty princess Idut, who was probably a daughter of Unas, is next to the southern wall of Zoser's complex. On the walls of its 10 chambers are colourful scenes of oxen, gazelle, ibex, hippopotamuses and other animals. The Mastaba of Queen Nebet and the Mastaba of Mehu are also beautifully decorated; and the Tomb of Nebkau-Her, which may be closed, is worth visiting if you can gain access.

Egyptologists debate whether the huge, sculpted boat pits, made of stone and located south of the causeway, actually held the royal barges which took the Pharaoh on his journey to the afterlife, or whether they merely represented these solar boats. Nothing was found when the 40 metre long crescent-shaped trenches were excavated.

Persian Tombs

The tombs of three Persian noblemen, just south of the Pyramid of Unas, are some of the deepest subterranean burial chambers in Egypt. The entrance is covered by a small inconspicuous wooden hut, to which a guard in the area has the key. If you don't have your own torch he will lead you the 25 metres down the winding staircase to the vaulted tombs of Psamtik, Zenhebu and Pelese. According to the ancient wall drawings, which are colourful and fantastic, Zenhebu was a famous Persian admiral and Psamtik was chief physician of the Pharaoh's court. The tombs were built to prevent grave robbers from stealing the contents. It didn't work: it was thieves who cut the spiral entrance passage.

Monastery of St Jeremiah

The half-buried remains of this 5th century AD monastery are up the hill from the Causeway of Unas and south-east of the boat pits. There's not much left of the structure because it was ransacked by invading Arabs in 950 AD, and more recently the Egyptian Antiquities Department took all the wall paintings and carvings to the Coptic Museum in Cairo.

Pyramid of Sekhemket

The unfinished Pyramid of Sekhemket is a short distance to the west of the ruined monastery. It was abandoned before completion, for unknown reasons, when it was only three metres high. There's an unused alabaster sarcophagus in one of the underground passageways, but no-one is permitted to enter this pile of rubble because of the danger of a cave-in.

Tomb of Akhti-Hotep & Ptah-Hotep

Akhti-Hotep and Ptah-Hotep, who were father and son officials during the reign of Djedkare (a 5th dynasty Pharaoh), designed their own tomb complex, which consists of two burial chambers, a chapel and a hall of pillars. The Hotep duo were judges, overseers of the priests of the pyramids, and chiefs of the granary and treasury. The reliefs in their chambers are some of the best at Saqqara and depict everyday life during the 5th dynasty. You'll see: Akhti-Hotep in the marshes building boats, fighting enemies and crossing rivers; a splendid scene of wild animals with Ptah-Hotep and other hunters in hot pursuit; people playing games, collecting food and eating; and Ptah-Hotep having a manicure while being entertained by musicians. The dual tomb is south of the main road, between the Step Pyramid and the rest house.

Philosophers' Circle

Down the slope in front of the rest house are several statues of Greek philosophers and poets, arranged in a circle beneath a protective roof. From left to right, the statues are Plato (standing), Heraclitus (seated), Thales (standing), Protagoras (seated), Homer (seated), Hesiod (seated), Demetrius of Phalerum (standing against a bust of Serapis) and Pindar. The circle was set up, during the Ptolemaic period, at the eastern end of a long avenue of sphinxes running from the temple, where a live Apis bull was worshipped, to the Serapeum, where the bulls of this strange animal cult were buried.

Serapeum

The sacred Apis bulls were by far the most important of the cult animals entombed at Saqqara. The Apis, it was believed, was an incarnation of Ptah, the god of Memphis, and was the calf of a cow struck by lightning from heaven. Once divinely impregnated, the cow would never again give birth and her calf was kept in the temple of Ptah and worshipped as a god. The Apis was always portrayed as black, with a distinctive white diamond on its forehead, a sun disc between its horns, the image of an eagle on its back and a scarab on its tongue. When it died, the bull was mummified, then carried on an alabaster bed to the subterranean galleries of the Serapeum at Saqqara, and placed in a huge sarcophagus.

The Apis catacombs date from the 13th century BC, when Ramses II began the first gallery, which reached a length of 68 metres. In the 7th century BC Psammetichus I cut a new gallery, which was extended by the Ptolemies to a length of 198 metres, and used till around 30 BC. Twenty-five Apis were embalmed and stabled in perpetuity here in monolithic granite coffins weighing up to 70 tonnes each. Only one mummified bull, now in the Cairo Agricultural Museum, was found when the Serapeum was excavated.

Until 1851, the existence of the sacred Apis tombs was known only from classical references. Having found a half-buried sphinx at Saqqara, and following the description given by the Greek historian Strabo in 24 BC, the French archaeologist

Auguste Mariette began digging, and uncovered the avenue of sphinxes leading to the Serapeum. His great discovery sparked the extensive and continuing excavation of Saqqara. In 1856 Mariette wrote that he'd been so profoundly struck with astonishment on first gaining access to the Apis vaults, five years before, that the feeling was still fresh in his mind. Only one chamber, walled up during the reign of Ramses II, had escaped the notice of tomb robbers. Finding it intact, Mariette wrote:

The finger marks of the Egyptian who had inserted the last stone in the wall built to conceal the doorway were still recognisable on the lime. There were also the marks of naked feet imprinted on the sand which lay in one corner of the tomb chamber. Everything was in its original condition in this tomb where the embalmed remains of the bull had lain undisturbed for 37 centuries.

The entrance to the Serapeum is near the rest house, on the main road, west of the Philosophers' Circle. It's very likely you'll experience the same feeling as Mariette, for this place is definitely weird and gets stranger still as you wander along galleries lit only by tiny lanterns that cast a murky light over the vaults and the enormous, macabre black sarcophagi they contain. The largest sarcophagus, at the end of the main gallery, was carved from a single piece of black granite and is covered in hieroglyphs.

Mastaba of Ti

This tomb, or mastaba, is one of the main sources of knowledge about life in Egypt towards the end of the Old Kingdom. Ti, an important court official who served under three Pharaohs, collected titles like his kings collected slaves. He was Lord of Secrets, Superintendent of Works, Overseer of the Pyramids of Abu Sir, Counsellor to the Pharaoh and even Royal Hairdresser. He married a woman of royal blood and the inscriptions on the walls of his tomb reveal that his children were rated as royalty. One of the best reliefs depicts Ti standing regally on a boat sailing through papyrus marshes, while others show men and women at various jobs like ploughing, ship-building, reaping grain and feeding cranes. The tomb, discovered by Mariette in 1865, is a few hundred metres north of the Philosophers' Circle.

Tombs of Teti, Mereruka & Ankhma-Hor

The avenue of sphinxes excavated by Mariette in the 1850s has again been engulfed by desert sands, but it once extended as far east as the Tomb of Teti. To get to this somewhat weathered tomb now, you must follow the road from the rest house, heading a little to the north once you've passed the Step Pyramid. The interior is often closed to the public but is worth seeing if you can get in.

Nearby is the Tomb of Mereruka, which has 30 rooms, many with magnificent wall inscriptions. Egyptologists have learned a great deal about the wildlife of ancient Egypt from these drawings. As you enter the tomb, notice on one of the walls the large-mouthed, sharp-tusked hippo-potamuses. The Tomb of Ankhma-Hor, a little further east, contains some very interesting scenes depicting 6th dynasty surgical operations, including toe surgery and a circumcision.

Mummified Animals

Excavations in this area have also uncovered several temples. They include the Anubieion, sacred to the jackal-headed Anubis, god of embalming and the dead, which has a gallery for dogs; the Bubasteion, sacred to the cat-goddess Bastet, which is filled with mummified cats; and other galleries with thousands of mummified birds and monkeys.

Abu Sir

The three pyramids of Abu Sir, at the edge of the desert, surrounded by a sea of sand dunes, formed part of a 5th dynasty necropolis. There were originally 14 pyramids at Abu Sir. Those that remain are mostly just mounds of rubble, though

at least one can still be entered. They are not easily accessible, but may be more so in the future.

Pyramid of Neferirkare Neferirkare's tomb is one of the best in the area and stands 45 metres high. It now resembles Zoser's Step Pyramid but, like the Giza pyramids, originally had an outer casing of stone.

Pyramid of Nyuserre Though the most dilapidated of the three, the Pyramid of Nyuserre has a causeway that runs to what's left of his mortuary temple to the south-east.

Pyramid of Sahure This is the most complete and the northernmost of the group. The entrance is open but it's only half a metre high – you have to crawl along for about two metres through Pharaonic dust and spider webs to get into the Pharaoh's tomb. The remains of Sahure's mortuary temple still stand nearby. From his pyramid, on a clear day, you can see as many as 10 pyramids stretching out before you to the horizon.

Other Monuments

North of the temple there are several interesting monuments, including several mastabas and the Tomb of Ptahshepses, who was a court official and relative of King Nyuserre. If you happen to be going to Abu Sir by camel, horse or donkey across the desert from Giza, then stop off at the 5th dynasty Sun Temple of Abu Ghorab. It was built by King Nyuserre in honour of the sun-god Ra. The huge altar is made from five big blocks of alabaster and once served as the base of a large solar obelisk. Very few travellers ever make it this far off the beaten track.

Mastabat el Faraun

The oldest structure in the South Saqqara area is the unusual mortuary complex of the 4th dynasty king Shepseskaf, believed to be a son of Mycerinus. Shepseskaf's tomb is neither a mastaba nor a pyramid.

The Mastabat el Faraun, or 'Pharaoh's bench', is an enormous stone structure resembling a sarcophagus topped with a rounded lid. The complex once covered 700 square metres and the interior consists of long passageways and a burial chamber. It is possible to enter the tomb if you can find a guard.

Southern Pyramids

The pyramids of the 6th dynasty Pharaohs Pepi I, Merenre and Pepi II, who made the move to South Saqqara, have been cleared of sand and feature some interesting hieroglyphic texts. The crumbling southernmost pyramids, built of sun-dried bricks, belong to 13th dynasty Pharaohs.

Pyramid of Pepi II A little north of the Mastabat el Faraun is the pyramid of this 6th dynasty Pharaoh, who allegedly ruled for 94 years. Pepi II's tomb contains some fine hieroglyphs. The ruins of his mortuary temple, which was once connected to the pyramid by a causeway, can also be explored. Nearby, to the west, are the remains of the pyramids of Queen Apuit and Queen Neith.

Pyramid of Djedkare North of what's left of Pepi II's valley temple is the tomb of Djedkare, a 5th dynasty Pharaoh. Known as Ahram esh Shawaf, or 'pyramid of the sentinel', it stands 25 metres high and can be entered through a tunnel on the north side.

Getting There & Away

Saqqara is about 32 km south of Cairo and three km west of Memphis. If you are coming from Memphis, take the Giza road north, then turn west and Saqqara will be straight ahead. If you're coming from Cairo or Giza, you have several options. Refer to the Memphis Getting There section for details on the train, taxi and Kamal minibus service from Cairo. The train from Cairo to the village of El Badrashein also goes to Dahshur – a taxi from either to North Saqqara should cost about E£5. A taxi from Giza to Saqqara should cost about E£15 to E£20. There are plenty of taxis available for the return journey.

One of the cheapest ways of getting to Saqqara without going via Memphis is to take bus No 800 (25 pt) from Midan Tahrir or a minibus (30 pt) from in front of the Mogamma building (also on Midan Tahrir). Get off at the Maryutia Canal stop. The minibus terminus is one stop beyond the canal and the bus terminus is up closer to the pyramids and the Hotel Mena House. From the canal (also called Saqqara Road) take a minibus 4 km to the village of Shoubra-ment, which is usually the end of the line for these buses. Then you either have to make a deal with the driver or try hitching a ride the rest of the way to Saqqara (about 16 km). Occasionally, there is a minibus that continues on to Abu Sir, but don't count on it. Good luck!

The most adventurous, though physically strenuous, option is to hire a camel, donkey or horse and cross the desert from the Great Pyramids of Giza to Saqqara. This takes at least eight hours for a round trip so make sure you're prepared for it. Unless you're accustomed to it, that amount of time spent on an animal will make sitting down rather difficult for a few days.

Animals can be hired from the stables near the Hotel Mena House and the Giza pyramids.

Getting Around

If you haven't already crossed the desert from Giza on your own beast of burden, the ideal way to visit the sights would be to hire a camel, horse or donkey at North Saqqara.

They can be hired at the rest house near the Serapeum in North Saqqara. A trip around North Saqqara should cost, after bargaining, E£2 for a camel or horse and E£1.50 for a donkey. Many of the animals wear blanket saddles emblazoned with the logos of various foreign tour operators and airlines, so don't be surprised to see a camel flying past with a Lufthansa or TWA sign on its side.

DAHSHUR

If you want to go to Dahshur, first check with the tourist office in Cairo to see if you still need permission from the Ministry of the Interior offices in Abbassiya (Cairo), as Dahshur is considered a military zone.

This southern extension of the necropolis of Memphis is a field of royal tombs, about 3.5 km long, just west of the village of Dahshur.

The Bent and Red pyramids were both built by Pharaoh Sneferu, the father of Cheops and founder of the 4th dynasty. Why Sneferu had two pyramids, and possibly a third at Meidum, is a mystery that has not been altogether solved by Egyptologists. If the purpose of a pyramid was to be a container for the Pharaoh's ka, then why would one Pharaoh with one ka need more than one tomb?

The other two dilapidated pyramids at Dahshur, which belong to 12th dynasty Pharaohs Amenemhet III and Sesostris III, are less interesting and really only for those with pyramid fever. Around all the pyramids there are also the customary tombs of the members of the royal families, court officials and priests.

Bent Pyramid

This is the most conspicuous of the four pyramids at Dahshur. Although its rather strange shape seems to suggest otherwise, this tomb and the Pyramid of Meidum, also built (or at least completed) by Sneferu, demonstrate the design transition from step pyramid to true pyramid.

For some reason, though, just a little over halfway up its 105 metre height, the angle of its exterior was reduced from 52° to 43.5°, giving it its distinctive blunt shape. The reason for the change in design is not known, but perhaps it was believed the initial angle was too steep to be stable. If it was considered unsafe it could explain

why Sneferu built another tomb only two km away, the so-called Red Pyramid, which rises at a constant angle of 43.5°.

Most of the Bent Pyramid's outer casing is still intact and it is unique in having two entrances. Nearby are the remains of the mortuary temple and further north are the ruins of Sneferu's valley temple, which yielded some interesting reliefs.

Getting There & Away

See the Saqqara Getting There & Away section for details.

HELWAN

Helwan, an industrial suburb of some 40,000 people, is about 25 km south of Cairo. At one time this was probably quite a pleasant place, but as a factory city it grew quickly and is now probably the most polluted area in Egypt. There are, however, a few unique things that are worth seeing.

Japanese Gardens

Strange as it may seem, Helwan is home to the only Japanese gardens in the Middle East. Although most of the grounds are scruffy and overgrown with weeds, and the once-grand duck ponds now have more squawking human bathers than quacking ducks, it is still obvious that this was once a magnificent place. Recently, there have been some efforts to restore the gardens to their former splendour. Weeds are being pulled and Buddhas are getting nose jobs and being repainted bright red. It's worth seeing if only to check out the row of red Buddhas – probably one of the last things you expect to see in Egypt. The gardens are close to the centre of town, down the street to your right as you leave the train station.

Wax Museum

Helwan's Wax Museum, which depicts Egypt's history from Ramses II to Nasser in lifelike tableaus, is also worth seeing. Displays include the death of Cleopatra,

Roman soldiers stabbing Christians with spears, a man being hanged, scenes of peasant life and Nasser's leadership of the 1952 Revolution. Fans whir at the feet of the figures to keep them cool, although most of them look as if they've already melted once and been remoulded. The caretaker usually insists on guiding you through the museum. It's open from 9 am to 5 pm and admission costs E£1, or 50 pt for students, plus a 50 pt tip for the caretaker.

Getting There & Away

The easiest way to get to Helwan from Cairo is to take a minibus from Bab el Louk Market, opposite the Tele-communications building. You can also take the metro from Midan Tahrir station to Helwan, which is the end of the line (50 pt).

To get from Helwan to Saqqara you can take a taxi for the ferry for 50 pt. There is also a minibus which leaves from the Helwan metro station and takes you to the ferry for 10 pt. The ferry is a green motorboat called *Markib Badrashein*. It costs 10 pt to cross the Nile to the village of El Badrashein, from where there are taxis and minibuses which go to Abu Sir.

Getting Around

If you don't feel like walking around Helwan you can take a *hantour*, or horse-drawn carriage, from the station to both the Japanese Gardens and the museum.

EL FAIYUM

About 100 km south-west of Cairo is El Faiyum, Egypt's largest oasis. The El Faiyum region is about 70 km wide and 60 km long, including the lake known as Birket Qarun. Home to more than 1.3 million people, it is an intricately irrigated, extremely fertile basin watered by the Nile via hundreds of capillary canals.

The region was once filled by Birket Qarun, which is fed by the Bahr Yusef, or 'river of Joseph', a tributary which leaves

Sobek

the Nile at Dairut. The lake now occupies only about one fifth of El Faiyum, on the north-western edge.

The Pharaohs of the 12th dynasty reduced the flow of water into the lake and reclaimed the land for cultivation by regulating the annual flooding of the Nile. The oasis became a favourite vacation spot for Pharaohs of the 13th dynasty, and many fine palaces were built. The Greeks later called the area Crocodilopolis, because they believed the crocodiles in Birket Qarun were sacred. A temple was built in honour of Sobek, the crocodile-headed god, and during Ptolemaic and Roman times pilgrims came from all over the ancient world to feed the sacred beasts.

El Faiyum has been called the garden of Egypt: lush fields of vegetables and sugar cane, and groves of citrus fruits, nuts and olives produce abundant harvests; the lake, canals and vegetation support an amazing variety of bird life; and the customs, living conditions and agricultural practices in the mud-brick villages throughout the oasis have changed very little in centuries. All this tradition and fertility, however, surrounds the rather grimy Medinet el Faiyum, or 'town of the Faiyum', which sadly is a microcosm of everything that is bad about Cairo: horn-happy drivers, choking fumes and dust, crowded streets and a population of more than 350,000.

Information

There are tourist offices opposite the water wheels in Medinet el Faiyum, at the lake and at Ain es Siliin. The people in the office near the wheel don't speak much English, but they can direct you to the train, bus or service taxi station.

There is a police station on Midan Qa'oun, the GPO is on Sharia Saad Zaghloul and there's a telephone office on Sharia al Hurriya, all in Medinet el Faiyum.

Water Wheels

Three functioning models of the actual water wheels still in use around El Faiyum can be seen opposite the tourist office. Irrigation water has to be obtained from the Nile rather than from Birket Qarun, as the lake is salty.

El Faiyum Market

This is an interesting local market which sells fruits, vegetables, and household goods such as huge aluminium pots and copper pans. You won't get hassled here – no-one speaks English.

Hawara Pyramid & Labyrinth

About 10 km south-east of Medinet el Faiyum, on the road to Beni Suef, is the dilapidated 58 metre mud-brick Pyramid of Amenemhet III. His once vast mortuary complex is now nothing but mounds of rubble, and even his temple, which had quite a reputation in ancient times, has suffered at the hands of stone robbers. Herodotus said the temple was a 3000 room labyrinth that surpassed even the pyramids; while Strabo claimed it had as many rooms as there were provinces, so

that all the Pharaoh's subjects could be represented by their local officials in the offering of sacrifices. In 24 BC, Strabo wrote:

. . . there are long and numerous covered ways, with winding passages communicating with each other, so that no stranger could find his way in or out of them without a guide. The roofs of these dwellings consist of a single stone each, and the covered ways are roofed in the same manner with single slabs of stone of extraordinary size, without the intermixture of timber or any other material.

The area was also used as a cemetery by the Greeks and Romans, who here adopted the Egyptian practice of mummification. Now, all that remains are pieces of mummy cloth and human bones sticking through the mounds of rubble. There's also a crocodile cemetery north-east of the pyramid.

The buses between Beni Suef and Medinet el Faiyum pass through Hawaret el Makta, from where it's a short walk to the pyramid. Just ask the driver to let you off.

Pyramid of Lahun

About 10 km south-east of Hawara, on the Nile side of the narrow fertile passage through the desert that connects El Faiyum to the river, are the ruins of a small mud-brick pyramid. Once cased in limestone, it was built by Senusert II back in the Middle Kingdom period around 1885 BC. This monument is definitely off the beaten track. Although there's not much of it left, you can climb to the top for a great view of the surrounding area. The people in the neighbouring village will probably be so surprised to see you that they'll invite you to tour their fields and houses.

You can probably hitch from Beni Suef or Medinet el Faiyum to the dirt road leading to the village of El Lahun; or take the local bus between the two cities and tell the driver where you want to stop.

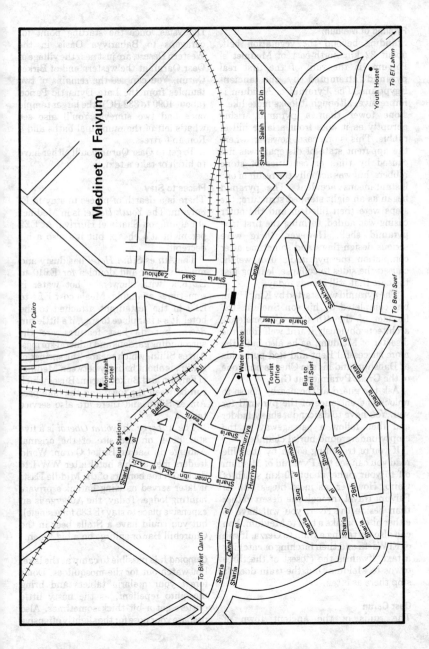

Medinet el Faiyum

To El Lahun
Youth Hostel

Sharia Salah el Din

To Cairo

To Beni Suef

Sharia Saad Zaghloul

Canal

Sharia el Nasr

Salakhana

Montazah Hotel

Water Wheels

Tourist Office

Bus to Beni Suef

Sharia el Birol

Sharia Amr

Bus Station

Sharia el Badd

Sharia el Aziz

Sharia Omar ibn Abd el Aziz

Sharia Tewfik

Sharia Gomhurriya

Sharia Hurriya

Sharia Suq el Samak

Sharia el Shut

Sharia 26th

Sharia el Canal

To Birket Qarun

Pyramid of Meidum

Standing beyond the vegetation belt, about 32 km north-east of Medinet el Faiyum, is the ruin of the first real pyramid attempted by the ancient Egyptians. The Pyramid of Meidum is impressive, although it looks more like a stone tower than a pyramid, rising abruptly as it does from a large hill of rubble. This is one case, however, where the apparent state of disrepair was not caused by time or centuries of stone robbers, but was actually the result of one instantaneous accident. The pyramid began as an eight stepped structure; the steps were then filled in and the outer casing was added, forming the first true pyramid shell. However, there were serious design flaws and sometime after completion the pyramid's own weight caused the sides to collapse, leaving just the core that still stands today.

The pyramid was started by King Huni, but completed by his son Sneferu, the founder of the 4th dynasty. Sneferu's architects obviously learnt well from the disaster of Meidum, as he also built the more successful Bent and Red pyramids at Dahshur, and his son Cheops built one of the Great Pyramids at Giza.

Ask the guard at the nearby house to unlock the entrance of the pyramid for you. You have to descend a shaky ladder and then follow a passageway to the empty underground burial chamber.

If you're travelling south by the Nile road you can see the Pyramid of Meidum off to your right, about 70 km south of Cairo. However, as most buses into El Faiyum travel through the desert rather than beside the river, you will have to either hitch or take a taxi to Meidum. You can also try taking a train to Gerza, Ifwah or El Wasta and then hitching or catching a taxi. Ifwah is the closest of the three towns to Meidum, but the train doesn't stop there as often.

Qasr Qarun

The ruins of the ancient town of Dionysias, once the starting point for caravans to Bahariyya Oasis in the Western Desert, are just near the village of Qasr Qarun at the western end of Birket Qarun. You can see the remains of two temples from the Late Dynastic Period (about 1090 to 332 BC); the larger temple once had two storeys. You'll also see what's left of the municipal baths and a Roman fortress.

To get to Qasr Qarun you'll either have to hitch or take a taxi.

Places to Stay

There is a dearth of places to stay in El Faiyum. The *Youth Hostel* is in Medinet el Faiyum, on Sharia el Hurriya. At E£2 per night it's cheap, but it's also a bit decrepit.

The *Ain es Siliin Hotel* has dusty and musty singles and doubles for E£10 to E£16.50 with showers – hot water is sometimes available. Meals cost E£4 to E£9 in the restaurant attached to the hotel. It's a fair place to stay, if a little run-down, but its best features are the surrounding gardens and mineral springs. Ain es Siliin, which means 'the springs of Siliin', is about halfway between Medinet el Faiyum and Birket Qarun. Buses which run between the town and the lake pass Ain es Siliin and there are also service taxis.

The *Auberge Fayyoum Oberoi* is a five star hotel on the site of the original Auberge du Lac on Birket Qarun. World leaders met at this hotel after WW I to decide on the borders of the Middle East; it later served as King Farouk's private hunting lodge. Today, the Auberge is an expensive place to stay (E£85 for a single), but you could have a Stella beer in the Churchill Bar or splurge on a big lunch.

Camping It is possible to camp at the lake, but watch out for the mosquitoes. Don't forget your malaria tablets and bring mosquito repellent, as the nasty little critters get a bit thick sometimes. Also prepare your nose for the slightly offensive smell of the lake; it is possible to get used to it.

Places to Eat

Aside from the standard fuul and ta'amiyya and kushari stands, there are also a couple of restaurants in Medinet el Faiyum. The *Cafeteria al Medina* opposite the water wheels serves shish kebab and a few other meat and chicken dishes for about E£5. Near the Montazah Hotel (see the Medinet el Faiyum map), the *Nadi el Muhavsa* serves just about every type of Egyptian food.

Things to Buy

Throughout El Faiyum, especially at Ain es Siliin, you will see lots of colourful basketwork and rugs. The baskets come in all shapes and sizes and cost as little as E£5. The rugs are made in cooperatives in and around Medinet el Faiyum. If you're interested in visiting the cooperatives, ask at the tourist booth for locations.

Getting There & Away

To get to El Faiyum from Cairo take bus No 8 from Midan Tahrir to Midan Giza, then look for the minibus terminal near the overpass. A service taxi or minibus from there to El Faiyum costs about E£2.50 per person and the trip takes 1½ hours.

There are other buses to El Faiyum every half-hour from Ahmed Hilmi Station (behind Ramses Station in Cairo). The buses run from 6 am to 6 pm and cost E£2 per person. These buses also stop at Midan Giza. During the high season (October to April) the buses tend to be quite full.

Getting Around

The bus terminal in Medinet el Faiyum is near the train tracks on Sharia el Badd el Ali. Buses run every hour to Cairo and other points in and around El Faiyum. To get to Ain es Siliin or Birket Qarun take a bus to the town of Sanhur from Mahattit el Ba'udiyya, in town. You can also take a

horse-drawn carriage for about E£5 return or a taxi for E£6 to E£7 return. To get to the pyramids of Hawara and Lahun, take the Beni Suef bus and tell the driver where you want to get off.

WADI NATRUN

Wadi Natrun is a partly cultivated valley, about 100 km north-west of Cairo, that was important to the Egyptians long before the Copts took refuge there. The natron used in the mummification process came from the large deposits of sodium carbonate left when the valley's salt lakes dried up every summer.

A visit to the monasteries of Wadi Natrun should explain the endurance of the ancient Coptic Christian sect. It is the desert, in a sense, that is the protector of the Coptic faith, for it was there that thousands of Christians retreated to escape Roman persecution in the 4th century AD. They lived in caves, or built monasteries, and developed the monastic tradition that was later adopted by European Christians.

In Wadi Natrun alone there were once more than 50 monasteries, built as fortresses to protect the isolated communities from marauding Bedouins. The focal point of the monasteries was the church, around which were built a well, storerooms, a dining hall, kitchen, bakery and the monks' cells. The whole complex was surrounded by walls about 14 metres high and four metres thick, and guarded by the keep – a tower which also served as an internal fort during sieges. While only four of the monasteries survived the Romans, the Bedouin raids and the coming of Islam, the religious life they all protected is thriving. The Coptic pope is still chosen from among the Wadi Natrun monks, and monasticism is experiencing a revival, with younger Copts again donning hooded robes to live within these ancient walls in the desert.

You can visit the monasteries as a side trip en route between Cairo and Alexandria or as a day tour from either city. Before you make the journey, however, you should check with the Coptic Orthodox Patriarchate. In Cairo the Patriarchate (tel 825863, 821274) is next to St Mark's Church, 222 Sharia Ramses, Abbassiya; in Alexandria it's on Sharia Nabi Daniel. Women are not allowed to stay overnight at the monasteries and if men wish to do so they need written permission from one of these offices. If you can't stay at one of the monasteries then you'll have to either camp or return to Cairo or Alexandria.

Deir Amba Bishoi

St Bishoi founded two monasteries in Wadi Natrun, this one (which bears his name) and the nearby Deir el Suriani. Deir Amba Bishoi – a great place to watch a desert sunset – contains the saint's body, which is said to be perfectly preserved under a red cloth, and the remains of Paul of Tamweh, who made quite a name for himself by committing suicide seven times. The monks there claim that it is not uncommon for St Bishoi to perform miracles for true believers.

Deir el Suriani

Deir el Suriani, or the 'monastery of the Syrians', is named for the many Syrian monks who once lived there; it's about 500 metres north-west of Deir Amba Bishoi. There are several domed churches in the gardens and courtyards of this tranquil monastery. Ask the monks to show you St Bishoi's private cell where he stood for nights on end with his hair attached to a chain dangling from the ceiling. It was during one of these marathon prayer vigils that Christ is said to have appeared and allowed Bishoi to wash His feet and then drink the water.

Deir Abu Makar

This monastery is south-east of Deir Amba Bishoi. Though structurally it has suffered worst at the hands of raiding Bedouins, it is perhaps the most renowned of the four monasteries, as over the centuries most of the Coptic popes have been selected from among its monks. It is the last resting place of many of those popes and also contains the remains of the '49 Martyrs', a group of monks killed by Bedouins in 444 AD.

Deir el Baramus

The most isolated of the Wadi Natrun monasteries is that of St Baramus, which is across the desert to the north-west. It's probably the best one to stay at if you can get to it, and have permission, as it's a little less austere than the others. The special feature of its church is a superb iconostasis of inlaid ivory.

Getting There & Away

Getting to Wadi Natrun may be difficult if you don't have your own transportation. You can take one of the regular buses along the desert road between Cairo and Alexandria and ask the driver to drop you off at the rest house, about 95 km from Cairo. From there you might find a private taxi or minibus to take you out to Deir Amba Bishoi. At the very least you should be able to get a ride to the village of Bir Hooker and arrange for additional transport from there.

If you have your own vehicle and you're coming from Cairo, take Pyramids Rd (Sharia al Ahram) through Giza and turn onto the desert road just before the Hotel Mena House. At about 95 km from Cairo (just after the rest house) turn left into the wadi, go through the village of Bir Hooker and continue on, following the signs indicating the monasteries. The first one is Deir Amba Bishoi, Deir el Suriani is about half a km to the north-west, Deir Abu Makar is a few km via a paved road to the south-east, and Deir el Baramus is quite a hike through the sands to the north-west.

THE NILE DELTA

If you have the time, it's well worth the effort to explore the lush fan-shaped delta of Egypt between Cairo and Alexandria. This is where the Nile divides in half to flow north into the sea at the Mediterranean ports of Damietta and Rashid (Rosetta). The delta is also laced with several smaller tributaries and is reputedly one of the most fertile and, not surprisingly, most cultivated regions in the world.

The delta region played just as important a part in the early history of the country as did Upper Egypt, though few archaeological remains record this. While the desert and dryness of the south helped preserve the Pharaonic sites, the amazing fertility of the delta region had the opposite effect. Over the centuries, when the ancient cities, temples and palaces of the delta were left to ruin, they were literally ploughed into oblivion by the fellahin. The attraction of this area, then, is the chance of coming across communities rarely visited by foreigners, where you can gain a little insight into the Egyptian peasant farmer's way of life.

Though service taxis and buses crisscross the region from town to town, the best way to get off the beaten track and wander through this incredibly green countryside is to hire a car. Along the back roads and canals you can visit the quaint farming villages that thrive amongst the fields of cotton, maize and rice. Theoretically, you're not supposed to leave the main roads, but in the unlikely event of you being hassled by the police you can always say you're lost.

Nile Barrages & Qanater

The Nile Barrages and the city of Qanater lie 16 km north of Cairo where the Nile splits into the eastern Damietta Branch and the western Rosetta Branch. The barrages, begun in the early 19th century, were successfully completed several decades later. The series of basins and locks, on both main branches of the Nile and two side canals, ensured the vital large-scale regulation of the Nile into the delta region, and led to a great increase in cotton production.

The Damietta Barrage consists of 71 sluices stretching 521 metres across the river; the Rosetta Barrage is 438 metres long with 61 sluices. Between the two is a one km wide area filled with beautiful gardens and cafes. It's a superb place to rent a bicycle or a felucca and take a relaxing tour.

The town of Qanater, at the fork of the river, is officially the start of the delta region.

Getting There & Away To get to the barrages from Cairo you can take a ferry for 50 pt from the water-taxi station in front of the Radio & Television building (Maspero Station), just north of the Ramses Hilton. The trip takes about two hours. A bus to Qanater leaves from in front of the Nile Hilton, on the Midan Tahrir side.

Zagazig

Just outside this town, founded in the 19th century, are the ruins of Bubastis, one of the most ancient cities in Egypt. There's not much to see in Zagazig itself, but as it's only 80 km north-east of Cairo it's an easy day trip to the ruins. The train heading for Port Said from Cairo takes about 1½ hours to Zagazig and a service taxi takes about one hour.

Bubastis The great deity of the ancient city of Bubastis was the elegant cat-goddess Bastet. Festivals held in her honour are said to have attracted more than 700,000 revellers, who would sing, dance, feast, consume great quantities of wine and offer sacrifices to the goddess. The architectural gem of Bubastis was the Temple of Bastet, sited between two canals, surrounded by trees and encircled by the city, which was built at a higher level to look down on it. The temple was begun by Cheops and Chephren during the 4th dynasty, and Pharaohs of the 6th, 12th, 18th, 19th and 22nd dynasties made their additions over about 17 centuries. Herodotus wrote:

Although other Egyptian cities were carried to

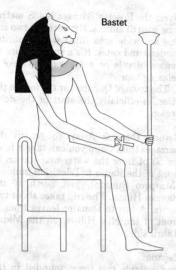

Bastet

a great height, in my opinion the greatest mounds were thrown up about the city of Bubastis, in which is a temple of Bastet well worthy of mention; for though other temples may be larger and more costly, none is more pleasing to look at than this.

The temple is now just a pile of rubble, and the most interesting site at Bubastis is the cat cemetery 200 metres down the road. The series of underground galleries, where many bronze statues of cats were found, is perfect for a bit of exploration.

Tanis

Just outside the village of San el Hagar, 70 km north-east of Zagazig, are the ruins of ancient Tanis, which many believe to be the Biblical city where the Hebrews were persecuted by the Egyptians before fleeing through the Red Sea in search of the Promised Land. It was certainly of great importance to a succession of powerful Pharaohs, all of whom left their mark through the extraordinary buildings or statues they commissioned, and for several centuries Tanis was one of the largest cities in the delta.

Tanis covers about four square km, only part of which has been excavated. The monuments uncovered date from as early as the 6th dynasty reign of Pepi I, around 2330 BC, through to the time of the Ptolemies in the 1st century BC. The excavation of the city so far has revealed sacred lakes, the foundations of many temples, a royal necropolis and a multitude of statues and carvings.

Although it's less impressive than other archaeological sites in the country, the Egyptian government has recently begun promoting Tanis as a tourist destination. A few tour groups have begun including it in their itineraries.

Tanta

Tanta, the largest city in the delta, is 90 km from Cairo and 110 km from Alexandria. There's nothing much of interest there, though it is a centre for Sufism, a form of Islamic mysticism. A mosque in Tanta is dedicated to Said Badawi, a Moroccan Sufi, who fought the Crusaders from there in the 13th century and then went on to assist in the defeat of Louis IX at Damietta.

In this area of the western delta, though there are no actual structural remains, are the sites of three ancient cities. North-west of Tanta, on the east bank of the Nile, is Sais, Egypt's 26th dynasty capital. Sacred to Neith, the goddess of war and hunting and protector of embalmed bodies, Sais dates back to the start of Egyptian history and once had palaces, temples and royal tombs.

West of Tanta, about halfway along the road to Damanhur, is the site of Naucratis, an ancient city where the Greeks were allowed to settle and trade during the 7th century BC. The city of Buto, east of Damanhur and north of Tanta, was the cult centre of Edjo, the cobra-goddess of Lower Egypt, always represented on a Pharaoh's crown as a uraeus.

Mansura

At the centre of Egypt's cotton industry is Mansura, one of the most important cities in the delta. The best thing about a visit to Mansura is the chance to taste the city's delicacy – buffalo milk ice cream.

Mansura is known as the 'city of victory' for the part it played in Egypt's early Islamic history. In 1249, the Egyptians retreated from the coast and set up camp at Mansura after the Crusader forces, under Louis IX of France, had captured the Mediterranean port of Damietta. When the Crusaders decided to make their push inland, they charged straight through the Muslim camp, only to be cut down on the other side of Mansura by 10,000 Mameluke warriors. Louis himself was captured and ransomed for the return of Damietta.

Damietta
Once a prosperous Arab trading port, Damietta's fortunes suffered greatly with the construction of the Suez Canal and the subsequent development of Port Said. During the Middle Ages, its strategic position on the north coast of Egypt, at the mouth of Nile, meant it was regularly being threatened by foreign armies. Over the centuries it was taken by the Germans, English and French, and defended by, among others, Salah al Din and Mohammed Ali. When it wasn't being attacked by marauding Crusaders, Damietta was doing a roaring trade in coffee, linen, oil and dates, and was a port of call for ships from all over the known world.

Ras el Bar
The small town of Ras el Bar, north of Damietta, is right at the point where the eastern branch of the Nile meets the sea, 170 km north-east of Cairo. It is a pleasant beach resort with several hotels and restaurants, and if you're planning on staying anywhere in the delta region this would be the best choice.

There are other quiet little beach resorts to the west of Ras el Bar at Gamasa, Baltim and El Burg.

Places to Stay *Abou Tabl*, 4 Sharia 17, is a basic hotel with singles for E£18 and doubles for E£25, plus 20% tax. Its restaurant is well known for its fiteer and other types of Oriental food.

Other OK hotels are the *Marine Fouad*, the *Marine el Nil* and the *Marine Ras el Bar*.

Getting There & Away Buses leave Cairo every hour, from 7.15 am to 5.15 pm, and travel direct to Ras el Bar. They leave from Ulali Station, which is near Ramses Station (see the Central Cairo map). During summer you need to book at least one day in advance. The trip takes 3½ hours and costs E£8 on an air-conditioned bus.

The Nile Valley – Beni Suef to Qus

The ancient Greek traveller and writer Herodotus described Egypt as 'the gift of the Nile'; the ancient Egyptians likened their land to a lotus – the delta being the flower, the oasis of El Faiyum the bud and the river and its valley the stem. Whichever way you look at it, Egypt is the Nile. The river is the lifeblood of the country and the fertile Nile Valley is its heart. And whether you journey down the valley by felucca, train, bus or plane you'll discover that even an outsider cannot ignore the power of the Nile and the hold it has always had over Egyptian life.

Rain seldom falls in the Nile Valley, so the verdant stretch of land, ranging from a couple of metres to a few km wide on either side of the river, is rendered fertile only by the winding Nile as it makes its way through the barren desert. The countryside is dotted with thousands of simple villages where people toil, day in day out, using tools and machinery modelled on designs thousands of years old. Even the region's large towns and cities, like El Minya, Asyut, Luxor and Aswan, are in some ways merely modernised extensions of these villages.

Travelling south from Cairo you pass through a world where ancient and medieval monuments almost seem to be part of the present. From Saqqara to Luxor, while you marvel at the remarkable history of the Pharaonic tombs and their builders, you'll realise that the daily labour and recreation of the fellahin in the 20th century differs very little from the images depicted in the wall paintings of the ancient monuments. The colourful scenes of Egyptians building, hunting, fighting, feasting, harvesting and fishing more than 2500 years ago are repeated daily on the banks of the Nile and in the valley's fertile fields.

BENI SUEF

Beni Suef is a provincial capital 130 km south of Cairo. Even with a population of 150,000 and a few multistorey buildings it isn't a big town, but is typical of the large Egyptian country towns that are basically overgrown farming villages. There are more donkey carts and hantours in the streets than cars and buses. While there's nothing of particular interest in Beni Suef itself, it is a good base for visiting El Faiyum.

Places to Stay

The *Semiramis Hotel* is really the only hotel in town worth mentioning. It has six singles and 24 doubles. Two of the singles have bathrooms and cost E£9; the other four cost E£7. Of the doubles, 20 have bathrooms and cost E£18; the rest cost E£12.50. Hot water and TVs are included, the 12% service charge is not. A continental breakfast is an extra E£2.50, and various other big meals are E£5 to E£6. The hotel faces the train tracks and is opposite the GPO.

There is also a *Teachers' Club* down the street towards the Nile (see the Beni Suef map) which has a few cheap rooms. It's a bit run-down, but you're bound to meet some interesting characters there who speak some English.

Places to Eat

Aside from the usual assortment of fuul and ta'amiyya stands, there is the *Nadi Shurta* on the Corniche along the Nile. Meals of fish and typical Egyptian fare cost about E£6 to E£8.

The *Semiramis Hotel* serves a variety of filling meals that include kufta and chicken kebab for about E£4. Other dishes average about E£5 to E£6.

Getting There & Away

There are frequent buses, trains and service taxis to Beni Suef from Cairo and

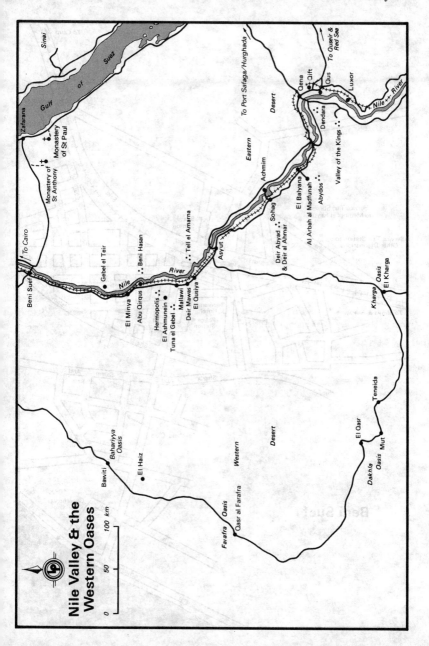

Nile Valley & the Western Oases

0   50   100 km

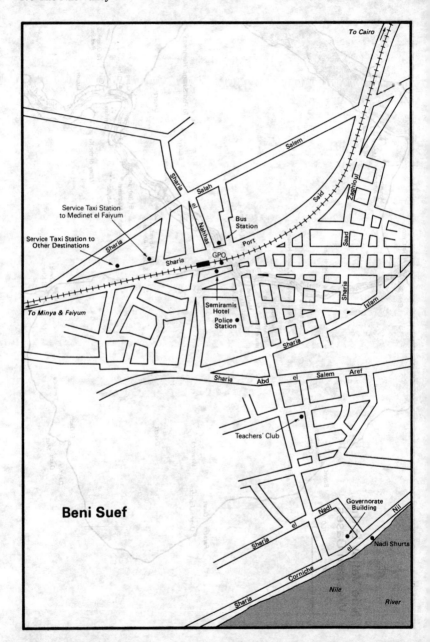

Beni Suef

Helwan. From Beni Suef there are buses to Cairo for E£3.50, to Medinet el Faiyum for E£1 and to El Minya for E£1.25. Service taxis for the same locations cost E£4, E£1.25 and E£1.50 per person. The Beni Suef bus station is opposite the GPO and the service taxi station is a little further down Sharia Port Said.

The buses tend to be crowded and occasionally the best 'seats' are on the roof. While travelling atop one of these buses a couple of 19 year old soldiers from the countryside told me why they were already married, or rather their graphic gestures and ear-to-ear grins explained why. I asked them how many kids they planned to have. 'Six or seven,' they said. 'And how will you feed all of these kids?' I asked. '*Allah, Allah, Allah hu-akbar,*' they said. That means 'Allah, Allah, Allah is great'. Hmmm!

Beni Suef is also a departure point for the trek across the desert to the Monastery of St Anthony, which is about 150 km east, near the Gulf of Suez. You'd really need your own truck or 4WD to make this journey, as it might be difficult to hire a service taxi in Beni Suef for the whole trip.

GEBEL EL TEIR

The main feature of this small Christian hamlet, 93 km south of Beni Suef, is Deir el Adhra – the 'monastery of the Virgin'. Established as a church/monastery in the 4th century AD by the Byzantine empress Helena, it was built on one of the sites where the Holy Family supposedly rested while fleeing Palestine. Gebel el Teir and its church are perched on a hill 130 metres above the east bank of the Nile.

Getting from the main Nile road to the east side of the river is definitely an adventure. In the west bank village opposite Gebel el Teir you ask for *il markib li Gebel el Teir*, which means 'the boat to Gebel el Teir'. You then walk to the Nile and wait for a shaky little canoe to appear and ferry you to the other side. Once across you walk through a field to

some stairs cut into the side of the cliff. They go up to the hamlet, where someone will probably lead you to the priest, but if not just ask for the *kineesa*, or church. The priest speaks some English and can give you a short tour of the monastery and the hamlet.

There's a *Guest House* which provides accommodation. Back at the foot of the stairs you can hitch a ride either north or south to a bigger ferry crossing. A ferry boat 24 km south of Gebel el Teir crosses the river to El Minya.

EL MINYA

A semi-industrial provincial capital 247 km south of Cairo, El Minya is a centre for sugar processing and the manufacture of soap and perfume. There are several hotels, which make this a convenient place to base yourself for day trips to the Pharaonic tombs and temples of Beni Hasan, Tuna el Gebel and Hermopolis.

There's not much to see or do in town, except just walk around and meet some of the friendly local people, most of whom will be extremely interested in whether or not you're married. The tree-lined Corniche along the Nile is a pleasant place for a picnic or a ride in a hantour.

Information

There's a tourist information office (tel 320150) at the corner of the Corniche (also known as Sharia Ramadan and Sharia el Nil at this point) and Sharia Abdel Monem. They can give you the latest information on getting to the Beni Hasan tombs, Tell el Amarna, Hermopolis and Tuna el Gebel. Hours are 8.30 am to 2 pm and 4 to 10 pm daily.

The telephone office is on Midan Palace and is open 24 hours.

Zawiyet el Mayyiteen

This is a large Muslim and Christian cemetery across the river from El Minya, near the ferry landing. Its name means 'corner of the dead'. The cemetery consists of several hundred mud-brick

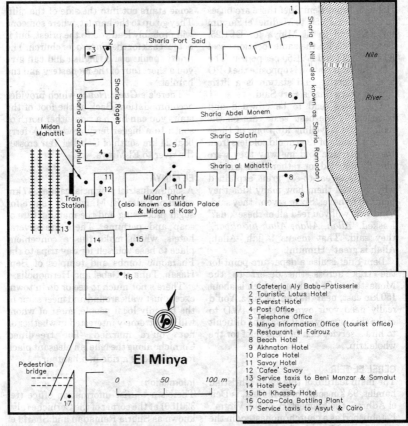

1 Cafeteria Aly Baba—Patisserie
2 Touristic Lotus Hotel
3 Everest Hotel
4 Post Office
5 Telephone Office
6 Minya Information Office (tourist office)
7 Restaurant el Fairouz
8 Beach Hotel
9 Akhnaton Hotel
10 Palace Hotel
11 Savoy Hotel
12 'Cafee' Savoy
13 Service taxis to Beni Manzar & Samalut
14 Hotel Seety
15 Ibn Khassib Hotel
16 Coca—Cola Bottling Plant
17 Service taxis to Asyut & Cairo

El Minya

0   50   100 m

mausolea stretching for four km from the road to the hills. It is said to be one of the largest cemeteries in the world.

Places to Stay

The *Ibn Khassib Hotel* (tel 224535) is in an ageing building on a side street near the train station. It has plenty of rooms, all with high ceilings and Victorian-style furniture. Bathrooms/showers are crammed together. Single/double/triple rooms are E£19.70/26.50/33. There are four relatively new rooms on the ground floor. Breakfast is included and other meals are available. Tour groups use this hotel and it's sometimes easy to get a ride with them to the local attractions.

The *Beach Hotel* (tel 322307) is a clean, pleasant place three blocks from the train station and overlooking the river. Singles with or without bath cost from E£8 to E£15. All the rooms there have full carpeting, air-conditioning and clean bathrooms.

The *Hotel Seety*, 71 Sharia Saad Zaghloul, is half a block south of the train station. It looks seedy from the outside, but several of the rooms are clean, comfortable and airy. The best part is a central living room full of antique furniture and an out-of-tune piano. A double room with/without bath costs E£15/10; a single is E£8/12.

The *Savoy Hotel* (also called the *Hotel Savoy*) is directly across from the train station. It has large, clean room with very high ceilings for E£5 single and E£8 double. Bathrooms are near the rooms.

The *Everest Hotel* is old and decrepit, a place to avoid – unless, of course, they renovate it.

The *Touristic Lotus Hotel* (tel 324541) is on Sharia Port Said, about a 10 minute walk from the train station. It's a modern brown structure with a restaurant on top, which serves simple meals such as chicken, salad, oily vegetables and chips for about E£6 to E£7. Singles cost E£15.80, doubles E£22.15; all have air-conditioning and include breakfast.

The *Akhnaton Hotel* (tel 325918), on the Corniche near the Beach Hotel, has 42 clean, carpeted rooms with air-conditioning on the 3rd and 4th floors, some with great views of the Nile. Singles/doubles are E£9.65/12.05.

The *Palace Hotel* (tel 324071/21) is on Midan Palace. It's similar to the Savoy with clean high-ceilinged rooms and a big, airy central lobby. Rooms are E£8.70 with bath and E£7 without. The rooms with bathrooms are better.

A few km north of town is the *ETAP*, a four star hotel that is one of the newest in the area. Single/double rooms are about E£104/130. It's popular mostly with tour groups.

Camping It's possible to pitch a tent at the El Minya Stadium, which is north of the station, directly up the tracks.

Places to Eat

The restaurant and cafeteria on top of the *Lotus Hotel* serves simple but filling meals for E£6 to E£8. However, they tend to serve their vegetables in a pool of oil. The views of the Nile and surrounding fields are fantastic.

The *Cafeteria Aly Baba – Patisserie*, on

the Corniche just north of Sharia Port Said, serves shwarma sandwiches and tiny hamburgers with tomatoes for 60 pt each. They also have a variety of typical Egyptian pastries. This is a good place to come in the morning for a cup of coffee and a pastry.

The *Restaurant el Fairouz* is on the Corniche at the corner of Sharia Salatin (see the El Minya map). The walls inside are garishly painted with peasant farming scenes that give the place a definite character. The menu is on a piece of papyrus and includes such things as hamburgers (frozen from Cairo, as they will gladly show you), sausages, chicken shish kebab and grilled 'Chinese' liver. Most of the items are under E£1.

Getting There & Away

Bus Buses of various prices and standards leave regularly from the bus station, which is near the Cairo and Asyut service taxi row, for destinations north and south of El Minya. There are buses to Cairo every hour from 5 am to 5 pm for E£4.15 with air-conditioning and E£3.50 without (four hours). Buses to Asyut (2½ hours) cost about E£2.50 and leave every half-hour from 7.30 am to 5 pm. From Asyut, there are at least nine buses daily to El Minya with fares starting at E£2.50.

Train The trip from Cairo takes about four hours and costs E£9.50 in 1st class, E£5.15 in 2nd class with air-conditioning, E£2.50 in 2nd class without air-con and E£1.10 in 3rd class.

Trains heading south depart fairly frequently, with the fastest trains leaving El Minya between about 11 pm and 1 am. Fares (1st class/2nd with air-conditioning/2nd without) from El Minya are: Asyut E£5.15/3/1.30; Sohag E£8.45/4.75/2.15; Qena E£12.80/7.05/3.35; Luxor E£14.25/7.85/3.75; and Aswan E£19.15/10.15/4.90.

Taxi From Ramses Station in Cairo the three to four hour trip to El Minya costs E£5. From El Minya service taxis cost

E£1 to Mallawi and E£2.50 to Asyut. The depot is about a 10 minute walk from the train station (see the El Minya map).

BENI HASAN

Beni Hasan is a necropolis on the east bank of the Nile about 20 km south of El Minya. More than 30 distinctive Middle Kingdom tombs of varying sizes are carved into a limestone cliff. Only a few of them are accessible.

The Beni Hasan necropolis is open from 7 am to 5 pm, but you should get there by 3 pm at the latest. It's a good idea to start earlier because it can get quite hot here towards the end of the day. Admission is E£3.75, including the boat trip and minibus ride to the tombs. You should also give the guard a bit of baksheesh for unlocking the tombs, although that's his job anyway. Photography is prohibited inside the tombs.

There are various tombs at Beni Hasan, the best of which are:

Tomb of Kheti (No 17)

Kheti was a governor of the nome, or district, of Oryx during Egypt's 11th dynasty (about 2000 BC). Wall scenes in his tomb show daily life in the Middle Kingdom, as well as two copulating cows and an attack on a fort.

Tomb of Baqet (No 15)

Baqet was the father of Kheti. His tomb has some strange wall paintings: wrestlers doing more than just wrestling with each other, gazelles doing the same, and a hunt for unicorns and winged monsters.

Entrance to Beni Hasan

Tomb of Khnumhotep (No 3)

This is a beautiful tomb. Khnumhotep served as a governor under Amenemhet III (about 1820 BC). The walls show colourful scenes of Khnumhotep's family life, and above the door are some interesting scenes of acrobats.

Tomb of Amenemhet (No 2)

This has the unusual addition of a false door facing west. The dead are supposed to enter the underworld only from the west. Amenemhet was a nomarch, or governor, and commander in chief of the Oryx nome.

Getting There & Away

To get to Beni Hasan from El Minya, or from Mallawi, which is further south, you take a minibus or service taxi to Abu Qirqus for about 25 pt. From there it is a 15 minute walk to the Nile. You then cross the Ibrahimiya Canal and take the boat across the river, which costs E£3.75 and includes the round-trip boat ride, the ticket and minibus transportation to the tombs. There's a great view of the Nile from the tombs further up the slope.

MALLAWI

Mallawi is 48 km south of El Minya. There is not much in town, except for a museum, one hotel and two restaurants, but it's a convenient departure point for the ancient sights of Hermopolis, Tuna el Gebel and Tell el Amarna.

Archaeological Museum

The small museum in town has a collection of artefacts from Tuna el Gebel and Hermopolis. It is open daily, except Wednesday, from 9 am to 2 pm and 4 to 6 pm. It closes at 12 noon on Friday. Admission is 50 pt, or 25 pt for students.

Places to Stay & Eat

There is only one – the *Samir Amis Hotel* on the west bank of the Ibrahimiya Canal, just north of the train station. The rooms aren't bad, but the bathrooms are a bit grimy. Rooms are E£3/4/6 for a single/double/triple. The hotel's restaurant has the best meals in town: meat, chicken, rice, vegetables and beer. A full meal costs about E£4.

There's another restaurant, just down the street from the Samir Amis, called the *El Hourriya*; look for the fly-covered cow carcasses hanging in front! It costs E£4 for a full meal.

Getting There & Away

A service taxi from El Minya costs E£1; from Asyut it's E£2 for the one hour trip.

HERMOPOLIS

Little remains of this ancient city, eight km north of Mallawi, that was once the centre for the cult of Thoth, the ibis-headed god of wisdom, healing and writing. The Greeks associated Thoth with their own Hermes – hence the city's Hellenic name – but in ancient times the city was known as Khmunu. Khmun was one of the eight all-powerful deities of the primordial chaos that preceded creation, and this city was believed to be sited where the sun first rose over the earth. The Arabic name for the present-day village, and the area surrounding the ruined city of Hermopolis, is El Ashmunein – a derivation of Khmun.

Apart from a few Middle and New Kingdom remains, the only real monument at Hermopolis is a ruined Roman agora and its early Christian basilica – the largest of its type still standing in Egypt. A museum is being built near two large sandstone statues of Thoth unearthed in the area.

Getting There & Away

To get to Hermopolis from Mallawi, take a local bus or taxi to the village of El Ashmunein; the turn-off to the site is one km from the main road. From the junction you can either walk the short distance to Hermopolis or coax your driver to go a bit further. Hitching around the area shouldn't

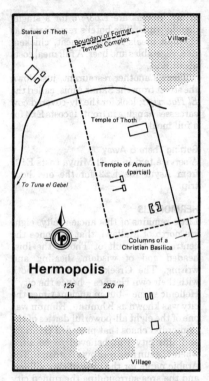

Hermopolis

Statues of Thoth

Boundary of Former Temple Complex

Village

Temple of Thoth

Temple of Amun (partial)

To Tuna el Gebel

Columns of a Christian Basilica

0   125   250 m

Village

be a problem, as the sight of a foreigner walking down the road is bound to attract quite a lot of attention.

TUNA EL GEBEL

Tuna el Gebel is seven km west of Hermopolis. The site is open from 6 am to 5 pm and admission costs E£1.25, or 50 pt for students. It gets very hot here, even in winter, so bring plenty of water, a hat and sunscreen if you plan to trek across the desert to the sites.

Apart from bordering on Akhetaten, the Pharaoh Akhenaten's short-lived capital, Tuna el Gebel was also the necropolis of Hermopolis. The oldest monument in the area is one of the six stelae which marked the boundary of

Akhetaten – in this case the western perimeter of the city's farm lands and associated villages. The stela, a rock-hewn shrine and some statues show Akhenaten and Nefertiti in various poses.

To the south of the stela, which is about five km past the village of Tuna el Gebel, are the catacombs and tombs of the residents and sacred animals of Hermopolis. Cairo University has an archaeological team at Tuna el Gebel excavating the complex.

The most interesting things to see there are the dark catacomb galleries filled with thousands of mummified baboons, ibises and ibis eggs – baboons and ibises were sacred to Thoth. Most of the mummi-fication was done in the Ptolemaic and Roman periods. The subterranean cemetery extends for at least three km, though Egyptologists suspect it may stretch all the way to Hermopolis. You definitely need a torch if you're going to explore the galleries.

Tomb of Petosiris

This is an interesting Ptolemaic tomb chapel; a sign directs the way. Petosiris was a high priest of Thoth; his family tomb, in the design of a temple, is entered through a columned vestibule. The tomb paintings show a mixture of two cultures: although they depict typical Egyptians farming scenes, the figures are wearing Greek dress.

Mummy of Isadora

In a small building behind the Tomb of Petosiris is the extremely well-preserved mummy of a woman who drowned in the Nile in about 150 AD. Isadora's teeth, hair and fingernails are clearly visible. You'll need to give the guard a bit of baksheesh to see her, though.

Well

The *sakiya*, or well, is next to a water wheel that once brought water up from its depths. The well was the sole source of

A Pharaoh and his queen making offerings to the sun-god

water for the priests, workers and sacred baboons of Tuna el Gebel. For a bit more baksheesh the guard will unlock the door and let you walk down to the bottom of the well. Watch out for the bats!

Getting There & Away

There's a fair amount of traffic between the Hermopolis junction and the village, so it should be fairly easy to hitch.

TELL EL AMARNA

The scant remains of this once-glorious city, 12 km south of Mallawi, may be a little disappointing when compared to its fascinating, albeit brief, moment in history.

In the 14th century BC, the rebellious Pharaoh Akhenaten and Queen Nefertiti abandoned the gods, temples and priests of Karnak at Thebes to establish a new city, untarnished by other gods. There they and their followers, through their worship of Aten, god of the sun disc, developed what many scholars believe was the first known form of monotheism.

The city, in the area now known as Tell el Amarna, was built on the east bank of the Nile on a beautiful, yet solitary, crescent-shaped plain, extending about 12 km from north to south. Except for the side bounded by the river, the palaces, temples and residences of the city were surrounded by high cliffs, broken here and there by wadies. The royal couple named their city Akhetaten, or 'horizon of the sun disc', and it served as the capital of Egypt for about 14 years.

It was abandoned for all time shortly after Akhenaten's death, when the priests of Karnak managed to regain their religious control. They desecrated the temples of Aten and generally did their best to obliterate all record of the heretic Pharaoh's objectionable new religion. Polytheism again predominated throughout

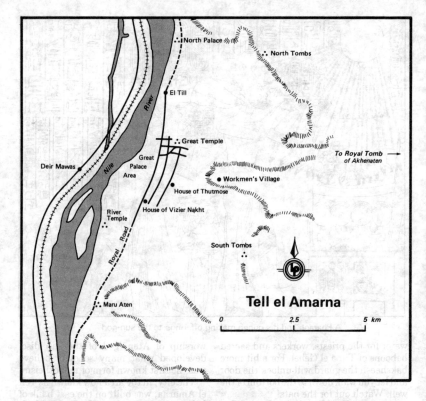

Tell el Amarna

0   2.5   5 km

North Palace

North Tombs

El Till

Great Temple

To Royal Tomb of Akhenaten

Great Palace Area

Deir Mawas

Nile

Workmen's Village

House of Thutmose

House of Vizier Nakht

River Temple

Royal Road

South Tombs

Maru Aten

the land as the Karnak priests persuaded Akhenaten's son-in-law and successor Tutankaten, or Tutankhamun as he became known, to re-establish the cult of Amun at Thebes. Akhetaten fell into ruin, and the stones of its palaces and temples were used for buildings in Hermopolis and other cities.

The Tell el Amarna necropolis comprises two groups of cliff tombs, one at each end of the city, which feature colourful wall paintings of life during the Aten revolution. Akhenaten's royal tomb is in a ravine about six km up Wadi Abu Hasah el Bahri, the valley that divides the north and south sections of the cliffs. He was not buried there, however, and no other tomb bearing his name has ever been found.

Due to the city's sudden demise, many of the tombs were never finished and very few were actually used. There are 25 tombs cut into the base of the cliffs, numbered from one to six in the north, and seven to 25 in the south. Those worth visiting are:

Tomb of Huya (No 1)
Huya was the superintendent of Akhenaten's royal harem. The Pharaoh and his family are depicted just inside the entrance on the right.

Tomb of Ahmose (No 3)
Ahmose was one of the king's versatile fan-bearers; his statue is at the back of the tomb.

Tomb of Merirye (No 4)

Merirye was the high priest of Aten. The tomb paintings show the Pharaoh riding around town in his chariot and visiting the Temple of Aten.

Tomb of Panehse (No 6)

Panehse was vizier of Lower Egypt and a servant of Aten. Most of the scenes in this tomb show Akhenaten and his family attending ceremonies at the Sun Temple.

Tomb of Mahu (No 9)

This is one of the best preserved, and the wall paintings provide interesting details of Mahu's duties as Akhenaten's chief of police.

Tomb of Ay (No 25)

This is the finest tomb at Tell el Amarna. The wall paintings show street and palace scenes, and one depicts Akhenaten and Nefertiti presenting Ay and his wife with golden collars.

Getting There & Away

To get to Tell el Amarna from Mallawi, take a service taxi from the south depot, or a local train to Deir Mawas from where you can walk or take a pick-up truck to the Nile boat landing. There you can try talking a felucca captain into ferrying you across for 25 pt; or you can take the motorboat for E£2, which includes transportation to the tombs. Once on the other side, a minibus or tractor takes you the five km trek across the desert to the northern tombs. The other tombs are about a 10 km round trip from the ferry landing. Tell el Amarna is open from 7 am to 5 pm and admission is E£1, or 50 pt for students. Bring a torch.

EL QUSIYA

Just outside the small rural town of El Qusiya, 35 km south of Mallawi, is the Coptic complex of Deir el Muharraq – the 'burnt monastery'. There is a large guest house just outside the pseudo-medieval crenellated walls of the monastery and the monks sometimes allow travellers to stay there.

Deir el Muharraq

The 70 monks who reside in the monastery claim that Mary and Jesus inhabited a cave on this site for six months and 10 days during their flight into Egypt. For seven days every year (starting at different times in June), thousands of pilgrims attend feasts to celebrate the consecration of the Church of Al Adhra, or the Virgin, the church built over the cave. Coptic Christians believe Al Adhra to be one of the first churches in the world.

The monks will show you the cave, its large stone altar and a special pillar which stands in front over an ancient water well. The religious significance of this place, they say, is given in the Old Testament.

In that day there will be an altar to the Lord in the midst of the land of Egypt, and a pillar to the Lord at its border. It will be a sign and a witness to the Lord of Host in the land of Egypt; when they cry to the Lord because of oppressors he will send them a saviour, and will defend and deliver them. And the Lord will make himself known to the Egyptians; and the Egyptians will know the Lord in that day and worship with sacrifice and burnt offering, and they will make vows to the Lord and perform them. (Isaiah 19:19).

Next to Al Adhra is a tower, a 5th century structure built for the monks to use as added protection in case of attack. It has four floors and a church inside.

The Church of St George, built in 1880, is lavishly decorated with paintings of the 12 apostles, each one with a wooden frame of inlaid ivory. The painting of St Mark with the lion is particularly interesting. Mark is always represented with a lion at his feet because once, when one attacked his father and Mark ordered it to go away, the great beast lay down at his feet instead.

Getting There & Away

A service taxi will take you from Asyut to

El Qusiya for 60 pt and there are occasionally minibuses between there and Deir el Muharraq. You could also take a service taxi from Mallawi.

ASYUT

Asyut, settled during Pharaonic times on a broad fertile plain bordering the west bank of the Nile, is unofficially the point where Upper (southern) and Lower (northern) Egypt meet. These days it's the largest town in Upper Egypt and the chief agricultural centre, dealing in camels, cotton, grain and its local speciality – carpets.

It has been an important trading town since ancient times and was once head of the great caravan route to the Western Desert oases and across the Sahara. For several centuries, the camel caravans that travelled up the 40 Day Road from Darfur province in the Sudan ended their trip in Asyut, and as recently as 150 years ago the town boasted the largest slave market in Egypt.

Though never really politically important, Asyut was once the capital of the 13th nome – the Sycamore province – and cult centre of the wolf-god Wepwawet, the avenger of Osiris (god of the dead). In the 4th century AD Christianity became the dominant religion and today there are often confrontations in the city between the Copts and Muslim fundamentalists.

The Asyut Barrage was built across the Nile in the late 19th century, under British supervision, to regulate the flow of water into the Ibrahimiya Canal and assist in the irrigation of the valley as far north as Beni Suef. Asyut is still a major departure point for trips to the Western Oases, or the New Valley as the region is now known.

Information

There is a tourist office (tel 322400) on Sharia el Mohafaza in the Governorate building.

The GPO is next to the Asyut Tourist

Hotel, facing the train station, and the telephone office is inside the station.

Things to See

There is a small museum of Pharaonic and Coptic artefacts in the American College on Sharia Gomhurriya. The museum, which includes a mummy display, was renovated in 1986.

On the way to the museum you'll pass a Coca-Cola bottling plant. It's a bit strange to watch the mechanised bottling process through one of the front windows and then turn around and watch the donkey carts pass by.

Gezira il Mohz, or 'banana island', is in the Nile at the end of Sharia Salah Salem. The island's lush tropical forest is a very pleasant place to picnic or even camp. A felucca ride to the island quay costs 50 pt.

Places to Stay

The *Youth Hostel* (tel 324846) is at Lux Houses, 503 Sharia el Walidiya. It costs about E£2 a night.

The *Zamzam Hotel* used to be a good deal, but it seems to have deteriorated. It's around the corner from the train station on Sharia Salah Salem. At E£3/6 for a single/double room, it's a fair last resort if there aren't rooms at the El Haramain Hotel, which is just down the street. Supposedly, there are hot showers. Be sure to wear rubber sandals because the bathrooms flood.

The *Semiramis Hotel*, just down the street from the Zamzam, is a dark, dirty place that is probably best avoided. Single/double rooms are E£4/8.

The *Lotus Hotel* is down the street from the Zamzam. Rooms cost from E£3.50, but stay there only if you can't afford anything better.

The *Asyut Tourist Hotel* (tel 322615) is a surprising hotel directly across from the train station. From the outside, it looks like a dilapidated house of cards ready to crumble in the slightest breeze. However, the rooms and bathrooms are quite clean. Although the hotel is on the crowded,

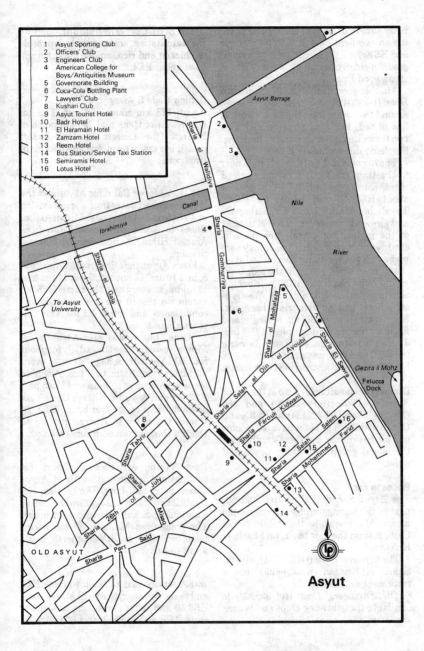

1 Asyut Sporting Club
2 Officers' Club
3 Engineers' Club
4 American College for Boys/Antiquities Museum
5 Governorate Building
6 Coca-Cola Bottling Plant
7 Lawyers' Club
8 Kushari Club
9 Asyut Tourist Hotel
10 Badr Hotel
11 El Haramain Hotel
12 Zamzam Hotel
13 Reem Hotel
14 Bus Station/Service Taxi Station
15 Semiramis Hotel
16 Lotus Hotel

Asyut

noisy square in front of the train station, it's an excellent deal at E£6 for a single and E£10 for a double. It's run by a small group of elderly townsfolk, a few of whom speak good English.

Another good deal is the *El Haramain Hotel* (tel 320426) on Sharia Salah Salem, around the corner from the Badr Hotel. It has 18 beds in clean, carpeted rooms on two floors in a quiet apartment building. Single/double rooms are E£4/6.

The *Reem Hotel*, on Sharia Nahda next to the train tracks, is a medium-priced place with singles for E£17.50, doubles for about E£34.50 and triples for E£41. Towels, breakfast, a colour TV, bathrooms and air-conditioners are included in most of the rooms, but overall this place is shoddy and overpriced. If you do stay here make sure you keep your door locked at all times, even when you're in the room.

The *Badr Hotel* (tel 329811) is behind the train station. It is a deluxe, Western-style hotel and an expatriate hang-out. Room rates are E£30 for a single and E£36.20 for a double, plus 17% tax. There's a restaurant with an à la carte menu. The hotel was started by one of Egypt's biggest construction contractors.

Camping It's possible to camp at the *Asyut Sporting Club* (tel 322139) and the *Officers' Club* (tel 322134), as well as on Gezira il Mohz. The clubs have bathrooms and food available, but there's nothing on the island except refreshing peace and quiet.

Places to Eat
The *Asyut Sporting Club* (tel 322139), next to the barrage/bridge, serves simple meals. Also known as the Public Works Club, it is on the east bank, on Sharia el Khazan.

The *Officers' Club* (tel 322134), also on Sharia el Khazan (west bank), has a restaurant and casino.

The *Engineers' Club* (tel 325302) is similar to the other two clubs and is near the latter.

The *El Nil Cafe & Restaurant*, opposite the train station, serves good cheap meals of chicken and rice, among other things, from about E£4.

Getting There & Away
Asyut, 378 km south of Cairo, 142 km north-west of Qena and 240 km north of Kharga (the nearest Western Desert oasis), is a major terminus for all forms of transport.

Bus Buses leave Cairo for Asyut and the Western Desert oases from a small station at 45 Sharia al Azhar, near Midan Ataba. Buses to Asyut only leave Cairo from Ahmed Hilmi Station, behind Ramses Station.

From Asyut they depart for Cairo at 7, 8, and 10 am, 12 noon, 2, 9, 10, 11 pm and 12 midnight every day; the cost is E£5.50, except on the 10 pm bus which is air-conditioned and costs E£10. The trip takes about seven hours.

Other bus routes are: Asyut to El Minya – usually nine times daily for about E£2.50; Asyut to Sohag – at least every half-hour from 6 am to 6 pm; Asyut to Qena – departures at 7 am and 12.45 pm, E£3.50; and Asyut to Kharga Oasis – six buses daily, three to four hours, E£3.50. One of the buses to Kharga goes on to Dakhla Oasis for an additional E£3.50.

Train Trains arrive and depart for destinations north and south of Asyut almost every half-hour. The 1st class air-conditioned trains to Asyut leave Cairo at 8 and 8.30 pm and take about 5½ hours. The train from Mallawi, 80 km north, takes two hours; and it's another 6½ hours south to Luxor.

Taxi A service taxi to Mallawi costs E£2 and takes one hour; one to El Minya costs E£2.50 and takes two hours; to Qena it costs E£5; and to El Qusiya 60 pt.

The Western Oases

About 90% of Egypt is barren desert, lying relentlessly hot, unproductive and uninhabited on both sides of the fertile Nile Valley and Nile Delta, all the way from the Mediterranean to the Sudan border. Only about 1% of the country's total population lives in this wasteland and most of them reside in the five isolated, yet thriving, oases of the Western Desert.

Since the late 1950s, in an attempt to make use of all this spare land, the Egyptian government has been investing heavily in development projects in and around these oases. At the same time, to relieve the pressures of overpopulation, landless fellahin and families from crowded towns in the Nile Valley have been encouraged to resettle in this so-called New Valley Frontier District, a region centred on Kharga Oasis and covering about 376,000 square km.

Although the oases are attracting more and more travellers, their increased popularity has not diminished the adventure of exploring this remote region. The ideal time to visit is in winter, because summer temperatures can soar as high as 52°C (125°F). However, I visited in the middle of May and found the temperature tolerable. You have to register with the police at each oasis, usually through the rest house or hotel where you are staying. It used to be necessary to get permission to visit Farafra and Dakhla, but this is no longer so unless, perhaps, if you're travelling by service taxi or your own vehicle.

Kharga and Dakhla oases are easily visited from Asyut; the oases of Farafra and Bahariyya are best visited from Cairo, though it is possible to get there via Asyut and Dakhla; and access to Siwa Oasis, in the north-west of Egypt, is via Marsa Matruh. A paved road is being built between Bahariyya and Siwa which may be finished by the time this is published. Siwa is described in the Alexandria & the Mediterranean Coast chapter.

If you want in-depth information on the history and archaeological sites of the oases, there is a three volume work, published by The American University in Cairo Press, which is available at the AUC Bookstore and most hotel bookshops.

KHARGA OASIS

Kharga, the largest and most developed of the oases, lies in a desert depression about 30 km wide and 200 km long. The chief town is El Kharga, 233 km from Asyut; it's a boom town with a population of about 90,000. Most of these people are Nubians resettled from the Nubian lands inundated by the creation of Lake Nasser after the construction of the Aswan Dam. The present-day community of Berbers, however, whose ancestors were Kharga's original inhabitants, can trace their roots back to when the oasis was a way station on the 40 Day Road caravan route between the Sudan and Egypt.

Temple of Hibis

This 6th century BC structure dedicated to the god Amun was built mostly by the Persian emperor Darius I. The temple, a few km north of town near the road, has been reconstructed and there's a great view of the surrounding palm groves from the roof.

Necropolis of Al Bagawat

Most of the several hundred mud-brick tombs in this Christian cemetery date from the 4th to the 6th centuries AD. They are traditional domed Coptic tombs, some of which have interesting wall paintings of biblical scenes. Ask the caretaker, who will expect baksheesh, to unlock the doors of the most colourful tombs. The cemetery is half a km past the Temple of Hibis, on the road to Asyut.

Temple of Nadura

This small temple, to the north-east of the

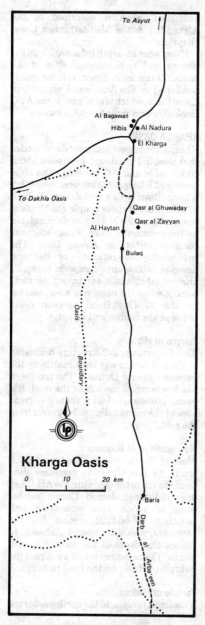

To Asyut

Al Bagawat
Hibis • Al Nadura
El Kharga

To Dakhla Oasis

Qasr al Ghuwaday
Al Haytan
Qasr al Zayyan
Bulaq

Oasis Boundary

Kharga Oasis

0   10   20 km

Baris

Darb al Arba'een

town, was built by the Roman emperor Antonius Pius in 138 AD. Look out for Kharga's duck farms nearby.

Also near the temple are the ruins of a 9th century Islamic mud-brick town, most of which was built underground so the inhabitants could escape the intense desert heat. Some of the buildings are still inhabited and the locals will gladly show you around and probably even invite you to their homes for tea.

Places to Stay

The *New Valley Tourist House* (tel 3728), near the Cinema Hibis, has cheap accommodation. Singles cost E£8 and doubles are E£12, although these rates have been known to go down. Fans are available and breakfast is served in the hotel's cafeteria.

The *Hotel Mut Balad el Shendi* has singles for E£18 and doubles for E£22.

The *Kharga Oasis Hotel* is the best in town. It's in a modern building at the north end of town and has 30 rooms, each with a bathroom. Singles cost E£20 and doubles are E£26. The hotel restaurant offers meals from E£2 to E£5. Room reservations can be made from Cairo through the Victoria Hotel (tel 918766).

The *Hamadalla Hotel* (tel 900638) has 54 rooms, with and without bathrooms, for rates ranging from E£10 to E£20. It's a good, basic hotel that is increasingly popular with groups.

Camping You can camp in the grounds of the *Kharga Oasis Hotel* for E£3 per person including access to showers.

Places to Eat

The best places to eat are the hotels, or you can shop for your own food in the town souk.

Getting There & Away

Air EgyptAir flights stop at Kharga en route between Cairo and Luxor on Wednesday and Saturday, with return flights on the same days.

Top: Pyramid of Meidum, El Faiyum (SW)
Bottom: Columns of the Basilica of Hermopolis, near Mallawi (SW)

Top: Temple of Dendara (SW)
Bottom: Hot spring in Bawiti, Bahariyya Oasis (SW)

Bus There are three buses a day from Cairo to Kharga via Asyut; fares range between E£7 and E£9. It is important to check departure times in advance, as they are subject to change. The trip takes from 10 to 11 hours.

Buses leave Cairo from the small bus station at 45 Sharia al Azhar (near Midan Ataba). The bus stops in Giza to take on additional passengers, but it's better to board at the Al Azhar Station, where it isn't crowded. Buy a reserved seat at least a day in advance.

From Asyut there are buses to Kharga at 7 and 8 am (continues to Dakhla) and 1, 2, 3 and 5 pm for E£3.50. The 8 am bus is the only one with air-con; it costs E£6. The trip takes three to four hours.

From Kharga there are at least four buses a day to Asyut. The trip costs E£3.50.

Taxi A service taxi is a convenient way to travel to Kharga from Asyut. The trip takes from three to four hours and costs about E£7 per person. Service taxis will also occasionally go to Dakhla Oasis.

DAKHLA OASIS
Dakhla, about 187 km west of Kharga and

311 km south-east of Farafra, was created from more than 600 natural springs and ponds. The bus from Asyut and Kharga drops you off at Mut, the largest town in the oasis, from where you can take a service taxi to El Qasr, the other town of interest in the area.

Sulphur Pools
The hot sulphur pools to the west of the main road between Mut and El Qasr are one of the dubious attractions of Dakhla. The pools smell like rotten eggs and look like bubbling mud holes with brown nodules floating on the surface, but are supposedly quite salubrious. An irrigation ditch near the pools has clean, clear water where you can rinse off the brown stuff afterwards.

El Qasr
The area just north of El Qasr is full of lush vegetation. The town itself is a charming little place that seems to have been barely touched by the development projects in other parts of the New Valley. The ancient architecture of this town looks as I imagine a medieval oasis village would have looked – narrow streets and carefully

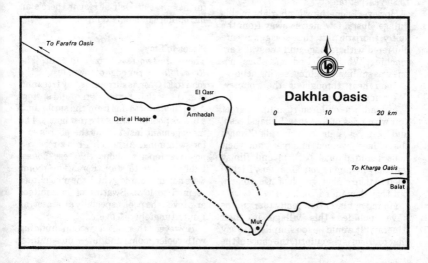

constructed mud-brick buildings. The people are still so unaccustomed to foreigners that you'll probably find their hospitality overwhelming. In the town centre you can watch the women doing laundry at the communal well.

Bashandi

Another so-called 'attraction' is the village of Bashandi, 27 km from Mut, just off the road to Kharga. A sign at the crossroads near the village announces that this is the site of a development project sponsored by an Egyptian university. In the village a more descriptive sign lists the projects: 'carpets project, girl's training centre for making and embroidering old clothes, basketmaking and dressmaking'. There has also been an attempt to make this a tourist site.

From an entirely material standpoint, everything seems to have worked. The projects are alive and well. The touristic part of the village is kept clean and tidy – no garbage on the passageways between the houses and smooth, rounded mud walls. The guardian of the local monuments gladly takes you to the village's 'Pharaonic' and 'Islamic' tombs and, when it's open, to the carpet factory.

However, something is not right in this village. Just a few metres away from the spiffy, touristic part, the passageways are cluttered with garbage and the walls are cracking. When I visited this place, no-one was smiling, laughing, saying hello or, as you hear throughout the country, 'Welcome in Egypt'.

Instead, the children rush up to greet you with cries of 'baksheesh, baksheesh' and 'pen, pen, pen'. As you walk through the village, women emerge from their houses and dangle baskets and flimsy jewellery in front of you. One of my friends tried to take a photograph of two women, but they demanded E£2.

I found out later that many tour groups have included this village in their itinerary. It would be too simplistic to say that tourism is the culprit, the cause of the

people's unusually sombre attitude. However, I think it must have had at least some negative impact on them. I would like to have seen this place before it was 'discovered'.

Getting there from Mut is easy. There are collective taxi pick-up trucks that go to at least the crossroads. We stopped an empty pick-up on the road in front of the Hamdy Restaurant and negotiated a round-trip fare of E£15 for the three of us. What the driver didn't tell us, though, was that he planned to cram as many people into the back as possible and stop practically every 100 metres. It took us more than an hour to go the 27 km to the village. To make matters worse, I watched a few of the other passengers pay only about 50 pt to go almost as far as Bashandi. The driver was really taking us for a ride.

Pharaonic Sites

There are several Pharaonic sites south-west of El Qasr. Near the village of Amhadah are several tombs dating from the 22nd century BC. A few km down the road there's a Roman cemetery with several colourful tombs; and a little further west at Deir al Hagar there's an intriguing sandstone temple.

Places to Stay

There are two rest houses in Mut. The *Rest House* at the edge of town, just off the road to El Qasr, is surrounded by trees and is at the outlet of an underground spring. A small viaduct runs from the spring into a brown pool in front of the rest house. The management insists that the pool is safe for swimming. Although I have received positive reports about the rest house, I didn't want to stay there. The rooms were hot and humid, which the mosquitoes seemed to love. Swarms of mosquitoes also loved the pool, especially at sunset, as I unfortunately discovered.

However, there is a second building with cooler rooms and fewer mosquitoes.

Single/double/triple rooms here are E£3.50/7/10.50.

The other *Rest House* is in the centre of town, across from the main mosque and next to the old bus station lot. It doubles as the 'tourist information office', which is really only a bulletin board and a rest house employee who speaks some English. There are rooms with and without bathrooms, for about the same price of E£5 per person. The rooms are a bit dusty and the mosquitoes a slight nuisance, but it's otherwise fine for a night.

Camping It's possible to camp in El Qasr, on a desert plateau just north of town, where the night sky is a spectacular field of stars; but be discreet and try not to attract too much attention. You can also camp at the sulphur springs near Mut, but the smell might be a bit much there.

Places to Eat
There are only three restaurant/cafes in Mut. *Dakhla's Sandwitch Cafeteria* is on the small square where the inter-city buses stop. It's a fair place for breakfast – tea, baked rice with milk, khounafa (sweet, stringy pastry) and a few other sickly sweet pastries. Sit outside in the 'garden' and count the passing cows.

Another place is the *Hamdy Restaurant*, which is on the main road through town, about a 10 minute walk from the central rest house. Hamdy serves chicken, kebab, vegetables and a few other small dishes. It may merely be a coincidence, but my Dutch friends and I and a group of Germans all ate there at the same time and we all got sick later that day.

We had better luck down the road towards El Qasr at the *Abu Mohammed Restaurant*. From a kitchen so clean it almost sparkled, Abu Mohammed and his cooks served us big helpings of chicken, green beans, rice, tomatoes and pickles for about E£5.50, including drinks.

Getting There & Away
Bus There is one bus a day between Cairo

and Dakhla (Mut) via Asyut and Kharga; the fare is around E£13. Another bus, which runs via Bahariyya and Farafra, goes to Dakhla a few times a week. Buses depart Cairo from a small station at 45 Sharia al Azhar, near Midan Ataba.

Because the Farafra to Dakhla buses run infrequently, it is important to get the most up-to-date information on schedules before planning your trip – else you could be held up in one of the oases, waiting for a bus out.

From Dakhla Oasis, there are buses to Kharga, Asyut and Cairo. An afternoon bus goes from Dakhla to Kharga in three hours for E£3.50; it then goes on to Asyut and Cairo. There may be earlier buses that go just to Kharga or to Kharga and Asyut. In any case, from Kharga there are more buses to Asyut.

Double-check the bus schedule because at the time of writing a new bus terminal was almost ready to open in Mut. This could mean a new schedule.

Upon arrival in Mut, we first went to the old bus station, which is in a square next to the central rest house. We wanted to find out about schedules, fares and reserved seats for the bus to Kharga. A driver told us to go to the new station, although none of the buses were using it yet.

At the new station, I approached a group of men who could have easily played 'B movie' lounge lizards in a cheap horror flick. A few had draped themselves over a low wall, others slouched in rattan chairs or lay sprawled on the ground. I asked them if they worked at the station and a few nodded and said they did.

'Tomorrow, when are there buses to Kharga?' I asked in Arabic.

'No buses from here,' one of them said.

'Yes, I know, but I was told that I can buy tickets here for the bus to Kharga. When is the first bus?'

'No tickets now,' another muttered.

They then chattered back and forth about departure times, but they couldn't agree. Finally, one man slid off the wall, sat up and said 8 am. Another slid off and said: 'No, no, it's 9 am.' Others chimed in with still other times.

At this point, I didn't care when. I just

wanted to buy us tickets. 'OK, we want to buy tickets for the bus to Kharga,' I said.

One of the guys who had slid off the wall, shrugged and said: 'No, the office is closed. Buy tickets in town.'

Back in town at the old bus station lot, another driver told us to buy tickets from the new station. Enough frustration for one day!

The next day we asked at least 10 people when the bus for Kharga was leaving from the old lot; the most usual reply was 'about 3.30 in the afternoon'. . .

Taxi Service taxis to Kharga, for about E£3.50 to E£4, are said to leave from the old bus lot in Mut.

FARAFRA OASIS

The main town of Farafra, the smallest oasis in the Western Desert, is Qasr al Farafra. Despite the relatively recent construction of a 310 km paved road linking it to Dakhla, and another 183 km stretch to Bahariyya, the 1500 people of this oasis are still quite isolated from most of the world.

Many of the people are Bedouin and still adhere to some of the age-old traditions of their culture. The small mud-brick houses of the town all have wooden doorways with medieval peg locks and the walls are painted with murals. The Bedouin women of Farafra produce beautifully embroidered dresses and shirts, though most of the work is for their own personal use and not for sale. Olives and olive oil are a speciality of the region.

The covered hot springs in town are a favourite among travellers. Women are permitted to bathe there only in the evening, but exceptions are sometimes made.

Museum

This is Farafra's only 'sight', so check it out. The museum consists of three stuffed gazelles, a dangerous snake behind glass, stuffed birds including an eagle and – unusually – a pelican, clay sculptures and paintings, a board game, and a catapult.

To Bahariyya Oasis

Ayn Bishawi

Plateau

Qasr al Farafra

Ayn Bisay

Oasis

Boundary

Farafra Oasis

0   25   50 km

To Dakhla Oasis

There's also usually a woman demonstrating how to make bread. The museum is owned by a man named Badr, a very expressive artist who paints and sculpts not-so-subtle works of village people.

White Desert

Saad (of Saad's Restaurant) organises overnight excursions into the White Desert for E£50 to E£60 per group, plus E£8 per person for food and supplies. The White Desert is an otherworldly region of blinding white sand and rock formations, about 45 km from town. (See also the Bahariyya Oasis Places to Stay section).

Places to Stay

The government *Rest House* in Qasr al Farafra has two clean rooms for E£2 per person. It's the red building next to Saad's Restaurant, on the right as you enter town from Bahariyya. Bring your own sheets, or a sleeping bag, and drinking water. There is electricity from 7 pm to 12 midnight. Near the main bus stop is another *Rest House* of similarly basic standards that charges about E£3.50.

Camping It's possible to pitch a tent at Well No 6, which is a hot spring six km west of the town. You can also go swimming in the concrete viaduct there.

Places to Eat
Saad's Restaurant is about the only place in Qasr al Farafra, although Saad's main 'dishes' seem to be jam, bread and cheese. Upon special request he will cook something, but that usually depends on the number of travellers squawking for food.

One or two fuul and cheese stands operate sporadically across from Saad's, and there are a few shops with some basic staples. There's no bakery in Farafra, so all bread must come from Bahariyya or Dakhla.

Getting There & Away
Two buses leave Cairo for Farafra on most days; they depart from the small bus station at 45 Sharia al Azhar (near Midan Ataba).

These buses travel via Bahariyya. They depart Bahariyya at around 11 am and 3 pm and take three hours to Farafra. About three times a week, one of them goes on to Dakhla, which takes an additional four hours and costs about E£6 from Farafra.

Because the Farafra to Dakhla buses run infrequently, it is important to get the most up-to-date information on schedules before planning your trip – else you could be held up in one of the oases, waiting for a bus out.

Sometimes you can hitch a ride from Farafra to Dakhla, but don't count on this.

The bus to Cairo from Farafra departs every day except Wednesday.

BAHARIYYA OASIS
Bahariyya is 330 km south of Cairo and is linked to the capital by a paved road across the desert. There are several little villages spread throughout the oasis but the main one, with a population of about 25,000, is Bawiti. This prosperous oasis is renowned for its dates, olives and turkeys.

Bawiti has a small town atmosphere, which you will soon feel when talking to the locals. Each place in town seems to have a story complete with plot and characters. After a few days there, you'll probably feel as if you've been watching, or even doing a 'bit part' in, an Egyptian soap opera.

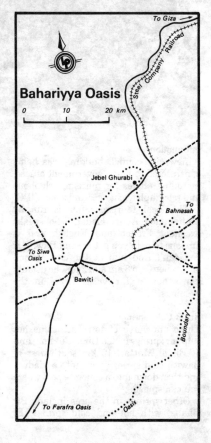

Information

A new city council building was being constructed to house government offices, including offices for tourism, telephone and telegraph exchanges and a new GPO.

The local tourism office is run by Mohammed Abdel Kader, who speaks excellent French and English and is anxious to help you get around Bawiti. If you can't find him at the city council offices between 8 am and 2 pm, he usually hangs out at the Oasis Hotel in the evenings.

Hot & Cold Springs

Three km north of town are some hot sulphur springs called Bir al Sukhna; and at Bir al Mattar, 10 km south-west of Bawiti, cold springs pour into a viaduct and then down into a concrete pool where you can splash.

Other springs in the area include Bir Ghaba, with hot and cold springs; El Bishmu (Roman springs), only about a 10 to 15 minute walk from the centre of town; Bir el Rumla, 2 km from town with 45° C slightly sulphurous springs; Bir el Muftella (also Roman springs); and El Howbaga (cold Roman springs).

White Desert

A one to two night trip to the White Desert 140 km away near Farafra can be easily made from Bawiti. It can be arranged with Ahmed Abdel Rahim Hassan, who is headmaster of one of the local secondary schools. He speaks good English and is happy to take you around the area in his bright yellow Toyota landcruiser. Ahmed introduced himself as I stepped off the bus and invited me to bounce around Bawiti with him in his landcruiser.

I went with him into the fields at the edge of town as the sun was setting behind the mountains in the distance. A parade of men in galabiyyas clip-clopped past us on donkeys. They were returning home from the fields with bundles of grassy stuff for their cows and goats. The overloaded donkeys coming out of the sunset over the horizon and marching towards the palm trees of the oasis were quite a sight.

His usual two day trip to the White Desert leaves Bawiti at about 1 pm and arrives in the desert well before sunset. You have about two hours to hike around the desert before continuing on to Farafra where you spend the night. Food, tea and a stop at a spring are also included. He charges E£20 per person.

Salah (of the Hotel Alpenblick) was also doing trips to the White Desert. After the uproar caused by his German trip (see the Places to Stay section), if he is still doing these trips he probably won't make the same mistake again.

Other Attractions

Bahariyya is not renowned for its ancient sites, although in Bawiti there are the remains of a temple and settlement dating back to the 17th dynasty. There is also a special hill, south-west of the town, known as Qarat al Firaki, or 'ridge of the chicken merchant'. The hill features several underground galleries containing signs of bird burials.

Places to Stay

At the time of writing there were only two places to stay in Bawiti, but that is likely to change as the influx of travellers increases. The two – the Hotel Alpenblick and the Oasis Hotel – have an ongoing rivalry, with the owners/managers of each bad-mouthing the other. During my visit, the *Hotel Alpenblick* was definitely considered the lesser of the two. Almost everyone I met in Bawiti who could speak some English insisted that the Alpenblick was a 'bad place'. I wondered why, because the rooms, toilets and showers were a bit less primitive than those at the Oasis and the price was only E£3/3.50 for singles/doubles compared to E£2 – not a big difference.

During my first evening at the Oasis, I listened to the Alpenblick story in between swatting away kamikaze contingents of bloodthirsty mosquitoes. Apparently, the owner, Salah Sherif, had once taken a group of German travellers into the White Desert near Farafra Oasis. The Germans mistakenly paid Salah for their trip before leaving Bawiti. When they arrived in the White Desert, Salah demanded more money for the return trip. They adamantly refused, so he drove off and left them with a few bottles of water and tins of food. The Germans somehow made it back to Bawiti and, eventually, to Cairo, where they complained to the West German Embassy. I heard a few versions of this story, but the ending was always that Salah was arrested and thrown in jail for a few months and the Alpenblick was temporarily closed down.

The Alpenblick has reopened, but it is on a small hill exposed to strong winds, so it's quite dusty. Perhaps, when the drooping plants and trees in the centre of the place have perked up, the hotel will be a more pleasant place. I felt a bit sorry for this hotel because the owner seemed to be such a black sheep, but I suppose Salah brought this upon himself. Just to be fair, at least give Salah, or whoever is now running the Alpenblick, a chance.

The *Oasis Hotel* is down the hill from the Alpenblick, on the left among a set of houses. It'll probably be your first stop when you get off the bus because there are signs pointing the way. The rooms are about as clean as is possible in a place built with painted mud bricks. Most rooms have electric fans, light, two beds and window screens. Rooms cost E£2 per person per night.

There are two bathrooms, but only one, where the toilet and shower are separate, is bearable. The hotel is enclosed by a wall; there is a shaded spot with a small gas stove for cooking and boiling water. Magdy, the manager, has a pick-up truck and can take small groups around the various springs in Bahariyya for a small negotiable fee.

In addition to camping facilities, there are two rooms with double beds, each with bathroom, at Ahmed Abdel Rahim Hassan's chicken farm and hot springs (see the Camping section).

Bir al Mattar, 10 km south-west of Bawiti, is a popular place to spend the night. There are eight bungalows there with two beds each, and 20 tents also with two beds each. Each bungalow has a fan and minifridge and costs E£5 per person; tents are E£3. Both rates include breakfast. Other facilities include eight shower/toilet stalls, a common kitchen and electrical generator. There's also a small market where you can buy bread, water and other staples. An expanded campground, tennis court and small restaurant are also planned.

Camping Camping is also possible at Ahmed Abdel Rahim Hassan's chicken farm and hot springs. Ahmed claims 'We start to make new paradise', but after the harvest, the surrounding garden and fields were somewhat sparse. It must be beautiful when everything is at its best – there are trees bearing pomegranates, sweet lemons, guava and mandarin oranges, mint plants, and palms with five types of dates. Various things still needed

to be fixed up, but the place does have potential.

Places to Eat

Unless you make your own meals, your food will be limited to the town's two 'restaurants' and rather meagre grocery stores. The first – *Abdel Hameed's Restaurant*, which serves 'Meat, livers, beans, chicken' – is in front of the bus stop, and charges about E£4 for a fairly filling meal. The other, called the *Popular Restaurant*, is owned and run by Mohammed Bayoumi Gash, a jovial guy in a big, brown galabiyya who seems to take his food seriously. He serves almost the same things as Abdel Hameed and at about the same prices. The Popular Restaurant is, as its name suggests, a popular hang-out both for travellers and locals.

At the time of writing, the *Restaurant Dabafou* was being planned for Bir al Mattar by a Cairo University geography student known as Reda Abed el Rasul. Reda has nicknamed himself 'The Desert Fox' and his personality matches his nickname – this becomes apparent when he greets you loudly with a slightly sly, but hearty, grin and hello. He isn't easy to forget.

Getting There & Away

Bus On most days there are two buses from Cairo to Bahariyya (Bawiti) and Farafra. They depart Cairo from a small station at 45 Sharia al Azhar (near Midan Ataba).

From Bahariyya, the bus takes three hours to Farafra.

The bus to Cairo departs Bahariyya at 7 am, 1 pm and, occasionally, 3 pm. On Wednesday, however, the only departure is at 7 am. Fares range from E£7 to E£9 depending on whether the bus is equipped with a video and/or air-con.

Taxi Supposedly, there's always a taxi going to Cairo between 3 and 4 pm, but this could be earlier or later and not every day. If and when it does go, the taxi costs

E£8 per person and takes three to four hours.

Motorcycle I met a group of Germans who rode motorcycles from Cairo to Bawiti and then on through the rest of the oases. Be extremely careful of the road! Two of the riders hit a patch of sand and fell off their bikes. One of them had concussion and briefly lost her memory. If she had not been wearing full motorcycle leathers and a helmet, she might have been more seriously injured.

Camel Before the paved road linked Bahariyya to Cairo, camel caravans were not uncommon. According to the local tourism representative, Mohammed Abdel Kader, the typical caravan took about 16 days. Once in a while, an intrepid foreigner organises a small caravan to make this trip.

SOHAG

The city of Sohag, 93 km south of Asyut, is an administrative centre for the governorate of Girga and one of the major Coptic Christian areas of Upper Egypt. The only real reason to go there, however, is to see the White and Red monasteries just outside Sohag, and to visit the town of Achmim across the river.

White Monastery

Deir Abyad was built in 400 AD, by the Coptic saint Shenouda, with chunks of white limestone from a Pharaonic temple. The White Monastery, as it is called, once supported a community of 2000 monks. Its fortress walls still stand, but most of the interior is in ruins, though you can see the several types of arches used in its construction. The monastery is 12 km north-west of Sohag; there's a cafeteria across the road.

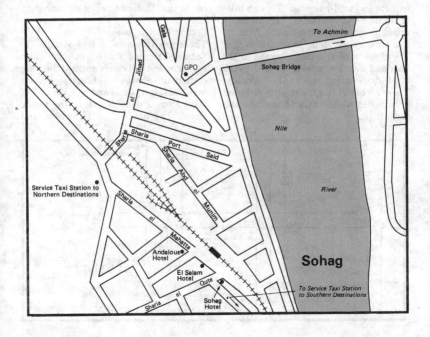

Red Monastery

Deir al Ahmar, the Red Monastery, was founded by Bishoi, a thief who converted to Christianity, built this and two monasteries in Wadi Natrun and eventually became a Coptic saint. There are two chapels on the grounds, Santa Maria Chapel and the St Bishoi Chapel. Be sure to see the remains of a 10th century fresco on the central altar – it contains a 1000 year old icon. There are interesting though fading frescoes on the walls, unusual pillars and old wooden peg locks on the doors.

Unless you're visiting sometime during the first two weeks of July, when you can catch a bus to the monasteries for 75 pt with thousands of other pilgrims, your only option is to take a taxi, which should cost about E£6.

Achmim

The town of Achmim, on the east bank of the Nile, is renowned for its unique woven carpets and wall-hangings. Though little of its past glory remains, except for an extensive, unexcavated cemetery, Achmim was once a flourishing provincial centre. There are several rockcut tombs in the area and a rock chapel dedicated to the local deity Min, the god of fertility. There's a bus across the river to Achmim from Sohag which takes 15 minutes and costs 15 pt.

Places to Stay

There is a *Youth Hostel* at 5 Sharia Port Said in Achmim.

The *Sohag Hotel* in Sohag is a dirty place with singles for E£3.50 and doubles for E£6. Each room has three beds and a shower, supposedly with hot water.

The *El Salam Hotel* is directly in front of the train station. It has basic singles for E£3.50 and doubles for E£6. In 1989 the place was being renovated and hot water heaters were being installed.

The *Andalous Hotel* is also opposite the train station. Singles are E£4.75 and doubles are E£7 including breakfast. Most of the rooms have fans and small tables. The bathrooms are basically clean and there's hot water.

Places to Eat

As well as the usual fruit and vegetable stands, there are also a few fuul and ta'amiyya places near the train station. There are no restaurants in Sohag, at least not in the Western sense of the word.

Getting There & Away

There are two service taxi stations in Sohag. The one for Asyut and other northern destinations is north of the train station on Sharia el Mahatta. Service taxis for Luxor, Qena and Nag Hammadi leave from a depot south of the Sohag Hotel. The bus station is nearby, and

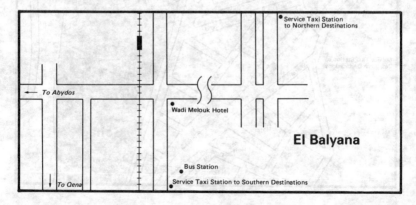

- Service Taxi Station to Northern Destinations
- ← To Abydos
- Wadi Melouk Hotel
- Bus Station
- Service Taxi Station to Southern Destinations
- To Qena

El Balyana

there are buses from Asyut at least every half-hour from 6 am to 6pm. The train also often stops at Sohag.

EL BALYANA

The only reason to go to this town is to visit the nearby village of Al Arbah al Madfunah. There you'll find the necropolis of Abydos and the magnificent Temple of Seti.

Abydos

The temples at Abydos served several dynasties of Egyptians and its huge necropolis was, for a long time, *the* place to be buried. Excavations indicate that it was a burial place of the last Pre-Dynastic kings, before 3100 BC. Seti I and Ramses II built the most important temples of the

complex in the 13th century BC; and Abydos was still important during Roman times.

The centre of the walled town of Abydos was a mound called Kom el Sultan; nearby was the all-important Temple of Osiris, of which little remains. Abydos maintained its importance for so many centuries because of the cult of Osiris, god of the dead.

The area was a natural shrine for the worship of this ruler of the netherworld because, according to mythology, it was here that the head of Osiris was buried after his brother Seth had murdered him, cut his body into several pieces, and scattered the bits all over Egypt. Osiris' wife and sister, the goddess Isis, searched

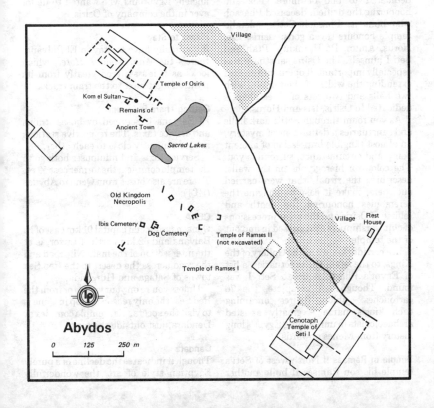

Abydos

0   125   250 m

for and found all the pieces and put him back together again, building temples wherever she found the dissected parts. Osiris and Isis then begat Horus, the falcon-god, who killed his uncle Seth. The temple at Abydos was the most important of the shrines to Osiris and became a place of pilgrimage. Most Egyptians would make the journey there at least once in their lifetime.

Abydos is open from 9 am to 5 pm daily. The admission fee for both temples is E£1, or 50 pt for students. Bring a torch.

Cenotaph Temple of Seti I The first structure you'll see at Abydos is one of Egypt's most complete temples. A cenotaph temple was a secondary mortuary temple dedicated to one or more gods and honouring the deified, deceased Pharaoh who built it. Pharaoh Seti's splendid temple honours seven gods: Osiris, Isis, Horus, Amun, Ra-Harakhty, Ptah and Seti I himself. The Osiris sanctuary was especially important; it opens into an area extending the width of the temple, with two halls and two sets of three chapels dedicated to Osiris, Isis and Horus.

As you roam through Seti's dark halls and sanctuaries a definite air of mystery, an almost tangible impression of ancient pomp and circumstance, surrounds you. The colourful hieroglyphs on the walls, describing the rituals that were carried out there, make it easy to imagine the ceremonies honouring the death and rebirth of Osiris and the great processions of cult worshippers that passed in and out of the temple.

In a corridor known as the Gallery of the Kings, to the left of the sanctuaries, a list of Egypt's Pharaohs up to Seti I was found. Though not complete, the 76 cartouches – oblong figures containing each king's name – greatly assisted archaeologists in unravelling Egypt's long history from Menes onwards.

Temple of Ramses II North-west of Seti's temple his son Ramses II built another temple dedicated to Osiris – and himself. The roof of the Temple of Ramses II has collapsed, but the hieroglyphs on the walls are interesting, though you have to get the guard to unlock the gate. The local villagers will let him know that a khahwagah, a not-so-complimentary way of saying 'foreigner', wants to get into the temple. The same villagers will probably also send a young stranger bearing 'gifts' for the khahwagah. Watch out: you'll quickly discover that these 'gifts' cost money.

Cemetery The extensive cemetery between Kom el Sultan and Seti's temple includes buried dogs, falcons and ibises as well as the cenotaphs or actual graves of those ancient Egyptians who wanted to lie for ever in the company of Osiris.

Places to Stay

If you really have to stay in El Balyana, there's the *Wadi Melouk Hotel*, which looks as if it's suffered greatly from its position right next to the train tracks.

Getting There & Around

El Balyana is serviced by buses, trains and service taxis. The respective stations are conveniently close to each other.

Service taxis and minibuses both go to the temple complex; the former cost 50 pt. There are also buses from Qena to Abydos (E£1).

QENA

Qena, a provincial capital 91 km east of El Balyana and 62 km north of Luxor, is at the intersection of the main Nile road and the road across the desert to the Red Sea towns of Safaga and Hurghada.

Unless you're on your way to or from the Red Sea, the only reason to stop in Qena is to visit the spectacular temple complex at Dendara, just outside the town.

Dendara

Though it indicates the decline of a purely Egyptian style of art, the wonderfully

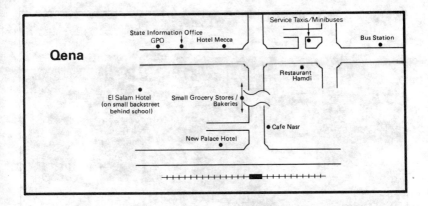

Qena

State Information Office
GPO • • Hotel Mecca

Service Taxis/Minibuses

Bus Station •

Restaurant
Hamdi

El Salam Hotel
(on small backstreet
behind school)

Small Grocery Stores /
Bakeries

• Cafe Nasr

New Palace Hotel

preserved complex at Dendara is a sight to behold. Complete with a massive stone roof, dark chambers, underground passages and towering columns inscribed with hieroglyphs, the main Temple of Hathor is almost intact.

While the Dendara necropolis includes Early Dynastic tombs and evidence that Cheops and later Pharaohs built there, the temple complex, as it stands today, was built by the Ptolemies and the Romans. Its very design, however, suggests that it was built on the site of an older temple and, as was the custom of the day, reproduces the character and mythology of the original. So, despite the apparent shortcomings in the quality of its design and decoration, and the fact that it was raised during foreign occupation, it is an impressive, beautiful monument to an ancient goddess of great renown.

Hathor was the goddess of pleasure and love; she was usually represented as a cow, or a woman with a cow's head, or a woman whose headdress was a sun disc fixed between the horns of a cow. She was the beneficent deity of maternal and family love, of beauty and light; the Greeks associated her with Aphrodite.

Hathor was also the wet nurse of Horus, before becoming his mate and bearing Ihy, the youthful aspect of the creator-gods.

Dendara was the ritual location where Hathor gave birth to Horus' child, and her temple stands on the edge of the desert as if waiting her return.

Hathor's head forms the capital of all 24 columns in the temple's Outer Hypostyle Hall. On the walls, there are strange scenes showing the Roman emperors Augustus, Tiberius, Caligula, Claudius and Nero as Pharaohs, making offerings to Hathor. The ceiling shows vultures flying amongst the sun, moon and stars of the Egyptian zodiac, with the sky-goddess Nut and other deities sailing their solar boats across the heavens.

The hieroglyphs in the Inner Hypostyle Hall deal with the temple's foundation. Beyond is the Hall of Offerings and Sanctuary of the temple proper, surrounded by a gallery of chapels and the east and west staircases to the roof.

The Hall of Offerings, where the daily rituals of the cult were carried out, shows the Pharaoh and others making offerings to Hathor. During the New Year Festival, images of the goddess were carried from here to the roof to be looked on by Ra, the sun-god. The views of the surrounding countryside from the roof are magnificent. The graffiti on the edge of the temple was left by Napoleon's commander Desaix, and other French soldiers, in 1799.

The Sanctuary was usually kept bolted

Temple complex at Dendara

and only the Pharaoh, or priests acting on his behalf, could enter. Reliefs on the walls show the special rituals of the Pharaoh entering the Sanctuary to show his adoration for the goddess.

From the Chapel behind the sanctuary Hathor would embark each New Year on her annual journey to Edfu, where she would lie in blissful union with Horus.

The reliefs on the exterior of the temple's south wall show various Roman emperors such as Nero and Caesarian – son of Julius and Cleopatra – and the great Egyptian queen herself making offerings to the head of Hathor.

Behind the main temple is the smaller Temple of the Birth of Isis built by Emperor Augustus. North of the main temple, the second structure on your left is a Roman *mammisi*, or birth-house, dedicated to Hathor and her son Ihy.

A 5th century Coptic basilica is squeezed in between the mammisi, the court of Hathor's temple and another birth-house. The birth-house was begun

by Nectanebo, a 30th dynasty Pharaoh, and completed by the Ptolemies.

The Dendara complex is open from 6 am to 6 pm and admission is E£2, or E£1 for students.

Dendara is four km west of Qena along the Nile. Local buses and service taxis run there from the town. From the road you can either walk, or hitch a ride with peasants from the village next to the temple.

Places to Stay

The *El Salam Hotel* is a quiet place behind the school and around the corner from the GPO. The bathrooms are dreary but the prices are rock bottom. It costs E£2.25 for a single and E£4 for a double without bath.

The *New Palace Hotel* (tel 2509) is just off Midan Mahattat, opposite the train station. A double with/without bath is E£8/6. The place is a bit drab but basically clean; there's no hot water.

There is supposedly a *Youth Hostel* on

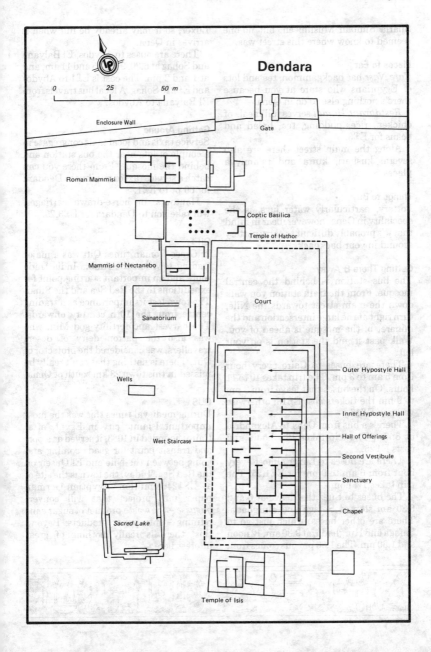

Dendara

0   25   50 m

Enclosure Wall

Gate

Roman Mammisi

Coptic Basilica

Temple of Hathor

Mammisi of Nectanebo

Court

Sanatorium

Wells

Outer Hypostyle Hall

Inner Hypostyle Hall

Hall of Offerings

West Staircase

Second Vestibule

Sanctuary

Chapel

Sacred Lake

Temple of Isis

Sharia Shuban Muslimeen, but no-one seemed to know where this street was.

Places to Eat
Cafe Nasr has backgammon, tea and lots of Egyptians who stare at you because there's nothing else to do in Qena.

Restaurant Hamdi serves full meals of chicken, rice, pudding, tea, bread and beans for E£3.

Along the main street there are also several kushari, kufta and ta'amiyya places.

Things to Buy
Pottery, particularly water jugs, is the speciality in Qena; however, bear in mind that it's probably difficult to carry pottery around in your backpack.

Getting There & Away
The bus station is behind the central mosque. From the train station you walk down the main street towards the Nile, turn right at the large intersection and the minaret of the mosque is ahead of you. Walk past it and the station is on your left.

There are buses to Cairo every hour from 5 am to 3 pm. The trip takes 10 to 11 hours. On the buses that leave from 3 pm to 9 pm the tickets cost E£16; otherwise you pay E£18.

There's a bus from Qena to Alexandria at 6 am. The trip takes 13½ hours and costs E£25.

There are buses to Luxor almost every hour from 6 am to 9 pm for E£1.25. The trip takes 1¼ hours.

The buses to Suez that leave at 6 and 6.30 am stop at Safaga and Hurghada. There are other buses, which just go to Safaga and Hurghada, at 9.30 am, 12 noon and 1.30 pm. The 1.30 pm bus comes from

Luxor, so it may already be full when it arrives in Qena.

There are buses to Abydos, El Balyana and Sohag at 6.30, 9, 10.15 and 11 am, and at 1 and 2 pm. The cost is E£1 to Abydos and E£2 to Sohag. A local bus travels from El Balyana to Abydos.

Getting Around
Service taxis and local taxis congregate in a couple of lots near the bus station and behind the mosque. From there you can catch a service taxi or minibus to Dendara for 60 pt to E£1.

Hantours, or horse-drawn carriages, will take you to Dendara for E£3.25.

QIFT
In Greco-Roman times Qift was a major trading town on the Arabia-India trade route and an important starting point for expeditions to the Red Sea and the Sinai. The town lost its importance as a trading centre from the 10th century onwards. The harvest and fertility-god Min, who was also the patron deity of desert travellers, was considered the protector of Qift. There is nothing that can't really be missed in this town 23 km south of Qena.

QUS
During medieval times this was the most important Islamic city in Egypt, after Cairo. Founded in 1083, it served as a port and transit point for goods coming and going between the Nile and El Quseir on the Red Sea. Today, the town is the site of a US$246 million Egyptian-German paper mill project that will convert *bagasse* – the waste product of sugar cane refining – into paper products. Beyond this, there is really nothing of great interest here.

The Nile Valley - Luxor

The sheer grandeur of Luxor's monumental architecture, and its excellent state of preservation, have made this village-city one of Egypt's greatest tourist attractions. Built on and around the 4000 year old site of ancient Thebes, Luxor is an extraordinary mixture of exotic history and modern commercialism.

Here the fellahin work the fields as they have done since time immemorial; mundane daily business is carried on as if there weren't hordes of foreigners walking the streets; modern hotels are full of Westerners; the souks are full of fake antiquities made just for the tourists; and modern Egyptians make a fine living out of the legacy of their ancestors.

It is one of the world's greatest open-air museums, a time capsule of a glorious long-gone era. Yet at the same time this overgrown village, with a population exceeding 100,000, thrives and bustles with life.

Its attraction for tourists is by no means a recent phenomenon: travellers have been visiting Thebes for centuries, marvelling at the splendid temples of Luxor, Karnak, Ramses II and Hatshepsut. As far back as Greco-Roman times visitors would wait in the desert to hear the mysterious voice of Memnon emanating from the colossal statues of Amenophis III; and in the past 100 years or so, since archaeology became a respectable science, curious travellers have been following the footsteps of the excavators into the famous tombs of the Valley of the Kings.

What most visitors today know as Luxor is actually three separate areas: the city of Luxor itself, the village of Karnak a couple of km to the north-east, and the monuments and necropolis of ancient Thebes on the west bank of the Nile.

Along the river, which for some reason seems even more majestic here, the rows of feluccas and antiquated barges share the east bank quays with the posh hotel ships of the Hilton and Sheraton.

Behind the tourist facade, the dirt streets are crowded with mud-brick tenements, pocked with mud puddles and filled with ordinary, friendly people. Luxor is definitely one of the highlights of a visit to Egypt.

History

Following the collapse of centralised power at the end of the Old Kingdom period, the small village of Thebes, under the 11th and 12th dynasty Pharaohs, emerged as the main power in Upper Egypt. Rising against the northern capital of Heracleopolis, Thebes reunited the country under its political, religious and administrative control and ushered in the Middle Kingdom period.

The strength of its government also enabled it to re-establish control after a second period of decline; liberate the country from foreign rule and bring in the New Kingdom dynasties.

At the height of its glory and opulence, from 1570 BC to 1090 BC, the New Kingdom Pharaohs made Thebes their permanent residence; the city had a population of nearly one million and the architectural activity was astounding.

Because so many kings left their mark at Thebes it can quickly become very confusing trying to keep track of who built what temples or tombs and when they did so. For detailed information on the history of Thebes, see the reference books listed in the Facts for the Visitor chapter.

Orientation

There are only three main thoroughfares in Luxor, so it's easy to find your way around – as long as you don't ask for street names. Some streets have signs, some have names but no signs and some have no names at all. If you ask the locals what the name of a particular street is they're quite likely to make one up on the spot, which is why nearly every map of Luxor is different. So, it's best to ask directions to a specific location rather than to the street or road it's on. The three main roads are Sharia al Mahattit, Sharia al Karnak and the Corniche.

Sharia al Mahattit – the street directly in front of the train station – runs perpendicular to the Nile all the way to the gardens of Luxor Temple. Sharia al Karnak runs one block in and parallel to the river, from Luxor Temple to Karnak Temple. Sharia al Karnak meets Sharia al Mahattit and runs around the southern end of Luxor Temple, which overlooks the Nile, to the corniche road.

To confuse matters Sharia al Karnak, where it meets Sharia al Mahattit, is also known as Sharia el Markaz; to the south, around the temple to the river, it's known as Sharia el Lokanda. The corniche road is known variously as Sharia el Bahr, Sharia Bahr el Nil or simply the Corniche.

Information

Tourist Offices
The tourist office and the State Information Office are in the Tourist Bazaar on the Corniche, next to the New Winter Palace Hotel. They're open from 8 am to 7 pm and the staff can fill you in on what the official prices for various services should be, as well as the most recent schedule and prices of the sound & light show at Karnak Temple (at the time of writing, tickets were E£10). They also have a handy booklet titled *Upper Egypt by Night & Day*. Lastly, travellers can leave messages taped to one of the columns next to the main information counter.

Post & Telecommunications
The GPO is on Sharia al Mahattit and there's a branch office in the Tourist Bazaar.

The telephone office is at the resplendent entrance of the Winter Palace Hotel. The central telephone office is on Sharia al Karnak and is open 24 hours. Three-minute

telephone calls to the USA are (8 am to 7.59 pm/8 pm to 7.59 am) E£17/13; UK E£15.20/11.50; Australia E£24.20/18.20; Canada E£18.20/13.70; West Germany E£15/11.50; and France E£18.20/13.70.

American Express The American Express office is next door to the Winter Palace Hotel and operates from 8 am to 9 pm. All the usual services are available. If you are heading south, this is the last American Express office where you can cash personal cheques and buy travellers' cheques until you get to Nairobi.

Thomas Cook There's also a Thomas Cook money exchange office across from American Express.

Airline Offices The EgyptAir office is on the Corniche, next to the entrance of the Winter Palace Hotel.

Film Film can be bought and processed at a few shops in town. The Cleopatra Studio, which is one of several shops in the arcade behind the tourist office, has Fujichrome 100 (36 exposures) for E£10, Kodachrome 64 (36 exposures) for E£20, Kodacolor 100 (36 exposures) for E£7 and Kodacolor 200 (36 exposures) for E£7.

According to the shopkeeper, these prices fluctuate quite often, so just use this as a general guide. Processing costs E£1 plus 30 pt per print and takes 24 hours.

Books & Maps Aboudi's Bookshop has an excellent selection of books, guidebooks and maps and is in the same complex as the tourist office and State Information Office. A few doors down towards the old Winter Palace Hotel is A A Gaddis where you can also find books and even aerogrammes embellished with mug shots of Tutankhamun. The bookshop in the ETAP Hotel also has an good selection of guidebooks and books on Egypt but their prices tend to be slightly higher.

Amun Festival During the winter, in either January or February, the Amun Festival is celebrated with a recreation of the ancient Amun-Ra (the sun-god and patron god of Thebes) procession from Luxor Temple to Karnak Temple and back again. Participants all wear what is believed to be typical Pharaonic dress as ascertained from hieroglyphics. For a schedule of events, write well in advance to the Luxor tourist office.

East Bank

Luxor Museum
This wonderful little museum on the Corniche, about halfway between the Luxor and Karnak temples, has a small but well-chosen collection of relics from the Theban temples and necropolis. The displays, which include pottery, jewellery, furniture, statues and stelae, were arranged by the Brooklyn Museum of New York.

On the 1st floor is a well-preserved cow-goddess head from King Tutankhamun's tomb. Exhibit No 61 is a finely carved statuette of Tuthmosis II that dates from at least 1436 BC.

The most interesting exhibit is the Wall of Akhenaten on the 2nd floor, which is actually a set of 283 sandstone blocks found within the 9th Pylon of the Karnak Temple. The reliefs show the rebel Pharaoh and his queen, Nefertiti, making offerings to Aten.

Also on the 2nd floor, check out the canopic jars which once contained the internal organs of the priest of the god Montu and King Tutankhamun's well-preserved funerary boats. There are a few other relics in the small garden outside.

The museum is open from 3 to 9 pm in winter, 5 to 10 pm in summer, and 10 am to 2 pm during Ramadan. Admission costs E£2, or E£1 for students.

Luxor Temple
Amun, one of the gods of creation, was the most important god of Thebes and head of the local triad of deities. As Amun-Ra, the fusion of Amun and the sun-god Ra, he was also a state deity worshipped in many parts of the country. Once a year from his Great Temple at Karnak the images of Amun and the other two gods in the local triad – Amun's wife, the war-goddess Mut, and their son, the moon-god Khons – would journey down the Nile to Luxor Temple for the Opet Festival, a celebration held during the inundation season.

Built by the New Kingdom Pharaoh Amenophis III, on the site of an older sanctuary dedicated to the Theban triad, Luxor Temple is a strikingly graceful piece of architecture on the banks of the Nile. Amenophis rededicated the massive temple as Amun's sacred 'harem of the south', and retained what was left of the original sanctuary built by Tuthmosis III and Hatshepsut 100 years earlier.

Ramses II, Luxor Temple

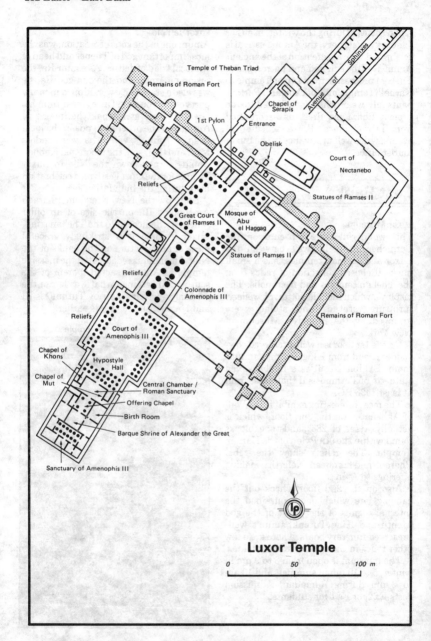

Luxor Temple

0   50   100 m

The Luxor Temple was added to over the centuries by Tutankhamun, Ramses II, Nectanebo, Alexander the Great and various Romans. At one point the Arabs built a mosque in one of the interior courts, and there was also once a village within the temple walls. Excavation work has been going on since 1885, and has included removing the village and clearing the forecourt and 1st Pylon of debris, and exposing part of the Avenue of Sphinxes leading to Karnak.

Fronting the entrance to the temple is the enormous 1st Pylon, about 24 metres high, in front of which are some colossal statues of Ramses II and a pink granite obelisk. There were originally six statues, four seated and two standing, but only two of the seated figures and the westernmost standing one remain. The obelisk too was one of a pair; its towering counterpart now stands in the Place de la Concorde in Paris.

Behind the pylon, which is decorated with Ramses' victorious exploits in battle, is another of his additions to the main complex. The Great Court of Ramses II is surrounded by a double row of columns with lotus-bud capitals, more reliefs of his deeds of daring-do and several huge statues. In the western corner of the court is the original Middle Kingdom Temple of the Theban Triad and south of that is the 13th century AD Mosque of Abu el Haggag, dedicated to a local sheik and holy man.

Beyond the court 14 papyrus columns form the splendid Colonnade of Amenophis III. The walls behind the columns were decorated during the reign of the young Pharaoh Tutankhamun and celebrate the return to Theban orthodoxy. The Opet Festival is depicted in great detail, with the king, the nobility and the common people joining the triumphal procession of Amun, Mut and Khons from Karnak.

The colonnade takes you into the Court of Amenophis III. This was once enclosed on three sides by double rows of towering columns, of which the best preserved,

with their architraves extant, are those on the east and west sides.

The Hypostyle Hall on the south side of the court is the first inner room of the temple proper and features four rows of eight columns each.

Beyond are the main rooms of the Temple of Amun, the central chamber of which was once stuccoed over by the Romans and used as a cult sanctuary. Through this chamber, on either side of which are chapels dedicated to Mut and Khons, is an Offering Chapel with four columns.

The interesting inscriptions in the Birth Room, to the eastern side of the chapel, show scenes of how mortal Amenophis claimed divine status by coming up with the notion that Amun had visited his mother Mutemuia in the 'guise' of his father Tuthmosis IV, with the result that he, Amenophis III, was actually the god's son.

Alexander the Great rebuilt the Barque (Boat) Shrine, beyond the Offering Chapel, adding reliefs of himself being presented to Amun. The last chamber on the central axis of the temple is the Sanctuary of Amenophis III.

The Luxor Temple is open from 6 am to 10 pm in summer; from 7 am to 9 pm in winter; and from 6 am to 6.30 pm during Ramadan. Admission costs E£2, or E£1 for students. The best time to visit is at night, when the temperature is lower and when the illuminated temple is an amazing, eerie spectacle beside the silent shimmering black of the Nile.

Temples of Karnak

The Amun Temple Enclosure (sometimes referred to as the Precinct of Amun) is the central enclosure of the numerous temples that make up the enormous Karnak complex; it was the main place of worship of the Theban triad. Its ancient name was Ipet-Isut, or 'the most perfect of places'.

Although the original sanctuary of the Great Temple of Amun was built during the Middle Kingdom period, when the Theban Pharaohs first came to prominence, the rest of the temples, pylons, courts, columns and reliefs were the work of New Kingdom rulers.

Karnak was built, added to, dismantled, restored, enlarged and decorated over a period of nearly 1500 years. During the height of Theban power and prosperity it was the most important temple in all Egypt.

The complex can be divided into three distinct areas: the Amun Temple Enclosure, which is the largest enclosure; the Mut Temple Enclosure, on the south side, which was once linked to the main temple by an avenue of ram-headed sphinxes; and the Montu Temple Enclosure, to the north, which honoured the original local god of Thebes.

A canal once connected the Amun and Montu enclosures with the Nile providing access for the sacred boats in the journey to the Luxor Temple during the Opet Festival. A paved avenue of human-headed sphinxes also once linked Karnak, from Euergetes' Gate on the south side of the Amun Temple Enclosure, with Luxor Temple.

Only a small section of this sacred way, where it leaves the Great Temple of Amun and enters the forecourt of his Southern Harem, has been excavated. The rest of the three km avenue lies beneath the city and paved roads of modern Luxor.

The Karnak site measures about 1.5 km by 0.8 km, which is large enough to hold about 10 cathedrals, and the 1st Pylon, at the entrance, is twice the size of Luxor Temple's. The further into the complex you venture the further back in time you go.

The oldest part of the complex is the White Pavilion of Sesostris I and the 12th dynasty foundations of what became the most sacred part of the Great Temple of Amun, the Sacred Barque Sanctuary and Central Court of Amun (located behind the 6th Pylon). The limestone fragments of the demolished pavilion, or chapel, were recovered from the foundations of

the 3rd Pylon, built five centuries after Sesostris' reign, and expertly reconstructed in the Open Museum to the north of the Great Court.

The major additions to the complex were constructed by Pharaohs of the 18th to 20th dynasties, between 1570 BC and 1090 BC. The Pharaohs of the later dynasties extended and rebuilt the complex, and the Ptolemies and early Christians also left their mark on it.

You'll need to visit Karnak at least twice to fully appreciate the size and magnificence of the complex. A return visit in the evening for the sound & light show would complete the picture.

General admission to the temples of Karnak is between 7 am and 5.30 pm and tickets cost E£3, or E£1.50 for students.

Amun Temple Enclosure – main axis From the entrance you pass down the processional avenue of ram-headed sphinxes, which once led to the Nile, to the massive 1st

Karnak Temple, Luxor

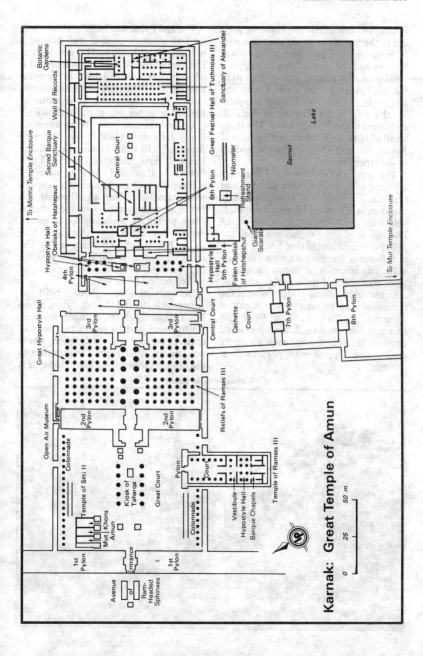

Karnak: Great Temple of Amun

0   25   50 m

To Montu Temple Enclosure

To Mut Temple Enclosure

Botanic Gardens

Wall of Records

Sacred Barque Sanctuary

Obelisks of Hatshepsut

Hypostyle Hall

Great Festival Hall of Tuthmosis III

Sanctuary of Alexander

Central Court

Sacred Lake

Nilometer

6th Pylon

Refreshment Stand

5th Pylon

Hypostyle Hall

Fallen Obelisk of Hatshepsut

Giant Scarab

4th Pylon

Great Hypostyle Hall

3rd Pylon

3rd Pylon

Central Court

Cachette Court

7th Pylon

8th Pylon

Open Air Museum

2nd Pylon

2nd Pylon

Reliefs of Ramses III

Colonnade

Temple of Seti II

Kiosk of Taharqa

Great Court

Mut Khons Amun

Colonnade

Temple of Ramses III

Vestibule

Hypostyle Hall

Barque Chapels

Court

Pylon

1st Pylon

1st Pylon

Entrance

Avenue of Ram-Headed Sphinxes

Pylon. You can climb the stairs on your left to the top of the pylon's north tower, from where you'll get an amazing view of Karnak and the surrounding country.

Back on the ground you emerge from the 1st Pylon into the Great Court, the largest single area of the Karnak complex. To the left is the Temple of Seti II, dedicated to the Theban triad. The three small chapels held the sacred barques of Amun, Mut and Khons during the lead-up to the Opet Festival.

The north and south walls of the court are lined with columns with papyrus bud capitals. The south wall is intersected by the Temple of Ramses III, which was built before the court. Obligatory scenes of the Pharaoh as glorious conqueror adorn the pylon of this 60 metre long temple which also features an open court, a vestibule with four columns, a hypostyle hall of eight columns and three barque chapels.

In the centre of the Great Court is the one remaining column of the Kiosk of Taharqa. A 25th dynasty Ethiopian Pharaoh, Taharqa built his open-sided pavilion of 10 columns, each rising 21 metres and topped with papyrus-form capitals.

The 2nd Pylon was built by Horemheb, an 18th dynasty general who headed a military dictatorship and became the last Pharaoh of his dynasty. Ramses I and II added their names and deeds to the pylon above that of Horemheb. Ramses II also raised two colossal pink granite statues of himself on either side of the entrance.

Beyond the 2nd Pylon is the awesome Great Hypostyle Hall. It was begun by Amenophis III while he was also building Luxor Temple, continued by Seti I and finished by Ramses II. Covering an area of 6000 square metres (which is large enough to contain Notre Dame Cathedral), the hall is an unforgettable forest of towering stone pillars. It is impossible to get an overall idea of this court; there is nothing to do but stand and stare up at the dizzying spectacle. You'll notice that the papyrus-form capitals seem to sway and jostle each other for space.

Between the 3rd Pylon, built by Amenophis III, and the 4th Pylon, raised by Tuthmosis I, is a narrow court. Tuthmosis I and III raised two pairs of obelisks in front of the 4th Pylon, which was, during their reign, the entrance to the temple proper. Only one of the four is

Karnak Temple, Luxor

Amun

still standing but parts of the others lie in the court.

Beyond the 4th Pylon is the oldest preserved part of the complex, its 14 columns suggesting that it was originally a small hypostyle hall. It was constructed by Tuthmosis III in his attempt to eradicate or hide all signs of the reign of his stepmother, Queen Hatshepsut. (See the section on Deir el Bahri further on in this chapter.) In this hall, around the two magnificent Obelisks of Hatshepsut, the vengeful king built a 25 metre high sandstone structure. The upper shaft of one of the obelisks, which she raised to the glory of her 'father' Amun, lies on the ground by the Sacred Lake; the other obelisk still stands, reclaimed from the sandstone, in front of the 5th Pylon. It is the tallest obelisk in Egypt, standing 29.5 metres high, and was originally covered in electrum from its pyramidal peak to halfway down the shaft.

The 5th Pylon was constructed by Tuthmosis I, with little space between it

and the now ruined 6th Pylon (built at a later date). The latter, the smallest pylon at Karnak, was raised by his son Tuthmosis II (Hatshepsut's husband and half-brother). In the small vestibule beyond the 6th Pylon are two pink granite columns on which are the emblems of Egypt carved in high relief – the lily of Upper Egypt on the north pillar and the papyrus flower of Lower Egypt on the south pillar. Nearby are two huge statues of Amun and his female counterpart Amunet which date from the reign of Tutankhamun.

Also amongst the ruins of this area around the temple's original Central Court are a Sacred Barque Sanctuary and at least two well-preserved walls.

Hatshepsut's wall and its colourful reliefs survived the years well because once again Tuthmosis III chose to cover her structure with one of his own rather than destroy it once and for all.

Although the king was no match for his powerful though peace-loving stepmother, he made up for Hatshepsut's domination of him during his teenage years by setting out, almost immediately after her death, to conquer the known world. His reputation as a great hero and empire builder was justly deserved, as the relief work on what is known as the Wall of Records demonstrates. Though unrelenting in his bid for power, he had a penchant for being fairly just in his treatment of the people he conquered. This wall was a running tally of the organised tribute he exacted in honour of Amun from his subjugated lands.

East of the foundations of the original Temple of Amun stands the Great Festival Temple of Tuthmosis III. It contains several fine reliefs of plants and animals in the so-called Botanic Garden. Twenty of the temple's many columns are unique in Egypt in that they are larger at their peak than their base.

Between the Festival Temple and the eastern gate of the enclosure are the ruins of two other structures, a portico built by

Taharqa and a smaller temple built by Tuthmosis III. The world's largest obelisk once stood on the base in front of this temple. The so-called Lateran Obelisk, which was 32.2 metres high, was removed from Karnak in 357 AD on the orders of the Roman emperor Constantine. Although it was bound for Constantinople, it ended up in the Circus Maximus in Rome and finally, in the 1580s, was re-erected in the Piazza San Giovanni in Laterano.

Against the northern enclosure wall of the precinct of Amun is the cult Temple of Ptah, started by Tuthmosis III and finished by the Ptolemies. Access to the inner chambers is through a series of five doorways which lead you to two of the temple's original statues. The headless figure of Ptah, the creator-god of Memphis, is in the middle chapel. To his left is the eerily beautiful, bare-breasted and lioness-headed, black granite statue of his goddess-wife Sekhmet, the 'spreader of terror'.

Montu Temple Enclosure A usually locked gate on the wall near the Temple of Ptah (Amun Temple Enclosure) leads to the Montu Temple Enclosure. Montu, the falcon-headed warrior-god, was the original deity of Thebes. The main temple was built by Amenophis III and modified by others. The complex is very dilapidated.

Amun Temple Enclosure – southern axis The secondary axis of the Amun Temple Enclosure runs south from the 3rd and 4th Pylons. It is basically a processional way, bounded on the east and west sides by walls, and sectioned off by a number of pylons which create a series of courts. Just before you get to the 7th Pylon, built by Tuthmosis III, is the Cachette Court, so named because of the thousands of stone and bronze statues discovered there during excavation work in 1903. Seven of the statues, of Middle Kingdom Pharaohs, stand in front of the pylon. Nearby are the remains of two colossal statues of Tuthmosis III.

The well-preserved 8th Pylon, built by Queen Hatshepsut, is the oldest part of the north-south axis of the temple. Four of the original six colossi are still standing, the most complete being the one of Amenophis I.

The 9th and 10th Pylons were built by Horemheb, who used some of the stones of a demolished temple that had been built to the east by Akhenaten (before he decamped to Tell el Amarna).

To the east of the 7th and 8th pylons is the Sacred Lake, where the priests of Amun would purify themselves before performing ceremonies in the temple. On the north-west side of the lake is the top half of Hatshepsut's fallen obelisk, and a huge statue of a scarab beetle dedicated by Amenophis III to Aten, the disc of the rising sun.

There are the ruins or remains of about 20 other chapels within the main enclosure. In a fairly good state of repair in the south-west corner is the Temple of Khons, god of the moon and time, and son of Amun and Mut. The pylon faces Euergetes' Gate and the avenue of sphinxes leading to Luxor Temple, and provides access to a small hypostyle hall and ruined sanctuary. The temple was started by Ramses III, and added to by other Ramessids, Ptolemies and also Herihor. Herihor, like Horemheb, had pushed his way up through the ranks of the army to claim power, declaring himself not only Pharaoh but high priest of Amun as well.

Nearby is the small, finely decorated Temple of Opet, dedicated to the hippopotamus-goddess Opet, who was the mother of Osiris.

Mut Temple Enclosure From the 10th Pylon an avenue of sphinxes leads to the partly excavated southern enclosure – the precinct of Mut. The badly ruined Temple of Mut was built by Amenophis III and consists of a sanctuary, a hypostyle hall and two courts. The Temple of Ramses III stands south-west of the crescent-shaped lake which partly surrounds the main temple. Throughout the area are granite statues of Sekhmet, with her leonine head crowned by a solar disc.

Sound & Light Show Karnak Temple's sound & light show easily rivals the one at the Great Pyramids. The 90 minute show recounts the history of Thebes and the lives of the many Pharaohs who built the sanctuaries, courts, statues or obelisks in honour of Amun. The show starts at the avenue of ram-headed sphinxes, passes through the 1st Pylon to the Great Court and on through the Great Hypostyle Hall to the Sacred Lake, where there's a grandstand for the show's finale.

There are two performances a night, in either English, French, German or Arabic, and the show costs E£10. The first show is at sunset (around 6 pm) and the second is at 8 pm. The following is the language schedule:

	1st show	*2nd show*
Monday	English	French
Tuesday	French	English
Wednesday	English	German
Thursday	Arabic	English
Friday	French	English
Saturday	English	French
Sunday	French	German

This schedule is subject to change, so first check with the tourist office or a hotel reception desk.

Getting There & Away To get to Karnak you can take a small covered pick-up truck from Luxor station for 15 pt or hire a horse-drawn carriage (known as a *hantour* or *caleche*) for around E£5 per hour. Give the driver baksheesh if you want him to wait. It's a quick bicycle ride to the temple or you can easily walk there.

West Bank

The west bank of Luxor was the necropolis of ancient Thebes, a vast City of the Dead where magnificent temples were raised to honour the cults of Pharaohs entombed in the nearby cliffs, and where queens, royal children, nobles, priests, artisans and even workers built tombs which ranged, in the quality of their design and decor, from the spectacular to the ordinary.

During the New Kingdom, the necropolis also supported a large living population. In an attempt to protect the valuable tombs from robbers, the artisans, labourers, temple priests and guards lived permanently in the City of the Dead, their lives devoted to its construction and maintenance. They perfected the techniques of tomb building, decoration and concealment, and passed the secrets down through their own families.

The desire for secrecy greatly affected tomb design. Instead of a single mortuary monument like a pyramid, which was both a venue to worship the immortal Pharaoh and the resting place of his mummified remains, the New Kingdom Theban rulers commissioned their funerary monuments in pairs.

Magnificent mortuary temples were built on the plains, where the illusion of the Pharaoh's immortality could be perpetuated by the devotions of his priests and subjects, while the king's body and worldly wealth were laid in secret tombs excavated and splendidly decorated in the hills. The prime location for the latter was an isolated canyon to the north-west, surrounded on three sides by high rugged cliffs.

However, even though there was only one way into the Valley of the Kings and the tombs were well hidden, very few escaped the vandalism of the grave robbers.

From the canal junction it is two km to the Valley of the Queens, seven km to the Valley of the Kings, and one km straight ahead to the student ticket office, past the Colossi of Memnon.

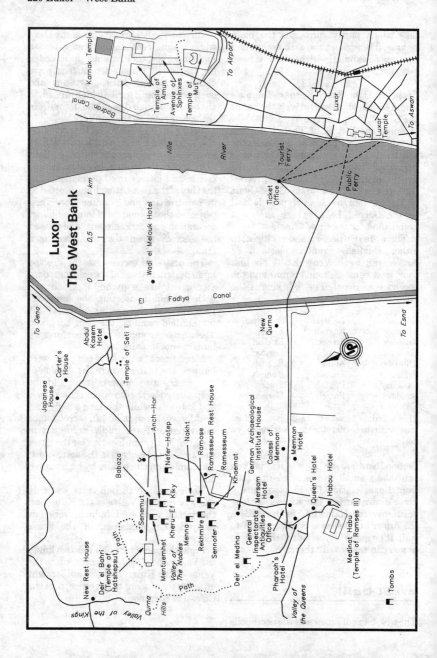

Luxor
The West Bank

0   0.5   1 km

Karnak Temple

Temple of Amun
Avenue of Sphinxes
Temple of Mut

To Airport

Badran Canal

Nile   River

Luxor

To Aswan

Luxor Temple

Tourist Ferry

Public Ferry

Ticket Office

To Qena

El   Fadlya   Canal

To Esna

Wadi el Melouk Hotel

New Qurna

Japanese House

Carter's House

Abdul Kasem Hotel

Temple of Seti I

Anch-Hor

Nefer-Hotep

Nakht

Ramose

Ramesseum Rest House

Ramesseum

Khaemat

German Archaeological Institute House

Colossi of Memnon

Memnon Hotel

Babaza

Valley of Kheru-Ef Kiky

Menna

Rekhmire

Sennofer

Mentuemhat

Valley of The Nobles

Senemut

Deir el Medina

General Inspectorate Antiquities Office

Mersam Hotel

Queen's Hotel

Pharaoh's Hotel

Habou Hotel

New Rest House

Deir el Bahri (Temple of Hatshepsut)

Qurna Hills

Path

Valley of the Kings

Path

Valley of the Queens

Medinat Habu (Temple of Ramses III)

Tombs

What to Bring

Bring a torch and, more importantly, your own water because although drinks are available at some sights, they can be relatively expensive. In the Valley of the Kings, for instance, drinks (including bottled water) at the rest house are overpriced.

Lastly, bring plenty of small change for baksheesh. The tomb and temple guards will often try to pretend to show you something hidden or mysterious. Apparently, they want you to think that whenever they are whispering in their best tomb, temple and tourist English that they are telling or showing you something special. (See the Tipping section in the Facts for the Visitor chapter.)

The best way to avoid these guys is to tag along with a group in each tomb or temple. Unfortunately, that also diminishes the aura of mystery surrounding solitary visits to these ancient sights.

Tickets

The ticket system for the west bank temples and tombs is awkward and annoying. Tickets for the sites must be bought at either the kiosk at the downstream 'tourist ferry' landing or the General Inspectorate/Antiquities Ticket Office (for student discounts), which is three km inland from the local ferry landing. They are sometimes reluctant to sell nondiscounted tickets at the latter office.

You cannot pay for admission at the sites, and individual tickets are required for each tomb, temple or group of sites, so you need to know just what you want to see before you set off. Tickets are valid only for the day of purchase and no refunds are given. Student prices are half the following.

Valley of the Kings E£5; Deir el Bahri – Temple of Hatshepsut E£2; Medinat Habu – Temple of Ramses III E£2; the Ramesseum E£1; Valley of the Queens E£1; Deir el Medina E£1; Tombs of the Nobles – Ramose, Userhet and Khaemhet

E£1, Sennofer and Rekhmire E£1; Assasif Tombs – Kheru-Ef, Nefer-Hotep, KiKy and Anch-hor E£1; Nakht and Menna Tombs E£1; Temple of Seti I E£1.

Getting Around

It's unrealistic to attempt to explore all of the attractions of the west bank in one day. The incredible heat and the desolate and mountainous landscape make it an expedition not to be taken lightly. The ideal time to visit is between sunrise and 1 pm, so a series of morning trips is the best way to go about it.

For getting around the west bank, you can walk (not recommended on hot days), rent a bicycle or donkey, or hire a taxi. By taxi, you can visit most of the sights in about five hours. There are plenty of taxis shuttling back and forth so it is not absolutely necessary to have one wait for you. All transportation and guides can be arranged from the town landing.

Bicycles are E£5 to E£6 per day, donkeys cost about E£7 per day (plus E£2 for the guide), and taxis E£5 per hour. Obviously, these prices could change, so use them as a guideline only. A good way of making the circuit is to take a taxi from the ferry landing to the Valley of the Kings. After exploring the tombs you can then walk up and over the hill to the Temple of Hatshepsut, the Valley of the Nobles and the Ramesseum. You can then catch another taxi to the Valley of the Queens and the Temple of Ramses III, or even continue on foot.

Temple of Seti I

Seti I, the father of Ramses II, expanded the Egyptian Empire to include Cyprus and parts of Mesopotamia. His imposing mortuary temple, dedicated to Amun, was an inspiring place of worship for his own cult and also served as a treasure house for some of the spoils of his military ventures.

Though the first two pylons and courts are in ruins, the temple itself is in reasonable repair and the surviving

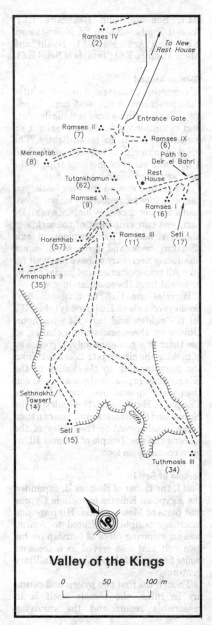

Ramses IV
(2)

To New
Rest House

Entrance Gate

Ramses II
(7)

Ramses IX
(6)

Merneptah
(8)

Path to
Deir el Bahri

Rest
House

Tutankhamun
(62)

Ramses VI
(9)

Ramses I
(16)

Horemheb
(57)

Ramses III
(11)

Seti I
(17)

Amenophis II
(35)

Cliffs

Sethnakht/
Tawsert
(14)

Seti II
(15)

Tuthmosis III
(34)

Valley of the Kings

0   50   100 m

reliefs, in the hypostyle hall, chapels and sanctuary, are superbly executed and some of the finest examples of New Kingdom art. This temple, just off Sharia Wadi el Melouk (the road to the Valley of the Kings), is seldom visited by tourists, so is well worth the effort.

On a barren hill, where the road from Deir el Bahri to the Valley of the Kings meets the road from Seti's temple, there is a domed house where Howard Carter lived during his search for the tomb of Tutankhamun.

Valley of the Kings

Once called the Gates of the Kings or the Place of Truth, the canyon now known as the Valley of the Kings is at once a place of death, for nothing grows on its steep, scorching cliffs, and a majestic domain befitting the mighty kings who once lay there in great stone sarcophagi, awaiting immortality.

The isolated valley, behind Deir el Bahri, is dominated by the natural pyramid-shaped mountain peak of El Qurn, or 'the horn'. The valley consists of two branches, the east and west valleys, with the former containing most of the royal burial sites.

All the tombs followed a similar design, deviating only because of structural difficulties or the length of time spent on their construction. The longer the reign of the Pharaoh, the larger and more magnificent his tomb. Two groups of workers and artisans would live, in alternating shifts, in the valley itself for the duration of the work, which usually took many years.

The tombs were designed to resemble the underworld, with a long, inclined rock-hewn corridor descending into either an antechamber or a series of sometimes pillared halls, and ending in the burial chamber. Once the tomb was cut its decoration was started; this dealt almost exclusively with the afterlife and the Pharaoh's existence in it.

The colourful paintings and reliefs are

Tutankhamun

extracts from ancient theological compositions, or 'books', and were incorporated in the tomb to assist the Pharaoh into the next life. Texts were taken from the *Book of Amduat* – 'the book of him who is in the netherworld'; the *Book of Gates*, which charted the king's course through the underworld; and the *Book of the Litany of Ra*, believed to be the words spoken by Ra, the sun-god, on his own journey through the caverns of death.

The worshippers of Amun or Amun-Ra (the fusion of the two deities and king of the gods) believed that the Valley of the Kings was traversed each night by Ra, and it was the aim of those who had been buried that day to secure passage on his sacred barque.

To do this, they had to be well equipped with a knowledge of the magic texts (hence the tomb decorations) before they could enter the boat of the god. Once aboard, they were brought to the kingdom

of Osiris, god of the dead, where they were judged. Those kings who passed the ordeal would then board a second sacred barque for the journey to the east, where having overcome the powers of darkness and death, they would live again, immortal in the company of Amun-Ra.

Tuthmosis I was the first Pharaoh to have his tomb cut in the barren cliffs, around 1495 BC, and in all 62 tombs have been excavated in the valley, though not all belong to Pharaohs.

Each tomb is numbered in order of discovery but not all are open to the public and there are often some tombs closed for renovation work. It's worth having your own torch (flashlight) to illuminate badly lit areas. Sometimes the guards have the endearing habit of switching off the lights if you won't give them baksheesh – and they wait till you're halfway in to leave you in the dark.

The road into the Valley of the Kings is a

gradual, dry, hot climb, so be prepared if you are riding a bicycle. There is a rest house in the valley where you can buy mineral water and soft drinks. It's expensive, usually crowded and closes at 2 pm.

If you want to avoid the inevitable crowds that tour buses bring to the tombs, head for the tombs outside the immediate area of the rest house. There are many to choose from, but some of my favourites are the tombs of Ramses VI (No 9), Queen Tawsert/Sethnakt (No 14) and Tuthmosis III (No 34).

Tomb of Ramses IX (No 6) The first on the left as you enter the Valley of the Kings, just before the rest house, this tomb consists of a long, sloping corridor, a large antechamber decorated with animals, serpents and demons, then a pillared hall and short hallway before the burial chamber. The goddess Nut is the feature of the ceiling painting; she is surrounded by sacred barques full of stars. Just before the staircase down to the burial chamber are the cartouche symbols of Ramses IX.

Tomb of Merneptah (No 8) Reliefs of Isis, the wife of Osiris and divine mourner of the dead, and Nepthys, the sister of Isis and guardian of coffins, adorn the entrance to this tomb, which is north-west of the rest house. Merneptah was the son of Ramses II and the Pharaoh mentioned in the Biblical book *Exodus*. The walls of the steep corridor, which descends 80 metres to his burial chamber, are decorated with texts from the *Book of Gates*.

Tomb of Ramses VI (No 9) The early excavation of this tomb forestalled the discovery of Tutankhamun's tomb below it. Originally built for Ramses V but usurped by his successor, who saved time and money by appropriating the site, this tomb extends 83 metres into the mountain. The passageway is decorated with scenes from the *Book of the Dead* and the *Book of*

the Caverns and the complete text of the *Book of Gates*.

Ramses VI's smashed sarcophagus lies in the pillared burial chamber at the end of the corridor. The burial chamber has a beautiful and unusual ceiling which details the *Book of Day & Night* and features the goddess Nut twice, stretched across the morning and evening sky.

Tomb of Ramses III (No 11) The burial chamber of this tomb, which is one of the largest in the valley, remains unexcavated and is closed to the public.

There is, however, plenty to see in the three passageways and 10 side chambers in the first part of the tomb. Also known as the Tomb of the Harpers, because of the painting of two musicians playing to the gods in a room off the second passage, it is interesting because the colouring of its sunken reliefs is still quite vivid. The sidechambers are decorated with pictures of their former contents, while other walls depict daily happenings.

Tomb of Ramses I (No 16) Although the tomb next to Seti's belongs to the founder of the 19th dynasty, it is a very simple affair because Ramses I only ruled for a couple of years.

The tomb, which has the shortest entrance corridor of all the royal resting places in the valley, has a single almost square burial chamber, containing the king's open, pink granite sarcophagus. The chamber is the only part of the tomb that is decorated; it features the Pharaoh in the presence of deities such as Osiris, Ptah, Anubis and Maat set on a blue-purple background.

Tomb of Seti I (No 17) The longest, most splendid and best preserved tomb of the Theban necropolis is the burial site of Seti I, which plunges over 100 metres down into the hillside. The detail of the enchanting, finely executed reliefs rivals even the renowned decorations in his Cenotaph Temple at Abydos.

Top: Street scene, Luxor (TW)
Bottom: The Ramesseum, Luxor (SW)

Top: The Colossi of Memnon, Luxor (HF)
Left: Donkeys overlooking the Valley of the Kings (GB)
Right: Statue of Ramses II in Karnak Temple, Luxor (HF)

Three long passages, intersected by decorated chambers, culminate in the large, two-part burial chamber. Colourful scenes include Seti appearing before Ra-Harakhty (god of the morning sun) beneath a ceiling of flying vultures and texts from the *Litany of Ra*.

In the first chamber Seti is shown in the presence of deities and in another passage the walls feature the Opening of the Mouth ritual which ensured that the mummy's organs were functioning.

The first section of the burial chamber is a pillared hall decorated with texts from the *Book of Gates*, while the second part, which contained Seti's magnificent alabaster sarcophagus, features texts from the *Amduat* and an astronomical ceiling. The tomb is east of the rest house.

Unfortunately, at the time of writing, this tomb was closed indefinitely for restoration.

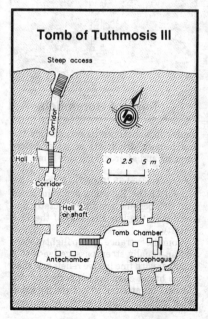

Tomb of Tuthmosis III

Steep access

Corridor

Hall 1

Corridor

Hall 2 or shaft

0   2.5   5 m

Antechamber

Tomb Chamber

Sarcophagus

Tomb of Tuthmosis III (No 34) Hidden in the hills between high limestone cliffs and reached only via a steep staircase that crosses an even steeper ravine, this tomb demonstrates the length the ancient Pharaohs went to thwart the cunning of the ancient thieves.

Tuthmosis III was one of the first to build his tomb in the Valley of the Kings. As secrecy was his utmost concern, he chose the most inaccessible spot and designed his burial place with a series of passages at haphazard angles and a deep shaft to mislead or catch potential robbers – all to no avail, of course.

The shaft, now traversed by a narrow gangway, leads to an antechamber supported by two pillars, the walls of which are adorned with a list of over 700 gods and demigods.

The burial chamber, which is oval-shaped like a cartouche, is decorated in a fairly restrained manner. The roof is supported by two pillars, between which is the king's empty, red sandstone sarcophagus; his mummy was found at Deir el Bahri.

Tomb of Queen Tawsert/Sethnakt (No 14) Queen Tawsert was the wife of Seti II. Her tomb was later taken over by Sethnakt after he had trouble building his own tomb. The tomb is decorated with well-preserved paintings showing scenes from the *Book of the Dead*, the *Book of Gates* and the ceremony of the Opening of the Mouth. Sethnakt's granite sarcophagus is in the tomb.

Tomb of Seti II (15) Adjacent to Queen Tawsert's tomb is that of her husband, Seti II. The tomb entrance starts with some fine reliefs but it was abruptly abandoned before completion. During the excavation of Tutankhamun's tomb it was used by Howard Carter for preliminary storage and restoration work on the finds. Today the mummy of an unknown person can be seen in the tomb.

Tomb of Amenophis II (No 35) One of the deepest structures in the valley, this tomb has more than 90 steps which take you down to a modern gangway built over a deep pit designed to protect the inner, lower chambers from thieves.

Stars cover the entire ceiling in the huge burial chamber and the walls feature, as if on a giant painted scroll, the entire text of the *Book of Amduat*. This was indeed the final resting place of Amenophis II, for although thieves did manage to make off with everything of value, they did no damage to the interior and left the king himself undisturbed.

When the huge tomb was excavated, by the French in 1898, 13 mummies were found, including that of Amenophis lying *in situ* in his sarcophagus, a garland of flowers still around his neck. Nine of the other mummies were also of royal blood, hidden there by priests, and included the bodies of Tuthmosis IV, Seti II, Amenophis III and his wife Queen Tiy. Warning: this

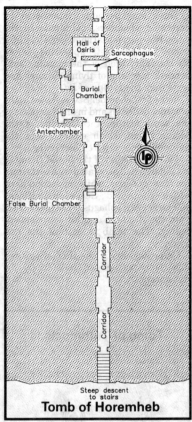

Tomb of Horemheb

tomb can sometimes be exceedingly hot and humid; drink lots of water before entering and after leaving this tomb.

Tomb of Horemheb (No 57) Horemheb, a general of the Egyptian army in about 1320 BC, became a military dictator and eventually the last Pharaoh of the 18th dynasty.

From the entrance a steep flight of steps and an equally steep passage leads to a chamber with fine festive reliefs and then a false burial chamber supported by two pillars. This attempt to fool any potential grave robbers didn't work, as ancient

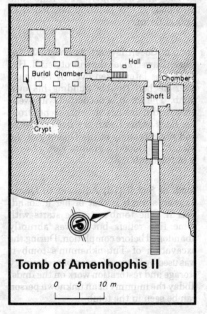

Tomb of Amenhophis II

0   5   10 m

thieves managed to find and uncover the stairway which leads steeply down to the real tomb; they left nothing but Horemheb's red granite sarcophagus.

The wall paintings of the burial chamber were never finished, indicating an untimely death, but are interesting because they reveal the different stages of decoration.

Tomb of Tutankhamun (No 62) The story behind the celebrated discovery of this, the most famous tomb in the Valley of the Kings, and the fabulous treasures it contained, far outshines its actual appearance.

Tutankhamun's tomb is neither large nor impressive and bears all the signs of a rather hasty completion and inglorious burial. The extraordinary contents of this rather modest tomb built for a fairly insignificant boy-king, however, can only make you guess at the immense wealth that must have been laid to rest with the likes of the powerful Seti I or Ramses II.

For years archaeologists believed that, if in fact Tutankhamun was buried in the valley, his tomb would contain little of interest. The nephew of Akhenaten, he was merely a puppet Pharaoh of the priests of Amun, supporting their counter-revolution against the parvenus of the late rebel king's desertion from Thebes.

During his brief reign Tutankhamun was seen to re-embrace the cult of Amun, restoring its popularity with the people, and then he died, young, with no great battles or buildings to his credit.

The English Egyptologist Howard Carter, however, believed he would find the young Pharaoh buried amongst his ancestors with his treasures intact. He slaved away for six seasons in the valley, excavating thousands and thousands of tonnes of sand and rubble from possible sites, until even his wealthy patron, Lord Carnarvon, tired of the obsession.

With his funding about to be cut off Carter made one last attempt at the only unexplored area that was left – a site

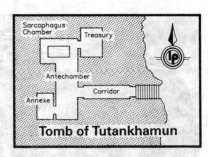

Tomb of Tutankhamun

covered by workers huts just under the already excavated tomb of Ramses VI.

On 4 November 1922 he uncovered steps and then a door, its seals untouched, and wired Lord Carnarvon to join him immediately for the opening of what he believed was the intact tomb of Tutankhamun.

The discovery proved sceptics wrong, and the tomb's priceless cache of Pharaonic treasures, which had remained undisturbed by robbers, vindicated Carter's dream beyond even his wildest imaginings.

Sadly, in perhaps the last great irony in the history of tomb robbing in the Valley of the Kings, evidence came to light some years later to suggest that prior to the tomb being officially opened in the presence of experts from the Metropolitan Museum of Art, Carter and Carnarvon themselves broke in, stole several articles and resealed the door.

The tomb, which is opposite the rest house, is small and for the most part undecorated. Three small chambers were crammed with furniture, statues, chariots, musical instruments, weapons, boxes, jars and food, all of which are now in the Egyptian Museum in Cairo.

The second coffin of gilded wood, the solid gold mummy case and of course the magnificent funerary mask, found on the king's body, are also in Cairo. The innermost coffin of gilded wood containing the decaying, mummified body of Tutankhamun, still lies within the carved granite sarcophagus in the burial chamber

Wall paintings in the Tomb of Horemheb

of his tomb, the walls of which are decorated with texts from the *Book of the Dead*.

Walk to Deir el Bahri From the tombs of Seti I and Ramses I you can continue south-east and hike over the hills to Deir el Bahri (or vice versa of course). The walk takes about 45 minutes through an amazing lunar-type landscape.

It offers various views of the Temple of Hatshepsut in the amphitheatre setting of Deir el Bahri below and excellent views across the plain towards the Nile.

In summer you should start this hike as early as possible, partly to catch the changing colours of the barren hills as the sun rises, but also because it gets mighty hot there later in the day. If you tire on the ascent there are donkeys available to carry you to the top!

If you plan to visit the sights, however, you will need tickets, which can only be obtained when the office opens at about 6.30 or 7 am. There's also a much longer trail from the Valley of the Kings to the Valley of the Queens via Deir el Medina.

Temple of Hatshepsut (Deir el Bahri)
Rising out of the desert plain, in a series of terraces, the Mortuary Temple of Queen Hatshepsut merges with the sheer limestone cliffs of the eastern face of the Theban Mountain as if nature herself had built this extraordinary monument.

The partly rockcut, partly free-standing structure is one of the finest monuments of ancient Egypt, though its original appearance, surrounded by myrrh trees, garden beds and approached by a grand sphinx-lined causeway, must have been even more spectacular.

Discovered in the mid-19th century by Auguste Mariette, it wasn't completely excavated till 1896 and is still being restored. The third terrace is currently closed to the public while a team of Polish archaeologists clear and repair it. Unfortunately, over the centuries the temple has been vandalised. Akhenaten

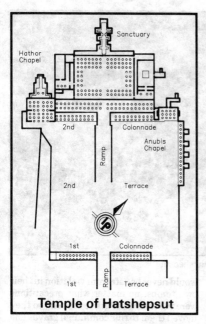

Temple of Hatshepsut

succession. The struggle for ultimate control was eventually won by the formidable Hatshepsut. As well as being only the third queen ever to rule ancient Egypt, Hatshepsut declared herself Pharaoh – which made her the first woman ever to reign as king.

Hatshepsut had married her father's son, her own half-brother Tuthmosis II, and she held many titles, including 'Pharaoh's wife and daughter' and of course 'queen'. She failed, however, to bear any sons, so it was Tuthmosis III, the son of one of the king's concubines, who became heir presumptive.

Following the death of her sibling/husband, Hatshepsut became regent to the new Pharaoh Tuthmosis III, but such was her power that the young boy had little chance of ruling in his own right.

Despite the backing of the army, Tuthmosis was no match for his aunt/stepmother/co-ruler, and Hatshepsut eventually overshadowed him enough to proclaim herself absolute monarch as both queen and king. She still, however, had to win over the priesthood and this she managed by claiming divine birth (as most Pharaohs did), by assuming the dress and manner of a man and by having herself depicted wearing the traditional Pharaonic beard in reliefs.

Hatshepsut ruled for 20 years, and for Egypt it was a time of peace and internal development. It is not known how she died, whether it was of natural causes or something more sinister. Almost as soon as Tuthmosis III finally took his place on the throne he led his country into war with Palestine.

removed all references to Amun, before taking his court off to Tell el Amarna; and the early Christians who took it over as a monastery (hence the name Deir el Bahri, or 'monastery of the north'), also defaced the pagan reliefs.

The worst damage, however, was done out of pure spite by Hatshepsut's successor, Tuthmosis III, who developed a fairly strong hatred of the queen in the 20 years he waited to ascend the throne of Egypt. Within weeks of her death he had obliterated or covered her name or image wherever he found it. Even in her own mortuary temple, where he and Hatshepsut were always represented together, as co-rulers, he hacked out her likeness, leaving only his own.

Following the death of Tuthmosis I in 1495 BC, a great controversy arose, between the late Pharaoh's daughter Hatshepsut and his grandson Tuthmosis III, over the rights of

The temple's 37 metre wide causeway leads onto the three huge terraced courts, which are each approached by ramps and are separated by colonnades. The renowned delicate relief work of the lower terrace features scenes of birds being caught in nets and the transport to Thebes of a pair of obelisks commissioned by Hatshepsut from the Aswan quarries.

The central court contains the best preserved reliefs. There Queen Hatshepsut recorded her divine birth and told the story of an expedition to the Land of Punt to collect myrrh trees needed for the precious myrrh incense used in temple ceremonies.

Temple of Hatshepsut

There are also two chapels at either end of the colonnade. At the northern end the colourful reliefs in the Chapel of Anubis show the co-rulers Hatshepsut and Tuthmosis III (with the queen's image again disfigured by her nephew) in the presence of Anubis, the god of embalming, Ra-Harakhty, the falcon-headed sun-god, and his wife Hathor. In the Chapel of Hathor you can see (if you have a torch) an untouched figure of Hatshepsut worshipping the cow-headed goddess.

Although the third terrace is out of bounds, you can see the pink granite doorway leading into the Sanctuary of Amun, which is hewn out of the cliff.

In 1876 the greatest mummy find in history was made just north of the Temple of Hatshepsut. After many antiquities began showing up in the marketplace the authorities realised someone had found, and was plundering, an unknown tomb. After investigations they discovered a massive shaft at the foot of the cliffs which contained the mummies of 40 Pharaohs, queens and nobles.

It seems that the New Kingdom priests realised that the bodies of their kings would never be safe from violation in their own tombs, no matter what precautions were taken against grave robbers, so they moved them to this communal grave. The mummies included those of Amenophis I, Tuthmosis II and III, Seti I and Ramses I and III.

You can hike over the mountain to the Valley of the Kings from here (see Valley of the Kings section). It should take about 45 minutes, but be prepared for a strenuous trek on hot days. Take plenty of water. The view of Deir el Bahri from above is spectacular.

The Ramesseum
The Ramesseum is yet another monument raised by Ramses II for the ultimate glory of himself. The massive temple was built to impress his priests, his subjects, his successors and of course the gods, so that he, the great warrior king, could live forever.

Many of his other works were rather crudely constructed but in this, his mortuary temple, he demanded perfection in the workmanship so that it would stand as an eternal testimony to his greatness.

Sadly, the Ramesseum, which was dedicated to Amun, is mostly in ruins. This fact no doubt disappoints Ramses II more than it does modern-day visitors to the site. He dared all those who questioned his greatness in future centuries to gaze on the magnificence of his monuments in order to understand his power over life and death. How the mighty fall!

The scattered remains of the colossal statue of the king and the ruins of his temple prompted the English poet Shelley to cut this presumptuous Pharaoh down to size by using the undeniable fact of Ramses' mortality to ridicule his

immortal aspirations. In the early 19th century Shelley wrote 'Ozymandias':

I met a traveller from an antique land
Who said: Two vast and trunkless legs of stone
Stand in the desert... Near them, on the sand,
Half sunk, a shattered visage lies, whose frown,
And wrinkled lip, and sneer of cold command,
Tell that its sculptor well those passions read
Which yet survive, stamped on these lifeless things,
The hand that mocked them, and the heart that fed:

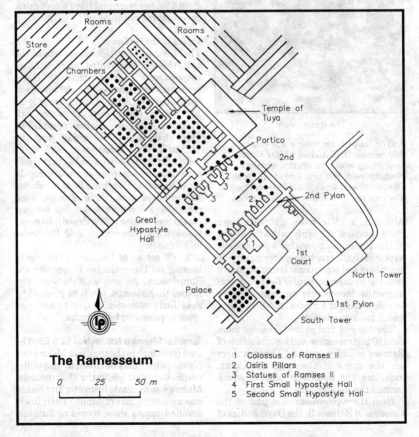

The Ramesseum

0   25   50 m

1   Colossus of Ramses II
2   Osiris Pillars
3   Statues of Ramses II
4   First Small Hypostyle Hall
5   Second Small Hypostyle Hall

The Ramesseum

And on the pedestal these words appear:
'My name is Ozymandias, king of kings:
Look on my works, ye Mighty, and despair!'
Nothing beside remains. Round the decay
Of that colossal wreck, boundless and bare
The lone and level sands stretch far away.

Although a little more elaborate than other temples, the fairly orthodox layout of the Ramesseum, with its two courts, hypostyle hall, sanctuary, accompanying chambers and storerooms is uncommon in that the usual rectangular floor plan was altered to incorporate an older, smaller temple – that of Ramses' mother, Tuya, which is off to one side.

The 1st and 2nd pylons measure more than 60 metres across and feature reliefs of Ramses' military exploits. Through them are the ruins of the huge 1st Court, including the double colonnade which fronted the royal palace.

Near the western stairs is part of the Colossus of Ramses II, the Ozymandias of

Shelley's poem, lying somewhat forlornly on the ground. When it stood, it was 17.5 metres tall. The head of another granite statue of Ramses, one of a pair, lies in the 2nd Court. Twenty-nine of the original 48 columns of the Great Hypostyle Hall are still standing, and in the smaller hall behind it the roof, which features astronomical hieroglyphs, is still in place.

There is a rest house/restaurant next to the temple which is called, not surprisingly, the *Ramesseum Resthouse*. It is owned by Sayed Hussain, whose father was a friend of Howard Carter. The rest house is a great place to relax and have a cool drink or something cheap to eat.

Tombs of the Nobles

The Tombs of the Nobles are one of the best, though least visited, attractions on the west bank. Nestled in the foothills and amongst the houses of the old village of Qurna (Sheikh Abd el Qurna) are at least 400 tombs which date from the 6th dynasty to the Greco-Roman period. The tomb chapels in the area date from the 18th to the 20th dynasties.

Of the 100 or so tombs that have something of interest, seven are highly recommended. They have been numbered and divided into three groups, each requiring a separate ticket, as follows: Nakht and Menna (often closed); Ramose, Userhet and Khaemhet; and Rekhmire and Sennofer.

You'll see signs leading to the tombs leading off the main road, opposite the Ramesseum. As you walk between the houses to the tombs, you'll be pursued by avid little salesmen, eager to sell you crudely produced handicrafts.

Tombs of Menna & Nakht (Nos 52 & 69) The wall paintings in the tombs of Menna and Nakht (which may be closed to the public) emphasise rural life in the 18th dynasty. Menna was an estate inspector and Nakht was an astronomer of Amun. Their finely detailed tombs show scenes of farming,

Tomb of Nakht

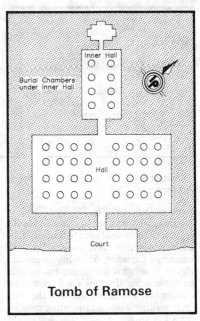

Tomb of Ramose

hunting, fishing and feasting. The Tomb of Nakht has a small museum area in its first chamber. Although this tomb is so small that only a handful of visitors can squeeze in, the walls have some of the best known examples of Egyptian tomb paintings including familiar scenes like the three musicians which now grace a million T-shirts, posters, postcards and papyrus paintings.

Tomb of Ramose (No 55) This is the Tomb Chapel of Ramose, who was a governor of Thebes during the reigns of Amenophis III and Akhenaten. It's a fascinating tomb and one of the few monuments dating from that time, when the cult power of the priests of Karnak was usurped by the new monotheistic worship of Aten.

Exquisite paintings and low reliefs grace the walls, showing scenes from the reigns of both kings and the transition between the two forms of religious worship. The reliefs of Ramose, his wife and other relatives are extraordinarily lifelike and clearly show their affectionate relationships. The tomb was never actually finished because Ramose deserted Thebes to follow the rebel Pharaoh

Reliefs in the Tomb of Ramose

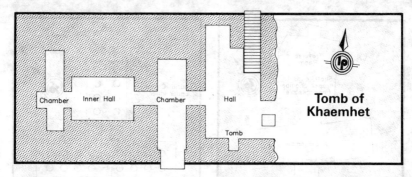

Tomb of Khaemhet

Chamber   Inner Hall   Chamber   Hall

Tomb

Akhenaten to his new city at Tell el Amarna.

Tomb of Userhet (No 56) The Tomb of Userhet, who was one of Amenophis II's royal scribes, is right next to Ramose's. Its most distinctive features are the wall paintings depicting daily life in ancient Egypt. Userhet is shown presenting gifts to Amenophis II; there's a barber busy cutting hair on another wall; and there are men making wine, and hunting gazelles from a chariot.

Tomb of Khaemhet (No 57) This tomb belonged to Khaemhet, who was Amenophis III's royal inspector of the granaries and court scribe. Scenes on the walls show Khaemhet offering sacrifices; the Pharaoh depicted as a sphinx; the funeral ritual of Osiris; and images of daily country life and official business.

Tomb of Sennofer (No 96) Prince Sennofer of Thebes worked for Amenophis II as a supervisor of the gardens of the Temple of Amun. The most interesting parts of his tomb are deep underground in the main chamber. The ceiling there is covered with clear paintings of grapes and vines, while most of the scenes on the surrounding walls and columns depict Sennofer with his sister. The guard usually has a kerosene lamp, but bring a torch just in case.

Tomb of Rekhmire (No 100) The Tomb of Rekhmire, a governor during the reigns of Tuthmosis III and Amenophis II, is one of the best preserved in the area. In the first chamber, to the extreme left, are scenes of Rekhmire receiving gifts from foreign lands. The panther and giraffe are gifts from Nubia; the elephant, horses and chariot come from Syria; and the expensive vases come from Crete and the Aegean Islands.

Deir el Medina

The small Ptolemaic temple of Deir el Medina is one km off the road to the Valley of the Queens and up a short, but very rocky, road that would be difficult for bicycles. The temple was built between 221 BC and 116 BC by Philopator, Philometor and Euergetes II.

It was dedicated to Hathor, the goddess of pleasure and love, and to Maat, the goddess of truth and the personification of cosmic order. However, the temple is called Deir el Medina, which means 'monastery of the town', because it was occupied by early Christian monks.

If you have the energy and the inclination, hike southward a short distance to see the remains of a New Kingdom village occupied by the artists and workers who built some of the tombs in the area. Archaeologists have been excavating this settlement for most of this century and at least 70 houses have been uncovered.

One of the two tombs in this area which can be visited is the Tomb of Sennedjem (No 1). Sennedjem was a 19th dynasty servant in the so-called Place of Truth – the Valley of the Kings. The tomb has only one chamber, but the wall paintings are magnificent. One of the most famous scenes shows a cat killing a snake; it's above the doorway to the burial chamber. There is no light, but the guard has a lantern if you haven't brought your own torch.

Most of the other tombs in the area belonged to the servants, overseers and labourers who worked in the valley.

Valley of the Queens

There are at least 75 tombs in Biban el Harim, the Valley of the Queens. They belonged to queens of the 19th and 20th dynasties and other members of the royal families, including princesses and the Ramessid princes. Only tomb Nos 43, 44, 52 and 55 are open.

The top attraction here is No 55, the Tomb of Amunherkhepshep. Amun, who was the son of Ramses III, was nine years old when he died. The scenes on the tomb walls show his father grooming him to be Pharaoh by introducing him to various gods.

Amun's mother was pregnant at the time of his death and in her grief she aborted the child and entombed it with Amun. A five month old mummified fetus was discovered there. Wall paintings also show Ramses leading his son to Anubis, the jackal-headed god of the dead, who then takes the young Prince Amun down to the entrance of the Passage of the Dead.

The Tomb of Queen Titi (No 52), who was wife and consort to one of the Ramses, is also interesting.

Medinat Habu

The temple complex of Medinat Habu was one of the first places in Thebes to be closely associated with the local god Amun. Hatshepsut, Tuthmosis III and Ramses III constructed the main buildings of the complex, which is second only to the Temples of Karnak in size and complexity,

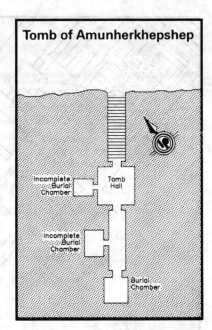

but Medinat Habu was added to and altered by a succession of rulers right through to the Ptolemies.

At its height there were temples, workshops, storage rooms, administrative buildings and accommodation for the priests and officials. It was the centre of the economic life of Thebes for several centuries and was still inhabited as late as the 9th century AD.

The original Temple of Amun, built by Hatshepsut and Tuthmosis III, was later completely overshadowed by the enormous Mortuary Temple of Ramses III, which is the dominant feature of Medinat Habu.

Ramses III was inspired in the construction of his shrine by the Ramesseum of his father. His own temple and the smaller one dedicated to Amun are both enclosed within the massive outer walls of the complex.

Also just inside, to the left of the gate, are the Tomb Chapels of the Divine Adorers, which were built for the principal

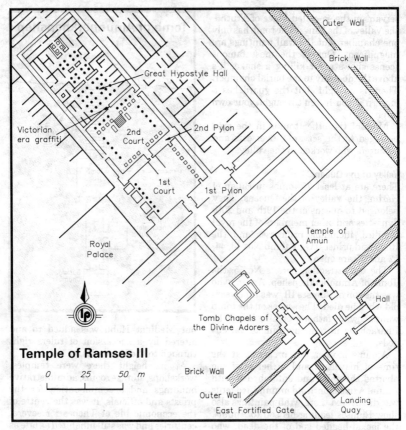

Temple of Ramses III

0   25   50 m

Outer Wall

Brick Wall

Great Hypostyle Hall

Victorian era graffiti

2nd Court

2nd Pylon

1st Court

1st Pylon

Royal Palace

Temple of Amun

Hall

Tomb Chapels of the Divine Adorers

Brick Wall

Outer Wall

East Fortified Gate

Landing Quay

priestesses of Amun. Outside the eastern gate, one of only two entrances, was a landing quay for a canal which once connected Medinat Habu with the Nile.

The well-preserved 1st Pylon marks the front of the temple proper. Ramses III is portrayed in its reliefs as the victor in several wars. To the left of the 1st Court are the remains of the Pharaoh's palace; the three rooms at the rear were for the royal harem. There is a window between the first court and the palace known as the Window of Appearances, which allowed the king to show himself to his subjects.

The reliefs of the 2nd Pylon feature Ramses III presenting prisoners of war to Amun and his vulture-goddess wife, Mut. The 2nd Court is surrounded by colonnades and reliefs showing various religious ceremonies.

Medinat Habu is off the road on your right as you return from the Valley of Queens. After you have finished wandering around the complex treat yourself to a cold Stella beer at the *Habou Hotel* opposite.

Colossi of Memnon
The massive pair of statues known as the Colossi of Memnon are all that remain of

the temple of the hedonistic Amenophis III. Rising about 18 metres from the plain, the enthroned, faceless statues of Amenophis have kept a lonely vigil on the changing landscape around them, surviving the rising flood waters of the Nile which gradually, through annual inundation, destroyed the temple buildings behind them.

Over the centuries, the crumbling rubble of what was believed to have been one of the most splendid of the Theban temples was ploughed into the fertile soil. A stela, now in the Egyptian Museum, describes the temple as being built from 'white sandstone, with gold throughout, a floor covered with silver, and doors covered with electrum'. (Electrum was a commonly used alloy of gold and silver.)

The colossi were amongst the great tourist attractions of Egypt during Greco-Roman times because the Greeks believed they were actually statues of the legendary Memnon, a king of Ethiopia and son of the dawn-goddess Eos, who was slain by Achilles during the Trojan War.

It was the northern statue which attracted most of the attention because at

Colossi of Memnon

sunrise it would emit a haunting, musical sound which the Greeks believed was the voice of Memnon greeting his mother each day. Eos in turn would weep tears of dew for the untimely death of her beautiful son.

Actually the phenomenon of the famous vocal statue was probably produced by the combined effect of a simple change in temperature and the fact that the upper part of the colossus was severely damaged by an earthquake in about 30 BC. As the heat of the morning sun baked the dew-soaked stone, sand particles would break off and resonate inside the cracks in the structure.

Certainly, after a well-meaning Roman governor repaired the statue some time in the 2nd century AD, Memnon's plaintive greeting to his mother was heard no more.

The colossi are just off the road, west of New Qurna – you won't miss them.

Amenophis III had quite a reputation for high and fast living. The ruins of his amazing palace are about one km south of Medinat Habu. The royal residence featured a lake, a banquet hall, private state rooms for Amenophis, a separate residence for his beloved queen Tiy, and quarters for court officials, servants, guests and of course the Pharaoh's extensive harem, which numbered over 300. Although the palace is badly ruined, the remains are quite substantial.

Places to Stay

Unless otherwise indicated, room rates include breakfast.

Places to Stay – bottom end

East Bank Luxor is full of 'bottom end' places to stay. Most of them are concentrated on or around the main streets south-west of the train station. If you can manage to avoid the squawking hotel touts who verbally pounce on as many travellers as possible as they get off the train, leave the station and you'll see

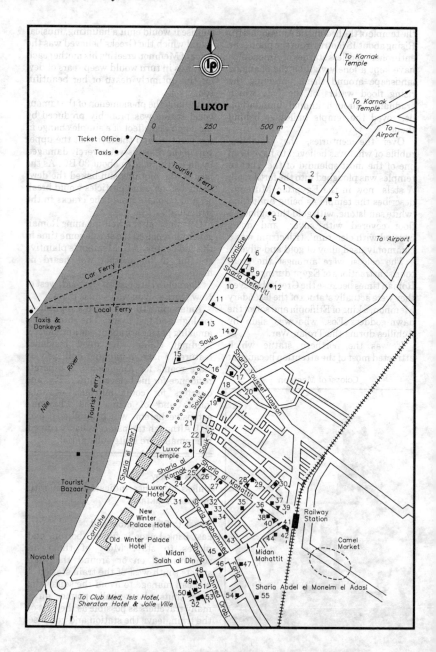

Luxor

0   250   500 m

To Karnak Temple

To Karnak Temple

To Airport

To Airport

Ticket Office

Taxis

Tourist Ferry

Car Ferry

Local Ferry

Taxis & Donkeys

Corniche

Sharia Nefertiti

Souks

Sharia Youssef Hassen

Souks

Souks

Sharia el Bahr

Luxor Temple

Sharia al Karnak

Tourist Bazaar

Luxor Hotel

New Winter Palace Hotel

Old Winter Palace Hotel

Sharia al Mahattit

Sharia Mohammed

Railway Station

Camel Market

Novotel

Midan Salah al Din

Midan Mahattit

Sharia Farid

Sharia Abdel el Moneim el Adasi

To Club Med, Isis Hotel, Sheraton Hotel & Jolie Ville

Sharia Ahmed Orabi

Nile River

•	PLACES TO STAY	53	Princess Pension
2	Youth Hostel	54	Grand Hotel
3	YMCA Campground	55	New Palace Hotel
6	Windsor Hotel		
7	Nile Hotel	▼	PLACES TO EAT
8	Philippe Hotel	21	Amoun Restaurant
10	ETAP Hotel	28	Mensa Restaurant
13	Savoy Hotel	36	Kushari Place
15	Mina Palace Hotel	39	El Hattey Restaurant
17	Emilio Hotel	40	Limpy's Restaurant
19	Nefertiti Hotel	41	New Karnak Restaurant
20	St Catherine Hotel	42	Salt & Bread Cafeteria
	(also spelled Cathrine/Catreen)	46	Restaurant Abu Hager
22	Horus Hotel		
24	Abu el Haggag Hotel	•	PLACES OF INTEREST
29	Salam Hotel	1	Hospital
30	St Mark's Pensione	4	Service Taxi Station
32	Golden Pension	5	Luxor Museum
33	Akhnaton Hotel	9	Misr Bank
34	Nour Home	11	Luxor City Council
35	Happy Home	12	Coptic Church
37	Ramoza Hotel	14	Central Telephone Office
38	Amoun Hotel	16	Police Station
41	New Karnak Hotel	18	Church/School
44	Thebes Hotel	23	Bus Stop
47	Oasis Hotel	25	Corner Bicycle Rental Stand
48	Salah el Din Hotel	26	GPO
49	Mubarak Hotel	27	Boulos' Bicycles
50	Families Hotel	31	Service Taxis to Armant
51	New Student Pension	43	Mosque
52	New Home Pension	45	Bicycle Rentals

the *New Karnak Hotel* on the left side of the station square.

This hotel, which is on Sharia Abdel el Moneim el Adasi (also known as Manches St), has long been a favourite among travellers, more for its low prices and convenient location than for its rooms. Hot water is available for short periods. Showers and bathrooms get flooded easily, so you may want to wear thongs. All rooms have fans, and singles/doubles cost E£6/8.

Also on Sharia Abdel el Moneim el Adasi, further down the road and on your left, you'll come across the *Thebes Hotel*. It is one of several small hotels that needs to send touts to the train station to get people to stay there. They promise hot water, air-con, TV and a few other 'treats', but just because they have these things

doesn't mean that they work or work well. Try to avoid this place if you can.

If you walk straight out of the train station and towards the Nile, you'll come across the *Ramoza Hotel* (tel 382270). It's on the right-hand side of Sharia al Mahattit. It was renovated a few years ago, so it no longer looks as old as its namesake (an 18th dynasty noble), although it does still have a slightly worn appearance.

This hotel seems to be popular with low-budget student tour groups. It costs E£10/20 for a single/double room with private bathroom, hot water, and air-con that varies from mediocre to good. This is one of the few hotels where rates have actually decreased over the last three years.

If you keep walking along Sharia al Mahattit and then turn left at the first street, which is Sharia el Madrassa el Miri, you'll find the *Happy Home*. This has long been a good place to stay for budget travellers. Rooms are quite clean, with shower stalls separate from toilets. There are several bulletin boards on the walls with useful information about Luxor. Singles/doubles/triples cost E£4/6/9. Payment in advance is required.

St Mark's Pensione, which is at 19 Sharia Michael Boulos, is on the first street on the right after the Ramoza Hotel. It's a tiny tucked-away pension with only a few rooms. There's a common room with two cushioned benches that can sleep two more people. The kitchen and bathroom are usually kept spotless and dry. Doubles cost E£10.

This place is run by the amiable Mr Atta, government worker by day, pension owner by night. He speaks enough English to help you get around. Mr Atta can be found either at St Mark's Pensione or in the lobby of the Ramoza Hotel.

Sharia Abdel el Moneim leads to Sharia Mohammed Farid – the first street marked with small hotel signs and arrows. It's about a five to 10 minute walk from the train station.

If you turn left on Sharia Mohammed Farid, there are several small hotels/pensions including the following. The *Oasis Hotel*, on your left, is a relatively new and clean hotel with 15 rooms. Unlike most places in this area, the shower doesn't extend over the toilet and flood the bathroom. Small fans are available. Single/double rooms without bath cost E£10/15.

At the end of the third alley on your right (you'll see signs) is a long-time budget travellers' haven – the *Grand Hotel*. There's a small but pleasant rooftop garden. The rooms are clean if somewhat small – they're basically adequate for budget travellers. Hot water is available. Singles cost E£4 to E£5; doubles E£8 to E£10; and triples E£12.

For more than 13 years, this hotel has been owned and run by Mr Abdo

Sulieman. He can often be found nestled among a pile of cushions in the hotel lobby/dining room, alternately sipping tea and puffing on a water pipe and always smiling.

Whenever possible, Mr Sulieman will take travellers to local weddings. His friend and sidekick, Ahmed Omar, is also often there, waiting to take you across to the west bank and plop you on a donkey.

Back on Sharia Mohammed Farid, a few metres down the road, on your left, is the *New Palace Hotel*. It is quite similar to the Grand Hotel but has somewhat larger rooms and less character.

If you turn right onto Sharia Mohammed Farid from Sharia Abdel el Moneim, you'll see the highly recommended *Nour Home* on the right. Rooms are clean and quiet, with fans and throw-rugs. One of the five rooms has a private bathroom. The shared bathrooms and showers are kept quite clean and hot water is available most of the day. You can't beat their price: E£3/6/9 for a single/double/triple.

It is run by a bright, capable accounting student named Ayman Ahmed el Saman and, occasionally, his partner Fayez. Both speak excellent English and can help you arrange just about anything around Luxor.

Just next to the Nour Home is the *Akhnaton Hotel* (tel 83979), which looks fancier on the outside than most other hotels and pensions around here, but has quite modest rooms. The bathrooms could be cleaner and the rooms lighter, but carpet in the hallways and rooms, overhead fans and hot water somewhat compensate for the negatives. Singles with/without bath cost E£10/8; doubles with/without bath cost E£15/13.

The *Golden Pension*, which is simple and very clean, is next door. It has only four rooms. A kitchen and washing machine are available for guests. Single/double/triple rooms cost E£6/10/12.

The 14 room *Princess Pension* (tel 383997) is one of several places just off

Sharia Ahmed Orabi, which runs parallel to Sharia Mohammed Farid. It seems a bit dusty, in part because of its balconied rooms and a nearby construction site. Most rooms have fans. Single/double/triple rooms cost E£4/7/9. Breakfast costs 50 pt and includes an omelette, bread, jam and tea.

Next door to the Princess is the relatively new *New Home Pension* (tel 383059), a place which seems destined to become a budget travellers' favourite. There's a washing machine, and free access to a kitchen with a refrigerator and stove. The bathrooms are toilet/shower combinations outside the rooms. Singles/doubles cost E£6/12. Tarek, the manager, will gladly show you the favourable comments in the guestbook and letters from guests.

Opposite the New Home Pension is the *New Student Pension*, which has quiet rooms with small balconies. Bathrooms are toilet/shower combinations; hot water is usually available. Breakfast includes an omelette, cheese, bread and jam. Tea is supposedly available at all times. They charge E£5 per person.

Across the alley form the New Student Pension is the *Families Hotel*, which is somewhat dirty; however, the people who run it seem friendly. Rooms are simple, with overhead fans. They charge E£3 per person and breakfast costs E£1.

At the bottom of the list (and the barrel) is the *Youth Hostel* (tel 382139) in a lane just off Sharia al Karnak. Rooms are clean and have at least two sets of bunk beds, but the showers tend to get swampy and stinky, so wear thongs. For their 'deluxe' room, you pay E£3 with a IYHA card; E£4 without. Frankly, it is inconvenient to stay there unless you are planning to take an early morning service taxi from the taxi station, which is about 100 metres from the hostel.

Other places to avoid are: the *Mubarak Hotel*, which is a dirty disgrace to the name of Mubarak; the *Salah el Din Hotel*, which has dirty rooms almost attached to

a mosque, thus making the call to prayer a convenient pre-sunrise alarm clock; the *Salam Hotel* with dirt, steam and locker-room odour; and the *Nefertiti Hotel*, a haven for flies and other creepy-crawlies.

West Bank On the west bank there are only six bottom end places to stay.

The *Memnon Hotel* is across the road from the Colossi of Memnon. It has hot water and dark, dingy rooms which cost E£10/14 for a single/double. The 2nd floor has less drab rooms, a few of which have balconies overlooking Medinat Habu. Overhead fans are available only in the ground floor rooms.

Opposite the Medinat Habu temple complex is the *Habou Hotel* (sometimes spelt 'Habu'). It has dark, dingy, and rather overpriced rooms (compared with what is available in Luxor). Singles/doubles cost E£10/20. You're really paying for the great location overlooking Medinat Habu.

The nearby *Queen's Hotel* has slightly better rooms, somewhat less of a view and an interesting owner, Hajj Ali Hassan Khalifa. He charges E£7/14 for a single/double room.

The *Mersam Hotel* (tel 82403), also known as the *Ali Abd el Rasul Hotel* or the *Sheik Ali Hotel*, is opposite the Antiquities Office. Rooms in the main building are somewhat better than the primitive mud-wall rooms in an adjacent building. Singles/doubles with an 'English' breakfast cost E£10/20; lower rates apply in the summer.

This hotel was once home to Sheikh Ali Abdul Rasul, a cantankerous old guy with a bone-cracking handshake and an aggressive sense of hospitality that kept you riveted to your seat, whether you liked it or not. Sheikh Ali actually helped discover the tomb of Seti I and if you've read Richard Critchfield's book *Shahatt*, then you'll know about this guy already. His son has now taken over the hotel.

The *Abdul Kasem Hotel* has singles/doubles for E£10/20. The rooms have fans, and are basic but OK. The best ones are on the top floor and there's a great view from the roof. The owners, the Kasem family, also have an alabaster factory attached to the hotel and rent bicycles for E£3 a day.

To get there, follow the road inland from either of the ferry landings, turn right on the road just after the canal, which is parallel to it, and follow the signs to 'Wadi el Melouk' (Valley of the Kings); the hotel is before the Temple of Seti I on Sharia Wadi el Melouk.

The *Wadi el Melouk Hotel* still exists on the east side of the canal, but excavation of the canal has almost completely isolated it. You're really not missing much because the hotel was somewhat of a dive.

Camping There used to be free camping in the garden in front of the Luxor Hotel, but not any more. Supposedly, camping is permitted across the street in the small park next to the Luxor Temple. Ask around the park, though, before setting up your tent.

The *YMCA* campground (tel 82425), on Sharia al Karnak, costs E£2 per night, including the use of its 20 showers. They also charge E£2 per vehicle. This is popular with overland travel groups such as Encounter Overland.

Places to Stay – middle
East Bank From the train station, walk to the end of Sharia al Mahattit. About a block to the left on Sharia al Karnak is the *Abu el Haggag Hotel*. It is opposite Luxor Temple, and there are great views of the temple from the upper floor rooms. All the rooms have bathrooms and air-con, but you have to pay E£3 extra for the latter. With singles/doubles/triples for E£15/20/25, this isn't the special bargain that it used to be.

Also on Sharia al Karnak, about a block north of Sharia al Mahattit, you'll see the *Horus Hotel* (tel 382165). It was completely revamped and upgraded to three stars in 1989. Rooms are clean and comfortable,

with air-con and bathrooms that no longer require swamp boots.

The hotel has an excellent location – it's near the souks and Luxor Temple. The only drawback is that a few of the rooms face a mosque, which could mean waking up with the early morning call to prayer. At E£15 to E£20 for a single with bath and E£25 to E£30 for a double with bath, this is a good deal. Fortunately, the tour groups have not yet discovered this place.

Further along Sharia al Karnak and about half a block to the right is the *Emilio Hotel* (tel 383570). This is one of the best middle and upper-middle price range hotels in town. It was built in 1987 and has 48 rooms, all with bathrooms, air-con, TV and a hotel video channel; some rooms have Nile views. The astroturf roof terrace has plenty of shade and several reclining chairs. Singles/doubles cost E£45. Lunch/dinner costs E£6.85/7.50. Prices do not include the 21% taxes and service charges. Reservations are essential here because it is often taken over by travel groups.

The two star *St Catherine Hotel* (sometimes spelled 'Catreen' or 'Cathrine'; tel 382684), 2 Sharia Youssef Hassan, is popular with German groups. Some of the bathrooms are somewhat small, but the rooms are otherwise fine. A double room for two costs E£26; for one person the cost is E£21. Room rates do not include the 21% for taxes and service.

The *Mina Palace Hotel* (tel 382074) is on the Corniche, north of Luxor Temple and near the landing for local ferries to the west bank. It has singles/doubles with air-con and private bathrooms for E£26/30. In summer, or when the hotel isn't full, rooms may be available for up to 50% less. Most rooms have Nile views.

The *Savoy Hotel* is also on the Corniche. It looks scruffy on the outside, but the bungalow rooms around the main building are quite pleasant. Bungalows are in the upper-middle price range, while the rooms without air-con in the main building fall in the middle range. The bungalows cost about E£62 for a single and E£82 for a double; main building rooms, which are older than the bungalows, cost from about E£26 to E£37.

The *Windsor Hotel* (tel 384306, 382847) is in a small alley just off Sharia Nefertiti. It's a generally excellent 72 room hotel although some of the rooms are a little shoddy and some are decidedly gloomy and dark. Most of the rooms are fully carpeted and have wallpaper, modern tiled bathrooms, TV and air-con. This place is popular with European tour groups. Singles/doubles/suites cost E£45/70/90. No credit cards are accepted.

The 40 room *Philippe Hotel* (tel 382284) is on Sharia Nefertiti, between the Corniche and Sharia al Karnak. It's an upper-middle range hotel with clean, carpeted rooms. All the rooms have powerful air-con and bathrooms with bathtubs, and there are some rooms with balconies. There's a pleasant roof garden with a small bar. Including breakfast a double room costs about E£70 and reservations are recommended.

Next door to the Philippe is the relatively new *Nile Hotel* (tel 382859), which has 50 double rooms of varying quality. There seems to be two hotels in the one building and the better, slightly pricier rooms are towards the front of the building. Most of these rooms have balconies, powerful air-con and bathrooms with bathtubs. Singles/doubles cost about E£25/35, with a few price differences depending on the room. In the future, as this hotel becomes increasingly popular with groups, reservations will probably be needed.

West Bank On the west bank, *Pharaoh's Hotel* is the only middle-range place to stay. It's near the Antiquities Office and is the newest and best hotel in the area. There are 14 rooms, most with air-con or strong overhead fans, wallpaper and tiled floors. Three of the rooms have private bathrooms.

There's a small restaurant and bright flower garden in front. The restaurant is popular with a few tour groups and is especially renowned for its sun-baked bread. Single/double/triple rooms cost E£20/40/60.

Places to Stay – top end
The hotels in this price range start at about E£70 for a single room or possibly higher because rates are linked to international standards and exchange rate fluctuations.

The *Mövenpick Hotel Jolie Ville* is on Crocodile Island, four km from town. It's a Swiss-managed place with a swimming pool, tennis courts and sailboats. The pool is open to the public for E£5. There are 320 modern, well-appointed rooms set out in bungalow-style amidst tropical and semitropical gardens. Singles/doubles cost US$84/109.

A shuttle bus runs between the Jolie Ville and the Winter Palace hotels. You can also take a taxi into town for E£3.50 (officially set rate) or the hotel motorboat for free. The boat departs from the hotel dock five times daily between 7.30 am and 4 pm.

The *ETAP Hotel* (tel 382166) is a four star place managed by a French-Egyptian company. The lobby is a nice cool place to hang out. Nonresidents can go to the disco for E£5, including drinks, and use the swimming pool for E£5. Single rooms cost E£75 and doubles cost E£90.

The *Winter Palace & New Winter Palace* (tel 382222) on the Corniche are attached. The new side is not nearly as interesting and romantic as the old, which was built to attract the aristocracy of Europe. Rooms cost over US$100, and there's a swimming pool, table-tennis tables and a tennis court. The pool is open to the public for E£10.

The *Luxor Wena Hotel* (tel 382405, 382769) on Sharia al Karnak faces Luxor Temple. It's recently been extensively renovated and upgraded and as a result it's now much more expensive, with rooms from US$49 for doubles. There's a swimming pool and a variety of restaurants.

Places to Eat

The *New Karnak Restaurant* is next to the New Karnak Hotel. Although the portions are small, the food is good and cheap. You can eat chicken for E£1.50, rice and salads for 50 pt, or spaghetti with a tablespoon of sauce for 75 pt – all to the sounds of '50s and '60s American rock 'n' roll music. The menu includes several other dishes such as *molochia* (spelt 'molokhiyya' in this book), but the restaurant often seems out of these. Also, don't get your hopes up about the chicken soup – not a chunk of chicken in sight. Try the Turkish coffee.

Limpy's gives you more food for almost the same prices as the New Karnak. Sitting outside in front of the restaurant gives you a ringside view of the noisy stream of people, hantours, donkey carts, cars and buses. When the outside kebab grill is fired up full blast, you get to watch the action through a haze of shish kebab smoke. It's quite popular with travellers and well-fed flies. A plate of kebab costs about E£3.50; fish costs E£3.50. Try either dish with tahina. It faces the train station; you'll see the sign and, sometimes, hear the blaring rock music.

The *Salt & Bread Cafeteria* is on your left as you leave the train station. They serve many entrees, including kebab, pigeon and chicken. A full meal costs about E£4 or E£5. Service is good.

Next to the Ramoza Hotel is a place to avoid – the *El Hattey Restaurant*. I felt sorry for this place because it was without customers every time I passed by. I went there and discovered why. I tried their so-called speciality – Tagen el Hattey 'Special' – for E£3.50; it was a bland stew that needed generous amounts of salt and pepper to make it edible.

The *Mensa Restaurant*, on Sharia al Mahattit, has cheap basic food. Dishes include chicken, pigeon stuffed with rice, sandwiches, and chicken with French fries and mixed vegetables. You can have almost a full meal for under E£3.

There is a juice stand on Sharia al Mahattit, opposite the GPO. It has great freshly squeezed drinks, but bring your own glass or paper cup. This street also has a number of good sandwich stands and other cheap eats possibilities.

The *Mina Palace Hotel*, on the Corniche, has a good restaurant which serves cheap grilled fish, rice pilaf, chicken and spaghetti. A full meal will cost about E£5.

The *Savoy Hotel* also has a restaurant. You can sit on the outside terrace overlooking the garden and the Nile and have a delicious meal of Egyptian goulash (I'm not quite sure what it's supposed to be!), fish or chicken for E£8 to E£10.

The *Amoun Restaurant*, on Sharia al Karnak, serves Oriental kebab, chicken, fish and various rice and vegetable dishes for E£3 per meal.

The ETAP Hotel has a snack bar and a coffee shop, named *Le Champollion* after the brilliant French Egyptologist who 'broke' the code of the Rosetta Stone. It's a pleasant, cool place to retreat for lunch. You can get spaghetti and salad for E£8.50, sandwiches from E£2 right up to to E£10 for a club sandwich, omelettes for E£5 to E£6 and ice cream for E£4. One traveller reported that even the lettuce in his salad was microwaved but they do make very good cappuccinos.

The *Marhaba Restaurant* is an Oriental-style dining room on the roof of the Tourist Bazaar building on Sharia al Karnak, near Luxor Temple. This place commands great views of the river. It serves entrees of kufta, kebab, pigeon and Nile perch for E£6.50 each. Heaps of rice is served with almost every dish. Don't joke with the waiter about there not being enough rice – or, as he did with me, he'll dump a trayful of rice on your plate and smother whatever you were trying to eat. The only dishes I can recommend here are the shakshouka and moussaka.

When it's hot, the windows stay closed for the restaurant's meagre air-con. As the sun filters through yellow glazed windows, the entire restaurant becomes a hothouse, perfect for growing tropical plants but unbearable for eating.

Restaurant Abu Hager is on Sharia Abdel el Moneim el Adasi, just past Sharia Mohammed Farid. It serves only shish kebab and kufta and seems to be popular with Egyptians who work in tourism-related businesses. A filling meal averages about E£5 to E£6.

For a truly decadent treat, dive into the relatively pricey buffet (E£25) at the *Mövenpick Hotel Jolie Ville*. A variety of superbly made international and typical Egyptian dishes are served, including curried chicken, torshi, fuul and great dips such as tahina and hoummos.

Entertainment
The *Mövenpick Hotel Jolie Ville* presents a quite extravagant floor show. For E£33 they will dress you up in a galabiyya, take you for a felucca ride at sunset, introduce you to 'peasants', and then feed and entertain you in a tent by the Nile.

The *ETAP and Winter Palace* hotels have folkloric and belly dance performances as well as discos.

Activities
The best thing to do in Luxor in the late afternoon or early evening is to relax aboard a felucca. Local feluccas cruise the river throughout the day and cost around E£3 per person per hour or E£10 per boat per hour.

An enjoyable outing is the trip upriver to Banana Island. The tiny isle, dotted with palms, is about five km from Luxor and the trip takes two to three hours. Plan it in such a way that you're on your way back in time to watch a brilliant Nile sunset from the boat.

Getting There & Away
Air EgyptAir flies daily between Cairo, Luxor and Aswan. A one-way ticket to Luxor from Cairo costs E£135. There are frequent daily departures.

There are also daily flights from Luxor to the following places (prices shown are one way): Aswan, Abu Simbel (E£135); the New Valley (Kharga, not always daily flights); Hurghada (E£60); Sharm el Shaykh (E£145); and St Catherine's Monastery (E£200).

Bus From Cairo, there's a comfortable air-con bus for Luxor that departs at 5.30 am from Midan Ahmed Hilmi, behind Ramses Station. The fare costs E£25 and the trip takes from nine to 11 hours. Buy the ticket at least a day in advance. In Luxor, the inter-city buses leave from in front of the Horus Hotel on Sharia al Karnak.

From Luxor to Hurghada, on the Red Sea coast, there are air-con buses at 10.30 am and 4 pm. The five hour trip costs E£10. There is a bus at 7 am but it is not air-conditioned and costs E£6.25. A traveller who took this bus in July reported that it was better to sit on the left side in order to avoid the sun.

From Luxor to Aswan, there are buses at 6, 8 and 10 am, 12 noon, and 1 and 2 pm. The trip takes four hours and costs E£3.50.

From Luxor to Cairo, there's one bus daily at 7 pm with video and air-con. The trip costs E£25 and takes about nine to 11 hours. You can buy the ticket the same day, but during the peak season, I suggest that you try to buy it at least one day in advance. I say 'try' because sometimes the ticket seller is somewhat reluctant to sell tickets in advance.

Train Sleeper cars between Cairo, Luxor and Aswan range from the luxurious 1st class deluxe (wagons-lits) to the standard, but still adequate, regular sleepers.

The wagon-lit fare between Cairo and Luxor is E£140 per person for a two person compartment. Each compartment has a sink with hot running water, piped-in music, a small clothes closet and adequate lighting. Dinner and breakfast are served directly to your compartment.

If you're craving a bit of comfort, then this is an extremely civilised way to travel although it actually costs more than flying. There are daily departures for Luxor from Cairo at 7 and 7.35 pm; and from Aswan at 2 and 5.45 pm. Refer to the Egypt Getting Around chapter for the wagon-lit schedule.

Other much less expensive overnight trains, some with sleeper compartments, also depart Cairo daily for Luxor and Aswan and vice versa. Reservations are needed for all sleeper cars.

Apparently, reservations for the economy sleepers are quite hard to come by because I have never met a traveller who managed to get a ticket.

Obtaining accurate fares for ordinary sleepers also seems to be a bit of a problem. In Cairo, Luxor and Aswan, the stationmasters and tourist offices gave me radically different fares for the same sleeper arrangements. Cairo to Luxor fares would seem to be about E£2.60 in 3rd class, E£6 in 2nd class ordinary, E£12.50 in 2nd class with air-con, E£25 in a 2nd class sleeper, E£24 in 1st class air-con and E£40 in a 1st class sleeper. If you do manage to travel on an ordinary sleeper, please let us know about your trip.

From Luxor to Aswan there are several trains daily, starting from 4.10 am; most of these originate in Cairo. From Luxor to Cairo there are trains around the clock.

As schedules do change from time to time, it is advisable to consult the posted timetables in Luxor, Aswan and Cairo train stations for the latest schedules. Although original departures are usually on time the trains often seem to run late by the time they complete the journey. Even the wagon-lit trains may be an hour or two late and the ordinary trains may run much later.

Taxi The service taxi station is on Sharia al Karnak, one block inland from the Luxor Museum.

A service taxi to Aswan costs E£4.50 and takes three hours; to Esna it costs E£1 and takes 45 minutes; to Edfu it costs E£2.50 for the two hour trip; and to Qena E£1.25.

You can hire a special taxi for E£75 to take you and seven others to Aswan, with stops en route at Esna, Edfu and Kom Ombo.

Felucca Lonely Planet author Hugh Finlay, who is renowned for going 'against the current', took a felucca between Luxor and Aswan:

A trip to Egypt would not be complete without a ride in a felucca – the traditional lateen-rigged boats that ply the waters of the Nile. Once upon a time they were the most important form of transport and communication in the country and were used for ferrying produce and goods up and down the river. They still carry a certain amount of local produce but these days the most lucrative cargo is tourists out to experience a bit of life on the river.

The ideal trip is the three day journey from Aswan to Luxor. We foolishly, however, tried to do it in the opposite direction. After four consecutive days of light winds that died out by 11 am, *and* with the current against us, we had covered less than half the distance to Aswan. If you're travelling downstream from Aswan to Luxor, then you can still make progress even if the wind dies out.

A quick check around the travellers' hangouts will usually turn up plenty of people wanting to make the trip, so getting a group together should be no problem. Obviously, the more people there are, the cheaper it's going to be. Remember, though, that conditions on the feluccas are fairly cramped so with any more than about six people you'll spend more time trying to keep out of each other's way than you will enjoying the ride.

There is no shortage of boats ready to take you – the cries of 'Hello, boat?' from the water's edge will follow you as you walk along the waterfront. Find a boat and haggle ruthlessly. Get firm answers from the owner as to what you are getting. Make sure he has plenty of blankets, as the nights are freezing, and that he will only be using bottled water for cooking. If you can arrange to visit a few small villages en route so much the better – he may well invite you to his own village to meet his family and have a meal.

Once you finally get out on the water, sit back, relax and enjoy the quiet side of Egypt as you drift slowly past mud-brick villages, young girls tending flocks of sheep on the banks and women washing clothes and collecting water in enormous earthenware pots (the men will be off somewhere else, busily drinking tea and talking). All the while, as you sail peacefully along, the barren hills of the desert beyond the water's edge and the cultivated fields are a reminder of how much these people of Upper Egypt depend on the Nile for their livelihood.

Hugh Finlay

Cruise Ship More than 55 boats offer Nile cruises between Luxor and Aswan, lasting for three to five nights. There are also 11 different night cruises to Luxor which start in Cairo.

The average rates range from E£130 to E£316 per day on a four star boat; and E£351 to E£572 per day on a five star boat (possibly even more during Christmas).

The Hilton, Sheraton, Club Med and Marriott all have luxurious floating hotels which travel the Nile.

Many of the boats, even the more inexpensive ones, are booked up several months in advance.

Getting Around

Airport Transport The airport (tel 82306) is seven km east of Luxor and the official price for a taxi between there and town is E£5 per car load.

Felucca There are, of course, a multitude of feluccas to take you on short trips or day tours from Luxor. They leave from various points all along the riverside. See the Activities section earlier in this chapter for more information.

Ferry Three ferries and a car ferry cross over to the Theban necropolis on Luxor's west bank. The boat landing near Luxor Temple is for the local ferry, which costs only 25 pt plus 10 pt for bicycles. It takes you to the west bank town landing, where there are plenty of service taxis and mini-buses, but no tickets to the monuments. If you take the road inland for three km you'll come to the Antiquities Office, where students can purchase discount tickets to the sites. (See the West Bank section earlier in this chapter.)

The other two ferries are 'tourist' boats which drop you off at the 'tourist' landing, about one km north of the town landing. The tourist ferries cost 50 pt but will not take bicycles. They are, however, quicker and take you to the ticket kiosk. The tourist ferry landings are in front of the Savoy and the Winter Palace hotels.

Bicycle Boulos' Bicycles is at 52 Sharia al Mahattit, next to a shoe store. There are many other bicycle rental places around town, all with similar prices. Bicycle rental typically costs E£5 or E£6 per day. They often ask you to leave your passport or student identification card.

Most hotels, including the ETAP and the Windsor, will rent bicycles. Their

bicycles are newer and in better condition but cost E£10 a day. It's possible to rent children's bicycles if you enquire. Bicycles can also be rented on the west bank, near the public ferry landing, but the choice of bicycle is better in the town itself.

Hantour or Caleche For about E£3 per hour you can get around town by horse and carriage. It's the most common means of transportation in Luxor. Rates are, of course, subject to haggling, squabbling and, sometimes, screaming!

AROUND LUXOR
An increasingly popular side-trip from Luxor is a visit to the supposedly typical village of Armant, on the west bank slightly south of Thebes. You can go by service taxi for 50 pt or, if you're feeling a bit athletic, by bicycle. I have not yet visited this village, but I met a few travellers who did and enjoyed it.

The Nile Valley – Esna to Abu Simbel

Following the death of Alexander the Great his huge empire was divided between his Macedonian generals. For 300 years the Greek-speaking Ptolemies ruled Egypt in the guise of Pharaohs, respecting the traditions and religion of the Egyptians and setting an example to the Romans who succeeded them.

Their centre of power tied them to Alexandria and the coast but they also pushed their way south, extending Greco-Roman power into Nubia through their politically sensible policy of assimilation rather than subjugation.

In Upper Egypt they raised temples in honour of the local gods, building them in grand Pharaonic style to appease the priesthood and earn the trust of the people. Somehow though these archaic imitations lost something in the translation; in many ways they were stilted, unimaginative edifices lacking the artistic brilliance that marked the truly Egyptian constructions they copied.

In southern Upper Egypt, south of Luxor, the major Greco-Roman works were a series of riverside temples at Esna, Edfu, Kom Ombo and Philae, admirable as much for their location as their actual artistic or architectural merit.

Beyond Edfu the ribbon of cultivation on the east bank gives way to the Eastern (Arabian) Desert. At Silsileh, 145 km south of Luxor, the Nile passes through a gorge, once thought to mark a cataract. In this area, there are Early Dynastic and New Kingdom ruins, including Elephantine and Abu Simbel; there's also the city of Aswan, the great High Dam and Lake Nasser, which mark the end of Egypt proper, for beyond them lie the forbidding, infertile desert lands of Nubia and the border with Sudan.

ESNA

The Greco-Roman Temple of Khnum is the main attraction of Esna, a small, busy farming town on the west bank of the Nile, 54 km south of Luxor. All that actually remains of the temple is the well-preserved Great Hypostyle Hall built during the reign of the Roman emperor Claudius. This sits, rather incongruously, in its huge excavation pit amongst the houses and narrow alleyways in the middle of town.

Dedicated to Khnum, the ram-headed creator-god who fashioned humankind on his potter's wheel, the temple was begun by Ptolemy VI and built over the ruins of earlier temples. The hall, as it stands today, was built later; it was excavated from the silt that had accumulated through centuries of annual Nile floods and is about nine metres below the modern street level.

The intact roof of the hall is supported by 24 columns decorated with a series of

Khnum

249

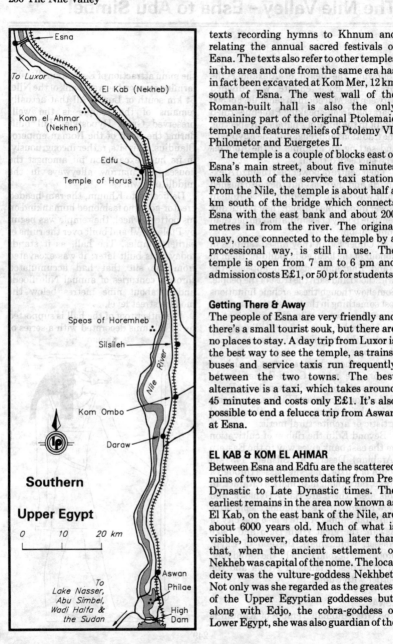

Southern

Upper Egypt

0   10   20 km

To Luxor

Esna

El Kab (Nekheb)

Kom el Ahmar (Nekhen)

Edfu

Temple of Horus

Speos of Horemheb

Silsileh

Nile River

Kom Ombo

Daraw

Aswan

Philae

High Dam

To Lake Nasser, Abu Simbel, Wadi Halfa & the Sudan

texts recording hymns to Khnum and relating the annual sacred festivals of Esna. The texts also refer to other temples in the area and one from the same era has in fact been excavated at Kom Mer, 12 km south of Esna. The west wall of the Roman-built hall is also the only remaining part of the original Ptolemaic temple and features reliefs of Ptolemy VI, Philometor and Euergetes II.

The temple is a couple of blocks east of Esna's main street, about five minutes walk south of the service taxi station. From the Nile, the temple is about half a km south of the bridge which connects Esna with the east bank and about 200 metres in from the river. The original quay, once connected to the temple by a processional way, is still in use. The temple is open from 7 am to 6 pm and admission costs E£1, or 50 pt for students.

Getting There & Away

The people of Esna are very friendly and there's a small tourist souk, but there are no places to stay. A day trip from Luxor is the best way to see the temple, as trains, buses and service taxis run frequently between the two towns. The best alternative is a taxi, which takes around 45 minutes and costs only E£1. It's also possible to end a felucca trip from Aswan at Esna.

EL KAB & KOM EL AHMAR

Between Esna and Edfu are the scattered ruins of two settlements dating from Pre-Dynastic to Late Dynastic times. The earliest remains in the area now known as El Kab, on the east bank of the Nile, are about 6000 years old. Much of what is visible, however, dates from later than that, when the ancient settlement of Nekheb was capital of the nome. The local deity was the vulture-goddess Nekhbet. Not only was she regarded as the greatest of the Upper Egyptian goddesses but, along with Edjo, the cobra-goddess of Lower Egypt, she was also guardian of the

Pharaohs and one of the deities associated with royal and divine births.

The town of Nekheb was enclosed by massive mud-brick walls and still contains the remains of a Roman temple, a sacred lake and cemeteries, and the ruins of the main temple of Nekhbet with its several pylons, hypostyle hall and birth-house. The temple was probably begun before 2700 BC but was enlarged considerably by 18th to 30th dynasty Pharaohs including Tuthmosis III, Amenophis II and the Ramessids.

A few km east of the town enclosure are three desert temples. At the entrance to Wadi Hellal is the rock-hewn Ptolemaic Sanctuary of Sheshmetet. To the south-east of that is a chapel built during the reign of Ramses II, restored under the Ptolemies and dedicated to a number of deities. About 3½ km from Nekheb is the Temple of Hathor and Nekhbet; it was built by Tuthmosis IV and Amenophis III. North of Nekheb are a number of rockcut tombs with fine reliefs.

On the opposite side of the river, the remains of the ancient town of Nekhen, which pre-dated Nekheb as capital of the nome, stretch for about three km along the edge of the desert. Now known as Kom el Ahmar, or 'the red mound', the area features the ruins of Pre-Dynastic settlements and cemeteries, and in the nearby wadis there are several Middle and New Kingdom tombs. The local god was Nekheny, a falcon with two long plumes on his head, who was later associated with Horus.

El Kab and Kom el Ahmar are 26 km south of Esna and north of Edfu.

EDFU

The largest and most completely preserved Pharaonic, albeit Greek-built, temple in Egypt is the extraordinary Temple of Horus at Edfu. One of the last great Egyptian attempts at monument building on a grand scale, the structure dominates this west bank riverside town, 53 km south of Esna. The town and temple were established on a rise, above the broad river valley around them, and so escaped the annual Nile inundation which contributed to the ruination of so many other buildings of antiquity. Edfu, a sugar and pottery centre, is also a very friendly place – even though it seems that no-one in town, except the pharmacist, speaks English.

Temple of Horus

Construction of this huge complex began under Ptolemy III Euergetes I in 237 BC and was completed nearly 200 years later during the reign of Ptolemy XIII (the father of Cleopatra) in the 1st century BC. In conception and design it follows the traditions of authentic Pharaonic architecture, with the same general plan, scale and ornamentation, right down to the 'Egyptian' attire worn by the Greek kings depicted in the temple's reliefs. Though it is much newer than the temples of Karnak, Luxor and Abydos, its excellent state of preservation fills in a lot of historical gaps because it is, in effect, a 2000 year old replica of an architectural style that was already archaic during Ptolemaic times.

Horus

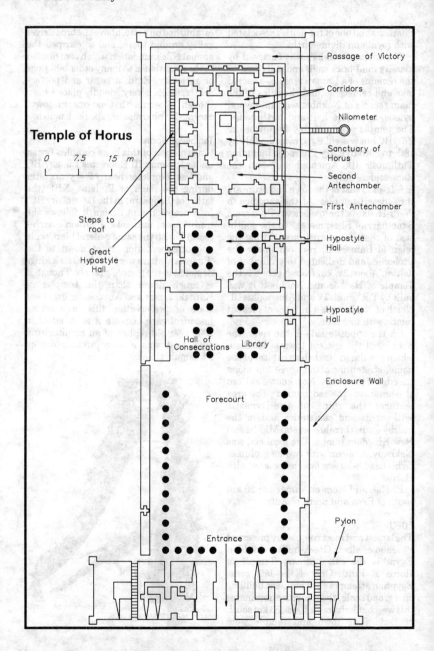

Temple of Horus

0 7.5 15 m

Passage of Victory

Corridors

Nilometer

Sanctuary of Horus

Second Antechamber

First Antechamber

Steps to roof

Great Hypostyle Hall

Hypostyle Hall

Hypostyle Hall

Hall of Consecrations

Library

Enclosure Wall

Forecourt

Pylon

Entrance

Being a copy it lacks artistic spontaneity. Where the Greek influence does penetrate, however, it produces a strangely graceful effect, which is most obvious in the fine line of the columns.

Dedicated to Horus, the falcon-headed son of Osiris, who avenged his father's murder by slaying his uncle Seth, the temple was built on the site where, according to legend, the two gods met in deadly combat. Ancient festivals at Edfu celebrated the divine birth of Horus and the living king (as all Pharaohs were believed to be incarnations of the falcon-god), as well as the victory of Horus over Seth and the yearly conjugal visit of the goddess Hathor. Another ritual was the annual recoronation of the Pharaoh to symbolise his oneness with Horus. During the proceedings, a live falcon was taken from the sacred aviary, crowned in the central court and placed in an inner chamber, where it 'reigned' in the dark for a year as the living symbol of Horus. As with the image of Hathor at Dendara, an image of Horus was taken each year to the roof of the temple for a rejuvenating sun bath.

Excavation of the temple from beneath sand, rubble and part of the village of Edfu, which had been built on its roof, was started by Auguste Mariette in the mid-19th century. The entrance to the temple is through a massive 36 metre high pylon guarded by a huge and splendid granite falcon and decorated with colossal reliefs of Pharaoh Ptolemy XIII pulling the hair of his enemies while Horus and Hathor look on. Beyond the pylon is a court surrounded on three sides by a colonnade of 32 columns covered in reliefs.

Before you enter the temple proper, through the 12 enormous columns of the first of two hypostyle halls, check out the areas on either side. On your left is the Hall of Consecrations where, according to the wall inscriptions, Horus poured sacred water on the king; on your right is the so-called Library, which features a list of books and a relief of Seshat, the goddess of

Osiris

writing. On either side of the second hall are doorways leading into the narrow Passage of Victory, which runs between the temple and its massive protective enclosure walls.

Once through the magnificent Great Hypostyle Hall there are two antechambers, the first of which has a staircase of 242 steps leading up to the rooftop and a fantastic view of the Nile and surrounding fields. You may have to pay the guard a bit of baksheesh if you want to go up because the stairs are usually closed.

The second chamber, which is beautifully decorated with a variety of scenes, leads to the Sanctuary of Horus, where the live falcon, the god and his wife reigned and received offerings. Around the sanctuary, there are a number of smaller chambers with fine reliefs and, off the Passage of Victory, a staircase leads down and passes under the outer wall of the temple to a Nilometer. The Temple of Horus is open from 7 am to 6 pm and admission costs E£2, or E£1 for students.

Places to Stay & Eat

The *El Medina Hotel*, just off the main square, costs E£6 a double. There is no hot water and the cold water is turned off after 9 pm, but you can ask the owner or his family, who live on the 1st floor, to turn it back on. From the top floor you can see something different every day, as most of the houses in town don't seem to have roofs, just lots of baskets. Breakfast costs 75 pt and the owner will gladly serve tea and biscuits in your room.

As for meals, you can buy canned goods, fruit and vegetables in the souk. The only places in town where you can get a Stella beer are at the train station across the river or at the cafeteria by the temple.

Getting There & Away

Trains, buses and service taxis stop frequently in Edfu. However, the train station is on the east bank of the Nile, about four km from town, and the buses which travel between Luxor and Aswan are usually so crowded by the time they get to Edfu that they're not worth the effort. Service taxis are again the best option. From Esna, the trip takes about an hour and costs E£1.50, direct taxis from Luxor take about two hours and cost E£2.50 and from Aswan they take 1½ hours and cost E£1.50. Feluccas will also stop at Edfu on their way north from Aswan. Very patient travellers who prefer to travel against the current can get a felucca heading south.

SILSILEH

At Silsileh, about 42 km south of Edfu, the Nile narrows considerably to pass between steep sandstone cliffs which are cluttered with ancient rock stelae and graffiti. Known in Pharaonic times as Khenu, which means 'the place of rowing', the gorge also marks the change from limestone to sandstone in the bedrock of Egypt. The local Silsileh quarries were worked by thousands of men throughout the New Kingdom and Greco-Roman

periods to provide the sandstone used in temple building.

On the west bank of the river is the Speos of Horemheb, a rock-hewn chapel dedicated to Pharaoh Horemheb and seven deities, including the local god Sobek.

KOM OMBO

The fertile, irrigated sugar cane and corn fields around Kom Ombo, 60 km south of Edfu, support not only the original community of fellahin but also a large population of Nubians displaced from their own lands by the encroaching waters of Lake Nasser. It's a pleasant little place easily accessible en route between Aswan and Luxor but possibly best visited on a day trip from Aswan, which is 40 km to the south.

In ancient times Kom Ombo was strategically important as a trading town on the great caravan route from Nubia and was the meeting place of the routes from the gold mines of the Eastern Desert and the Red Sea. During the Ptolemaic period it served as the capital of the Ombite nome, and elephants were brought up from Africa to Kom Ombo to train with the armies to defend the region. The main attraction these days, however, is the unique riverside Temple of Kom Ombo, about four km from the centre of town.

Temple of Kom Ombo

Kom Ombo or, more precisely, the dual Temple of Sobek and Haroeris, stands on a promontory at a bend in the Nile, where in ancient times sacred crocodiles basked in the sun on the river bank. Although substantially ruined by the changing tides of the river and by later builders who used many of its stones for new buildings, Kom Ombo is, nevertheless, a stunning sight.

It is also unusual in that, architecturally, everything is doubled and perfectly symmetrical along the main axis of the temple. There are twin entrances, twin courts, twin colonnades, twin hypostyle halls, twin sanctuaries and, in keeping

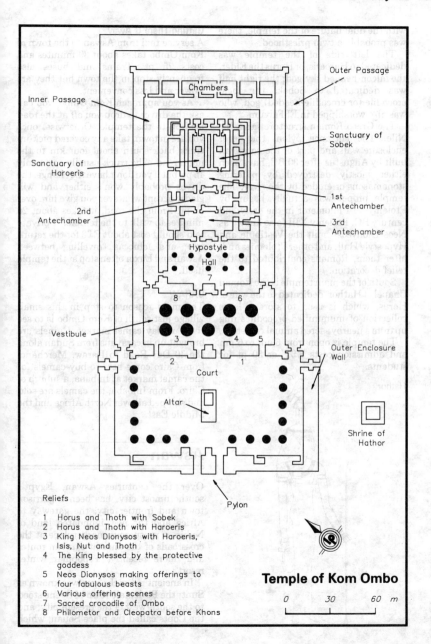

Reliefs

1 Horus and Thoth with Sobek
2 Horus and Thoth with Haroeris
3 King Neos Dionysos with Haroeris, Isis, Nut and Thoth
4 The King blessed by the protective goddess
5 Neos Dionysos making offerings to four fabulous beasts
6 Various offering scenes
7 Sacred crocodile of Ombo
8 Philometor and Cleopatra before Khons

Temple of Kom Ombo

0   30   60 m

with the dual nature of the temple, there was probably a twin priesthood.

The left side of the temple was dedicated to Haroeris, or Horus the Elder, the falcon-headed sky-god; the right half was dedicated to Sobek, the local crocodile (or crocodile-headed) god, who was also worshipped in El Faiyum.

The Greco-Roman structure faces the Nile. The entrance pylon, the outer enclosure wall and part of the court, all built by Augustus after 30 BC, have been either mostly destroyed by pilfering stonemasons or eroded by the river. The temple proper was actually begun by Ptolemy VI Philometor in the early 2nd century BC; Ptolemy XIII (also known as Neos Dionysos) built the Vestibule and Hypostyle Hall; and other Ptolemies and, after them, Romans contributed to the relief decoration.

South of the main temple is the Roman Chapel of Hathor, dedicated to the wife of Horus, which is used to store a large collection of mummified crocodiles dug up from a nearby sacred animal cemetery.

The temple is open from 6 am to 6 pm and admission costs E£1, or 50 pt for students.

Hathor

Getting There & Away

A service taxi from Aswan to the town of Kom Ombo takes about 30 minutes and costs 75 pt. Trains and buses also frequently stop in the town but they are slower and less convenient.

As you approach Kom Ombo, you can ask the driver to drop you off at the road leading to the temple. Otherwise, once you are in town, take any covered pick-up truck back south about four km to the main road. The truck usually costs only 15 pt, but if you don't have the change, the driver probably won't either and will gladly accept whatever you give him over 15 pt. From the road, it takes about 20 minutes to walk to the temple. A private taxi should cost about E£3 for the return trip; and feluccas travelling between Aswan and Luxor often stop at the temple itself.

DARAW

The main reason to stop in this small village just south of Kom Ombo is to see the Tuesday camel market. Camels are brought up in caravans from Sudan along the 40 Day Road to Daraw. Merchants from Cairo come here to buy camels for the camel market at Imbaba, a suburb of Cairo. From Imbaba, the camels are sold and shipped all over North Africa and the Middle East.

Aswan

Over the centuries Aswan, Egypt's southernmost city, has been a garrison town and frontier city, the gateway to Africa and the now inundated land of Nubia, a prosperous marketplace at the crossroads of the ancient caravan routes and, more recently, a popular winter resort.

In ancient times the area was known as Sunt; the Ptolemaic town of Syene stood to the south-west of the present city; and the Copts called the place Souan, which

Top: Overlooking Kitchener's Island, Aswan (TW)
Bottom: Feluccas on the Nile, Aswan (SW)

Top: Temple of Philae, near Aswan (SW)
Left: Reliefs in the Temple of Kom Ombo (GB)
Right: Statues of Ramses II, Abu Simbel (GB)

means 'trade', from which the Arabic 'Aswan' is derived.

The main town and temple area of Sunt was actually on the southern end of the island called Yebu, which means both 'elephant' and 'ivory', and which the Greeks later renamed Elephantine Island. A natural fortress, protected as it was by the turbulent river, Aswan was then capital of the first Upper Egyptian nome and a base for military expeditions into Nubia, the Sudan and Ethiopia. From those foreign parts, right up into Islamic times, the city was visited by the great caravans of camels and elephants laden with slaves, gold, ivory, spices, cloth and other exotic wares.

Pharaonic and Ptolemaic leaders took their turn through history to guard the southern reaches of Egypt from the customary routes of invasion; their fleets patrolled the river as far as the Second Cataract at Wadi Halfa and their troops penetrated several hundred km into the Sudan. Aswan was also, to a certain extent, the 'Siberia' of the Roman Empire, one of those far-flung garrisons where troublesome generals were sent to protect the interests of the emperor while staying out of the Forum.

The modern town of Aswan, which is the perfect place for a break from the rigours of travelling in Egypt, lies at the northern end of the First Cataract, on the east bank of the Nile opposite Elephantine Island.

Although its ancient temples and ruins are not as outstanding as others in the country, Aswan does have a few things to offer the traveller, one of which is the town's superb location on the river. The Nile is magically beautiful here as it flows down from the great dams and around the giant granite boulders and palm-studded islands that protrude from the cascading rapids of the First Cataract. The Corniche is one of the most attractive of the Nile boulevards.

So, while you can visit Pharaonic, Greco-Roman, Coptic, Islamic and modern monuments, an excellent museum, superb botanical gardens, the massive High Dam, Lake Nasser and one of the most fascinating souks outside Cairo, by far the best thing to do in Aswan is sit by the Nile and watch the feluccas gliding by at sunset.

The best time to visit Aswan and, if possible, to continue into the Sudan, is in winter, when the days are warm and dry, with an average temperature of about 26°C. In summer, the temperatures are around 38°C to 45°C and it's too hot to do anything other than just sit by a fan and swat flies or stay in a swimming pool.

Orientation

It's quite easy to find your way around Aswan because there are only three main avenues and most of the city is along the Nile or parallel to it. The train station is at the north end of town, only three blocks east of the river and its boulevard, the Corniche el Nil.

The street which runs north-south in front of the station is Sharia al Souk (also occasionally signposted as Sharia Saad Zaghloul), Aswan's splendid market street, where the souks overflow with colourful and aromatic wares and where merchants and traders from all over the region jostle and bargain with each other.

One block in from the Nile is Sharia Abtal el Tahrir where you'll find the youth hostel, a few hotels and some pricey tourist souks. On the Corniche itself are most of Aswan's banks, government buildings, travel agencies, restaurants and top hotels, and from there you can see the rock tombs on the west bank, as well as the islands of Elephantine (the larger one) and Kitchener.

Information

The tourist office is two blocks north of the Abu Simbel Hotel, which is one street in from the Corniche. The staff can give you official prices for taxis and felucca trips, but lower prices are usually obtainable

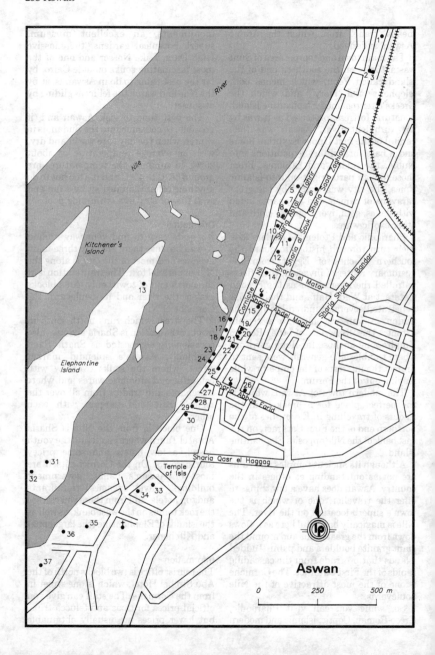

Aswan

0   250   500 m

1	Mena Hotel
2	Rosewan Hotel
3	Hotel El Saffa
4	Restaurants
5	Youth Hostel
6	El Amin Hotel
7	Tourist Office
8	Restaurant Carré Ace
9	Ramses Hotel
10	Abu Simbel Hotel
11	Cleopatra Hotel
12	Bus Station
13	Aswan Oberoi Hotel
14	GPO
15	Happi Hotel
16	Isis Hotel
17	Tourist Map Kiosk
18	Saladin Restaurant
19	El Salam Hotel
20	Hathor Hotel
21	Restaurant Maxime's
22	Horus Hotel
23	Aswan Moon Restaurant
24	Monalisa Restaurant
25	Philae Hotel
26	Abou Shelib Hotel
27	El Nile Restaurant
28	Hotel Continental
29	Thomas Cook
30	Police Station
31	Aswan Museum
32	Temple of Khnum
33	EgyptAir
34	Telephone Office
35	Hotel Pullman Cataract
36	New Cataract Hotel
37	Kalabsha Hotel

with some haggling. The main information counter is manned by Farag Gomaa, a helpful guy who seems to be quite knowledgeable about Egyptology. Gomaa is also a good photographer. For those travellers interested, he offers some tips on which photographic subjects to avoid in Egypt. Official government policy, which Gomaa can explain in greater detail, is to avoid certain subjects – such as anything military.

The office is open Sunday to Thursday from 9 am to 2 pm and 6 to 8 pm; and on Friday from 10 am to 12 noon and 6 to 8 pm. During Ramadan hours can be somewhat erratic.

Post & Telecommunications The GPO is also on the Corniche, adjacent to the municipal swimming pool and opposite the Police Rowing Club. There's another post office on the corner of Sharia Abtal el Tahrir and Sharia Salah al Deen, about a block east of the Horus Hotel, but not many foreigners seem to use this branch.

International telephone calls can be made from the telephone office, which is on the Corniche towards the southern end of town, just past the EgyptAir office. Current rates are clearly posted on signs above the telephone booths. Write the number, city and country on a slip of paper and hand it over the counter to the operator who places international calls.

There's also a post office stamp counter here that is occasionally open.

A fax machine is available at the Oberoi Hotel. Between 8 pm and 8 am, you can fax a one page message to the USA for about E£6.

Film Film is available at a few stores in Aswan. At Photo Sabry on the Corniche, it takes about one to two days to develop colour prints for 50 pt each. Kodacolor 100 (24 exposures) costs E£10, 200 (36 exposures) E£12 and 100 (36 exposures) E£12. One hour or overnight processing is also available at a few places.

Sharia al Souk

The exotic atmosphere of Aswan's backstreet souks is definitely one of the highlights of the city. Even though the fabulous caravans no longer pass this way, the colour and activity of these markets and stalls recall those romantic times. Just wander through the small, narrow alleyways off this street and you'll see, hear, smell and, if you want, taste life as it has been for many centuries in these parts. Note that there were too many of these small passageways to show on the Aswan map.

Best of all, you probably won't be hassled by merchants hungry for the tourist buck because most of the market is for the locals. So far just the spice shops and a few souks have succumbed to tourism.

Fatimid Cemetery

Just south of the city's public gardens and over a small hill is a collection of low stone buildings with domed roofs topped by crescents. Some of these early Islamic tombs also feature figures of local holy people, or the more widely revered Sayeida Zeinab, granddaughter of the Prophet.

Unfinished Obelisk

In the desert south of the Aswan train station are the northern quarries, which supplied the ancient Egyptians with most of the hard stone used in pyramids and temples, and a huge discarded obelisk. Three sides of the shaft, which measures nearly 42 metres long, were completed except for the inscriptions and it would have been the largest single piece of stone ever handled if a flaw had not appeared in the granite. So it lies there, where the disappointed stonemasons abandoned it, still partly attached to the parent rock and with no indication of what it was intended for.

The quarries are about one km from town past the Fatimid Cemetery and entry costs 50 pt.

Aswan Cultural Centre

Aswan's world-famous folkloric dance troupe performs here between October and February from 9.30 to 11 pm. Admission is E£3. The centre also presents traditional Upper Egyptian and Nubian music performances and exhibits the instruments used in them. Other exhibits in this two storey centre include a few display cases with material covering Arab-Muslim culture, and a British-sponsored exhibit about Charlie Chaplin.

There's also a library, language centre with courses in English and French, and a computer class with five computers.

Elephantine Island

Perhaps elephants once roamed the banks of the Nile here. They certainly passed through in the great caravans or with various armies, but it is more likely that Aswan's longest inhabited area was named Yebu after the numerous giant grey granite boulders, in the river around the island, which resemble a herd of elephants bathing.

Apart from being Egypt's frontier town, where the island officials were known as 'Keepers of the Gate of the South', Elephantine also produced most of the Pharaohs of the 5th dynasty and was the centre of the cult of the ram-headed Khnum, god of the cataracts and creator of humankind, and his companion goddesses Anukis and Satis.

Excavation of the ancient town, which began at the start of this century, is still going on and the jumbled remains of the fortress and three temples are visible. There's also a small 3rd dynasty step pyramid; a tiny chapel reconstructed from the Temple of Kalabsha, which is just south of the High Dam; and, taking up the entire northern end of the island, the deluxe and incongruous Aswan Oberoi Hotel which, most sensibly, has its own private ferry and a three metre fence around it to keep the tourists in, and away from the local Nubians.

The inhabitants of the three colourful Nubian villages on the west side of Elephantine are friendly and the alleyways are worth exploring.

To get to Elephantine Island you can take a felucca, for 10 pt to 25 pt, from the landing just north of the Cataract Hotel; or catch the Oberoi ferry, though you may not be able to get beyond the hotel compound.

Aswan Museum On the south-east end of the island, overlooking the ruins of the original town and surrounded by an attractive flower and spice garden, this modest little museum houses a collection of antiquities discovered in Aswan and Nubia. Most of the Nubian artefacts were found and rescued before the construction of the old Aswan Dam. The weapons, pottery, utensils, statues, encased mummies and sarcophagi date from Pre-Dynastic to late Roman times and everything is labelled in Arabic and English. The sarcophagus and mummy of a sacred ram, the animal associated with Khnum, dominates the centre of the downstairs mummy room.

The museum is open in winter from Sunday to Thursday between 8 am and 5 pm, and on Friday from 9 am to 1 pm; in summer it's open on the same days from 8.30 am to 5 pm. Admission to the museum and the ruins outside is E£1, or 50 pt for students.

Nilometer Heavenly portents and priestly prophecies aside, the only sure indication in ancient times of the likelihood of a bountiful harvest was that given by the Nilometer. Descending to the water's edge from beneath a sycamore tree near the museum, the rock-hewn shaft of the ancient Nilometer measured the height of the Nile. Although it dates from Pharaonic times, and bears inscriptions and cartouches from the reigns of Amenophis III and Psammetichus II, it was rebuilt by the Romans and restored last century.

When the Nilometer recorded that the level of the river was high it would mean that the approaching annual flood would be heavy and therefore sufficient for the irrigation vital to a good harvest. It also affected the taxation system, for the higher the river, the better the crop season and the more prosperous the fellahin and merchants – and therefore the higher the taxes.

You can enter the Nilometer from the river or down steps from above or just view it from a felucca on the water.

Temple of Khnum Amongst the ruins of the ancient town are the remains of a large temple built by Nectanebo, a 4th century BC Pharaoh, and dedicated to Khnum, the patron of Elephantine and the god who created humankind on his potter's wheel. At the gateway to the temple Ptolemy XI Alexander II, who ruled around 80 BC, is shown worshipping the ram-god. A team of German archaeologists has been excavating and restoring the temple.

Nearby are the remains of a small portion of the Temple of Satis, dedicated to Khnum's goddess daughter. The Temple of Heqaib, an interesting stone shrine honouring a prince of the nome, is also close by. A 6th dynasty official, Heqaib was deified after his death and remained a cult figure for many centuries. A small Ptolemaic temple discovered on the tip of the island has been restored.

Kitchener's Island

One of the most delightful places in Aswan, this island to the west of Elephantine was given to Lord Horatio Kitchener in the 1890s when he was consul-general of Egypt and commander of the Egyptian army. Indulging his passion for beautiful flowers, Kitchener turned the entire island into a botanical garden, importing plants from the Far East, India and other parts of Africa. The gardens, which are perfect for a peaceful stroll, attract an amazing variety of colourfully exotic birds. The hundreds of white ducks in the small out-of-bounds cove at the southern end of the island, however, belong to a biological research station.

There are no ferry services to Kitchener's Island but it's easy enough to hire a felucca for a return trip or incorporate the gardens on a river tour. The price for a felucca is negotiable and starts to come down quickly if you first show that you are interested and then begin to walk away. I hesitate to quote prices because everybody I met seemed to pay a different price, but an average of E£4 per hour seems reasonable. Entry to the island itself costs E£5, however, and this is definitely not reasonable.

Dr Ragab Papyrus Museum

Dr Ragab is well known throughout Egypt for mass producing high quality papyrus paintings. His Aswan papyrus museum/ shop is actually a two storey barge moored to the shore. Beautiful papyrus paintings of various sizes hang from the walls and are displayed in glass cases on both levels. The cheapest painting is comparable in size to the cover of a Lonely Planet book and cost about E£5.

Papyrus painting

Tombs of the Nobles

The high cliffs opposite Aswan, a little north of Kitchener's Island, are honeycombed with the tombs of the princes, governors, 'Keepers of the Gate of the South' and other dignitaries of ancient Yebu. They date from the Old and Middle Kingdoms and although most of them are in a sorry state of repair, there are a few worth visiting.

To get to the west bank tombs, you can either take the ferry from a landing near

the Abu Simbel Hotel for 25 pt or include them on a felucca tour of the river. Admission to the tombs is E£1, or 50 pt for students. Hours are 8 am to 5 pm.

Tombs of Mekhu & Sabni (Nos 25 & 26)

These tombs are of rough 6th dynasty construction. The reliefs in No 26 record a tale of tragedy and triumph. Mekhu, one of the 'Keepers of the Gate', was murdered on an expedition into Africa, so his son Sabni led the army into Nubia to punish the tribe responsible. Sabni recovered his father's body and sent a messenger to the Pharaoh in Memphis to inform him that the enemy had been taught a lesson. On his return to Aswan he was met by priests, professional mourners and some of the royal embalmers, all sent by the Pharaoh himself to show the importance that was attached to the keepers of the kingdom's southern frontier.

Tomb of Prince Sarenput II (No 31)

This dates from the 12th dynasty and is one of the best preserved tombs. There are statues of the prince and wall paintings depicting Sarenput and his son hunting and fishing.

Tomb of Prince Sarenput I (No 36)

This tomb also dates from the 12th dynasty but it's older than No 31. On the rear wall of a columned court, to the left of the door, the prince is shown being followed by his dogs and sandal-bearer, and there are other scenes of his three sons and women bearing flowers.

Tomb of Heqaib (No 35)

The Tomb of Heqaib, the deified official whose temple stood on Elephantine, has a columned facade and some fine reliefs showing fighting bulls and hunting scenes.

Kubbet al Hawa

Also on the west bank is Kubbet al Hawa, a small tomb constructed for a local sheikh at the top of the hill. If you climb up to it, you'll be rewarded with fantastic views of the Nile and the surrounding area. From there you can also try to rent a donkey or camel for the trek across the desert to the Monastery of St Simeon.

Mausoleum of the Agha Khan

Aswan was the favourite wintering place of Mohammed Shah Agha Khan, the 48th imam, or leader, of the Ismaili sect of Islam. When he died in 1957 his wife, the Begum, oversaw the construction of his domed granite and sandstone mausoleum, which is part of the way up the hill on the west bank opposite Elephantine Island. Modelled on the Fatimid tombs of Cairo, the interior, which incorporates a small mosque, is more impressive than the exterior. The sarcophagus, of Carrara marble, is inscribed with texts from the Qur'an and stands in a vaulted chamber in the interior courtyard.

The Begum still lives for part of the year in the white villa, below her husband's mausoleum, which used to be their winter retreat. Every day she places a red rose on his sarcophagus; a ritual that is carried on in summer by her gardener.

The tomb is open Tuesday to Sunday from 9 am to 5 pm and admission is free (the guards are not supposed to accept baksheesh). Remember to remove your shoes. There is a felucca dock just below the mausoleum.

Monastery of St Simeon

Deir Amba Samaan is a 6th century monastery which, although it hasn't been used for more than 700 years, is one of the best preserved of the original Christian strongholds in Egypt. It is not known who St Simeon was exactly but his monastery survived until the monks were driven out or murdered by Arabs in the 14th century.

Surrounded by desert sands, except for a glimpse of the fertile belt around Aswan in the distance, the monastery bears more resemblance to a fortress than a religious sanctuary. It once provided accommodation for about 300 resident monks plus a further 100 or so pilgrims. Built on two levels, the lower of stone and the upper of mud-brick, it was surrounded by 10 metre high walls and contained a church, stores, bakeries, offices, a kitchen, dormitories, stables and workshops.

If you don't fancy a camel or donkey ride from the Tombs of the Nobles then there is a paved pathway to the monastery from the Mausoleum of Agha Khan. The monastery is open from 9 am to 6 pm and admission is E£1.

Places to Stay

The hotel rates given in this section include breakfast, unless otherwise specified. Don't expect much – usually it's just coffee or tea, two pieces of bread or rolls, jam and butter.

Places to Stay – bottom end

North of Aswan Station Square The 27 room *Rosewan Hotel* (tel 24497) has been popular with low-budget travellers for several years. It has clean, simple, rather small doubles with shower/toilet combinations for E£12.30; singles are E£8.20. All rooms have fans and tiled floors.

To get there, turn right as you leave the train station, take the first street on the left (Sharia el Shahid Kamal Noureldin Mohammed), and the hotel is in the middle of the block, just past the Hotel El Saffa. The reception desk manager, Regab, can help arrange group taxi or minibus trips to Abu Simbel for about E£17 per person.

The *Hotel El Saffa* is next to the Rosewan. Singles/doubles are E£3/5 with sinks and balconies in each room. A few rooms also have showers with hot water. The toilets could be cleaner.

A few blocks north of the Rosewan and the Saffa is the partly air-conditioned *Mena Hotel* (tel 324388). The cool, carpeted rooms have telephones, showers, toilets and balconies. A few rooms have either poor air-con or just fans. Singles are E£8.50, doubles E£14, and doubles without air-con are E£12.

The best deal in the hotel is a comfy suite with two bedrooms and a 'salon' that can sleep five people for E£30. For those with student cards, student reductions are available.

To get there, turn right as you leave the train station and follow the street that is parallel to the tracks for about 10 minutes. You'll see a sign for the hotel.

South of Aswan Station Square The *Youth Hostel* (tel 322313) is on Sharia Abtal el Tahrir, not far from the train station. It's not in the greatest shape, with dirt, noise and crowded rooms being its 'special' features. With rates at E£2 per night, you could stay at a bottom end hotel for only very little more. There's a special section for foreigners, and entrance is on the north side of the building.

Across the street from the Youth Hostel is the *Marwa Hotel*, which is entered from an alley on the south side of the building. Be careful of the open manholes in the alley.

Another floor is being added and the cafeteria is being expanded. The rooms are simple, but clean and comfortable, a great bargain at only E£2.50 for a single and E£4 for a double. The reception manager, Mohammed Ali Stohy, is an amiable guy who speaks excellent English and doubles as a lawyer for the Bank of Agriculture & Development in Aswan.

The *El Amin Hotel* (also signposted as *Elamin Hotel*) is a good, inexpensive hotel that lists itself as being on Sharia Abtal el Tahrir, but is actually on a side street just across from the Ramses Hotel and the Carré Ace restaurant. A few rooms are somewhat dusty and the toilet/shower combinations are rather small, but it's still a good deal at E£7 for a single, E£11 double for one person, and E£13 for two.

The *Hotel Continental* (tel 322311) is still one of the most popular places to stay in Aswan despite continual reports of hungry cockroaches and slimy toilets. The main redeeming feature is its simple and clean rooms, which have Nile views

for the rock-bottom price of E£2.50 per double for two people or E£1.75 for one person. The hotel is on the Corniche. It is a 20 minute walk from the train station. The cafe downstairs is a great place to meet other travellers and to arrange felucca trips down the Nile or taxis/minibuses to Abu Simbel.

Around the corner from the Continental, near the heart of the souk, is the one star *Abou Shelib Hotel* (tel 323051). Its central location is an advantage for exploring the souk, but the hotel is also near a mosque. If your room faces the mosque, you'll probably be shaken out of bed by the first call to prayer. Rooms are clean and simple, with fans and toilet/shower combinations (big bathrooms in some). Doubles with big bathrooms are E£12, singles E£10; doubles with showers are E£10, singles E£8; doubles without showers are E£8.50.

The *Molla Hotel*, on a side street near the souk, has been recommended. Each room has a sink with hot water and there are hot showers just off the hall. Doubles cost E£5.

Camping There's an official, but somewhat basic, camping ground near the Unfinished Obelisk, which is a 20 minute walk from the area around the Hotel Continental. There are cold showers crammed in next to toilets. Although there are enough grassy spaces for setting up tents and a few bushes and small trees, there really isn't any shade. Bright lamps and guards keep the place secure, but the former can make it difficult to sleep. It costs E£1 per person.

Places to Stay - middle
The *Ramses Hotel* (tel 324119), on Sharia Abtal el Tahrir, is a good deal and, according to some travellers, is one of the best places to stay in Aswan. Doubles with showers, toilets, air-con, colour TV, minirefrigerators and Nile views cost about E£45, singles with the same amenities E£32. Older double rooms without Nile views and other amenities cost about

E£20, singles E£14. During the summer, the rooms are discounted by as much as 50%. This hotel is popular with tour groups from all over Europe.

The *Happi Hotel* (tel 322028) is also on Sharia Abtal el Tahrir, a few blocks down from the Ramses Hotel. It has clean doubles with bathrooms for E£26.50; singles are E£19.50. The rooms have fans and the tiled bathrooms are clean. Some rooms also have balconies. It's very popular with European tourists and the food is quite decent at E£5 for a three course dinner. The owner also runs the Cleopatra Hotel.

The 66 room *Abu Simbel Hotel* (tel 322888, 322327) is on the Corniche, not far from the tourist office. Doubles with showers cost E£26 for two people and E£19.50 for one person. There are also six rooms with big bathrooms for E£22.50. The view of the Nile from the balcony of each room is fantastic. The reception manager, Adel Abdel Aty Masry, speaks good English and will try to answer most questions about Aswan and Abu Simbel.

The 109 room *Cleopatra Hotel* (tel 324001, 322983), on Sharia Saad Zaghloul just south of the railway station, is well situated for exploring the old market area. With doubles for about E£60, it's really an upper-middle end hotel. All rooms are clean, comfortable and air-conditioned, with private bathrooms and telephones.

On the Corniche is the *El Salam Hotel*, which can be considered a fair deal for the price; doubles cost about E£20, singles E£10. Most rooms have fans and Nile views.

Next to the El Salam Hotel is the 36 room *Hathor Hotel* (tel 322590), which has some rooms with air-con and hot showers crammed in next to toilets for E£25. Doubles/singles without air-con are E£20/E£13. Rooms are clean and some have tiled floors. There's an inexpensive restaurant in the lobby that serves chicken, fish and freshly squeezed juices.

The *Philae Hotel*, also on the Corniche,

is similar to the Abu Simbel, but the rooms are uncarpeted. Nile views, decent air-con and a central location are fair compensation. Singles are E£16, doubles E£22. All rooms have air-con.

Places to Stay – top end
The *Hotel Pullman Cataract* (tel 322016, 322510, 322233) was formerly known as the Cataract or Old Cataract Hotel. It is an impressive Moorish-style building surrounded by gardens on a rise above the river, with splendid views of the Nile and across the southern tip of Elephantine Island to the Mausoleum of the Agha Khan. Doubles there cost US$55 (standard room, Nile view), US$47 (standard room, garden view), US$69 (super room, Nile view), and US$57 (super room, garden view). The hotel is worth visiting just to partake of a cool Stella or a cocktail on the veranda, but the minimum charge is E£8 for nonresidents. The hotel's exterior was used in the movie of Agatha Christie's *Death on the Nile*, in part because Christie once did some of her writing here.

Everything about the Pullman Cataract bespeaks turn-of-the-century elegance, from its finely bevelled glass elevator to its large, well-furnished rooms. Both standard and 'super' rooms are equally super – high ceilings, hard wood floors, Oriental carpets, antique furniture.

The *New Cataract Hotel PLM Azur* is next door. Its swimming pool is open to the public for about E£5 per day from 9 am to 9 pm.

The four star *Kalabsha Hotel* (tel 322999) nearby is another high class affair, with an excellent view of the First Cataract. Singles are US$30, doubles US$37, excluding taxes; breakfast is E£4, lunch E£11 and dinner E£13.50 (buffet meals cost more). Guests can use the swimming pool at the Cataract Hotel for free.

The *Aswan Oberoi* (tel 323455) on Elephantine Island has two hotel launches that ferry guests and visitors from the east bank. The views from the Oberoi tower are magnificent and the gardens are a pleasant place to just hang around and watch the feluccas. The swimming pool is open to the public for about E£5 per day from 9 am to 9 pm. Rooms there, however, start at E£100.

The four star *Isis Hotel* (tel 324744, 324905) is ideally situated between the Corniche and the Nile. The rooms are more like stuccoed cabins; they are fully carpeted and have powerful air-con, large bathrooms, colour TV and telephones.

There are also shops, two restaurants (one serves decent Italian dishes) and a swimming pool which is open to the public for a small fee. Singles cost US$60 and doubles are US$71 including taxes. They are hoping for five star status, which means that room rates will probably increase.

Places to Eat

There are a few restaurants and cafes on the south side of the Aswan Station Square including the *Restaurant Gomhoreya*, which has been recommended by some travellers. Try their grilled pigeon, when they have it, for about E£3.50 (plus 10% service). Along Sharia Saad Zaghloul (Sharia al Souk) in the block or two from the station you pass a number of eating places with decidedly odd names. You could eat at the *Commoner Restaurant*, have a drink at *Roxy Milks* and finish up at the *Station Sweeter*.

A block back from the station on Sharia Abtal el Tahrir is the *Carré Ace Restaurant*, which is adjacent to the Ramses Hotel. It serves a full meal of food such as kufta and kebab (E£3.25), Egyptian dips (tahina, baba ghanough), spaghetti, and cooked vegetables for about E£5 to E£6. Taxes (6%) and service (12%) are added on. The head waiter, Essmat-Abd el Malek, doubles as one of the curators of the Aswan Museum. The other waiters are a happy-go-lucky lot, always smiling and telling jokes.

Back towards the station, just past the youth hostel, is the *Aswan Sweet Corner*,

which has a good selection of honey-soaked cakes.

The *Monalisa Restaurant* on the Corniche has good and cheap but basic food. You can have breakfast or a main meal of fish and kebab, on the stone terrace overlooking the Nile, for about E£5.

The *Aswan Moon Restaurant*, next to the Monalisa, offers big meals for two people for about E£8 to E£10.

The *Restaurant el Nil* (or *El Nile Restaurant*) is on the Corniche a few doors away from the Hotel Continental. A full meal with fish, chicken or meat, rice, vegetables, tahina and bread should cost about E£5.50.

Also on the Corniche are the *Philae Restaurant*, which seems to be popular, and *Restaurant Maxime's*, whose menu in English attracts travellers. The latter restaurant can't be recommended, however. As you wait for a E£5 plate of greasy chicken and undercooked fries, don't lean on the placemats and tablecloth. They seem to keep both coated with a thin but sticky coat of jam, perhaps to feed the gregarious gang of flies that buzzes overhead.

For grilled, rather than overly greasy, chicken and fish, try the *Saladin Restaurant* on the Nile side of the Corniche. For about E£2.50 you can get chicken or fish with cooked vegetables.

The *Medina Restaurant* on Sharia al Souk, across from the Cleopatra Hotel, has been recommended for its kufta and kebab deals – E£2 for a quarter kg of kufta and E£3 for a quarter kg of kebab.

In the Isis Hotel, by the river, is the pleasant *Ristorante Italiano*, a good place to make an expensive escape from yet another meal of kufta and kebab. Pasta dishes are E£14, main courses E£16 to E£20.

Activities

As you will quickly discover if you spend any time near the Nile, feluccas are the traditional canvas-sailed boats of the

Egyptian part of the Nile. They have probably changed little in centuries. A visit to Aswan wouldn't be complete without at least an hour ride on a felucca between the islands in the Nile.

For advice about hiring a felucca, see the Getting There & Away section.

Getting There & Away

Air EgyptAir flies from Cairo to Aswan daily. The flight takes 1½ hours and costs about E£185 one way.

The return flight between Aswan and Abu Simbel costs about E£161.

Sudan Airways used to fly from Aswan to Khartoum every Tuesday at about 4 am for E£170. They shared an office in Aswan with Emeco Travel on Sharia Abtal el Tahrir and were open from 9 am to 4 pm daily except Friday. At the time of writing, however, service had been suspended indefinitely.

Bus The bus station is behind the Abu Simbel Hotel on Sharia Abtal el Tahrir. The air-con bus to Abu Simbel costs E£16 return and leaves at 8 am daily.

There are at least five buses per day from Aswan to Kom Ombo (45 minutes), Edfu (1½ hours), Esna (two hours) and Luxor (around four hours). Check the bus station for schedules.

The green buses are more basic, cheaper and less reliable than the green-and-yellow buses. Fares are: Luxor E£5; Esna E£3 (green-and-yellow bus)/E£2.25 (green bus); Edfu E£1.50/E£1.25; and Kom Ombo E£1/16 pt (I asked three times about this last fare because it seemed oddly low). There are also two direct buses to Cairo for E£28 (with air-con and video) and E£25 (air-con only).

Train There are at least five trains a day from Aswan to Cairo, including two deluxe wagon-lit trains. Check the timetables posted at the train stations for the latest schedules.

Express train No 85, from Aswan to Luxor, Cairo and on to Alexandria, has air-con, sleepers and a restaurant. Express No 87, which also stops at Qena, has sleepers and a restaurant. Train No 981 has 1st and 2nd class, air-con and a restaurant; and train No 89 has sleepers, air-con, a restaurant, a bar and a buffet.

The trip from Aswan to Cairo is scheduled to take about 16 hours but often takes more than 20.

The most expensive sleeper cars are the wagons-lits – E£140 to Cairo, which is the same as from Luxor; see the Getting Around chapter for the wagon-lit schedules. First class and 2nd class sleepers, both of which are quite adequate, are cheaper. Reservations are necessary for all three types of sleepers, especially during the winter season.

The cheapest way to get to the High Dam, 13 km south of Aswan, is to take a train to Sadd al Ali Station, the end of the Cairo to Aswan line. The train departs Aswan for Sadd al Ali at 6, 8 and 10 am daily (Ramadan schedule: 7, 8 and 9.45 am). Check with the tourist office for the latest schedule.

Taxi The service taxi station is across the train tracks on the east side of town. Just off Sharia al Souk, one block south of the train station, is an overpass over the tracks. Climb the overpass and walk to the end of the street on the other side (about 10 minutes). Turn right and walk about half a km to the service taxi station. Taxis frequently depart north to most major destinations.

In Luxor you can hire a special taxi for a total of E£75 to take you and seven others to Aswan with stops en route at Esna, Edfu and Kom Ombo.

Felucca The most popular felucca trip is a three day, two night trip from Aswan to Edfu. From there, you take a service taxi to Luxor for about E£2.50, although some travellers have reported paying as much as E£5 each. Another alternative is a one or two night trip to Kom Ombo, returning by service taxi to Aswan. The only

Felucca

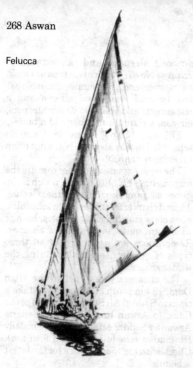

problem with the latter is that you may have to walk about two km from the Nile to the main road, but it's usually easy to hitch a ride. The last option is three nights, four days to Esna, returning by service taxi to Luxor. The felucca captains are quite adamant about not continuing on to Luxor.

A felucca that can hold six to eight passengers charges a total of about E£150 for the trip to Edfu. The captain helps you register at the police station, where each passenger must also pay a E£5 registration fee.

Finding a felucca is easy – as soon as you approach the Corniche, you will be swamped with offers. However, finding a good captain can occasionally be a problem, especially if you are a single woman or a group of women. On overnight trips, a few women travellers have reported sailing with felucca captains who had groping hands and exhibitionist tendencies.

However, there was one captain in particular whose name was often mentioned by travellers as an honest, no-nonsense guy: Noury-Dawi Mohammed.

Noury is a young, slightly built Nubian from the village of Jebel Takok, which is just south of the New Cataract Hotel. He is soft-spoken almost to the point of shyness, but if you ask him he will tell you in good English (or French, German or Italian) about his family and village. Noury will also take groups for private visits to his village, but he limits the number because he says that he doesn't want Jebel Takok to become a tourist sight.

Noury can be contacted through the Bazaar Abu Salah, which is on the Corniche just south of the main Aswan police station. He used to sail a felucca named the *Amsterdam*, but was about to get a new one called the *Oregon*.

If you are trying to assemble a group for this trip, try the Hotel Continental. Actually, any of the low and middle-range hotels are good sources for assembling a group.

Take plenty of bottled water for the trip; otherwise the captain will dip into the Nile for cooking and drinking water. A mosquito net is helpful, more for your peace of mind than for warding off hungry swarms. Most travellers I've met who have done the trip to Edfu didn't seem bothered by the mosquitoes. It can also get cool at night, even in the early summer when daytime temperatures reach 40° C (104° F) or sometimes higher, so bring a sleeping bag or something else to keep warm. A hat is essential to protect you from the sun during the day.

Steamer The Sudanese Maritime Office (also known as the Nile Valley Navigation Office) is next to the tourist office, one street in from the Corniche. This is the place to buy tickets to Wadi Halfa. The steamer leaves from the Aswan docks, near the Sadd al Ali train station south of the High Dam, on Monday, Thursday and Saturday, between 11 am and 3 pm.

The trip takes about 20 hours in either direction and costs E£53 for 2nd class and E£88 for 1st class, which usually includes six to eight cups of tea. There is no longer any deck class. Although food is available on the boat, no travellers have spoken highly of it, so take plenty of food with you. As soon as you board, try to find a space to stretch out on the deck rather than worrying about your seat inside. Foreigners are usually permitted to stake out the deck area around the bridge. Inside, the wooden seats are uncomfortable, impossible to sleep on and it's hot, crowded and stuffy. It may also be crowded outside but the scenery is better and you'll get a cool breeze.

I have yet to meet a traveller who didn't like this trip. Although the steamer doesn't make any stops before Wadi Halfa, except once overnight so the captain can sleep, it's a relaxing journey that takes you past Abu Simbel.

Coming from Wadi Halfa, the boat docks near the High Dam and passport officials check passports before the passengers disembark. Foreigners are allowed off the boat first and into the customs depot, which is adjacent to the train station (end of the line). There are taxis just outside the customs depot.

See the Sudan Getting There chapter for more details of this trip.

Getting Around
Airport Transport The airport is 25 km from the town and the taxi fare is about E£12.

Taxi A taxi tour that includes the Philae Temple, the High Dam and the Unfinished Obelisk costs around E£20 for five to six people.

Felucca Apart from a few buses, taxis and horse-drawn carriages, feluccas are the most common form of transportation to the attractions around Aswan. There is an official government price for hiring feluccas (check with the tourist office), but with a bit of bargaining you should be able to hire a boat for five or six hours for a reasonable price. A shorter three or four hour tour costs about E£20.

Ferry A ferry shuttles across the Nile from near the GPO on the town side of the river to just below the Tombs of the Nobles on the west bank. The fare is 50 pt each way. Note that the boat is divided into two sections – women up front, men in the back.

AROUND ASWAN
The Aswan Dam
When the British constructed the Aswan Dam above the First Cataract at the turn of the century it was the largest of its kind in the world. The growing population of Egypt had made it imperative to put more land under cultivation and the only way to achieve this was to regulate the flow of the Nile. Measuring 2140 metres across, the dam was built almost entirely of local Aswan granite between 1898 and 1902. Although its height had to be raised twice to meet the demand, it not only greatly increased the area of cultivable land but provided the country with most of its hydroelectric power. Now completely surpassed in function, and as a tourist attraction, by the more spectacular High Dam six km upstream, it is still worth a brief visit, as the area around the First Cataract below it is extremely fertile and picturesque. All trips to Abu Simbel include a drive across this dam.

Sehel Island
Sehel, the large island north of the old Aswan Dam, was sacred to the goddess Anukis and her husband Khnum. As a destination for an extended felucca trip on this part of the Nile Sehel Island is a good choice, although there isn't much to see apart from a friendly Nubian village and a great many rock inscriptions, dating from Middle Kingdom to Greco-Roman times.

One Ptolemaic inscription, on the

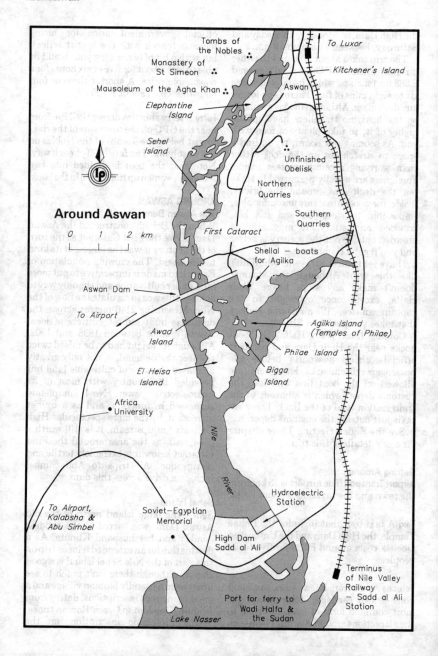

Around Aswan

Tombs of
the Nobles

To Luxor

Monastery of
St Simeon

Kitchener's Island

Mausoleum of the Agha Khan

Aswan

*Elephantine
Island*

*Sehel
Island*

Unfinished
Obelisk

Northern
Quarries

Southern
Quarries

First Cataract

0   1   2 km

Shellal — boats
for Agilka

Aswan Dam

To Airport

*Agilka Island
(Temples of Philae)*

*Awad
Island*

Philae Island

*Bigga
Island*

*El Heisa
Island*

Africa
University

Nile

River

To Airport,
Kalabsha &
Abu Simbel

Soviet–Egyptian
Memorial

Hydroelectric
Station

High Dam
Sadd al Ali

Terminus
of Nile Valley
Railway
– Sadd al Ali
Station

Port for ferry to
Wadi Halfa &
the Sudan

Lake Nasser

south-eastern side of the island, records the story of a seven year famine that plagued Egypt during the much earlier time of Pharaoh Zoser. It seems that Khnum, god of the cataracts, had withheld the inundation of the Nile for seven years and Zoser finally travelled to Aswan to ask the local priests why the god was punishing the Egyptians. Apparently some land belonging to Khnum's traditional estates had been confiscated; as soon as Zoser returned the land and raised a temple to Khnum on Sehel, the Nile rose to its accepted flood level.

Temple of Philae

Philae is pronounced 'feel-i'. The romantic and majestic aura surrounding the temple complex of Isis on the island of Philae has been luring pilgrims for thousands of years; during the 19th century the ruins were one of Egypt's most legendary tourist attractions. Even when it seemed that they were destined to be lost forever beneath the rising waters of the Nile, travellers still came, taking to row boats to glide amongst the partly submerged columns and peer down through the translucent green to the wondrous sanctuaries of the mighty gods below.

From the turn of this century, Philae and its temples became swamped for six months of every year by the high waters of the reservoir created by the construction of the old Aswan Dam. In the 1960s, when the approaching completion of the High Dam threatened to submerge the island completely and forever, the massive complex was disassembled and removed stone by stone from Philae in an incredible rescue organised by UNESCO. The temples were reconstructed on nearby Agilka Island, which was even landscaped to resemble the sacred isle of Isis, in positions corresponding as closely as possible to their original layout.

The oldest part of Philae dates from the 4th century BC but most of the existing structures were built by the Ptolemies and the Romans up to the 3rd century AD.

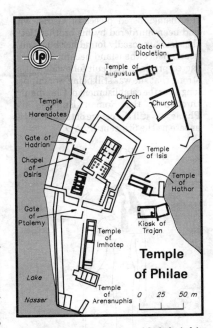

Temple of Philae

The early Christians also added their bit to the island by transforming the main temple's hypostyle hall into a chapel, building a couple of churches and of course defacing the pagan reliefs; their inscriptions were in turn vandalised by the early Muslims.

At first, however, it was the cults of Isis, Osiris and Horus, and the Greco-Roman temple raised in honour of the goddess, that drew devotees not only from all over Egypt but the whole Mediterranean.

Isis, the sister and wife of the great Osiris, was the Egyptian goddess of healing, purity and sexuality, of motherhood and women, of the promise of immortality and of nature itself. She was worshipped so passionately and her popularity was so great that she became identified with all the goddesses of the Mediterranean, finally absorbing them to become the universal mother of nature and protector of humans.

It was on Philae, during her search for

the dismembered pieces of Osiris, who had been murdered by his brother Seth, that Isis supposedly found her husband's heart; hence the island became her most sacred precinct. Her cult following was so strong that she was still being worshipped long after the establishment of Christianity throughout the Roman Empire, and Philae was still the centre of the cult of Isis as late as the 6th century AD.

Isis

The boat to Agilka Island, which is where the temple is located, leaves you at the base of the Hall of Nectanebo, the oldest part of the Philae complex. Heading north, you walk down the Outer Temple Court, which has colonnades running along both sides, to the entrance of the Temple of Isis marked by the towers of the 1st Pylon.

In the Central Court of the Temple of Isis is the mammisi, or birth-house, dedicated to Horus. Successive Pharaohs reinstated their legitimacy as the mortal descendants of Horus by taking part in the mammisi rituals, which celebrated the god's birth.

The 2nd Pylon provides access to the Vestibule and the Inner Sanctuary of Isis;

a staircase, on the western side, leads up to the Osiris Chambers, which are decorated with scenes of mourners; and everywhere there are reliefs of Isis, her husband and son, other deities and, of course, the Ptolemies and Romans who built or contributed to the temple.

On the northern tip of the island are the Temple of Augustus and the Gate of Diocletian; east of the 2nd Pylon is the delightful Temple of Hathor decorated with reliefs of musicians; and south of that, the elegant, unfinished pavilion by the water's edge is the Kiosk of Trajan. The completed reliefs on the kiosk feature Emperor Trajan making offerings to Isis, Osiris and Horus.

The temple complex is open from 7 am to 6 pm and admission is E£3, or E£1.50 for students. There is a sound & light show in the evenings which costs E£10 for the ticket and E£1 to E£6 for the boat to Agilka Island. Double-check the schedule at the tourist office or the Aswan Cultural Centre:

	1st show	2nd show
Saturday	English	French
Sunday	French	German
Monday	English	Italian
Tuesday	French	English
Wednesday	English	Spanish
Thursday		French
Friday	English	French

Some travellers have reported being disappointed by their visits to the temple because of the hassles involved in first arranging the taxi and then the boat to the island. Perhaps by the time this book is published, the boats to Philae will be better regulated. The lack of a guide to explain certain parts of the temple also didn't help.

Getting There & Away The boat landing for the Philae complex is at Shellal, south of the old Aswan Dam. The only way to get there is by taxi or organised trip (arranged by most travel agencies and major hotels in town, but possibly for more money than you may pay otherwise). In one case, the round-trip taxi fare for a group of six cost E£30 without bargaining. A small motorboat to the island will cost about E£12 return for the whole boat (this seems to be negotiable). The boat fare should be a reasonable fixed rate, but apparently the government hasn't imposed this condition on the boat owners yet.

High Dam

Egypt's contemporary example of building on a monumental scale contains 18 times the amount of material used in the Great Pyramid of Cheops. The controversial Sadd al Ali, the High Dam, is just over four km across and 111 metres high at its highest point. The water contained by the dam has backed up nearly 500 km, taking it well into the Sudan and creating Lake Nasser, the world's largest artificial lake. The rising level of this incredible reservoir has inundated the land of Nubia with waters as deep as 200 metres, forced the relocation of thousands of Nubians and Sudanese and washed away 45 villages along the banks of the Nile south of Aswan.

While the old Aswan Dam successfully regulated the flow of the Nile during the course of a year, it was realised, as early as the 1940s, that a much bigger dam was needed to counter the unpredictable annual flooding of the great river. However, it wasn't until Nasser came to power in 1952 that plans were drawn up for a new dam six km south of the British-built one.

The proposed construction created international political tension and focused worldwide attention on the antiquities that would be lost by the creation of a huge lake behind the dam.

In 1956, after the USA, the UK and the World Bank suddenly refused the financial backing they had offered for the project, Nasser ordered the nationalisation of the Suez Canal as a means of raising the capital. This move precipitated the Suez Crisis in which France, the UK and Israel invaded the canal region; they were eventually restrained by the United Nations. The Soviet Union then offered the necessary funding and expertise, and work began on the High Dam in 1960 and was completed in 1971.

While the old dam simply controlled the flow of the Nile, the High Dam collects and stores water over a number of years so that a high or low annual flood can be regulated at all times. The area of Egypt's cultivable land was increased by 30%; the High Dam's hydroelectric station has doubled the country's power supply and a rise in the Sahara's water table has been recorded as far away as Algeria.

On the other hand, artificial fertilisers now have to be used because the dam hinders the flow of silt that was critical to the Nile Valley's fertility, and it's estimated that in the next 40 years or so that silt will have filled the lake. In recent years, the extremely high rate of evaporation from the lake, coupled with low annual floods, has reduced the water level in the reservoir forcing a reduction in the amount of water released for irrigation and power generation. The greatest fear is that should the dam ever break or be sabotaged most of Egypt would be swept into the Mediterranean.

Another consequence of the dam's construction was the fact that a great many valuable and irreplaceable ancient monuments were doomed to be drowned by the waters of Lake Nasser.

Teams from the Egyptian Department of Antiquities and archaeological missions from many countries descended on Nubia to set in motion the UNESCO-organised projects aimed at rescuing as many of the threatened treasures as possible. Necropoli were excavated, all portable artefacts and relics were removed to museums and, while some temples disappeared beneath the lake, 14 were salvaged and moved to safety. Ten of them, including the temple complexes of Philae, Kalabsha and Abu Simbel, were dismantled stone by stone and rebuilt on higher ground in Egypt. The other four were donated to the countries which contributed to the rescue effort; they include the splendid Temple of Dendur, which has been reconstructed in a glass building in the Metropolitan Museum of Art in New York.

The Visitors' Pavilion, on the east side of the dam, has exhibits detailing the construction of the High Dam and the dismantling of Abu Simbel. It's open from 7 am to 2 pm and 3 to 6 pm and admission is free if you come by foot. If coming by car or minibus each passenger must pay E£1.50 for the privilege of driving to the pavilion. I chatted with several travellers at the pavilion and they all seemed to have the same reaction – 'Hmph, so this is what we paid E£1.50 for, to see a big piece of concrete!'

On the west side of the dam, there is a stone monument honouring Russian-Egyptian friendship and cooperation; and the view from the top of Sadd al Ali is spectacular.

Getting There & Away The cheapest way to get to the High Dam, which is 13 km south of Aswan, is to take a train to Sadd al Ali Station, the end of the Cairo to Aswan line. The station is near the docks for the boat to the Sudan and from there you can either walk for a long way or take a service taxi to the dam. The train departs Aswan for Sadd al Ali at 6, 8 and 10 am daily (Ramadan schedule: 7, 8 and 9.45 am). Check with the tourist office for the latest schedule.

If you're planning to take a taxi across the top of the dam, then you might also consider continuing on to the Temple of Kalabsha, which is another 10 km south, on the west side of Lake Nasser. If you get a group together, it should only cost about E£15 to E£20 per person for four or five hours.

Kalabsha, Beit al Wali & Kertassi

As a result of the massive UNESCO effort to rescue the doomed monuments of Nubia,

these three temples were transplanted from a now submerged site about 60 km south of Aswan. Until recently the new site, on the west bank of Lake Nasser a little upriver from the dam, was considered a military area and you needed special permission to visit these monuments – which is, perhaps, one of the reasons why these temples were (and still are) seldom visited.

The Temple of Kalabsha was erected during the reign of Emperor Augustus, between 30 BC and 14 AD, and was dedicated to the Nubian god Mandulis. Isis and Osiris were also worshipped there and during the Christian era the temple was used as a church.

The West German government financed the transfer and reconstruction of the 13,000 blocks of the temple, and was presented with the temple's west pylon, which is now in the Berlin Museum. During the rescue operation, evidence was found of even older structures, dating from the times of Amenophis II and Ptolemy IX.

An impressive stone causeway leads from the lake up to the 1st Pylon of the temple, beyond which are the colonnaded court and the Hypostyle Hall, which has 12 columns. Inscriptions on the walls show various emperors and Pharaohs cavorting with the gods and goddesses. Just beyond the hall are three chambers, with stairs leading from one up to the roof. The view of Lake Nasser and the High Dam, across the capitals of the hall and court, is fantastic. An inner passage, between the temple and the encircling wall, leads to a well-preserved Nilometer.

The Temple of Beit al Wali, which means 'house of the holy man', was rebuilt with assistance from the US government and placed just north-west of the Temple of Kalabsha. Most of Beit al Wali, which was carved from the rocks, was built during the reign of Ramses II. On the walls of the first chamber are several interesting reliefs, including scenes of the Pharaoh's victory over the Cushites and his wars against the Libyans and Syrians. Ramses is shown pulling the hair of his enemies while women plead for mercy.

Just north of the Temple of Kalabsha are the remains of the Temple of Kertassi. Two Hathor (cow-headed) columns, a massive architrave and four columns with intricate capitals are the only pieces which were salvaged from Lake Nasser.

The government price for the taxi between Kalabsha and Aswan is around E£10; you should double-check with the tourist office for the latest information.

ABU SIMBEL

While the fate of his colossal statue and the Ramesseum in Luxor no doubt gnaws at the spirit of Ramses II, the mere existence, in the 20th century AD, of his Great Temple at Abu Simbel must make him shake with laughter and shout 'I told you so!'.

The Abu Simbel temples were threatened with being swallowed forever beneath the rising water and silt of Lake Nasser. Their preservation, 280 km south of Aswan, must rank as the greatest achievement of the UNESCO rescue operation. And, hewn as they were out of solid rock, the modern technology involved in cutting, moving and rebuilding the incredible temples and statues at least paralleled the skill of the ancient artisans who chiselled them out of the cliff face in the first place.

In the 1960s, as work progressed on the High Dam, UNESCO launched a worldwide appeal for the vital funding and expertise needed to salvage the Abu Simbel monuments. The response was immediately forthcoming and a variety of conservation schemes were put forward. Finally, in 1964 a cofferdam was built to hold back the already encroaching water of the new lake, while Egyptian, Italian, Swedish, German and French archaeological teams began to move the massive structure.

At a cost of about US$40 million the

Abu Simbel

temples were cut up into more than 2000 huge blocks, weighing from 10 to 40 tonnes each, and reconstructed inside a specially built mountain 210 metres away from the water and 65 metres higher than the original site. The temples were carefully oriented to face the correct direction and the landscape of their original environment was recreated on and around the concrete, dome-shaped mountain. You can enter the dome either through a door next to the Great Temple of Ramses II or through a door across from the ticket office on the opposite side of the dome.

The project took just over four years. The temples of Abu Simbel were officially reopened in 1968, while the sacred site they had occupied for over 3000 years disappeared beneath Lake Nasser.

The Great Temple of Ramses II was dedicated to the gods Ra-Harakhty, Amun and Ptah and, of course, to the deified Pharaoh himself; while the smaller Temple of Hathor was dedicated to the cow-headed goddess of love and built in honour of Ramses' favourite wife, Queen Nefertari. They were carved out of the mountain on the west bank of the Nile between 1290 BC and 1224 BC. By the mid-1800s, the sandstone cliff face and temples were all but covered in sand; although they were partially cleared many times, it wasn't until the British began excavating, around the turn of this century, that their full glory was revealed.

From the Great Temple's forecourt, a short flight of steps leads up to the terrace in front of the massive rockcut facade, which is about 30 metres high and 35 metres wide. Guarding the entrance, the four famous colossal statues of Ramses II sit majestically, staring out across the desert as if looking through time itself. Each statue is over 20 metres high and is accompanied by smaller, though much larger than life-size, statues of the king's mother Queen Tuya, his wife Nefertari and some of their children.

Above the entrance to the Great Hypostyle Hall, between the central throned colossi, is the figure of the falcon-headed sun-god Ra-Harakhty. Unfortunately, the sun-god has been subjected to the trials of time and now lacks part of a leg and foot. The roof of the hall is supported by eight columns, each fronted by a 10 metre high statue of Ramses; the roof is decorated with vultures representing Osiris; and the reliefs on the walls depict the Pharaoh in various battles, victorious as usual. In the next hall, the four columned Vestibule, Ramses and Nefertari are shown in front of the gods and the solar barques that carry the dead to the underworld.

The innermost chamber is the sacred Sanctuary, where the four gods of the Great Temple sit on their thrones carved in the back wall and wait for the dawn. The temple is aligned in such a way that on 22 February and 22 October every year, the first rays of the rising sun reach across the Nile, penetrate the temple, move along the Hypostyle Hall, through the Vestibule and into the Sanctuary, where they illuminate the somewhat mutilated figures of Ramses II, Ra-Harakhty, Amun and Ptah. (Until the temples were moved, this phenomenon happened one day earlier.)

The other temple at the Abu Simbel complex is the rockcut Temple of Hathor, which is fronted by six massive standing statues, about 10 metres high. Four of them represent Ramses, the other two represent his beloved wife Queen Nefertari and they are all flanked by the smaller figures of the Ramessid princes and princesses.

The six pillars of the Hypostyle Hall are crowned with Hathor capitals and its walls are adorned with scenes depicting: Nefertari before Hathor and Mut; the queen honouring her husband; and Ramses, yet again, being valiant and victorious. In the Vestibule and adjoining chambers there are colourful scenes of the goddess and her sacred barque. In the Sanctuary there is a striking statue of a cow, the sacred symbol of Hathor, emerging from the wall.

The admission fee for both temples is E£6, or E£3.50 for students.

Places to Stay

There are two hotels at Abu Simbel. The privately owned *Nefertari Hotel* is about 400 metres from the temples. It has singles/doubles for US$34/42, with air-con, full carpeting and, in some rooms, mini-refrigerators. There's also a swimming pool. A 50% discount is often available in the summer. The restaurant stays open all year. During the winter, most of the hotel's 76 rooms and suites are full, so reservations are recommended.

The government-run *New Ramses Hotel* is in the town of Abu Simbel, about 1½ km from the temples.

Getting There & Away

Until July 1985, when the road between Aswan and Abu Simbel was officially opened, the only way to visit the temples of Ramses II and Hathor was by flying in. (See the Aswan Getting There & Away section.) These days the 280 km can be covered in a variety of ways.

Air-con buses leave for Abu Simbel from the Aswan bus station every day at 8 am. Tickets cost E£16 return and the trip takes about 3½ hours one way. The bus leaves Abu Simbel at about 2.30 pm, or earlier if people wish. You should buy your ticket at least one day in advance.

A possibly cheaper alternative would be to get a group together and hire a taxi or minibus for a tour of the temples at Philae and Kalabsha as well as the High Dam and Abu Simbel. A minibus should cost about E£18 per person (transportation only). But be forewarned – a visit to Abu Simbel alone is quite enough for one day.

Some hotels in Aswan can arrange minibuses and taxis for you. Most of these trips depart at about 5 am in order to arrive at Abu Simbel by 8 to 8.30 am before it gets too hot. They will return you to Aswan any time from 1 to 3 pm, depending on how long a sheesha break the driver decides to take at the roadside 'rest house' on the way back and how much time is spent at the High Dam. The admission fees for Abu Simbel (E£6, or E£3.50 for students) and the High Dam (E£1.50) aren't included.

Abu Simbel is 50 km north of the Sudanese border but overland travel between the Sudan and Egypt is only possible if you have your own transportation. Check to see if the last section of the road between the two countries has opened, and remember that travel in the Sudan is not recommended while the civil war is still being fought.

The Suez Canal & the Red Sea Coast

The Suez Canal, one of the greatest feats of modern engineering, links the Mediterranean with the northern end of the Red Sea. Among the area's many highlights are the ancient monasteries of St Anthony and St Paul. The Red Sea is renowned for its spectacular marine life, and a visit to this region offers the chance to sample some of the best snorkelling and diving you'll find anywhere in the world.

The Suez Canal

The Suez Canal represents the culmination of centuries of effort to enhance trade and expand the empires of Egypt by connecting the Red Sea and the Mediterranean. Although the modern canal was by no means the first project of its kind, it was the only one to bypass the Nile as a means of connecting the two seas and excavate across the Isthmus of Suez to provide a major shipping route between Europe and Asia.

The first recorded canal was begun by Pharaoh Necho, between 610 and 595 BC, and stretched from the Nile Delta town of Bubastis, near present-day Zagazig, to the Red Sea via the Bitter Lakes. Despite his oracle's prophecy that the canal would be of more use to invading barbarians than to the Egyptians, Necho persevered until, having caused the death of more than 100,000 workers, he was forced to abandon the project.

His canal was completed about a century later under Darius, one of Egypt's Persian rulers, and was maintained by the Ptolemies. Cleopatra, in a bid to save what was left of her fleet after the Egyptian defeat at Atrium, attempted to pass up the canal to the Red Sea, failing only because of the low flood level of the Nile that year.

The canal was improved by the Romans under Trajan, but over the next several centuries it was either neglected and left to silt up, or was dredged by various rulers for limited use, depending on the available resources.

In 649 AD it was restored by Amr, the Arab conqueror of Egypt, to facilitate the export of corn to Arabia. Twenty years later, it was filled in by another caliph to stop the supply of grain to Mecca and Medina, so he could starve the people against whom he was waging war.

Following the French invasion in 1798, the importance of some sort of sea route south to Asia was again recognised. For the first time the digging of a canal directly from the Mediterranean to the Red Sea, across the comparatively narrow Isthmus of Suez, was considered. The idea was abandoned, however, because Napoleon's engineers mistakenly calculated that there was a 10 metre difference between the two sea levels.

British reports corrected that mistake several years later, but it was the French consul to Egypt, Ferdinand de Lesseps, who pursued the Suez Canal idea through to its conclusion.

In 1854 de Lesseps presented his proposal to the Egyptian khedive, Said Pasha, who authorised him to excavate the canal but, although de Lesseps had financial backing from private investors, the project was initially hindered by the British and French governments. Finally, in 1855, the scheme was approved and the Suez Canal Company, headed by Ferdinand de Lesseps, was formed and began issuing shares to raise the necessary revenue. Said Pasha granted the Company a 99 year concession to operate the canal, with the Egyptian government to receive 15% of the annual profits.

Construction began in 1859, but it was not an easy project. At one stage,

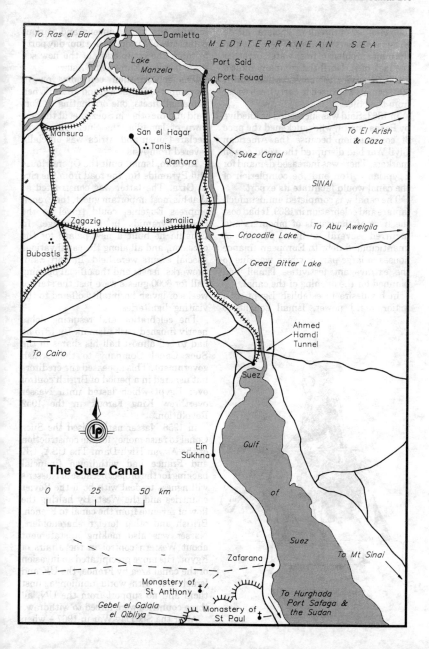

The Suez Canal

0   25   50 km

following an outbreak of cholera, all de Lesseps' workers ran away. There was also the major problem of fresh water, or rather the lack of it. Until the company built a canal to service the construction works, 3000 camels were used to carry fresh water from the Nile.

In 1863, Said was succeeded as khedive by Pasha Ismail, who quickened the pace of construction because the American Civil War had disrupted the world cotton markets. There was increased demand for Egyptian cotton and the completion of the canal would facilitate its export.

The canal was completed amidst much fanfare and celebration in 1869. It had cost the lives of thousands of labourers and incurred several million pounds of unanticipated debt to European finance houses, a large part of which was due to the extravagant festivities Ismail had planned for the opening of the canal.

In his desire to establish Egypt as a major world power, Ismail sought to impress the kings, queens and various potentates of Europe with a four day party to mark the completion of the new sea route between Europe and Asia.

The inauguration ceremony on 16 November 1869 was a grand affair. When two small fleets, one originating in Port Said and the other in Suez, met at the new town of Ismailia, the Suez Canal was declared open and Africa was officially severed from Asia.

In Cairo, Ismail built the Opera House and Pyramids Rd, the road from the city to Giza. The latter was constructed so that his most important guest, the French empress Eugénie, could travel to the Great Pyramids in her carriage. In Ismailia he built a new palace for the occasion, and all along the canal various special events were held. In Port Said, fireworks, feasts and the official opening ball for 6000 guests were just the start of weeks of lavish hospitality offered to the visiting dignitaries.

The celebration and resulting debts nearly finished Pasha Ismail. By 1875 he had to sell almost half his shares in the Suez Canal Company to the British government. This appeased the creditors but ushered in a period of British control over Egypt which lasted until Nasser overthrew King Farouk in the 1952 Revolution.

In 1956 Nasser nationalised the Suez Canal to raise money for the construction of the Aswan High Dam. The USA, UK and France had withdrawn financial backing for the project because of Nasser's willingness to deal with both the Soviet countries and the West. By halting the flow of revenue from the canal to French, British and other foreign shareholders, Nasser was also making a statement about Western control in the affairs of Egypt. His move precipitated an invasion of the canal area by France, the UK and Israel; but with world opinion against them and no support from the UN, all three countries were forced to withdraw.

After the Six Day War in 1967 – when

Israel returned to the area after Egypt tried to block the Straits of Tiran, the former's only outlet to the Red Sea – the canal was closed for about eight years.

The Israelis entrenched themselves along the eastern bank of the canal by building a line of fortifications called the Bar Lev Line. In 1973 Egypt tried, but failed, to take the Sinai and Suez Canal back from Israel by blasting the Bar Lev Line with water cannons. By this time the canal was full of sunken ships and sea traffic remained paralysed until 1975, when Sadat reopened the canal.

Following the 1978 Camp David Agreement and the 1979 peace treaty signed between Egypt and Israel, the Suez Canal has been filled with a constant flow of maritime traffic. It is 163 km long but is still not wide enough to accommodate modern ships sailing in opposite directions. There are plans to widen the canal but, for now, ships can pass at only two points – the Bitter Lakes and Al Ballah. With a depth of 19.5 metres, the canal is deep enough for most ships other than supertankers.

The canal is a prime source of hard currency for Egypt's beleaguered economy. Each ship that passes through the canal is charged a fee based on its size and weight. The average fee is about US$70,000. Over 50 ships make the 15 hour journey daily; the canal's daily capacity is 80 ships.

PORT SAID

The main attraction of Port Said, and the reason for its establishment on the Mediterranean, is the Suez Canal. Its status as a duty-free port also makes it the most flourishing of the canal cities. There are some mediocre beaches along the Mediterranean which are good for swimming and, along some of the original city streets, there are some fine old buildings with wooden balconies.

The spectacle of the huge ships and tankers lining up to pass through the northern entrance of the canal is certainly something to be seen, but there's not really all that much to do.

Port Said was founded in 1859 by its namesake, the khedive Said Pasha, as excavation for the Suez Canal began. Much of the city is an island, created by filling in part of Lake Manzela, to the west, with sand from the canal site. The city continued to grow until 1956, when much of it was bombed during the Suez Crisis. It suffered again during the 1967 and 1973 wars with Israel. Damage can still be seen but most of the city has been rebuilt.

Today, Port Said is a city of 257,000 people, connected to the mainland by a bridge to the south and a causeway to the west. There is also a ferry across Lake Manzela to Matariyyah, and another between Port Said and its sister town, Port Fouad, on the other side of the canal.

Egyptians think of Port Said as a summer resort, and hundreds of beach bungalows line the Mediterranean coast along the city's northern edge. However, unlike Alexandria, Port Said has not yet been overrun by throngs of Egyptians seeking sun, sand and sea.

Information

Most of the banks and important services are either on Sharia Palestine, which runs along the canal, or on the New Corniche, which runs along the beach front at right angles to the canal.

Customs As Port Said is a duty-free port, everyone must pass through customs when entering and leaving the city, so be sure to have your passport with you. Also, be sure to declare cameras, lenses, radios, cassette players or anything else that a bored customs official might think you bought at a discount in Port Said. If you don't, you may get slapped with a 12% customs duty tax on the undeclared goods when you leave.

Tourist Office The tourist office, at 43 Sharia Palestine, has maps, some

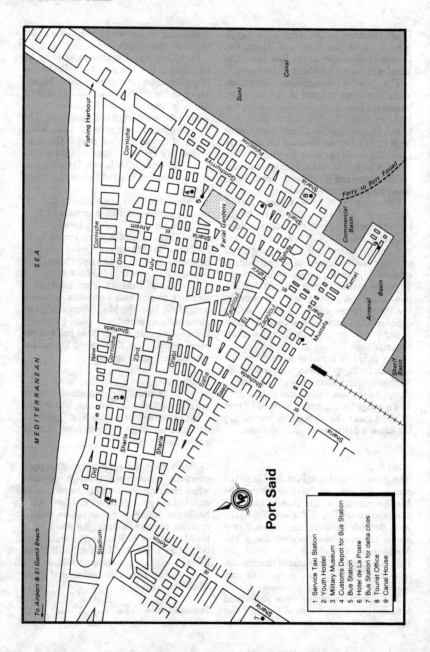

Port Said

1 Service Taxi Station
2 Youth Hostel
3 Military Museum
4 Customs Depot for Bus Station
5 Bus Station
6 Hotel de La Poste
7 Bus Station for delta cities
8 Tourist Office
9 Canal House

information about the Suez Canal and the port, and a very complete hotel list – just in case the ones listed here are full. Zenatte Nour, one of the officials there, speaks English and French and is full of facts about the canal. The office is open from 8 am to 2 pm Saturday to Thursday and 8 am to 12 noon on Friday.

Post & Telecommunications The GPO is opposite the Farial Gardens, one block from Sharia Gomhurriya.

The telephone and telegraph office is on Sharia Palestine, two blocks north of the tourist office.

Money There are numerous money-changing offices around town which offer better rates than the banks. Thomas Cook, on Sharia Gomhurriya, is conveniently situated.

Consulates The US Consulate (tel 22154, 23886) is at 11 Sharia Gomhurriya.

The West German Consulate is on the corner of Sharia Gomhurriya and Sharia Tahr el Bahr, in the Hamza building.

Canal House

One of the best views of the canal used to be from the large white-columned building south of the ferry terminal and tourist office. The dome of the Canal House is now off-limits because, according to the gate guards, it 'contains great secrets'. Even a promise to keep my eyes shut as I passed by the 'secret' offices to the dome didn't get me in. You might try to talk your way in, however, as security at the front gate seems arbitrary.

Port Fouad

This is really a suburb of civil servants, across the canal from Port Said. It was founded in 1925. The yacht club in Port Fouad is the place to go to find a passage or work on a vessel through the canal, as the captains are often looking for crew members. The free ferry from Port Said to Port Fouad, which offers a great view of

the canal, leaves about every 10 minutes from a terminal one block south of the tourist office.

Military Museum

The small military museum on Sharia 23rd July has some interesting relics from the 1967 and 1973 wars with Israel. There are captured American tanks with freshly painted Stars of David, a couple of unexploded bombs and various other unpleasant reminders of recent wars, as well as exhibits of ancient Pharaonic and Islamic conflicts. The museum costs E£1 to get in; it is open from 9 am to 2 pm and occasionally from 5 to 8 pm.

Farial Gardens

If you get tired of watching ships cruise in and out of the canal, the Farial Gardens offer a pleasant refuge for a stroll or a picnic. They're in the centre of town next to the bus station.

Places to Stay – bottom end

The *Youth Hostel*, near the stadium, is the cheapest place to stay in Port Said, but as hostels go it's not such a good deal. It's E£2 per night with an IYHA card and E£3 a night without. I've no idea what the rooms are like. When I dropped in at 4.30 pm and asked to see the rooms, the manager stuttered and said, 'No, the *shababs* and *shababettes* (male and female hostellers) are sleeping'. Sleeping! At 4.30 in the afternoon? Let me know if you stay there.

The Akry Hotel and the El Ghazal Hotel are a couple of the best deals in town. The Greek-owned *Akry Hotel* (tel 21013), at 24 Sharia Gomhurriya, has clean singles and doubles without bath for about E£8; and doubles with bath for E£10. The *El Ghazal Hotel*, at 23 Sharia 23rd July, has doubles for E£9 with bath or E£7 without.

Places to Stay – middle

The *Hotel de la Poste*, on Sharia Gomhurriya, has a fading elegance which the management has attempted to salvage through careful renovation. Doubles with bath cost from E£9 to E£15 per night and some rooms have a TV and refrigerator. There's a restaurant, bar and patisserie downstairs. It's worth having a chat with the hotel manager, Mr Salem Sakra, if you can catch him in the evenings. One of the 'Heroes of Port Said', he fought off invading British troops in the 1956 Suez Crisis and later became city manager and governor of Sohag province.

The *Vendome Hotel* (tel 20802), at 37 Sharia Gomhurriya, has clean, simple rooms at E£8/6 for a single with/without bath; or E£12/9 a double with/without bath. All prices include breakfast.

The *Regent Hotel*, a few doors down from the Vendome, has large, charming rooms with hardwood floors, armoires and balconies. They cost E£13 a double without bath or E£15 with.

The *Abu Simbel Hotel*, 15 Sharia Gomhurriya, is a modern, almost European-style establishment with shower/toilet stalls, TV, fans and refrigerators in all rooms. There is supposed to be hot water but the Italian water heaters in each room don't seem to work. At E£16 for a double and E£12 for a single (including breakfast), it's slightly overpriced.

Places to stay – top end

The *Holiday*, on Sharia Gomhurriya opposite the Hotel de la Poste, has doubles for E£35 and singles for E£28, including taxes and breakfast.

The *ETAP*, on the beach front, gets a four star rating from the tourist office, mostly because of the views. Singles are E£35 and doubles are E£28, plus a 14% tax and E£3 for breakfast. You must show official exchange receipts for payment.

Places to Eat

Not surprisingly, there are plenty of fish restaurants in Port Said. One of the best and cheapest is *Galal*, on the corner of Sharia Gomhurriya and Sharia Gaberti, one block from the Hotel de la Poste. You

pay E£5 for a fish, complete with head and bulging eyes, and a couple of Egyptian salads.

The *Geanola*, next door to the Abu Simbel Hotel, has big meals of fish, meat, salad and chips, etc for about E£6. The owner is Italian and the menu is in French.

In front of the *Hotel de la Poste* there's a bar, a cafe and a restaurant. The latter has cheap hamburgers, sandwiches, salads and what is called pizza.

Opposite the ETAP there's the *Hati al Medina* restaurant, which serves the best and cheapest kufta, kebab and salads in town.

For a splurge try *Maxim*, the best restaurant in town, where you can get a full fish dinner for E£15. It's on the corner of the Old Corniche and Sharia Gomhurriya and has a splendid view of the ships entering the canal.

Things to Buy

Almost anything can be bought in Port Said, from the latest Western fashions to Sony walkmen and VCRs, at duty-free prices. The best deals can be found along Sharia Gomhurriya, one of the main shopping streets.

Getting There & Away

Bus The bus terminal is on a small street next to the Farial Gardens. Remember to get there early because you must first pass through customs. Inside the terminal, you pass to the left if you have nothing to declare.

Buses to Cairo leave every hour from 7 am to 6 pm. Tickets with the Superjet company cost E£7; E£5 with the Golden Rocket company. The Delta bus company charges E£5.50 for a bumpy ordinary bus; E£6 for a bumpy ordinary bus with air-conditioning; or E£7 for the express bus, which gets to Cairo in 2½ hours – 30 minutes faster than the others.

The Golden Rocket company's Cairo-bound buses are the only ones which stop in Ismailia. The trip there takes 1½ hours; the buses also stop at Qantara.

Delta buses are the only ones which go to Alexandria. The E£7 Express and the E£6 air-conditioned buses leave at 8 and 10 am and 12 noon. The ordinary Delta bus costs E£5 and leaves at 2.30 pm.

Delta buses leave for Suez at 1 and 4 pm and cost E£4 for the 3½ hour trip.

Buses to the delta towns of Mansur, Damietta, Tanta and Zagazig leave from a bus station on Sharia Stalingrad, just past the Salah Salim Mosque near Sharia al Amin.

Train There are at least four trains a day to Ismailia and Cairo (four hours). Check departure times in advance.

Taxi Service taxis to all the previously mentioned destinations leave from the old train station square on Sharia al Amin. The fares are: Qantara – E£1; Cairo – E£4; Ismailia – E£2; Suez – E£5; and Zagazig – E£4.

Boat Unless you are a merchant sailor, getting a passage on a merchant vessel going through the canal is nearly impossible. However, you may be able to get a passage or work on a private yacht from Port Fouad.

The North African Shipping Company (NASCO), 83 Sharia Nabi Daniel, Alexandria (or 171 Sharia Mohammed Farid, Cairo), represents the Louis Cruise Lines' ships *Princesa Cypria* and *Marissa*, both of which usually travel between Alexandria, Port Said, Israel and Cyprus. Departures from Alexandria every Tuesday and Friday.

Getting Around

The horse-drawn carriages known as hantours are the best and most enjoyable way to tour Port Said, especially around sunset. The carriage and driver can be hired for about E£3 to E£4 per hour.

QANTARA

The only reason to visit the town of Qantara, 80 km south of Port Said, is so that you can cross to the east side of the canal and leave again as quickly as possible. The service taxis, which cross the Sinai to the Egypt-Israel border, leave from the east bank.

Most of Qantara was destroyed during the 1973 war with Israel and the town's buildings are still pocked with bullet holes. A free boat ferries passengers from one side of the canal to the other. Be prepared to join a stampede of people, chickens, and donkeys for a space on the boat. It can be fun if your sense of humour is still intact after trying to talk a donkey out of your seat.

ISMAILIA

Ismailia was founded by and named after Pasha Ismail, the ruler of Egypt during the construction of the Suez Canal in the 1860s. Ferdinand de Lesseps, the director of the Suez Canal Company, lived in the city until the canal was completed.

Ismailia is perhaps the most picturesque of the new canal towns, yet it has been quickly developing, or rather devolving, into an urban mess. The city of 500,000 people is divided in two by the railway line, which marks a boundary between well-tended streets on one side and a veritable disaster area on the other.

The streets and squares on the eastern side of the city are lined with trees and dotted with malls and parks. The Sweetwater Canal, named for its fresh water connection with the Nile, weaves through this half of Ismailia, around lush thickets of trees to Lake Timsah, or Crocodile Lake, which is the smallest of the Bitter Lakes.

On the other side of the tracks you'll find the main bus and service taxi station – a microcosm of the surrounding neighbourhood, which features muddy, potholed streets, horn-honking maniacs and smoking piles of garbage.

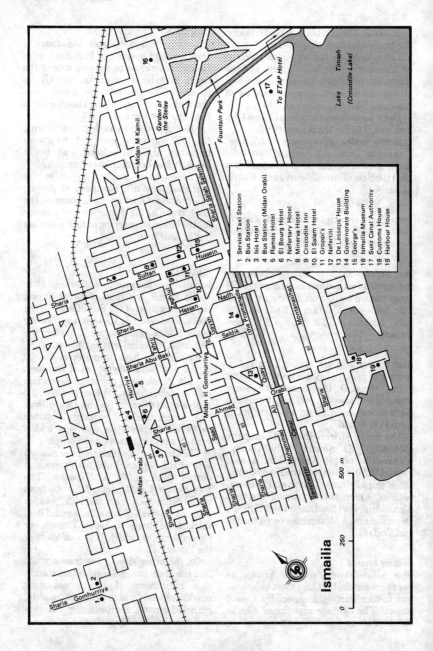

Ismailia

1 Service Taxi Station
2 Bus Station
3 Isis Hotel
4 Bus Station (Midan Orabi)
5 Ramsis Hotel
6 El Bourg Hotel
7 Nefertary Hotel
8 Minerva Hotel
9 Crocodile Inn
10 El Salam Hotel
11 Groppi's
12 Nefertiti
13 De Lesseps' House
14 Governorate Building
15 George's
16 Ismailia Museum
17 Suez Canal Authority
18 Customs House
19 Harbour House

Lake
Timsah
(Crocodile Lake)

Orientation

Ismailia's main street runs diagonally from the station, around the gardens of Midan el Gomhurriya, to Mohammed Ali Quay, the street which runs beside the Sweetwater Canal. The quay is also known as the Promenade and Sharia Salah Salem.

Information

Registration You must register with the police if you intend to stay in Ismailia for more than 24 hours.

Tourist Office The tourist office is at the end of a 1st floor hall, in the Governorate building on Mohammed Ali Quay. It is open from 8 am to 2 pm daily except Friday and, apart from being somewhat of an educational experience, is next to useless. The slack hours give the sluggish bureaucrats who work there plenty of time to read their newspapers and watch the faded tourist posters peel off the walls. If you really want a lesson in Egyptian bureaucracy, try asking for a street map of Ismailia; I tried and the following happened:

An official from the State Information Office had taken me downstairs to the tourist office after unsuccessfully searching for a map himself by opening and closing a lot of drawers. I saw a colourful wall map just outside the door as we entered the tourist office, but realised all the street names were in Arabic. There were two women in the office, so I asked them for a smaller version of the wall map. They briefly looked up from their newspapers and bare desktops, sighed and shrugged their shoulders.

I looked to the official for help. He also shrugged, so I went back to the wall map outside and started drawing it. The official hovered behind me watching.

Me: What's the name of this street? _
Official: Hmmm, do you have a car?
Me: No. What's the name of this square?
Official: Well, if you had a car then I could show you around Ismailia.

He sounded really disappointed. As a final test

I pointed to another street on the map – the street right in front of the Governorate building. He didn't know, so I asked if he knew someone in the building from Ismailia.

Official: I'm from Ismailia.

Another man appeared and the official asked him for a map. We followed the second official into the tourist office. He opened a drawer and pulled out a beautifully drawn map of the city. I asked if they had a photocopier so that a copy could be made.

Official: No.
Me: OK, I'll trace it then. Do you have a sheet of paper?
Official: No.

I didn't believe him. After all, this was a government office. No paper, ha! I remembered that I had some, so I started tracing the map myself.

Official: Why are you doing that?
Me: Because you said that you didn't have a copy machine.
Official: We have a copy machine upstairs.

He disappeared with the map but returned after a few minutes without copies.

Official: The map was too big.

I'm not sure what finally prompted her, but one of the women with her nose in a newspaper suddenly opened a drawer and handed me a dusty tourist map of Ismailia. I dashed out of the office with the official closely following me.

Official: Are you sure that you don't have a car?

Post & Telecommunications The GPO and the telephone office are on the south-west corner of Midan el Gomhurriya.

Ismailia Museum

This small but interesting museum on Mohammed Ali Quay, several blocks north-east of the Governorate building, has more than 4000 objects from Pharaonic and Greco-Roman times. There are statues, scarabs and stelae, and details of the completion of the first canal, between the Bitter Lakes and Bubastis, by Darius. The 4th century AD mosaics are the highlight of the collection.

Garden of the Stelae

Near the museum is a garden containing sphinxes from the time of Ramses II. You need permission from the museum to visit the garden.

De Lesseps' House

The residence of the one-time French consul to Egypt used to be open to the public, but now you can only see the interior if you're a VIP of some sort. If you really want to see the outside of the house where de Lesseps lived while directing the construction of the Suez Canal, it's on Mohammed Ali Quay near the corner of Sharia Ahmed Orabi.

Beaches

There are several good beaches around Lake Timsah but using them involves paying to get into one of the resort clubs that dot the shore. Entrance fees vary, as some include a buffet lunch as part of the admission price, but all include access to a private swimming beach. Supposedly the lake was once full of crocodiles, but there have been no sightings for a good many centuries and certainly no record of any swimming tourists being mistaken for lunch.

According to the locals, the best beach is Le Jardin des Enfants which is two km north of Ismailia. It belongs to the Suez Canal Authority, but is open to the public for a E£5 entrance fee.

Places to Stay – bottom end

The *Minerva Hotel*, 29 Sharia Saad Zaghloul, charges E£6 for a bed in a somewhat dark and gloomy double room. The benevolent manager really needs to do something, though, about the faulty water heaters and somersaulting fleas.

The *Isis Hotel* on Midan Orabi, opposite the train station, is very clean and reasonably priced. Singles without

bath are E£7 or E£8.50 and with bath are E£11. Doubles are E£15/12 with/without bath. Breakfast is about E£2.25.

The *Nefertary Hotel*, 41 Sharia Sultan Hussein, is similar to the Isis. They have doubles with a bath for E£9 and doubles without a bath for E£7.50. Breakfast costs E£2.

There's a relatively new 400 bed *Youth Hostel* in the El Sheikh Zayid area northwest of Ismailia. Sheikh Zayid bin Sultan al Mahayan, the ruler of Abu Dhabi and president of the United Arab Emirates, financed much of the construction in this area. A bed costs E£3.50 per night.

Camping There is no official campground in the Ismailia area; however, it is possible to camp on the beach around Lake Timsah.

Places to Stay – middle

The *Ramsis Hotel* is on Sharia el Hurriya about two blocks to your left as you leave the train station. It has very clean doubles, with a TV, telephone and air-con in every room, for E£15 per night. Breakfast is, according to the manager, 'almost whatever you want' and costs E£3.

The *El Salam Hotel*, on Sharia el Gaysh, has clean singles and doubles with baths for E£20 and E£25 respectively.

The *El Bourg Hotel*, on Midan Orabi, has 27 suites each with colour TV, bathroom and air-con. Rooms cost E£20 to E£30 per night.

Places to Stay – top end

The *Crocodile Inn*, on the corner of Sharia Saad Zaghloul and Sharia Sultan Hussein, seems to have everything except crocodiles. There are various lounges and restaurants including a 24 hour coffee shop. Singles are E£23 and doubles E£30.

The *ETAP*, right on the lake at Gezira el Fursan, has all the amenities of an expensive hotel. For around E£10 you can use their swimming pool and beach, and for E£15, on Friday and Sunday, you can make a pig of yourself at their buffets.

Top: Entrance to the Suez Canal, Port Said (SW)
Bottom: Waiting for fuel on the Qena-Hurghada road (HF)

Top: The Mediterranean at Marsa Matruh (SW)
Left: Midan Saad Zaghloul, Alexandria (SW)
Right: The British War Cemetery, El Alamein (SW)

Places to Eat

The *Social Club* is a garden restaurant and cafeteria in Milaha Garden, run by the Ismailia Governorate, where you can get good, inexpensive meals.

George's and the *Nefertiti*, both on Sharia Sultan Hussein, serve fish and meat dishes for about E£6 to E£10.

Groppi's is across the street from George's. It's a smaller version of the Cairo Groppi's, but with just as good a selection of pastries and ice cream.

Getting There & Away

Bus Buses for Cairo and Port Said depart from Midan Orabi every 30 to 45 minutes. Express buses leave for Cairo at least three times a day.

Buses for Suez, Alexandria and El Arish depart from the Sharia Gomhurriya terminal just west of the train tracks. Buses to Suez leave hourly; buses to Alexandria take five hours and leave at 7 am and 2.30 pm; buses to El Arish leave at 8 and 11.30 am and also at 1 pm, and take three hours.

Bus times can vary, so it is wise to check them in advance.

Train Every day there are eight trains to Cairo, four to Port Said and nine to Suez.

Taxi Service taxis depart frequently from the Sharia Gomhurriya terminal for Cairo (E£3), Port Said and Suez.

Getting Around

Ismailia's parks and tree-lined streets are good bike riding territory. There are a few bike shops on the side streets off Mohammed Ali Quay – just ask around for the best deal.

SUEZ

Suez is a city going through a metamorphosis. It was all but destroyed during the 1967 and 1973 wars with Israel and traces of the devastation are still visible. The revamped main streets are mostly a facade hiding a sordid mess of back street slums, though they are a sign that things are gradually changing for the better. The bombed-out hulls of buildings (some occupied by squatters), walls peppered with bullet holes and streets littered with debris remain amongst the reconstruction works, while three US-made Israeli tanks squat on the Corniche as a memorial to the wartime victories.

Suez sprawls around the shores of the gulf where the Red Sea meets the southern entrance of the Suez Canal. There is nothing much to do there except take in the best view of the ships passing in or out of the canal, and there's very little in the way of tourist facilities. Suez is basically just a transit point, not only for the great tankers, cargo vessels and private yachts en route to or from the Mediterranean, but for travellers and the Muslim faithful as well. The Gulf of Suez is one of the departure points for the haj, or pilgrimage to Mecca; most other people just pass through Suez on their way to the Sinai or the Red Sea beaches.

Information

Tourist Office The staff at the Port Tewfik tourist office, on the eastern side of Suez Bay, are helpful almost to the point of being obsequious. They are more than eager to provide information about the city, canal and surrounding sites. The office is open from 8.30 am to 2.30 pm daily, except Friday.

Post & Telecommunications The GPO is on Sharia Hoda Shaarawi. The telephone office is on Sharia Salaam between Sharia Abdul el Sarawat and Sharia Haleem.

Money There are plenty of moneychanging offices in Suez, especially at Port Tewfik.

Places to Stay – bottom end

The *Youth Hostel*, on Sharia Tariq el Horeya facing the stadium, is often full of stampeding kids. Only stay at this place, which is a long walk from the bus station,

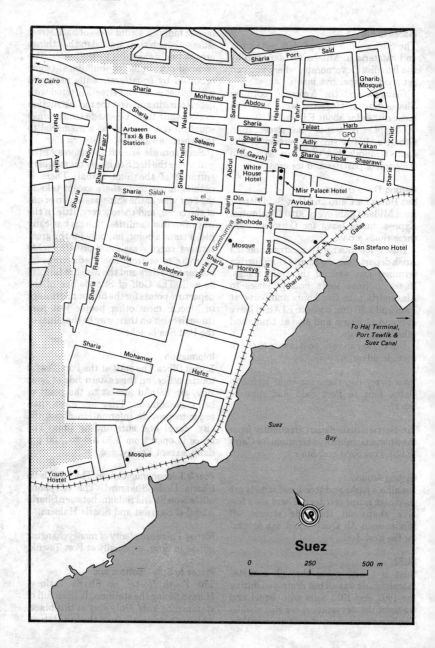

To Cairo

Sharia Port Said

Gharib Mosque

Sharia

Sharia

Mohamed

Abdou

Sarawat

Haleem

Tahrir

Sharia el Faarz

Arbaeen Taxi & Bus Station

Waleed

Sharia Khalid

Salaam

Sharia el

Sharia

Talaat Harb

GPO

Adly Yakan

Hoda Shaarawi

Khidr

Raouf

Sharia

Ataka

Sharia Salah

el

Abdul Din el

White House Hotel

Misr Palace Hotel

Sharia Salah el Din el Ayoubi

Sharia

Sharia Rashed

Sharia

Shohoda

Gomhurriya

Mosque

Zaghloui

Galaa

San Stefano Hotel

Sharia el Baladeya

Sharia el Horeya

Saad

el

Sharia

To Haj Terminal, Port Tewfik & Suez Canal

Sharia Mohamed

Hafez

Suez Bay

Mosque

Youth Hostel

Suez

0 250 500 m

as a last resort if you're desperate. It costs E£2 per night for members or E£3 for nonmembers.

The similar but more civilised *Haj Terminal*, on the north shore of Suez Bay, is a good deal for E£2 a night. It's on the Corniche (also called Sharia el Galaa), between the city and Port Tewfik, and is basically four large rooms, each with 150 beds. The showers are clean and there's a cafeteria.

The *Misr Palace Hotel*, 2 Sharia Saad Zaghloul, has 101 beds in single and double rooms of varying prices, standards and degrees of cleanliness. Singles/ doubles without showers are E£6.25/8; with showers they're E£7/13. Check the room they offer before you decide to stay.

Places to Stay – middle

The *Hotel Beau Rivage*, 44 Sharia Saad Zaghloul, has singles with showers from E£9 to E£10.25 and doubles with showers from E£11 to E£13. Breakfast is an additional E£2.50.

The *White House Hotel*, 322 Sharia Salaam, is a very clean, respectable and popular place. Singles with showers range from E£29 to E£34; without showers they're E£18. Doubles with/without bath are E£38/26. They charge you E£2.50 for air-con even when it's cold outside. The hotel restaurant serves a variety of filling meals for E£5 to E£9.

The *Bel Air Hotel* on Sharia Saad Zaghloul, opposite the Misr Palace, has also been recommended. It costs E£14 for a double with bath and it has a good restaurant.

Places to Stay – top end

The *Red Sea Hotel*, 13 Sharia Riad, Port Tewfik, claims to be one of the best in town, although foreigners who have stayed both there and at the White House Hotel might dispute that. Singles/doubles with bath are E£27/32.

Places to Eat

El Magharbel, next door to the White House Hotel, is one of the few restaurants in town. It serves reasonably good meals for about E£7.

You might also try the sandwich shops for cheap, impromptu meals of meat sandwiches with side orders of pickled vegetables.

The *Social Club*, on the Corniche, has inexpensive fish as well as hazy views of the Gulf of Suez and the surrounding mountains.

Getting There & Away

Bus All buses to Cairo, Ismailia, the Red Sea beaches and the Sinai leave from Arbaeen Station on Sharia el Faarz, near the centre of town.

Buses to Cairo (E£2.50) and Ismailia leave frequently between 7 am and 5 pm. The trip to Cairo takes two hours.

Buses to Ein Sukhna (E£1) depart frequently.

There are three air-conditioned buses a day to Zafarana, Ras Gharib and Hurghada and they should be booked well ahead. The trip to Hurghada takes five hours.

Buses to Oyun Musa, Ras el Sudr, Hammam Fara'un and El Tor leave at 10 am, 12 noon, 1 and 2 pm. The trip takes one hour, 1½ hours and 2½ hours respectively.

Buses to Sharm el Shaykh leave at 7 and 10 am and 2 pm, and take six hours.

Buses to Wadi Feran and St Catherine's depart at 9.30 and 11 am and take three and four hours respectively.

Buses to Nuweiba leave at 9.30 and 10 am and the bus to Taba leaves at 9.30 am.

Buses to the Sinai use the Ahmed Hamdi Tunnel, which goes under the Suez Canal 17 km north of the city. An expatriate in Suez suggested that travellers heading for the Sinai should go to the entrance of the tunnel and wait for the faster, more comfortable Sinai bus from Cairo. The only problem with this is that you must either pay E£13 for a taxi from Suez or talk the driver on the Suez-

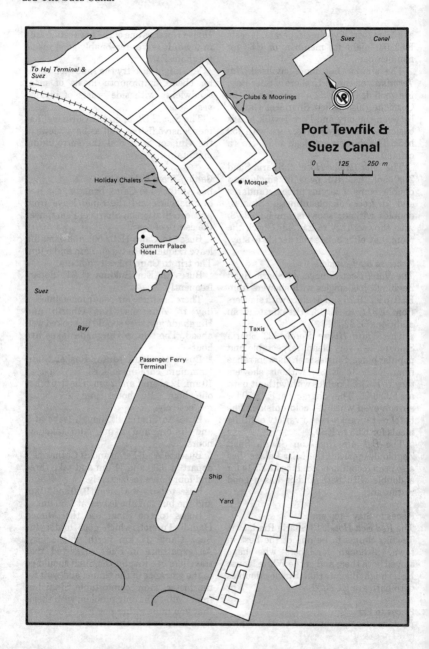

Port Tewfik &
Suez Canal

0   125   250 m

To Haj Terminal &
Suez

Clubs & Moorings

Holiday Chalets

● Mosque

● Summer Palace
Hotel

Suez

Bay

Taxis

Passenger Ferry
Terminal

Ship

Yard

Ismailia bus into dropping you off at the road junction. The Cairo bus has to pass through the junction but the driver may not stop for you there. Hitching might be possible.

Bus times are always subject to change, so remember to check them in advance.

Train There are four or five trains a day to Cairo – check at the station for departure times. The trip takes approximately 3½ hours.

There are also four trains daily to Ismailia, where you can connect with other trains going to Cairo or Port Said.

Taxi Service taxis go to all the destinations serviced by buses and trains. They take seven passengers, are faster than buses over long distances and the fares are usually about the same.

Boat It is possible to travel by boat between Suez and Jeddah. The trip from Suez (via Aqaba in Jordan) takes three days. Single fares from Egypt are E£165 in 1st class, E£145 in 2nd class and E£105 on deck. Contact the Egyptian Navigation Company on Sharia el Nabi Mousa in Suez or Menatours on Sharia Talaat Harb in Cairo for details, as the schedule is a bit erratic.

There's also a boat called the *Saudi Moon* that goes from Suez to Jeddah. As Gordon Robinson, a writer who covers Saudi Arabia and the Gulf for Lonely Planet, discovered, getting on this boat can be an adventure:

The departure system at Suez is not equipped to deal with the presence of a foreigner on the boat. Having cleared Security, we were loaded into minibuses for the trip to the other side of the docks. Once there we piled out and into a long, narrow room with pale green walls. The Egyptians were each handed a yellow departure card and a piece of paper with a tax stamp on it. The clerk stared at me for a moment, and then began rummaging through a drawer for the pink foreigners' departure card.

After I had filled out the card, an officer came along, inspected it and pronounced it incomplete. I would have to take the card down to the Immigration Office at the other end of the dock, he said. It could not be processed here (in the departure lounge, at passport control).

'Why not?'

'It is incorrect. You must go. Not possible here.'

'Well, where do I go?'

'There.'

'Where there? What is the name of the office? The office of the police?'

'No, you must go to the other one.

At the far end of the dock I found the 'other' police post where I was made to fill out another card. The first one, it seemed, had not been signed by a particular (absent) official. I waited while the official was located (he was, it appeared, back in the departure hall) to sign the card. This accomplished, I filled it out, waited while it and the official signature were again checked, and was then told to go to Immigration to have the passport stamped. Where, I asked, was Immigration?

'There.' Oh no, I thought, here we go again. . .

Of course, wherever Immigration might be it was most certainly *not* in the building marked 'Immigration/Passports' (that would have been too easy). The official there looked at my duly signed card, and pointed me back toward the police post from which I had just come: 'There,' he said. I protested that the people 'There' had sent me 'Here'. After hurried consultation, the officers decided that I should return to the long, narrow green room. They would, they said, figure out what to do about me and send someone around to take care of it.

To my surprise someone did appear in the departure room about 15 minutes later (being the only non-Arab in the room I was not difficult to locate) and informed me that I could now proceed through passport control. Another ride in an overcrowded minibus followed, and I was soon boarding the *Saudi Moon* – at last. Now all I had to do was make it through the next three days on the boat.

More of Gordon's experiences can be found in Lonely Planet's *West Asia on a shoestring*. He adds that if you thought departure formalities in Suez were fun, wait until you get to Jeddah. . .

On Saturday and Wednesday, the boat

to Aqaba departs at 12 noon; check-in starts at 9 am. Fares for the 17 hour trip range from E£70.50 to E£113.50. The boat from Aqaba to Suez departs on Monday and Saturday.

Getting Around

There are regular minibus services along Sharia Salaam from Arbaeen Station to Port Tewfik. They stop to pick you up or drop you off wherever you want along the route and cost 25 pt.

The Red Sea Coast

WARNING: Much of the coastline is mined. Use only designated beaches and roads and if you're unsure ask the local military authorities.

EIN SUKHNA

Ein Sukhna, which means 'hot eyes', is the site of springs originating from within Mt Ataka, the highest mountain on the Red Sea coast. There's not much to Ein Sukhna, except a wonderfully deserted beach and the hot springs, but the area is gradually being developed as a resort.

There are several buses from Suez, 55 km north, so it's possible to visit Ein Sukhna on a day trip from the canal city.

If you want to stay longer there is the *Ein Sukhna Hotel*, which has 80 rooms and 30 bungalows from E£40 to E£55 a double.

ZAFARANA

This town, 62 km south of Ein Sukhna and 150 km east of Beni Suef on the Nile, is little more than a way stop for visits to the isolated Coptic monasteries of St Anthony and St Paul in the mountains overlooking the Gulf of Suez.

Buses running between Suez and Hurghada will take you to Zafarana.

MONASTERIES OF ST ANTHONY & ST PAUL

The Coptic Christian monasteries of St Anthony and St Paul are open for day trips between 9 am and 5 pm; permission to stay overnight must be obtained from the Coptic Patriarch in Cairo, at 222 Sharia Ramses, Abbassiya. St Anthony's guest house is for men only. St Paul's has accommodation for men and women but the monks won't take any visitors at all during Lent.

The monasteries are only about 30 km apart, but thanks to the cliffs of the Gebel el Galala el Qibliya they're around 82 km apart by road.

Monastery of St Anthony

Hidden away in the barren cliffs of the Eastern Desert, the fortified religious community of St Anthony's represented the beginning of the Christian monastic tradition. Built in the 4th century AD by the disciples of St Anthony, the walled village at the foot of Mt Kalalah is the largest of the Coptic monasteries.

This founding monastic order sprang up around the son of a merchant who had given up his worldly possessions to devote his life to God. Anthony actually retreated into the desert, in about 294 AD, to escape the disciples he had attracted to his hermit's cave by the Nile. While his followers adopted an austere communal life at the foot of the mountain, Anthony took himself off to a cave, high above the developing monastery village, where he lived to the ripe old age of 105.

Despite its isolation, the monastery suffered Bedouin raids in the 8th and 9th centuries, attacks from irate Muslims in the 11th century and a 15th century revolt by bloodthirsty servants that resulted in the massacre of the monks.

Following the example set by St Anthony, St Paul and their followers 16 centuries ago, the 25 monks and five novices who live at St Anthony's today have dedicated their lives to poverty, chastity, obedience and prayer.

St Anthony's has several churches, chapels, dormitories, a bakery, vegetable garden and a spring. The oldest part of the

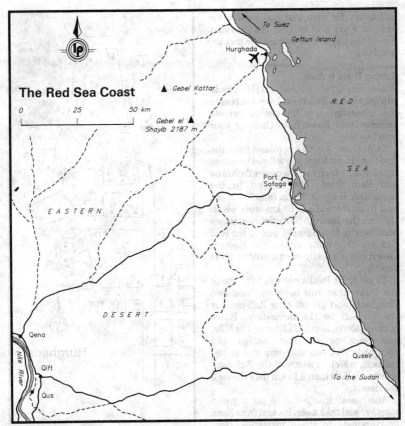

The Red Sea Coast

0   25   50 km

To Suez

Geftun Island

Hurghada

▲ Gebel Kattar

Gebel el ▲
Shayib 2187 m

RED

SEA

Port
Safaga

EASTERN

DESERT

Qena

Nile River

Qift

Qus

Quseir

To the Sudan

monastery is the Church of St Anthony, built over the saint's tomb. There is a *Guest House* for men only.

If you're hiking in from the main road make sure you're properly equipped, especially with water, as it's a long, hot and dry walk. If you do get this far you should also hike up to the Cave of St Anthony, which is north-east of the monastery. The medieval graffiti on the walls is fascinating and there is a breathtaking view of the hills and valley below.

Monastery of St Paul

The most fascinating part of this large complex, in the cliffs of the Gebel el Galala el Qibliya, is the Church of St Paul, cluttered with altars, candles, ostrich eggs (the symbol of the Resurrection) and colourful murals. It was built in and around the cave where Paul lived for nearly 90 years, during the 4th century, after founding the monastery as a show of devotion to St Anthony. The fortress, above the church, was where the monks retreated during Bedouin raids.

Visitors are more than welcome and a couple of the monks, who speak excellent English, give guided tours. St Paul's has two *Guest Houses*, one inside the monastery for men and one outside for women. Food and lodging are provided free of charge, so don't abuse the monks' hospitality.

Getting There & Away

Buses running between Suez and Hurghada will take you to Zafarana. Direct access to the monasteries is limited to private vehicles, tour buses from Cairo or your own two feet.

St Anthony's is 45 km inland from the Red Sea. To get there you follow the rather rough road which runs between Zafarana and Beni Suef. The turn-off to the monastery is about 35 km from Zafarana and from there it's a 10 km walk south through the desert to St Anthony's. Buses occasionally travel from Cairo to the Red Sea via this route across the Eastern Desert but it's really more suited to 4WD vehicles.

To get to St Paul's you can take one of the buses that run between Suez and Hurghada and get off after Zafarana at the turn-off to the monastery. Buses between Qena, north of Luxor on the Nile, and Suez go via Port Safaga and Hurghada and can also drop you at the turn-off, which is south of the Zafarana lighthouse. It's then a 13 km hike through the desert.

Another alternative is to get a group together and take a service taxi from Suez or Hurghada to the monasteries. Beni Suef is also a departure point for the 150 km trek across the desert to the monasteries. You'd really need your own truck or 4WD to make this journey, as it might be difficult to hire a service taxi in Beni Suef for the whole trip.

HURGHADA (GHARDAKA)

The only attractions of this one-time isolated and modest fishing village are the warm and brilliant turquoise waters of the Red Sea, the amazing colours of the splendid coral and exotic creatures of the deep, and the soft white sand beaches backed up by the mountains of the

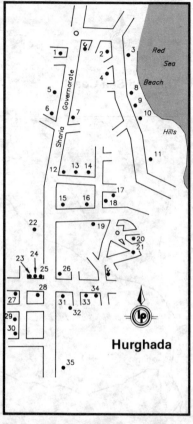

Hurghada

Eastern Desert. There are no ancient tombs and no Pharaonic temples or crumbling monasteries, just nature at its best.

While the crystal-clear waters and fascinating reefs have made Hurghada, or Ghardaka as the Egyptians call it, a popular destination amongst diving enthusiasts the world over, if you're not into beaches, swimming or snorkelling then this developing resort town probably has little to offer.

The beaches near town are marred by chunks of concrete, iron rods and empty oil drums – the results of an ongoing hotel

1	EgyptAir
2	Seahorse Hotel
3	Hurghada Hotel
4	El Gezira Hotel
5	Tourist Information Office
6	Telephone Office
7	GPO
8	Shedwan Golden Beach Hotel
9	Hotel Construction Site
10	Geisum Camping/Seafood Restaurant
11	Apartments
12	Bicycle Rental
13	Ta'amiyya Stand
14	(Blackhorse) Seahorse Trips
15	Red Sea Restaurant
16	Abak Pastries
17	Aladin's Lamp Restaurant
18	Grocery Stores & Restaurant Telknae
19	Abak Restaurant
20	Happy House Two
21	Old Bus Station
22	Minibus to beaches near Giftun Village, the Sheraton & Moon Valley Village
23	Sunshine House
24	Sunshine Sea Trips
25	Sunshine Restaurant
26	Weshahy Restaurant
27	Ramoza Seatrips
28	Luxor Tourist Flat
29	Ramoza Hotel
30	Barracuda Hotel
31	Service taxis to Suez/Cairo/Luxor/Aswan
32	Happy Home
33	Happy House
34	Red Sea Wonderland (Captain Mohammed)
35	New Bus Station

construction boom. New hotels, resort villages, campgrounds, a big youth hostel and more dive centres were all in various stages of construction at the time of writing. With more competition among hotels, the prices listed in the hotel section will most likely change, perhaps drastically, in the coming years. It's possible that the beautiful beaches south of Hurghada (mainly south of the Sheraton) will also change, perhaps for the worse, because of development. Most of the best beaches have already been claimed by resort complexes in the three to five star range, beginning with the Sheraton and going 15 to 20 km south.

Aside from the beaches, there's also, of course, good swimming and excellent diving around the coral reefs and offshore islands; an increasing number of places in town and at the hotels provide equipment for most aquatic sports.

Information

Tourist Office The tourist office (tel 439337) is on Sharia Governorate but the staff aren't very helpful. The GPO and the telephone office are near the big town mosque. The latter is open 24 hours every day except Friday.

Airline Offices The EgyptAir office is also near the main mosque. Note that you can't use credit cards to buy tickets at the EgyptAir office in Hurghada; nor can you obtain a credit card cash advance from the local banks.

Marine Museum

The marine biology station, about five km north of town, has an interesting museum and aquarium. There is a huge collection of fantastically colourful fish, Red Sea sharks and the rare whalelike manatees. Entry to the museum is free and a bus there costs 50 pt.

Water Sports

Hurghada's underwater paradise really shouldn't be missed. The coral reefs are teeming with weird and wonderful exotic marine creatures that swim, float or just lie on the bottom in a variety of shapes, sizes and colours.

Although there is some easily accessible coral at the beach south of the Sheraton, the best reefs are offshore – the most popular ones are around Geftun Island – and the only way to see them is to take a boat and make a diving excursion of at least one day. There are plenty of places in town that organise trips, but first, a few words of caution.

Arrange your dive the night before and be sure that the proprietor of your hotel or tourist flat has correctly registered your name and passport number.

Take your passport to the dock with you because sometimes the authorities there will want to check it before you board the boat.

Wear a T-shirt to avoid sunburn while swimming and make sure you use sunblock while sitting in the boat.

Wear tennis shoes or reef shoes while exploring tide pools and reefs. The coral is very sharp and can easily cut your feet to pieces.

As pretty as they seem to be, there are some creatures that should be avoided, especially sea urchins, blowfish, fire coral, feathery lionfish, moray eels, turkeyfish, stonefish, parrotfish and, needless to say, sharks. Familiarise yourself with pictures of these creatures before diving.

Snorkelling A day trip, which includes transport to and from the harbour, visits to two diving sites, snorkels, masks and a barbecue lunch on Geftun Island, costs E£15 to E£20 per person.

A trip to the 'House of Sharks' costs E£8 per person (E£6 if you bring your own mask) for a minimum of 10 people. No food is included. The boat departs at 10 am and returns at 4 pm.

An overnight trip, which includes three meals, snorkels, masks, transport and a night on Geftun Island, costs E£30 per person. Bring your own sleeping bag. The boat leaves at 12 noon and returns at 5 pm the following day.

For information and bookings, you have several options. Most hotels and pensions can arrange these trips for you. Captain Mohammed of Happy House (see the Places to Stay section) takes people out in the *Mermaid* – E£25 per person for a day trip to Geftun and Abu Ramada islands and E£10 for the 'House of Sharks'. His son Emad works with his father on these trips from an office next to the Sunshine House (see the Places to Stay section).

There is also a four day, three night trip to several distant islands, for a minimum

of five people, which includes food, snorkels, masks and drinks. The cost is E£80 per person. A tent is available for rent, but take your own sleeping bag. Talk to Ali at the Red Sea Restaurant for more information.

Equipment Diving and snorkelling equipment can be rented at Saleem's, the Magawish Tourist Resort and the Sheraton. Prices are about E£4 for a mask and snorkel, and E£3 for flippers.

Places to stay – bottom end

The *Luxor Tourist Flat* has received mixed reviews. Some say it's dirty, others say it's clean but whichever way you look at it, it's definitely cheap. It costs E£3 per person for a bed and access to hot showers and a kitchen. There are overhead fans in all five rooms. It's on the main road through town, opposite the street to the old bus station. Sometimes the manager raises the price if he thinks he can.

The *Sunshine House*, across the road, is run by Captain Mohammed's entrepreneurial son Emad Mohammed. At the time of writing, he was adding a 2nd floor and hoped to add a rooftop cafe. The 1st floor has three clean, well-maintained rooms with window screens, rugs and powerful overhead fans. The bathrooms are kept spotless, with water, even hot water, available 24 hours. There's a common room and a kitchen with a refrigerator available for guests. The common room becomes a sort of dorm when travellers can't find another place to stay. Emad charges E£3 to E£4 per person.

The *Ramoza Hotel* is almost a two star place. It was being renovated when I visited, so it looked as if a hurricane had just passed through. The rooftop restaurant and cafe were also being renovated. When everything is finished, this should be quite a pleasant place. Single/double/triple rooms are E£10/20/30.

Next to the Ramoza is the *Barracuda Hotel* (tel 440625), which is slightly better for about the same price. Single/double/triple rooms with baths are E£10/20/25; doubles/triples without are E£15/19.

Captain Mohammed's *Happy House* on Midan el Dar Mosque has two double rooms with a kitchen and refrigerator. It is next to his Red Sea Wonderland souvenir shop. If you don't plan to stay here, it's still worth at least stopping by to see the souvenir store and listen to Captain Mohammed's fish stories. The store is a study in seashore kitsch – seashell lamps and picture frames, stuffed fish with protruding lips and sharp teeth, fish nets and cork floats. Fortunately, the rooms are devoid of souvenirs – the hotel is a clean basic place to stay for E£4 to E£5 per person.

Across from Captain Mohammed's is the *Happy Home*, which is run by a happy guy named El Sayed Mustapha. He has eight beds in three rooms with a pleasant common room in the centre. Signs, announcements and decorations cover the walls. He can help you make arrangements for the boat to Sharm el Shaykh. The room price is E£3 to E£4 per person.

Near the centre of town and the old bus station is the *Happy House Two*, a takeoff on Captain Mohammed's place. It has three very clean rooms with overhead fans, occasional rugs, a kitchen, a great common room for breakfast and a decent collection of used paperbacks. The bathrooms are clean and have hot showers. At only E£4 per person, this is a real bargain.

Another inexpensive place that travellers have recommended is the *Luxor Palace Hotel*, which is run by two guys, one Dutch and the other Egyptian. It's near the Shedwan Golden Beach Hotel and the 3 Corners Restaurant.

Camping The official campground is across the road from the Giftun Village and adjacent to the new youth hostel.

Camping is also possible on the beach in front of the Hurghada Hotel for E£2 per person per night.

Places to Stay – middle
The *Moon Valley Village* used to be called the Moon Valley Hotel, but they changed the name and increased the prices. They now have clean, comfortable rooms with fans and tiled floors rather than huts. At E£50/60 for a single/double, however, they are overpriced. Perhaps when the swimming pool and reception area are completed and the beach in front is cleared of construction materials, their room rates will seem fairer. The hotel is a 10 minute drive south of town on the road to the Sheraton.

Closer to town than the Moon Valley is the *Hotel Sherry* (tel 441709), which is set back about 100 metres from the same road. Although its rooms don't have much of a view – the hotel is surrounded by construction sites – they are clean, carpeted, comfortable and have air-conditioning. This is one of the most inexpensive places to stay with air-conditioning in Hurghada. The beach is within walking distance. Single/double/triple rooms are E£25/35/46.

Around the corner is the *Travel Star Hotel*, which is really more in the upper bottom end bracket than the middle one. They have 20 rooms, all with fans and without bathrooms. The bathrooms and showers are clean. Beds are simple, bunk-bed style with foam rubber mattresses and pillows. Singles/doubles are E£25/30. They are building a three star hotel across the road that should be completed by the time this is published. It will have 38 rooms with bathrooms and air-conditioning, a swimming pool, disco and restaurant.

The *Families Hotel* is a dirty deal that can't be recommended at any price.

The *El Gezira Hotel* is a relatively new place adjacent to the Seahorse Hotel. All the rooms have air-con, telephones, carpeting and private bathrooms. A few rooms also have TV. Single/double/triple rooms are E£42/65/87.

The *Seahorse Hotel* (tel 441704) is the cheapest hotel in town with air-conditioned rooms. The air-con is so powerful, you'll probably not want to keep it on all night. There are also rooms without air-con, but these can get quite hot in the summer. The beach is within close walking distance, although the better beaches are outside town. In the summer, singles/doubles without air-con are E£32/52; with air-con they are E£37/57. In the winter, rates are E£39/62 and E£44/67. They accept American Express cards, but a 5% surcharge is added.

On the beach in front of the El Gezira and the Seahorse is the *Hurghada Hotel* (tel 440393) with 10 bungalow-style buildings on the beach, each with three rooms. The beautiful view of the Red Sea compensates for the lack of an adequate beach. From the outside the bungalows look shabby, but inside they're OK – large rooms with clean bathrooms, overhead fans and one to three beds. Prices for singles/doubles/triples start at E£19/26/35.

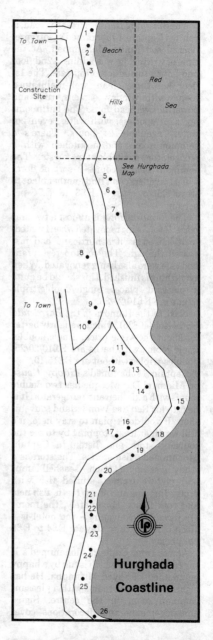

1	Shedwan Golden Beach Hotel
2	Hotel Construction Site
3	Geisum Camping/Seafood Restaurant
4	Apartments
5	New Giftun Hotel Complex
6	New Ferry Terminal
7	Port Area
8	New Tourist Information Centre
9	Red Sea Diving Centre
10	Families Hotel
11	Travel Star Hotel
12	Hotel Sherry
13	Coral Hotel
14	Moon Valley Village (hotel)
15	Sheraton Hotel
16	Youth Hostel
17	Badr Campground
18	Mashrabiyya Hotel
19	Giftun Village
20	Marine Sports Club
21	El Samaka Beach Hotel
22	Princess Club
23	Hor Palace Hotel
24	Magawish Resort Village
25	Jasmine Village (hotel)
26	New Hotel Complex

Places to Stay – top end

The hotels in this category mostly cater to groups, which usually means that their rates will be higher than similar hotels in other parts of Egypt. Travel agencies in Europe and Cairo offer reductions on these places if you book in advance. In Cairo many of the agencies along Sharia Talaat Harb and Midan Tahrir have signs in their front windows advertising special deals for these places.

The southernmost resort development in the area is 20 km from Hurghada – a sprawling complex that will most likely be in the four or five star range. Between that complex and Jasmine Village, which is five km north, there will probably be a Felfela's resort village – thus yet another addition to the Felfela empire (see the Cairo Places to Eat section).

The *Jasmine Village* (tel 760159, 744828) has 362 bungalow-style air-conditioned rooms and caters mostly to German groups. As with most of the other complexes, it has a full water sports

centre, including a diving and windsurfing centre. It's the sort of place that is purely for fun in the sun, thus with little other than Egyptian cuisine to distinguish it from similar resorts in other beach areas around the world. Singles/doubles range in price from E£114/218 to E£143/273 on a half-board arrangement.

Further north is the huge walled enclosure called the *Magawish Resort Village* (tel 40255, 40759), also known as *Tourist Village*; it was formerly associated with Club Med. As with the other resorts, it caters mostly to groups. Prices range from E£108 to E£164 for a single and E£239 to E£291 for a double (half and full-board rates). It's operated by Misr Travel, so additional information is easily obtainable in Cairo from their offices (the main offices are in Abbassiya).

One of this resort's distinguishing features is its dive centre run by Drs Wael and Hussam Nasef, two brothers who are both specialists in hyperbaric (diving-related) medicine. The centre is equipped with Hurghada's only decompression chamber, two 15 passenger dive boats and full diving and snorkelling equipment.

The brothers also run the Cairo Underwater & Hyperbaric Medicine Centre (tel 260 0850), 13 Sharia Seif el Din Barkook, Nasr City, District 1, Cairo; it's open from 6 to 10 pm daily, except Friday. They offer NOWI and CMAS (French-based) diving certification courses for about E£416, which is a good price.

The *Hor Palace Hotel* (tel 441710, 440603) is a smaller complex that charges about the same rates as the others, but the rooms don't have the same level of amenities. They have villas with full kitchens and 36 rooms, all air-conditioned. Single/double/triple rooms are E£114/151/229. Group rates are offered, probably for much less. It tends to be popular with groups of divers.

Next door is the *Princess Club* (tel 441717, 441818) with 25 villas and 68 rooms at a variety of rates depending on whether you want a view of the garden or swimming pool, neither of which is spectacular. Rates for single/double/triple rooms range from E£119/184/247 to E£145/216/281. In the villas, the showers aren't separate from the toilets. Not all the rooms have air-con.

The *El Samaka Beach Hotel* (tel 258 0678, 258 3028) is yet another group tourism place, but it seems to have one of the best windsurfing centres in the area. There's also a diving centre. Singles/doubles/triples are E£75/125/172 with half-board.

The *Giftun Village* has 358 bright whitewashed rooms with polished floors and air-con. There's also a diving and windsurfing centre known as the Barakuda International Aquanautic Club. Rates range from E£140/182/226 to E£112/142/208 for single/double/triple rooms.

The *Sheraton Hotel* (tel 988607), seven km south of town, charges E£104 to E£156 for singles and doubles. Check with Sheraton International for the latest rates because they are subject to change according to the seasons. If you use the Sheraton beach you'll supposedly have to pay E£5 for the privilege, but I met travellers who didn't.

In town along the waterfront is the *Shedwan Golden Beach Hotel* (tel 440240). Although the rooms are fine for a tourist group vacation, they are overpriced for individual travellers. The rooms have air-con, basic tiled floors and private bathrooms. Single/double/triple rooms are E£112/143/177. Many German tour groups stay here.

Places to Eat

The *Happy Land Restaurant* has seafood cocktails for E£2.50 to E£10, spaghetti for E£1.50 and calamari for E£4.

The *Red Sea Restaurant* serves various types of fish for about E£6. Their fish kebab is good. The tables on the rooftop terrace are more pleasant than the ones downstairs.

The *Aladin's Lamp*, a small restaurant on a side street in central Hurghada, is

Mosque, Hurghada

best known for serving seven kinds of lobster. Prices range from E£1 to E£20 for lobster and various other dishes.

The Belgian-owned and managed *3 Corners Restaurant* is considered the best restaurant in Hurghada. It's in front of the Shedwan Golden Beach Hotel, a 10 to 15 minute walk from the centre of town. The main dishes of shrimp (baked, fried or grilled) and lobster in garlic are relatively pricey at E£19.50 and E£28.50, but there are cheaper things on the menu, such as seafood pizza for E£6 and calamari at E£4.20.

Near the town market area is the *Abak Restaurant*, where you can get a filling meal of soup, tahina, rice and fish or meat for about E£4 to E£5. The fish is usually marinated and then grilled. The daily menu is whatever they can serve that day.

Getting There & Away

Air The daily 7 am flight from Cairo to Hurghada costs about E£165 one way.

There is a flight from Hurghada to Sharm el Shaykh on Friday at 7 am for E£104; and one to St Catherine's on Monday at 7 am for E£140 one way.

Bus There are frequent buses to and from Cairo every day. Times vary, so check them well in advance. Prices range from E£10 to E£18 according to the standard of the bus. Book your tickets at least one day in advance and be present 30 minutes before departure.

My friend and I were told the day before we planned to leave Hurghada that we didn't need reservations for either of the Cairo buses. The next day we trudged over to the bus station at 4.30 am and half an hour later a gleaming new bus pulled into the lot. Everything about it spelled comfort and, as we had ridden throughout Egypt crammed like sardines on 3rd class trains and local buses, this was certainly a welcome sight! We boarded the bus, plopped into a couple of cushy seats and promptly closed our eyes. But it was all too good to be true.

'Hey, you're in my seat.' Someone was poking my shoulder and I looked up to see an Egyptian woman, who started shoving plastic shopping bags under my legs.

'What do you mean?' I asked, 'These are our seats.'

'No,' she said and showed me her ticket.

My friend and I tumbled out of our seats and off the bus – it was full. Another bus was supposed to arrive in half an hour, so while my friend went across the lot to get a couple of glasses of tea, I stormed into the bus office to buy reserved places for the next bus.

'Impossible,' they said.

'No, it is possible. Sell me two tickets,' I squawked.

I think they sold me the tickets just to shut me up. I walked back to the centre of the lot proudly clutching two tickets for reserved seats to Cairo, or so I thought. In the next few moments I discovered otherwise.

As my friend walked out of the cafe with two glasses of tea on a tray, a windowless bus rumbled into the lot. People converged on the doors like vultures and mothers shoved their kids, along with plastic shopping bags and aluminium pots, through the windows. I yelled to my friend to watch our packs, so he dropped

the tray and ran over as I jumped through a window – and belly-flopped right onto the laps of a couple of soldiers. It was too late. The bus was full before it had even stopped.

My friend and I stood over the engine at the back for seven hours. Except for the man who puked on my foot, all the Egyptians around us were friendly. They kept smiling and saying 'Welcome in Egypt'.

Buses leave for Qena and Luxor at 6 and 11 am and at 4 pm (this bus has air-con). The trip takes four hours to Qena and five to Luxor; the latter costs E£6.25/10 with/without air-con. Try to take the air-conditioned bus, as several travellers have complained to me about the others

There are also several buses daily to Suez – they are often just the Cairo buses making a stop in Suez.

Taxi Service taxis go to all the same places as the buses but at least seven passengers are needed to get a good price: to Luxor – four hours, E£6; Aswan – six hours, E£9; Suez – four hours, E£10; Cairo – five hours, E£15.

Boat The *Moreen II* sails from Hurghada to Sharm el Shaykh three times a week, supposedly on Sunday, Tuesday and Thursday. Tickets can be bought, or at least arranged, from most hotels and travel agencies in town for E£51.

Getting Around
Airport Transport From the airport to central Hurghada, the taxi fare is E£5.

Bus In the mornings, minibuses full of day labourers go almost all the way to the Jasmine Village for about 35 pt. Throughout the day, minibuses regularly run at least as far south as the Sheraton, and often farther if there are enough passengers.

Taxi Taxis will take you as far south as the Sheraton for about E£4 (or more if there are plenty of tourists around). Hurghada taxi fares are the highest in Egypt.

Bicycle Bicycles can be rented in town for E£2.50 for the day or E£1.15 for half a day.

Hitching It's sometimes possible to hitch around town or out to the beaches, but the locals seem accustomed to receiving payment from travellers.

PORT SAFAGA

Port Safaga, 53 km south of Hurghada, is first and foremost a port for the export of phosphates from local mines. Secondly, it's a small resort with a pricey hotel. Free camping is possible at the beach. If you are headed south along the coastal road to the Sudan, you must complete customs formalities in Port Safaga.

Very few travellers seem to venture south of Port Safaga, so if you do make it past the port you'll be journeying through a seldom visited part of Egypt.

QUSEIR

Quseir, a medieval port town of 4000 inhabitants, is 85 km south of Port Safaga and about 160 km east of Qift on the Nile. Until the 10th century it was one of the most important exit points for pilgrims travelling to Mecca and was also a thriving centre of trade and export between the Nile Valley and the Red Sea. The Suez Canal put an end to all that. There's an old fort and a small souk which are worth checking out, and there's excellent snorkelling from the beach about five km north of town.

Places to Stay

It's possible to stay at *Samia's* for about E£3.50 per night. Samia is a very helpful guy who's building a few bungalows with cooking facilities, a little north of town.

Getting There & Away

There are daily buses to and from Cairo, via Hurghada, and service taxis travel west to Qift and north to Port Safaga.

MARSA ALAM

Marsa Alam is a fishing village 145 km south of Quseir. A road also connects the village with Edfu, 230 km across the desert to the west.

BERENICE

The military centre and small port of Berenice, 145 km south of Marsa Alam, was founded in 275 BC by Ptolemy II Euergetes I and was an important trading post until the 5th century AD. Near the town, the ruins of the Temple of Seramis can be seen. The US Navy occasionally brings its aircraft carriers here. Apparently, this is one of the staging areas for the US Rapid Deployment Forces.

BIR SHALATAYN

This tiny village 75 km south of Berenice is ostensibly the border post between Egypt and the Sudan. If you get this far, let us know what's there.

Alexandria & the Mediterranean Coast

On the north coast of Egypt, west of where the Rosetta branch of the Nile leaves the delta and where the barren desert meets the sparkling waters of the Mediterranean, is the charming, though somewhat jaded city of Alexandria, once the shining gem of the Hellenistic world. Nearby are the Mediterranean resorts of Sidi Abdel Rahman and Marsa Matruh and the famous town of El Alamein, where the tide of WW II was changed in favour of the Allies. The rest of this region is sparsely populated. The road westward to the Libyan border passes along an almost deserted coast that greets the sea with craggy cliffs or smooth sandy beaches.

between Europe and Asia. The city's library once contained 500,000 volumes, and its research institute, the Mouseion, produced some of the most scholarly works of the age. The Pharos lighthouse, built on an island just offshore, was one of the Seven Wonders of the World.

During the reign of Cleopatra, the last of the Ptolemies, Alexandria rivalled Rome in everything but military power. After a brief liaison with Julius Caesar, Cleopatra married Marc Antony, who was high on the list to replace the assassinated statesman as leader of the Roman Empire. But the union of the Egyptian queen and the Roman general was not popular in Rome, especially with Caesar's

Alexandria

Having conquered Greece, the Macedonian general who became known as Alexander the Great set his sights on Egypt and the Persian Empire. After leading his victorious troops south to Memphis in 332 BC, Alexander followed the Nile back to the Mediterranean and chose a fishing village as the site of his capital, Alexandria.

Alexander designed the city carefully, for he envisioned it as a naval base, a great trading port, and the political and cultural centre of his empire. Though he is buried there, Alexander did not see the gift he gave the classical world, nor probably did he imagine the greatness it would achieve. Its architecture was as impressive as that of Rome or Athens, and in the last three centuries BC it attracted some of the finest artists and scholars of the time, becoming a renowned centre of scientific, philosophical, and literary thought and learning.

Under the Ptolemies, who ruled Egypt after Alexander, Alexandria developed into a major port on the trade routes

Alexander the Great

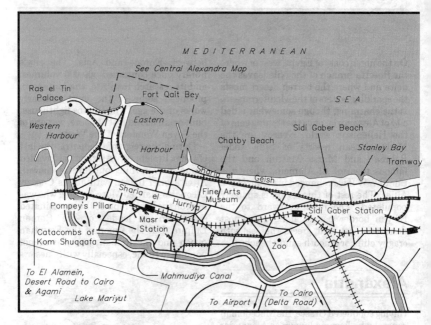

Map labels:
MEDITERRANEAN
SEA
See Central Alexandra Map
Ras el Tin Palace
Fort Qait Bey
Eastern Harbour
Western Harbour
Harbour
Sidi Gaber Beach
Chatby Beach
Stanley Bay
Tramway
Sharia el Geish
Sharia el Hurriya
Fine Arts Museum
Pompey's Pillar
Sidi Gaber Station
Catacombs of Kom Shuqqafa
Masr Station
Zoo
To El Alamein, Desert Road to Cairo & Agami
Lake Mariyut
Mahmudiya Canal
To Airport
To Cairo (Delta Road)

nephew Octavian, whose sister was already married to Marc Antony.

In the ensuing power struggle, the Egyptian fleet was defeated at Actium in 31 BC by the superior forces of Octavian, who later changed his name to Augustus and declared himself emperor of Rome. As Octavian led his forces towards Egypt, Cleopatra, rather than face capture, reputedly put an asp to her breast and ended the Ptolemaic dynasty.

Alexandria, the most powerful and prosperous provincial capital of the Roman Empire, remained the capital of Egypt for the next 600 years under Roman and Byzantine control. Although the original great library had been burned when the Romans had first tried to conquer Alexandria, Cleopatra had begun another collection in a new building alongside the famed Serapeum. The city was still regarded as the most learned place on earth.

But during the 4th century AD, Alexandria's populace was ravaged by civil war, famine and disease, and although the city later became a centre of Christianity, it never regained its former glory. At the end of the century, the city's cultural importance was almost wiped out by the destruction of the library and the Mouseion by the Christians.

The conquering Muslims abandoned Alexandria in the 7th century and established their new capital further south on the Nile. When the French arrived in the 19th century, Cairo had long since replaced Alexandria as Egypt's major city, and the latter was again little more than a fishing village.

Napoleon's invasion, however, reinstated Alexandria's strategic importance, and it underwent a revival during the reign of Mohammed Ali when new docks, an arsenal, and a canal linking the city with the Nile were built. The stage was set for Alexandria's return as a vital Mediterranean trade centre; when the Suez Canal

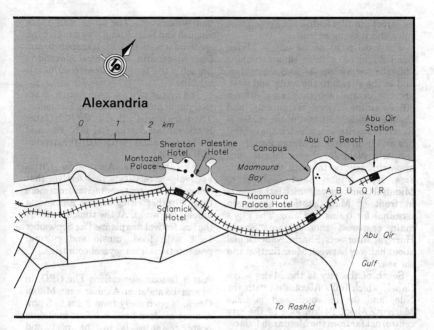

was completed in 1869, the city's position as a major modern port was assured.

The city also became cosmopolitan, attracting Europeans, Turks and wealthy Egyptians and providing the inspiration for Lawrence Durrell's novels known collectively as *The Alexandria Quartet*. During WW II the city was an Allied post, and part of the pivotal Battle of El Alamein was planned by Allied intelligence from the Hotel Cecil.

Today Alexandria is the largest port in Egypt, a major industrial centre, and the country's unofficial summer capital, with a population of three million. Every year the perfect Mediterranean climate, the relaxed atmosphere, and the city's reputation for the best food in the country draw thousands of holiday-makers to the waterfront cafes and beautiful beaches.

The port handles about 80% of Egypt's import and export trade; more than 5000 ships call at Alexandria annually. It is cleaner and less congested than Cairo,

and although it thrives to a certain extent on the romantic reputation of its past, it is still a warm and welcoming city.

Orientation
Alexandria is a true waterfront city, nearly 20 km long from east to west and only two km wide. The main port is on the western side of the Ras el Tin promontory, while the Eastern Harbour, in front of the Corniche, is used mostly by fishing and pleasure craft. The tip of the promontory was once Pharos Island, where the famous lighthouse stood, but silting gradually formed the causeway that now connects the island with the mainland.

Sharia 26th of July sweeps from the tip of the promontory east along the beaches towards Montazah Palace. Along the way its name changes to Sharia el Geish. These two seaside streets are referred to collectively as the Corniche.

Whereas in Cairo 'sharia' is translated

as 'street', in Alexandria it's French that rules and it becomes 'rue'.

The focal point of the city is Midan Saad Zaghloul, a large square running onto the waterfront. Around the midan, and in the streets to the south and west, are the central shopping area, tourist office, airline offices, restaurants, and cheaper hotels. Just east of the midan is Ramli Tram Station, which is the central bus and tram depot in Midan Ramli.

Sharia Nabi (or Nebi) Daniel runs approximately north-south through this area, from Midan Saad Zaghloul to Midan el Gomhurriya, which is the square in front of Masr Station, the main terminal for trains to Cairo. The city's main east-west thoroughfare, Sharia Hurriya, intersects Sharia Nabi Daniel about halfway between Masr Station and the sea.

South of the city is the Mahmudiya Canal, which links Alexandria with the Nile, and to the south-west is Lake Mariyut. About 24 km east of the city centre, not far from the Montazah Palace, is the town of Abu Qir, famous as the site of two historic battles between the French and British, and now famous for its seafood restaurants.

Information

Registration If Alexandria is your first port of call in Egypt, remember that you have to register within seven days of arrival. You don't have to go through the process yourself if you're staying in a hotel, as the management will register for you. If you do need the passport office, it's at 28 Sharia Talaat Harb.

Tourist Office At the main tourist office (tel 807611, 803929), on the south-west corner of Midan Saad Zaghloul, you can pick up a free copy of the pocket-size information book *Alexandria by Night & Day*, published every year for the local tourism industry by Nada Advertising Agency. The information about hotels, restaurants and things to see is sketchy, but it's not a

bad publication. The office staff speak English and French, and they can give you some information about transport to and from Alexandria. The central Alexandria branch of the Tourist Police (tel 807611) is upstairs.

The tourist office is open from 8.30 am to 6 pm; 9 am to 4 pm during Ramadan. There are tourist offices at the Sidi Gaber Station, Masr Station (tel 492 5985), and the Maritime Station (tel 800100, extension 258) as well.

Ask about the Alexandria Cities Festival – a relatively new festival that brings together representatives from more than 40 other cities named Alexandria around the world. At the time of writing, the first festival was planned for September 1989, with food, music and cultural presentations from several countries.

Post & Telecommunications The GPO, in Sharia Iskander el Akhbar near Midan Orabi, is open daily from 8 am to 8 pm. A more modern branch office, including poste restante, is in the post and telephone building adjacent to Masr Station. It's open daily from 9 am to 3 pm. There is another branch at Ramli Tram Station, open from 8 am to 2 pm, and one at Masr Station, open from 8 am to 5 pm.

The telephone office at Ramli Tram Station is open 24 hours a day. The other two branches, at Masr Station and Sharia Saad Zaghloul, are open from 9 am to 11 pm.

Money Several major international banks have offices in Alexandria. The main branches are as follows:

Bank Misr
   9 Sharia Talaat Harb (tel 807429)
   18 Sharia Talaat Harb (tel 807031)
   Hotel Cecil, Midan Saad Zaghloul (tel 807055)
Bank of America
   Sharia Lomomba (tel 21257)
Banque du Caire (Bank of Cairo)
   16 Sharia Sisostris (tel 807087)
   5 Sharia Salah Salem (tel 32895)

Barclays International
    10 Sharia Fawotur (tel 21307)
Chase Manhattan International
    19 Sharia Dr Ibrahim Abdel el Said
Citibank
    95 Sharia 26th of July (tel 806376)

American Express American Express (tel 30084) is at Sharia Hurriya, in the Isis Travel office. Hours are 9 am to 1 pm and 5 to 7 pm Monday to Thursday, and 9 am to 1 pm on Friday and Saturday.

Thomas Cook There are Thomas Cook offices at:

Main Office
    15 Midan Saad Zaghloul (tel 27830, 35118)
Hotel Cecil
    Midan Saad Zaghloul (tel 807055)
Palestine Hotel
    Montazah Gardens (tel 861594)
Metropole Hotel
    52 Sharia Saad Zaghloul (tel 21467)
Hotel San Stefano
    Sharia el Geish, San Stefano (tel 63580)

Books & Bookstores *Guide to Alexandrian Monuments* describes the main attractions and details the city's history. It's available from the Greco-Roman Museum for E£2.

Newcomers' Guide to Alexandria was written by resident Americans to help new arrivals cope with the practicalities of life in the city. It's available at some bookstores and from the American Cultural Center.

E M Forster's *Alexandria: A History & a Guide*, written during WW I, is still regarded as the best historical guide to the city. In a collection of short essays, Forster recreates the 2250 years of Alexandria's existence and then takes the visitor on a guided tour of the city's attractions as they were early this century. An annotated edition of the book recently published by Michael Haag Ltd brings the guide up to date for the modern traveller.

Lawrence Durrell's *The Alexandria Quartet* offers an fascinating insight into the cosmopolitan community of Alexandria before and during WW II.

You should be able to find these publications in Alexandria in the following English-language bookstores: Library Mustakabal, 32 Sharia Safia Zaghloul; El Ahram Library, on the corner of Sharia Hurriya and Sharia Nabi Daniel; and Dar el Maaref on Midan Saad Zaghloul.

Maps The best map of the city is published by Lehnert & Landrock. The *Clyde Leisure Map No 6 (Egypt & Cairo)*, published by Clyde Surveys, England, is another excellent map that includes places of interest, hotels, restaurants, and facts about the city and surrounding areas.

Emergency If you have a real emergency, telephone the special 'urgent help' number, 123. Other emergency services are as follows:

Fire
    (tel 180)
Hospitals
    University Hospital, Chatby (tel 420 1573)
    Al Moassa Hospital, Sharia Hurriya, Elhadara (tel 421 6664)
Police (Police Secours)
    tourist office, Midan Saad Zaghloul (tel 122)
Tourist Police
    tourist office, Midan Saad Zaghloul (tel 807611)
    Montazah (tel 863804)

Consulates The addresses of some of the foreign consulates in Alexandria are:

France
    2 Midan Orabi (tel 807518); open from 8.30 am to 2 pm daily, except Friday and Saturday
Greece
    63 Sharia Iskandar el Akhbar (tel 482 5896)
Israel
    207 Sharia Abdel Salam Aref, Louran District (tel 586 3873)
Italy
    25 Midan Saad Zaghloul (tel 482 7292)

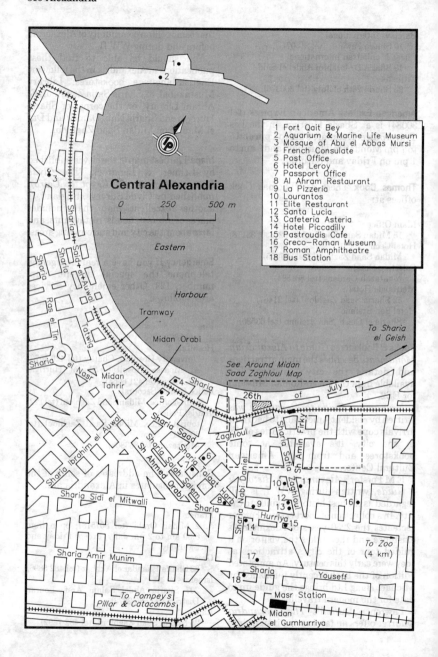

Central Alexandria

0   250   500 m

1 Fort Qait Bey
2 Aquarium & Marine Life Museum
3 Mosque of Abu el Abbas Mursi
4 French Consulate
5 Post Office
6 Hotel Leroy
7 Passport Office
8 Al Ahram Restaurant
9 La Pizzeria
10 Lourantos
11 Elite Restaurant
12 Santa Lucia
13 Cafeteria Asteria
14 Hotel Piccadilly
15 Pastroudis Cafe
16 Greco-Roman Museum
17 Roman Amphitheatre
18 Bus Station

Eastern

Harbour

Tramway

Midan Orabi

See Around Midan Saad Zaghloul Map

To Sharia el Geish

26th   of   July

Sharia   Said + el Auwi

Sharia Ras el Tin

Totwig

Sharia el Nasr

Midan Tahrir

Sharia

Zaghloul

Sh Amin Firky

Sharia Safia Zaghloul

Midan Orabi

Sharia Saad

Sharia Ibrahim el Auwal

Sharia Saida Salem

Sharia Talaat

Sharia Ahmed Orabi

Sharia Nabi Daniel

Harb

Sharia Sidi el Mitwalli

Hurriya

Sharia Amir Munim

To Zoo
(4 km)

Sharia   Youseff

To Pompey's
Pillar & Catacombs

Masr Station

Midan
el Gumhurriya

Sudan
Silsila Building, Sharia 26th of July,
Azharita (tel 483920)
Turkey
11 Sharia Selvago (tel 26879)
UK
3 Sharia Mena, Rushdy District (tel 546 7171);
open from 8 am to 1 pm, Sunday to Thursday;
open on Saturday for emergencies only
USA
110 Sharia Hurriya (tel 482 1911); open
from 9 am to 12 noon, Sunday to Thursday
West Germany
5 Sharia Mena, Rushdy District (tel
845443)
Yugoslavia
Sharia Pharaon (or Pharana) (tel 806536)

Cultural Centres The American Cultural
Center (tel 482 4117, 482 1009) is at 2
Sharia Pharaon, behind the consulate;
hours are 8 am to 4 pm, Monday to Friday.
American films are shown every Monday
and Wednesday at 6 pm. American
speakers are invited here every month.

The British Council (tel 481 0199, 482
9890) is at 9 Sharia Batalsa, Bab
Sharki.

The French Cultural Centre (tel 492
2503) is at 30 Sharia Nabi Daniel; hours
are 9 am to 1 pm and 4 to 8 pm daily,
except Friday and Saturday.

Ancient Alexandria

There is little left of ancient Alexandria –
the modern metropolis is built over or
amongst the ruins of the great classical
city. A few archaeological sites, often
discovered accidentally, have been
excavated and preserved, but for the most
part only an odd column or two or a
gateway marks the location of legendary
Ptolemaic or Roman edifices.

Much of the romance of Alexandria lies
in the past, not the present, and it's often a
case of simply using your imagination. If
you stand at the intersection of Sharia
Nabi Daniel and Sharia Hurriya, for
instance, you are also at the crossroads of
the ancient city, then acclaimed as one of
the most glorious places in the world. In
those days, Sharia Hurriya was known as

the Canopic Way, and it extended from
the city's Gate of the Sun in the east to the
Gate of the Moon in the west. According to
a 5th century bishop, 'a range of columns
went from one end of it to the other'.

Just south of this intersection, on
Sharia Nabi Daniel, you will find what is
believed to be the site of the renowned
Mouseion and library, where the greatest
philosophers, writers and scientists of
ancient times gathered to exchange ideas.

Nearby is the modern, fairly uninteresting Mosque of Nabi Daniel, built on the
site of Alexander's tomb. Rumour has it
that the great Macedonian still lies
wrapped in gold in his glass coffin,
somewhere in the unexplored cellars below.

Greco-Roman Museum

The 21 rooms of this excellent museum
contain about 40,000 valuable relics dating
from as early as the 3rd century BC.
The museum's own guide book gives little
indication of where to find anything other
than the rooms and some numbered
exhibits. The collection includes a
splendid black granite sculpture of Apis
(the sacred bull revered by Egyptians),
many statues of Serapis (the fusion Apis
and Osiris, the god of the underworld and
lord of the dead), and busts and statues of
various Greeks and Romans. There are
also mummies, sarcophagi, pottery, tiny
terra cotta figures, bas reliefs, jewellery,
coins and tapestries.

The museum is at 5 Sharia al Mathaf al
Romani, just north-west of Sharia Hurriya
and 10 blocks from Sharia Nabi Daniel.
It's open from 9 am to 4 pm daily, except
on Friday, when it closes at 11.30 am.
Admission costs E£1, or 50 pt for students.

Roman Amphitheatre

The 13 white marble terraces of the only
Roman theatre in Egypt were discovered
only recently, when the foundations for a
new apartment building were being dug.
The terraces, arranged in a semicircle
around the arena, are excellently preserved.

The site, which is still being excavated,

is on Sharia Youseff, east of Sharia Nabi Daniel. It's open from 9 am to 4 pm. Admission costs 50 pt, or 25 pt for students, but it will cost you an extra E£10 to take photographs.

Pompey's Pillar & the Serapeum

This massive yet unimpressive 25 metre high pink granite column, which the Crusaders mistakenly credited to Pompey, rises out of the disappointing remains of the far more splendid and acclaimed Serapeum. What was once an acropolis, topped by the Temple of Serapis and surrounded by subsidiary shrines and buildings, including Cleopatra's library, now merely features excavated subterranean galleries, the ruins of the Temple of Isis, a few sphinxes and Pompey's Pillar.

The pillar, which has a circumference of nine metres, was erected amidst the Serapeum complex around 297 AD for Diocletian, not Pompey. During the final assault on the so-called pagan intellectuals of Alexandria in about 391 AD, the Christians destroyed the Serapeum and library, leaving only the pillar.

To get to the pillar and the ruins of the Serapeum, which are in an archaeological park south-west of the city centre, near the Mahmudiya Canal, take yellow tram No 16 from Midan Saad Zaghloul. The site is open from 9 am to 4 pm. Admission costs 50 pt, or 25 pt for students.

Catacombs of Kom el Shuqqafa

These catacombs, the largest known Roman burial site in Egypt, were discovered accidentally in 1900 when a donkey cart fell through a part of the roof. They consist of three tiers of tombs and chambers cut into the rock to a depth of about 35 metres. Constructed in the 2nd century AD, probably as a family crypt, they were later expanded to hold more than 300 corpses. There is even a banquet hall where grieving relatives paid their last respects with a funeral feast.

The eerie nature of the catacombs is accentuated by the weird blend of Egyptian and Roman features in the sculptures and reliefs. The catacombs have been excavated, but the bottom level is usually flooded and inaccessible.

Kom el Shuqqafa is about 10 minutes walk south of Pompey's Pillar, or you can take yellow tram No 16 from Midan Saad Zaghloul. The catacombs are open from 9 am to 4 pm. Admission costs E£1, or 50 pt for students, plus E£4 for taking photographs.

Fort Qait Bey

This 15th century medieval fort guards the entrance to the Eastern Harbour. It is built on the foundations of the Pharos lighthouse, one of the ancient Seven Wonders of the World.

The lighthouse, Alexandria's original sentinel, stood about 150 metres high. It had a square lower storey with 300 rooms, a double spiral staircase leading up

Fort Qait Bey

through the octagonal 2nd storey, and a circular 3rd storey leading to the lantern room, topped by a statue of Poseidon. It was built during the reign of Ptolemy Philadelphus in about 280 BC, on what was then Pharos Island. A causeway, formed when silt blocked the channel between the island and the mainland, now connects the island with the mainland and divides the harbour in two.

It is not known exactly what reflected the firelight out to sea to guide and warn approaching ships, but writings of the time suggest it was a mysterious mirror or a lens through which the Pharos keeper could detect ships not seen by the naked eye. If the scientists of ancient Alexandria had discovered the lens then its secret was lost when the two upper storeys were wrecked. Legend has it that the Byzantine emperor could not attack Alexandria because of the lighthouse, so he instructed his agents in the city to spread rumours that it was built on top of the treasure of Alexander the Great. Before the Alexandrians could do anything to stop him, the Egyptian caliph had demolished the top half of the lighthouse, sending the mechanism into the sea.

Several Muslim leaders attempted its restoration, but the lighthouse was eventually completely destroyed by an earthquake in the 14th century, and left in ruins. In about 1480, the Mameluke Sultan Qait Bey fortified the peninsula, using the foundations and debris of the Pharos lighthouse to build his fort, incorporating a castle and mosque within the walls. Mohammed Ali modernised the fort's defences in the 19th century, but the minaret and castle were severely damaged by a British bombardment in 1882.

Today, the three floors of the fort house a small naval museum, with model ships, paintings and recreations of historic naval scenes. The views of the city from the fort are superb. To get to the fort and the nearby aquarium, take yellow tram No 15 from Midan Ramli or bus No 116 along Sharia 26th of July. Admission is only

E£1, but it will cost you an extra E£5 to take photographs.

Aquarium & Marine Life Museum

This poor excuse for a museum and aquarium is on the causeway near Fort Qait Bey. It has a large variety of stuffed and lacquered fish, a few live specimens, a whale skeleton, sponges and coral. Some of the displays were being renovated and upgraded, so perhaps this will be a better museum in the future. It's open from 9 am to 2 pm. Admission costs E£1, or 50 pt for students.

Ras el Tin Palace

The palace buildings, built by Mohammed Ali on the western side of the peninsula, are closed to the public, but the surrounding gardens are open. King Farouk owned the palace until 1952. The 300 rooms have been kept as they were in the '50s, and are used for state guests and other VIPs.

Mosque of Abu el Abbas Mursi

Dominating the main square on Sharia Tatwig, about one km south of the fort, is one of the best examples of Islamic architecture in Alexandria. This mosque, with its four domes and high minarets, was built by Algerians in 1767 over the tomb of a 13th century Muslim saint. It's worth visiting, but don't enter during official prayer times. Yellow tram No 15 from Midan Ramli stops nearby.

Synagogue

Built just over 100 years ago, this last vestige of what was once a thriving Jewish community now serves only about 70 people. It is the home of the Jewish Community of Alexandria (tel 26189). Before the wars with Israel there were about 15,000 Alexandrian Jews, who could trace their ancestry back to the founding of the city by Alexander the Great. The synagogue, a fabulous Italian-built structure with pink marble pillars, is at 69 Sharia Nabi Daniel. It's open from

8 to 10 am on Saturday and from 10 am to 1 pm on other days.

Cavafy Museum

On the top floor of the Greek Consulate, 63 Sharia Iskander el Akhbar, is a museum dedicated to the great Alexandrian poet Constantine Cavafy. The museum recreates the rooms in which Cavafy lived from 1908 until his death in 1933. The building in which he lived still stands, at 4 Sharia Sharm el Shaykh; this street runs off Sharia Sultan Hussein, just east of Sharia Nabi Daniel and two blocks north of Sharia Hurriya.

Fine Arts Museum

A limited but interesting collection of modern Egyptian art, and Alexandria's public library, are housed in this museum at 18 Sharia Menasha, east of Masr Station and south of the tracks. It's open from 8 am to 2 pm daily, except Friday; on Wednesday it's also open from 7 to 9 pm. Admission is free. Yellow tram No 14 will take you to the museum from Midan Ramli.

Zoo

The surprisingly clean Alexandria zoo, on a small hill surrounded by the Nouzha and Antoniadis gardens, is a pleasant place to spend a couple of hours. There is a large outdoor cafe which offers light meals and refreshments. It's about 30 minutes walk from Midan Saad Zaghloul, or you can take bus No 303 from Sharia 26th of July.

Montazah Palace

Montazah Palace, at the eastern end of Sharia el Geish, was built by Khedive Abbas II. It was the summer residence of the royal family before the 1952 Revolution and King Farouk's abdication. The adjacent Salamlek Hotel, also built by Abbas II, was designed in the style of a chalet to please his Austrian mistress.

The magnificent gardens and groves and the semiprivate beach make this an ideal place to spend a relaxing day,

although the palace and its museum are apparently no longer open to the public. The grounds, which once featured a menagerie of lions, tigers and bears, include the rather tasteless but high-class Palestine Hotel, which is a little west of the Salamlek.

Admission to the palace grounds costs E£1, or E£1.25 on holidays, Sunday and Monday. Bus Nos 211 and 220 and minibus No 725 leave for the palace from Midan Orabi, and can be caught from anywhere along the Corniche. Bus No 220 continues to Maamoura.

Royal Jewellery Museum

The Royal Jewellery Museum, 21 Sharia Ahmed Yehia Pacha, Zizinia (or Zezeniya), is one of Alexandria's newest attractions. Formerly one of King Farouk's palaces, it now houses a stunning collection of jewels from Mohammed Ali's early 19th century rule in Egypt, including diamond-encrusted garden tools, jewelled watches with hand-painted miniature portraits, and necklaces. Take blue tram No 2 from Ramli Tram Station or any bus on the Corniche going towards Montazah, and get off at Zizinia. The museum is open from 9 am to 4 pm. Admission is E£1, or 50 pt for students.

Beaches

There are several public or semipublic beaches along Alexandria's waterfront, but most of the ones between the Eastern Harbour and Montazah are usually crowded and grubby. These include Sidi Gaber, Mandarra (not recommended) and Montazah. At most beaches you can rent chairs and umbrellas for about E£1 per day.

Maamoura Beach, about one km east of Montazah Palace, is one of the best; it even has a few small waves rolling in. You can get there on bus No 220, which runs along the Corniche.

However, the beaches at Agami and Hannoville, about 17 km west of central Alexandria, are the best, as they're cleaner and less crowded. Bus Nos 450 and

460 go to both beaches from the north side of the Corniche. Minibus No 750 goes to Agami from Masr Station, or you can take a service taxi for 50 pt.

Canopus

On Maamoura Bay, near Abu Qir, is the site of ancient Canopus, famous in Greek legends long before the founding of Alexandria. The settlement, at the end of a limestone ridge extending from the Western Desert, overlooked the Canopic mouth of the Nile (which has long since dried up), and was for a time a noted religious centre. In 450 BC, Herodotus claimed to have seen a temple to Hercules on the site, and was informed that Paris and Helen had sought refuge at Canopus during their escape to Troy. Another Greek legend claims that the district was named after a pilot of Menelaus' fleet who died there by the Nile on the Greeks' return journey from the Trojan War. Egyptian mythology, however, claims that Canopus was a god whose body was an earthenware jar!

Abu Qir

This coastal town, 24 km east of central Alexandria, is historically important for two major 18th century battles between the French and English. During the Battle of the Nile in 1798, Admiral Nelson surprised and destroyed the French fleet in the bay at Abu Qir. Although Napoleon still controlled Egypt, his contact with France by sea was effectively severed. The British landed 15,000 Turkish soldiers at Abu Qir in 1799, but the French force of 10,000 men, mostly cavalry led personally by Napoleon, forced the Turks back into the sea, drowning at least 5000 of them.

There are plenty of buses from central Alexandria to Abu Qir every day. It's best to go during the week to avoid the crowds of Alexandrians who flock there on the weekends. If you're into seafood, this is definitely the place to go (see the Alexandria Places to Eat section).

Places to Stay

Summer is the high season in Alexandria. August is particularly busy, so you may have difficulty finding a hotel room even at some of the bottom end places.

Places to Stay – bottom end

The *Hotel Piccadilly* (tel 492 4497) is on the 8th floor, 11 Sharia Hurriya, three blocks north of Masr Station. Rooms plus breakfast cost E£8 for a single or E£12 for a large double with bath; some rooms have balconies, and you can order breakfast. It's sort of a last resort, because no one has ever recommended it.

The *Youth Hostel* (tel 597 5459), 32 Sharia Port Said, costs E£2 for members or E£5 for nonmembers. To get there, take any blue tram from Ramli Station and get off at the Chatby Casino, in front of the College of St Mark. It's open from 7 to 10 am and 2 to 11 pm.

The *Hotel Acropole* (tel 805980), 4th floor, 1 Sharia Gamal al Din Yassin, is one of the best deals in Alexandria. It's clean, pleasant and centrally located, one block west of Sharia Saad Zaghloul and right next to the Hotel Cecil. Some rooms have great views of the Mediterranean. None of the rooms has a bathroom, but the shared bathrooms are kept clean. It usually costs between E£5 and E£10 per person (including taxes and breakfast) in a single, double or triple room. The hotel is popular, so you may need to make a reservation during the summer high season.

Across the street is the *Hotel Triomphe*. Its rooms are almost decrepit, with sagging beds and bathrooms that usually seem to require swamp boots. I can't even recommend this place as a last resort.

A few doors down from the Triomphe, on Sharia Gamal al Din Yassin, is a building with three pensions. On the 5th floor is the *New Hotel Welcome House*, which is neither new nor very welcoming. It's an overpriced dive with nails sticking out of the floor.

The *Hotel Gamil* (tel 815458), on the

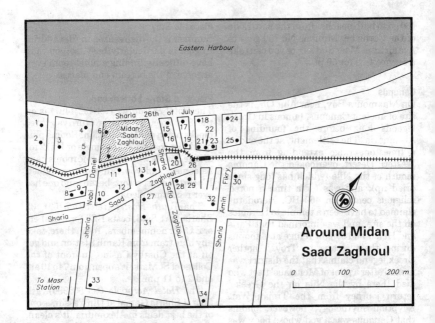

Eastern Harbour

Sharia 26th of July

Midan Saan Zaghloul

Sharia Nabi Daniel

Sharia Zaghloul

Sharia Safia Zaghloul

Sharia Amin Fikry

Sharia Saad

Sharia

To Masr Station

Around Midan Saad Zaghloul

0   100   200 m

4th floor of the same building, has seven rooms, but not all the rooms are the same, so you'll have to do some comparing. The shared bathroom is kept clean. It's a family-run pension; the current owner/manager, Said Gamil, took it over from his father. Single/double rooms are E£11/15, not including breakfast.

The *Hotel Normandie* (tel 806830) is across the hall from the Gamil; some rooms have views of the harbour. Most of the pension is furnished with French antiques, a reminder of the French lady who owned this place until her death. Although the hotel is now run by an Egyptian named Mohammed Awaadullah, a 1950s' photo of the lobby shows that none of the furnishings have changed. Single/double rooms are E£10/12.50.

Around the corner from these last three pensions is the *Hotel Union* (tel 807312/771). The hotel is quite clean and well maintained, and great value. Some rooms have TVs, sparkling tiled bathrooms,

balconies and fantastic harbour views. Single rooms cost between E£13 and E£21, and doubles are between E£18 and E£28. It's slightly more than other bottom end places, but it's definitely worth the extra cost.

Hotel Ailema, 7th floor, 21 Sharia Amin Fikry, just south of Ramli Station, is associated with the Hotel des Roses and Oxford Pensione in Cairo. The rooms and bathrooms are clean and some rooms have views of the sea. A single/double room with a bath costs E£10/13. Singles/doubles without a bath are E£9/12. There's a TV room and restaurant, so it's quite a decent place for the price.

Hyde Park House (tel 35666) is one floor up from the Ailema. The rooms are clean, but a bit dark. Singles/doubles without bathrooms are E£5/8; doubles with a bath are E£12.50. A continental breakfast with an egg costs E£2.50.

Hotel Leroy (tel 809099) is opposite the passport office, on the top floor of an office

1	New Hotel Welcome House, Hotel Gamil & Hotel Normandie
2	Hotel Triomphe
3	Hotel Acropole
4	Hotel Cecil
5	New Imperial Restaurant
6	West Delta Buses
7	Golden Rocket Buses (to Cairo)
8	New Capri Hotel
9	Tourist Information Office
10	Brazilian Coffee Store
11	Patisserie Delices (second entrance)
12	Patisserie Delices
13	Hotel Metropole
14	Trianon Cafe
15	Hotel Semiramis
16	Italian Consulate
17	Athineos & Crazy Horse Nightclubs
18	Restaurant Oriental
19	Patisserie Athineos
20	Post Office & Telephone Office
21	Egypt Air
22	Hannoville Egypt Tours
23	Restaurant Darwish (annexe)
24	Restaurant Darwish
25	Thomas Cook Money Exchange & British Airways
26	Ramli Tram Station
27	Bank
28	Ala Kefak Pizzeria
29	Taverna Restaurant
30	Hotel Ailema & Hyde Park House
31	Fuul Mohammed Ahmed Restaurant
32	Admiral Hotel
33	Synagogue
34	Al-Ekhlass Restaurant

building at 25 Sharia Talaat Harb. Most of the rooms are clean and have balconies. Singles/doubles cost E£12/19 for half-board, or E£8/14 for bed & breakfast only.

The *New Capri Hotel*, 8th floor, 23 Sharia el Mina el Sharkiya, is in the same building as the tourist office. Singles with/without a bath cost E£13/17, and doubles cost between E£17 and E£25. Prices include breakfast and taxes.

Places to Stay – middle

The *Admiral Hotel* (tel 480 5343), 24 Sharia Amin Fikry, is just off Midan Ramli. The rooms are clean but the bathrooms are a bit grimy. Singles with/

without bathrooms cost E£20/15; doubles with/without are E£25/20. All prices include breakfast.

The *Salamlek Hotel*, in the grounds of Montazah Palace, once served as the guest palace for King Farouk's visitors but these days it's being renovated to serve common folk. Singles cost E£20 and doubles are E£26. The place has air-conditioning, although it's so close to the beach and sea breezes that it's really not necessary. One traveller described this place as 'derelict'.

The *Semiramis Hotel* (tel 482 6837, 482 7837) is a tourist-class hotel on the Corniche that has several rooms with an ocean view. There's also a rooftop restaurant with a commanding view of the Mediterranean. Single/double rooms are about E£27/33.

The *Agami Palace Hotel* (tel 430 0230/386), Agami Beach, 17 km west of Alexandria, is well situated on the beach. Single/double rooms are E£56/64.

The *Hannoville Hotel*, Hannoville Beach, is a little further west of the Agami Palace Hotel, and somewhat better. Single/double rooms are E£50/60.

The *Maamoura Hotel* (tel 865401) is the only hotel at Maamoura Beach. It has single/double rooms for E£70/90.

Places to Stay – top end

The *Hotel Cecil* (tel 807055/463), overlooking Midan Saad Zaghloul, is a grand and elegant place and something of an institution in Alexandria. Its history is one of romance and intrigue. Its guests over the years have included Somerset Maugham, Lawrence Durrell and Winston Churchill, and during WW II it was the headquarters of the British Secret Service. These days, single rooms are E£65 and doubles are E£70. Many rooms have splendid views of the Eastern Harbour. There's a charming tea lounge, bar and casino, and you can get breakfast, lunch and dinner for between E£7 and E£25, not including a 17% service charge and tax.

The *Metropole Hotel* (tel 492 1465), 52 Sharia Saad Zaghloul, is a three star hotel; some rooms have fantastic views, and they all have telephones and TVs. Single/double rooms with a bath cost E£45/50; without a bath they cost E£28/35. Meals are served downstairs in the hotel's restaurant. Breakfast is E£4, lunch is E£8, and dinner is E£13. None of these prices include the 17% tax and service charge.

The *Palestine Hotel* (tel 431 0500/282) is a four star hotel in the Montazah Palace complex. Single/double rooms are E£175/290, but prices are higher from 1 May to 30 September.

The five star *Sheraton*, across the street from the Montazah Palace grounds, is situated so that most of the rooms have decent views of the Mediterranean. The rooms, various amenities, restaurants and facilities are of a quality that you would expect from most Sheraton hotels. Single/double rooms start at E£200/250.

Places to Eat
Around Midan Saad Zaghloul There are many places to eat along Sharia Safia Zaghloul. At the Ramli Station end of the street, close to the seafront, there are a number of cafes, juice stands, shwarma stands and bakeries. The *Trianon Cafe* in the Metropole Hotel, at the corner of Midan Saad Zaghloul and Sharia Safia Zaghloul, is one of Alexandria's superb cafes. They have ice cream sodas, a yummy chocolate mousse and cappuccinos, but there is a minimum charge of E£2 per person plus a 12% service charge.

Moving up the street you come to *Al-Ekhlass* (482 4434), 49 Sharia Safia Zaghloul, which serves very good Egyptian food. Kebab and kufta cost about E£7. There's a variety of meat dishes with Oriental rice and salad for E£8, and the tahina is excellent. A full dinner special for four people costs E£30.

Next is *Lourantos*, 44 Sharia Safia Zaghloul, which serves kufta, roast beef,

kibda and chicken sandwiches for 50 pt, and full meals for E£6.

Elite, a Greek restaurant at 43 Sharia Safia Zaghloul, next to the Cinema Metro, has a bit of class and culture at reasonable prices, but not much in the way of Greek food. The walls are decorated with prints by Chagall, Picasso and Toulouse-Lautrec and originals by famous Egyptian artists such as Seif Wanly and Ahmed Moustafa. The restaurant is popular with artists, actors and journalists. The usual menu is quite long, but unfortunately the waiters prefer to give travellers the shorter, more expensive one. Look for the full menu on the wall. They serve pizza, moussaka, espresso, and a special dessert called Rock & Roll – ice cream blended with jelly and slices of banana and orange, topped with whipped cream. Prices range from E£6 to E£15.

Across the road from the Elite the *Santa Lucia* (tel 482 2293) at 40 Sharia Safia Zaghloul is one of Alexandria's best restaurants. A full seafood meal costs under E£20. Next to the Santa Lucia is *Cafeteria Asteria* (482 2293) which serves good light meals. Small tasty pizzas cost E£5, sandwiches are E£1, and salads are 75 pt. They also serve ice cream, espresso and hot chocolate.

Turn right off Sharia Safia Zaghloul to find *Pastroudis Cafe* (492 9609) at 39 Sharia Hurriya. This is one of Alexandria's institutions, and is still a fine place to watch the passing parade while drinking Turkish coffee or fresh lemonade. Their cakes are superb.

La Pizzeria (483 8082), 14 Sharia Hurriya, has pizza and other cheap dishes, including spaghetti for E£4 and steak with chips and fresh vegetables for E£5.50. A few doors away the sandwich shop opposite the Hotel Piccadilly has good sandwiches for 50 pt.

Fuul Mohammed Ahmed, 317 Sharia Shakor, is one block south of Midan Saad Zaghloul and one street east of Sharia Nabi Daniel; the sign is in Arabic, but it's easy to find. All the food is typically Egyptian and very cheap; meals cost as little as E£1. Fuul dishes are served with a green salad, and the tahina and hoummos come with olive oil. Try the desserts, especially the mahalabiya and crème caramel. The restaurant is open from 6 am to 12 midnight.

Ala Kefak, 1 Sharia Saad Zaghloul, is a clean pizzeria. The inexpensive menu includes pizza, spaghetti and steaks. Service is lousy; you have to remind the waiter that you have ordered.

Restaurant Denis (483 0457), 1 Sharia Ibn Basaam, three blocks east of Ramli Station, serves fresh seafood by weight. Prices are between E£7 and E£12 for various types of fish, E£30 per kg for shrimp, and 75 pt for salad.

There are a number of interesting places around Ramli Station. *Taverna Diamantakis* (482 8189), opposite the station, serves fried or grilled fish, squid, shellfish, and a fairly good Greek salad. The *Athineos Cafe*, which like the Pastroudis is part of Alexandria's cafe history, also looks across to the station.

Other Parts of Alexandria The *San Giovanni Restaurant* (848178), jutting out over the sea at 205 Sharia el Geish, Stanley Beach, is one of the best eating places in Alexandria. A full seafood meal costs about E£20. The restaurant is open from 1.30 to 4 pm and 8.30 to 11 pm, and features an after-dinner nightclub with live music.

The *Delta Hotel* (tel 482 9820), 14 Sharia Champollion, Mazarita, has excellent French-style food at reasonable prices, including Coquilles St Jacques, fish soup, steak with Béarnaise sauce, and Shrimp Provençal. The Delta is open from 12 noon to 4 pm and from 7.30 to 11.00 pm.

Tikka Grill, on the waterfront near the Mosque of Abu el Abbas, has great views. Meals cost between E£8 and E£14, and you can pile your plate up with extras from the salad bar.

Alexander's Restaurant (tel 866111), in the Ramada Renaissance Hotel, 544 Sharia el Geish, Sidi Bishr, is a comparatively expensive but elegant restaurant. Their specialities include smoked salmon, crab and cheese soufflé, and grilled fish kebab. Prices range from E£4 to E£15.

The *New China Restaurant* (tel 548 0996), in the Hotel Corail, 802 Sharia el Geish, Mandarra Bay (near Montazah Palace), has splendid views of the Mediterranean. Chinese food is the speciality here; dinner costs less than E£15. The restaurant is open from 12 noon to 4 pm and 6 to 11 pm.

The *Zephyrion* (tel 560 1319) in Abu Qir is probably one of the best restaurants in Egypt. Its location alone warrants that honour. Zephyrion is Greek for 'breeze of the sea', and this restaurant, on a magnificent terrace overlooking the ocean with waves breaking below, certainly has that. The menu features Greek-style fish, giant shrimp, shrimp with lemon and oil, fried squid, and beer or wine. To order, go to the cashier, choose the fish yourself, and indicate how you want it cooked. You can have a tremendous meal for a moderate price (about E£15 to E£20, plus a 10% service charge).

Abu Qir Coffeeshop, in the Landmark Hotel, Midan San Stefano, serves ravioli, seafood, chicken and various other dishes. It's open 24 hours a day.

Ras el Tin Restaurant, also in the Landmark Hotel, is managed by Britons and has international food at fair prices. A plate of hoummos, tahina, baba ghanough, olives and pickles is a particularly cheap favourite.

The *Seagull Restaurant* (tel 445 5575) is reputedly one of the best seafood restaurants in the Alexandria area. It's west of the city, on the way to Agami Beach. Locals claim that it is now better than the Zephyrion. To get there, take the Agami bus and get off at the El Max bus stop. The restaurant is in a huge, castlelike building overlooking the waterfront.

There are three *Wimpys* in Alexandria: in Montazah, Maamoura and Rushdy. There's also a *Kentucky Fried Chicken* in Montazah.

Entertainment

Most of Alexandria's major hotels have nightclubs and discos, and live music is a feature of the many clubs along the Corniche. The most popular include the *Crazy Horse* and a small Greek venue called the *Athineos*.

There are several good cinemas in Alexandria that show English-language films for about E£1 admission. They are all around Midan Saad Zaghloul. Check with the tourist office for details of cinemas and films.

For one week every September, Alexandria hosts an International Film Festival of uncensored films from at least 10 countries. The tourist office will have the details.

If you don't have anything better to do with your money, there are casinos in the *Hotel Cecil* and the *Palestine Hotel*.

Getting There & Away

Air Air travel to Alexandria from within Egypt is expensive; the one-way fare for the 40 minute flight from Cairo is about E£70. Unless you are in a tremendous hurry, it is best to get to and from Alexandria by bus, taxi or train.

Bus Two bus companies, West Delta and Golden Rocket, operate services between Alexandria and Cairo. On average, two buses travel in each direction every hour between 5 am and 7 pm. Both companies also run buses in the very early hours for those catching early flights from Cairo. The West Delta bus leaves at 12.30 am, and the Golden Rocket bus leaves at 1 am.

Buses for Cairo leave from Midan Saad Zaghloul; the ticket offices are opposite the Hotel Cecil.

West Delta buses travel on both the desert and delta roads to Cairo, so if you have a preference you need to say so when buying your ticket. The trip takes about three to 3½ hours and costs from E£7 to E£8 depending on the route; E£10 to E£12 if you wish to continue to the Cairo airport.

The Golden Rocket company offers a deluxe service with light refreshments served on board during the trip. You can order tea, coffee, soft drinks, sandwiches and snacks from a steward or stewardess on the bus, but accept only what you have ordered. Tickets are E£7 to E£10, or E£15 to E£20 if you want to go to Cairo airport. The cheaper fares apply to buses leaving before 4.30 pm.

Between 8 am and 1 pm, hourly buses make the four to five hour trip between Alexandria and Marsa Matruh; two buses stop in El Alamein and Sidi Abdel Rahman. Buses depart hourly from Midan Saad Zaghloul between 8 am and 1 pm during the summer, but less frequently the rest of the year.

Buses to Rashid (Rosetta) leave every half-hour. Some are faster than others, so if you're in a hurry ask for the *otobees sareeha*, which means the 'fast bus'.

Buses to Damietta depart at 8 am, 12 noon and 3.30 pm from Midan Saad Zaghloul. The four hour trip costs E£3.50.

Train Cairo-bound trains leave Alexandria at least hourly, nearly 24 hours a day, from Masr Station, stopping at Sidi Gaber Station. The trip is via Damanhur and Tanta, takes about three hours and costs E£9.50 in 1st class, or E£6 in 2nd class; a student discount is available in 1st class.

The train from Alexandria to Marsa Matruh, which is as far west along the coast as foreigners are permitted to travel, takes an uncomfortably long eight hours. The bus service on this route is faster and more comfortable.

As with all trains in Egypt, check for the latest schedules and fares before making your travel arrangements.

Taxi The service taxi depot is opposite

Masr Station. The fares are about E£6 to Cairo or to Marsa Matruh. Service taxis to Rashid leave from Midan Tahrir; the fare is about E£4.

Boat There are regular ferry services between Alexandria and Heraklion (Crete), Piraeus, Venice and other destinations around the Mediterranean. The ferries usually offer a choice of two or three berth cabins, with or without private showers and toilets.

The ticket prices vary according to the cabin you choose and the time of year. There are also special youth and student fares, and Eurail Pass holders are entitled to a 30% discount.

The approximate fares given here are representative of Adriatica Line's cheapest and most expensive berths.

The fares from Alexandria to Heraklion range from US$95 to US$195 in the low season, and from US$105 to US$215 in the high season.

To Piraeus the low season fares range from US$135 to US$260, and the high season fares from US$150 to US$290.

To Venice it costs from US$240 to US$495 in the low season, and from US$265 to US$550 in the high season.

A line between Yugoslavia and Alexandria was also being considered.

You must confirm your reservation at least 48 hours in advance at the shipping agencies in Cairo or Alexandria and report to the maritime station at least three hours before the ship's departure.

Adriatica's shipping agents in Alexandria are De Castro & Co (tel 35770), 33 Sharia Salah Salem; and Menatours (tel 809676), Midan Saad Zaghloul. Menatours also represents other shipping lines and has an office in Cairo, at 14 Sharia Talaat Harb.

Adriatica Line's ships have two main itineraries, given in the following table, throughout the year. The second itinerary is more common between July and October (the high season):

From	To	Duration
Venice	Dubrovnik	22½ hours
Dubrovnik	Piraeus	30 hours
Piraeus	Heraklion	15 hours
Heraklion	Alexandria	56 hours
Venice	Piraeus	48 hours
Piraeus	Heraklion	13 hours
Heraklion	Alexandria	34 hours

The North African Shipping Company (NASCO), 83 Sharia Nabi Daniel, Alexandria (or 171 Sharia Mohammed Farid, Cairo), represents the Louis Cruise Lines' ships *Princesa Cypria* and *Marissa*, both of which usually travel between Port Said, Israel and Cyprus with departures every Tuesday and Friday. The *Princesa Cypria* departs Alexandria every Saturday for Limassol (Cyprus), Rhodes, Tinos and Piraeus.

Amoun Shipping, 71 Sharia Hurriya, in front of the Governorate building, represents Russian ships that go to Greece, Cyprus and Syria.

All these itineraries are also followed in reverse. Also, you should be aware that travelling by ship will not save you money. In fact, flying to the same destinations will often be cheaper. There are, of course, a few exceptions, especially if you have an International Student Identity Card (ISIC) or if you are under 31. You must present bank receipts showing that you officially exchanged the amount of the fare or credit card receipts showing that you spent an equivalent amount in Egypt.

The tourist office in Alexandria can provide information on other shipping lines and destinations.

Getting Around

Airport Transport To get to Alexandria airport from the city centre you can take bus No 203 from Midan Saad Zaghloul or a taxi for E£10.

West Delta bus company buses to Alexandria leave from the lot in front of Cairo airport's old terminal at a quarter to the hour, every hour, from 4.45 am to

7.45 pm. During the day the fare is E£12, but at night it's E£15.

Bus Most of Alexandria's local buses leave from Ramli Station, but some leave from Midan Orabi. Services operate between 5.30 am and 1 am. Single trips around Alexandria cost between 5 pt and 25 pt.

The most important routes are serviced by the following buses: No 203, between the airport and Midan Saad Zaghloul; Nos 211 and 220, up and down the Corniche to Montazah Palace (No 220 continues on to Maamoura Beach); No 260, between Midan Orabi, Montazah Palace and Abu Qir; No 500, between Ramli Station, Midan Orabi and Agami; and Nos 450 and 460, between Midan Saad Zaghloul, Agami and Hannoville.

Minibus No 750 goes to Agami and Hannoville; No 725 goes to Montazah Palace; Nos 720 and 726 go to Maamoura; and No 728 goes to Abu Qir.

Tram You can get to most places around central Alexandria by tram. Ramli Station is the main tram station. Yellow trams go west from Ramli Station: No 14 goes to Masr Station, No 15 goes to the Mosque of Abu el Abbas Mursi and Fort Qait Bey, and No 16 goes to the Catacombs of Kom el Shuqqafa and Pompey's Pillar. Blue trams go east from Ramli Station: No 2 goes to Montazah via Zizinia. Some trams have two carriages, in that case the front carriage is for women, the back one for men. It causes considerable amusement when an unsuspecting foreigner gets in the wrong carriage! The standard fare is 10 pt.

Taxi The baksheesh you pay to the taxi driver will probably exceed the cost of a bus or tram ticket for the same journey. Without baksheesh, a taxi will cost from about E£1 per person for a short trip, and E£4 for a trip to the eastern beaches.

RASHID (ROSETTA)

The ancient city of Rashid, also known by its former name of Rosetta, is 65 km east of Alexandria, where the western (Rosetta) branch of the Nile empties into the Mediterranean. Founded in the 9th century, Rashid is most famous for the Rosetta Stone, an inscribed stone that was unearthed by Napoleon's soldiers in 1799. The basalt slab, which dates from the reign of Ptolemy V (about 196 BC), was inscribed in Egyptian hieroglyphs, demotic Egyptian and Greek. The combination of written languages enabled a Frenchman, Jean-François Champollion, to finally decipher the ancient Pharaonic language.

Rashid became one of the most important ports in Egypt when Alexandria declined between the 8th and 19th centuries. It reached its height in the 17th and 18th centuries, but as modern Alexandria began to develop, Rashid became a backwater.

Rashid has a certain charm, though its beautiful palm groves tend to shelter a city besmirched with garbage and manure. The main attractions are its fine old buildings with colourful facades and

Nile kingfisher

superbly intricate mashrabiyya screens. The best of these include Bait Qili, which has been turned into an interesting museum, Al Amaciali and the House of Ali al Fatairi. The Mosque of Zaghloul, at the bottom of the main street, was founded in 1600 AD, and the Mosque of Mohammed al Abbas, near the Nile, was built in 1809.

Getting There & Away

Although buses and trains operate between Alexandria and Rashid, the easiest way to get there and away is by hire car or service taxi. The latter should cost about E£4.

You can catch a train from Sidi Gaber Station in Alexandria to Maamoura, just east of Montazah Palace, and then another train from there to Rashid.

Buses for Rashid leave Alexandria every hour.

The Mediterranean Coast

The 105 km stretch of coastline between El Alamein and Alexandria is slated for massive tourist development. Beach resort projects, such as the Hotel Arik and the massive Marakia resort, have begun popping up along the beautiful beaches of this region.

EL ALAMEIN

The small coastal village of El Alamein, 105 km west of Alexandria, is most famous as the scene of a decisive Allied victory over the Axis powers during WW II. The massive battle of El Alamein, between the Allied tank divisions under the command of Field Marshal Montgomery and the German-Italian armoured force of Field Marshal Rommel's Afrika Korps, altered the course of the war in North Africa.

In June 1942, Rommel, nicknamed the Desert Fox, launched an offensive from Tobruk in Libya in an attempt to push his troops and 500 tanks all the way through the Allied lines to Alexandria and the Suez Canal. The Allied forces initially thwarted the advance of the Afrika Korps with a line of defence stretching southward from El Alamein to the Qattara Depression. Then, on 23 October 1942, Montgomery's 8th Army swooped down from Alexandria with 1000 tanks, and within two weeks routed the German and Italian forces, driving Rommel and what was left of his Afrika Korps back to Tunis.

More than 80,000 soldiers were killed or wounded at El Alamein and the subsequent battles for control of North Africa. The thousands of graves in the town's three huge war cemeteries, the area's main tourist attractions, are a bleak and moving reminder of the war.

Today El Alamein is a busy construction area. An oil pipeline and new port facilities for shipping Egypt's oil from throughout the country are being built, and there are plans for a canal across the Qattara Depression from the Nile. The canal project is designed to open up new areas of arable land for Egypt's expanding population, but is being delayed by the many WW II mine fields in the Western Desert. These unexploded mines are also a hazard to wandering travellers, so stick to the beaten tracks.

Things to See

The War Museum, on the western side of town, features detailed displays of the El Alamein battles, profiles on Rommel and Montgomery, and various tanks, heavy artillery and other implements of destruction. One section of the museum is dedicated to Egypt's victories in the 1973 war with Israel and the smashing of the Bar Lev Line. The museum is open from 9 am to 1 pm; admission is 50 pt.

The British Military Cemetery, on the eastern side of town, is a haunting place where more than 7000 tombstones cover a slope overlooking the desert battlefield of El Alamein. The plaques on the walls of the entrance building honour soldiers from the UK, Australia, New Zealand,

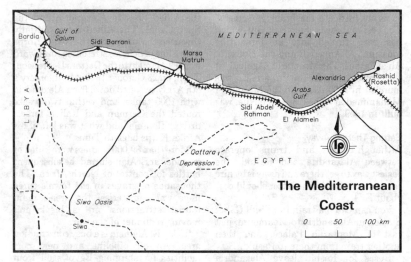

The Mediterranean Coast

France, Greece, South Africa, east and west Africa, Malaysia and India who fought for the Allied cause. The cemetery is maintained by the War Graves Commission, and admission is free.

The Italian War Memorial is about six km west of El Alamein, and the German War Memorial is another four km on, on a hill overlooking the Mediterranean. They are both as chillingly interesting as the Allied cemetery.

Places to Stay & Eat

The *El Alamein Rest House* has single/ double rooms for E£8/10. Meals at the restaurant cost between E£5 and E£7. The menu includes spaghetti with seafood sauce, fried or grilled shrimps, jelly with fruit, and home-made cake. There is also a cafeteria at the bus stop.

Hotel Arik, 15 km east of El Alamein, has double rooms and four person bungalows for E£75 plus 12% service.

Getting There & Away

El Alamein can be reached by train, bus or service taxi from Alexandria's Masr Station or Midan Saad Zaghloul, but the train takes twice as long as a bus or taxi

and the El Alamein station is inconveniently located across the desert from the town.

Buses leave Alexandria for Marsa Matruh between 8 am and 1 pm; two buses stop in El Alamein. Getting off the Marsa Matruh bus in El Alamein should be no problem, as most of the coastal buses from Alexandria and Cairo stop at the Rest House; but getting on it in the first place is another thing altogether, as it's nearly always full.

A service taxi to El Alamein is probably the best option, though you may have to pay the full fare to Marsa Matruh (E£6). The fare for either a bus or service taxi to El Alamein is only E£3 or E£4. Hitching is possible, as the volume of traffic along the coast road is increasing, but it is not advised. This is a hot, dry, and sparsely populated region.

From Cairo, the buses leave from next to the telephone office on Midan Tahrir, and service taxis leave from Ramses Station and from in front of the Nile Hilton.

SIDI ABDEL RAHMAN

The fine, white sandy beach and the sparkling blue-green of the Mediterranean make this stunning little resort, 23 km west of El Alamein, one of the most beautiful stretches of coastline you're ever likely to visit.

Bedouins occasionally congregate in a small village about three km inland. They belong to the Awlad Ali tribe, who came into the region several hundred years ago from Libyan Cyrenaica and subdued the smaller local tribes of the Morabiteen. There are now five main tribes subdivided into clans, each of which has several thousand members. The Egyptian government has been attempting to settle these nomads, so nowadays most of the Bedouin have forsaken their tents and herd their sheep and goats from the immobility of government-built stone houses.

Apart from the spectacular beach, the Bedouin village, and the expensive hotel and camping ground, there is not much else to Sidi Abdel Rahman.

Places to Stay & Eat

The *Al Alamein Hotel*, a semideluxe place right on the beach, has single/double rooms for E£36/44, plus 22% taxes and service charges.

You can hire a tent at the hotel for E£16 for one person or E£19 for two, plus 17.5% taxes and service charges. There are 23 tents, 12 of which are equipped for overnight stays.

The only place to eat in the area is the hotel's restaurant, where lunch costs E£15 and dinner E£20, so unless you plan to catch and cook your own fish it's a good idea to bring food and water with you.

Getting There & Away

There are buses twice a day between Alexandria and Sidi Abdel Rahman. The trip takes about three hours.

MARSA MATRUH

The large waterfront town of Marsa Matruh, built around a charming bay of clear Mediterranean waters and clean white sand beaches, is the Egyptian equivalent of the French Riviera. It's a relaxing place, a little less expensive than

the other north coast resorts and popular with holidaying Egyptians. Relatively few foreign tourists seem to get this far west but if you have the time it's a good spot to take a break from the busy cities and ancient monuments.

There is a strong military presence in the area due to the town's proximity to Libya. It's not a good idea to go there when tensions with that country are on the rise, but it's quite safe most of the time. At the time of writing, full diplomatic relations between the two countries had been restored and the border reopened.

Orientation & Information

There are really only two streets in Marsa Matruh that you need to know: the Corniche, which runs right round the waterfront, and Sharia Alexandria, which runs perpendicular to the Corniche, towards the hill behind the town.

The tourist office, on the ground floor of the Governorate building on the corner of Sharia Alexandria and the Corniche, is open from 9 am to 2 pm daily except Friday, when it's usually open from 4 to 8 pm. However, I was there after 4 pm on a Friday and found it closed, and three other travellers arrived before 4 pm and found it open!

There is only one post office in Marsa Matruh; it's in Sharia al Shataa, one block south of the Corniche and two blocks east of Sharia Alexandria. The hours are from 8 am to 3 pm except on Friday and Saturday, when it's closed. The 24 hour telephone office is across the street from the GPO.

Most of the hotels are on the Corniche, and the restaurants and shops are on or around Sharia Alexandria.

Siwa Permits

Permission to travel to Siwa is easily obtained, sometimes on the spot, from the Military Intelligence Office at the eastern end of Sharia al Shataa, which is parallel to the Corniche. The office is easy to find, but if you need directions, ask a local for *ta'asree siwa*, which means 'Siwa permit', and you'll be shown the way to a large green door. Bring a photocopy of your passport identity pages and Egyptian visa pages. You can get photocopies made at El Faham Kodak, in Sharia Alexandria.

Rommel Museum

Built into the caves that Rommel used as his headquarters during the conflicts at El Alamein, this museum details the exploits of the famous field marshal during his WW II campaigns in North Africa. The museum is on the Corniche, east of Sharia Alexandria. It is open in summer only, every day except Friday, from 10 am to 4 pm. Although it's officially closed during winter, you might be able to arrange to see it through the tourist office.

Rommel's Beach

This beach, a little east of the museum, is supposedly where Rommel took time off from his tanks and troops to have his daily swim.

Other Beaches

As well as the beautiful bay beaches of Marsa Matruh there are several splendid, unspoiled beaches east and west of the town. Some of the more secluded beaches can only be reached by paddle board or surf kayak, which can be rented from some hotels in the town. The wreck of a German submarine lies offshore, and sunken Roman galleys are reputedly lying in deeper waters off the eastern beaches.

About 10 km west of Marsa Matruh is Obayyid Beach, a developing resort with overpriced tent accommodation (see the Places to Stay section).

Shatit el Gharam, which means the 'beach of lovers', can only be reached by paddle board across the bay, but the trip is easy. The large rock formations at this beach are certainly worth seeing.

About 16 km from Marsa Matruh, on the ocean side of the bay, is Cleopatra's Beach. Nearby is Cleopatra's Bath, where the great queen and Marc Antony are supposed to have bathed.

Agiiba means 'a miracle of nature', and Agiiba Beach, about 20 km west of Marsa Matruh, is just that. It is a small but spectacular beach, accessible only by a path leading down from the clifftop. There is a cafe nearby where you can get light refreshments.

Places to Stay

Accommodation prices vary greatly from winter to summer, and substantial discounts are sometimes available until early June.

The *Arous el Bahr Hotel* (tel 944419) is on the Corniche, facing the water. The hotel name means 'bride of the sea'. Most rooms have balconies overlooking the bay. Good, clean single/double/triple rooms with a bath cost E£14/18/23. The hotel also has bungalows available nearby for about E£20 per night for up to four people. Breakfast is another E£3. Be careful when you have a shower: the bathrooms tend to get flooded. The staff are extremely helpful, especially about arranging transportation. I was a little taken aback when one of the desk clerks told me that breakfast included 'eggs, bread, tea and shit'. It turned out that she thought 'shit' meant cheese!

The three star *Hotel Beau Site* (tel 942066), on the waterfront, has received rave reviews, even though it looks rundown and weather-beaten. Single rooms cost between E£12 and E£25, and double rooms cost between E£15 and E£31, plus 12% taxes and service fees. The hotel is closed during winter.

Rommel House Hotel (tel 945466) is a clean, 60 room hotel. Single/double rooms cost E£21.50/26.50, plus 14% taxes and service charges. All rooms have bathrooms, TV and (in summer only) refrigerators, and some have air-conditioning. Breakfast is available, and there's a cafeteria.

The three star *Hotel Negresco* (tel 942252), behind the Sidi Alwan Mosque on the Corniche, has spotless rooms with air-conditioning, clean bathrooms and TV. In winter, single/double rooms are E£38/45; in summer the prices are about E£64/80. Breakfast is included and is served whenever you want in the morning.

The *Hotel Shepheard* (tel 944295) isn't like its Cairo namesake, but it's still a good place to stay for a moderate price. Most rooms have a balcony with Mediterranean views, a bath with soap and fresh towels each days, TV and wall-to-wall carpeting. Single/double/triple rooms are E£27/36/51.

The *Riviera Palace Hotel* (tel 942051) has 32 rooms. It is officially a three star establishment, but its rooms seem only up to two star standard. The halls are freshly painted, but a few beds were missing, and the top sheets and bathrooms could be cleaner. Single/double/triple rooms are E£20/28/35.

The *Hotel des Roses*, run by a Greek family, has clean single/double rooms for E£6/8.50. Breakfast is another E£2.50. The hotel is closed during winter.

The *Matruh Hotel* (also known as the *Hamada Hotel*) is a dusty dive on the main road. There is no hot water or breakfast. Rooms are a ridiculous E£18 a double, so stay there only as a last resort.

The *New Lido Hotel* is a rather decrepit place that is closed in winter. Some rooms overlook the sea; single/double rooms cost E£5/8.

The *Hotel Rio*, near the centre of town, has single/double rooms for E£5/7.

The *Hotel Ghazal* is a clean place which costs E£2.25 for a bed – but that's about all you get.

If you want to rough it a little, the tents on the shore at Obayyid Beach, 10 km west of town, cost between E£18 and E£33 per person per night, including three meals and access to showers and toilets. Camping here is popular among Egyptians in the summer.

Places to Eat

The *Alexandria Tourist Restaurant* serves complete meals of fish, salad and rice for E£5, and great tahina for only 50 pt.

The *Restaurant Panayotis Greece* is opposite the Alexandria. According to the chef, everything is good. Try the *scotalia*, which is a fantastic Greek salad that's only available when there's enough fetta cheese. A meal of fish, bread and salad costs E£5 to E£6.

The *Beau Site Restaurant* is in the Beau Site Hotel, so it's closed in winter. The food is fairly good, but beware of the prices. Three tourists said they were charged over E£70 for a fish dinner; the food is good, but not that good!

The *Camona Restaurant*, in Sharia Galaa, serves one kg of kebab and kufta for E£10 to E£15 – enough for a big meal for at least four people.

The *Anji Restaurant*, in a side street off Sharia Alexandria, serves a big breakfast of cornflakes, omelette, yogurt, bread, cheese and peppermint tea at a reasonable price.

For delicious, freshly baked pastries, try *El Sharbatly's Confectionery* in Sharia Alexandria, next to the Matruh Cafe and the Matruh Hotel.

Getting There & Away

Air Although you can get an EgyptAir flight between Cairo and Marsa Matruh for about E£100, buses and service taxis are much cheaper and easier ways to make the trip.

Bus Buses leave for Marsa Matruh from Midan Saad Zaghloul in Alexandria. The trip takes four or five hours. Buses depart hourly between 8 am and 1 pm, and the fare is about E£10.

There is usually only one bus per day from Cairo to Marsa Matruh, though several make the trip in summer. The regular bus usually leaves at 8 am from Midan Tahrir. You should buy your ticket at least one day in advance from the ticket kiosk closest to the Mogamma building.

The six or seven hour trip costs between E£10 and E£20, depending on the type of bus.

If you are continuing on to Siwa Oasis, there are two daily buses: one at 7 am and one with air-conditioning at 3 pm. The four or five hour trip costs E£4. To visit Siwa Oasis you need a permit, which is easily obtainable in Marsa Matruh (see the Siwa Permits entry in the Marsa Matruh section).

Train There are several daily trains between Alexandria and Marsa Matruh, but it's a long and tedious trip taking up to eight hours. You may save some money, but it will take at least twice the time to get to your destination if you go by train instead of by bus and taxi.

Taxi Service taxi is probably the most convenient way to get to Marsa Matruh, especially if you can get a group together. Service taxis frequently leave Alexandria from a stand in the park in front of Masr Station. They take about the same time as the buses and cost E£6 per person.

If you're coming from Cairo, the taxi goes via Alexandria, adding about five hours to the trip. Taxis leave from Ramses station and from in front of the Nile Hilton.

Taxis to Siwa and Alexandria from Marsa Matruh can be arranged in a lot across from the bus station for E£6 per person.

Hitching It shouldn't be too difficult to get a lift from Alexandria to Marsa Matruh, but it is not wise. The area is hot, dry, and sparsely populated. If you do intend hitching, take plenty of water and be careful about sun exposure.

Getting Around
Caretas, or donkey carts, are the most common form of transport around the streets of Marsa Matruh. Some are like little covered wagons with colourful canvas covers. A ride across town should cost between 75 pt and E£1.25.

Private taxis can be hired for the day for E£20 to E£30 but you must negotiate and bargain aggressively, especially in the summer.

During the summer there are regular bus services from town to Cleopatra, Obayyid and Agiiba beaches. They leave every 15 minutes from 8 am until sunset.

Bicycles can be rented next to the Riviera Palace Hotel for E£5 per day.

SIWA OASIS
The lush and productive Western Desert oasis of Siwa, famous throughout the country for its dates and olives, is 300 km south-west of Marsa Matruh and 550 km west of Cairo, near the Libyan border.

The original Berber settlers were attracted to this island of green in a desolate sea of sand many centuries ago, when they discovered several freshwater springs in the area. Although Islam and Arabic eventually reached this far into the desert, Siwa's solitary position has allowed the predominantly Berber-speaking inhabitants to preserve many of their ancient traditions and customs.

Until recently, Siwa was so isolated that, apart from the desert caravans of ancient times or the occasional pilgrim who journeyed there to visit the famed Temple of Amun, very few outsiders ventured there.

But now there is a paved desert road into the Siwa area and microwave stations linking it to the rest of the country. At the time of writing, a paved road for the stretch between Siwa and Bahariyya Oasis had been partially completed. Visiting Siwa today is not as adventurous as it used to be, because hordes of travellers come here. For example, in May 1989, in the low tourist season, the Military Intelligence Office in Marsa Matruh issued over 500 Siwa travel permits.

The most illustrious of Siwa's early visitors was the young conqueror Alexander, who led a small party on an eight day trek through the desert in 331 BC to seek out the Oracle of the Temple of Amun. Alexander's goal, which he apparently attained, was to seek confirmation that he was the son of Zeus, and also to uphold the traditional belief that, as the new Pharaoh of Egypt, he was also the son of Amun.

Apart from a Greek traveller who visited in 160 AD, the people of Siwa did not see another European until 1792.

It takes about four to five hours to get to Siwa Oasis from Marsa Matruh – quite an improvement on Alexander's journey from the coast.

Siwa Permits

Because of its proximity to Libya, you must have written permission from the military to visit the oasis. This procedure is easy in Marsa Matruh (see the Siwa Permits entry in the Marsa Matruh section).

Things to See

Siwa's greatest attraction is the oasis itself, which boasts more than 200,000 palm trees, 50,000 olive trees and a great many fruit orchards. The vegetation is sustained by more than 300 freshwater springs and streams and the area attracts an amazing variety of bird life, including quails and falcons.

On the hill of Aghurmi, four km east of the town of Siwa, are the ruins of the 26th dynasty Temple of Amun, built between 663 and 525 BC. The temple, was dedicated to Amun, the ram-headed god of life, who was later associated with Egypt's sun-god, Ra, and the king of the Greek gods, Zeus.

Gebel al Mawta, also known as the Mount of the Dead, is an interesting site one km north of the town. There are several tombs in the area, many of which have not yet been excavated and explored. Most of the tombs date from Ptolemaic and Roman times, and there seem to be pieces of mummies and mummy cloth scattered all over the place. You can climb the hill to see a few of the tombs, but don't take photographs of the surrounding military bases.

Cleopatra's Bath, a spring that pours into a stone brick pool, is a popular bathing hole for the locals, but the scum floating on the surface doesn't make it very appealing.

There is a similar pool on Fantasy Island, an oasis ringed by the Salt Lake, which is accessible across a narrow causeway. The island seems isolated, because it takes about an hour for the careta ride to the island, six km from the town. The pool is in an idyllic setting amidst palm trees and lush greenery. It's hardly the setting for a picnic with a TV, but that's what I found when I got there – a TV hooked up to a car battery and a group of soldiers behind it munching chunks of watermelon.

Places to Stay

There are three hotels in town, but one, the *Siwa Hotel*, was closed when I was there, perhaps permanently.

The *El Madina Hotel* is in the centre of town, near the mosque. It has clean beds and bathrooms, but the pit toilets are rather stinky. The hotel charges E£2 per night per person.

You'll find better rooms at the *Arous El Waha*, which is about half a km from the town centre on the road to Marsa Matruh. The rooms, with private bathrooms and balconies overlooking a small palm garden, cost E£5 per person.

Camping is possible near Cleopatra's Bath, one of Siwa's many freshwater springs.

Places to Eat

The most popular place to eat in town is *Restaurant Abdu*, which is around the corner from the mosque. Abdu and his assistant serve a tasty vegetable stew, roast chicken (obtained fresh from the chicken store next door), rice, and beans in tomato sauce. They will gladly show you the kitchen so you can see what's cooking.

The only other restaurant in town is *Restaurant Kelani* two doors down from the Abdu. They serve spongy ta'amiyya and French fries dripping with oil. Yuck!

Getting There & Away

Siwa can be reached by bus, minibus or service taxi. There are two daily buses to Siwa Oasis from Marsa Matruh: one at 7 am and the other (air-conditioned) at 3 pm. The four or five hour trip costs about E£4. Buses from Siwa to Marsa Matruh leave at 5.30 am and 2 pm. The 5.30 am bus sometimes leaves earlier or later, so you should be in front of the Arous El Waha or the main mosque by at least 5 am; the bus stops at both places.

Supposedly, you can buy a ticket the night before from the main bus office, but I couldn't find the driver, so I couldn't buy a ticket. I also couldn't find the bus station, which is supposedly about one km from the centre of town. I asked five people in Arabic where the station is, but no-one seemed to know. The last man I asked didn't want to or couldn't tell me; he just wanted to know how he could get to the USA from Siwa!

A taxi to Siwa from Marsa Matruh costs E£6.

Getting Around

Bicycles can be rented from a small shop near the El Madina Hotel, but hiring a careta is a much more amusing way to get around. Adel and his brother, sons of the chicken store owner, both have carts, and will probably approach you while you're at the Restaurant Abdu. A three hour tour of the oasis, including the Temple of Amun, Cleopatra's Bath, the Oracle Temple, Salt Lake and Fantasy Island, costs E£2 per person.

The Sinai

The Sinai, a region of awesome and incredible beauty, has been a place of refuge, conflict and curiosity for thousands of years. Wedged between Africa and Asia, its northern coast is bordered by the Mediterranean Sea, and its southern peninsula by the Red Sea gulfs of Aqaba and Suez. Row upon row of barren, jagged, red-brown mountains fill the southern interior, surrounded by relentlessly dry, yet colourful, desert plains. From the palm-lined coast, dunes and swamps of the north to the white-sand beaches and superb coral reefs of the Red Sea, the Sinai is full of contrasts.

In Pharaonic times, the quarries of the Sinai provided enormous quantities of turquoise, gold and copper. The great strategic importance of the 'Land of Turquoise' also made it the goal of empire builders and the setting for countless wars.

The Sinai is a land of miracles and holy places. Elijah, Jacob and Abraham, the prophets of Judaism, Christianity and Islam, wandered through its hills and deserts. It was here that God is said to have first spoken to Moses from a burning bush and, later, delivered the Israelites from the Egyptian army with the celebrated parting of the Red Sea.

And Moses stretched out his hand over the sea; and the Lord caused the sea to go back. . .And the children of Israel went into the midst of the sea upon the dry ground: and the waters were a wall unto them on their right hand, and on their left. And the Egyptians pursued. . .and the Lord overthrew the Egyptians in the midst of the sea. And the waters returned and covered the chariots, and the horsemen, and all the host of Pharaoh that came into the sea after them; there remained not so much as one of them. . .Thus the Lord saved Israel that day out of the hand of the Egyptians; and Israel saw the Egyptians dead upon the sea shore. (Exodus 14: 21-30)

The Sinai is the 'great and terrible wilderness' of the Bible, across which the Israelites journeyed in search of the Promised Land, and it was from the summit of Mt Sinai that God delivered his Ten Commandments to Moses:

Tell the children of Israel; Ye have seen what I did unto the Egyptians. . .If ye will obey my voice and keep my covenant, then ye shall be a peculiar treasure unto me above all people: for all the earth is mine. And ye shall be unto me a kingdom of priests, and a holy nation.

And Mount Sinai was altogether in smoke, because the Lord descended upon it in fire; and the whole mount quaked greatly. . .And the Lord came down upon Mount Sinai. . .and called Moses up to the top of the mount. . .And God spoke all these words, saying, I am the Lord thy God, which have brought thee out of the land of Egypt, out of the house of bondage. Thou shalt have no other gods before me. . . (Exodus 19-20)

History

In the 16th century BC, the soldiers of the Egyptian army, under Pharaoh Tuthmosis III, were far more fortunate than their biblical ancestors – they successfully crossed the Red Sea and the Sinai to conquer Palestine and Syria. Alexander the Great marched across the Sinai to conquer Egypt in 332 BC and, in 48 BC, just east of present-day Port Said, the opposing armies of Cleopatra and Ptolemy, her brother, battled for the Egyptian throne. Throughout the Sinai, holy places mark the spots where Mary, Joseph and Jesus supposedly rested during their flight into the Sinai to escape King Herod.

The Arab general Amr led his forces through the Sinai in 639 AD to conquer Egypt and bring Islam to Africa. In 1160, Salah al Din (known to the West as Saladin) built a fortress at Ras el Gindi, to protect Muslim pilgrims and to guard Egypt against the invading Crusaders. In

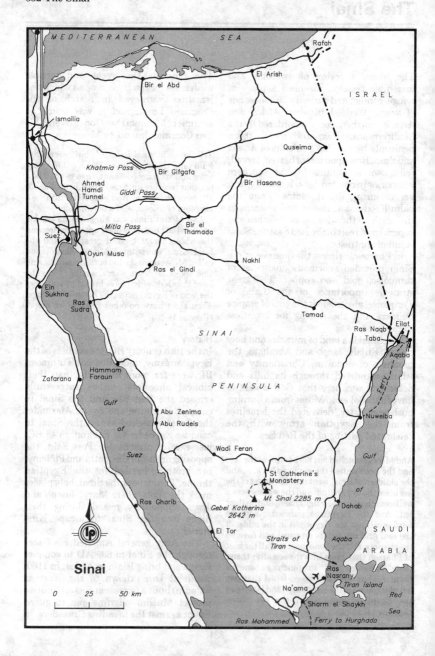

MEDITERRANEAN SEA

Rafah

El Arish

Bir el Abd

ISRAEL

Ismailia

Quseima

Khatmia Pass

Bir Gifgafa

Ahmed
Hamdi
Tunnel

Giddi Pass

Bir Hasana

Mitla Pass

Bir el
Thamada

Suez

Oyun Musa

Ras el Gindi

Nakhl

Ein
Sukhna

Ras
Sudra

Tamad

SINAI

Ras Naqb

Eilat
Taba

Zafarana

Hammam
Faraun

Aqaba

PENINSULA

Gulf
of
Suez

Abu Zenima
Abu Rudeis

Nuweiba

Wadi Feran

Gulf
of

Ras Gharib

St Catherine's
Monastery

Mt Sinai 2285 m

Dahab

Gebel Katherina
2642 m

El Tor

Aqaba

SAUDI

ARABIA

Sinai

Straits of
Tiran

0   25   50 km

Ras Nasrany

Na'ama

Tiran Island

Sharm el Shaykh

Red
Sea

Ras Mohammed

Ferry to Hurghada

the 16th century, the Ottomans crossed the Sinai to make Egypt part of their empire.

The Ottomans' power struggle with the French under Napoleon and with the British under Allenby continued to see the passage of armies back and forth across the Sinai, right up to the beginning of this century. The international border of the Sinai, from Rafah to Eilat, was actually drawn up by the British, prior to WW I, to keep the Germans and Turks away from the Suez Canal. In 1948, 1956 and from 1967 to 1979 the battle for the Sinai was fought between Egypt and Israel.

Israel briefly took the Sinai in its 1948 War of Independence, but was pressured, by the UK, into returning it to the Egyptians. In 1956, Israel, with the support of the UK and France, took control of the canal and the Sinai. Although Israel held the region for four months, a lack of US and UN support forced its return to Egypt.

In 1967, Egypt's President Nasser closed the strategic Straits of Tiran, at the southern tip of the Sinai, blocking Israel's access to the sea. The Israelis again captured the Sinai, and kept it by building a series of fortifications along the eastern bank of the Suez Canal. The Sinai remained impregnable until 1973, when the Egyptians, under President Sadat, used water cannons to blast the sand-dune barriers of the so-called Bar Lev Line. Today, Egyptians continue to speak of their 'secret weapon' and the great victory over Israel, even though their celebrations were short-lived.

Within two weeks, the Israelis had mustered their forces for a counterattack. Crossing the Suez Canal, they encircled the 30,000-strong Egyptian Third Army, took the city of Suez and came within striking distance of Cairo. Peace negotiations began at the now-famous Km 101, culminating in President Sadat's historic visit to Jerusalem, the Camp David Agreement and, in March 1979, the signing of a peace treaty by Begin and Sadat in Washington, DC.

In accordance with the treaty, Israel withdrew from most of the Sinai by 1982. A UN Multinational Force & Observers group, the MFO, was established to ensure adherence to the treaty by both Egypt and Israel. Most of the peacekeeping force, comprised of American, Canadian, French, Italian, British and Dutch personnel, is stationed at Na'ama Bay and El Arish to monitor Egyptian compliance with the military limits

imposed by the treaty. Basically, however, MFO members spend their days going to the beach, in between counting jeeps, tanks, Bedouin camels and other modes of transport.

Since the departure of the Israelis, more and more Egyptians are settling in the Sinai, taking advantage of the burgeoning tourist trade. For the most part, however, the region is populated by Bedouins.

Climate

It gets quite hot in the Sinai, so remember to always carry water, use copious amounts of sunblock cream, wear sensible clothes to avoid sunburn (a T-shirt is advisable while snorkelling), and use a hat or scarf. While summer temperatures can reach 50°C (120°F), it gets very cold at night and the mountains can be freezing even during the day; come prepared with warm clothing. In winter, you'll definitely need a sleeping bag, especially if you're camping out.

The Bedouins

The nomadic lifestyle of the 14 Bedouin tribes of the Sinai is rapidly changing as the 20th century encroaches on the age-old customs of these desert people. Once, they moved on, with their black goatskin tents, camels and goats, whenever the wells, wadis or other desert watercourses ran dry, and their tradition of hospitality used to be one of the major attractions for many of the travellers who visited the region. Now, as tourism and hotel projects continually spring up along the Sinai coasts, contact with Bedouins who don't work with tourists is becoming increasingly rare.

Most of their ancestors came from the Arabian peninsula, but the Bedouins' laws, customs and religion (which blends Islam and pagan beliefs), as well as their resilience and amazing hospitality, were born of their lifestyle in the Sinai – the isolation, the harsh, dry climate and the need to keep moving on in search of water.

The wealth of a Bedouin is still measured in camels and children, although Western technology is slowly making its presence felt. While you may see the traditional Bedouin goatskin tents and camels in the Sinai, there are also pick-up trucks and settlements of crude stone huts, or palm-frond shacks, with corrugated roofs and TV antennae.

Ever since the reign of Mohammed Ali, early in the 19th century, governments have been trying to settle the Bedouin tribes. Like the Israelis before them, the Egyptians have built schools, medical clinics and social centres for the Bedouins. They have also placed hundreds of 200 litre barrels of water strategically, at points where they wish to create stable settlements. Many of the Sinai's 50,000 Bedouins now harvest dates, cultivate grain, grow vegetables and cater to the tourists.

Information

Visas If you're entering Egypt by way of the Sinai from Israel, you will need an Egyptian visa. This can only be obtained before you get to the border. On arrival in Egypt, you must register with the police within seven days.

Special Sinai-only visas, valid for seven days, are issued at the Taba border, and at the Egyptian consulates in Israel. Travel with these visas is limited to the east coast and St Catherine's. For more information on entering Egypt from Israel, refer to the Getting There chapter at the beginning of the book.

Money As changing money in the Sinai can be awkward, it's best to take as much in E£ with you as possible. The banks and hotels in Sharm el Shaykh, Na'ama Bay, Dahab, Taba, St Catherine's and El Arish will change any sort of travellers' cheques but, anywhere else, only US$ (cash) will be bought.

Books *The Red Sea Coasts of Egypt – Sinai & the Mainland* by Jenny Jobbins

(The American University in Cairo Press) has good route descriptions of the coastal road around the Sinai.

The Rubbishing of the Sinai

Egypt is not exactly garbage free but modern litter is most evident and most sad in the Sinai. It's a combination of attitude and environment. The Bedouin were used to moving on and leaving their debris behind them. No matter, it was all biodegradable and if it took a little longer to rot away in the dry desert environment that was no problem – after all there weren't many people in the Sinai to see it. Now there are a lot more people and their modern plastic garbage doesn't decay at all. The whole Sinai is becoming covered in a scattering of plastic bags and some places are real horror stories. The popular budget travel centre of Dahab would be a beautiful little bay if the whole place wasn't one big garbage dump. And Moses would have no trouble at all finding his way to the top of Mt Sinai today – he could just follow the empty plastic mineral water bottles and used toilet paper. It's a pity he didn't bring down one more commandment – Thou Shalt Not Litter.

Getting Around

The few paved roads through the desert and hills link only the permanent settlements, so the most practical way of getting around is by bus or service taxi. There are frequent bus connections between most Sinai destinations.

Water Sports

Don't be completely fooled by the undeniable beauty of the Red Sea coast's blue-green waters and coral reefs – they do have their share of hazards. Always wear sandshoes or fins when you're exploring the reefs, and avoid bumping into the coral, especially fire coral, as it is extremely sharp and can cause a painful, burning sensation where it breaks your skin. Before diving or snorkelling, you should learn to recognise such potentially dangerous creatures as the stonefish, lionfish and scorpionfish. Barracuda and Moray eels are also prevalent, though seldom threatening. There are sharks in the Red Sea, but it's been a long time since

sharks have bothered humans in the Sinai waters. If you do see one, don't panic – nothing attracts sharks more than a terror-stricken human flailing about in their territory.

Treat the Sinai, above and below the sea, with care. Don't ruin a beautiful place by leaving garbage in the water, on the beach or in the mountains. When diving or snorkelling, do not touch the coral and plants, nor turn over rocks. Unfortunately, not enough people have respected this part of the world. On a single day in 1989, volunteers from the Cairo Divers Club collected almost a tonne of garbage from beaches near three Sharm el Shaykh dive sites. So clean up after yourself and do what you can to preserve the natural beauty of this very special place.

Conservationists and environmentalists are also concerned that extensive tourism and related development in the area between Ras Mohammed and Na'ama Bay will upset the delicate coastal and marine ecosystems. They are particularly worried that Ras Mohammed, the 'crown jewel' of world diving sites, will be ruined by its transformation into Egypt's first national marine park. The region currently attracts 60,000 visitors each year. However, a paved road has made the area more accessible, and a visitor centre was due to open by early 1990. The number of visitors is, therefore, expected to increase.

Diving If you have never dived before, the Sinai is the perfect place to learn. The average certification course takes about five days and usually includes several dives. The total cost of a five day open-water course leading to PADI or NAUI certification is usually around US$200.

Na'ama Bay has the greatest concentration of dive operators but the rates are fairly similar at all the Sinai's dive centres. Daily rental costs for a mask, snorkel or fins will be around US$1 to US$2. All other equipment is available including wet suits, regulators, buoyancy compensators, tanks and so on.

Introductory dives including equipment cost around US$40, advanced open-water courses including equipment cost US$150. Full-day diving trips including equipment and air fills cost US$45 to US$60 a day depending on the operator. From Na'ama Bay the trips to the Straits of Tiran or to Ras Mohammed are usually a little more expensive than dives at closer sites. Discounts are available on five day and 10 day packages and can bring the daily diving cost down to around US$30.

OYUN MUSA

Oyun Musa, or the 'springs of Moses', is said to be the place where Moses, on discovering that the water there was too bitter to drink, took the advice of God and threw a special tree into the springs, miraculously sweetening the water.

Seven of the 12 original springs still exist and, around them, a small settlement has grown up. The palm trees are a bit unusual, as most have had their crowns blown off in various Sinai wars and still haven't quite returned to their previous state.

Oyun Musa is about 40 km south of the Ahmed Hamdi Tunnel, which goes under the Suez Canal near Suez. Camping is possible but, as the spring water is too brackish, there is no drinkable water – and there's no sign of the special tree that Moses used.

Getting There & Away

There are half a dozen buses each way between Cairo and Sharm el Shaykh every day and they travel via Oyun Musa. Departures are from the Sinai Terminal (Abbassiya Station) in north-east Cairo.

The buses from Suez to El Tor also pass through Oyun Musa. They leave Suez at 10 am, 12 noon, 1 and 2 pm, and take one hour.

RAS EL GINDI

Eighty km south-east of the Ahmed Hamdi Tunnel is Ras el Gindi, which features the 800 year old Fortress of Salah

al Din. In the 12th century AD, Muslims from Africa and the Mediterranean streamed across the Sinai on their way to Mecca. As the three caravan routes they followed all converged at Ras el Gindi, Salah al Din built a fortress here to protect the pilgrims making their Haj. He also planned to use the fort as a base from which to launch attacks on the Crusaders, who had advanced as far as Jerusalem. As it turned out, Salah al Din managed to evict the Crusaders from the Holy City even before the completion of his fortress.

Ras el Gindi is definitely off the beaten track and, because it is rarely visited, most of the fortress is still standing. There is no public transport, so you must either have your own vehicle or hire a taxi.

RAS EL SUDR

Ras el Sudr, or Sudr, is about 60 km south of the Ahmed Hamdi Tunnel. The town developed around one of the country's biggest oil refineries, yet for some strange reason the Egyptians decided to build a tourist resort here. The *Sudr Beach Inn* (tel 70752) has furnished apartments and chalets, near the refinery and on the beach, for between E£34.50 and E£43 per night.

Near Sudr, there is a favourite rest stop for the Sinai bus drivers. This disastrous place has a flooded men's bathroom that is close to the worst I've ever seen. The urinal pipes leak into cans underneath, and onto the floor. Puddles are everywhere. Even with good shoes, you're inclined to tread very gingerly through here. Egyptian and foreign bus passengers alike complain about this place, apparently to no avail.

Getting There & Away

Buses from Suez to El Tor travel via Sudr; they leave Suez at 10 am, 12 noon, 1 and 2 pm. The trip takes 1½ hours. The Cairo to Sharm el Shaykh bus also goes via Sudr.

HAMMAM FARA'UN

Hammam Fara'un, or 'the Pharaoh's

bath', is about 55 km south of Sudr. The Egyptians who travel here to relax in the hot springs and streams and lie on the beautiful, isolated beach rant and rave about the place. Alas, this splendid isolation won't last much longer, as plans are underway for the development of a resort and a rheumatism treatment centre.

Getting There & Away
The Sinai bus from Cairo can drop you off at the turn-off to Hammam Fara'un and the beach is not too far from the main road. There are also buses from Suez to Hammam Fara'un at 10 am, 12 noon, 1 and 2 pm; they take 2½ hours.

FROM ABU ZENIMA TO EL TOR
Several of Egypt's development schemes in the Sinai are being implemented along this 90 km stretch of coastline beside the Gulf of Suez. Most of the projects relate to the offshore oil fields; consequently, the area is marred by jumbled masses of pipes, derricks and machinery.

El Tor, the administrative capital of southern Sinai, is something of a boom town, with a broad, clean, central avenue bordered by new apartment buildings. There are a couple of hotels in town.

NA'AMA BAY & SHARM EL SHAYKH
The southern coast of the Gulf of Aqaba, between Tiran Island in the straits and Ras Mohammed at the tip of the Sinai, features some of the world's most brilliant and amazing underwater scenery. The crystal-clear water, the rare and lovely reefs and the incredible variety of exotic fish darting in and out of the colourful coral have made this a snorkelling and scuba diving paradise, attracting divers from all over the globe.

If you've never had the chance to explore the living treasures of the deep, this is the place to do it. The reefs are easily accessible and you'll find all the necessary diving equipment, as well as accommodation, restaurants, bars and public services, around Na'ama Bay and in nearby Sharm el Shaykh.

As a place to stay, Na'ama Bay is the better of the two – there isn't much on offer in Sharm el Shaykh, which was initially developed by the Israelis during their occupation of the peninsula.

Budget travellers should be warned that Na'ama Bay and Sharm el Shaykh are in the throes of a hotel construction boom. Most of the hotels will be in the four to five star deluxe range and the range of budget accommodation is very limited. See the Places to Stay section for more information.

Information
Sharm el Shaykh is about six km south of Na'ama Bay, where the coast road south from the Egypt-Israel border town of Taba turns the corner to run north to Suez and Cairo.

Most of the public services, such as the GPO, telephone office, Tourist Police, bus station and banks, are in Sharm el Shaykh, while the main dive shops and the Sinai's best supermarket are at Na'ama Bay. There are also banking facilities in Na'ama Bay; they're usually open 9 am to 12 noon and 6 to 9 pm. The Fayrouz Village Hilton has a surprisingly good bookshop.

If you've just arrived in Egypt, you can register at the main police station near the port, about one km from Sharm el Shaykh. However, the hotel or campground at which you're staying will register your passport with the police.

Water Sports
Obviously, the main attractions here are underwater and are best seen with a mask and snorkel or scuba gear. For those who don't want to get their feet wet, there are also glass-bottom boats.

Na'ama itself has no reefs, but the stunning Near Gardens and the even more incredible Far Gardens are an easy walk from the bay. The Near Gardens are about 45 minutes north of Na'ama, near the

point at the end of the bay, and the Far Gardens are another half hour along the coast. Take plenty of drinking water with you. Other dives to the north of Na'ama Bay include the Cathedral, Tiger Bay and the Canyon.

South of the bay are dive sites like the Tower (an incredible drop off only a couple of metres from the shore), Amphoras (they've all gone if there ever were any there), Paradise Bay, Turtle Bay and Fiasco. Pinkie's Wall has a sheer wall with pink soft coral.

Ras Umsid, near Sharm el Shaykh, is easily accessible. Prime diving is a three minute walk from the Clifftop Hotel and a simple wade from the beach, to the right of the small military outpost. The beautiful coral garden has lots of colourful fan coral, a great variety of fish, including barracuda and at least two resident Napoleon wrasse (which love hard-boiled eggs!). It's a good dive with a deep, sloping wall.

Diving at the other, more spectacular, diving sites in the area require a little more organisation and, as you need to go with one of the dive centres, will also cost you more.

Ras Mohammed, the southernmost point of the Sinai is, without doubt, one of the best diving sites in the world. The splendid coral gardens, with fish of every imaginable shape, size and brilliant colour, provide a stunning visual feast. There is also a shipwreck (which scattered hundreds of toilet bowls on the bottom) and a hang-out for sharks which, fortunately, don't seem to be too hungry. Sadly, however, Ras Mohammed is no longer a secret spot, inaccessible to most divers. In the high season, as many as 10 dive boats a day each bring an average of 20 divers into the area. Conceivably, that means 200 or more divers a day, churning up the water, bumping into coral and disturbing the fish. Environmentalists fear that this daily human invasion is causing irreparable damage to one of the world's most beautiful underwater ecosystems. If you do dive here, try not to disturb the flora and fauna; in other words, do your best not to touch *anything*. Popular Ras Mohammed dive sites include the Shark Observatory, Sting Ray Alley and the Eel Garden – descriptive names!

Tiran Island, in the Straits of Tiran, is also an excellent site, once again accessible only by boat. It's not as popular as Ras

Mohammed, partly because of the strong current and sizeable shark population. Jackson and Gordon reefs are the popular dives here; there are above-water wrecks on these reefs. Thomas Reef has canyons, lots of soft coral and you may see turtles or sharks. Woodhouse Reef is nice too.

Dive Shops There are a number of dive shops at Na'ama Bay, all with similar services and equipment. The Aquamarine Dive Centre offers numerous dive courses throughout the year and is attached to a resort complex that has been taken over by the Wagons-Lits company, so the dive centre will probably be expanded. Alain Sobol, the centre's enthusiastic Belgian manager, hopes to create a diving education centre with Scuba Pro International that specialises in one of the world's best diving curricula.

Also popular is the Aquanaute Diving Centre, in front of the Shamandura Supermarket. It's smaller than the Aquamarine, so classes also tend to be somewhat smaller. Occasionally, the Aquanaute organises one day diving excursions to Dahab, particularly for their students. Prices are similar to those at the Aquamarine.

There are several other good centres, including the Camel Diving Centre and the DTM Diving Centre at Fayrouz Village Hilton. Windsurfing is supposedly available at the DTM Centre, but during my visit they had only one board that could be used.

The Cairo Diving Club organises monthly trips, rents equipment and offers plenty of information on the dive sites. The British Sub-Aqua Club, also in Cairo, offers BSAC and PADI certification and instruction. For details, see the Dive Clubs entry in the Cairo Information section.

Emergency Centre At the Na'ama Bay jetty, a fully equipped diving emergency centre, including a decompression chamber, is being built with US government aid.

Places to Stay & Eat
Na'ama Bay and Sharm el Shaykh are experiencing a hotel boom that will probably convert the area into a four and five star hotel paradise. There's even a small forest of palm trees being planted on the beach. Several new hotels opened in 1989 and more were under construction. New projects at Na'ama Bay include a 200 room Sheraton Hotel (in place of the Marsa Alaat campground); redevelopment of the Aquamarine Hotel as a Pullman Hotel; a 200 room Victoria Company hotel development; and even a 600 room hotel in the grounds of the Environmental Institute. In Sharm el Shaykh developments include a Hilton (with 48 apartments and 68 chalets) and two or three resort villages between the Clifftop Hotel and Ras Umsid.

Na'ama Bay *Gafy's Camp*, at the north end of the bay, is the cheapest place to stay. With your own tent it costs E£3 per person, in their tents the cost including breakfast is E£6 per person in a small tent or E£10 in a large one. Although most of the camp consists of shoddy, patchwork tents, which flap about in the wind and become dust receptacles, Gafy plans to build more permanent structures and upgrade the tents. The bathrooms only have fresh water for two hours a day; salt water is available for the rest of the day. Have you ever tried brushing your teeth with salt water? It's not a pleasant experience. The campsite restaurant has a bar and offers dinner for E£10.

Next to Gafy's is *Marsa Alaat*, the Egyptian government campground, but this will probably become the site of the forthcoming Sheraton hotel complex. Unofficial camping is possible around the point of the north end of the bay, next to the Near Gardens diving area.

The campground next to the Shamandura supermarket and snack bar has now been replaced by an expanded snack bar and some permanent buildings. Ali el Dib, the jovial, big-bellied owner, plans to build a two star, 30 room hotel on the grounds. For now, though, he has the best supermarket in the area, and a great snack bar with a super-clean kitchen. Breakfast, including cornflakes and pancakes, costs E£5, and the variety of food served throughout the day ranges from spaghetti to calamari, fresh fish and vegetables.

The beachfront *Naama Beach Hotel* has the most interesting architecture at Na'ama Bay. It's a desert fantasy painted white throughout except for dashes of blue and green. The nightly cost including breakfast and dinner is US$47/80 for singles/doubles. Back from the Naama Beach Hotel is the *Tiran Hotel*, another recent addition with doubles at E£130 including breakfast.

Also behind the Naama Beach Hotel is the *Sanafir*, which is excellent value at E£88/108 for singles/doubles with bathrooms; the cost includes breakfast. It's the Moorish-style brainchild of the dashing Adly el Mestekawi, who is a combination of Indiana Jones and Omar Sharif. Once in a while, he rides his horse through the arched hotel entrance and into the central courtyard cafe, bar and restaurant area. The Sanafir has only 30 rooms, each with whitewashed walls, domed ceilings, and beds raised two or three steps above the floor. There are also clean, though very small, concrete-floored huts at E£25/30. The shared showers and bathrooms are very clean. Breakfast is a treat – an all-you-can-eat buffet with cornflakes, lots of juice and fruit, scrambled eggs, pancakes, yogurt, bread, jam and plenty of coffee and tea.

The *Fayrouz Village Hilton* (tel (062) 770504) is a sprawling 'village' of deluxe air-conditioned bungalows. It has almost everything you'd expect of a Hilton hotel, including high prices – singles/doubles are US$95/105 and larger suites are even more expensive. The breakfast buffet is included but lunch or dinner will cost about E£35.

The four star *Ghazala Hotel* (tel (062) 770217) is a medium-size complex offering rooms and cool bungalows with carpeting and polished wood-slat walls. The architecture is as ugly as the nearby Naama Beach Hotel's is attractive. Prices are a little less than the Hilton at US$75/85 for singles/doubles. The beachfront bar and restaurant are popular, particularly at night.

Overlooking the bay from the south end the 90 room *Marina Sharm Hotel* (tel (062) 770175) was the Israeli hotel which pioneered Na'ama Bay as a resort. The complex includes three restaurants, two cafeterias, a bakery and a ping-pong room. The cheaper rooms are domed, prefabricated, plexi-glass structures in front of the hotel. They are clean and carpeted, with good air-conditioning, and cost E£73 a night. Rooms in the main building are of a similar standard, but somewhat larger, and cost E£104. The 5th floor rooms are fully carpeted and have bigger beds, stronger air-conditioning and a TV for E£152 per night.

The Youth Hostel in Na'ama Bay was taken over by the University of Suez for use as an Environmental School. The school, in turn, was bought by the president of the United Arab Emirates, to be transformed eventually into a three storey, 600 room hotel. At the north end of the bay, just beyond the Hilton, the Aquamarine Hotel was another Na'ama Bay pioneer but in early '90 it was being totally rebuilt as a Pullman Hotel.

Apart from the hotels, which tend to be expensive, the dining possibilities are limited. There's the campsite restaurant, the snack bar beside the supermarket and the *White House*, a pizzeria and barbecue restaurant where Sadat and Begin met while the Israeli air force bombed an Iraqi nuclear power plant. (The meeting was considered an embarrassment to Sadat.) Today, the White House offers a very filling meal of kufta, kebab and salad for about E£10. In the evenings, the terrace is a pleasant place for dinner, or just for tea or a beer. Their pizzas are terrible.

Sharm el Shaykh The *Youth Hostel*, next to the Clifftop Hotel, is fine if you can stand meeting a lot of noisy Egyptian teenagers who insist on having their picture taken with you. At E£5 per night, this youth hostel is pricier than others in Egypt, but that's because the rooms have air-conditioning. It's open from 6 to 10 am and 2 to 8 pm. Alcohol and card-playing are banned.

The *Clifftop Village Hotel* (tel (062) 770448) offers good accommodation, with doubles for about E£100. It's a bit out of the way, but convenient if you're visiting Ras Umsid.

If you have your own tent or sleeping bag, it is possible to camp on the beach at Ras Umsid, near the Clifftop Hotel. Just go down the hill to the beach, but be discreet and, once again, be aware of the dangers – especially for women.

The *Atfet el Mesk* teahouse seems to be in cahoots with at least one Sinai bus driver. There are also a few similar places in the warehouse-like building that houses one of the town's commercial centres. These include the *Sinai Star Restaurant*, the *Brilliant Restaurant* and the *Fisherman's Cafe*. Sharm el Shaykh offers few other places to eat.

Getting There & Away

Air Ras Nasrany, the airport for Sharm el Shaykh and Na'ama Bay, is some distance north of Na'ama Bay. At 12 noon on Monday and Saturday, an Air Sinai flight leaves Sharm el Shaykh, arriving at St Catherine's Monastery at 12.30 pm. The one-way fare is E£94. On Friday, there are flights between Sharm el Shaykh and Hurghada, in both directions, for E£104, one way.

Air Sinai also flies from Cairo to Sharm el Shaykh daily, except Monday and Wednesday, for E£150 one way. Flights leave Sharm el Shaykh for Cairo seven times a day, at 7 and 10 am, 1, 4.30, 5 and 11.30 pm and 12 midnight.

Condor, a charter subsidiary of Lufthansa German Airlines, has at least one direct flight a week from West Germany to Sharm el Shaykh throughout the year and several flights weekly during the high season (which lasts from about October to April).

Bus There are half a dozen buses a day between Cairo and Sharm el Shaykh and Na'ama Bay; they leave Cairo from Abbassiya Station (also known as the Sinai Terminal) at Midan Abbassiya. The trip takes an average of six to seven hours; the fares vary with the departure time and range from around E£15 to E£22. The night buses are the most expensive. They even serve refreshments on these deluxe buses – but take care, they're very expensive.

The 7 am bus from Cairo arrives in Sharm el Shaykh at about 1.30 pm, continues to Na'ama Bay and returns by 2 pm to Sharm el Shaykh, where it stays until about 3 pm. In Sharm el Shaykh everyone gets off the bus in front of the Aftet el Mesk teahouse, where the driver tells all Dahab-bound passengers to stay until 3 pm (although the bus may leave before 3 pm). However, the manager won't let you stay there unless you buy something. Sharm el Shaykh-Dahab buses are around E£5; it's about E£10 to St Catherine's.

The buses arrive and depart from in front of the bus ticket office in Sharm el Shaykh, and will pick up from any of the hotels at Na'ama Bay. If you want a reserved seat (and this is a good idea on the overnight bus), you have to buy a ticket from the Sharm el Shaykh office, next to the bus lot. The hotels will do this for you, for a fee.

Boat The *Moreen II* sails from Sharm el Shaykh to Hurghadha three days a week. The fare for the five hour trip is E£51, one-way. The schedule is somewhat erratic because the boat occasionally breaks down, the wind can be strong and, sometimes, there aren't enough passengers.

Getting Around

Public transport between Sharm el Shaykh and Na'ama Bay basically consists of an open-sided yellow *tof-tof* which, supposedly, runs hourly until 7 pm. If you happen to see it, just flag it down for the 25 pt ride between the two towns. In addition to the usual warnings about hitchhiking, note that the MFO vehicles (which you will see often in this area) are not allowed to carry civilian passengers and, therefore, cannot give you a lift.

DAHAB

The village beach resort of Dahab is 85 km north of Sharm el Shaykh on the Gulf of Aqaba. Dahab means 'gold' in Arabic, and the Bedouins named the beach after its glimmering sands, which resemble gold dust. There are two parts to Dahab – in the new part is Dahab's only government-sanctioned hotel, as well as the dive centre, the bus stop and well-maintained tourist huts. The other part of Dahab is a Bedouin village, about 2½ km north of town, which now seems to have more low-budget travellers than Bedouins in residence. The village (its proper name is Assalah) has become a haven for budget travellers – where else can you find accommodation virtually on the beach for only E£4 a night?

For a few travellers, these savings have meant that money can be spent on other things, such as hash and marijuana. If the glazed eyes and dizzying swaggers of several foreigners I saw there are any indication, both are potent and popular. Stay away from this stuff! Several foreigners are arrested and jailed each week for possession and use of drugs. In an effort to deter the spread of drug use, the Egyptian government, encouraged by the USA, has initiated tough antidrug campaigns which they take very seriously. It isn't unusual to read, in the *Egyptian Gazette*, that several foreigners are to be executed for drug dealing.

Dahab's Bedouin village certainly has great potential as a pleasant place to spend some time swimming among the beautiful coral reefs, lazing around the beach and, perhaps, learning something about traditional Bedouin life. Unfortunately, however, although some travellers will probably disagree with me, this was not my experience of the place. Instead, I saw a village swarming with flies, no doubt attracted by the mounds of garbage and dead animals left on the beach to fester in the sun. Naturally, rats, mice and other bothersome little creatures love this environment. Under such circumstances, the restaurants probably find it difficult to keep their kitchens and food clean. It is, therefore, hardly surprising that people get sick – diarrhoea and nausea are the most frequent complaints, but there's also the occasional case of dysentery or hepatitis. While a few of the camps are basically well maintained, many reminded me of dog-houses and stables.

Until (and if) the village is cleaned up, I can only advise that you stay there at your own risk. The MFO base in Na'ama Bay goes even further, forbidding American MFO soldiers from visiting either Dahab or the village. The Egyptian government prevents Egyptians spending the night in Dahab. The other half of Dahab is another world – cleaner, healthier and, of course, somewhat costlier.

Information & Orientation

Dahab is off the Sharm el Shaykh-Nuweiba-Taba road, and in turn the Bedouin village of Assalah is off the Dahab turn-off road. The post office, bank (open 8 am to 2 pm and 5 to 8 pm), dive shop and other amenities are in Dahab where you also find the Dahab Holiday Village and a campsite. All the other Dahab accommodation, the numerous 'camps', are in Assalah, where there are also many small restaurants and 'supermarkets'.

Water Sports

Diving is, of course, the most popular activity in Dahab. The best sites are north and south of the resort motel. Either look for the waves breaking on the offshore coral, or check the map at the dive shop.

The Blue Hole is an infamous deep dive, recommended only for experienced divers. The 'hole' is an 80 metre deep pool in the reef, only a few metres out from shore. The most popular challenge is to dive to a depth of about 60 metres and swim through a tunnel to the outer edge of the reef. This is most definitely not a dive for the inexperienced and the Dahab dive shop tells lurid tales of fatalities due to nitrogen narcosis or improper use of equipment (which isn't difficult at such a depth).

An easier and probably more enjoyable approach to the Blue Hole is to dive to a much more reasonable depth and work your way around the edge of the hole to a dip in the reef known as 'the bridge'. This part of the reef seems to attract a greater assortment of bright, colourful fish, perhaps because of the noticeably warmer waters. Since this is quite close to the surface, it can also be viewed using nothing more than snorkelling gear.

The Canyon is also a popular shore dive but, to an inexperienced diver, it will seem somewhat harrowing at first. From the shore, you snorkel along the reef before diving, past a wall of coral, to the edge of the Canyon. It is dark, narrow and seems capable of swallowing you. With less than 10 dives logged, I shook my head in refusal when Mohammed Kabany, the divemaster, pointed to this foreboding place and urged me to dive in.

The International Diving Centre in Dahab is run by Mohammed and Ingrid Kabany, both highly experienced Sinai divers, who are also quite knowledgeable about travel in the rest of the Sinai. They have created a great dive centre from a once poorly run operation. A full day of diving costs US$35, plus US$10 for all equipment, while a half-day is US$20. An introductory dive costs US$40, a diving excursion to Ras Mohammed US$50, a

five day diving package US$160 and a five day diving course US$175.

Many snorkellers head for the Garden, just north of the village.

Camel Treks

Many of the local Bedouins organise camel trips to the interior of the Sinai. In the morning, camel drivers and their camels congregate along the waterfront in the village. Register with the police before beginning the trek, and don't pay the camel driver until you return to the village. A one day trip costs E£15. The best of these treks is to Wadi Nay, where there is a small oasis and a Bedouin village. The wadi begins about four km south, along the shore from the dive centre.

Places to Stay

You can stay in Dahab or in the Bedouin village.

Dahab It is possible to camp out, either in one of the clean, pleasant huts at the official Egyptian campground, next to the dive centre, or with your own gear on the beach. Huts cost E£16.50 per person, while camping with your own gear is E£3 per person. These prices include access to bathrooms and showers from 8 am to 8 pm.

The three star *Dahab Holiday Motel* (tel 770788) is owned and operated by the Sinai Hotels & Diving Clubs company, but the Wagons-Lits company is in the process of taking over and expanding the facilities. The rooms are a bit overpriced but adequate, with showers and air-conditioning. Singles/doubles/triples cost around E£68/90/115, but prices are sometimes discounted if there is a high vacancy rate.

Bedouin Village - Assalah Most travellers on limited budgets head for the Bedouin village 2½ km north of the town of Dahab, where you can stay in a thatched hut at one of the 40 Bedouin-run encampments. The average price of E£4 per person per night includes a foam mat on the ground

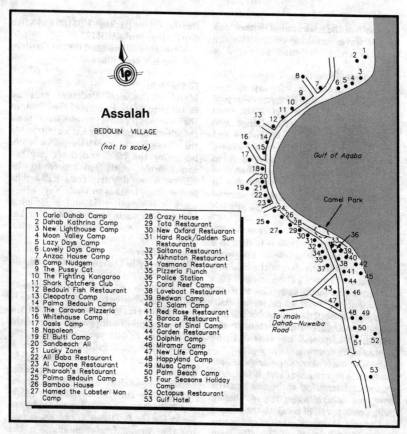

Assalah

BEDOUIN VILLAGE

(not to scale)

Gulf of Aqaba

Camel Park

To main
Dahab–Nuweiba
Road

1 Cario Dahab Camp
2 Dahab Kathrina Camp
3 New Lighthouse Camp
4 Moon Valley Camp
5 Lazy Days Camp
6 Lovely Days Camp
7 Anzac House Camp
8 Camp Nudgem
9 The Pussy Cat
10 The Fighting Kangaroo
11 Shark Catchers Club
12 Bedouin Fish Restaurant
13 Cleopatra Camp
14 Palma Bedouin Camp
15 The Caravan Pizzeria
16 Whitehouse Camp
17 Oasis Camp
18 Napoleon
19 El Bulti Camp
20 Sandbeach Ali
21 Lucky Zone
22 Ali Baba Restaurant
23 Al Capone Restaurant
24 Pharaoh's Restaurant
25 Palma Bedouin Camp
26 Bamboo House
27 Hamed the Lobster Man
Camp

28 Crazy House
29 Tota Restaurant
30 New Oxford Restuarant
31 Hard Rock/Golden Sun
Restaurants
32 Soltana Restaurant
33 Akhnaton Restaurant
34 Yasmana Restaurant
35 Pizzeria Flunch
36 Police Station
37 Coral Reef Camp
38 Loveboat Restaurant
39 Bedwan Camp
40 El Salam Camp
41 Red Rose Restaurant
42 Baraca Restaurant
43 Star of Sinai Camp
44 Garden Restaurant
45 Dolphin Camp
46 Miramar Camp
47 New Life Camp
48 Happyland Camp
49 Musa Camp
50 Palm Beach Camp
51 Four Seasons Holiday
Camp
52 Octopus Restaurant
53 Gulf Hotel

(or nothing, if you want to pay even less), a roof over your head and access to a toilet and shower (which are sometimes crammed together). Compare camps because some are cleaner than others although none of them are anything more than basic.

The *Mohammed Ali Camp* seems to be one of the better camps. This relatively clean place, which has a 24 hour guard, charges E£2 for a mattress in a carpeted hut. There are also stone-walled huts with electricity and window screens. Other camps recommended by travellers include the *Sheikh Ali*, the *Star of Sinai* and the *Palm Beach*.

The one place which is any different to the 'camps' is the *Gulf Hotel*, about a km south of the village, where the rooms sleep three and are a little more luxurious. Rooms cost E£13.50, have a few pieces of furniture, a real window and you don't have to supply your own sleeping bag.

Places to Eat

Dahab There is a cafeteria/kiosk on the beach and another at the bus stop; they sell basic canned staples, mineral water, ice cream, candy bars and sometimes bread. The restaurant at the *Holiday Motel* serves a E£1 breakfast while lunch or dinner cost E£6. There's also a restaurant at the dive centre which offers some of the best inexpensive food in Dahab. For about E£8, you get a big, filling meal of fish, tahina and rice.

Bedouin Village - Assalah The cheapest places to eat are the Bedouin restaurants in the village, but be very careful. I met many travellers who got sick here and heard numerous reports of restaurant patrons becoming ill. In the space of a few months, there were several cases of dysentery, and even a few cases of hepatitis, one of which resulted in the death of a Swiss man. On the other hand, I met travellers who stayed in the village for a few weeks, ate at the restaurants almost every day and were afflicted with no more than the usual 'Pharaoh's revenge' diarrhoea.

Under the circumstances, however, I refuse to recommend any of these restaurants. I looked at several and, at best, the sanitary conditions were dubious. One had leashed monkeys swinging around near the kitchen. Others had fish and meat sitting in the sun. There were mounds of rotting garbage crawling with flies. A few had no electrical generators and, thus, no refrigeration. As an alternative, there are a number of grocery stores selling fruit, vegetables and canned foods.

Getting There & Away
The regular daily buses between Sharm el Shaykh and Taba, in either direction, travel via Dahab and Nuweiba. Service taxis operate regularly from the village to Taba, St Catherine's, Sharm el Shaykh and other destinations.

Getting Around
A taxi from the Dahab bus stop to the Bedouin village costs 50 pt.

NUWEIBA
The beach resort town of Nuweiba is 87 km north of Dahab. During the Israeli occupation, it was also the site of a major

cafeteria moshav (farming settlement), which has now been converted into a residence for Egyptian government officials.

Although it is one of the Sinai's most popular beaches, Nuweiba is certainly not the most attractive; the area has become something of a major port, with a continual flow of people and vehicle traffic on and off the ferry between Nuweiba and Aqaba. The town offers little more than a holiday village, a kiosk, a police station behind the kiosk, a bus stop next to the kiosk, a couple of restaurants and a dive shop. The mountain scenery, however, is beautiful and the coral reefs, for which Nuweiba is renowned, are spectacular.

Water Sports
Once again, underwater delights are the feature attraction and scuba diving and snorkelling the prime activities.

The Diving Centre offers the necessary equipment at much the same prices as in Na'ama Bay. The centre also hires out windsurfers, kayaks and pedal boats, by the hour. If you can get 10 people together, you can rent a glass-bottom boat.

Camel Treks
Check with the Diving Centre about camel trips into the mountains. The shortest trek, to Ein Furtaga, takes eight hours for the round trip. The E£30 cost includes an English-speaking guide and lunch.

There are also overnight treks to the Bedouin encampment at Ein Machmed, and to the Coloured Canyon. The Coloured Canyon is between St Catherine's and Nuweiba. Few tourists visit the area, and getting there is something of an adventure. As it's about 5 km from the main road, you will need a 4WD vehicle. Even then, you have to park your vehicle and walk for about 1½ hours. This surrealistic place derives its name from the layers of bright, multicoloured stones that resemble paintings on the canyon's very steep, narrow walls. Total silence (the canyon is sheltered from the wind) adds to the eeriness. The canyon is sometimes known as the Blue Valley because a Swiss man painted the whole valley blue a few years ago.

Other camel trips can be arranged by talking to Aish Sliman, or members of his family, who live in the village of Tarabin, two km from Nuweiba.

Places to Stay

Camping at the official grounds costs E£20 for a three or four person tent. You can also camp on the beach near the tents for E£2, but it can get quite windy at night. A set rate is charged for three visits to the nearby bathroom and shower facilities.

Alternatively, you can take your sleeping bag south down the beach and sleep under the palm trees for free, although this practice could expose you to danger and is not recommended for female travellers.

The two star *Nuweiba Holiday Village* and *New Nuweiba Holiday Village* have 126 air-conditioned rooms and bungalows, as well as a bar, a private beach, tennis courts and a VCR. Single bungalows cost from E£65 to E£130, and double bungalows from E£78 to E£164.

There's also the four star, 66 room *El Sayadeen Tourist Village* (tel 757398, 92634), where singles/doubles average around E£65/96.

Places to Eat

There are cheap seafood restaurants and cafes along the beach.

Getting There & Away

Bus Buses from Cairo arrive in Nuweiba in time to connect with the ferry to Aqaba. You can buy a Cairo to Aqaba ticket from the Sinai Terminal (Abbassiya Station) in north-east Cairo for E£69.40. If bought separately, the bus portion of the ticket costs E£25.

Boat Two ferries a day travel from Nuweiba to Aqaba in Jordan. The ferries are scheduled to depart at 10 am and 3 pm but, in fact, they wait for the buses from Cairo, which usually leave the Sinai Terminal (Abbassiya Station) at 7 am and 11 pm. The ferries will also be delayed until all passport and customs formalities are completed. A 3rd class ticket for the three hour trip costs E£37 (with bank receipts).

Some travellers report that it's cheaper to buy two one-way tickets than to buy a return ticket in Egypt. The 3rd class ticket from Aqaba to Nuweiba costs JD 7.5, or about US$21. In Jordan, you can also change E£ for US$ at a better exchange rate than applies in Egypt.

BASATA

The encampment of Basata is about 30 km (a 30 minute drive) north of Nuweiba. Basata, which means 'simple' in colloquial Egyptian Arabic, is a simple, but clean, travellers' settlement of bamboo huts, very well maintained by a German-educated Egyptian named Sherif. The settlement has a common kitchen hut, an electrical generator and a campground. The kitchen is probably unique in Egypt – you take whatever you want from the cabinets and refrigerator and pay for it before you leave. Sherif emphasises honesty and trusts that his guests will do the same. This friendly, carefree atmosphere attracts a variety of people, ranging from backpackers to employees of foreign embassies. At the time of writing, Basata charged E£7.50 per person per night. The Sinai needs more such places, and two similar villages are supposedly being constructed in the area.

TABA

Until 1989, a few hundred metres of beach, a luxury hotel and the Nelson coffee shop at Taba, a place on the Israel-Egypt border, represented a minor point of contention between the two countries. After several years of squabbling and formal arbitration, the land was returned and the hotel sold to Egypt. It's now the Taba Hilton. Egyptians regarded the event as a victory, of sorts, over the Israelis. Since 1982, when the rest of the Sinai was returned to Egypt, Taba has served as a busy border crossing between Egypt and Israel.

A special Sinai-only visa for US$6 is available at Taba. It can also be obtained from Egyptian consulates in Israel, including the one in Eilat.

Getting There & Away

Crossing the border from Israel you go through immigration and customs and then have a km walk past the Taba Hilton to the bank, the border tax collection point (E£13) and then the bus and taxi stand. Cairo buses take 6½ to seven hours and cost E£35. You can charter a whole service taxi for about E£250. It takes about 2½ hours by service taxi to St Catherine's at a fare of E£15 per person. The bus is slightly cheaper but much slower.

ST CATHERINE'S MONASTERY

Fifteen Greek Orthodox monks live in this ancient monastery at the foot of Mt Sinai. The monastic order was founded in the 4th century AD by the Byzantine empress Helena, who had a small chapel built beside what was believed to be the burning bush from which God spoke to Moses.

The chapel is dedicated to St Catherine, the legendary martyr of Alexandria, who was tortured on a spiked wheel and then beheaded for her Christianity. Her body was supposedly transported by angels to Mt Catherine, the highest mountain in Egypt, which is about six km south of Mt Sinai. There, the body was 'found', about 300 years later, by monks from the monastery.

In the 6th century, Emperor Justinian ordered the building of a fortress, with a basilica and a monastery, as well as the original chapel, to serve as a secure home for the monks of St Catherine's and as a refuge for the Christians of the southern Sinai.

Despite the isolated setting, the monastery and Mt Sinai attract a great many tourists and pilgrims. When you visit, remember that this is still a functioning monastery, not just a museum piece. The only parts of the monastery to which members of the public are admitted

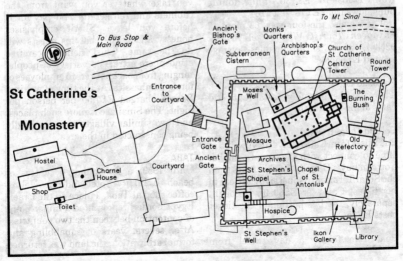

are the chapel and a rather macabre room full of the bones of deceased monks; you are also permitted to view part of a splendid collection of icons and jewelled crosses. St Catherine's is open to visitors from 9.30 am to 12 noon daily except on Friday, Sunday and holidays, when the monastery is closed.

Information & Orientation

The airport for St Catherine's is some km north of the village. Near the monastery there's a large roundabout where you turn east to the monastery itself, a couple of km further on. Right beside the roundabout is the large St Catherine's Tourist Village and the Al Fairoz Hotel. Continue south from the roundabout and the road ends a couple of km further on at the village of Al Milga, where there is a bank, phone office, police station and a variety of shops and cafes. The bank will change cash or travellers' cheques.

Mt Sinai

Although some archaeologists and historians dispute Mt Sinai's biblical claim to fame, it is revered by Jews, Christians and Muslims, all of whom believe that God delivered his Ten Commandments to Moses from its summit.

At a height of 2285 metres, Mt Sinai (Gebel Musa is the local name) towers over St Catherine's Monastery. It is easy to climb and there are two well-defined routes to the summit – the camel trail and the Steps of Repentance. Mt Sinai is not, however, the mountain directly up the valley behind the monastery, that one is far lower! From the top you can look across to the even higher summit of Mt Catherine.

The camel trail is the easier route and this climb takes an average of about two hours. Along the way, you'll probably be greeted by Bedouin camel cowboys anxious to put you in the saddle, although they can take you only as far as the final steps leading to the summit. Usually, there are at least four or five tea and Coca-Cola stands on the trail, catering to those

St Catherine's Monastery

in need of a caffeine fix. At the stand where the camel trail meets the steps, a full breakfast is sometimes available.

The alternative path to the summit, the taxing 3000 Steps of Repentance, was laid by one monk as a form of penance. If you want to try both routes, it's best to take the path up and the steps down, particularly if you want a great view of the monastery.

During the summer, you should avoid the heat by beginning your hike at 2 or 3 am. This way, you'll also see the sunrise. The trail can be a bit difficult in parts, so a torch (flashlight) is essential.

If you plan to spend the night on the summit, make sure you have plenty of food and water. As it gets cold and windy there, even in summer, you will also need warm clothes and a sleeping bag (there is no space to pitch a tent). As late as mid-May, be prepared to share the summit with hoards of tourists, some bearing ghetto-blasters, others carrying Bibles and hymn books. With the music and singing, and people nudging each other for a space on the holy mountain, don't expect to get much sleep, especially in the wee small hours before sunrise.

Just below the summit, along the Steps of Repentance, the small plateau known as Elijah's Hollow is dominated by a 500 year old cypress tree, marking the spot where the prophet Elijah heard the voice of God. On the summit itself is a Greek Orthodox chapel, containing beautiful paintings and ornaments, and a small mosque. Unfortunately, they'll probably be locked. The summit also offers spectacular views of the surrounding bare, jagged mountains and plunging valleys where, throughout the day, the colours of the rocks and cliffs change like those of stone chameleons.

Places to Stay

St Catherine's Monastery runs a hostel next door. It's open every day; check in between 4 and 7 pm. The hostel offers clean, basic facilities and access to a small kitchen for about E£5 per night. Even if you don't stay there, you can leave baggage in one of the rooms while you hike up Mt Sinai. This service will cost you about E£1 in baksheesh.

Right by the roundabout, two km west of the monastery, is the expensive *St Catherine's Tourist Village* where double rooms cost US$85 including breakfast and dinner. The dinners are a truly terrible, old fashioned British Army/institutional food at its very worst. Beside the tourist village is the somewhat grubby *Al Fairoz Hotel* where doubles cost E£35. They also have campground huts.

With the fairly frequent bus connections available between St Catherine's, other Sinai destinations and Cairo, you can easily avoid having to spend a night here and, frankly, that would be my advice – unless, of course, you're sleeping on top of Mt Sinai.

Places to Eat

The modern cafeteria right by the roundabout principally caters to tour bus groups. In the village, near the bus stop, there's a bakery and a host of small shops and cafes. The *Restaurant Welcome* and *Friends Cafeteria* are good for simple inexpensive meals.

Getting There & Away

Air Air Sinai has Monday and Saturday flights from Cairo to St Catherine's Monastery for about E£118, one way. A flight from Hurghada to St Catherine's, and vice versa, operates on Monday only and costs E£140 one way. There is also a flight from Luxor to St Catherine's. A one-way flight from Sharm el Shaykh to St Catherine's costs E£94.

Bus You can ask the driver to drop you off at the crossroads, which is closer to the monastery. Buses to Sharm el Shaykh cost about E£10.

Taxi Service taxis travel in and out of the village irregularly and infrequently. If you're lucky, you might be able to find a taxi driver who is willing to take you all the way to Cairo. If so, the trip will cost about E£60 (with three other people). You can often find service taxis at the monastery, they often wait for people coming down from Mt Sinai (not bearing the Ten Commandments) in the early afternoon. Count on E£8 to E£10 per person to Dahab.

WADI FERAN

The Bedouin outpost of Wadi Feran is between the west coast of the Sinai and St Catherine's Monastery. After many km of rough, barren desert and harsh, rocky hills, this lush, date-palm oasis is certainly a refreshing sight.

EL ARISH

El Arish, on the northern coast, is the capital of the Sinai peninsula and has a population of 35,000. Although the city is trying desperately to become a beach resort, it is seldom visited because there's not much of interest here.

Information

The police station and hospital are on Sharia 23 July, just off the main shore road.

The GPO, which is open from Saturday to Thursday between 9 am and 3 pm, is in the same building as the telephone & telegraph office (open 24 hours a day), near the hospital.

Things to See

The museum, on the outskirts of town (along the road to Rafah), is one of the few attractions of El Arish. Established a couple of years ago to inform people about life, human and animal, in the Sinai, the museum's displays include stuffed birds and Bedouin handicrafts and clothing.

Every Wednesday, when the souk is held, the Bedouins come in from the desert with their camels. The veiled women sell embroidered dresses, while the men sell camel saddles.

There is also, of course, the palm-lined beach. In summer, a makeshift city of tents is erected and the beach gets very crowded.

Places to Stay

You can camp on the beach at the official El Arish campground, seven km west of the city. This costs E£5 for a tent with two beds and lights, or E£2 if you have your own gear.

Near the beach in town, the *Moon Light Hotel* has rooms without bath for E£4 per person, and rooms with bath for E£6.

The *El Salaam Hotel* is on Sharia 23 July, above the Aziz Restaurant on Midan Baladiya. Rooms here range in price from E£8 to E£10 per person.

The *Sinai Beach Hotel* is a little more up-market and charges E£20 for a double with bath.

The *Oberoi El Arish* is a relatively recent four star addition to the growing El Arish resort accommodation scene. Singles/doubles with bath cost a mere E£40/50, plus 20% taxes and services.

Places to Eat

Good cheap meals of fuul and ta'amiyya are available at the *Aziz Restaurant* on Sharia 23 July.

At the *Sammar Restaurant*, also on Sharia 23 July, you can get kebab and kufta.

A couple of other decent restaurants, both with bars, are the *Sinai Rose Cafeteria* and the *Mashribiyya Cafeteria*. They are right on the beach and serve good salads and fish.

Getting There & Around

There is a Sinai bus from Cairo to the Israeli border at Rafah. It travels via El Arish and takes about five to six hours. Buses departing Cairo at 7 and 8 am go all the way to Rafah, while the 3 pm bus goes only as far as El Arish. Service taxis also make the trip from Cairo. For more information on the border crossings, see the Getting There chapter at the beginning of the book.

A taxi from the El Arish bus station to the beach costs 50 pt.

THE
SUDAN

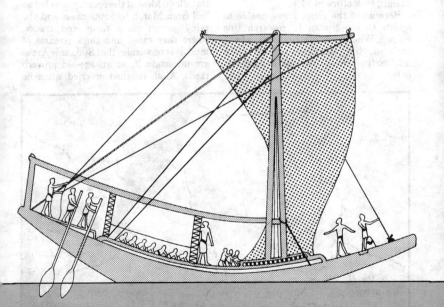

Introduction

WARNING: When this book was going to press, international aid agencies were withdrawing their personnel from the Sudan due to the escalating civil war. The situation may have improved by the time you read this – but at present travel in the Sudan cannot be recommended and is at your own risk.

On 30 June 1989 the government of Sudan was overthrown by army officers in a bloodless coup. According to the coup leader, Brigadier Omar Hassan Ahmed Bashir, the army seized power to 'end the conflicts, partisan chaos and. . .anarchy' that have beleaguered Sudan since the now deposed prime minister, Sadiq al Mahdi, took office in 1986.

Because of the coup, I was unable to return to the Sudan to research this edition. Where possible, prices have been updated, but travellers should treat information about costs as a guideline only.

Although the Sudan is a fascinating place to visit, whether conflicts in the west and south will end soon is uncertain. If and when political and economic stability return and the famines, civil war, refugee crises and intertribal raids end, hopefully it will again be safe to travel through the Sudan – however, that is not the case at present.

Travel beyond the following routes and places is unsafe and/or extremely difficult: Wadi Halfa to Khartoum by road (difficult) and train; Khartoum and Omdurman; Khartoum to Kassala and on to Port Sudan.

When the Sudan is again more accessible, it will likely be – as in the past – only for the hardiest and most adventurous travellers. Most of the country is as hot as hell from March to September, and the rainy season turns roads and tracks, where they exist, into thick streams of mud. It is no wonder that Sudanese Arabs are uncertain if, as an age-old proverb reads, Allah laughed or cried when he

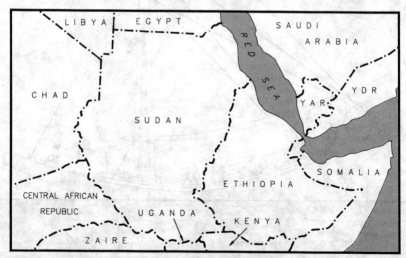

354

created the Sudan. He probably did both.

The Sudan is Africa's largest country – about a third of the size of the USA. There are only 24 million people in this vast area but they comprise more than 300 tribes and speak more than 100 languages and dialects. Traditional culture has mostly been preserved. In Khartoum, the capital, and other towns this is evident in the dress, speech and facial scars of the people.

Much of the adventure in the vast expanses of the Sudan lies in getting from place to place. Some buses and trains function, but the most common mode of transport is hunching and huddling in the back of a rugged Bedford truck. These trucks travel to wherever there are people who have something to buy or sell. The Bedfords almost always get through, unless swirling sandstorms blind the driver or choke the engine, or the roads turn to gooey mud. Even if you are temporarily stranded in some village on the edge of the world, Sudanese hospitality means you will always be offered food and shelter.

In the past, it was power and great hidden treasures which made the Sudan the object of numerous invasions and explorations throughout its long, jumbled history. Today, much of the Sudan still remains to be explored. It is one of the world's last frontiers.

Facts about the Country

HISTORY

For historical purposes the Sudan can be divided into three regions, each made up of loosely defined kingdoms or sultanates bordered by the Nile, the mountains, the wide expanses of desert or the swamps. Most of what is known of the Sudan before the 15th century AD relates to northern Sudan, which stretches from present-day Khartoum to Wadi Halfa.

Knowledge of northern Sudan's ancient history comes from Egyptian sources. To the Egyptians of the Old Kingdom (2600-2100 BC) the Sudan was known as the Land of Cush: the source of ivory, incense, ebony, gold and slaves.

As Egyptian trading and raiding parties increased their forays into the Sudan, the imperialist designs of Egypt's Middle and New Kingdom pharaohs (2050-1085 BC) also increased. Like 20th century European imperialists, the conquering pharaohs did their best to Egyptianise the Sudanese. Egyptian political control dominated the arts, language and religion of the Sudan. Signs of this influence can still be seen in the ruins of many Egyptian structures and temples along the Nile in northern Sudan, such as the Temple of Barkal near present-day Karima.

But, as has happened many times throughout history, the colonies that powerful kingdoms or countries create often become big headaches as they turn on their creators, or invaders, and sometimes conquer them. That is what happened with Egypt and the Land of Cush.

By the 8th century BC, Cush was a great power. Under the ruler Piankhi, the Cushites conquered Egypt, establishing the 25th Dynasty (712-663 BC). Cush control, however, was short-lived. In 671 BC, less than 50 years after Piankhi's triumph, Taharqa, the last ruler to build at Luxor's celebrated Karnak Temple, lost Egypt to invading Assyrians. By 654 BC the Cushites were back in their old capital of Napata, far to the south of Egypt, near present-day Merowe.

Over the next century the capital was moved from Napata to Meroe (north of present-day Shendi) and a new, less Egyptian kingdom arose. Temples, tombs and pyramids influenced by Greek, Roman and Indian architecture were built at Naqa and Musawwarat, and a cursive Meriotic script replaced Egyptian hieroglyphics. This writing remains undeciphered, so much of Meroe's history is mysterious.

However, it is known that marauding Romans came down from Egypt in 23 BC, sacked Napata and generally weakened the Meriotic Empire. The nomadic Blemmya people, ancestors of the Beja tribe, moved in like vultures and gradually picked away at the empire until an invasion in 350 AD by the Axumite Kingdom of Ethiopia ensured the demise of Meroe.

By the 4th century AD most of the inhabitants of northern Sudan were Christian. They spoke Nubian (whose origin still baffles linguists), and they wrote in Coptic script, which is still read by Egyptian Coptic priests. Small Christian kingdoms eventually superseded the Axumites and ruled until the 7th century AD, when the followers of the Prophet Mohammed swept into Africa on a conversion rampage.

Over the next several centuries northern Sudan came under Arab influence. By the 16th century Arab tribes were in control, most of the population was Muslim, and Islam had spread to the western Sudan regions of Kordofan and Darfur.

In Darfur the Arab-African Fur people were in control. The exact origins of this tribe, who possessed the darker skin of the Africans and the thin-lipped faces of the

Arabs, are unknown, as their history before conversion to Islam is a mystery.

For centuries the vast desert of the Kordofan isolated the Fur from the political whims and follies of the Nile kingdoms and dynasties. Even with conversion to Islam they remained isolated, and as late as the 16th century they established an independent sultanate which lasted until 1916. Today, vestiges of this sultanate can be seen in the old Fur capital of El Fasher and, in the town of El Geneina to its west, there is still a man who claims to be sultan.

Around the same time, another sultanate emerged under the Fung people, whose kingdom streched from the Sixth Nile Cataract, north of Khartoum, southward to Sennar. Their moment of glory, however, was short-lived. They reached their pinnacle of power in the 18th century after repulsing a Shilluk invasion from the south and scoring victories in wars against the Abyssinians (the former name of the Ethiopians) and the Fur.

A French doctor named Poncet who visited Sennar in 1699 gave the following description of the Fung:

. . .they were a crafty, suspicious and deceitful people. . .A good deal of the Fung's wealth was said to come from the fabulous gold mines at Fazughli, on the Ethiopian border, and the king kept up considerable state. Once every week he would ride out to one of his country houses, accompanied by three or four hundred horsemen and footmen, who sang his praises and played the *tabor* (a small drum) while they marched. . .the king, who never appeared in public without a piece of coloured gauze over his face, presided at his court of law with the authority of a Roman governor. Criminals, on being convicted, were thrown to the ground and beaten to death with clubs.

By the end of the 18th century the Fung Empire was fragmented and ripe for pillage and plunder by the Ottoman ruler of Egypt, Mohammed Ali.

Mohammed Ali was a ruthless and power-hungry army officer who gained control of Egypt with the help of the Mamelukes, a mercenary military class who were originally Turkish slaves. Later, when the Mamelukes themselves posed a threat to Mohammed's power, he promptly eliminated the Mameluke leaders in one fell swoop by inviting them all to dinner and murdering them afterwards. Then, to quell the understandable disquiet in the Mameluke ranks and to furbish his coffers, he sent them to the Sudan to bring back gold and 40,000 black Sudanese slaves to build up a new army.

Led by Ismail, Mohammed's 25 year old son, the ragtag army of 10,000 soldiers penetrated the swamps of the Sudd, which had long been a natural barrier to Arab expansion. With the promise of 50 pt each for every human ear they won in war, Mohammed's determined troops managed to open up the south. For the Sudan the results were disastrous.

Three thousand ears were sent back to Mohammed. Ismail also sent his father 30,000 slaves, mostly women and children, though only half of them survived the trip to Cairo. When no gold was found, Ismail started for home but got only as far as Shendi with his band of not-so-merry mercenaries who had, of course, been taking more than just ears from the Sudanese people. Ismail died a fiery death in a tent set alight by the locals, who had had enough of being raped, pillaged and plundered.

When Mohammed heard about his son's death, he too wanted more than ears. By 1823, 50,000 Sudanese had been killed and Mohammed Ali had control of the Sudan.

Egypt remained in control for the next 50 years, until the time of Khedive Ismail, who ruled Egypt from 1863 to 1879. Britain and France became increasingly interested in the region, especially with the completion of the Suez Canal in 1869. This expensive project placed Egypt in heavy debt to many foreign powers and initiated European intervention in the affairs of Egypt and the Sudan.

The British were the dominant European

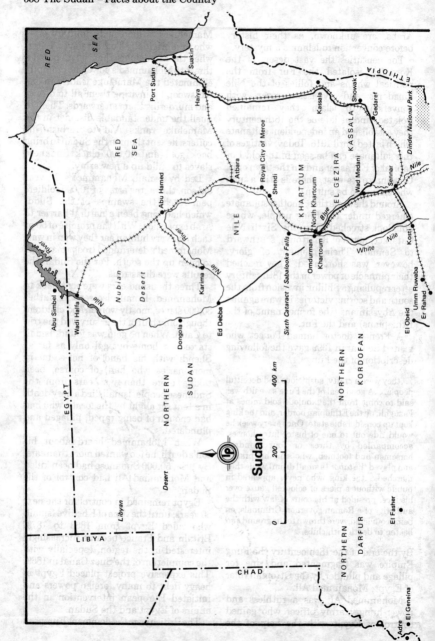

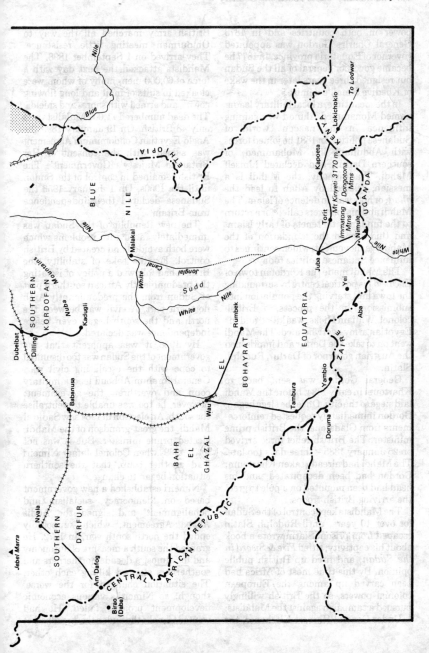

power in both countries and in 1873 General Charles Gordon was appointed governor of Equatoria province. In 1877 he became governor general of all the Sudan but resigned three years later in the wake of Khedive Ismail's demise.

In the meantime, a local military leader named Mohammed Ahmad was gaining influence in the nascent world of Sudanese politics. In 1881 he joined forces with Abdullahi ibn Mohammed, of southern Darfur, and declared himself Mahdi. Traditionally, the Mahdi is a messiah, selected by Allah to lead the *jihad*, or holy war, in defence of Islam. The Mahdi and his followers called for a return to the fundamental tenets of early Islam, and this formed the foundation of the Mahdiyya movement, which continues to influence Sudanese politics today.

The Mahdi made the Kordofan town of El Obeid his political centre by surrounding the town and starving the population into submission. In the process, a British colonel, William Hicks, was killed and his Egyptian army overwhelmed. The Mahdi went on to take the Darfur and imprisoned the Austrian governor of Darfur, Rudolph Slatin.

General Gordon was sent back to Khartoum in early 1884, before the Mahdi laid siege to the city. Once the siege began, Gordon immediately requested reinforcements from Gladstone, the British prime minister. The British relief force arrived on 25 January 1885 – three days too late. The Mahdi had already taken Khartoum; Gordon had been decapitated, and his head had been mounted on a pole to greet the arriving British troops.

The Mahdists kept control of the Sudan for over 10 years, until Rudolph Slatin escaped from prison. Slatin wrote a book about his captivity, titled *Fire & Sword in the Sudan*, and fired up British public opinion. By this time most of Africa had been carved up among the European colonial powers, so the British willingly pursued a campaign against the Mahdists.

Under General Herbert Kitchener, the British army marched all the way to Omdurman meeting little resistance. They arrived on 1 September 1898. The Mahdists attacked the next day with a force of 60,000 men, many of whom were cloaked in suits of mail and long flowing gowns, and armed with sabres and shields. The dead numbered 11,000 Mahdists and only 48 British. On 19 January 1899 the Anglo-Egyptian Condominium Agreement was signed 'with the consent of Her Britannic Majesty's Government'. The British remained in control of the Sudan until the 1950s. On 1 January 1956 the Sudanese declared their independence from Britain.

The new Republic of the Sudan was immediately faced with problems which were both avoided and created by British control. For the sake of stability, the British had followed a policy of isolating the predominantly African southern part of Sudan from the predominantly Arab northern part. A civil war between the north and the south began even before independence was declared.

By 1958 it was apparent that the government of the Sudan was too disunited to cope with the escalating civil war. General Ibrahim Abboud lead a military coup and overthrew the government; however, he too was unable to neutralise the south. An election in 1964 saw Sadiq al Mahdi, the great-grandson of the Mahdi, elected prime minister. But it was not until 1969, when Colonel Jafaar Nimeiri lead another coup, that the southern situation began to change.

Nimeiri established a new government based on 'democracy, socialism and nonalignment' and signed the Addis Ababa Agreement, which supposedly ended the north-south war, in 1972. He granted the south a measure of autonomy and for almost a decade northerners and southerners stopped killing each other. The situation changed for the worse, though, as Nimeiri's various economic development projects failed. He had wanted to make the Sudan the 'breadbasket of the Middle East' by encouraging Arab and Western investment in projects such as the Gezira Scheme and the Jonglei Canal.

The Gezira is a 25,000 square km marshy region south of Khartoum between the White and Blue Niles. Much of the region is devoted to cotton but it's far from being a breadbasket. The purpose of the Jonglei Canal was to divert a 560 km stretch of the White Nile that would otherwise flow into the wide marsh south of the Gezira. The additional Nile water could have then been used for further irrigation and cultivation of the Gezira. But Nimeiri invested too heavily and too quickly, amassing a mountain of external debts in the process.

The International Monetary Fund and the US government pressured Nimeiri into increasing the prices of commodities such as bread, sugar and petrol. In the early 1980s he began to turn to Muslim fundamentalists for support, much to the chagrin of the predominantly Christian and animist south. For southerners, the last straw was Nimeiri's symbolic declaration of *sharia*, or Islamic law. In September 1983, a month all Nile perch will remember with drunken delight, Nimeiri dumped the capital's entire liquor stocks into the Nile.

The disaffected south again took up arms and a rebel leader named John Garang went into hiding to reactivate the Sudanese People's Liberation Movement, or SPLM. Within a few months the government virtually lost control of the south and Nimeiri declared a state of emergency and suspended the constitution.

Less than two years later, in April 1985, Nimeiri was deposed in a coup engineered by the Sudanese army. A transitional military government under General Abdul-Rahman Swareddahab took power. He set about purging the extremist Islamic fundamentalists and promised elections within 12 months.

The elections in April 1986, the first in 20 years, saw the return of the former prime minister deposed by Nimeiri in 1969. Sadiq al Mahdi promised to return Sudan to a democratic and pluralist society, but continued to support sharia. In June 1989 he was deposed by a military coup.

THE SUDAN TODAY

The Sudan today is a nation fraught with political turmoil, economic chaos, civil war, drought, famine, disease and refugee crises.

Government & Economy

In theory, the Sudan has a British-style parliamentary system. In practice, the system breaks down. There are too many groups with different interests, ethnic backgrounds and cultural traditions. Occasionally coalitions form which temporarily overlook their differences, but they quickly crumble with the slightest disagreement. In the 1986 elections over 30 political parties originally campaigned for support, but only a few survived the campaign trail. The reasons for this messy political situation stem from more than just divergent interests.

Sudan's economy can be equally blamed, as it is both a cause and an effect of the political situation. Without a strong economy, the Sudanese find it difficult to create a base for a stable government. However, with a per capita income of less than US$400 a year and an external debt of more than US$12 billion, neither a stable government nor a stable economy seems possible in the near future.

The weak economy, in turn, cannot be blamed entirely on political instability. The Sudan is predominantly an agricultural country, its main crops being cotton and sorghum, but both earn insufficient amounts of hard currency and are subject to the whimsical world commodities market. At one time when the price of cotton plummeted, thousands of bales of cotton wasted away in the overflowing warehouses of Port Sudan.

In 1989, the only good news about Sudan's economy was that it was about to become Africa's largest producer of sunflower seeds – not exactly a major source of hard currency.

The Civil War

The war between the SPLM and the Sudanese government was sparked by Nimeiri's declaration of Islamic law. The southerners interpreted this as an abrogation of the Addis Ababa Agreement. John Garang, an Iowa State University alumnus and member of the southern Dinka tribe, went into self-imposed exile to lead a revolt against the government. He founded the SPLM with plenty of support from disgruntled southerners and the Ethiopian government across the border.

Most of Garang's arms and supplies come from Ethiopia (or, in other words, Gorbachev and Castro), although in recent years some assistance was also coming from Israel and Kenya. About the same time, the SPLA (the army wing of the SPLM) began overrunning government army convoys. Garang himself described these victories in great detail on his daily radio broadcasts over the Voice of the Sudanese People's Liberation Movement. In one broadcast he went so far as to recite the serial numbers of the army trucks and blood types of the officers captured. If you want to find out what's happening with the SPLM, tune in to the Voice of the SPLM on the short-wave frequency of approximately 9500 kHz. Garang broadcasts in English almost every day from about 2.30 to 3 pm.

Mahdi restored democracy to the Sudan, but his continued adherence to and support for sharia helped perpetuate the war in southern Sudan. Adherence to sharia placated the predominantly Muslim government and thus kept Mahdi in power. However, the non-Muslim Dinkas of the south were against sharia.

Although the government pumped an estimated US$1 million a day into war efforts, they consistently lost ground to the SPLM. By March 1989, the SPLM was estimated to have won control over about 90% of southern Sudan. Some estimates put Garang as far north as the southern base of the Nuba Mountains and the town of Malakal. Government troops were surrounded in Juba and a few other towns by SPLA troops and mined roads. The Nile steamer hasn't run for a few years because river traffic was declared fair game for target practice. Air traffic was also threatened. A Sudan Airways passenger jet en route to Juba was shot down.

For the hundreds of thousands of southern Sudanese whose towns and villages became battlegrounds, life was totally disrupted. According to an *Economist* Intelligence Unit report on the Sudan, 'over 500,000 civilians have been killed [and] millions have been displaced'. In 1988, the report said, 'over 250,000 people died in southern Sudan as a direct and indirect result of the civil war'. Southerners were forced to flee to Wau, Juba and even Khartoum, where sprawling refugee camps of makeshift huts and tents have sprung up. To make matters worse, on 4 August 1988 about a million refugees were left homeless when floods hit the Khartoum camps and most of the city.

Famine

The war-caused refugee crisis spawned a host of other problems throughout much of the country south of Khartoum. Mass famine on an almost unprecedented scale, which was even worse than the drought-caused famine of 1985-1986, was the chief result.

In 1985-1986 the western Sudan regions of the Kordofan and Darfur and part of the eastern region near Kassala and Gedaref experienced severe drought and, subsequently, widespread famine. Six to seven million people were threatened with starvation or severe malnutrition. In the Kordofan, 400,000 Sudanese were forced to leave their villages to go in search of food. The United Nations, as well as the United States Agency for International

Development and other world aid agencies, rushed food and supplies to as many parts of the country as possible. During the summer months the efforts of the aid agencies were hindered by temperatures as high as 48°C and ferocious *haboobs*, or sandstorms.

In a 1989 article in the *New Yorker* magazine, journalist Raymond Bonner detailed the horrendous effects of the more recent war-caused famine on the Sudanese. He also examined the often futile efforts of various governments and international aid organisations to get food and medical assistance to the people. Their efforts were obstructed, in part, because assistance had become a contentious issue between the SPLM and the Sudanese government. Neither wanted the other's troops to be resupplied with food and medical equipment. Consequently, whatever supplies existed, especially in the towns, went to government troops first, not to the refugees.

According to Bonner, in the village of Abyei, north of Wau, there were 'thousands of children. . .suffering from malnutrition' in October 1988. In July and August, the village was hit with a measles epidemic. Bonner wrote:

Fifty or sixty children died each day – at least two thousand altogether. Hyenas dragged some bodies away before they could be buried. There is a military garrison in Abyei. . .the soldiers had medicine, but they wouldn't share it with the dying children. . .The military commander in Abyei said in October that more than ten thousand people had died of starvation since the beginning of the year, half of them children. . .

This was only one example of many that he cited in his article.

Even if medicines were available, doctors and other medical personnel are in drastically short supply. According to some of the latest statistics, there are only about 4000 doctors in the Sudan, which means there is approximately one for every 6000 people. These trained medical practitioners are concentrated in or near Khartoum, so the situation in southern Sudan is even more critical. In the south there is one doctor for every 83,000 people.

With a shortage of doctors and medicines, the Sudanese are blighted by an assortment of diseases and ailments that reads like a litany of woes. There are various strains of malaria, tuberculosis, meningitis, hepatitis, trachoma, glaucoma, bilharzia, measles, dysentery. . .the list goes on and on.

The United Nations was aware of the famine and the medical situation, but wasn't able to get aid into southern Sudan until April and May 1989. A massive airlift and overland convoy were organised after a temporary cease-fire was arranged between the Sudanese government and the SPLA. Negotiations and peace talks began in Addis Ababa, but little if any progress was made. The June 1989 coup doesn't seem to have changed things for the better; at the time this book was going to press, the civil war had flared up once again.

The Refugee Crises – how to help

The rock concerts have come and gone, raising millions of dollars for refugee relief supplies in the Sudan, and the media blitz asking for more help has long since subsided. Yet there are still millions of refugees in desperate need throughout the Sudan.

If you are concerned about the situation and are seriously interested in helping, then it's possible to volunteer for a three to six month stint as a relief worker. Doctors, nurses, medical technicians, mechanics and administrators, usually with experience in developing countries, are desperately needed.

However, when this book was going to press international relief agencies were withdrawing their personnel from the Sudan due to escalating violence. Check to see if this has changed – but at present working with an aid agency cannot be recommended.

If it is safe to get involved, keep in mind that previous experience with refugee problems is highly desired by most of these groups. Working in the refugee camps of Sudan is not for the uninitiated. Otherwise any of the following nonprofit organisations would be happy to receive greatly needed donations of money, clothing and food for the Sudanese:

The American Refugee Committee Objectives: the improvement of the general health conditions of refugee settlements and camps in eastern Sudan. One of its largest assistance programmes is in the Fau Five settlement where it operates medical clinics and feeding centres, but the organisation was considering downgrading its operation. Postal address: PO Box 48 (c/o the Acropole Hotel), Khartoum.

Christian Outreach This organisation operates the Shegarab refugee camps Nos 1 and 2 just north of Showak, which are quickly becoming permanent settlements because of the difficulty involved in repatriating some of the refugees. Christian Outreach has an office in a flat in Khartoum next to the Islamic Bank, Sharia el Qasar. Postal address: PO Box 220 (c/o Acropole Hotel), Khartoum.

Concern Concern is an Irish humanitarian group that is working with refugees in Muglad. It has an office (tel 222617) at House 3, Block 14 Riyadh area. Postal address: PO Box 3277.

International Committee of the Red Cross Totally nonpolitical and nonreligious with extensive operations in the Sudan, this organisation has an office (tel 47866) at House No 50, Street 35, Khartoum 2.

International Rescue Committee This organisation operates 16 camps mainly in eastern Sudan. Postal address: PO Box 8263 (c/o Acropole Hotel), Khartoum (tel 43895).

LALMBA Association Objectives: to operate and maintain a medical unit, three village clinics and dispensaries, and three feeding centres for malnourished people. The association's main centre is in the eastern Sudan town of Showak. The village clinics and feeding centres are to the east, near the Ethiopian border, in the villages of Wad Hileau, Abuda and Um Ali. The association is based at 7685 Quartz St, Golden, Colorado, 80403 USA (tel (303) 420 1810). Sudan postal address: PO Box 233, Kassala.

Médecins Sans Frontières Objectives: to provide emergency medical assistance to refugees. The organisation is based at 68 Blvd St Michel, 75005 Paris, France. Its main operations are in the eastern Sudan refugee reception centre of Wad Sherifa, which once had the dubious distinction of being one of the largest in the world. Today, there are approximately 60,000 refugees in the two camps that comprise the centre. This organisation has also been instrumental in bringing aid to southern Sudan. Sudan address: Street 33, New Extension (tel 47128).

OXFAM This organisation has offices throughout the world and extensive aid programmes throughout the Sudan. The Khartoum office is next to the UNICEF offices in Khartoum 2. Postal address: PO Box 3182, Khartoum 2.

Save the Children Fund Based in the UK and the USA, this organisation's involvement in refugee problems in the Sudan is extensive. Recently, it has concentrated its efforts on long-term development projects in order to provide substantial health care programmes.

UNICEF (UN World Food Programme) A major force behind aid efforts in the Sudan, UNICEF has a Sudanese office (tel 46381) opposite Farouk Cemetery in Khartoum. Postal address: PO Box 1358, Khartoum.

Other Organisations Other organisations providing assistance in the Sudan include Adventist Development Relief Agency, Euro Action Accord, CARE, Mercy Corps International, VSO (UK) and the World Health Organization.

GEOGRAPHY

The Sudan, the largest country in Africa, is bordered by Egypt, Libya, Chad, the Central African Republic, Zaire, Uganda, Kenya and Ethiopia. A country of contrasts, it stretches from the deserts of Nubia to the equatorial rainforests and swamps of the Sudd, just north of the great lakes and the source of the Nile.

In the north, the Nile slices through seemingly endless and lifeless desert plains. In some places the desert comes right up to the banks of the river, while in others a narrow band of vegetation separates the water from the barren sands.

In Khartoum, the two sources of the mighty Nile River become one. The Blue Nile flows down from Lake Tana, through the highlands of Ethiopia and via the Sudanese towns of Er Roseires and Wad Medani before joining the much longer White Nile, which starts from Lake Victoria on the Kenya-Uganda-Tanzania border.

There are several mountain ranges in the Sudan. In the far west is the Jebel Marra range – the highest in the country and a favourite hiking area among travellers. Closer to Khartoum are the Nuba Mountains – home to the intriguing and long-isolated tribes of the Nuba people. In the east are the Red Sea Hills and the mountain resort of Erkowit, which dates from British colonial days. In the south are the beautiful mountain ranges of Matong and Dongotona. Mt Kinyeti in the Immatong Mountains is the highest peak in the Sudan at 3170 metres.

In the northern and western regions, most of the country is sparsely populated desert.

CLIMATE
The climate and weather vary greatly from north to south. The northern two-thirds of the Sudan is hot and dry most of the year. South of Khartoum, the temperatures tend to be lower but humidity and rainfall are greater.

The best time to visit the Sudan is between November and March, before the rains and after the heat. If you decide that you must go there at any other time, then be prepared for very hot weather. Temperatures of 48°C (118°F) are not unusual in the north, and even in the cooler south the maximum temperature is

up around 37°C (96°F). In winter, from November to March, it is still hot but it usually gets no higher than the mid-30s.

Throughout the year you will encounter the infamous haboob, or khamsin, in all but the mountains and tropical regions. During these sandstorms of monstrous proportions, the sun disappears from the sky as a thick curtain of sand falls over the land and the winds begin howling. Everything and everyone in the storm's path gets coated with fine grains of dust.

POPULATION & PEOPLE
The Sudan's population numbers only about 24 million, yet the country has more than 300 distinct tribes from more than 150 ethnic groups, and more than 100 languages and dialects. The ethnic groups range from the predominantly Muslim Arabs, Nubians and Fur in the north and west, to the predominantly Christian or animist African peoples in the south. It is interesting to travel from north to south to see the transition from Arab to African cultures.

In the north, adherence to Islamic strictures is strong. Alcohol and pork are outlawed and clothing is conservative. The men wear long flowing gowns called *galabiyyas* and loosely wrapped turbans called *emmas*. The women wear *tobes*, which are nothing more than several metres of sheer, brightly coloured material wrapped around their heads and upper bodies and usually worn over a gown.

In Khartoum, women office workers wear only white tobes because, as one woman told me, 'We don't want a carnival atmosphere in our offices'.

In eastern Sudan, the women tend to wear brown or black tobes; some, such as the Rashaida women, also wear the ever-mysterious veils that reveal only their dark, piercing eyes and curly, black fringes.

As you travel south, the people become darker skinned, culturally more African and generally less conservative than the northern Muslims. They usually wear less clothing and· some tribes, such as the Nuba from the Nuba Mountains, wear no clothing at all. South of El Obeid you will also find a forlorn porkchop or two and a few varieties of bootleg spirits – things which are definitely in short supply to the north.

Although northerners and southerners are often culturally distinct, some are very similar in appearance as there has been much intermarriage between Arabs and Africans in the Sudan. Consequently, it is often possible to meet a person who looks African yet professes to be Arab. The prevalence of decorative facial scarring also makes it hard to distinguish between the two groups.

The practice is common among Africans and Arabs of both sexes. The purposes and meanings of different scar patterns vary from group to group, though scarring is usually a sign of tribal identification or, for some women, a sign of beauty.

Another practice which crosses ethnic groups and tribes is female circumcision. Westerners find this barbaric and incomprehensible, but for many Sudanese it is still an accepted part of their culture. The government and many parents supposedly try to discourage it; they are, however, fighting an age-old tradition. An elderly women in each village is usually assigned the role of circumcising girls when they reach the age of five. Despite the controversy surrounding this practice, many Sudanese women proudly regard their circumcision as a sign of womanhood and a means of pleasing their husbands.

The Sudanese are some of the poorest, yet most generous and hospitable people in Africa. As you travel through the country they will welcome you into their homes to sip tea, break bread, chat and sometimes to stay for a few days. On buses, trains, ferries and even camel caravans, people will share whatever food and drink they have.

On a bus from Khartoum to Kassala, I sat opposite a Sudanese woman and her two young sons. She made a small lunch of cheese sandwiches and olives and, without a word, wrapped a sandwich and a couple of olives in paper and placed it on my lap.

RELIGION

More than 70% of the population is Muslim, while 20%, or more, adheres to various indigenous religions and 5% is Christian.

Islam

Most Sudanese Muslims, like the Egyptians, belong to the Sunni sect. But, more so than in Egypt, various mystical and political currents of Islam have gained significant followings in the Sudan.

Generally, the mystical side of Islam is referred to as Sufism. Throughout the Sudan various Sufi orders or fraternities follow their own *tariqa*, which is a path or way to God. The members of a tariqa attain a closer relationship with Allah through special spiritual exercises conducted by the *sheikh*, or leader, of the tariqa. The exercises vary from simply reciting Qur'anic passages to singing, dancing and whirling oneself into a state of ecstasy. The whirling dervishes of Omdurman (near Khartoum) are renowned for their weekly whirls.

The more political currents of Islam in the Sudan are not necessarily detached from mainstream Sunni Islam or the various Sufi orders; however, they can be considered as separate groups under the rallying flag of Islam.

One of the most important politico-religious movements in the Sudan is called Ansar. It has its roots in the Mahdiyya movement of the late 19th century, and the thrust of it has not changed much since then. The members of Ansar believe that a Mahdi, a messenger of God and representative of Mohammed, will come to lead the people. The movement has become quite a political force among a variety of tribal groups ranging from the nomadic Baggara

Arabs to the sedentary tribes of the White Nile.

A related organisation is the Ikhwan al Muslimiyya, or 'Muslim brotherhood'. Essentially, this is a political organisation which seeks religious ends by encouraging the institution of Islamic society and polity based on sharia. The organisation's popularity and influence seems to increase as economic conditions worsen, and its developing power was probably a major reason behind Nimeiri's declaration of sharia in 1983. The brotherhood continues to be a major and, some would say, potentially destabilising influence on Sudanese politics.

Indigenous Religions

At least 20% of the population adheres to some form of indigenous or local religion. The forms vary by ethnic group and tribe but, in general, they relate to certain forces of nature and ancestor worship.

The Dinka, Nuer and other Nilotic tribes of southern Sudan, for example, see human beings as ants in relation to God, though certain men and women among them are sometimes considered to have special godlike powers. They are often accused of being sorcerers or witches, of practising black magic and inflicting illness upon people or animals.

In the north, the notion of the 'evil eye' is prevalent among the Arabs. One who expresses too much interest in the affairs of another can be suspected of deliberately causing harm to that person. As protection against witches, sorcerers and the evil eye, each group has its versions of diviners, witch doctors and exorcists who provide amulets, medicinal concoctions and advice.

Christianity

Only 5% of the population is Christian. Most of the Christians are Roman Catholics but there are some Anglicans. Missionary incursions over the last two centuries, especially in southern Sudan, account for most of the Christian population. Missionaries continue to

actively 'spread the word' throughout that region.

HOLIDAYS & FESTIVALS

For a rundown of Islamic holidays and festivals refer to the Egypt Facts about the Country chapter. Other holidays in the Sudan are:

1 January
Independence Day; commemorates the birth of the independent Republic of the Sudan in 1956. On this day the soldiers who are not fighting civil war battles in the south get to line up and parade through the streets of Khartoum.
27 March
Unity Day; commemorates the signing of the Addis Ababa Agreement, which ostensibly unified northern and southern Sudan in 1972.
25 December
Christmas Day

LANGUAGE

Although there are more than 100 languages and dialects in the Sudan, Arabic is the main language. Dinka is prevalent in southern Sudan, and English is spoken throughout the country.

English should suffice for travel in most parts of the Sudan but, as in Egypt, knowledge of even a few words of Arabic brings instant smiles from the locals. Sudanese Arabic is, however, slightly different from Egyptian Arabic.

Pronunciation

The hard 'g' sound does not exist. It is pronounced as a 'j'. For example, the word 'galabiyya' (the long cotton gown worn by men), is pronounced 'jalabiyya' in the Sudan.

Secondly, the 'sh' sound is generally not used at the end of a verb to negate it. Thus, the Egyptian phrase *mafeesh* – which means 'there is not' or 'there are not' – becomes 'mafee' in the Sudan.

Vocabulary

There are also a few differences in vocabulary between the two countries.

How are you?

   – to a man   *kayf hallak?*
                      (pronounced
                      'aleck')

   – to a woman   *kayf hallik?*
                      (pronounced
                      'alick')
   – to a foreigner   *hawadja*

The word lists in the Egypt section are, for the most part, applicable to the Sudan. *Hawadja* is a word which you will hear often as you travel through the Sudan.

Top: Suakin, eastern Sudan (SW)
Bottom: Bus stop on the road to Port Sudan (SW)

Facts for the Visitor

VISAS & DOCUMENTS

Visas are required by everyone, but the requirements vary from embassy to embassy and are liable to change at any time. Restrictions relating to South Africa and Israel, however, hold for all applications.

Anyone whose passport contains signs of having visited Israel, such as an Israeli stamp or an Egyptian border stamp, will be denied a Sudanese visa. If you crossed overland to or from Israel, then you are doomed unless you have a second passport. Some embassies will readily issue you a second passport, so check with your own government's passport office or embassy. But obtaining a new passport doesn't always work because the Sudanese then assume that you may be trying to hide the fact that you have been to Israel. The American Embassy in Cairo, for example, issues second passports in a day or two for US$35. However, sometimes the Sudanese won't issue you a visa if your passport doesn't have an Egyptian entry stamp. South African nationals cannot obtain Sudanese visas.

Visas must be obtained from a Sudanese Consulate or a Sudanese Embassy. They cannot be obtained at Sudanese borderposts, airports or ports.

According to expatriates in the Sudan, emergency visas used to be issued upon arrival at the airport – so you never know, it may just depend on the mood of the government or the official at the time.

Generally, the requirements for 90 day tourist visas are: US$10 in cash or money order; three passport-size photographs; two copies of the application form (five forms and photos in Cairo); a letter of recommendation from your embassy; and proof of a return air ticket or the means to buy one (this can be a credit card or letter from your bank).

Bear in mind that these requirements can change and are not absolute!

According to some travellers, the Sudanese Embassy in London (tel 839 8080), Cleveland Row, SW1, grants visas in 24 hours.

The embassy in Washington, 2210 Massachusetts Avenue, NW, Washington, DC 20008, grants visas in two to three weeks, though it has been known to take as long as two months.

The latest reports about the embassy in Cairo were fair. With a letter of recommendation from your embassy it could take as little as two or three hours to get the visa, though at the time of writing the average wait was three weeks.

Americans can get their letters of recommendation from the consular section of the US Embassy in Cairo. The French Embassy in Cairo will not issue letters of recommendation for French nationals and Sudanese visas should be applied for in France.

Proof of cholera and yellow fever vaccinations is required if you're arriving from an infected area. African countries south of latitude 12°N are considered infected areas, as are many South American countries.

Registration

All visitors are required to register within three days of arrival in the country, at the Aliens' Office in Khartoum.

You must also register with the police within 24 hours of your arrival in other towns and cities. According to travellers' reports, though, Kassala seemed to be the only town where the police abided by this rule.

Visa Extensions

Visa extensions can also be obtained in one day at the Aliens' Office for S£10.

Travel Permits

Travel permits are required for travel anywhere outside Khartoum. They can be obtained for S£10, with two passport-size photographs, in two to seven days from the Aliens' Office. You must indicate only one town or city per permit, although you can apply for more than one permit at the same time. Travellers have been arrested and deported for travelling outside Khartoum without the proper permits. At the time of writing, permits were only being issued for destinations north of Khartoum and some cities and towns in eastern Sudan. Civil war, border disputes and many other related problems have made southern and western Sudan indefinitely off limits to travellers without special permission.

Visiting Archaeological Sites

A permit from the Department of Antiquities in Khartoum is required for visits to all historical sites. Be sure that the authorisation is legible, otherwise the guards at each site are apt to refuse entry.

CUSTOMS

The Sudan is a 'dry' country. The customs officials are strict about alcohol and will confiscate any liquor you have.

MONEY

Drastic economic measures were expected as a result of the coup, including a revamping of the monetary system. By the time you read this, there is a strong possibility that Sudan will have a new currency or at least a different pricing structure. Prices could be higher or lower than those listed here, so just use these as a guideline.

At the time of writing, the official rate was US$1=S£12.80. The black market rate was as much as US$1=S£20. Changing money on the black market in Sudan is considered risky business, so be careful if you plan to do this.

Sudanese currency is divided into pounds (S£) and piastres (pt); 100 pt = S£1.

Theoretically, you are supposed to declare the amount of foreign currency that you bring into the Sudan, but I haven't heard of anyone ever being asked for a currency declaration form or official exchange receipts. It is, therefore, hardly surprising that the black market for foreign currency, especially US$ and British pounds, is flourishing in the Sudan.

At some hotels bank receipts showing that you have changed money officially must be presented if you want to pay your bill in Sudanese pounds. Most of the hotels which require this, however, are so outrageously priced that they're out of the average traveller's budget anyway. Airlines also require bank receipts for international ticket purchases.

If you're coming overland from Egypt, you can buy Sudanese pounds in the Aswan bazaars, from the stalls, curio shops and camel traders. The rate is less than the black market rate in the Sudan but better than the bank rate.

Money from Home

The best way to have money sent to you in Khartoum is through Citibank. Call home or send a telex to your bank and give them your passport number. To claim your

money in Khartoum you will need to show an onward air ticket and your passport, and pay a commission of US$11.

American Express has an office in Khartoum but they do not offer any financial services such as cashing cheques or money transfers.

TOURIST INFORMATION
Foreign Embassies
The telephone numbers of some of the embassies in Khartoum are:

Austria	77170
Belgium	75564
China	73651
Denmark	80489
France	77619
West Germany	77990
Greece	73155
India	80341
Italy	45270
Japan	44549
Jordan	45893
Netherlands	47271
Niger	78420
North Yemen	43918
Pakistan	42434
Saudi Arabia	41938
Somalia	44800
South Yemen	44947

Sweden	76308
Switzerland	71161
Turkey	73894
UK	70760
USA	74611

Egypt Tourist visas for Egypt take one to two days to be issued. The Egyptian Embassy (tel 77646/7, 72836) is on Sharia el Gama'a, Mogran, Khartoum. Visas cost S£26 for Americans and S£75 for other nationalities. You will need two photographs.

Central African Republic The embassy of the Central African Republic (tel 44167) is in the New Extension in Khartoum, near Street 35. A 10 day visa costs S£70 and you need three passport photos. Some travellers have received their visas in a day, but it can take up to two weeks. At the time of writing, relations between the Sudan and the Central African Republic had been severed.

Chad One month visas for Chad can be obtained in half an hour from the embassy (tel 42545) in Street 19, the New Extension, Khartoum. Take a yellow fever certificate and two photographs.

Uganda Visas for Uganda are not necessary for Commonwealth passport holders. Other nationalities should apply for visas at the embassy (tel 43049) in Street 35, the New Extension, Khartoum. They take three weeks and cost S£2.60. You will need two photographs.

Zaire The Zaire Embassy (tel 42451), in the New Extension in Khartoum, between Streets 21 and 23, issues multiple entry visas but will not accept Sudanese pounds. Visas cost US$27 for one month, US$53 for two months and US$66 for three months, and can take from a couple of days to a few weeks to be issued. Three passport photos are required.

GENERAL INFORMATION
Post
The GPO in Khartoum is open from 7.30 am to 1 pm and from 5.30 to 6.30 pm. Mail to the USA takes about two weeks but from the USA can take up to a month.

There is a poste restante service in the GPO of every major town and city.

Electricity
The electric current is 240 volts AC, 50 Hz.

Time
There is only one time zone in the Sudan and that is two hours ahead of Greenwich Mean Time. So, when it's 12 noon in Khartoum it is: 10 am in London; 5 am in New York and Montreal; 2 am in Los Angeles; 1 pm in Moscow; and 8 pm in Melbourne and Sydney.

Business Hours
Most shops are open from 8 am to 2 pm and from 6 to 8 pm. Government offices are officially open from 8 am to 2.30 pm. If you must visit a government office, it's better to show up after 9 am to give the busy bureaucrats enough time to have tea and read the newspaper.

Banks are open from Saturday to Thursday between 8.30 am and 12 noon.

Fridays are holidays for Muslims; and Sundays are holidays for Christians.

MEDIA
Newspapers & Magazines
Five to six day old copies of the *International Herald Tribune*, and week old editions of *Time*, *Newsweek* and the *Economist* can be bought at most of Khartoum's big hotels, such as the Meridien and the Hilton.

One of the best sources of current information on the Sudan is the English-language magazine *Sudanow* published in Khartoum by the Ministry of Culture & Information. Although it is a government publication, it is surprisingly frank and critical of the government. Recent articles have included discussions of 'Sudan's paraplegic economy', the problems of Sudan Railways and why southern Sudan is rebelling.

Another informative publication is the *Sudan Times*, a daily four page English-language newspaper that offers very frank appraisals of government affairs.

Radio & Television
The Sudan has one TV station and a few radio stations. The TV news in English is at 7.25 pm and there are occasional English-language programmes.

For the latest radio news in English tune into the Voice of America or the BBC. Both operate on several short-wave frequencies and a couple of medium-wave frequencies at various times throughout the day and night.

HEALTH
Refer to the Health section in the Egypt Facts for the Visitor chapter for: detailed information on the more common ailments and diseases in this part of the world and how to avoid or treat them; the suggested items for a first-aid kit; and advice on travel insurance.

There is a severe shortage of trained medical personnel and equipment in the Sudan and most of the country's doctors and facilities are in Khartoum. There are doctors and hospitals in most towns but the level of medical care is a far cry from Western standards.

If you become seriously ill, first try to see a doctor from one of the relief agencies. If that doesn't work and you need to be hospitalised, try to leave the country as quickly as possible. Unfortunately, this can be a problem because Sudan lacks the facilities for speedy medical evacuations. I realise this sounds a bit alarmist, but after seeing a few wards and hearing a couple of horror stories about hospital conditions from expatriate teachers and doctors, I believe it is sound advice.

An expatriate teacher who was hospitalised for a knife wound (he was stabbed in the arm one night in Khartoum) told me that they allowed him to stay in the hospital as long as he wanted because most of the ward was being emptied out. The patients who had been there were being moved to the tuberculosis ward because they had all contracted TB after entering the hospital for other, unrelated ailments. The teacher left the hospital as quickly as possible.

Another possibility for medical treatment is through the International Association for Medical Assistance to Travellers (IAMAT). The local IAMAT representative is Dr W Williams at the Khartoum Clinic (tel 44479, 44133). Check with the USA or British embassies for further information.

Vaccinations

The war in the Sudan has left the country with a severe shortage of doctors and medicines. Diseases such as malaria, tuberculosis, meningitis, hepatitis, trachoma, glaucoma, bilharzia, measles and dysentery are common. You must have yellow fever and cholera vaccinations if you have come from an infected area, which includes most African countries south of the Sudan. Other recommended vaccinations include typhoid, tetanus and meningitis and you should also consider gamma globulin for protection against infectious hepatitis.

You should check for reports of current epidemics and see a doctor for advice on vaccinations before you travel in the Sudan.

Food & Water

Unless your stomach has already been introduced to the revengeful cuisine of other developing countries, then the chances are that diarrhoea will strike. Once again, refer to the Health section in the Egypt Facts for the Visitor chapter for info on how to cope.

Tap water in Khartoum and Kassala is generally safe to drink; in other parts of the country you should boil the water or use water purification tablets or iodine. Sometimes the water may be so cloudy that it's definitely a good idea to filter it through a handkerchief or piece of cloth. Some travellers rely on local advice for deciding whether to drink the water, but I am suspicious of this.

FILM & PHOTOGRAPHY

Permits are required for photography in the Sudan and can be obtained free from the Sudanese Tourism Corporation office. The permit is merely a formality, as you will rarely, if ever, be asked to produce it.

It is still, of course, a good idea to exercise discretion when taking photographs in the Sudan. Do not point your camera at anything which might be considered military or high-security related. This includes airfields, bridges, soldiers and government buildings. The list has recently grown to include souks, or public markets. When taking photographs of the locals it is always better to ask first, as some people simply don't like being photographed and others are offended by it.

Film is expensive in the Sudan so stock up before you arrive. Processing, on the other hand, is relatively cheap. Expatriate residents in Khartoum recommend the Fantastic Colour Lab, which is on the ground floor of the building which houses the French Cultural Centre, around the corner from the Taysir Bus Company. They can process a 36 colour print film in two hours for about S£60.

ACCOMMODATION

Hotels

Khartoum has its fair share of luxury hotels, such as the Hilton and the Meridien, and like luxury hotels in any country they are comfortable but expensive.

The cheaper hotels in the Sudan are usually run by Greeks or Sudanese and do not require bank receipts proving that you changed your money officially. They have most of the amenities of semidecent hotels, such as bugless beds, running water, maybe even rooms that have both a sink *and* a bathroom, and occasional meals. They usually have a big fan whirling over the bed or an air-conditioner which drips and circulates the air with a lot of noise. Room prices tend to range from S£20 to S£200.

Government Rest Houses

These are also common throughout the Sudan. They are one step above the *lakondas* and sometimes even cheaper. Outside of Khartoum, Kassala and Port Sudan, these are some of the best places to stay. Prices and arrangements for accommodation vary from town to town.

Lakondas

The most common form of accommodation in the Sudan, lakondas are usually a series of basic rooms around an open courtyard. Beds tend to be closely woven rope nets stretched over a wooden frame. When it is hot – which is often – the beds are put in the courtyard. They are simple, but cheap and comfortable places to stay. Prices are usually less than S£15 per night.

Youth Hostels

There are two youth hostels in the Sudan – one in Khartoum and the other in Port Sudan. At S£3 per night (slightly less with an International Youth Hostel Association card) they are the cheapest places to stay, though conditions are very basic. They have lots of bunk beds crammed in a room and bathrooms are dirty, but if you are on an extremely tight budget, then you may not mind getting what you pay for.

FOOD

Sudanese food is very simple. Few spices are used and most dishes are seasoned with only lemon juice, salt, pepper and broth. The following are some of the most common dishes.

Vegetables

Fuul is stewed beans served in a variety of ways – sometimes with a sprinkling of cheese and mixed with salad. It is eaten by first mashing the beans with the salad and scooping the result into your mouth with a piece of pita bread.

Fassoulia is a dish of smaller, stewed beans which taste a bit like Heinz baked beans without the sauce.

Bit-tatas are boiled potatoes.

Salata is a salad of tomatoes, lettuce, onions, green peppers, and lime juice dressing.

Sherifa is a green vegetable similar in texture to spinach.

Addis is the ever-popular yellow lentil, one of the most common vegetables in the Sudan.

Bamiyya, also known as ladies' fingers or okra, is a long green vegetable with red tips often used in soups and stews.

Mashay are tomatoes or aubergines stuffed with rice and minced lamb.

Many vegetable dishes are served with a lump of meat, a splash of oil and a watery broth.

Fish

Nile perch is a speciality of Khartoum and Omdurman and is served with a coating of fried batter and red peppers. It is usually available only in the mornings.

Meat & Poultry

Kebab is stewed or skewered meat, usually lamb.

Kalawi is chopped kidney, usually served with a bit of bread and a dash of lemon juice.

Kibda is stewed or skewered liver.

Shia is strips of beef or lamb, cooked on a bed of coals and served with salad.

Lahma is a large, almost indistinguishable lump of beef or lamb served in soup.

Gammonia is stewed sheep's stomach, often served with tomatoes and onions.

Chicken is usually stewed and served in a soup or broth.

Breads

Kisera is a thin, unleavened bread made from *durra*, which is a type of maize.

Gurassa is a thick, unleavened bread not often found in Khartoum but common elsewhere.

Dessert

Hoshab is a cold, red cocktail made from chopped bananas, figs and raisins. It is the only Sudanese dessert I know of and it's superb.

DRINKS
Tea & Coffee

Laban, which is hot sweetened milk, is very popular with the Sudanese but is served only in the evenings.

Shai saada is a sweet tea, served in small glasses without milk and sometimes spiced with cloves, mint or cinnamon.

Shai bi-laban is sweet tea with milk, usually served only in the early morning or early evenings.

Shai bi-nana is a sweet, mint-flavoured tea.

Gahwa fransawi literally means 'French coffee' but it generally refers to Western-style instant coffee, such as Nescafe.

Gahwa turki is very strong Turkish coffee, served in very small coffee cups.

Jebbana is very strong coffee served from a tin or earthenware container with a conical spout. It is drunk from small china bowls and is often spiced with cinnamon, ginger or other spices. 'Jebbana' refers to the name of the container.

Fruit Juices

A variety of freshly squeezed juices is available throughout the Sudan. Some of the best include *kakaday* (a drink made from the hibiscus plant), *limoon* (lemonade), *burtuaan* (orange juice) and *manga* (mango juice). Guava juice and grapefruit juice are also good.

Alcohol

Although alcohol is officially banned under Islamic law, it is still possible to find a few bootleg concoctions.

Aragi is a clear, strong drink made from dates. It tastes a bit like Bacardi rum and can easily knock you off your feet.

Merissa is a beer made from sorghum which looks gross but tastes fine.

Tedj is the name for a variety of wines made from dates or honey, some of which aren't too bad.

BOOKS

Not many books have been written about the Sudan but there are a few which are highly recommended.

Nick Worrall's *Sudan* (London Times Press) is an excellent summary, in words and photographs, of the diversity of cultures in contemporary Sudan.

Alan Moorehead's classics, *The Blue Nile* and *The White Nile* (New English Library, 1982 and Random House, 1983), should be read by anyone planning a trip to Egypt or the Sudan. Both books are certain to whet your appetite for exploration and adventure.

Mike Asher's book *In Search of the 40 Days Road* recounts his search for the trail which Sudanese camel-traders follow when taking their camels north to Aswan. It was published in 1984 by Longman Publishers and in 1987 (paperback) by Penguin Books.

The Sudan: A Country Handbook is

the best general reference on the Sudan. It is published by the American University Press in Washington, DC and updated every three to five years.

The London Times publication *With Geldof in Africa* recounts Bob Geldof's 1985 Band Aid trips to refugee camps. The photographs are a superb and very moving presentation of the peoples of Sudan.

Leni Riefenstahl's book *The People of Kau* (Collins, 1976) is also recommended for its photographs. This book caused a bit of controversy a few years ago because it drew a lot of attention to the Nuba people. The Sudanese government was embarrassed by the nakedness and 'primitive ways' of the Nuba people. The development-conscious government did not want the Sudan presented to the world as a country of naked tribespeople who paint themselves with red mud, wrestle and hunt with spears. Yet it is the ability of these people to continue their traditional way of life that is one of the beautiful things about the Sudan.

Tayib Saleh's books are also recommended. He writes fictionalised literary accounts of life in the Sudan. One can learn much from his books about life in northern Sudan. Some of his titles include: *The Wedding of Zein & Other Stories* and *The Season of Migration to the North* (3 Continents Press, Washington DC, 1978).

MAPS

Michelin Map No 154 of North-East Africa is excellent for the Sudan but lousy for Egypt. The Land Survey office near the Government Palace in Khartoum sells some of the best maps on the Sudan.

THINGS TO BUY

On the streets of Khartoum and Kassala, men and boys cloaked in gowns and turbans will rush up to you clutching swords, daggers and knives. Each weapon is sheathed in stained leather and ready for use – or rather sale. As many Sudanese men still wear daggers and swords at their sides as part of their dress, these little demonstrations are a bit scary. As a form of protection they have been superseded by modern weaponry.

When I arrived in Khartoum I didn't realise that these sword-bearing characters merely wanted to sell me their wares so I ran away down the street the first time one of them waved his sword in my face. However, if you're a budding Lawrence of Arabia or Mata Hari or if you've just always wanted an exotic blade, then this is definitely the place to buy it.

In the Omdurman souk you can buy some beautiful pieces of ivory jewellery for half the price you'd pay in Europe or the USA – that is if you don't object to contributing to the decline of the elephant population. Elephants in the Sudan and other parts of Africa are being massacred for the sake of pretty jewellery, so avoid buying ivory. Other ideologically unsound artefacts include stuffed crocodiles, and wallets or purses made from crocodile skin. The World Wildlife Fund would have a fit here.

Many places in the souk also sell beautiful ebony carvings.

WHAT TO BRING

Since it is warm in the Sudan throughout the year, bring light clothing. If you are planning a trek into the cooler climes of Jebel Marra, then bring a sweater or light jacket.

During the rainy season you must have a poncho or cool, loose-fitting rain jacket, though it is still warm even when it rains.

It is also a good idea to have a bandanna (the large, usually chequered handkerchief often seen on the bad guys in Westerns) to cover your mouth and nose during sandstorms or wild rides on the backs of lorries.

Other suggested accessories include: sunglasses, a hat, a big plastic rubbish bag to cover your pack during rain and sand storms, insect repellent, a mosquito net, a bed sheet (sleeping bags are useful only as something to sleep on) and nylon cord to string up your mosquito net and use as a laundry line.

Most toiletries and first-aid supplies are readily available in Khartoum and Port Sudan.

Getting There

Travel to the Sudan is subject to the state of the civil war. All or some of the means of entering the country discussed in this chapter may not be feasible when you read this. Check the current situation.

AIR

Flying is the most expensive way to get to the Sudan. Ironically, it costs only a bit less for a one-way flight to Khartoum from Nairobi or Cairo than it does to buy a return ticket from London. That is due, in part, to the currency exchange regulations in Egypt and Kenya.

On the other hand, because the troubles in southern Sudan make travelling overland through there impossible, flying is really the only way to enter the country from any of the southern African countries.

If you buy airline tickets in the Sudan you must produce bank receipts to prove you changed the money officially, which makes the tickets quite expensive. You will also need a Civil Aviation Permit, available from most travel agents for S£75. Also, if you are flying on any airline

other than Sudan Airways or EgyptAir, you will need an exit visa.

For more detailed general information on types of tickets and the best places to buy them, refer to the Getting There chapter in the Egypt section.

From the UK

Several airlines fly from London to Khartoum, including EgyptAir (via Cairo), British Airways, Lufthansa (via Frankfurt/ Munich/Cairo), Aeroflot (via Moscow, but they are not the cheapest), Balkan Air (via Sofia, in Bulgaria), Kenyan Airways and Sudan Airways. The best deals on flights to Khartoum can be found in the London magazines *Time Out, LAM* or the *News & Travel Magazine* (*TNT*).

From Europe

Amsterdam Some of the best fares in Amsterdam are through the student travel bureau NBBS Reiswinkels (tel (020) 237686), Dam No 17. KLM has reasonably priced return flights to Khartoum which the NBBS can arrange.

Brussels From Brussels you can fly to Cairo, or Khartoum via Cairo, for reasonable fares that are comparable to those from London bucket shops, if you buy your tickets through NBBS Reiswinkels (student travel agency) or Acotra (tel 513 4480), 38 Rue de la Montagne, Brussels.

Switzerland In Zurich, check with the Air Ticket Service AG (tel (01) 252 6464) at Seilergraben 49. They are especially good at arranging unique round-the-world fares.

From Africa

Sudan Airways, Kenyan Airways, Ethiopian Air, Tunis Air, British Airways and KLM are some of the airlines which fly between the Sudan and other African countries.

KLM flies between Khartoum and Mt Kilimanjaro and Dar es Salaam in Tanzania. They sometimes offer student discounts of 25%.

Sudan Airways used to fly from Aswan to Khartoum every Tuesday at about 4 am for E£170. They shared an office in Aswan with Emeco Travel on Sharia Abtal el Tahrir and were open from 9 am to 4 pm daily except Friday. At the time of writing, however, service had been suspended indefinitely.

From the USA & Australia

There are no direct flights to the Sudan from the USA and Australia. Make your way to one of the countries listed in this section and travel to the Sudan from there.

Leaving Sudan

When you buy your ticket or confirm your reservation in a Khartoum travel agency, you will need to buy a Civil Aviation Permit for S£75. If you are flying any airline other than Sudan Airways or EgyptAir, you will also need an exit visa. Double-check these requirements with the travel agent and, as a backup measure, the owners/managers of the Acropole Hotel. The latter are probably some of the best informed people in the Sudan, especially about travel-related matters.

OVERLAND

Currently it is possible to enter the Sudan safely from only one of the eight countries on its borders: Egypt. Conditions on all borders, except Egypt's, are apt to change for the worse because civil war in southern and western Sudan and in Chad has made travel by land extremely difficult or impossible.

There are a couple of ways of going overland to the Sudan from Egypt. If you have your own 4WD vehicle it's possible to drive along the Red Sea coast; or you can try and join the camel herders on 'The 40 Day Road' from western Sudan, through the Sahara to Aswan (see Michael Asher's book *In Search of the 40 Days Road*, Penguin Books 1987).

For more information refer to the Egypt Getting There chapter and the Aswan Getting There section.

BOAT

There used to be a ferry service four times a month between Jeddah (Saudi Arabia), Port Sudan and Suez but at the time of writing it had been indefinitely suspended. For more information, see the Port Sudan Getting There section.

The easiest and most popular route from Egypt to the Sudan is by Nile steamer from Aswan to Wadi Halfa. The steamer leaves from the docks south of the High Dam between 11 am and 3 pm on Monday, Thursday and Saturday. The journey takes about 20 hours and costs E£53 for 2nd class and E£88 for 1st class. The steamer ride can be hot and uncomfortable, but it is an interesting way to enter the country.

The Thursday steamer arrives in Wadi Halfa on Friday morning and, as Sudanese offices are closed on Friday, you cannot disembark until Saturday morning.

Upon arrival, you need to buy a pink exit form from the police for S£1. See the Wadi Halfa section in the Northern

Sudan chapter for information about where to stay.

In Cairo you can buy steamer tickets at the Sudanese Maritime Office (also called the Nile Valley Navigation Office) at Ramses Station. The ticket price includes eight cups of tea. (See also the Egypt Getting There chapter and the Aswan Getting There & Away section.)

Getting Around

Whichever route you take through the Sudan, you'll end up having to use an interesting collection of trucks, riverboats, trains, international agency jeeps, mail vans, camels, donkeys and even the occasional free flight, as baggage, in a light plane. Apart from flights, all travel is slow and many routes are impassable during the rainy season from June to September, so allow plenty of time to get through this country. It isn't just road transport which takes time, though – even the trains are notoriously slow and subject to long delays.

AIR
Sudan 'Insha'allah' Airways is the only airline which makes internal flights and, theoretically, it flies to all of the Sudan's major cities. However, most of its planes are grounded and in need of repair. Check the latest issue of *Sudanow* for up-to-date flight information.

It is difficult, if not impossible, to make reservations for any internal flights from Sudan Airways offices in other countries. Waiting lists for most flights can be as long as three weeks. In Khartoum I met a United Nations development programme official who waited two weeks before he got on a flight to El Obeid, which is only about 340 km as the crow, or plane, flies.

Some travellers have managed to hitch rides around the country with cargo planes but the chances of this are fairly slim and depend entirely on the whims of the pilots themselves.

Although it's not recommended with the current political situation, we have heard of some people hopping cargo planes from Khartoum to Juba. The *only* reason to go to Juba at the moment would be the very unlikely possibility that you could get another free or cheap cargo plane out of the Sudan. It's not advisable to go to Juba just for the hell of it. The government still holds the town but the rebels have it surrounded and the whole region is under their control. Once, a Sudan Airways passenger jet was shot down en route to Juba.

BUS
Travelling by bus is very common throughout the Sudan, even though only 2% of the country's roads are paved. The most common type of bus is built a bit like a raised tank with an open frame and several rows of slatted benches. The sides have canvas flaps which fold down to keep the dust out. There are also 'luxury' buses but these only run between Khartoum, Kassala and Port Sudan. A couple of the luxury bus lines have air-con or partly air-con buses, comfortable seats and shock absorbers. This is luxury indeed if you're going to be spending eight to 10 hours on a bus.

If you intend to travel by bus in the Sudan, you should be forewarned that buying tickets might be a slight hassle. Foreigners are required to have travel permits for any destinations outside of Khartoum and must present these permits at all checkpoints during the trip. For the bus driver, this means the presence of foreigners could greatly slow the trip. Consequently, drivers can sometimes make it difficult for you to buy tickets. It is better to have a Sudanese buy tickets for you.

TRAIN
Sudan Railways runs an extensive but somewhat rundown collection of trains. The system dates back to General Kitchener's rush to clobber the Mahdi in the late 1890s. He laid track from Wadi Halfa to Abu Hamed across 370 km of harsh Nubian desert in 1897 at the rate of half a km a day. For details of this line's

schedule today and other train services see the Getting There sections of the relevant towns.

There are three classes on Sudanese trains – 1st, 2nd and 3rd. First-class compartments officially carry six passengers but more passengers usually squeeze in. Second and 3rd-class compartments seem to have no limit to the number of passengers. The 2nd and 3rd classes also have subclasses called *mumtaz*, which translates as 'excellent'. So, presumably, 2nd-class mumtaz is better than regular 2nd class. The differences are usually barely noticeable, though.

It is also possible to ride on top of the trains for free, although this is not officially condoned because people have been known to fall off. It is often difficult to plant yourself firmly on top and it can get quite hot and dusty, so protect yourself from the elements and tie your pack down.

Student discounts of 50% to 75% are available for those under 26 years. Permission can be obtained from the Ministry of Youth in Khartoum or the Area Controller's office in other towns. Travellers report, however, that the discounts are not available on the train from Wadi Halfa.

The southbound train from Wadi Halfa is usually more crowded than the northbound train because it's packed with Sudanese and huge bundles of things bought in Egypt.

BOAT

As of mid-1986, the civil war hostilities had stopped the Nile steamers and most other Nile boat traffic, except the steamer from Aswan to Wadi Halfa. Garang has threatened to shoot at any boats moving south of Kosti.

TRUCK

Souk lorries, which are big Bedford market trucks, transport goods and people between almost every town and village in the Sudan. For a minimal amount of money you get to share the back of a truck with as many as 40 people, sacks of grain, live goats, bags of sugar and bundles of cotton or whatever else needs to be transported and sold. Some travellers I met in the Sudan swear by this economical form of travel but you never know what might be in that large, putrescent bundle next to you. My travel companions on one truck trip were a pile of dead, desiccated goats with eyes bulging and mouths agape. All 10 goats stared at me from Showak to Kassala, where I thankfully got off.

If you do travel by truck, there are a few things to keep in mind. Take plenty of water for desert trips (you can buy large, plastic Thermos jugs in Khartoum), and it's a good idea to take something to eat as well. Food could be a problem along the way, depending on your destination, although bread is usually available in most villages. Make sure you have a hat or something to cover your head during the day. The nights can be cold, so be prepared. A torch (flashlight) is also useful. Lastly, you must be in fairly decent physical shape to endure travel by truck.

A traveller named Penny Xarwalyczha of Cumbria, UK, wrote the following about her truck trip through northern Sudan:

You must be mentally and physically tough to stand truck trips in northern Sudan. . .One traveller [told me] that after a two day trip in the back of a Bedford truck across the desert to Khartoum, he ended up with a cut head, two cut feet and a very, very sore arse. It's not funny when it's happening. It's exhausting and I've never ever had a rougher journey in my life. Please prepare others and spread the word. Now I look back and I laugh at it all. In my opinion, Sudan is for the intrepid, hardy traveller who must have no expectations, but live with whatever comes along from day to day. . .

BICYCLE

Bicycles are not used much in the Sudan

because most of the roads are so bad. However, in 1984 a couple of British cyclists built a contraption which allowed them to ride their bikes on the railway tracks and they travelled all the way from Wadi Halfa to Khartoum.

HITCHING

Hitching rides for free is uncommon in the Sudan, as most drivers will ask for some sort of compensation.

CAMEL

In western and northern Sudan camels are a common beast of burden and transport. Most of them are bred in western Sudan, so it is there that you will probably get the best deal on a camel – approximately US$150 for the latest model. But be warned if you have never ridden a camel – they can be smelly, temperamental and very difficult to handle.

DONKEY

These contrary, sometimes adorable, critters are used throughout the Sudan as a mode of transport. Souks in most towns and villages sell them quite cheaply so you can even own your own donkey and travel at will, if you can get it to go where *you* want.

LOCAL TRANSPORT
Bus & Box

Buses and 'boxes' are common transport in most cities. Boxes are small pick-up trucks with two benches and a canvas covering over the back. They usually travel prescribed routes and are much cheaper than taxis.

Taxi

Taxis are prevalent in Khartoum, Omdurman, Kassala, Port Sudan and Wadi Halfa. Fares are subject to the whims of the drivers and the bargaining abilities of the passengers. Flagging down a taxi is simple – just stick your arm out and wave.

Khartoum

The sun was rising as I hopped into a taxi at the Khartoum airport terminal to go 'downtown'. Ten minutes later, the taxi stopped on a dirt street cluttered with trash and lined on one side by small, two storey buildings and on the other by a low white wall topped with shards of glass.

'We're here,' the driver said.

'Where?' I asked.

'Downtown, downtown Khartoum. *Ahlan wa Sahlan*,' he replied, which means 'welcome'.

Actually, the 'real' downtown was around the corner on Sharia el Gamhuriyya. Here, the buildings were taller, the street was paved and there was almost enough traffic to merit traffic lights. Nevertheless, my first impressions stuck; Khartoum is a quiet city.

Khartoum lacks the congestion and squalor of other Third World capitals, and the tree-lined streets near the river are a very peaceful place to stroll. The population of just four to five million is spread between Khartoum and its sister cities, Omdurman and North Khartoum, across the Nile.

Established in 1821 as a military outpost by Ismail, Mohammed Ali's son, Khartoum derives its name from its site at the confluence of the Blue and White Niles on a spit of land which resembles an elephant's trunk, or *khartoum*. The city grew and prospered, especially between 1825 and 1880 when many of the inhabitants made their fortunes through the roaring slave trade. The slaves were captured from regions south of Khartoum and sold to traders in Egypt, Turkey and other northern countries.

Khartoum became the capital of the Sudan in 1834 and was used as a base by many European explorers of Africa. However, during the latter part of the 19th century, the city's prosperity declined and it was ransacked twice – first by the Mahdi to oust Gordon and then by Kitchener to get rid of the Mahdi.

Cook's *Traveller's Handbook for Egypt & the Sudan*, published in 1929, had this to say about Gordon's defeat:

In 1884 General Gordon went to Khartûm to withdraw the Egyptian garrison, but very soon after the city was besieged by the Mahdi and his followers, and Gordon's position became desperate; famine, too, stared him in the face, for he distributed daily among the destitute in the city the supplies which would have been ample for the garrison. . .During the whole of January Gordon continued to feed all the people in Khartûm; 'for that he had, no doubt, God's reward, but he thereby ruined himself and his valuable men'. . .On the night of 25th January (1885) Gordon ordered a display of fireworks in the town to distract the people's attention, and in the early dawn of the 26th the Mahdists crossed the river, and, swarming up the bank of the White Nile where the fortifications had not been finished, conquered the Egyptian soldiers, who made but feeble resistance, and entered the town. Numbers of Egyptians were massacred, but the remainder laid down their arms and, when the Mahdists had opened the gates, marched out to the enemy's camp. The Dervishes rushed to the palace, where Gordon stood on the top of the steps. . .and in answer to his question, 'Where is your master, the Mahdi?' their leader plunged a huge spear into his body. He fell forward, was dragged down the steps, and his head having been cut off was sent over to the Mahdi in Omdurmân. The fanatics then rushed forward and dipped their spears and swords in his blood, and in a short time the body became 'a heap of mangled flesh'.

The Mahdi professed regret at Gordon's death, saying that he wished he had been taken alive, for he wanted to convert him. . .Khartûm was given up to such a scene of massacre and rapine as has rarely been witnessed even in the Sudan.

Thirteen years later, Sir Herbert Kitchener and his troops recaptured the city, raising the British and Egyptian flags 'amid cheers for Her Majesty Queen Victoria, and the strains of the Khedival Hymn'. Kitchener began rebuilding Khartoum in 1898, designing the streets along the lines of the Union Jack so that the city would be easier to defend. At about the same time, North Khartoum, on the other side of the Blue Nile, was developed as an industrial area.

Before his defeat, the Mahdi established Khartoum's sister city Omdurman across the confluence of the two Niles. Laid out in a more traditional fashion, with many small narrow streets, mud-brick buildings and a huge souk, this area has managed to resist many 20th century changes and retains its Islamic character.

It's not difficult to imagine how life in Khartoum may have been at the turn of the century, as the arcaded sidewalks and colonial-style architecture of some of the government buildings are still reminiscent of the British Empire at its height. In typical British imperialist fashion, however, the description in Cook's *Traveller's Handbook* of 1929 is a little over the top:

The rebuilding of the city began immediately after the arrival of the British, and the visitor can judge for himself of the progress made in this respect during the twenty-three years of peace which have followed its occupation by a civilised power.

Orientation
The British put their indelible mark on Khartoum by laying out the streets in the shape of the British flag. The city centre lies on the south bank of the Blue Nile. There, you'll find the cheap hotels, restaurants and government offices.

South of the centre, across the railway line, the New Extension contains most of the embassies, the expatriates' clubs and the airport.

The city of Omdurman is to the north, across the White Nile, and North Khartoum is on the other side of the Blue Nile.

Information
Registration Everyone is required to register with the Aliens' Registration Office in Khartoum within three days of arrival. The office is on the left-hand side of Sharia el Khalifa, down from the GPO towards the Nile.

Tourist Office The Tourist Information Office (tel 74664) is on the corner of Sharia el Huriyya and Sharia el Baladaya in the Sudan Tourist & Hotels Corporation building. It's open from 8.30 am to 2.30 pm. Photo permits are issued free there and also available is a colourful map of the Sudan.

Post & Telecommunications Postal, telegraph and telephone services are all in a building on the corner of Sharia el Gama'a and Sharia el Khalifa.

The GPO is open daily, except Fridays, from 8.30 am to 1 pm. It costs 75 pt for ordinary international letters. Poste restante is located there.

The telephone office is also open daily, except Fridays, from 8.30 am to 8 pm. Calls should be booked several hours or even a day in advance.

The telegraph and telex office is open 24 hours a day, seven days a week, including holidays. Telex numbers in Khartoum have become five digit, so any previously three digit numbers are now prefixed by 22.

American Express The American Express office is opposite the British Airways office on a small side street just off Sharia el Gamhuriyya, between Sharia el Taiyar Morad and Sharia el Khalifa. The office is upstairs, above the KLM office, and is open daily, except Fridays and Sunday evenings, from 8.30 am to 1.30 pm and 5.30 to 7.30 pm. This American Express office does not offer any financial services (such as cheque cashing or cash exchange).

Mail can be collected from the box on the front counter; after-hours access to the box is sometimes possible because

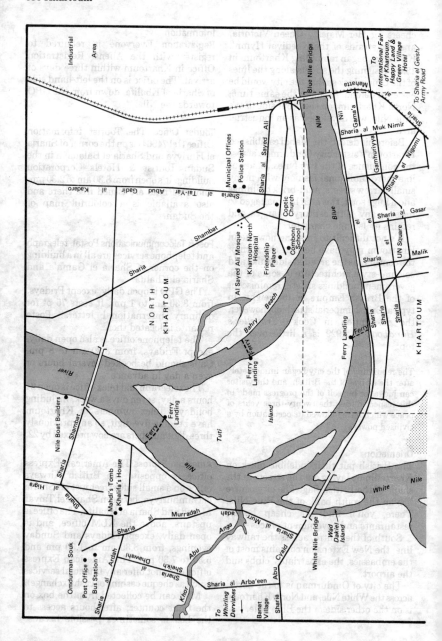

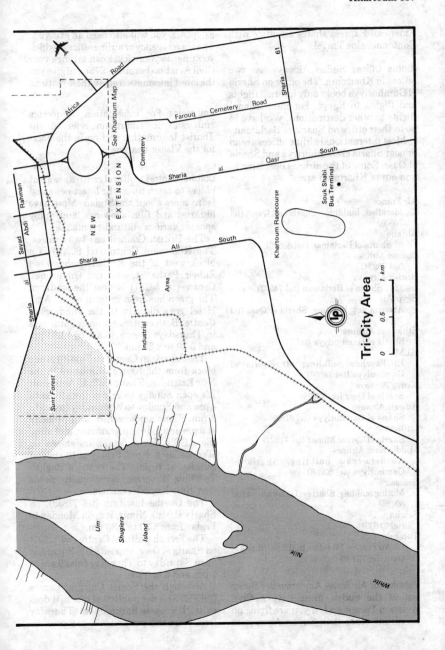

Tri-City Area

American Express shares an office with Contomichalos Travel.

Airline Offices Sudan Airways has two offices in Khartoum. The office on Sharia el Gamhuriyya books only internal flights and flights to Egypt. For international flights to other destinations, you have to go to their office on Sharia el Barlaman.

Most international airline offices are on or near Sharia el Gamhuriyya and Sharia el Qasr. Some of the airlines operating in and out of Khartoum are:

Air France
 Meridien building, Sharia el Qasr (tel 76606)
Alitalia
 87 Sharia el Barlaman (tel 80526)
Balkan Airlines
 (tel 76234)
British Airways
 3241 Sharia el Barlaman (tel 74577)
EgyptAir
 Abouela new building, Sharia el Qasr (tel 70259)
Ethiopian Airlines
 Sharia el Gamhuriyya (tel 77180)
KLM
 El Fayehaa building, off Sharia el Gamhuriyya (tel 74066)
Kenya Airways
 Sharia el Qasr (tel 73429)
Kuwait Airways
 Sharia el Gamhuriyya (tel 81826)
Lufthansa
 Sharia el Taiyar Morad (tel 71322)
Middle East Airlines
 Abouela new building, Sharia el Gamhuriyya (tel 80968)
Swissair
 Morhig building, Sharia el Gamhuriyya (tel 80196)
Saudia
 (tel 71633)
Tunisair
 c/o Air France, Meridien building, Sharia el Qasr (tel 75726)

Permits for Air Travel Any traveller flying out of the Sudan must have a Civil Aviation Permit and, if you are flying on an airline other than Sudan Airways or EgyptAir, you will also need an exit visa. The travel agency or airline office at which you finalise your ticket can arrange your Civil Aviation Permit (S£75) and give you the latest information about these matters.

Embassies For information on foreign embassies in Khartoum refer to the Tourist Information section in the Facts for the Visitor chapter.

Cultural Centres Cultural centres are great places to catch up on the latest news and learn more about the Sudan. Most have libraries and film showings, and many sponsor various cultural events.

The British Council has two centres. The Khartoum Centre (tel 80269) is a block west of the British Embassy on Zubeir Pasha St, and the Omdurman Centre (tel 53281) is near the stadium. The green bus from in front of the Arak Hotel goes directly to the Omdurman Centre. Both centres are open Saturdays to Thursdays from 8.30 am to 12.30 pm and 5.30 to 8.30 pm.

The American Center (tel 40876) is one block from the Kenyan Embassy in the New Extension, Khartoum 2, El Ammarat. It's open Sunday to Friday from 9 am to 1 pm and Sunday to Wednesday from 5 to 8 pm. Films are screened each Monday at 6 pm and video programmes, including the ABC's *World News*, are shown on Wednesday at 6 pm, Friday at 10 am and Sunday at 6 pm. The centre's English Teaching Program occasionally needs part-time English teachers.

The Goethe Institute (tel 77833), on Sharia al Muk Nimir, is open Monday to Friday from 5.30 to 8.30 pm.

The French Cultural Centre (tel 72837) on Sharia el Qasr, opposite UN Square, is open Saturday to Thursday from 9 am to 1 pm and 6 to 8 pm.

Although the Soviet Cultural Centre (tel 81258) is not publicised much, it does exist. It's open Saturday to Thursday from 9 am to 2 pm and 5.30 to 9 pm.

Bookstores Three bookstores in Khartoum have fairly good selections of English-language books and current magazines.

The Khartoum Bookshop is on Zubeir Pasha St, one block from the Arak Hotel towards Sharia el Qasr.

The Sudan Bookshop is at the corner of Sharia el Taiyar Morad and Sharia el Barlaman.

The Nile Bookshop (tel 43749) in the New Extension, Street 41, has books and magazines in French and German, as well as in English.

Maps The Sudan Survey Department publishes excellent maps of almost every corner of the country, including Khartoum. The departmental office is next to the Government Palace, on the right-hand side when facing the Nile. Their *General Map of Greater Khartoum* is also sold in the English-language bookstores.

Clubs Various ethnic, religious and national clubs form the backbone of Khartoum social life, especially for the city's expatriate residents. Although entry to all clubs requires membership, it is sometimes possible to arrange temporary membership or enter with a member. The clubs' activities vary from music, film presentations and athletics to serving food, conducting tours and providing accommodation.

The American Club (tel 70114) is around the corner from the Youth Hostel, near the train tracks (refer to the Khartoum map). Holders of US passports can obtain a one day membership to the American Club for S£5 and anyone is welcome to come with a member. There's a restaurant/snack bar, swimming pool and a couple of tennis courts. A few expatriates claim, however, that the club's drinking water has made them sick.

The Sudan Club (tel 72044) is actually the Commonwealth Club. Official membership is essential for entrance, accommodation and use of the club swimming pool and squash courts. Exceptions are occasionally made for members of the British East India Club, the Turf Club of Cairo and similar 'old empire' establishments. Commonwealth passport-holders may be granted entry for S£5 a day and entrance is sometimes also granted to other nationalities, for a fee.

Even if you are without the proper connections, it is worth visiting the Sudan Club to check out the information boards inside the gate. Occasionally, there are movies, lectures, cultural events and tours (led by old retired officers) to such places as Colonel Hicks' last battleground, and these events are sometimes open to the public.

The Sudan Club is on the corner of Sharia el Barlaman and Contomichalos St. The manager's office – a terribly bureaucratic place – opens at 8.30 am. The club was bombed in mid-1988, so expect security here to be quite tight.

The Syrian and Armenian Clubs, opposite each other in the New Extension area of Khartoum, both serve delicious Middle Eastern food and have music on Thursday nights. They are a cross between a hotel lounge and a student pub without the alcohol. Call the Syrian Club (tel 42660) or the Armenian Club (tel 43165) for details of what's on. Boxes (small pick-up trucks) from UN Square pass near the clubs.

If you're an inveterate socialiser, there's also the German Club (tel 42438), the Hellenic Club (tel 43757) and the Italian Club (tel 42322).

National Museum

The National Museum is the best of Khartoum's four museums. The 1st floor exhibits feature artefacts and antiquities from prehistoric Sudan and later periods, including the kingdoms of Cush and Napata. On the 2nd floor, there are colourful frescoes and mosaics from the ruins of ancient churches in northern Sudan.

In the garden outside are the recon-

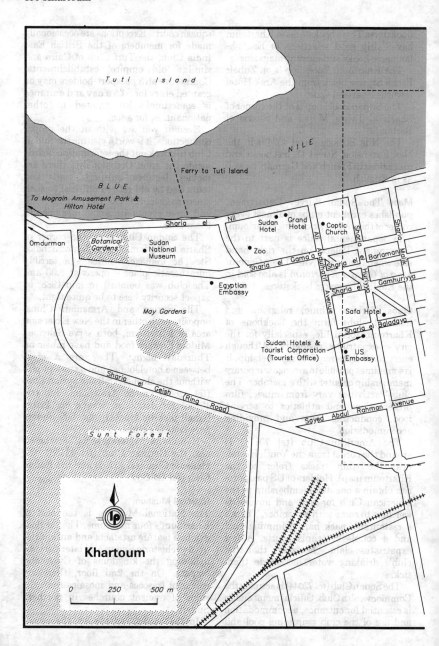

Khartoum

0   250   500 m

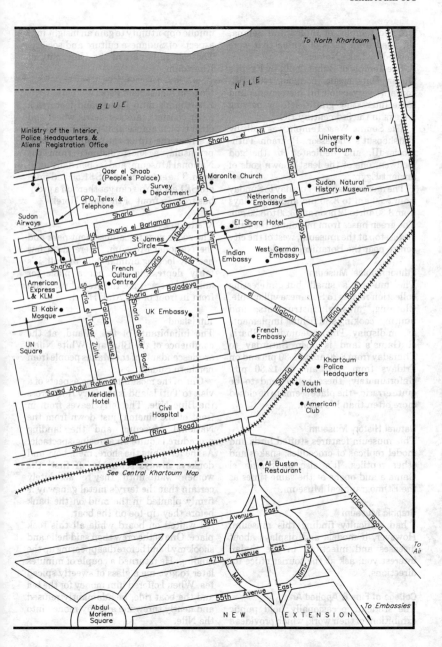

structed temples of Buhen and Semna, salvaged from parts of Nubia that were flooded by Lake Nasser.

The Temple of Buhen, built by Egypt's Queen Hatshepsut in about 1490 BC, contains very colourful hieroglyphs and some interesting graffiti left by passing Greeks in the 3rd century BC.

The Semna West Temple was built by Hatshepsut's successor, Pharaoh Tuthmosis III, and dedicated to the god Dedwen, one of the least known gods of ancient Egypt.

The museum is open Tuesday to Sunday from 8.30 am to 8.30 pm and on Fridays from 8.30 am to 12 noon and 3.30 to 8.30 pm. The green buses from in front of the Arak Hotel stop at the museum, west of the city centre near the Botanical Gardens.

Ethnographical Museum

The museum's small but interesting collection relates to Sudanese village life. Clothing, musical instruments, and hunting, cooking and fishing implements are on display. The museum is on Sharia el Gama'a and is open Saturday to Thursday from 8.30 am to 1.30 pm and on Fridays from 8.30 am to 12.30 pm. Unfortunately, these hours tend to be quite erratic – the place seems to be closed more often than it's open.

Natural History Museum

This museum features stuffed birds and model replicas of crocodiles, snakes and other reptiles. It's also on Sharia el Gama'a and opens at the same times as the Ethnographical Museum.

Graphic Museum

I had difficulty finding this museum. However, if models and displays about diseases and infections in the Sudan interest you, ask at the tourist office for directions.

College of Fine & Applied Arts

The students occasionally hold public exhibitions of their work, which provides a unique opportunity to gain an insight into aspects of Sudanese culture and society. The college is part of the University of Khartoum.

Mograin Amusement Park

Khartoum's mini-Disneyland features a roller coaster, carousel, ferris wheel and other typical amusement-park attractions. It's near the tip of the 'elephant trunk' peninsula, a short distance from the National Museum, and is open daily until 9 pm. The entrance fee is S£1.50 and rides are S£1 each. You can get there on a green bus from in front of the Arak Hotel.

Khartoum Zoo

The zoo is near the amusement park and the National Museum. There are a few healthy-looking animals but, overall, it's fairly depressing and not a place for animal lovers. Take the green bus, again from in front of the Arak Hotel.

Tuti Island

The inhabitants of this island, at the confluence of the Blue and White Niles, are descendants of the Mahas people from northern Sudan.

One of the most interesting aspects of a visit to Tuti Island is the ferry ride across the Blue Nile. The ferry leaves from in front of the cinema, just down from the National Museum, and the landing procedure is quite an amusing spectacle. As the ferry hits the shore, men, boys and donkeys always scramble off first; the women wait until they're absolutely certain that the ferry's metal gangway is firmly planted in the mud on the bank before they tip-toe off the boat.

I waited on board while all this took place. One of the crew then said hello and shook my hand before disappearing up the landing. He returned a couple of minutes later to give me a glass of sweetly spiced tea. When I offered him money for the tea and the boat ride, he adamantly refused and nearly threw me and my money into the Nile.

At the Tuti Island landing, a bus picks up passengers for the trip to the small, brick village in the centre of the island. It offers nothing much of interest.

A 10 minute walk from the village is the landing from which the small, leaky sailboat takes you across the other branch of the Blue Nile to Bahry Beach in North Khartoum, not far from the Friendship Palace Hotel. Ask someone in the village for directions.

Two boys work on the boat, one paddling with a big stick while the other furiously tries to scoop the water out faster than it seeps in through cracks patched with bits of rag. If you happen to fall into the Blue Nile, you needn't worry about bilharzia. There might be crocodiles, but bilharzia is confined to the White Nile.

If you survive the boat trip, and most people do, the beach in front of the Friendship Palace Hotel is a good place to go swimming.

Race Track

Khartoum's race track is south of the city near Souk Shabi. There are races on Fridays and Sundays from 4 pm, and polo matches on Wednesdays and Saturdays at 4 pm. Boxes for Souk Shabi and the race track leave from Sharia el Taiyar Zulfa near UN Square.

Verona Fathers

The Verona Fathers is an Italian-based Jesuit missionary order which has been working in the Sudan for several years. The order operates a unique secondary school in Khartoum, on Sharia el Qasr near the Meridien Hotel, and also helps run a refugee camp on the outskirts of the city.

The school has no walled classrooms; students simply sit in groups, around the large interior courtyard, with their teacher and a blackboard.

The Fathers don't mind having visitors. They often present BBC video shows on various aspects of the Sudan, such as the construction of the Jonglei Canal.

Omdurman

Across the confluence of the two Niles is Khartoum's sister city, a world apart from the capital. At first, Omdurman has the appearance of a large, scattered village. There is no skyline of gleaming high-rise offices (most of the buildings are mud constructions), the streets are narrow and goats wander the dusty alleys between the houses. Little seems to have changed here since the Mahdi made Omdurman his capital after decapitating General Gordon and defeating the British in 1885.

Souk The Omdurman Souk, the Sudan's largest market, attracts people from all over the country to sell an amazing variety of wares. In the shops and stalls, craftspeople carve and shape pieces of ebony and ivory into candlesticks and statuettes, goldsmiths and silversmiths crouch over glimmering bits of metal, pounding and cutting out jewellery, and other merchants hang shrivelled crocodiles and zebra heads in their store windows. Some of the jewellery is nice but Cairo's Khan el Khalili bazaar is more extensive. The green buses in front of the Arak Hotel terminate at the souk.

Whirling Dervishes Every Friday afternoon, about an hour before sunset, a group of dervishes, dressed in galabiyyas and brightly coloured patchwork gowns, gathers in front of the Hamed al Niel Mosque in Omdurman. These men come together to venerate, in a most unusual way, a 19th century sheikh who was the head of their tariqa, or path of Islam.

The various tariqas have their origins in 16th century Sufism and their members follow an ascetic, more mystical form of Islam. The sheikh of each tariqa teaches its members his own particular path to Allah, which may involve simply studying the Qur'an or taking part in a frenzied ceremony called a *dhikr*. As most Sudanese Muslims today belong to an order of some sort, you may see quite a variety of dhikrs as you travel through the Sudan.

The whirling dervishes of Omdurman follow the teachings of the late Sheikh Hamed al Niel. He is venerated as a saint because it is believed that he was, and is still, able to perform miracles and act as an intermediary between the members of the tariqa and Allah.

As a show of respect for the sheikh, some of the men who have gathered at the mosque begin beating steadily on big drums. This is a signal for the dervishes to begin their march across the field to the mosque. They enter the circle of observers which forms in front of the mosque and begin chanting and walking slowly around a pole. As the drum beat and chanting speed up they, and anyone who wants to join them, attempt to whirl themselves into a detached state of mind. The object of this dhikr is 'oneness with Allah', and it lasts until sunset or complete dizziness, whichever comes first.

As dervishes begin their initiation into the ways of the tariqa at the age of 10, there are usually a few young boys mimicking their elders outside the circle of whirling men.

To get to the Hamed al Niel Mosque, take a green bus from in front of the Arak Hotel to the Al Murradah Stadium on Sharia el Arbein (pronounced 'arba'een'). Walk past the stadium and through the village to a field; from here, it's only a 10 minute walk to the mosque on the other side.

The Mahdi's Tomb The Mahdi and his 50,000 warriors were responsible for instigating the first uprising against the British in the 1880s. After capturing Khartoum from the British in 1885, however, the Mahdi apparently retired to a life of amazing decadence and grew tremendously fat, while his harem of 30 women attended to his every whim. The only interruptions he allowed were the occasional councils of war.

The Mahdi died on 22 June 1885, only five months after General Gordon was beheaded, and was entombed in a mosque with a shiny silver dome. The Khalifa Abdullahi, who had taken over the Mahdi's residence after his death, declared that Omdurman was the 'sacred city of the Mahdi' and that a pilgrimage to the Mahdi's tomb was an obligation of Sudanese Muslims, in place of the haj to Mecca (which was prohibited).

General Kitchener destroyed the mosque when he recaptured Khartoum in 1898. Cook's 1929 *Traveller's Handbook to Egypt & the Sudan* described the desecration as 'necessary'.

The tomb was badly injured in the bombardment of Omdurmân on the 22nd, and after the capture of the town it was destroyed by the British, the Mahdi's body being burnt in the furnace of one of the steamers and his ashes thrown into the river. This was considered to be necessary as the building had become a symbol of rebellion and fanaticism, the goal of pilgrimages and the centre of fraudulent miracles.

The mosque and tomb were rebuilt in 1947 by the Mahdi's son. Foreigners are not permitted to enter, but the green bus from the Arak Hotel passes close to the mosque and the Khalifa's house nearby. The tomb is the building with the more conical dome.

Beit el Khalifa This house was built in 1887 as the home of the Mahdi's successor. The mud and brick building has changed little from the time when the Khalifa Abdullahi lived there, before his defeat at the hands of General Kitchener's forces in the 1898 Battle of Omdurman.

The house is now a museum featuring relics from the Mahdi's various battles and the British occupation of the Sudan. The steel boat used by the French leader General Marchand to 'occupy' Fashoda in 1897 and the Arrol motor car of Sir Wingate, governor of the Sudan in 1902, are on display in the courtyard. There is even a 'water room', where there were facilities for hot baths. Interesting suits of mail from the Battle of Atbara in 1898 and numerous Mahdiyya war banners and guns can also be seen.

Beit el Khalifa is opposite the Mahdi's tomb, so you can take the same bus. It's open Tuesday to Sunday from 8.30 am to 8.30 pm, and on Friday from 8.30 am to 12 noon and 3.30 to 8.30 pm. Entry costs 22 pt.

Nile Boat Builders

On the Omdurman side of the Nile, just north of the Shambat Bridge, a group of workers can be seen sawing and hacking at long planks of wood. They are building the broad-sailed boats which are seen up and down the Nile.

Places to Stay - bottom end

The *Youth Hostel* is in Khartoum 2 on 47th Ave, near the eastern end of El Mek Nimir Circle, across from the Tokyo Bookshop. It's a clean, pleasant place with a big shady garden and costs S£7 per night with an IYHA card.

The *Port Sudan Hotel* on Kulliyat el Tibb St, about five minutes walk from the train station, offers beds in a courtyard for S£1.75 each and a room in which you can lock up your gear. The hotel also has clean and airy rooms for S£2.

The *Bahr el Ghazal Hotel*, near Souk Arabi off Sharia Malik (the sign is in Arabic), is also cheap, but don't expect much from this place. A bed in one of the four to five bed rooms costs S£2.50 a night. The windowless rooms are a bit dark and gloomy but, as the showers and toilets are combined in the same stall, they at least are kept fairly clean. During the summer, you can sleep on the roof. If you are just looking for a place to sleep, this is certainly one of the cheapest.

Opposite the bus station on Sharia el Baladaya, near UN Square, is the *El Khalil Hotel*. It charges S£3/5.50 for singles/doubles.

The *El Nowyi Hotel* on Sharia el Isbitalya is good value – doubles are S£14 to S£20 for two, S£7 to S£10 for one, and

there are also a couple of singles with bath. The rooms are cleaned every day.

The *Asia Hotel* is popular with travellers. It's next to the Safa Hotel on Sharia el Baladaya, around the corner from the tourist office. Dusty singles cost S£12 per night; the rooms on the roof are the best and have good views of UN Square.

Places to Stay - middle

The *Nakiel Hotel* is an excellent choice and especially popular with Sudanese honeymooners. It's centrally located opposite the Souk Arabi, a couple of blocks from UN Square. Although the sign is in Arabic, the hotel is easy to find – just go up the lane next to the *mubkhar* (incense seller) marked on the Central Khartoum map. Rooms cost S£28.60 for a single, S£40 for a double. The hotel has been renovated and all rooms have air-con, overhead fans and typically dungeonlike toilet stalls. The lobby is furnished with a TV and fuzzy sofas.

The *El Sawahli Hotel* has 24 clean, simply furnished rooms with air-coolers and overhead fans. Doubles/triples cost S£28/42, and showers and toilets are shared on each floor. The hotel is on Zubeir Pasha St, about a block north-east of UN Square.

Another popular place with travellers is the *Safa Hotel* on Sharia el Baladaya, near the tourist office. It costs S£20 for a single with overhead fan and air-cooler and, although the rooms are simply furnished and a bit dark, they are clean. If you get claustrophobic, seek refuge in the lobby among the potted plants and cushioned chairs.

The *El Sharq Hotel* is a place of last resort. You'll pay S£33 for a single bed in a dark, grimy room with peeling walls, stained sheets, a sink and an overhead fan. The smaller front rooms share a common bathroom in which it's a good idea to wear shoes or sandals. The rooms surrounding the courtyard at the rear each have bathrooms which resemble medieval torture chambers, but the doors

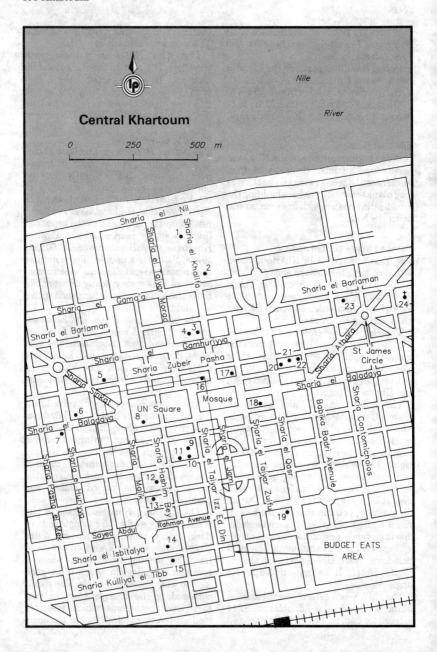

Central Khartoum

0   250   500 m

Nile

River

Sharia el Nil
Sharia el Taiyar Moraq
Sharia el Khalifa
Sharia el Gama'a
Sharia el Barlaman
Sharia el Barlaman
Sharia el Gamhuriyya
Sharia Zubeir Pasha
Sharia el
Sharia Sinkat
UN Square
Sharia el Baladaya
Sharia el Baladaya
Sharia el Hurriya
Sharia Prasha el Mek
Sharia Malik
Sharia Hashim Bey
Sharia el Taiyar Izz Ed Din
Sharia el Jami
Sharia el Taiyar Zuful
Sharia el Qasr
Sharia Attara
Sharia el Baladaya
Sharia Contomicholos
Babika Badri Avenue
Mosque
Sayed Abdul Rahman Avenue
Sharia el Isbitalya
Sharia Kulliyat el Tibb

St James
Circle

BUDGET EATS
AREA

1	Aliens' Registration Office
2	GPO
3	British Airways
4	American Express/KLM Airlines
5	El Sawahli Hotel
6	Safa Hotel
7	Tourist Office
8	Bus to Sanghat
9	Nakiel Hotel
10	Mubkhar (Incense Seller)
11	Hotel Nilein
12	Souk Arabi – buses to Souk Shabi
13	Bahr el Ghazal Hotel
14	El Nowyi Hotel
15	Garden Restaurant
16	Maxim's Burgers
17	Arak Hotel & buses to Omdurman
18	Boxes to Souk Shabi
19	Meridian Hotel
20	French Cultural Centre
21	Metropole Hotel
22	Acropole Hotel
23	Sudan Club
24	Greek Church

do have locks. Be insistent if you have a preference for one of these rooms.

The *Metropole Hotel* (tel 71166), 4 Zubeir Pasha St, has a certain mystique. Like the more expensive Acropole two doors down, the Metropole is a favourite among expatriates and seems to attract an odd assortment of characters fit for a spy novel, including journalists, Bombay pipe salesmen, mysterious Belgian-Turkish businessmen with cases full of money, Sudanese entrepreneurs and ex-politicians. Rooms are S£47 a single and S£80 for a double (S£60 for single occupancy), including three meals, and all rooms have big whirling overhead fans. Most rooms also have a sink, an air-cooler, a desk and a dresser. The meals are much the same every day – bread, tea and eggs for breakfast, murky soup, bread, salad and meat for lunch and, usually, cold leftovers from lunch for dinner.

The *Sudan Club* offers limited accommodation to members and associate members (see the Clubs section earlier in this chapter). A single or a bed in a double room costs S£51 a night. The rooms are clean, cool and comfortable. Meals are also available.

The *Falcon Hotel* has been recommended by some travellers. Rooms cost S£150.

An overland group suggested a hotel (the name of which they had forgotten) on Sharia el Qasr, near the Meridien. The hotel charged S£50 for a single, and S£101 for a double with a shower-toilet combination, small water bottles and fans. A few rooms are also said to have air-coolers that generate more noise than cool air. A lunch of chicken or fish with chips and bread costs S£25. Breakfast is not usually available.

Places to Stay – top end

The *Acropole Hotel* (tel 72680, night calls on 72026; telex 22190 ACROP SD) is run by George, a Greek guy who invariably smiles when you meet him. He must be happy – his hotel is the unofficial centre for many of the development aid and refugee relief workers and nearly always full of expatriates. George has greatly assisted several international agencies in expediting communications and providing information. Rooms cost S£121 a single and S£160 a double, including full board. Rates are official, so bank receipts showing official money exchange must be presented.

If you are not staying there, it's worth stopping by for tea and a chat with some of the guests. Everybody there seems to have an interesting story to tell about some part of the Sudan. Unfortunately, much of the main building was damaged when the hotel was bombed in mid-1988. At the time of writing, only the annexe was open.

Khartoum has four international category hotels: the *Hilton*, the *Meridien*, the *Grand* and the *Friendship Palace*. All have similarly high standards, and their rates range from US$110 to US$130 a single and US$130 to US$150 a double. The Friendship Palace is renowned for its concerts and has fantastic rooftop views of the Blue and White Niles. Once again, official exchange receipts must be shown if you're paying in Sudanese pounds.

Places to Eat

Most restaurants in Khartoum are simple, nameless places which serve a single dish or a small variety of dishes. When you eat in these places, you first buy tokens at the cash register for the dishes you want. Then, you take the tokens to the kitchen window and hand them to the 'cooks'. The Sudanese use bread to scoop up their food so you won't be offered eating utensils.

Also plentiful in Khartoum are Eritrean restaurants, mostly run by refugees from the northern Ethiopian province of Eritrea. Most of the restaurants are small rooms hidden behind unmarked metal doors. Furthermore, many disappear as quickly as they appear and, as they don't advertise, you must ask Eritreans to show you the way. They usually serve *ngira* – a spicy vegetable and meat concoction served with soft, flat bread.

Budget Eats There is a group of drinks bars on Sharia Malik, between Zubeir Pasha St and UN Square. One juice stand here specialises in freshly squeezed orange juice, another serves both orange and lemon juices and a third sells lemon drinks. drinks. There is also a stand which offers hot sweetened milk, mostly in the evenings.

Also in this group is a restaurant from which you can get grilled Nile perch in the mornings.

North-east of UN Square, near the Arak Hotel, *Maxim's Burgers* is Sudan's first attempt at Western-style fast food. The hamburgers are meagre, but tasty if you drown the meat in ketchup.

A cafe near the Nakiel Hotel specialises in hoshab, a Sudanese fruit cocktail. It's directly opposite the shop with the Arabic Coca-Cola signs.

Excellent spiced tea is available opposite the post office off Sharia Hashim

Bey, a couple of blocks south of UN Square. This place is very busy between 9 and 10 am.

The *Garden Restaurant*, in front of the El Kabani Hotel, is a popular place, although the 'garden' is small with only a couple of trees.

On Sayed Abdul Rahman St, just west of the Sharia Malik corner, is a great place for fresh milk and yogurt. A stand in front sells fried fish in the evenings.

A block further north you'll find an Eritrean tea house where specially spiced Eritrean tea is served from 7 am. You sit on rope beds under a thatched bamboo awning and watch squawking chickens scramble away from the woman stirring a big pot in the corner. The tea house entrance is the last unmarked blue metal door on your left.

Around the corner, back towards Sharia Malik, you'll find freshly baked bread for sale at night and in the morning.

Nearby is a great eating place for those on a tight budget who want a taste of typical Sudanese cuisine. It's the place with the bright purple doors and a Michael Jackson photograph on the wall. They serve fuul, addis, kebab and kalawi. As with all Sudanese eating places, there are no knives and forks.

A chewing tobacco shop, a little to the north up Sharia Malik, is popular with Sudanese men. They buy the tobacco eagerly – the vendor can hardly cram the sludgelike product into little plastic bags fast enough to meet the demand. Almost next door is a typical Sudanese bakery.

A fish restaurant opposite the Bulgarian Trade Mission serves fresh fish with cucumbers and yogurt every morning, while the *Casa Blanka* serves decent omelettes and great ice cream. Try the mango ice cream.

Another ice cream place recommended by travellers is the *Silvermoon* in Souk Two. It's clean, well maintained and even has an espresso machine. They serve generous scoops of four types of ice cream.

Restaurants There is a Chinese restaurant in the New Extension on Street 15, near the airport. A complete, typically Chinese meal costs about S£50 to S£60.

Nearby, a Korean restaurant serves traditional Korean food, including octopus. It's in the *Africa Hotel*, just past the entrance to the airport road and near the exit to Street 30. Look for the hotel sign and red lantern.

You can also get a meal at the *Sudan Club* at 7 am, 1 pm and 6 pm. The Nubian cook makes a mean but delicious beef curry with bananas, vegetables and peanuts for S£8. (See the Clubs section for information about this place.)

Some of the big hotels have Western-style restaurants. The *Grand Hotel* has chicken and roast beef sandwiches that are renowned among some expatriates. But breakfast, served in a large, mysteriously quiet dining room, is overpriced.

At the Hilton Hotel, the *Ivory Room*'s S£27 all-you-can-eat Friday buffet is one of the best deals in town. The regular restaurant offers carefully prepared three course meals, with delicious European and Sudanese dishes ranging in price from S£30 to S£40.

The Friendship Palace Hotel serves club sandwiches and tuna fish sandwiches in the *Tuti Cafe*. There is also a nightly S£28 buffet in the restaurant.

Activities

Most of the major hotels operate two to three hour cruises for about S£30 and these are highly recommended by all who have taken them. The Acropole Hotel offers a cruise every Friday at 10 am for which you need to book, at least one day in advance, with George. The Hilton Hotel's sunrise cruise is available every Friday and Saturday, and the Grand Hotel also offers a cruise. Check with the hotels for their latest schedules.

Getting There & Away

In 1989, travel to western Sudan was becoming extremely difficult because of the possible civil war in Darfur and Kordofan provinces, border problems with Chad, Libyan intervention and the breaking of relations with the Central African Republic. Although foreign aid workers and related personnel were, at the time of writing, still able to gain access, travel permits were no longer being issued to travellers. However, if the situation improves, the information given in this section regarding travel to western Sudan will probably again be pertinent.

The civil strife also makes travelling from Khartoum to points south of Kosti impossible. Travel permits are not being issued. John Garang's SPLM forces have shot down planes to Juba, so that service has been discontinued.

Air For details of flights into, around and out of the Sudan, refer to the Getting There & Away and Getting Around chapters at the start of the Sudan section.

If you're arriving in Khartoum on an international flight, the entry procedure is simple. Before going through passport control, you have to fill out two arrival registration forms, which you'll find on the side counters next to the tourist information booth. Sometimes, the booth has maps and information about Khartoum.

The Sudan is a 'dry' country. The customs officials are strict about alcohol and will confiscate any liquor you have.

After customs, you can change money at the bank window on your right if you can't wait until you get into town.

Everyone flying out of Khartoum airport is required to have a Civil Aviation Permit (S£75) and, if you're flying with an airline other than Sudan Airways or EgyptAir, you also need an exit visa. These requirements are subject to change, so double check them with a travel agency or airline in Khartoum before departure.

For flights to Cairo, a Location Certificate must be obtained from the agency or airline office from which you bought your ticket or confirmed your reservation.

Bus The companies with the best buses are Safina (considered the best), Arrow and Taysir – their vehicles have comfortable seats, occasional air-conditioning and complimentary tea. (Bring your own cup for the tea, unless you want to share the 'public' cup with potential TB carriers!) Fares range from S£35 to S£50.

Taysir's tickets can be bought from the company's city office, in the same building as the French Cultural Centre on Sharia el Qasr. The other companies have their offices at Souk Shabi.

Book your bus tickets at least a day in advance.

It's advisable to have a Sudanese buy tickets for you because the bus companies aren't keen to have foreigners on their buses. With foreigners aboard, the bus is delayed at each checkpoint while the foreigners' permits are checked.

Heading north, a bus to Karima leaves from behind the GPO in Omdurman every Saturday and Tuesday at 10 am. The 24 hour journey across the desert and through oases to Karima, with stops at Shendi, Atbara and Abu Hamed, costs S£15 for a seat in the front and S£11 for a seat towards the back.

If you're heading east or north-east, Halfa Express seems to have the most frequent departures for Wad Medani, Gedaref and Kassala. The buses to Kassala, all of which stop at Wad Medani, Gedaref and Showak, take seven to 10 hours, depending on the number of police checkpoints along the way. Buses for Wad Medani, Gedaref, Kassala and Port Sudan leave from Souk Shabi in south Khartoum between 6 and 7.30 am each day. None of the buses go all the way to Port Sudan on the same day.

Two types of bus make the trip west to El Obeid. Local buses, which are Bedford truck chassis with windowless bodies, travel five days a week. When the sandstorms come, tarps are tied over the sides in a futile attempt to keep out the dust. The second type of bus, run by the Military Transport Corporation, leaves every two days and has real windows. Both buses cost about S£30, depending on fuel shortages.

Buses leave for El Obeid from the Omdurman souk five days a week, except during the rainy season. The buses can't be driven at night because the road is nothing more than a track in the desert, so the trip can take 24 hours if the bus doesn't reach El Obeid by sunset. Take warm clothing in case you have to camp in the desert with the rest of the passengers.

The Sugipto and Taysir companies operate daily buses to Kosti and Sennar. They leave daily from Souk Shabi in south Khartoum, take 4½ hours and cost S£10.

Train Four trains a week go north. The train to Wadi Halfa departs at 6.40 am on Sunday and Wednesday, stops at Abu Hamed, then continues across the Nubian Desert to Wadi Halfa. The other train goes to Karima, departing at 10.45 am on Sunday and Wednesday and takes seven to nine hours. You must book a day in advance for these destinations.

Where the east and north-east is concerned, there is a train from Khartoum via Sennar to Gedaref and points beyond, but the trip is agonisingly slow.

The train for El Obeid in western Sudan goes via Kosti and supposedly leaves on Tuesdays at 5.15 pm. It continues on to Nyala, leaving at 10.30 am on Mondays.

The journey to El Obeid usually takes 31 hours but, during the rainy season (May to September), it can take as long as 63 hours. Check with the Khartoum stationmaster for the latest details. The train to Wau has stopped running.

Truck If you travelling to the north, trucks for Karima and Dongola leave from Post Office Square in Omdurman. The trip to Dongola takes more than a day.

Trucks to all east and north-east destinations leave from Souk Shabi.

Top: Fruit market, Khartoum (SW)
Left: Tomb of the Mahdi, Omdurman (SW)
Right: A White Nile 'ferry', Khartoum (SW)

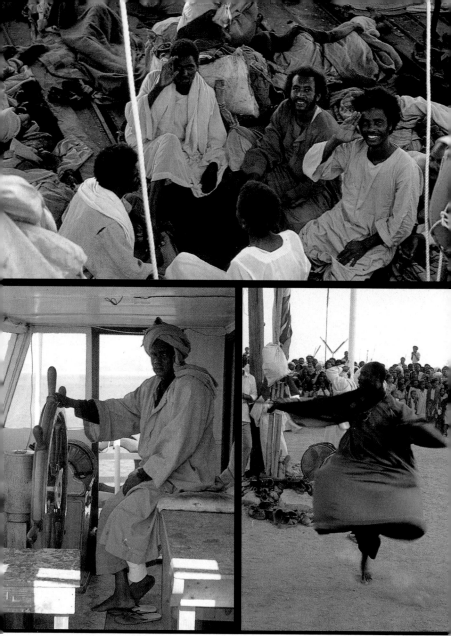

Top: Passing time on the ferry, Lake Nasser (SW)
Left: Mohammed the ferry driver, Lake Nasser (SW)
Right: A whirling dervish, Omdurman (SW)

Trucks for destinations in western Sudan leave from the souk in Omdurman.

Getting Around

Airport Transport The airport is 10 to 15 minutes from central Khartoum, about S£15 by taxi.

There are also buses to town from the main road – just flag one down. The trip costs 25 pt, but the buses are often full by this point because they are coming from the outlying suburbs.

Bus & Box Buses, boxes (pick-up trucks) and taxis are the main modes of transport around Khartoum. Most buses and boxes begin and end their trips in and around UN Square. I have attempted to indicate as clearly as possible the destinations of the transport available in each corner of the square. However, as I walked around the square and asked the drivers their routes, I got some very strange responses. My efforts in UN Square were not wasted though – I collected the following information. All buses on Sharia el Taiyar Zulfu, in front of the Arak Hotel, go to

Omdurman. That includes the big green bus mentioned in previous sections.

Boxes to Omdurman leave from the corner of Sharia el Gamhuriyya and Sharia el Huriyya.

Buses to Souk Shabi in south Khartoum leave from Souk Arabi, which is little more than a dirt lot near the Hotel Nilein.

Boxes to Souk Shabi leave from a dirt lot opposite the mosque on Sharia el Taiyar Zulfu.

Boxes to the New Extension and the airport leave from Sharia el Jami.

If in doubt, ask an intelligent-looking person for directions. If that person doesn't speak English, say *otobees* (for bus), or *box le*, then your destination, shrug your shoulders and look confused. The Sudanese are very helpful and you'll eventually get where you want to go.

Taxi If you're in a hurry (and that's a difficult state of mind in the Sudan) or just frustrated, take one of the battered yellow taxis. At S£20 for a ride across town, they're relatively cheap. The fare to the airport is usually about S£30 to S£40.

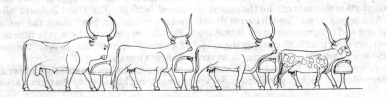

Northern Sudan

The 1628 km stretch of Nile between Wadi Halfa and Khartoum is often overlooked by travellers, yet some of the finest ruins of ancient Sudan can be found along this route. The kingdoms of Cush, Meroe and Napata all rose in this region and, although the pyramids, temples and palaces they left behind don't rival those of Egypt, they are untouched by the commercialism which surrounds the Egyptian monuments and are well worth visiting. You are left alone to wander, undisturbed by anxious guides and con artists selling trinkets and camel rides. It is this opportunity for solitary exploration that makes these sites so appealing.

Northern Sudan is also home to the distinctive people of Nubia and several Arab tribes. As much of Nubia was submerged by the waters of Lake Nasser (which was created by the construction of the Aswan High Dam), the Nubian people now live throughout Upper Egypt and northern Sudan. About 50,000 were resettled at Khashm el Girba, on the Atbara River, when the dam was being built. Despite the diaspora, the Nubians have retained their unique language and many of their traditions.

The two predominant Arab tribes in northern Sudan are the Shaigia and the Gaalyeen. The town of Shendi is the main centre of the Gaalyeen, who are scattered across the region from Atbara to the Sixth Cataract. The Shaigia are dispersed throughout northern Sudan amongst the Nubians and the Gaalyeen.

To truly experience this part of Sudan, you have to forgo the comparative comforts of the train trip for the rigours of truck or bus travel through barren desert plains and meagre oases on roads that are seldom more than faint tracks in the sand. Between Dongola and Karima, however, you can take a break from bouncing around in the back of a truck to cruise up or down the Nile on an old steamer for a few days.

WADI HALFA

There is not much to Wadi Halfa. Basically, it's a transit point where the the Lake Nasser steamer from Aswan meets the Sudan Railway's train for Khartoum. Near the dock, there is an ice plant and cold storage house built by the People's Republic of China in the 1970s for a then, and still, nascent fishing industry. The Chinese even provided 35 two tonne fishing boats.

You will be eagerly met at the quay by taxi drivers and moneychangers. The latter will happily change your excess Egyptian pounds at a better rate than the bank, while the former will try to take as many of your Egyptian pounds as possible for the ride into town. Try furious bargaining. Otherwise, just start the long, hot walk to town and hope someone takes pity on you and offers a free ride. It's a few km; just follow the tracks in the sand. Don't head for the buildings you see ahead and to the left – that's the fish processing plant. You can also change money with the shopkeepers in town.

Places to Stay & Eat

The town's two basic but clean hotels are near the train station. The *Hotel Nile* (also called the Nile Hotel) costs about S£13 a night; most travellers put their beds on the verandah. Simple meals of baked beans and a few chunks of meat cost S£4, tea is 50 pt, two eggs are S£6 and bread is 50 pt. The *Hotel Bohaera* also serves meals and costs about the same. Even if you don't stay here, take time out for a soothing cup of tea (75 pt) in the cool Bohaera lounge.

However, before dropping your gear at one of these hotels, go to the train station

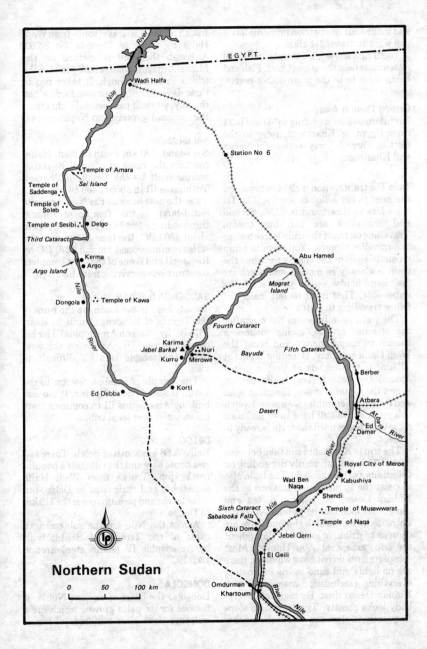

EGYPT

Nile River

Wadi Halfa

Station No 6

Temple of Amara
Sai Island
Temple of Saddenga
Temple of Soleb
Temple of Sesibi
Delgo
Third Cataract
Kerma
Argo Island
Argo
Dongola
Temple of Kawa

Abu Hamed

Mograt Island

Fourth Cataract
Karima
Jebel Barkal
Nuri
Kurru
Merowe
Korti
Ed Debba

Bayuda

Fifth Cataract

Berber

Atbara

Desert

Atbara River

Ed Damer

Royal City of Meroe

Wad Ben Naqa
Kabushiya
Shendi
Temple of Musawwarat
Temple of Naqa
Jebel Qerri
Sixth Cataract
Sabalooka Falls
Abu Dom

El Geili

Omdurman
Khartoum
Blue Nile

Northern Sudan

0   50   100 km

and make your reservation immediately if you want to travel 1st class.

You'll find a few juice stands and small restaurants near the market area. Fish and beans seem to be the main dishes here.

Getting There & Away

For information on getting to Wadi Halfa from Egypt or Khartoum, refer to the Getting There & Away sections for Aswan and Khartoum.

Train The train station is right in town and the boat ticket office is nearby. The 1st class fare to Khartoum is S£56. Second and 3rd class are bad but cheap. Travelling on top of the train is free but, as one traveller reports: 'You have to jump on out of sight of the conductor when the train is already in motion and there are few hand-holds. . .with your stuff it's impossible. That must be left inside for fellow travellers to watch.'

The train usually leaves the day after the steamer arrives, giving visitors a chance to spend money and boost the Wadi Halfa economy. Boarding begins at 10 am, but hundreds of people crowd around the gate several hours earlier. When the signal is given, the gates open and everyone scrambles for a seat. Even if you get one, you still have to sit and wait for several hours until the train is ready to leave.

The trip to Khartoum can take between 32 and 75 hours, primarily depending on the number of breakdowns. The train also stops at the 10 numbered stations in the Nubian Desert. At Station 6, tea and sometimes food can be purchased. Local untreated water, which the Sudanese are content to drink, is available throughout the trip, except at Abu Hamed. Most compartments do not have windows, there are no lights and sand swirls in, coating everything (including passengers) with Nubian Desert dust. By nightfall, everybody looks ghostly. The train also stops frequently to clear sand from the tracks.

Truck You can also travel south from Wadi Halfa by truck to Dongola for S£60. Although the road is marked on the Michelin map, it doesn't really exist so the trip is extremely rough. It takes two to three days, so bring your own food. Along the way, you will pass several sights from the ancient Egyptian and Napatan eras.

SAI ISLAND

Sai Island, 190 km south of Wadi Halfa, contains the ruins of a small Egyptian temple built by the Egyptian Pharaoh Tuthmosis III in about 1460 BC.

On the east bank of the Nile, opposite Sai Island, is the Temple of Amara. Superseding a fort built there by Seti I in about 1300 BC, the temple was one of a series commissioned around 1270 BC by Ramses II and is one of the most complete constructions surviving from his reign.

SADDENGA & SOLEB

Twenty km further south are the ruins of the Temple of Saddenga, built in about 1370 BC by Pharaoh Amenophis III for his consort Queen Tiy. As it's on the west bank, the temple is a bit difficult to visit.

The Temple of Soleb, a few km to the south, is also difficult to visit. It too was built by Amenophis III to commemorate his victories over local tribes.

DELGO

Delgo is 68 km south of Soleb. There is a rest house here and the village is a popular truck stop. Trucks from Wadi Halfa sometimes end their trips at Delgo, but other trucks and pick-ups cover the 110 km to Dongola.

Across the Nile are the subterranean ruins of the Temple of Sesibi, built by Amenophis IV (Akhenaten) around 1360 BC.

DONGOLA

Dongola, the heart of ancient Nubia, is famous for its palm groves, which are a welcome sight after hundreds of km of desert. The date harvest in September is quite a show. Young boys from the town scale the palms, knives clenched between their teeth, and cut down clusters of dates.

There's a colourful fruit and vegetable market behind the main square and, occasionally, nomads come in from the desert to buy and sell camels, sugar, tea and other goods.

On the east bank there are the ruins of the Temple of Kawa, which was the repository of gifts for the Cushite ruler Taharqa. Taharqa was king of the Land of Cush from 688 to 663 BC and was also the last Pharaoh of Egypt's 25th dynasty (he lost the country to invading Assyrians). A ferry takes you across the river.

Places to Stay & Eat

There is a *Rest House* and a couple of lakondas near the Dongola Hospital. Accommodation at the pleasant *Hotel El Mana* costs S£5 a night; rooms have fans and there are clean cold showers. You can also camp along the banks of the Nile.

Tea houses are found on every corner and you can buy cheap food at the cafes opposite the daily market.

The town also has a well-stocked pharmacy.

Getting There & Away

The steamer to Karima has an erratic schedule; it may not run at all from March to June when the level of the Nile is low. If you do get on it, the calm, four day journey to Karima is perfect for recuperating from the truck or bus trip. On the other hand, if there's no sign of the steamer and you don't feel like hanging around Dongola, you could always hop on another truck or bus. The bus between Wadi Halfa and Dongola follows desert tracks and costs S£60. A bus between Dongola and Ed Debba costs S£40 and the bus fare between Ed Debba and Karima is S£25. Bring a lot of water for the Ed Debba to Karima trip.

KARIMA

Karima is a busy market town with a population of over 15,000. The market is held twice a week and attracts people from the surrounding villages. But, apart from the souk and a couple of Coca-Cola stores offering a brief respite from midday summer temperatures of 50°C, there is little of interest in the town itself. Outside of town, however, there are several important archaeological sites dating from the ancient Egyptian and Napatan kingdoms.

Jebel Barkal

Two km south of Karima is Jebel Barkal, a 100 metre hill considered sacred by the 18th dynasty Egyptians. In the 13th century BC, Tuthmosis III and Amenophis II built the Temple of Amun at the foot of the hill and it remained a religious centre for the next 1000 years.

Pyramid Tombs

The pyramid tombs of Kurru, south of the Temple of Amun, were built by the Napatan King Piankhi long after Egyptian pyramid construction ceased. The pyramids are much smaller than those in Egypt and have suffered terribly from looting.

There are other pyramids opposite Karima in the village of Nuri, although the pyramidal section of these tombs has crumbled. Ferries cross the Nile regularly from Karima and the tombs are 10 km upstream and two km inland. There are usually boxes available to get you there.

Places to Stay & Eat

Accommodation in Karima is limited to a *Rest House* at the local canning company, the basic *Taharqa Hotel* in town and the *El Nassar Hotel*, which has dorm beds for S£4. The food at the restaurant on the main square is good.

Getting There & Away

Buses and trucks leave Karima a few times a week on the one day journey through the Bayuda Desert to Khartoum.

Twice a week, a 3rd class, 12 hour train trip to Abu Hamed meets the Wadi Halfa to Khartoum train.

The steamer from Karima to Dongola stops along the way at the ruins of Old Dongola.

ABU HAMED

Missing the train to Khartoum or Wadi Halfa is the only reason to stay at the railroad junction town of Abu Hamed. Next to the railway station is a government *Rest House* with a huge verandah and showers. To stay there, you need to obtain prior permission from the police station near the mosque.

The nightly arrival of the train is an interesting sight. A market, illuminated by little kerosene lanterns, suddenly materialises out of nowhere around the train. You can usually buy fruit, vegetables and bread.

There is also an hourly ferry to the former Christian stronghold of Mograt Island, the largest island in the Nile.

ATBARA

The Atbara River flows down from the Ethiopian highlands to meet the Nile here. Atbara is also the junction of two of Sudan's major train routes, the Khartoum to Wadi Halfa and the Atbara to Port Sudan lines.

The railway dominates life in this city of 75,000 people. It's not surprising then that Atbara is a major centre for the Sudanese railway unions and was the scene of an attempted coup by pro-Communist army officers in 1971.

The city figured prominently in Sudan's colonial history. The 1898 Battle of Atbara was the first major battle between the British and the Mahdists since the defeat of Gordon. In April of that year, the Mahdist army marched down the Nile to meet Kitchener's Anglo-Egyptian expedition at Atbara. The Mahdists were completely routed; 2000 of them were killed when Kitchener and his army attacked, with superior modern artillery, to the rousing music of Scottish pipes and English flutes, drums and brass instruments. The young Winston Churchill, who witnessed the battle as a war correspondent, later wrote a book about his experiences called *The River War*.

After the victory, Kitchener marched on to take Khartoum. British officials settled in Atbara, expanding the railway and building several large colonial-style houses which can still be seen. The Anglican church in Atbara is one of the few in northern Sudan.

Atbara is of particular interest to railway buffs because it's something of a graveyard for the steam locomotives that died during Nimeiri's rule. He supposedly ignored the railways, the railway unions and the city itself because the Communist Party was, and still is, very strong there.

An interesting camel and crafts market is held on Saturdays at nearby Ed Damer. To get there, take a box from Atbara.

There are ferries from town across the confluence of the Atbara and Nile rivers.

Places to Stay

Atbara offers few places to stay since the popular Hotel Astoria burned down in 1984. There is a small hotel next to the site of the former Astoria which costs 50 pt per night.

The *Hotel Atbara*, next to the Watania Cinema, is recommended. The nearby *Youth Hostel*, on the other hand, is run-down and dirty. The more up-market colonial-style *Rest House* on Main Ave is 10 minutes from the train station.

Getting There & Away

Bus The very bumpy daily bus to Khartoum costs S£13 and takes eight hours.

Train The 12 hour trip on the extremely crowded train to Khartoum costs S£18 in 1st class, S£12 in 2nd and S£8 in 3rd.

The train to Port Sudan takes 18 hours to cover the 474 km from Atbara, but the trip is not recommended. If you want to skip Port Sudan, you could leave the train at Haiya junction, but catching a bus from there might be difficult.

ROYAL CITY OF MEROE

The ruins of the capital of the ancient Kingdom of Meroe are about 100 km south of Atbara. The kings of Meroe lived here from 592 BC to 350 AD and gained fame in the Greco-Roman world for their prosperous iron industry and agricultural development. Their architecture was highly developed and reflected extensive Egyptian influence. Hieroglyphic inscriptions on the ruins of pyramids, palaces and temples in the area show that the Meroites worshipped Egyptian deities. The Meroites also developed their own script, which has been only partly deciphered.

The Kingdom of Meroe ended in 350 AD with the rise of King Ezana of the Abyssinian kingdom of Axum and his armies' subsequent invasion of Meroe.

In the 1820s, the Italian explorer Ferlini arrived in what was left of the royal city with the Turko-Egyptian forces of Mohammed Ali. Ferlini was specifically looking for treasure but managed to find only a single cache of gold in pyramid No 6, which he smuggled back to Milan for auction. In his greedy search, Ferlini hacked the tops off 40 pyramid tombs! Although his vandalism is still evident, these pyramids are in better shape than those at Nuri and Kurru.

Between the Nile and the train tracks stands the Temple of Amun, and traces of the nearby royal palaces and swimming pool. The ruins of another temple are about 1½ km east of the Temple of Amun, and the royal pyramids, where the Meroites buried their dead, are in the desert, five km to the east.

To get to the ruins, take the train to Kabushiya, then local transportation to Bagrawiya, the village near the site. There is a *Rest House* nearby.

SHENDI

The town of Shendi is 70 km south of the Royal City of Meroe. Shendi has a government *Rest House* and is the starting point for visits to the Meriotic temples of Musawwarat and Naqa. Local transport goes to both places from Shendi, as well as from Wad Ben Naqa, a village to the south. There is also frequent transport to and from Khartoum.

In 1988, a group of American aid workers set out to explore this area in two Land Rovers. While stuck on a soft, sandy part of the road, they were approached by a group of camel riders, faces covered by long scarves, who pulled out daggers and swords and stole all they could carry from the Americans and their vehicles.

Temple of Musawwarat

The site of the Temple of Musawwarat, about 20 km south of Shendi, features a reconstructed temple complex and the remains of a palace. Statues of elephants and lions are scattered in the sand near the reservoirs (*hafirs*) that the Meroites dug to provide the area with water.

Temple of Naqa

The Temple of Naqa is 40 km east of the Nile and 55 km south-west of Shendi. A kiosk at the temple reflects the extent of Roman influence in the Sudan – on the back wall of the temple, carvings show that the Meroites worshipped Apedemek, a lion-god.

SABALOOKA FALLS

These beautiful but seldom visited waterfalls are at the Sixth Cataract of the Nile, about 50 km north of Khartoum. If you enjoy kayaking and just happen to have a kayak with you, this place is recommended. A British expatriate kayaker in Khartoum visits Sabalooka regularly and has somehow avoided getting bilharzia. To get there, leave the bus at Jebel Qerri or Abu Dom and persuade a local to take you the rest of the way.

Western Sudan

Travel through western Sudan is rough, tough and absolutely fascinating. This diverse region covers an area of 549,579 square km, from the deserts and plains of Kordofan to the mountains and hills of Darfur, and is populated by more than six million people from as many as 23 tribes and ethnic groups. These include the Arab Baggara tribes of Northern Kordofan, the African Nuba people of the Nuba mountains and the black Saharan nomads of the Zaghawa tribe of Northern Darfur.

Most of the land is harsh desert nurturing only thorny *heskanit* grass and acacia bushes. The tiny heskanit thorns stick to your skin and clothes, and the grass is brutal to extract. In the midst of this apparent bleakness, however, there are beautiful lakes, mountains, hills and lush palm groves.

Little is known of the early history of the provinces of Kordofan and Darfur because the region has no ruins of ancient palaces and temples from bygone kingdoms and dynasties.

Until Islam was introduced here in the 16th century, most of the scattered tribes and groups were isolated from each other. By 1596, the dynasty of Sultan Suleiman Solong had established itself in Darfur and united the Fur people, converting them to Islam. The Fur Sultanate thrived for the next 320 years, fending off challenges from the Fung Sultanate and from the Abyssinians to the east. In 1916, it was overthrown by Anglo-Egyptian forces.

El Obeid, the capital of Kordofan, was the Mahdi's first political centre. It was there that he decimated the smaller, weaker forces of Colonel Hicks in 1883 and consolidated his political and military forces before marching to Khartoum.

Today, the towns and villages of Kordofan and Darfur are still strongholds

for Mahdiyism. Until the June 1989 coup, the Umma Party, one of Sudan's foremost political groupings, was headed by the great-grandson of the Mahdi, Sadiq al Mahdi; the party has a big following in western Sudan.

Over the last few years, drought and famine in Kordofan, Darfur and neighbouring Chad have displaced or killed hundreds of thousands of people. The United Nations estimated that over 400,000 Sudanese had to leave their villages in search of food and water. At the same time, thousands of refugees swarmed into Sudan, fleeing war and hunger in Chad. In 1985 and 1986, food and medical aid was rushed into the area from all over the world.

Even in the face of such persisting problems, numerous travellers and expatriate relief workers speak of the incredible hospitality and friendliness of the Sudanese. The people in this region, suffering such severe hardship, still share what little food and drink they have with visitors. Do not abuse the privilege of experiencing Sudanese hospitality. Give your host at least a token of thanks, such as a small gift. The gesture alone means a lot.

EL OBEID

El Obeid, a city of 200,000 people, is surrounded by inhospitable desert. Once the Mahdi's capital, El Obeid is also famous as the 'gum arabic capital of the world'; as well, it has the second and third best football teams in the Sudan.

For those yearning to know, gum arabic is used in the manufacture of ink and food thickeners. It's also one of the ingredients in the soluble capsules of some pain killers and other drugs. The gum arabic is extracted from little balls hanging from the branches of acacia trees.

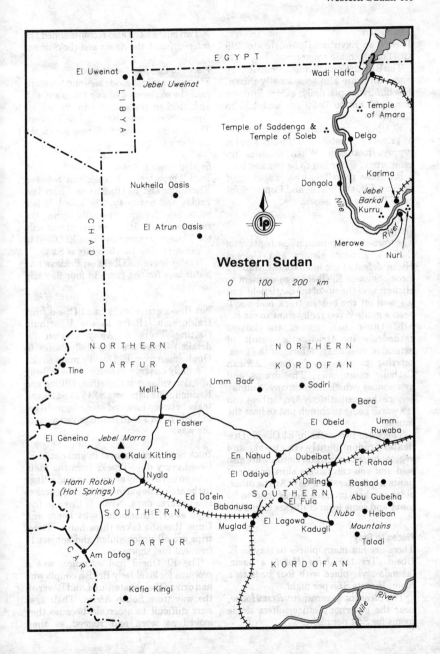

EGYPT

El Uweinat
Jebel Uweinat

LIBYA

Wadi Halfa

Temple of Amara

Temple of Saddenga & Temple of Soleb

Delgo

CHAD

Nukheila Oasis

Dongola

Karima

Jebel Barkal

Kurru

El Atrun Oasis

Nile River

Western Sudan

0   100   200 km

Merowe

Nuri

NORTHERN DARFUR

NORTHERN KORDOFAN

Tine

Mellit

Umm Badr

Sodiri

Bara

El Fasher

El Obeid

Umm Ruwaba

El Geneina

Jebel Marra

Kalu Kitting

Nyala

En Nahud

Dubeibat

Er Rahad

El Odaiya

Dilling

Rashad

*Hami Rotoki
(Hot Springs)*

Ed Da'ein

Babanusa

El Fula

SOUTHERN

Abu Gubeiha

Heiban

SOUTHERN DARFUR

Muglad

El Lagowa

Kadugli

Nuba Mountains

Talodi

C A R

Am Dafog

K O R D O F A N

Kafia Kingi

River

Information

There's an Egyptian Consulate (tel 249 4167) on the main square.

The British Council runs a small library where films are also occasionally shown. The library is open daily, except Fridays, from 8.30 am to 12.30 pm and 4.30 to 6.30 pm.

El Obeid's only electricity is provided by private generators and the city's water supply fluctuates. When it dries up completely, water has to be trucked in.

For those travellers who cannot exist without TV, the Syrian and Coptic clubs have TV sets and generators.

Things to See

The town's small museum has displays on Sudan's ancient history and Colonel Hicks' defeat at the hands of the Mahdi's forces. Outside El Obeid, a monument to Hicks marks the site of the battlefield, but it's well off the beaten track and you'll need a guide if you really want to see it.

El Obeid has one of the largest cathedrals in Africa, the result of extensive missionary efforts in the area, catering to the town's large African Catholic community. The drums and xylophones which accompany Sunday services have a distinctly African beat and it's worth going to church just to hear the music.

There are two souks in El Obeid. One deals predominantly in meat and vegetables, but cloth and clothing are also sold and you can have a shirt or pair of pants made there in a day. At the other, older market, produce prices tend to be lower and some local crafts are available.

Places to Stay

There are not many places to stay in El Obeid. Try the *John Hotel*, a basic, lakonda-style place with four beds to a room. It costs S£5 per night.

The pleasant government *Rest House*, near the governor's office, offers single rooms for S£7 per night.

Travellers have also recommended the *International*, the *Arous* and the *Shikan*.

Places to Eat

There are several good cafes and tea stalls near the souks, as well as a takeaway fish and chicken restaurant and an old ice cream shop which also sells beef burgers. The best place to eat Sudanese food is the *Banker's Club*.

Getting There & Away

Train Three trains a week run between Khartoum and El Obeid – on Thursday, Friday and Saturday. The schedule is a bit erratic though, especially during the rainy season, which often means that only the Thursday train runs from El Obeid to Khartoum. The 1st class fare is S£45.

Trains leave El Obeid on Fridays and Saturdays for the three to four day trip to Nyala.

Bus Buses arrive daily in El Obeid from Omdurman. (Refer to the Khartoum Getting There & Away section for details.) There are also daily buses to Omdurman from El Obeid's main souk.

A daily bus travels south to the railway junction villages of Dubeibat, Dilling and Kadugli. The trip costs S£15 to S£20 and takes between four and seven hours to get to Kadugli on a road that is paved most of the way.

Truck Souk lorries travel in and out of El Obeid every day. Trucks from the main souk go to virtually every town and village in the area. The journey to El Fasher takes two to three days, Nyala is three to five days away, Khartoum is 24 hours and Umm Ruwaba takes three hours. These trips are all unscheduled and subject to frequent fuel shortages.

The El Obeid fuel situation was a problem for an elderly British couple who had driven their beaten-up Land Rover all the way from South Africa. Their ages were difficult to ascertain because they looked as worn and rugged as their vehicle. They told me that, on arrival in El Obeid, they had to change money at the bank in order to buy diesel fuel for the Land Rover. However, there wasn't any fuel, so two of the bank managers took a rubber tube and siphoned fuel out of the bank's supply for them. The couple also said that when they were camping out, the lorry drivers would stop, toot their horns and ask, 'Are you OK?'.

UMM RUWABA

This little town is 135 km east of El Obeid along a terrible road but can also be reached by train from Khartoum. Umm Ruwaba has a small but interesting camel market at which members of the Arab Baza'a tribe sell their camels. The town is also home to some of the more African Jawa'ama tribe. The two groups seem to stay away from each other.

THE NUBA MOUNTAINS

Everyone who has travelled in this region raves about the beautiful scenery and the fascinating Nuba people. Scattered throughout the mountain villages where they practise terrace farming, the Nuba remained isolated from the modern world until quite recently and have managed to retain most of their traditional ways. Body painting and scarring, female circumcision and bloody wrestling matches are common.

The photo-journalist Leni Riefenstahl assembled a beautifully photographed account of the Nuba called *The People of Kau*. Her photographs of the naked Nuba and their wrestling matches and courting dances piqued the curiosity of many travellers and accelerated the Nuba's exposure to the outside world.

The Sudanese government, ever mindful of its development and modernisation efforts and embarrassed by this display of traditionalism, attempted to impede visits to the Nuba Mountains by insisting that foreigners obtain travel permits and leave their cameras in Kadugli. The government has also embarked on a programme to clothe the Nuba.

There are a few obvious points to take into consideration if you're visiting this region, the most important of which is to show respect for the traditional ways of these people. This is a rather contentious issue for travellers because the influx of inquisitive Westerners is already having an effect. These days, much to the displeasure of the Nuba elders, the younger men paint themselves and perform their dances for dollars with little regard for Nuba tradition.

If you wish to take photographs, always ask first and remember that the Nuba are people, not museum pieces or circus performers to be gawked at.

Er Rahad

The town of Er Rahad, although relatively commercialised and not particularly noteworthy, is a good starting point for treks into the Nuba Mountains. The best part of town is the lake. Here, you can buy wonderful eel steaks to eat by the water. Accommodation in Er Rahad takes the form of a lakonda-style hotel.

The trip on one of the daily souk lorries from El Obeid to Er Rahad costs S£5. A common truck route in this region runs south from Er Rahad through part of the Nuba Mountains to Sidra, Karling, Rashad, Abu Gubeiha, Kologi, Tosi and Talodi. All these towns and villages have good souks and most have some sort of rest house. The trucks run irregularly during the rainy season.

Jebel Ed Duair

Before reaching Sidra, the souk lorry will pass Jebel Ed Duair. It's a great mountain for climbing but only for the most intrepid.

Rashad

Rashad is a gorgeous place so, if you have the time, it's definitely worth a visit. You can catch a souk lorry from Rashad to Horad Delab.

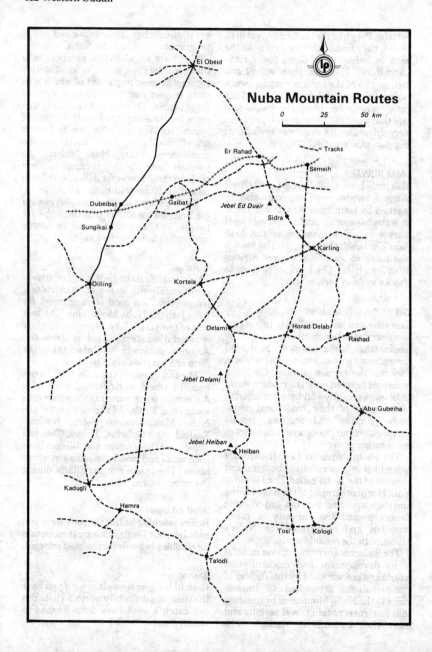

Nuba Mountain Routes

0   25   50 km

---- = Tracks

El Obeid

Er Rahad

Semeih

Dubeibat

Gaibat

Jebel Ed Duair

Sidra

Sungikai

Karling

Dilling

Kortala

Delami

Horad Delab

Rashad

Jebel Delami

Abu Gubeiha

Jebel Heiban

Heiban

Kadugli

Hamra

Tosi

Kologi

Talodi

Horad Delab

From the village junction of Horad Delab, it's possible to get lorry rides to most villages in the Nuba Mountains. You can sleep overnight on a rope-net bed in the cafes and, while you're here, check out the lush palm grove.

Abu Gubeiha

Abu Gubeiha is south of Rashad. The village's highlight is the pervasive aroma of mangoes and guavas from the nearby fruit groves.

Heiban

The village of Heiban is at the base of Jebel Heiban, the Sudan's third highest mountain (Mt Kinyeti is the highest), at the centre of the Nuba range. Heiban is said to be the coldest place in the country.

The village is predominantly African and Christian, which explains the large number of pigs running around. If you haven't seen a pork chop in a while, this is your chance to pig out (sorry!).

Heiban to Kadugli

Souk lorries regularly travel this rough but beautiful route. The scenery is magnificent, as the road meanders through a mountain pass and groves of baobabs, palms and prickly trees. For the more adventurous, hiking would take two to three days.

Talodi to Kadugli

A British teacher raved about his bicycle ride along this 75 km route. He said that the scenery was fantastic and the experience well worth the effort. Apparently, it is possible to borrow a bicycle in Talodi and then have it returned by lorry from Kadugli.

KADUGLI

Kadugli is an important market town of 30,000 people and has a popular souk where many traditional foods and spices are sold. Kadugli is also a good point from which to begin walks or excursions into the Nuba Mountains. Souk lorries travel to the mountain villages regularly, except during the rainy season.

Places to Stay

The lakonda-style *South Kordofan Hotel* costs S£5 per night. The only other option is the government rest house called *The Palace Resthouse*.

Getting There & Away

The daily bus from El Obeid to Kadugli costs about S£20 and takes from four to seven hours.

Two buses a day to El Obeid leave Kadugli from in front of the cinema. Between Kadugli and Dilling, you pass through sorghum and sesame country.

The souk lorry route from Kadugli to El Lagowa, El Fula and Nyala has been highly recommended for its spectacular scenery. You can catch the train at El Fula – if you don't mind waiting an indefinite number of days.

EN NAHUD

The noteworthy feature of the Southern Kordofan town of En Nahud, 215 km south-west of El Obeid, is its unique limestone architecture. The government *Rest House* is the only place to stay.

EL ODAIYA

The very beautiful town of El Odaiya is 83 km south of En Nahud. There are lots of trees and green hills, especially after the rains, and the 145 km lorry ride to Babanusa is another which has been recommended for its scenery.

BABANUSA

Babanusa is a railway junction village where you can catch trains to Nyala, Er Rahad and Khartoum.

MUGLAD

A few km south of Babanusa is Muglad, which was basically an oil exploration base, complete with an airstrip and a large compound full of foreigners. Today, this erstwhile Texas-style boom town is full of refugees who, in 1988, were starving and dying at an appalling rate (see the introduction to this chapter).

BARA

There is not much to this oasis town, just north of El Obeid, except a lot of vegetable gardens. Buses going between Khartoum and El Obeid stop at Bara.

SODIRI

Sodiri is a very bleak place in the middle of the desert, 167 km north-west of Bara. It used to be the site of a large camel market, but the market and the people of Sodiri suffered greatly during the 1985 famine.

UMM BADR

This mere dot on the map, seemingly in the middle of nothing but desert, is apparently quite a surprising little place. One intrepid traveller who ventured there described it as 'a very beautiful, very green lake area where a lot of camel nomads hang out'. It is a two to three day lorry trip from El Obeid.

ED DA'EIN

Ed Da'ein is a railroad village almost 200 km west of Babanusa and the 'capital' of the nomadic Rizeigaat tribe. It's a very laid-back place with a lakonda-style hotel and friendly, hospitable people.

NYALA

Nyala was the Fur Sultanate's capital from the late 16th century. With the Fur people united under the banner of Islam, the sultanate thrived and prospered for over 300 years, partly because of Nyala's isolation from the rest of Sudan. Despite the modern railroad connection to Khartoum, the town is still an isolated outpost on the edge of the desert, at the base of a mountain range dominated by the Sudan's second highest mountain, Jebel Marra.

Information

The staff at the government tourist office in Nyala can help you plan a trek to Jebel Marra, including the purchase of a donkey, camel or horse from the souk. The tourist and registration offices are just past the radio mast.

Another good source of information about treks to Jebel Marra are the British English teachers in Nyala.

Nyala has three souks but, because of the drought and famine in the region, the main market is now only a quarter the size it was in 1985. On the other side of the wadi, however, two souks have sprung up which the locals have dubbed 'Texas' and 'Korea'. Most of the souk lorries leave from the Texas souk.

Places to Stay

The government *Rest House*, opposite the main souk, is a good place to stay if you can get permission. The rooms surround a garden courtyard, all have wash basins and you can cook in the guest house kitchen if you bring your own food.

The cheap and basic *Darfur Hotel* costs S£1.50 for a mattress on rusty springs. It's difficult to store your gear there though.

Other hotels which have been recommended by travellers include the *Deenobee Hotel*, *Hotel Zaire* and the *Andafusu Hotel*.

Camping Nyala has two unofficial camping sites. Although the land is privately owned, it is sometimes possible to camp along Wadi Nyala, among the mango trees and monkeys. The other site is under the mango trees of the Kondua Forest, about four km further down the wadi.

Places to Eat

Topping the list of eating places is the *Camp David*, near the Darfur Hotel. It serves delicious cakes, tea and milk. At the 'hole-in-the-wall', near the mosque in the centre of town, you can get veal cutlets.

Fresh food is easily purchased in the

souk. Tinned food is available in town, although it is expensive.

Getting There & Away

Nyala is the rail terminus. The tedious trip back to Khartoum could take as long as five days; for fare information, see the Khartoum section. There are no buses.

Souk lorries leave from all three markets, but the majority depart from the Texas souk. They travel to practically every imaginable destination, including the Central African Republic, Khartoum, the villages near Jebel Marra, El Fasher and El Geneina. The popular trip to El Fasher takes 1½ days.

HAMI ROTOKI

On the way to the village of Kass, you might consider making a stop at the medicinal hot springs of Hami Rotoki, near Jebel Marra. The locals claim that the water there is hot enough to make tea, yet not too hot to bathe in.

JEBEL MARRA MOUNTAINS

This beautiful mountain region of rivers and orchards is fine, hilly walking country. No two people share the same experience here, but travellers agree that the hospitality in these mountains is unrivalled.

Nyala is the starting point for a visit to Jebel Marra, an extinct volcanic crater which, at 3071 metres, is the second highest mountain in the country and the feature attraction of this area.

Food and water are no problem and you can't really get lost because the local people are always pointing you in the right direction. The locals also insist that you visit their houses and will fill your arms with fruit.

To get to Jebel Marra, take a truck from Nyala to Nyatiti, then begin your walk – just head towards the mountains. Halfway to Quaila, just past the first village, is an excellent waterfall and pool where you can camp and swim. The schoolteacher in Quaila may be able to find accommodation

for you and point you in the direction of the crater. From Quaila, you walk to the hot springs and up to the crater of Jebel Marra. Once at the edge, you go halfway round the rim before heading down again, to the crater floor. From there, you walk out through the canyon to Taratonga to catch the weekly truck to Nyala.

If you have the time, stay in Taratonga and visit some of the nearby villages. Three which are worth a look are Sunni to the north and Gandator and Kalu Kitting to the south-west. From Kalu Kitting, you can get back onto the main road at Nyama, between Nyala and Nyatiti. Here, there's a camp for the German construction gang who have been building the road. They often have transport going to Nyala and some travellers reported that they were allowed to use the camp swimming pool.

It is also possible to trek to Jebel Marra in the opposite direction. The exact route you take will naturally depend on your objectives and the available time, but the following is one possibility:

Jebel Marra Trek

Take a truck from Nyala to Menawashi (S£4), which is basically just a truck stop where several people sell food. Menawashi has no rest house, but the locals will probably offer you accommodation in their huts.

From Menawashi, it's a two hour walk over flat, scrubby land to Marshing. There's usually an empty hut or two there; ask the village schoolteacher where you can sleep. At the cafe in Marshing, you can get soup and bread for S£1 and tea for 25 pt. There's also a market on Wednesdays and Sundays.

A five hour walk from Marshing brings you to the beautiful village of Melemm. The *Rest House* is next to the police station and the very friendly police will probably supply you with firewood, water and other necessities. Melemm's market takes place on Mondays and Fridays.

The all-night truck ride from Melemm

to Deribat costs about S£5 and takes you through beautiful hills, some of which are so steep that it may be necessary to winch the truck up. There's no rest house in Deribat but the village does have several tea houses, a cafe and a Monday market.

Jawa is a two hour walk from Deribat. You may be able to find accommodation in the huge hospital. Market day in Jawa is Thursday.

About 1½ hours away is Sunni, one of the Jebel Marra's most scenic settlements. One of the four beds in Sunni's large old *Rest House* costs S£1.50. There's no souk, but a small shop sells rice, nuts, dates, cigarettes and the occasional chicken. Don't miss the 35 metre high waterfall behind the power station.

From Sunni, it's a five hour walk/scramble to Lugi. The views en route are beautiful but it gets very cold, especially at night, and there are only a few huts in the fields along the way. There's no rest house or market at Lugi, but there is a small store with basic supplies.

The next leg is the 2¼ hour walk to Taratonga through a landscape of conifers and heather which is very similar to the Scottish highlands. Taratonga itself is a picturesque little village set on wooded, grassy slopes. There's a market on Saturday and a shop which sells basic supplies. The *Rest House* is in disrepair so, if you're there during the rainy season, it's better to look for an empty hut or try the schoolhouse. The village teacher speaks English and can arrange guides to the crater for you.

It's a good idea to get a guide up to the crater. The walk usually takes three hours with a guide but could take five to eight hours if you go it alone. The same applies between the crater and the next village of Kronga (also known as Kuela), which takes about five hours with a guide but much longer if you get lost.

The walk from Kronga to the village of Khartoum takes 1½ hours. Khartoum has a Saturday market. It's another 3½ hours

to Nyatiti, with its well-stocked market, cafes, *Rest House* and transport back to Nyala.

If you lack camping equipment and/or don't fancy walking, it's possible to buy donkeys and sell them again when you're ready to leave.

A Second View of the Jebel Marra Trek
A British teacher, who made the trek after working in Ed Da'ein, Southern Darfur, reported:

The Jebel is probably the most beautiful place in that part of Sudan not affected by war. . .For those hiking on the higher slopes above the villages. . .[this] is an area that I think is a potential death-trap. . .It can be a problem finding food, water and people to ask the way. . .I hiked on Jebel Marra from Nyatiti to the crater and back again. I've never heard of anybody starving to death, but I can assure you that of the six teachers I met on the mountain who were hiking in three groups, all of them had been lost between the crater rim and Quaila and two of them had run out of water and would very likely not have come down alive if they hadn't luckily met a local man who showed them the way. As for me, I ran out of water too and was in a pretty desperate state for a while. Once you run out of water and are lost, panic can set in very quickly. Furthermore, the mental and physical deterioration your body suffers when it's dehydrated is alarmingly quick! None of us were hiking novices at the time so the difficulties we had are likely to be shared by many if not most other people. . .

December is more than two months into the dry season, so water is not going to be over-abundant outside the villages. . .take as much as you can carry.

My advice to anyone walking from Nyatiti to the crater and then to the Hot Springs: for those based in Nyala, the best place to start your hike is Nyatiti. There is a paved road from Nyala to Zalingei and all buses to Zalingei will stop at Nyatiti. The rest house is situated beyond the village on the way to Quaila about half an hour's walk from the main road. Don't go straight there though, as you need to get a letter of permission which can be obtained from the centre of the village. Nyatiti has at least one restaurant, and shops where you can buy food for the walk and even saucepans.

Top: The jebels of Kassala (SW)
Bottom: A cattle drive in eastern Sudan (SW)

Top: A camel yard in eastern Sudan (SW)
Left: Ruins of a coral building, Suakin (SW)
Right: Medical clinic in a refugee camp, eastern Sudan (SW)

Before going further, I would suggest that, when in El Fasher or Nyala, you find out from a knowledgeable foreigner or Sudanese when the village souk days are. It is a good idea to time your hike in accordance with them. On these days, the villages are much more lively and colourful and you should be able to get hot meals. . .Furthermore, there are more people walking to and from the villages on these days. . .

If you're hiking from Nyatiti to Quaila, you should leave soon after sunrise so you can laze around Quaila during the hottest part of the day – very enjoyable on souk days. If you want to get to the crater the following day, you can either just walk up to the waterfall above the village and camp there or continue on to the hot springs. The springs aren't too hard to find as the path is fairly easy to follow. Beyond the waterfall there's a long narrow passageway in the rocks near the stream. The path then crosses the stream several times but the last part of the walk is quite an exhausting part from the right bank of the stream. If you are a little anxious about getting your bearings and your Arabic isn't too good, take heed of the following: as you look towards Jebel Marra, you will see a flat-topped mountain not far ahead of you to the left of Marra. This is Jebel Idwa, and provided you keep it to your left, you won't go far wrong. For directions, you should ask for Deriba, which is the local name given to the crater lakes. At the hot springs, the place to fill your water bottle is the stream just beyond them (straight ahead from the Quaila path) where you can see some palm trees. This is the last place you'll find water before you get to the crater bottom. From here onwards, the path is often quite hard to find, as the terrain is first stony and very steep and then ashy with stones and lots of ash ravines to fall into or get lost in. So take care! From the springs upwards there are no villages and few people around to help if you're in trouble.

The hardest part of the walk comes first, so start early when it's still cold and you won't have to drink much water. Looking at the springs coming from Quaila, the path is on the steep slope on your right (with Jebel Idwa straight ahead). It's very heavy going but it levels out and then you have to do a lot of clambering (sometimes on all fours) across the rocks. You need to concentrate hard, as it's a long way down in places.

After a couple of hours, the path starts to run parallel with the crater rim. The highest point of the mountain is on your right, but you'll probably be too tired to even contemplate the idea of attempting the very steep and probably dangerous ascent. Your first view of the crater takes about three hours from the hot springs as the path runs along the rim. It's a breathtaking sight. On the right is a green sulphur lake which fills a crater within the main crater, below almost vertical cliffs rising to the summit. On the left are two salt lakes. The grassy crater bottom is a startling contrast with the grey ash ravines below you on the other side. Apart from the livestock grazing on the crater pasture there are also baboons which live in the crater sides as well as in the ash ravines. I only heard one screaming above the green lake, but the other teachers spotted them in the ravines.

Assuming you want to get downhill, you'll have to be patient, as the path down is nearer to the far end of the crater. By the time you get to the bottom (about five hours after leaving the hot springs), you'll probably be running short of water. Fortunately, you won't have to go far, as you'll soon come to a muddy area where the cattle drink. If you look carefully, you'll find a spring very near the path where fresh, sulphur-free water flows out of the muddy ground. As far as I know, this is the only source of fresh water on the crater, although you can drink from the green lake if you're really desperate.

Those travelling in the opposite direction from the crater and/or Taratonga to Quaila are very likely to get lost unless they keep Jebel Idwa to their right and don't start descending towards the ravines. If the path you're on seems to be leading you down towards Idwa, it's better to retrace your steps towards the crater rim again. Otherwise, you'll probably get lost in the ravine without much water. You could come seriously unstuck. Coming from this side, Jebel Idwa is easy to spot. Looking ahead on the Quaila path, it's below you a little to the right. Once you get down to Nyatiti, you have the choice of going down the main road and taking a bus or lorry, or staying at the rest house. However, if you choose to stay there you must get permission, so you, or a representative of your group, will have to go down to the village and come back again. If you are in a hurry, it is possible to walk from the crater rim down to Nyatiti in a day as long as you start early.

DAGU JEBELS

These hills are a two day hike from Nyala

and feature prehistoric rock paintings. This is beautiful walking country, especially after the rains, but watch out for the heskanit burrs which are very thick and sticky in this area.

KAFIA KINGI

This village, in the south-west corner of Southern Darfur, is most interesting for the people who live in the area. The Fallata Umboro, members of a non-Arab nomadic group, are descended from the Fulani people of West Africa and are famous for their *fakis*. A faki is usually a teacher, but the Fallata give their teachers the status of magicians. These fakis travel around, for one month each year, collecting roots and herbs. When they return, people come to them for spells and secret potions. The fakis' love potions are popular, especially among old women. The women pour the potion into the tea of the men whose attention they are trying to attract.

The Sudanese government has declared the area around Kafia Kingi a national park. The park is barely accessible, but souk lorries occasionally travel into the region.

EL FASHER

El Fasher first gained prominence in the early part of the 18th century as a principal centre of the Fur Sultanate. It was also the starting point for one of Africa's most famous caravan routes, the Darb al Arba'een, or the '40 Day Road'. Incredibly wealthy camel caravans laden with ebony, spices, ivory and beautiful cloth, as well as hundreds of slaves captured from other parts of Africa, regularly made the long trip across the desert to the great bazaars of Aswan and Asyut in Egypt.

In the early 19th century, as if slavery itself wasn't horror enough, Mohammed Ali commissioned two Coptic priests in Asyut to carry out castrations on most of the young male slaves who survived the arduous journey.

Although Mohammed had managed to extend his military might into other parts of the Sudan, his ambition to conquer El Fasher and gain control of the Darfur and the great caravan route was never realised. It was not until 1874, long after his death, that Darfur became a province of Egyptian Sudan. Egyptian control lasted until the time of the Mahdi and the subsequent downfall of the Khalifa in 1898. A religious zealot named Ali Dinar then established an autonomous sultanate based in El Fasher. The sultanate lasted until 1916 when, on 6 November, a couple of British planes flew in and shot Sultan Ali Dinar dead from the air. The locals of El Fasher revere the sultan as a martyr.

During WW II, El Fasher was a small but important airbase for US C-47 cargo planes. It was basically a refuelling stop for planes flying the Miami to North Africa supply route.

Places to Stay & Eat

The government *Rest House*, in the building next to the palace, is a good place to stay. It was once the British commissioner's residence.

Buji's, one of the few restaurants in town, is on Palace Rd and serves decent roast beef and chips. Opposite Buji's is the only place in El Fasher to get ice cream.

Getting There & Away

Souk lorries and a few buses travel to most destinations near El Fasher. There is a weekly bus to Mellit, a twice weekly bus to Kutum, and daily buses and lorries to Nyala.

MELLIT

This village, north of El Fasher, is home to a large number of camel breeders and salt traders from the seminomadic Zaghawa tribe who, until recently, spoke only their own Saharan languages. They have now been Arabised and, today, most Zaghawa also speak some form of Arabic and profess Islam.

The salt traders of Mellit travel 140 km

north by camel through the Tabago Hills to the village of Malha, where they meet the salt miners who come down from the Meidob Hills. The salt is then taken back to Mellit and on to El Fasher.

Mellit's camel traders take a much more arduous route. They travel for 27 days, north from Mellit through the Tabago and Meidob hills, across the Sahara Desert to the oases of El Atrun and Nukheila and on to Jebel Uweinat on the Libyan border, where they sell their camels. If you dare, you may accompany the Zaghawa on this trek, but they do tend to lose camels and a few people along the way!

EL GENEINA

El Geneina, the Sudan's westernmost town, is little more than a principal border post for crossing into Chad. Once the centre of a powerful sultanate, El Geneina is now the seat of the 'powerless' Sultan of Massalit, the son of a ruler installed by the British in the first half of this century. Although his kingdom is divided between Chad and the Sudan, the sultan still holds court every day in a courtyard at the base of his palace. With a bit of diplomacy, you might be able to talk your way into the palace for an official audience.

There is a government *Rest House* in town. Souk lorries from El Fasher travel regularly to Chad.

TINE

The village of Tine is a two day lorry ride north of El Geneina. It used to be possible to cross into Chad from here but the war in Chad may have put an end to that, as well as causing increased banditry in the Sudan. To combat this, the Sudanese government formed a Camel Corps of armed nomads who have been quite effective in tracking down these bandits. Their presence has given the place a sort of Wild West atmosphere.

TO/FROM THE CENTRAL AFRICAN REPUBLIC

At the time of writing, the border between the Sudan and the Central African Republic had been closed. Should it reopen, most of the following information will again apply.

Occasionally, trucks from the Texas souk in Nyala go all the way to Bangui in the Central African Republic, via the Sudanese village of Am Dafog and the Central African Republic border town of Birao. The trip will cost between S£120 and S£250, depending on the driver; it can take from four to 17 days, as the truck drivers often spend a couple of days selling their wares in souks along the way.

Between August and December, the rains prevent trucks from operating between Nyala and Bangui. The police also refuse to grant travel permits to head west at that time.

An alternative way of travelling this route involves taking a truck from Nyala as far as Rahad el Berdi, where you can stay at the police station. The 12 hour trip costs around S£15.

Once in Rahad, ask around for a guide and animal transport to Am Dafog. Donkeys and guides are available for about S£50, but camel trains are the usual choice. This option should cost about S£5 for your bags, S£30 if you want to ride too. The 160 km trip through shallow swamps and coarse grass is tough, but shouldn't take longer than five days.

The police station at Am Dafog provides accommodation; food is available at a cafe. An interesting souk straddles the border between the Central African Republic and the Sudan, and the lake here has water even at the end of the dry season.

Birao, a town often referred to by the Sudanese as Daba, is a 1½ day journey from Am Dafog. You can hire camels for this trip in Am Dafog; two camels and a guide should cost S£25 per person. Along the way, you will ford at least five deep wadis (watercourses) and meet nomad cattle herders. The nomads are usually very helpful and hospitable. You stay with them, eat with them – prime steak, fresh milk and yogurt – and, if you're lucky, share some of their music with them.

I met a British couple who had driven this route in the opposite direction, seeing no other vehicles for three days. Their only comment about the trip was: 'What a horrible track of sand.'

Eastern Sudan

Eastern Sudan is one of the country's most accessible regions. A 1200 km stretch of good tarmac road links Khartoum with Kassala and Port Sudan, travelling through terrain that is basically flat, except in the Red Sea Hills area south of Port Sudan. The road, which was completed in 1980, has greatly facilitated the transport of goods and people. It was built in this region because much of the Sudan's sorghum, an important staple, is grown here.

Over the past few years, drought and pestilence have resulted in poor crops and have increased the great hardship faced by the locals and the thousands of refugees who have crowded into the region.

There is a great diversity of people in eastern Sudan. In the Red Sea Hills are the nomadic Beja people. They speak Bedawiya, a language without script; according to some experts, they bear a close resemblance to the ancient Egyptians. The Rashaida people, near Kassala, are nomadic camel and goat breeders who live in goatskin tents and drive Toyota pick-up trucks. In the Gedaref area, the Shukriya Arabs predominate and, throughout the region, there are Ethiopian refugees, fleeing drought, famine and war in Eritrea and Tigre.

The refugee crisis in eastern Sudan is an urgent problem. More than 300,000 refugees live in camps and settlements along the 439 km stretch of road from Wad Medani to Kassala. From the road, you cannot really see how bad conditions are in the camps. As many as 20% of the refugees, mainly women and children, are malnourished, disease is rife, and there are shortages of shelter, water and clothing.

If you have an opportunity, it is worth visiting a camp to increase your under-standing of the desperate problems of these people. Don't make a 'sightseeing' visit, though – the refugees need any help you can give. So do what you can, and make others aware of the situation.

WAD MEDANI

Wad Medani, on the Blue Nile, is the first major city south of Khartoum along the road to Port Sudan. It has a population of 145,000, but not much of interest to the visitor.

Opposite Wad Medani, on the other side of the Blue Nile (which is supposedly free of bilharzia), there's a good swimming beach. A box from the Wad Medani vegetable souk to the village of Hantub, just near the beach, costs 50 pt. Hantub has quite a good souk – plenty of fruit, vegetables, eggs, turkey and duck. In Wad Medani various staples, such as canned goods and toilet paper, are available from small grocery stores.

A couple of good bookshops near the Gulinar Restaurant sell English-language books, and you can buy interesting wedding drums in the souk.

Places to Stay & Eat

The *Gulinar Restaurant* near the GPO serves good Ethiopian curries, chicken and chips, yogurt and salads. Each table is painted with the name of a different African country.

The *Imperial Hotel*, at the traffic circle near the Nile bridge, is the biggest building in town – you can't miss it. The Imperial is a favourite with Sudanese honeymoon couples. It's also one of the few places in town with regular supplies of Pepsi and ice cream. The hotel is fairly new, with a TV in the lounge and air-conditioners and flush toilets in the rooms, and it has a small rose garden in front. The rates (S£140 per night) can increase substantially during holidays.

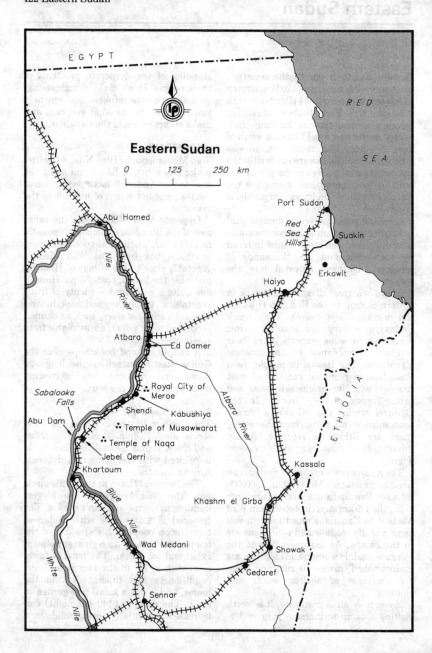

If you stay at this hotel, you will probably see many Sudanese newlyweds with intricate henna tattoos on their feet and arms. An American aid worker who got tattooed told me more about this traditional Sudanese practice:

Sudanese brides arrive at the hotel with henna designs on their feet and arms; the men have similar decorations, but only on their left hands. After a paste is made from the henna leaves and painted on the skin, it is left to dry and then scraped off. Then you are seated over a smoking hole and covered up for 'curing'. You are supposed to stay over the hole as long as possible. Foreigners usually can't last more than half an hour, although ideally you should stay at least an hour. It takes about half a day for the tattoos to completely cure and dry. To maintain the brown-maroon colouring of the designs, you should spread oil over the tattoo about two or three times a day. The result, of course, is continually slippery skin.

Getting There & Away
Most of the numerous buses and lorries operating between Khartoum, Kassala and Port Sudan stop in Wad Medani. For more information, see the Getting There & Away sections for those cities.

EL FAU
There are numerous refugee camps and settlements along the road between Wad Medani and Gedaref. Several new settlements have sprung up around El Fau, and the Sudanese government has been attempting to transfer refugees from other camps to these settlements.

GEDAREF
Gedaref is a dirty, semi-industrial city with a population of 30,000. It is renowned only for its sesame seeds, huge quantities of which are auctioned daily.

If you somehow get stuck in this sesame centre and need a place to stay, try the *Amir Hotel* or approach an expatriate. The souk and grocery stores are well stocked, so you won't go hungry.

As Gedaref is along the main road, there are frequent lorry and bus connections in both directions – west to Khartoum or north to Kassala and Port Sudan. The main road is a short distance from town. If you choose to hitch be aware of the dangers, particularly if you are female.

SHOWAK
The small town of Showak is the eastern Sudan headquarters for the United Nations High Commission for Refugees, and for a Colorado-based charity called LALMBA (pronounced 'la-lum-ba'). LALMBA operates a medical clinic, and a nationally renowned eye clinic that brings in visiting ophthalmologists. LALMBA also runs small medical clinics and feeding centres in the villages of Abuda, Um Ali and Wad Hileau, to the south and east of Showak, near the Ethiopian border. The following account of a day in Wad Hileau gives you some idea of life in a refugee camp:

Sister Bridget Haase, an American nun from Crystal City, Missouri, is one of the people responsible for seeing that the malnourished children of the Wad Hileau settlement get fed. She exudes an incredible enthusiasm for her work as, every morning, she marches across the field from the LALMBA compound to the mud rondavels (called *tukels*) and grass-mat huts of the refugees.

'These we call the defecation fields,' she told me, pointing around her at the flat and barren fields that were devoid of life, except for a few people squatting in the distance.

'There are latrines,' she explained, 'but they are too far and too few for many of the refugees.'

Water, too, is a problem in Wad Hileau. The only source of water is a tank, a couple of km from the huts and tents, on the periphery of the camp. The camp grew faster than the water supply could be extended, and many of the refugees, especially the women and children, have neither the containers nor the energy to fetch water. The shortage of available water means that many of the refugees cannot wash regularly. Consequently, disease of every kind is rife throughout the settlement.

Malaria is the most common disease in Wad Hileau, perhaps because the refugees lack the

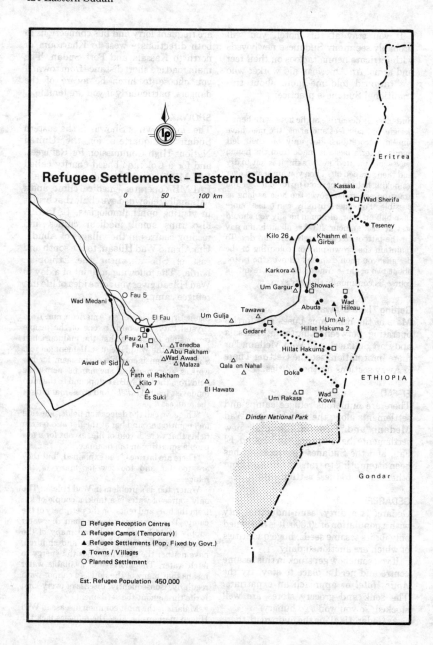

Refugee Settlements – Eastern Sudan

0   50   100 km

Eritrea

Kassala
□ Wad Sherifa

Teseney

Kilo 26 ▲   Khashm el
                 Girba

Karkora ●

Um Gargur ●   Showak □
               Abuda ▲   Wad
                          Hileau ▲

Wad Medani ○ Fau 5

El Fau ○

Um Gulja △   Tawawa ●
                      □ Gedaref   Hillat Hakuma 2 ●
Fau 2 □□
Fau 1 □
        △ Tenedba
        △ Abu Rakham   Hillat Hakuma ●□
Awad el Sid △ △ Wad Awad
            △ Malaza
        △ Fath el Rakham   Qala en Nahal
        △ Kilo 7   △   Doka ●   ETHIOPIA
        △
        Es Suki   El Hawata
                           △   Um Rakasa   Wad
                                           △ □   Kowli □

                           Dinder National Park

                                                        Gondar

☐ Refugee Reception Centres
△ Refugee Camps (Temporary)
▲ Refugee Settlements (Pop. Fixed by Govt.)
● Towns / Villages
○ Planned Settlement

Est. Refugee Population 450,000

seemingly inherent resistance of most Sudanese. The daily malaria mortality rate of 12 per 10,000 is considered high by world standards. Tuberculosis is still a problem, but somewhat less so than in recent years. Meningitis has also been a problem.

In one tent designed for two or three people, four women, one of whom was pregnant, and children of all sizes were sitting in the dirt. Wisps of smoke from a tin-can charcoal stove in front failed to deter the swarm of flies inside, and the flies clung to everything, including the mouths and eyes of the children.

A tiny baby boy and a thin, scraggly four year old girl wore the numbered plastic bracelets which LALMBA had given them to indicate that they were registered with the feeding centre. About 5% of the children at Wad Hileau are severely malnourished; a year ago, the statistics were much worse.

The feeding centre was just a flat, grass-roofed enclosure with mat walls. Here, a line of children waited to be weighed. Clusters of women and children sat off to the side, sipping cups of porridge, while opposite, in a roped-off section, some of the hundreds of severely malnourished children were trying to eat.

At the settlement's medical clinic, Ashagrie Kindie, one of the medical examiners, told me about another problem with which they must contend – the traditional medical beliefs and practices of the refugees.

'Parents burn their children with hot nails because they think disease can be burnt out,' he said. 'And when someone has malaria or hepatitis, they cut 44 places on his body. I tell them that it is bad because the bleeding will make them worse. It's a difficult job.'

Ashagrie is typical of many Ethiopian political refugees. He fled his country because, one day, the army came to his town of Gondar.

'They gathered all the students from little to big in front of the school and started shooting them. I saved my life by running.'

KHASHM EL GIRBA

Khashm el Girba is a relatively uninteresting town 62 km north of Showak. Several thousand Nubians have been resettled in the area, after being displaced from their own lands by the creation of Lake Nasser when the Aswan High Dam was built.

A dam, built on the Atbara River just outside town, has proven a classic example of a development project whose impact was miscalculated and underestimated. The dam caused a range of environmental problems by altering the flow of the Atbara. The river banks began to erode more quickly and large areas of date palms were destroyed. As the dates were a principal source of livelihood, many people were forced to migrate to other towns.

You can visit the area and swim in the lake that was created by the dam. However, this is supposedly a military area, so you can't stay overnight.

KASSALA

Kassala, a city of 150,000 people, is famous for its fruit and its jebels, or hills. The bizarre sugarloaf jebels can be seen on the horizon from several km away and add a certain mystical beauty to the place.

The souk is considered to be one of the best in the Sudan and sells grapefruits, oranges, dates, pomegranates, melons and bananas, as well as cloth, local crafts and jewellery. A lot of the silver jewellery is made by the veiled women of the Rashaida tribe.

The Rashaida came here from Saudi Arabia a little more than 150 years ago and have clung to their nomadic ways ever since. Most, if not all, of the Rashaida live in the goatskin tents which you will see by the roadside as you approach Kassala and Port Sudan. The women wear unique veils and thick silver bracelets and necklaces. Silver is a status symbol for the Rashaida.

A Rashaida girl announces her eligibility for marriage by wearing an intricately woven silver veil and several necklaces. When the girl finds a man she likes, she expresses interest by lifting the veil to expose her chin to him. (The Rashaida consider chins erotic!) If the man accepts the invitation to marry her, he then has to come up with 100 camels for her family, before the wedding. Take advantage of

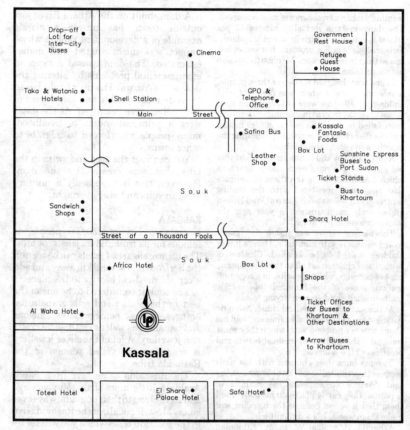

Main Street

Drop—off Lot for Inter-city buses

Cinema

Government Rest House

Refugee Guest House

Taka & Watania Hotels

Shell Station

GPO & Telephone Office

Kassala Fantasia Foods

Safina Bus

Box Lot

Sunshine Express Buses to Port Sudan

Leather Shop

Ticket Stands

Bus to Khartoum

Souk

Sandwich Shops

Sharq Hotel

Street of a Thousand Fools

Souk

Africa Hotel

Box Lot

Shops

Al Waha Hotel

Ticket Offices for Buses to Khartoum & Other Destinations

Arrow Buses to Khartoum

Kassala

Toteel Hotel

El Sharq Palace Hotel

Safa Hotel

any opportunity you have to attend one of the interesting Rashaida wedding ceremonies. The big wedding season is after Ramadan.

Kassala is also a favourite destination for honeymoon couples from other parts of the Sudan.

Information
You are required to register with the police upon arrival in Kassala. The police can also assist you with obtaining permission to visit the huge Wad Sherifa refugee camp nearby.

Places to Stay
The *Taka* and *Watania*, opposite the Shell station, are cheap, lakonda-style hotels. Beds in both places cost S£5 per night.

In a side street across from the souk and the Africa Hotel is the *Al Waha Hotel*, which is also popular with travellers. It's clean, with showers and toilets, and has a safe for keeping valuables. Dormitory beds cost S£4 per person.

Down the street from the Al Waha is the *Toteel Hotel*, which charges S£30 for a single. Each room has a ceiling fan and air-cooler.

The relatively new *El Sharq Palace Hotel* is around the corner and a block away from the Toteel. At the time of writing it was temporarily closed but, when it's open, clean double rooms with showers cost S£44 a night. The hotel's rooftop restaurant offers reasonably good meals. On a clear day, the hills and mountains of Eritrea are visible from here and, at night, it used to be possible to see the battle fireworks from across the border in Ethiopia.

A block further on from the El Sharq Palace, the new, sparkling-clean *Safa Hotel* has 35 rooms which start at S£88. Most rooms don't have showers, but all have overhead fans.

The *Salam Hotel*, near the souk, has been recommended by several British teachers working in the Sudan. It has clean rooms and showers and costs S£6 per night.

The *Africa Hotel* has decent rooms for S£3.50 a night. The showers and toilets are in the halls.

The *Khartoum Hotel* has also been recommended as a 'good travellers' hotel'.

Places to Eat

There are a few sandwich shops not far from the Africa Hotel, just off a popular market street known as the Street of a Thousand Fools. The shops serve excellent grilled meat.

Try *Kassala Fantastic Foods* for good sandwiches, fuul, cakes and pastries. A variety of drinks, including laban (hot sweetened milk), lemon juice and, sometimes, Pepsi, is also available. They are open all day.

Another popular souk area is an Eritrean marketplace diagonally across from the Taka and Watania hotels.

Getting There & Away

Several buses a day leave both Khartoum and Port Sudan for Kassala; they drop you off in a parking lot near the Shell station, about one km from the centre of Kassala. The buses from Khartoum also stop at Wad Medani, Gedaref, Showak and Khashm el Girba.

There are daily buses from Kassala to Khartoum and Port Sudan, stopping at the major towns along the way. Some buses even go to Teseney in Ethiopia, but foreigners usually aren't allowed to take these.

The Sunshine Express bus company operates buses to Port Sudan. Tickets for the eight hour trip cost S£18 and can be bought from a shed behind the El Sharq Hotel, down the street from the police station. Tea and iced water are served en route, but bring your own cup – sharing the public cup is not recommended.

The Taysir, Arrow and Safina companies have daily buses to Khartoum. Their ticket offices are near the souk (see the Kassala map). Sunshine Express is the best – their vehicles are big and air-conditioned, with shaded windows. The journey takes seven to 10 hours, depending on the number of police checkpoints along the way, and fares range from S£15 to S£22.

Boxes go to the village of Khatmiya and the refugee camp of Wad Sherifa.

KHATMIYA

You can begin a climb into the hills from the village of Khatmiya, at the base of the jebels. In the early evening, bats appear in the sky and baboons come down from the jebels to drink from the village well. On moonlit nights, the effect is quite eerie.

Married couples come to Khatmiya to drink from a well here. This is supposed to bring them good luck and help women become pregnant.

WAD SHERIFA

East of Kassala, near the Ethiopian border, the Wad Sherifa refugee camp must be one of the largest in the world. With a population of 60,000, it is a city in itself. If you want to visit the camp, you must first obtain permission from the police and the Sudanese Commissioner of Refugees in Kassala.

HAIYA

Haiya is a railway junction town, 351 km north of Kassala. From here, you can catch the train westward to Atbara.

ERKOWIT

This beautiful, isolated resort is in the Red Sea Hills, 30 km off the main road between Kassala and Port Sudan. The hotel is surrounded by picturesque hills, streams and vegetation. Somewhat incongruously, however, it now functions as a Palestinian training camp.

SUAKIN

The small island of Suakin, 58 km south of Port Sudan, is linked to the mainland by a short causeway. Once a major trading centre, Suakin today is noteworthy for its unique, but crumbling, architecture. Many of the buildings are made from coral.

Suakin's history is cloaked in myth and legend. One legend concerns the origin of the name Suakin, which translates as 'land of Ginn'. Apparently, Queen Balgies, of the Sabaa Kingdom of Yemen, sent seven virgin maidens to King Solomon in Jerusalem. On the way to the Holy City, however, a storm drove the ship off course to Suakin and, by the time it arrived in Jerusalem, all the girls were pregnant. They claimed that they had had sexual relations with the Ginn, a demon of Suakin.

As early as the 10th century BC, Suakin was an important commercial centre and was used by Ramses III as a port for his trade with the lands across the Red Sea. In subsequent centuries, it declined in importance and it was not until the 19th century, under Ottoman rule, that Suakin again prospered, this time as a slave-trading centre. In 1881, the Mahdi restored the coral buildings. Today the buildings are again crumbling for, with the establishment of Port Sudan in 1905, Suakin was superseded and deserted.

It may no longer be possible to stay overnight at Kitchener's old headquarters on Suakin Island. However, you might be able to stay at the police station in the village of El Geif, on the mainland. Supposedly, you need prior permission from the Red Sea Province Headquarters in Port Sudan, but I seriously doubt the necessity of this. The headquarters is full of somnolent bureaucrats, who will keep you waiting for hours and then tell you that, today, a permit is not required. The same applies to registration. Check with them first, though, just in case someone in the permit office wakes up momentarily.

There are frequent boxes and minibuses between Port Sudan and Suakin. It's also possible to visit Suakin on a day trip from Port Sudan.

PORT SUDAN

The harbour city of Port Sudan has a population of more than 200,000. It was established by the British in 1905 as a sea port to facilitate the export of raw commodities, such as cotton, sorghum and sesame. The city has fallen into disrepair and decay – even the carefully planned parks are now defoliated – but the beautiful lattice woodwork on the windows of many of the older buildings is one of the signs of a more elegant past. The main attractions in and around Port Sudan are the trip to Suakin, the possibility of Red Sea diving and great chocolate milkshakes.

Information

There is a tourist office near the Palace Hotel; the staff are very helpful. The registration and permit offices are at the Red Sea Province Headquarters nearby.

Diving

Hamido Travel Agency, Red Sea Enterprise (run by Captain Halim), Al Somkari Travel Agency and Juju Safari & Tourism Agency can help arrange diving trips in the area.

Alternatively, you could go to the yacht basin at the end of Suakin St and ask for Angelo Della Valle or Captain Abdul

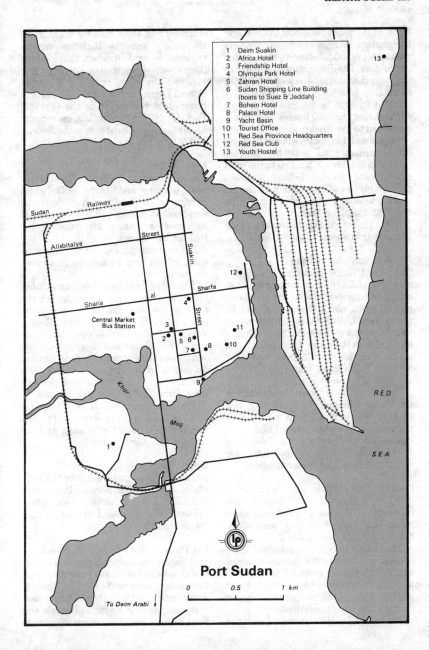

1   Deim Suakin
2   Africa Hotel
3   Friendship Hotel
4   Olympia Park Hotel
5   Zahran Hotel
6   Sudan Shipping Line Building
    (boats to Suez & Jeddah)
7   Bohein Hotel
8   Palace Hotel
9   Yacht Basin
10 Tourist Office
11 Red Sea Province Headquarters
12 Red Sea Club
13 Youth Hostel

Sudan Railway

Alisbitalya Street

Suakin Street

Sharfa

Sharia al Street

Central Market
Bus Station

Khor Mog

RED

SEA

Port Sudan

0   0.5   1 km

To Deim Arabi

Nabi, of the yacht *Felicidad*. Angelo and the captain take groups diving for very reasonable rates and also give basic diving instruction. The diving sites to which they take you include the wreck of the Italian cargo ship *Umbria*. (It was deliberately scuttled in 1940 by its crew to prevent surrendering the 3000 tonnes of bombs it contained to the British.

Angelo and the captain will also take you diving on Shaabrumi Reef (where Jacques Cousteau conducted his Precontinent II experiments, leaving behind a giant, podlike underwater hangar and several shark cages), Turtle Island and the beautiful Dolphins' Reef.

At the time of writing, the cost of a diving trip averaged about S£1050 a day.

Places to Stay – bottom end

The 50 bed *Youth Hostel* is a basic place with several dormitories, cooking facilities and a refrigerator. It's in the Salabona part of town, north of the port, and its position on the Red Sea is picturesque – if you ignore the garbage on the beach and the sludge in the water. It costs S£1.50 a night with an IYHA card and S£2 without. To get there, take a red bus from the central market bus station.

The *Africa Hotel*, down the street from the Sudan Shipping Line building, is a dive. However, it is cheap at S£1.50 a night and is, therefore, often full.

The *Zahran Hotel* and the *Friendship Hotel*, both near the Africa Hotel, are cheap and have been recommended.

Places to Stay – middle

The *Bohein Hotel* is one of the best deals in town. The clean, well-maintained rooms all have fans and air-coolers. Singles/doubles cost S£99.

The *Palace Hotel* is a pleasant, if fairly expensive, choice. An air-conditioned single with shower costs S£200 a night, and you have to show bank receipts when paying. Free video movies, usually in English, are shown nightly.

At the *Red Sea Hotel*, rooms of a similar standard cost about S£350 a night. Both the Palace and the Red Sea require payment in hard currency, thus making them relatively expensive.

Across the street from the statue of Osman Digna, at the corner of Sharia al Sharfa and Suakin St, is the *Olympia Park Hotel*. It's decent, but overpriced: rooms cost more than those at the Bohein, and they're not as clean.

Places to Eat

The restaurant at the *Palace Hotel* serves beef burgers and tasty milkshakes. Service is horrendous, but don't be surprised when they add 30% to your bill for service and taxes. Nevertheless, it's still not bad value.

In the evenings, you can get very good shish kebabs from a nameless place near the yacht basin.

The only other place to eat, apart from the local cafes scattered throughout the city, is the *Red Sea Club* (not to be confused with the Red Sea Hotel). Temporary membership costs S£50 per day, or S£120 for three days, and entitles you to use the swimming pool and snooker tables and to eat whatever the cook feels like serving. This is also a good place to meet divers and arrange a diving trip.

The *Customs Club* is primarily for customs officers. They serve good grilled fish and an excellent bean soup, and the cocoa is also worth trying.

Getting There & Away

Air It is fairly easy to get a seat on the daily Sudan Airways flight between Port Sudan and Khartoum. The Sudan Airways office in Port Sudan is around the corner from the Zahran Hotel.

Bus There are daily buses from Kassala to Port Sudan. Buses from Khartoum to Port Sudan take two days. For more details on these buses, refer to the Getting There & Away sections for Kassala and Khartoum.

Buses from Port Sudan to Kassala and Suakin leave from Deim Suakin (refer to the Port Sudan map), departing at 6, 6.30 and 7 am each day. The Sunshine Bus Company is one of the better companies. Tickets to Kassala cost about S£17, and you need to make reservations at least one to two days in advance.

Train The 'Superexpress' is the Sudan's 'nice' train. It leaves Port Sudan on Mondays at 8 pm and stops only at Atbara and Shendi. The connecting train between Khartoum and Wadi Halfa supposedly arrives in Atbara on Wednesdays.

The fare to Khartoum is S£90 for a sleeping car berth with full board, S£65 in 1st class, S£55 in 2nd class and S£45 in 3rd class. You must make reservations at least a day or two in advance.

The regular train leaves on Saturdays at 6 pm, but it is not unusual to wait up to 12 hours before the train actually departs. The 18 hour trip to Atbara costs S£26 in 1st class; 2nd class is almost always packed to the hilt. This train meets the northbound train in Atbara on Sunday.

Truck The souk lorry parks are in Deim Arabi, just south of the city's outskirts.

Boat It used to be possible to get a boat to/from Jeddah (Saudi Arabia), Port Sudan and Suez, but at the time of writing the Port Sudan stretch had been indefinitely suspended. If service has resumed, the following information will be pertinent.

The agent's office is in the Sudan Shipping Line building (see the Port Sudan map). In Khartoum, check with Sabra Travel and the Reservations Agency (tel 75349, 77083). All foreigners must show bank receipts to buy the tickets. There used to be approximately four trips a month, but be wary of the departure times which Sabra give you.

Fares to Jeddah range from S£120 in deck class to S£198 in 1st class A (double cabin with toilet and shower). Fares to Suez range from S$133 in deck class to S$234 in 1st class A.

AROUS
Arous, 50 km north of Port Sudan, used to be an overpriced resort but, at the time of writing, it was closed. If you do manage to get there, you'll find excellent diving in the colourful coral reefs offshore. You can camp near the resort hotel, but bring your own food.

Southern Sudan

WARNING: SOUTHERN SUDAN IS A WAR ZONE AND IS CLOSED TO TRAVELLERS. TRAVEL IN THIS REGION AT YOUR OWN RISK.

At the time of writing, travel south along the White Nile from Kosti to Juba, either overland or by steamer, was impossible for foreigners. The SPLM Anya-nya 2 rebels have been waging a guerrilla war against the government since 1983, when rebel leader John Garang went into hiding to reactivate the Sudanese People's Liberation Movement.

The main reason for the rebellion in the south was prime minister Nimeiri's declaration of sharia, which made Islamic law applicable to the entire country. The SPLM, which represents the predominantly Christian and animist southerners, kept up the hostilities even after the 1985 coup d'état, which ousted Nimeiri and brought in the one year rule of the Transitional Military Council. The rebels continued their fight against the government of Sadiq al Mahdi because, although the new leader regularly announced the 'imminent abrogation of sharia', he did not implement this promise. The 1989 coup doesn't seem to have changed things, as the war had flared up again when this book was going to press.

The central government lost control of the south when the railway line between Babanusa and Wau was sabotaged, the Kosti to Juba Nile steamer was blown up (in February 1984), and roads throughout the region were mined. Chevron-sponsored oil exploration projects in the Bentiu area were abandoned due to rebel attacks, and French engineers were forced to stop work on the building of the Jonglei Canal.

Travel to all southern towns and villages, including Juba, Torit and Wau, is unsafe and illegal. At the time of writing, travel permits were not being issued for these and most other southern destinations.

Travel to Kosti, and beyond to Sennar, Dinder, Dinder National Park, Ed Damazin and Er Roseires, is still possible but, as the civil war spreads northward, it's increasingly risky.

If the civil war is resolved, the roads cleared of mines, autonomous Arab tribal militias placated and the south reopened for travel, the following information will again be applicable.

KOSTI

Kosti, a relatively small city along the White Nile, was named after a Greek shopkeeper. There's not much of interest here except, perhaps, the Kenana sugar plant. The plant is a significant development project for the Sudan.

Places to Stay

The lakonda-style *Tabidi Hotel*, built around a courtyard, has been recommended by travellers. There are three beds to a room; a room costs S£12, whether or not you need all three beds. Ten metres from the hotel is an open field, leading to the Nile.

The *Abu Zayd Hotel* is very clean and costs S£5 per person. There's also a colonial-style government *Rest House*.

Getting There & Away

Frequent buses to Sennar and Khartoum leave from near the railroad tracks. The trip to Sennar, in a bus with padded seats, costs S£3.

For details of the boat trip between Kosti and Juba, refer to the Juba Getting There & Away section.

SENNAR

Sennar is a convenient transit point, from which it is easy to make a lorry connection to Suki or the village of Dinder.

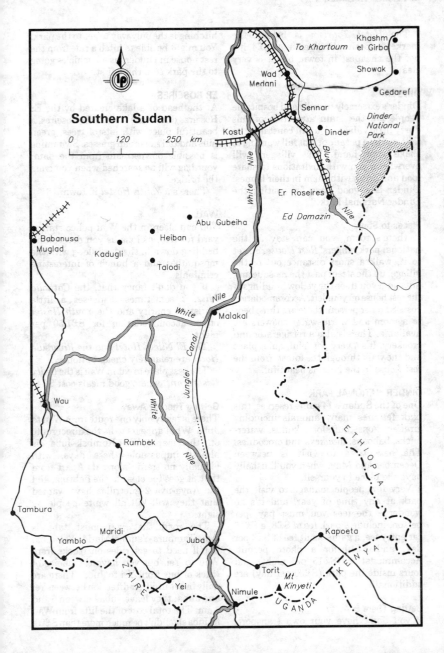

Southern Sudan

0   120   250 km

The *Hotel Tourism* is behind the market, opposite the cinema. At S£4, it's not the cheapest in town, but it is very clean.

DINDER
Dinder's extremely friendly and hospitable people are the main attraction of this dusty little village. You will constantly be followed by a parade of kids, all wanting to shake your hand. The villagers will overwhelm you with invitations to share food and drink with them in their homes. Dinder is a good base for visiting the Dinder National Park.

Places to Stay
If there's room, you can stay at the national park rangers' *Rest House*. To get to it, walk a short distance out of the village, up the street past the mosque and huts, and you'll see the yellow buildings of the rest house on your left. Accommodation costs S£5 per person; there are three beds to a room and warm-water showers are available. There's also a refrigerator and crockery. It's a very peaceful, quiet place and the walk through the forest, from the rest house to the Nile, is beautiful.

DINDER NATIONAL PARK
One of the Sudan's 14 game reserves, this park features many animals including giraffes, lions, buffaloes, kudus, water-bucks, baboons, monkeys and crocodiles. The best time to visit is between December and May, when you'll usually have the place to yourself.

Very few people manage to visit the park at any time of year, and it's no wonder – the fees you must pay, per person, include a park fee of S£8, a S£15 car entry fee, a game scout fee of S£3 per day, and S£10 for a photo permit. Accommodation (S£15 per night) and tours inside the park (S£30 per day) are additional!

Getting There & Away
If you don't have your own transport, hitching is the only way to get to the park. You might be able to hitch a ride from the rest house in Dinder, as all vehicles going to the park stop there first.

ER ROSEIRES
At the head of a lake created by the Er Roseires dam is the town of Er Roseires, a beautiful place with lots of trees, green hills and tall savannah grasses. Swimming is possible downstream from the dam; your bag will be searched when you cross the bridge.

There's a *Youth Hostel* in town.

WAU
You can sleep in the Wau police station yard for free, as long as you don't mind bedding down in the dust along with the mosquitoes and a bunch of interesting criminals.

If you don't fancy that, the *Catholic Mission* sometimes dispenses a little Christian charity and the *Youth Hostel* offers accommodation for S£1.50 per night.

The *El Nilein Hotel* and the *Riverside Hotel* are relatively cheap options.

The best place to eat in Wau is the *Unity Restaurant*, where good meals cost S£4.

Getting There & Away
There is really only one route from Wau to Juba. What appears to be the direct route on the maps, Wau-Rumbek-Juba, is almost impassable these days, with virtually no traffic along it. Apart from that, it goes too close to the fighting, and the Anya-nya 2 guerrillas have warned that they will kill all white people on sight.

The road that you must take is Wau-Tambura-Yambio-Maridi-Yei-Juba. You'll need to get rides on trucks from Wau to Yei, but you have the choice of truck or bus from Yei to Juba. There are daily buses in either direction between Yei and Juba; they leave Juba between 6 and 7 am. The total cost of the lifts from Wau to Juba shouldn't be much more than S£20.

The stretch between Wau and Tambura is pretty bad, but the section from Juba to Yambio is much better. Between Maridi and Yei, there are incredible views into the Nile and Zaire river basins.

The best people to approach for lifts along this route are the international aid agencies like UNICEF and FAO (the UN's Food & Agriculture Organization), Sudanese government departments and the Sudanese Council of Churches – but keep in mind that their first priority is to assist local inhabitants. If you find yourself stuck in Wau, there is a mail truck which leaves every Monday for Juba and takes three to five days – but there's a lot of competition for seats.

YAMBIO

A night at Yambio's beautifully located *Protestant Mission* will cost you S£2. From Yambio, you can cross the border into Zaire via the market village of Gongura. Trucks to Isorio are available in Gongura.

YEI

Ask at the *Agricultural Research Station* for a place to stay.

JUBA

Although the government still holds Juba, the SPLM controls the surrounding region. Many travellers do grow to like this 'one-horse town'. At the moment, however, it seems to have little to recommend it. Why go there?

If you do, you must register with the police on arrival – this costs 10 pt for a revenue stamp. If you're heading south, you must get an exit permit before you leave. These permits are obtainable from the Immigration Office, which is in the same building as the police, and cost 25 pt. Get this permit before you start looking for a lift. Photography permits can be obtained from the Ministry of Information, but they have to be countersigned by the police.

Malakia

Much of the life of Juba actually takes place here, in the traditional village of Malakia. The market is well worth visiting, especially if you're about to take the boat north to Kosti (if you can). Among other things, you can buy portable stoves for S£1 to S£2 and charcoal for 25 pt.

Malakia is two km from Juba. The main Juba lorry park is near the souk.

Immatong Mountains

Dominated by the Sudan's highest mountain, Mt Kinyeti (3170 metres), the Immatong Mountains were developed as a hill station resort by the British colonial authorities.

If you have time for a detour, it's worth visiting this region, east of Juba and south of Torit. Make your way to the *Gilo Guest House* in Gilo; although it was looted in the civil war, the guest house retains a lot of old world charm. There are no mosquitoes or tsetse flies in these hills, and it's wonderfully cool. You can forget about this place in the rainy season, however, when the road is impassable.

Places to Stay

For many years, the most popular hotel in Juba has been the *Hotel Africa*, where it costs 50 pt to sleep on the floor and S£1.25 if you want a bed. Because of its popularity, however, this hotel is often full, and the management has allowed the place to run down. It was recently described by one traveller as 'no better than the boat'. Another visitor drew attention to the 'cholera-style toilets'. The hotel food is good, but certainly not the cheapest in town.

If you don't like the Africa, or can't get in, try the *MTC* (Multi-Service or Medical Training Centre), behind the football stadium. It has 10 beds for S£1.50 each, and floor space for 50 pt.

For something more comfortable, try the *Juba Hotel*. A room here costs S£30. You may also be able to stay on the verandah of the Immigration Office, free of charge.

Places to Eat

For food, go to the *People's Restaurant* or the *Greek Club*. The latter has been recommended by many travellers. The *Unity Garden* on May St is also very popular.

Most of the tap water in Juba comes straight from the Nile and is not filtered. If you drink it, you'll get sick.

Getting There & Away

Road Going south from Juba, you have the choice of crossing into either Uganda or Kenya. Until Idi Amin was deposed in Uganda, the main route south went directly into Kenya via Torit, Kapoeta, Lokichoggio and Lodwar. If you're looking for a rugged trip, you can still go this way, but you should allow at least a week for the journey. It's not possible during the rainy season. The section between Lodwar and Kapoeta was being upgraded, but the civil war has probably put an end to this.

These days, most travellers take the road into Uganda via Nimule. To make this trip, you need to obtain a permit in Juba. Most days, trucks travel from Malakia, two km from Juba, to Kenya, via Uganda. They cost Kenyan Sh 300 (S£20). The drivers prefer Kenyan Sh, but they will also accept US$ and UK£.

The journey takes about 1½ days, with many army/police checkpoints en route, at which you will be thoroughly searched. Ugandan army and police officers will pressure you into giving them certain items of your baggage. A polite, but firm, refusal and a little humour may do the trick; otherwise, leave something you can do without in the top of your pack. As they seem to be particularly fond of medical supplies, they may take these and leave the rest of your pack alone. It's best to go through in the morning, when they're more likely to be sober.

There are also daily buses between Juba and Nimule. These cost S£3.05 and take about six hours.

Boat The following information about the Kosti to Juba Nile steamer refers to the period before the civil war flared up again. It should still give you a good idea of what to expect if the political situation permits travel in the region in the future.

The old Kosti to Juba steamer was sunk by SPLM rebels in February 1984. It was replaced by two new boats, the *Juba* and the *Nimule*, which make the journey in far less time than the old boat used to. They have 1st and 2nd class only.

The steamer trip should take six to eight days travelling upstream, and about four days going downstream. There are departures in either direction two or three times a week; the fares were S£55 in 1st class and S£40 in 2nd class. There won't be any spare berths on the day of sailing, so if you want a berth you must book in advance.

Meals can be bought on the boat, but they're not cheap – S£1.65 for lunch and S£1.75 for dinner. If you want to keep costs down, take some food and a portable stove. Putting your own food together also helps pass the time. Water comes straight from the Nile and is not boiled. The toilets get sluiced down once a day, but they don't stay clean for long. You will also need insect repellent.

If you're heading north from Juba, it may be worth hanging around the harbour for a while, talking to the crew members of boats docked there. Some travellers have managed to get free lifts as far north as Malakal. You can save a lot of money this way, as boats from Malakal to Kosti cost S£15 in 2nd class and S£19 in 1st class.

Depending on how you take to slow boats, this journey can be very interesting – there are plenty of tribal villages and lots of wildlife en route – or very boring. If it turns out to be the latter, you could always pass some time by writing us a letter and telling us about the latest developments. Be careful about taking photographs of tribespeople on the river banks. The boat crew, too, are especially sensitive to being photographed, and many travellers have had their film ripped from their cameras.

Egyptian Gods & Goddesses

Amun – one of the deities of creation and the patron god of Thebes. Amun, his wife Mut and their son Khons formed the Theban triad.
Amun-Ra – king of the gods; the fusion of Amun and the sun-god Ra.
Anubis – jackal-headed god of embalming and of the dead.
Anukis – wife of Khnum; wears a white crown flanked by two gazelle horns.
Aten – the disc of the rising sun, worshipped as the sole deity by Pharaoh Akhenaten and Queen Nefertiti.
Atum – god of the rising sun, identified with Ra.

Bastet – cat-goddess; local deity of Bubastis in the Nile Delta.

Edjo – cobra-goddess of Lower Egypt; she was the protector of the Pharaoh and was represented on his crown as a rearing cobra.
Eos – goddess of the dawn.

Geb – god of the earth and husband of Nut.

Haroeris – Horus the Elder, a form of Horus the falcon-god.
Hathor – goddess of pleasure and love. Represented as a cow, a woman with a cow's head, or a woman with a headdress of a sun disc fixed between the horns of a cow. She was the wet-nurse and lover of Horus, and the local deity of Dendara in the Nile Valley.
Horus – falcon-god; the offspring of Isis and Osiris. Identified with the living Pharaoh.

Ihy – the youthful aspect of the creator-gods.
Isis – powerful goddess of healing, purity, sexuality, motherhood and women. The sister and wife of Osiris and mother of Horus, she was also the divine mourner of the dead. She was worshipped so passionately that she became identified with all the goddesses of the Mediterranean, finally absorbing them to become the universal mother of nature and protector of humans.

Khnum – ram-headed god of the Nile cataracts and local god of Elephantine Island. He was often shown moulding humankind on his potter's wheel.
Khons – god of the moon and time; son of Amun and Mut.

Maat – goddess of truth and the personification of cosmic order.
Min – ithyphallic god of the harvest and fertility; local god of Achmim and patron deity of desert travellers.
Montu – falcon-headed war-god; the original patron deity of Thebes.
Mut – vulture or lioness-headed war-goddess; wife of Amun.

Neith – goddess of war and hunting, and protector of embalmed bodies.
Nekhbet – vulture-goddess of Nekheb; guardian (along with Edjo) of the Pharaohs and a deity associated with royal and divine births.
Nekheny – local falcon-god of ancient Nekhen, later associated with Horus.
Nepthys – guardian deity and sister of Isis.
Nut – sky-goddess, often depicted as a woman or a cow stretched across the ceilings of tombs, swallowing the sun and creating night. Each morning, she would give birth to the sun.

Opet – hippopotamus-goddess; the mother of Osiris.
Osiris – ruler of the Underworld. Osiris was murdered by his brother Seth and brought back to life by his sister Isis to rule as the judge of the dead.

Ptah – creator-god who formed the world with words from his tongue and heart; local deity of ancient Memphis.

Ra – the great sun-god. He was creator and ruler of other deified elements of nature and was often linked with other gods.
Ra-Harakhty – falcon-headed god, the fusion of Ra and Horus.

Sacred Animals – Apis bulls of Memphis, cats of Beni Hasan, crocodiles of Kom Ombo, cobra or uraeus, baboons, hippopotami, ibis, monkeys, rams, cows, goats, leopards, jackals, snakes and lizards.
Satis – daughter of Khnum and Anukis. This family was the triad of the First Cataract and was worshipped at Elephantine Island (Aswan).
Sekhmet – lioness-headed goddess; the 'spreader of terror' and wife of Ptah.

Serapis – Greco-Egyptian god; the fusion of Osiris and Zeus.

Seshat – goddess of writing.

Seth – evil brother and murderer of Osiris.

Shu – god of the air.

Sobek – crocodile or crocodile-headed god; local deity of El Faiyum and Kom Ombo.

Thoth – ibis-headed god of wisdom, healing and writing; local god of ancient Hermopolis in the Nile Valley.

Wepwawet – wolf-god and avenger of Osiris; local god of Asyut in the Nile Valley.

Glossary

Bab – gate.

Book of the Dead – ancient theological compositions, or hymns, that were the subject of most of the colourful paintings and reliefs on tomb walls. Extracts from these so-called books were believed to assist the deceased person safely into the afterlife via the Kingdom of the Dead. The texts were sometimes also painted on a roll of papyrus and buried with the dead.

Canopic Jars – pottery jars which held the embalmed internal organs and viscera (liver, stomach, lungs, intestines) of the mummified Pharaoh. They were placed in the burial chamber near the sarcophagus.

Capitals – in Pharaonic and Greco-Roman architecture the top, or capital, of a column was decorated with plant forms, such as the papyrus, palm or lotus, or other motifs, like the human face and cow's ears of the goddess Hathor.

Caravanserai – large inn enclosing a courtyard, providing accommodation for caravans.

Caretas – donkey cart.

Cartouche – oblong figure enclosing the hieroglyphs of royal or divine names.

Cenotaph – symbolic tomb, temple or place of cult worship that was additional to the Pharaoh's actual burial place.

Electrum – alloy of gold and silver used for jewellery, ornaments and decorating buildings.

Fellahin – the peasant farmers or agricultural workers who make up the majority of Egypt's population.

False Door – fake, seemingly half-open ka door in a tomb wall which enabled the Pharaoh's spirit, or life force, to come and go at will.

Galabiyya – full-length robe worn by men.

Haj – pilgrimage to Mecca. All Muslims should make the journey at least once in their lifetime.

Hantour – horse-drawn carriage.

Heb-Sed Festival – five-day celebration of royal rejuvenation, held after 30 years of a Pharaoh's reign and then every three years thereafter.

Heb-Sed Race – traditional re-enactment, during the festival, of a Pharaoh's coronation.

The king sat first on the throne of Upper Egypt and then on the throne of Lower Egypt to symbolise the unification of the country and the renewal of his reign.

Hieroglyphs – ancient Egyptian form of writing, which used pictures and symbols to represent objects, words or sounds.

Hypostyle Hall – hall in which the roof is supported by columns.

Iconostasis – screen with doors and icons set in tiers, used in eastern Christian churches.

Ithyphallic – denoting the erect phallus of a Pharaoh or god (usually used in reference to the god Min); a sign of fertility.

Ka – spirit, or 'double', of a living person which gained its own identity with the death of that person. The survival of the ka, however, required the continued existence of the body, hence mummification. The ka was also the vital force emanating from a god and transferred through the Pharaoh to his people.

Khedive – Egyptian viceroy under Ottoman suzerainty (1867-1914).

Kiosk – open-sided pavilion.

Kuttab – Qur'anic school for boys.

Liwan – vaulted hall, opening into a central court, in the madrassa of a mosque.

Lotus – white waterlily regarded as sacred by the ancient Egyptians, who likened their land to the lotus – the Nile Delta was the flower, El Faiyum the bud, and the Nile and its valley the stem. The lotus was specifically identified with Upper Egypt.

Madrassa – theological college that is part of a non-congregational mosque.

Mammisi – birth-house. In these small chapels or temples, erected in the vicinity of a main temple, the rituals of the divine birth of the living king were performed. All Pharaohs were believed to be incarnations of the falcon-god Horus.

Mashrabiyya – ornate carved wooden panel or screen; a feature of Islamic architecture.

Mastaba – Arabic word for 'bench'; a mud-brick structure above tombs from which the pyramids were developed.

Midan – town or city square.

Mihrab – niche in the wall of a mosque that indicates the direction of Mecca.

Minbar – pulpit in a mosque.

Mortuary Complex – a Pharaoh's last resting place. It usually comprised: a pyramid which was the king's tomb and the repository for all his household goods, clothes and treasure; a funerary temple on the east side of the pyramid which served as a cult temple for worship of the dead Pharaoh; pits for the solar barques; a valley temple on the banks of the Nile, where the mummification process was carried out; and a massive causeway from the river to the pyramid.

Muezzin – mosque official who calls the faithful to prayer five times a day from the minaret.

Natron – whitish mineral of hydrated sodium carbonate that occurs in saline deposits and salt lakes and acts as a natural preservative. It was used in ancient Egypt to pack and dry out the body during mummification.

Nilometer – pit descending into the Nile and containing a central column marked with graduations. The marks were used to measure and record the level of the river, especially during the inundation.

Nome – administrative division or province of ancient Egypt.

Obelisk – monolithic stone pillar, with square sides tapering to a pyramidal top, used as a monument in ancient Egypt. Obelisks were usually carved from pink granite and set up in pairs at the entrance to a tomb or temple. A single obelisk was sometimes the object of cult worship.

Opet Festival – celebration held in Luxor (Thebes) during the Nile inundation season, when statues of the Theban triad – Amun, Mut and Khons – would be transported by river from Karnak Temple to Luxor Temple to join in the festivities.

Papyrus – plant identified with Lower Egypt; writing material made from the pith of this plant; a document written on such paper.

Pylon – monumental gateway at the entrance to a temple.

Pyramid Texts – paintings and reliefs on the walls of the internal rooms and burial chamber of pyramids and often on the sarcophagus itself. The texts recorded the Pharaoh's burial ceremonies, associated temple rituals, the hymns vital to his passage into the afterlife and, sometimes, major events in his life.

Sabil – covered, public drinking fountain.

Sarcophagus – huge stone or marble coffin used to encase other wooden coffins and the mummy of the Pharaoh or queen.

Scarab – dung beetle regarded as sacred in ancient Egypt and represented on amulets or in hieroglyphs as a symbol of the sun-god Ra.

Serapeum – network of subterranean galleries constructed as tombs for the mummified sacred Apis bulls; the most important temple of the Greco-Egyptian god Serapis.

Serdab – hidden cellar in a tomb, or a stone room in front of some pyramids, containing a coffin with a life-size, lifelike, painted statue of the dead king. Serdabs were designed so that the Pharaoh's ka could communicate with the outside world.

Sharia – Islamic law, the body of doctrines that regulates the lives of Muslims. Arabic for 'road' or 'way'.

Solar Barque – wooden boat placed in or around the Pharaoh's tomb. It was the symbolic vessel of transport for his journey over the sea of death to the Kingdom of the Dead to be judged before Osiris, and for his final passage to the eternal afterlife.

Souk – market.

Speos – rockcut tomb or chapel.

Stele (plural: stelae) – stone or wooden commemorative slab or column decorated with inscriptions or figures.

Ulama – group of Muslim scholars or religious leaders; a member of this group.

Uraeus – rearing cobra with inflated hood, associated with the goddess Edjo. This was the most characteristic symbol of Egyptian royalty and was worn on the Pharaoh's forehead or crown. The sacred, fire-spitting serpent was an agent of destruction and protector of the king.

Wakala – inn for travelling merchants. It was built around a courtyard, with living quarters above the warehouses and stables.

Index

MAPS

Dear traveller

Prices go up, good places go bad, bad places go bankrupt...and every guidebook is inevitably outdated in places. Fortunately, many travellers write to us about their experiences, telling us when things have changed. If we reprint a book between editions, we try to include as much of this information as possible in a Stop Press section. Most of this information has not been verified by our own writers.

We really enjoy hearing from people out on the road, and apart from guaranteeing that others will benefit from your good and bad experiences, we're prepared to bribe you with the offer of a free book for sending us substantial useful information.

Thank you to everyone who has written and, to those who haven't, I hope you do find this book useful – and that you let us know when it isn't.

Tony Wheeler

Since Egypt & The Sudan travel survival kit was last published, little has changed in Egypt. Most of the reports we get from travellers are complaints of gross overcharging at monument sites, problems with felucca captains and continued hassles for Western women.

In the Sudan, however, the civil war is still raging and it is becoming more difficult to obtain travel permits for the regions near the border with the Central African Republic. Getting around is difficult and certain areas are off limits.

EGYPT

The current exchange rate is US$1 to E£3.21.

Since October 1991, currency declarations for arrivals are no longer required. People departing, however, may not take out more than US$5000. Sometimes higher amounts can be taken out, but that depends on the status of the traveller and the discretion of the customs officer.

Some travellers reported that it is no longer possible to obtain cash with a Eurocard or MasterCard in Cairo, but bills can be paid with these cards in most other places in Egypt.

THE SUDAN

All currency must be declared at borders. Customs at Khartoum airport are very strict. Without a declaration form you will not be able to change money legally as most hotels will ask for the form. Changing money on the black market is still very risky.

Photographic permits are still available, but using a camera in the Sudan is more dangerous than it used to be, despite the permit.

A curfew exists in Khartoum from 11 pm to 4 am, and during Ramadam from midnight to 4 am. Curfew passes are available for a valid reason and most hotels will issue them. Visitors arriving after 11 pm should attempt to get a lift into town with expatriates meeting the flight, as passes are only issued in the city.

There is a roadblock outside Nyala barring the way to Jebel Marra which you officially cannot visit. The Sudanese People's Liberation Army (SPLA) are apparently only 200 km south of Nyala and there is a danger that the vital road link to Am Dafog will be cut off. Also Nyala is surrounded by roving gangs of bandits who will not hesitate to attack.

People should be warned about Western Sudan. Tribes are heavily equipped with arms which they will use to stop trucks and buses. People have been gunned down!

Lonely Planet Guidebooks

Lonely Planet guidebooks cover virtually every accessible part of Asia as well as Australia, the Pacific, Central and South America, Africa, the Middle East and parts of North America. There are four main series: 'travel survival kits', covering a single country for a range of budgets; 'shoestring' guides with compact information for low-budget travel in a major region; trekking guides; and 'phrasebooks'.

Australia & the Pacific
Australia
Bushwalking in Australia
Papua New Guinea
Papua New Guinea phrasebook
New Zealand
Tramping in New Zealand
Rarotonga & the Cook Islands
Solomon Islands
Tahiti & French Polynesia
Fiji
Micronesia
Tonga
Samoa
New Caledonia

South-East Asia
South-East Asia on a shoestring
Malaysia, Singapore & Brunei
Indonesia
Bali & Lombok
Indonesia phrasebook
Burma
Burmese phrasebook
Thailand
Thai phrasebook
Philippines
Pilipino phrasebook

North-East Asia
North-East Asia on a shoestring
China
China phrasebook
Tibet
Tibet phrasebook
Japan
Japanese phrasebook
Korea
Korean phrasebook
Hong Kong, Macau & Canton
Taiwan

West Asia
West Asia on a shoestring
Trekking in Turkey
Turkey
Turkish phrasebook

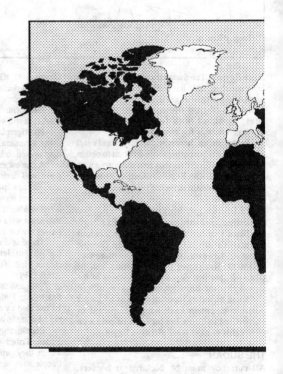

Indian Ocean
Madagascar & Comoros
Maldives & Islands of the East Indian Ocean
Mauritius, Réunion & Seychelles

Mail Order

Lonely Planet guidebooks are distributed worldwide and are sold by good bookshops everywhere. They are also available by mail order from Lonely Planet, so if you have difficulty finding a title please write to us. US and Canadian residents should write to Embarcadero West, 112 Linden St, Oakland CA 94607, USA and residents of other countries to PO Box 617, Hawthorn, Victoria 3122, Australia.

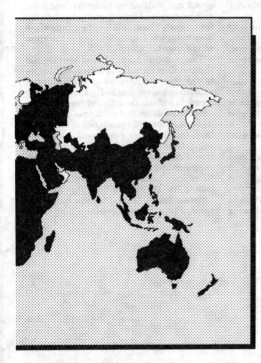

Europe
Eastern Europe
Trekking in Spain

Indian Subcontinent
India
Hindi/Urdu phrasebook
Kashmir, Ladakh & Zanskar
Trekking in the Indian Himalaya
Pakistan
Kathmandu & the Kingdom of Nepal
Trekking in the Nepal Himalaya
Nepal phrasebook
Sri Lanka
Sri Lanka phrasebook
Bangladesh
Karakoram Highway

Africa
Africa on a shoestring
East Africa
Swahili phrasebook
West Africa
Central Africa
Morocco, Algeria & Tunisia

North America
Canada
Alaska

Mexico
Mexico
Baja California

South America
South America on a shoestring
Ecuador & the Galapagos Islands
Colombia
Chile & Easter Island
Bolivia
Brazil
Brazilian phrasebook
Peru
Argentina
Quechua phrasebook

Middle East
Israel
Egypt & the Sudan
Jordan & Syria
Yemen

Lonely Planet

Lonely Planet published its first book in 1973. Tony and Maureen Wheeler had made a lengthy overland trip from England to Australia and, in response to numerous 'how do you do it?' questions, Tony wrote and they published *Across Asia on the Cheap*. It became an instant local best-seller and inspired thoughts of a second travel guide. A year and a half in South-East Asia resulted in their second book, *South-East Asia on a Shoestring*, which they put together in a backstreet Chinese hotel in Singapore in 1975. The 'yellow book', as it quickly became known, soon became *the* guide to the region and has gone through five editions, always with its familiar yellow cover.

Soon other writers came to them with ideas for similar books – books that went off the beaten track with an adventurous approach to travel, books that 'assumed you knew how to get your luggage off the carousel,' as one reviewer put it. Lonely Planet grew from a kitchen table operation to a spare room and then to its own office. Its international reputation began to grow as the Lonely Planet logo began to appear in more and more countries. In 1982 *India – a travel survival kit* won the Thomas Cook award for the best guidebook of the year.

These days there are over 70 Lonely Planet titles. Over 40 people work at our office in Melbourne, Australia and another half dozen at our US office in Oakland, California.

At first Lonely Planet specialised in the Asia region but these days we are also developing major ranges of guidebooks to the Pacific region, to South America and to Africa. The list of walking guides is growing and Lonely Planet now has a unique series of phrasebooks to 'unusual' languages. The emphasis continues to be on travel for travellers and Tony and Maureen still manage to fit in a number of trips each year and play a very active part in the writing and updating of Lonely Planet's guides.

Keeping guidebooks up to date is a constant battle which requires an ear to the ground and lots of walking, but technology also plays its part. All Lonely Planet guidebooks are now stored and updated on computer, and some authors even take lap-top computers into the field. Lonely Planet is also using computers to draw maps and eventually many of the maps will be stored on disk.

The people at Lonely Planet strongly feel that travellers can make a positive contribution to the countries they visit both by better appreciation of cultures and by the money they spend. In addition the company tries to make a direct contribution to the countries and regions it covers. Since 1986 a percentage of the income from each book has gone to aid groups and associations. This has included donations to famine relief in Africa, to aid projects in India, to agricultural projects in Central America, to Greenpeace's efforts to halt French nuclear testing in the Pacific and to Amnesty International. In 1989 $41,000 was donated by Lonely Planet to these projects.